Core Text Series

KT-486-328

- Written with authority by leading subject experts
- Takes a focused approach, leading law students straight to the heart of the subject
- Clear, concise, straightforward analysis of the subject and its challenges

Company Law: Alan Dignam and John Lowry

Constitutional and Administrative Law: Neil Parpworth

Criminal Law: Nicola Padfield

European Union Law: Margot Horspool, Matthew Humphreys and Michael Wells-Greco

Evidence: Roderick Munday

Family Law: Mary Welstead and Susan Edwards

Intellectual Property Law: Jennifer Davis

Land Law: Ben McFarlane, Nicholas Hopkins and Sarah Nield

Medical Law: Jonathan Herring

O'Sullivan and Hilliard's The Law of Contract: Janet O'Sullivan

The Law of Trusts: J E Penner

For further information about titles in the series,
please visit www.oup.co.uk/series/cts

OXFORD
UNIVERSITY PRESS

O'Sullivan & Hilliard's The Law of Contract

Eighth Edition

JANET O'SULLIVAN MA, (CANTAB), PHD (CANTAB)

Fellow of Selwyn College, Cambridge, and Senior Lecturer in Law,
University of Cambridge

OXFORD
UNIVERSITY PRESS

OXFORD
UNIVERSITY PRESS

Great Clarendon Street, Oxford, OX2 6DP,
United Kingdom

Oxford University Press is a department of the University of Oxford.
It furthers the University's objective of excellence in research, scholarship,
and education by publishing worldwide. Oxford is a registered trade mark of
Oxford University Press in the UK and in certain other countries

Fifth edition 2012
Sixth edition 2014
Seventh edition 2016

Impression: 1

Public sector information reproduced under Open Government Licence v3.0
(http://www.nationalarchives.gov.uk/doc/open-government-licence/open-government-licence.htm)

Published in the United States of America by Oxford University Press
198 Madison Avenue, New York, NY 10016, United States of America

British Library Cataloguing in Publication Data
Data available

Library of Congress Control Number: 2018932378

ISBN 978-0-19-880782-7

Printed in Great Britain by
Bell & Bain Ltd., Glasgow

Preface to the eighth edition

After writing seven editions of this book in collaboration with Jonathan Hilliard, this is the first that I have undertaken on my own. Jonathan's professional commitments as a QC, as well as his new family responsibilities as devoted father to baby Iris, meant that he has stepped away from detailed involvement in new editions of the book. So I want to begin this preface by expressing my huge gratitude to him for being the most wonderful co-author, collaborator, and friend (as well as an exceptionally brilliant former student) for two decades. I am so grateful for his wisdom, support, and hard work, both on the original text and subsequently.

The preface to the first edition of this book explained that its aim was to give students as sound an understanding of the basics of contract law as possible and, equally importantly, of why the law is the way it is, in order that they might not only understand the current state of the law but be stimulated to form their own views on whether it is justifiable. With that in mind, Jonathan and I made two choices when writing the first edition. These were, first, that the book would focus both on the fundamentals of contract law and the rationales underlying them; second, that where the law was controversial in some respect, we attempted to set out in detail our opinions, and the opinions of others, on whether the rule in question is correct. This structure seems to have worked well and has been preserved in this latest edition. The chapters on Incapacity and Illegality no longer appear within the book (as these topics do not generally form part of undergraduate courses on the law of Contract) but are available on the online resources.

I hope that this book will be of use both to students wanting a clear picture of the basics of the subject, and to those eager to explore the law and its controversies in greater depth. In particular, it remains my view that it is no longer feasible to study the 'core' of a legal subject without reading and thinking about the academic contributions to it, so this book aims to draw attention to academic writing that I hope students will enjoy and benefit from reading.

This edition incorporates, where possible, new authorities decided before 1 October 2017, and the courts have been as busy as ever in the contractual field over the last two years. It includes decisions from the Supreme Court in *Marks & Spencer plc v BNP Paribas Securities Services Trust Co (Jersey) Ltd* and *Trump International Golf Club Ltd v Scottish Ministers (Scotland)* (on implied terms), *Wood v Capita Insurance Services Ltd* and *Impact Funding Solutions Ltd v AIG Europe Insurance Ltd* (on interpretation), *Hayward v Zurich Insurance Co plc* (on fraudulent misrepresentation), *Lowick Rose LLP v Swynson Ltd* and *Globalia Business Travel SAU v Fulton Shipping Inc* (on mitigation and collateral benefits). It features numerous decisions of the Court of

Appeal, such as *Wells v Devani* and *Rollerteam Ltd v Riley* (on contractual formation), *MWB Business Exchange Centres Ltd v Rock Advertising Ltd* (on consideration and variation), *MSC Mediterranean Shipping Co SA v Cottonex Anstalt* (on repudiatory breach), *Wright v Lewis Silkin LLP* (on loss of a chance), *Wellesley Partners LLP v Withers LLP* (on remoteness of damage and concurrent liability in contract and tort), and *One Step (Support) Ltd v Morris-Garner* (on negotiating damages), as well as many significant first instance decisions.

When citing case law in this book, I have retained the style used in previous editions – that is to adopt the terminology introduced by the Civil Procedure Rules, calling the party bringing proceedings the 'claimant' not the 'plaintiff' (unless reproducing a quotation using the label 'plaintiff'), even where the relevant case pre-dates the introduction of the Rules. I can only apologise to those readers who find this a grating anachronism (like spotting a digital watch in a costume drama), but it seemed the best solution to the problem.

I would both like to offer my sincere thanks to the Contract 'team', past and present, in the Cambridge Law Faculty for their inspiration, particularly Neil Andrews, Jack Beatson, Paul Davies, Steve Hedley, Jonathan Morgan, Roderick Munday, Stelios Tofaris, and Graham Virgo. I am particularly indebted to the professionalism and helpfulness of David Wills and all his staff in the Squire Law Library. I would also like to thank my past and present supervision students, whose Contract supervisions road-tested the ideas in this book and whose thought-provoking questions inspired many a re-write. In addition, I am grateful to many other students, from Cambridge and elsewhere, who have taken the time and trouble to provide feedback on previous editions of this book, as well as pointing out errors and infelicities. I urge you to let us know of any that remain.

Finally, my heartfelt gratitude to those I love (I truly hope I have told you so often enough) for all your support for me, and above all to my three precious children Rob, Amy, and Hannah, for putting everything into perspective. I would like to dedicate this edition to my beloved parents Anne and Rob, who celebrated their Golden Wedding Anniversary during its preparation.

Janet O'Sullivan
Selwyn College, Cambridge

New to this edition

The eighth edition of The Law of Contract has been thoroughly revised to reflect recent developments in the law since the publication of the seventh edition, including the following important new cases:

- From the Supreme Court, *Marks & Spencer plc v BNP Paribas Securities Services, Trust Co (Jersey) Ltd* and *Trump International Golf Club Ltd v Scottish Ministers (Scotland)* (on implied terms), *Wood v Capita Insurance Services Ltd* and *Impact Funding Solutions Ltd v AIG Europe Insurance Ltd* (on interpretation), *Hayward v Zurich Insurance Co plc* (on fraudulent misrepresentation), *Lowick Rose LLP v Swynson Ltd* and *Globalia Business Travel SAU v Fulton Shipping Inc* (on mitigation and collateral benefits).

- From the Court of Appeal, *Wells v Devani* and *Rollerteam Ltd v Riley* (on contractual formation), *James-Bowen v Metropolitan Police Commissioner* (on intention to create legal relations), *MWB Business Exchange Centres Ltd v Rock Advertising Ltd* (on consideration and variation), *The Hut Group Ltd v Nobahar-Cookson* and *African Export-Import Bank v Shebah Exploration and Production Company Ltd* (on exclusion clauses), *Spar Shipping A/S v Grand China Logistics Holding (Group) Co Ltd* (on classification of terms as conditions or innominate terms), *MSC Mediterranean Shipping Co SA v Cottonex Anstalt* (on repudiatory breach), *Wright v Lewis Silkin LLP* (on loss of a chance), *Wellesley Partners LLP v Withers LLP* (on remoteness of damage and concurrent liability in contract and tort) and *One Step (Support) Ltd v Morris-Garner* (on negotiating damages).

Contents

Table of legislation

Table of cases

1 General themes and issues

SUMMARY

This chapter offers a general introduction to the law of contract and classical contract theory, with its themes of contract as bargain, the primacy of the parties' intentions and freedom of contract. It considers critical objections to classical contract theory, dealing with individualism, commercial issues and borderlines between contract and other subjects within the law of obligations, as well as European and international initiatives in the field of contract law.

1.1 This book is about the law relating to contracts. Contracts are made and performed every moment of every day and affect every aspect of life, whether you are purchasing food in a supermarket, taking a bus or train journey, booking tickets for the theatre on the internet, or leasing a flat. In our market economy, businesses make contracts to raise finance, employ staff, acquire premises and raw materials, and trade their services or goods, and consumers make contracts to purchase those services or goods. The law of contract provides the ground rules to make it clear what is needed for a contract to exist and be enforceable and indeed what it means to be 'enforceable', to resolve disputes about what the contract means, and to prescribe the consequences if one party does not do what he has contracted to do.

1.2 Notice that we have already referred to the law of 'contract' in the singular, even though a huge number of very diverse sorts of situations count as contracts. It is true that, though both are contracts, there is a world of difference between a simple cash sale in a shop and a complex commercial financing transaction recorded in a long, technical, legal document. It is also true that, increasingly, different types of contracts have their own specific sets of rules, often derived from statutes or other regulatory codes covering one sort of contract only. So, for some commentators, it is time to recognise that a system based on general rules, relating to all contracts and applied blindly regardless of context (so that a case about a contract to sell a house might be cited as authority for a particular rule in a case about a guarantee, employment, or shipping contract) is inappropriate and unhelpful, obscuring rather than highlighting important contextual differences. The response must be that judges and practising lawyers (and those who create law courses) still think in terms of a general 'Law of Contract' as the foundation on which the various specific regimes are built, so students need to know and understand this language and reasoning before they can form a view about whether it is time to change the conceptual frame-work. In any event, the courts tend not to apply the general rules of contract blindly, but by and large examine sensitively and in detail whether a decision reached in one context should properly be applied or distinguished in another context.

1.3 In the early common law (unlike Roman Law), there was no such systematic and sep-arate law of contract, because lawyers did not analyse disputes in terms of substantive rules, but by reference to the procedural question of which 'form of action' was ap-plicable. It was not until the nineteenth century that the first recognisable textbook on the Law of Contract was written, reflecting the fact that, for the first time, a unifying philosophy about contracts and contractual disputes had emerged and was accepted. This philosophy, often called 'classical' contract theory, remains extremely influential today and still provides a convincing justification for much of the contemporary law of contract.

1.4 Classical contract theory has three related threads. First, a contract is a bargain, which means a reciprocal agreement between the parties, almost invariably an exchange of promises (I promise to do X and you promise to do Y in return). So a one-sided gratuit-ous promise is not a contract. Second (and not always entirely consistent with the first thread), contracts are the product of the will of the parties, so that it is the parties' inten-tion to 'bind' themselves that justifies legal recognition of enforceable contractual rights and obligations. In contrast with other areas of law, for example the law of tort, the role of the courts is not to prescribe the content of contractual obligations but to give effect to the intention of the parties. Third, freedom of contract is paramount. Everyone is free to decide whether or not to contract at all, with whom they are willing to contract, and on what terms. Once again, the law must interfere as little as possible, ensuring only that improper tactics by one party, such as fraud or coercion, did not compromise the other party's negotiating freedom.

1.5 In many respects, the classical theory remains a good explanation of much of the current law of contract, though as is often pointed out, it is not a perfect model and does not ex-plain many aspects of the law and contemporary practice. The first thread is challenged, since many contracts do not involve an agreement in the form of a bilateral exchange of promises. For example, you will encounter unilateral contracts, where one party prom-ises something if the other party acts in a specified way, and formal contracts contained in a 'deed', which are binding even though gratuitous and with no element of bargain. Many simple bilateral contracts are made and performed instantaneously, so each party's notional *promise* to perform looks like an artificial legal construct. More fundamentally, it is pointed out that contracts made on printed standard terms, such as where a con-sumer acquires a car on hire purchase terms or books a package holiday, bear no resem-blance to a negotiated bargain.

1.6 Similar objections are levelled at the second thread, that contractual obligations are consensual and based on the intention of the parties. Critics point to the prevalence of the printed standard form and the frequent insertion of 'implied terms' into contracts, some justified as giving effect to the intentions of the parties but others, like the implied conditions that goods sold in the course of the seller's business are of satisfactory quality and fit for their purpose, are inserted by statute regardless of intention. Contracts are sometimes described as requiring a 'meeting of minds', but even in the nineteenth century, this was misleading. This is because the parties' intention is judged *objectively*—how would their words and actions have appeared to a reasonable person? So, although questions about the formation, contents, and interpretation of a contract are resolved by reference to the parties' intentions, this is not really an enquiry into what the parties subjectively intended or wanted. After all, as Rix LJ pointed out in *Procter & Gamble v Svenska Cellulosa Aktiebolaget SA* (2012), 'when it comes to a dispute the [subjective] question of actual intention is likely to be submerged in wishful thinking.'

1.7 The third thread, the principle of freedom of contract, receives the most critical scrutiny. Even in the nineteenth century, absolute freedom of contract did not exist, but was constrained, for example, by rules about illegal contracts and contractual incapacity, while the twentieth century was marked by restrictions, practical and legal, on all aspects of freedom of contract. The freedom whether or not to contract at all is inhibited by legal devices (like statutory rights for tenants to obtain a new lease or to purchase their council houses) and practical pressures (anyone who wants to have a telephone or use public transport must make a contract). The freedom to choose with whom to contract is restricted by statutes outlawing various forms of discrimination and where monopoly (and, at one time, nationalised) suppliers provide the only source of a particular product or service. Finally, the freedom to choose the contents and terms of a contract is qualified in a number of ways, by statutory controls on certain sorts of 'undesirable' terms (for example, the protective regimes in the Consumer Credit Act, the Unfair Contract Terms Act, and the Consumer Rights Act) and, once again, by the prevalence of non-negotiable printed standard contract terms, often almost identical across the particular market sector. All in all, the classic Victorian image of contract, perhaps involving two gentlemen negotiating and eventually shaking hands over the sale of a horse, does not look very promising as a model for the twenty-first century.

1.8 However, the reality is a lot more complex than just a simple choice between abandoning or advocating the classical model. For example, the model of contract as a bargain consisting of exchanged promises remains, as we will see, a central notion in legal reasoning today, as does the fact that, fundamentally, contracting is an expression of the free will of the parties. Just because, away from the core meaning of contract, there are cases that do not entirely resemble the core (and perhaps shade into other legal concepts, like tort), is no reason to dismiss the core model as useless. It is undeniable that the courts continue to emphasise the significance of the parties' intentions and, when it is understood that the objective test involves not a substitution of the judge's own ideas about what a reasonable solution would have been, but that of a reasonable person placed in the position of the parties and understanding the conventions and usage of that particular market, this seems a wholly appropriate way to approach contractual questions.

1.9   Freedom of contract, too, remains a central concept. It has been pointed out that, in economic and political terms, the pendulum has swung back in the direction of freedom of contract in the last two-and-a-half decades, matching the individualist, free market philosophy of recent governments. And it is certainly still the starting point of many judges and commentators, who treat the 'inroads' into freedom of contract discussed earlier as exceptions to the norm, not evidence of a different norm. Moreover, many of these inroads are tailored to a very specific problem, that of consumer protection. Consumer contracts raise particular problems, but these are generally (and better) controlled by targeted statutory provisions, not general common law restrictions (as, for example, the history of the common law 'doctrine of inequality of bargaining power' tells us: see paras **12.24**). Where contracts between businesses are concerned, the assumption is that the parties should be free to make the deals and on the terms they regard as desirable for their businesses, with access to legal advice on both sides and thus with minimal interference from the law later. So, duly qualified, the classic model remains a good basis on which to approach the rules and ethos of the law of contract, at least where commercial contracts are concerned. Indeed, recently the courts have explicitly relied on freedom of contract as a fundamental value in commercial contracts, when grappling with the conundrum of what should happen where the parties' original written contract contains a provision prohibiting any agreed *variation* of the contract unless it is also made in writing, but where the parties have subsequently orally agreed to vary their deal. Citing freedom of contract, the Court of Appeal (in both *Globe Motors Inc v TRW Lucas Varity Electric Electric Steering Ltd* (2016) and *MWB Business Exchange Centres Ltd v Rock Advertising Ltd* (2016)) upheld the subsequent oral variation, even though paradoxically this meant disregarding the original, very sensible, commercial term, designed to prevent difficult arguments about whether the contract had been changed by an informal conversation. The justification is that (like Parliament) contracting parties cannot fetter their future freedom, though setting procedural requirements for contractual variation is much less problematic than fettering a future sovereign Parliament. *MWB* is discussed further in paras **5.62–5.66**.

1.10   Closely related to these basic threads are two features of the English law of contract, both of which you will come across throughout your reading. The first is the so-called individualist ethos and the second is the commercial importance of clear, 'bright-line' legal rules. The individualist ethic means that contracting parties are expected to look after their own interests, not those of the other party. English law assumes an adversarial stance, with each party seeking, within the confines of permissible tactics, to make the best possible bargain in the short term. A number of contractual rules can be seen in this light. For example, although the law is scrupulous about false statements made in the run up to contracting (generally allowing the other party to escape from the contract), it imposes no active duty of disclosure of relevant information. One party can keep quiet, even if he knows that the other party is mistaken as to some quality of the contractual subject matter—he is not forced to give up what is regarded as his negotiating advantage. And English law (unlike, for example, French and German law) has no general doctrine of 'good faith' between the parties, either before or after contracting. One party can pull

out of negotiations at the last minute for any or no reason, insist on strict adherence to the terms of a contract and exercise a contractual right for whatever motive he pleases—there is no notion of 'abuse' of contractual rights.

1.11 This individualist stance is not universally accepted. Even putting to one side the consumer-welfare ethos now plainly operating in the regulation of consumer contracts, critics argue that it would not be disastrous for English law as a commercial system to acknowledge that contracting parties have some minimal obligations to cooperate with and accommodate each other. For example, civilian systems do not grind to an inefficient halt by virtue of recognising pre-contractual and contractual duties of good faith. Critics also point out that many contracts are not isolated, one-off transactions, but are either long-term ventures, more like a relationship than an adversarial bargain, or at least represent one transaction forming part of an ongoing course of dealing between the parties. In such circumstances, it is argued that limited duties of cooperation and good faith would better reflect the parties' assumptions when contracting and, paradoxically, might be a better basis on which to promote self-interest in the long term (by reassuring potential contractors and thus encouraging risk-taking). Finally, important empirical research has shown that commercial parties do not necessarily think or act as the individualist ethos presupposes, often favouring renegotiation and accommodation, rather than an insistence on strict legal rights backed up by legal action. The Canadian Supreme Court in *Bhasin v Hrynew* (2014) decided that Canadian contract law is subject to a general organising principle of good faith, although in reality this decision was not as radical as it might sound, since its application was confined to requiring the parties to behave honestly towards each other, which is usually an implied contractual term in any event.

1.12 On the other hand, English law's individualist ethos has much to recommend it. For example, a rule requiring disclosure of material information would require the better-prepared, more knowledgeable party to give up his negotiating advantages for nothing, discouraging research and penalising what ought to be rewarded. A general principle of good faith might lead to uncertainty—what does it mean to be in bad faith and by whose standards? Plus, such a principle may well be unnecessary, since English law already penalises specific instances of bad faith (such as duress and misrepresentation) and has numerous piecemeal devices at its disposal (like implying terms, applying principles of contractual construction, and insisting on mitigation of loss) to tailor 'good faith' solutions in appropriate cases. Finally, the empirical evidence that commercial parties generally act in a cooperative manner does not necessarily tell us anything about what the 'default' legal regime should be if their cooperative approach fails. After all, we would not consider changing the criminal law to reflect widespread ignorance (or flouting) of it and it may be that cooperative behaviour works best when understood as a concession, not a legal requirement.

1.13 Whatever your view on the individualist ethos, it is important to appreciate the undoubted advantages of clarity and certainty in the law of contract. Every area of the law experiences tension between the need for clarity and certainty, so that conduct can be regulated by reference to predictable rules, versus the desirability of flexibility, giving the courts enough discretion to respond to the merits of a dispute. In the law of negligence, for example, this tension is seen as the courts recognise the advantages of an objective standard of care but baulk at applying it across the board. In contract, this tension is particularly evident, but in most cases there is everything to be said for clarity and certainty, even if this means some harsh decisions on the merits. Commercial parties need to know where they stand and, on balance, would prefer to be the loser today if that means that, next time, they know precisely what to do to avoid being the loser again.

1.14   The most important thing to remember is that the law of contract is very definitely not just concerned with litigation and resolving disputes after the event, although (perhaps inevitably) the focus of commentators is on case law, which is, by definition, the product of litigation. It is also facilitative, a set of ground rules to enable parties to make and perform their desired bargains, and needs to be clear and accessible as such to practitioners drafting contracts and advising clients in negotiations. Concepts like 'good faith' and 'abuse of rights' are inherently (and deliberately) hard to define and thus problematic for those seeking clear advice in advance about their contracts and conduct.

1.15   Thus far, we have considered in very general terms some of the theoretical issues you will need to think about when studying the law of contract. But let us now put some flesh on the bones and consider, in the light of all the theory, how the law treats a fairly typical commercial contract. Imagine X is a soft drink manufacturer and Y is a commercial grower of tomatoes. X wishes to ensure a supply of tomatoes to make tomato juice, sales of which peak at Christmas time. So X makes a contract with Y in June, to purchase from Y a hundred tons of tomatoes to be delivered in October at an agreed price per ton—the price to be paid on delivery of the tomatoes. Both parties, being rational, make the contract for a good reason—X to feel secure about a supply of tomatoes in October at a price it is happy with, Y because it wants to make a profit and is confident that the cost of growing and harvesting the tomatoes will be less than the price. The contract allows both forward planning and risk allocation.

1.16   Notice a number of important features straight away. First, it does not matter whether the contract is made orally or in writing—with very limited exceptions (such as contracts for the sale of land or guarantee contracts), English law does not require writing, signature, or other formalities for a valid contract. Second, even if Y made a mistake in its final calculations and offered a lower price per ton than it intended, this will not affect the validity of the contract. Y will generally be held to the terms to which, objectively, it appeared to be agreeing, regardless of its innermost intentions. Third, many of the terms of the contract (such as obligations about the quality of the tomatoes) will be included automatically, by virtue of the Sale of Goods Act, not because of the express intentions of the parties. Fourth, notice the gap between the date the contract is made (June) and the date it is to be performed (October). The contract is valid and binding immediately in June, even before any part of the contract has been performed or any sums spent in preparation to perform the contract. So if X changes its mind the day after making the contract and pulls out, Y could in theory sue him for damages. As we will see, this theory is subject to the very important qualifications that Y must have suffered some loss and must act reasonably to keep that loss to a minimum ('mitigation'), but crucially notice the meaning of loss here. In contract, you suffer 'a loss' merely because you expected to be better off had the contract been performed but, as a result of the breach, you are not better off to the same extent (though you may be no worse off). This feature has been subjected to heavy criticism—why should one party be able to sue for damages when it seems to be no worse off as a result of the breach? But, as we will see, it reflects the essence of what is wrong with breaching a contract, which is that the party in breach has not done what he or she promised to do. Furthermore, commerce is built on the understanding that contracts create enforceable obligations and corresponding expectations *immediately*, not at some unidentifiable later date when the other party first acts or incurs expenditure in reliance.

1.17 If we enlarge on the facts slightly, other features can be illustrated. Imagine that there is an unexpectedly cold summer, Y's crop does very badly and he does not have a hundred tons of tomatoes to sell in October. Other tomato growers experience the same difficulties, so that by October the market price of a ton of tomatoes has risen way above the contract price. Y will wish to escape from his contractual obligation to deliver the tomatoes to X, but (assuming X and Y have not negotiated a right for Y to do so in circumstances of this kind) he stands little chance. Contractual obligations are generally strict—'You promised it, you do it!'—so it is irrelevant that Y is not 'at fault' in the tort sense of the word. Moreover, English law takes an extremely restrictive view of when unexpected external circumstances provide an excuse for escape from a contract. This may seem 'hard' on Y, but think back to the reasons why the parties wanted to make a contract in the first place. Y took the risk that he could perform for less than the contract price, hoping to make a profit (which he would have done if the market price had moved down instead of up). X made the contract to allow for forward planning, for the security of not having to worry about the risk of the market price moving up, for reasons like problems with the tomato harvest (and was prepared to take the risk of the market price moving down to achieve this security). So it is crucial that the law holds the parties to their contract in these unexpected conditions—otherwise, why bother to make a contract at all? X might just as well have taken his chances in October.

1.18 This simple example has raised a number of distinctive features that mark the law of contract off from other areas of the law of obligations. Finally, we should briefly explore the boundaries between the law of contract and these other areas. First, consider the differences between tort and contract, which in classical theory represent a very sharply delineated boundary. Traditionally, the law of contract is concerned with voluntarily assumed obligations, while the law of tort involves obligations imposed by law, regardless of the intention of the parties (it is pointless to drive around with a sign on the bonnet of your car, stating that you do not agree to owe a duty of care to your fellow road-users!). Tort is primarily concerned with fault, whereas contracting parties can, and frequently do, commit themselves to strict contractual obligations; damages for breach of contract protect financial expectations, whereas tort remedies are geared to compensating harm, usually to persons or property.

1.19 As you will discover, while the core contractual situation and the core tort situation are fundamentally different, the edges of the two concepts are not quite as sharp as this might suggest. Developments in the law of negligence relating to financial harm have muddied the distinction, with liability under *Hedley Byrne v Heller* (1964) justified because one party has 'undertaken responsibility' for the other, in a relationship resembling, but just falling short of, contract. For example, recovery under *White v Jones* (1995) uses tort to protect expectations of financial gain because contractual remedies are regarded, rightly or wrongly, as deficient. On the other side of the coin, many contractual obligations exactly reproduce tortious duties, as where professionals contract to take reasonable care, and the law now recognises concurrent liability in such cases (especially significant for procedural reasons, because the rules of limitation, or time limits for bringing a claim, are more favourable to claimants suing in tort rather than for breach of contract). Concurrent liability leads to its own difficulties, such as whether a defence of contributory negligence should be available in a contractual action and whether the tort or contract rules on foreseeability of loss should apply. Many situations dealt with in books on the law of contract, such as the effect of false statements, undue influence and 'estoppel' representations that induce detrimental reliance, might equally rationally be regarded as part of the law of tort. More fundamentally, it has been pointed out that certain implied contractual terms, imposed by operation of law without reference to the parties' intentions, are closer to tort duties than consensual contractual obligations—for example, a bus company's relationship with its passengers is contractual, with terms and conditions 'incorporated' into the contract via wording on a notice or the ticket, but is it really very different in kind from the tort duties that the bus company, via its driver, owes to other road-users and pedestrians?

1.20 Another important border is between the law of contract and the law of restitution, with the latter frequently said to be based, not on consensual obligations, but on the legal imperative to reverse unjust enrichment. It is often pointed out that the obligation to repay money paid under a mistake, historically justified by artificially implying a 'promise' to repay it, is now understood instead as based on a legal obligation to reverse unjust enrichment. And it is usually stressed that restitution is subservient to contract, so that restitution cannot be claimed when there is a subsisting contract governing the situation. But once again, the boundary between restitution and contract is not as distinct as this suggests and, indeed, it may not even be appropriate to think in terms of boundaries at all. A better metaphor might be a 'turf war', since it is not uncommon to find a particular legal issue being 'claimed' by some commentators as part of the law of restitution and by others as part of the law of contract. One example which we will consider in this book is what happens where one party does work for someone else pursuant to a very loose arrangement that it is to be paid for. For some, that situation is so far away from 'contract' that payment can only be justified on the basis of restitution; others have a broader concept of 'contract' that can stretch to such a case.

1.21 It is also increasingly common for public law issues to arise in contractual disputes, where one or both of the parties is a public or quasi-public body. For example, in *Hampshire County*

Council v Supportways Community Services Ltd (2006) the council terminated its contract with a company providing contracted-out housing services for it, having concluded that the services were too expensive. The Court of Appeal had to decide whether the company could seek the public law remedy of judicial review, or whether the appropriate remedy was a private law contractual remedy for breach of contract. Sometimes a public body makes a contract that obliges it to act 'reasonably', and the courts have to decide whether that means 'reasonably' in the public or private law meaning of the word (see *Krebs v NHS Commissioning Board* (2014)). Public and private law principles arise alongside each other where a public body seeks tenders from private companies with a view to awarding a contract for public works (see *Central Tenders Board v White* (2015)). In addition, the courts must consider the Human Rights Act whenever a contract made by a public authority is in issue. Moreover, in all cases the courts themselves, as public authorities, must act in a way that complies with the Human Rights Act, for example when exercising their discretion to grant or refuse the remedies of specific performance or an injunction.

1.22 Finally, it is worth thinking about the sources of contract law. You will find when reading this book that it is almost entirely about the home-grown English law of contract, found in the common law and in domestic legislation. But in our global age, it is also important to consider wider international aspects of the law of contract, not least because so many contracts are entered into across international borders or in cyberspace, potentially triggering difficult problems of which conflicting legal system applies to the contract (the 'conflict of laws').

1.23 The law of contract is one of the many areas which will be affected by the eventual Brexit deal, as yet unresolved. One of the aims of the European Commission has always been to bolster the single market in the EU and make cross-border and cyber transactions more straightforward, by reducing divergence in national contract laws. One way is by enacting Directives, such as the Unfair Terms in Consumer Contracts Directive (93/13/EEC), which member states must implement to provide a minimum harmonised level of consumer protection (this is considered in more detail in Chapter 8). Many such measures were implemented into UK national legislation, which will remain in force post-Brexit. Other initiatives are ongoing and therefore the UK's future participation is in doubt. For example, in 2015 the Commission launched its Digital Single Market initiative (see also the mid-term review of the initiative published in May 2017), which includes proposals to harmonise aspects of contract law relating to digital transactions and e-commerce. More controversially, there have been various research projects searching for shared principles of contract law across European systems, such as the Lando Commission, a group of academics who published the 'Principles of European Contract Law' (PECL). Then in 2009 a Draft Common Frame of Reference (DCFR) was published, building on the PECL, followed by a Green Paper from the European Commission on 'Policy Options for Progress towards a European Contract Law for Consumers and Businesses' (COM (2010) 348), which launched a public consultation on the DCFR.

1.24 Even putting Brexit to one side, the DCFR is a controversial proposal across the EU member states. At the weaker end of the scale, it might be used simply as a 'toolbox', a reference resource for the Commission when drafting future legislation or revising existing measures; or it could be offered as an optional alternative code for member states to adopt voluntarily; or for contracting parties to select as the applicable law of their contract. At the other end of the spectrum, the nuclear option would be to make the new rules mandatory and replace existing national contract law systems, even for purely domestic transactions. The Green Paper is cautious about this option, acknowledging that it would raise sensitive issues of subsidiarity and proportionality. But as commentators have pointed out, the DCFR has been drafted as a set of model rules, in the form of a codification of the law; much like a fully-fledged civilian 'civil code' and certainly nothing like a 'toolbox' (see Whittaker (2009) and Jansen and Zimmermann (2010)). It remains to be seen how the Green Paper is received, but it is likely that anything other than the weaker options would meet with fierce political and scholarly resistance in many member states, as happened to a subsequent 'weaker' proposal by the Commission for the introduction of a Common European Sales Law (COM (2011) 635 final), an optional code that contracting parties could select to govern their transactions, that met with a hostile response from governments, and was withdrawn in 2015. Now, of course, Brexit means that the UK will not implement the DCFR initiative in any form, though it remains a significant matter for any UK individual or company contracting in future with a party from an EU member state. (For further discussion of the potential implications of Brexit on domestic contracts, see para **14.34**.)

1.25 In addition to EU sources, there are a number of international examples of non-binding statements of principle and optional model terms in use in international commerce. The best known examples are, first, the Vienna Convention on International Sales of Goods, a hugely successful set of terms for business-to-business sales of goods, created by the United Nations Commission on International Trade Law, which applies by default whenever the parties have not chosen to apply another law. Secondly, there is a set of model rules for sale of goods and provision of services called the Principles of International Commercial Contracts created by UNIDROIT (the International Institute for the Unification of Private Law), which has also been very successful, as a resource for legislators and for contracting parties looking for acceptable terms and conditions.

1.26 So, overall, throughout your reading of this book, be aware of the very important and often wholly distinct core notion of a contract, but also keep a critical eye out for qualifications and exceptions, as well as the tension at borders with other areas of the law and potential international involvement in the contractual regime. (It might be worth coming back to this chapter at the end of your reading, armed with some information on which to formulate your own views about the questions raised!)

FURTHER READING

Atiyah 'Contracts, Promises and the Law of Obligations' Chapter 2 in *Essays on Contract* (1986)

Brownsword *Contract Law—Themes for the Twenty-First Century* (2006)

2 Offer and acceptance I: general principles

SUMMARY

This chapter deals with the traditional 'offer and acceptance' required for formation of a contract, introducing the principle of objectivity in contractual formation and contrasting bilateral and unilateral contracts. Offers are contrasted with invitations to treat and standard commercial situations are analysed, as is contracting by e-mail and online. Likewise the requirements of acceptance and of communication of acceptance are explored, as are revocation and the battle of the forms.

2.1 Traditionally, we require an offer and acceptance in order to form a contract. An offer is an indication of one party's willingness to enter into a contract with the party to whom it is addressed as soon as the latter accepts its terms, and an acceptance is an agreement to the terms of the offer. For example, if I am a car dealer and I say to you, 'Will you buy this rare sports car for £100?', I am indicating my willingness to enter into a contract to sell my car to you, and that I intend this contract to arise as soon as you agree to the terms of my offer. If you reply that you would be delighted to do so, you have agreed to the terms of my offer, and a contract is formed between us.

2.2 The offer and acceptance requirement suggests that a contract is an agreement. Taking this one stage further, the requirement suggests that the parties' *intentions* determine whether a contract is formed and what the contents of this contract are (what obligations it places on the parties and what rights it gives each party against the other). So in our car example, the contract of sale is formed because both parties intend to enter into such a contract. I am placed under an obligation to give you the car and am given a right to the £100 from you in return. Conversely, you are placed under the obligation to pay me the £100 and are given the right to have the car transferred to you by me. These rights and obligations arise because the parties intend them to.

2.3 All of this seems unproblematic, perhaps even intuitive. Indeed, many take the view that, by and large, it is (for example, Burrows (1983) and Birks (1983)). However, matters are not always so simple: sometimes we are happy to say that there is a contract despite it being extremely difficult to identify an offer and acceptance, and often we do not focus exclusively on the parties' actual intent.

2.4   First, as Atiyah (1986) points out, we often have an incorrect view of what constitutes a 'typical contract' and what features such a contract has. We tend to think that, typically, parties sit down and negotiate until they reach a clear agreement, which they often then write down. It is at this point that we tend to think that a binding contract arises, before the parties have started to perform the contract. So we form the view that a contract is formed by a clear agreement between the parties. They agree first and perform later. However, in many everyday contracts, the parties do not sit down and reach complete agreement before performing or focus on legal niceties like offer and acceptance. Therefore, it is often artificial to try to find an implied offer and acceptance. As Lord Wilberforce points out by way of example in *The Eurymedon* (1976), it is difficult to break down a simple purchase of goods in a supermarket into an offer and an acceptance, principally because we do not pay much regard to such legal concepts when doing the shopping! *The Satanita* (1897) provides another good example. There, the defendant entered a yacht race. It was held that by entering the race, he made a contract with the other competitors that he would be bound by the rules of the race in return for their being equally bound. However, it is hard to find an offer and acceptance between the competitors: in agreeing to enter the race, each competitor dealt only with the yacht club, not the other competitors. Similarly, in the commercial sphere, deals may be done face to face without sequential offer and acceptance, and sometimes with little formality, particularly if they have to be concluded quickly or the counter-parties trust each other.

2.5   Secondly, in order to ascertain whether a contract has been formed, and if it has, what its terms are, we often do not focus on the parties' *actual* intentions. Instead we focus on what each party's intention reasonably *appeared to be* to the other party. In order to work out whether there was a valid offer in our car example, we ask whether it should have appeared to you that I was offering to sell my car, not whether it was my actual intention to do this. This is known as the principle of '*objective intention*' and is discussed further later. So a party might be bound by a contract even though this is the last thing she intends. As the Supreme Court emphasised in *RTS Flexible Systems Ltd v Molkerei Alois Müller GmbH & Co KG* (2010):

> Whether there is a binding contract between the parties and, if so, upon what terms depends upon what they have agreed. It depends not upon their subjective state of mind, but upon a consideration of what was communicated between them by words or conduct.

2.6   Thirdly, in working out whether there is a valid offer and acceptance, factors other than the apparent intention of the parties may also be relevant. We shall see this later in this chapter (see para **2.24**), when examining the distinction between an offer and an invitation to treat, and in Chapter 3 when examining the doctrine of intention to create legal relations. Leggatt J gave a nice example of the inter-relation between the latter doctrine and the objective identification of a valid offer in *Blue v Ashley* (2017), to which we will return in Chapter 3:

> There can be circumstances in which a person uses the language of offer without expressing a genuine willingness to be bound. For example, if someone says at a party

'I will give you a million pounds, if you can speak for a minute on [a random subject] without hesitation, deviation or repetition', this is unlikely to be interpreted as an offer despite the literal words used. That is because it is unlikely that anyone would reasonably have thought that the words were meant seriously.

2.7 Fourthly, in some contexts we are happy to impose duties and bestow rights upon the parties that they have not agreed to. For example, we imply terms into a contract, despite the fact that the parties have not agreed to such terms (see Chapter 7). Take our car example: while we might not have agreed that the car will be of a certain quality or even thought about the matter at the time of entering the contract, a term will be implied into the contract placing me under an obligation to provide a car of a satisfactory quality. Similarly, in some circumstances, statute permits us to strike down terms of the contract that seem unfair, despite the fact that the parties have agreed to such terms (see Chapter 8). Moreover, contract law is happy to give one party various remedies against the other party when the latter breaches a term of the contract, despite the fact that the parties have not agreed to any such remedies (see Chapters 16–18).

2.8 Finally, if we take such a strict approach, by always requiring an offer and acceptance, the result will often be that no contract will be found between the parties. This is problematic, because the law is very unclear as regards when one party will have to pay for work done by the other, if there is no contract between them (see Chapter 5 for more on this). Moreover, if there is no contract, one party cannot recover for loss caused to him by the other party because there is no contract between them to be breached.

2.9 The following lessons can be drawn from the discussion. The first is that there is no conceptual reason why a contract must consist of an offer and acceptance. A contract is a legal concept that we invent to help us explain the law, so we can give it whatever meaning we want. We can adopt a narrow view, by focusing solely on the parties' intent and always requiring offer and acceptance, or a broader approach, by not always requiring an offer and acceptance and more generally, by looking at factors other than the parties' intent in determining what duties and rights (if any) they should have under the law of contract. The issue is whether it is *helpful* to explain a particular situation in terms of contract. Does it help to explain the law better? Are the consequences of doing so desirable?

2.10 The second lesson is that 'offer and acceptance' is a helpful way of analysing many situations and the presence of an offer and acceptance is certainly *sufficient* to establish a contract (providing the requirements discussed in Chapters 4 and 6 are also fulfilled). However, it is not a *necessary* ingredient of a contract, so while acceptance is a helpful tool for working out whether there should be a contract, we do not need to try to fit all situations into an offer and acceptance framework in order to find a contract. This point will be demonstrated later in two specific contexts (see discussion of the 'battle of the forms' at para **2.108** and 'work done in anticipation of a main contract that fails to materialise' at para **2.117**).

2.11 A final, more general lesson is that there is nothing wrong with taking into account factors other than the parties' intent when working out whether there should be a contract and what rights and duties it should give rise to. We shall see at various points in the book, including this chapter, that this is something that the courts do all the time without controversy.

Two preliminary points

2.12 Two important points must be made before we can embark upon an examination of the specifics of offer and acceptance. The first has already been touched upon: the principle of 'objective intention'. A clear definition of the principle is put forward by Spencer (1973):

> Words are to be interpreted as they were reasonably understood by the man to whom they were spoken, not as they were understood by the man who spoke them.

The matter was famously put in the following terms by Blackburn J in *Smith v Hughes* (1871):

> If, whatever a man's real intention may be, he so conducts himself that a reasonable man would believe that he was assenting upon the terms proposed by the other party, and that other party upon that belief enters into the contract with him, the man thus conducting himself would be equally bound as if he had intended to agree to the other party's terms.

So if A makes a statement to B, we work out whether the statement is an offer (or acceptance) and if it is an offer, what its terms are, by asking how things would appear to a reasonable person in B's position, rather than by looking at A's actual intent (see *Crest Nicholson (Londinium) Ltd v Akaria Investments Ltd* (2010) and *Destiny 1 Ltd v Lloyds TSB Bank plc* (2011) for a useful re-affirmation of this).

2.13 The scope of the principle is a matter of some controversy. It is often referred to as a general, universal principle (for example, Smith (1979)) but it is submitted that its ambit is more restricted. To determine its proper ambit, we must first understand its purpose, which is to protect B, the party to whom the offer or acceptance in question is made, by allowing him to rely on A's apparent intent. It prevents A from turning around and saying that they did not have the intent which they appeared to have, that secretly they had a different intention. So it guards against surprise. Going back to our car example, say that my offer to sell you the car was just a joke on my part, but you had no way of telling this. If you sought to enforce the contract, but I denied that I had made an offer because I was only joking, then the court would hold that I had made an offer because *it reasonably appeared that way to you.*

2.14 From this rationale we can begin to articulate the circumstances in which the principle applies. The following conditions are necessary for its application:

- B must be seeking to hold A to A's apparent intent. B must be saying 'A appeared to mean this, so A should be held to this meaning.'

- B must have actually believed that A's apparent intent represented A's actual intent (see for example, *The Agrabele* (1987)). Indeed, this emerges from the quotation from *Smith v Hughes*. The purpose of the principle is to protect B by allowing him to assume that A means what A says. Therefore, there is no need to protect B in this way where B does not believe or assume that (see Vorster (1987)), a view supported obiter by Leggatt J in *Blue v Ashley* (2017), 'There is, at least arguably, a limitation on the objective nature of the test where one party's subjective intention is actually known to the other.'

- It must be possible to work out what the apparent intent of A was.

- It must not be B's fault that A appeared to agree to something that A did not actually intend to (*Scriven v Hindley* (1913), on which see Spencer (1973)). If B's offer was confusing in some way, A should not be bound by their apparent intent. If B has relied on A's apparent intent, A is effectively to blame and should have framed the offer more clearly.

- If the purpose of the principle is to allow B to rely on A's apparent intent, it has been suggested that it should be necessary to show that B has relied in some way: see Atiyah (1986a). English law has generally not explicitly required this (although see *The Hannah Blumenthal* (1983)) and it is submitted that its stance is correct. In the commercial world particularly, it is extremely important that A knows if, at what moment and on what terms they become legally bound. Accordingly, it is undesirable for A to have to keep B's actions under review in order to be able to spot if and when B has relied, and so tell if, when and on what terms a contract has been formed with.

2.15 Let us take four examples to illustrate how these conditions operate in practice. In *Moran v University of Salford* (1993), the University of Salford sent a letter to Mr Moran offering him a place on the Physiotherapy course, which Mr Moran accepted. However, the University claimed that it did not mean to offer him a place and that the offer was the result of a clerical error. The Court of Appeal held that at the very least there was a strong and clear case for saying that a contract had been formed. The University's apparent intent was clearly to offer Mr Moran a place, and this is the way that Mr Moran interpreted the letter.

2.16 In *Raffles v Wichelhaus* (1864) the parties agreed a sale of 125 bales of cotton, to be delivered from Bombay on a particular ship, the *Peerless*. Unfortunately, there were two ships with this name, leaving Bombay at different times. One party thought the agreement referred to the ship leaving in October, but the other thought it referred to the ship leaving in December. The claimant brought an action for the price. It was held that the fact that the meaning of the agreement was ambiguous was capable of giving a defence. While little reasoning was given by the court, its approach appears to have been as follows. It was not possible to work out what the apparent intent of the defendant was, so the objective principle did not apply and the court had to look at the actual intent of the parties. If the actual intention of one party was different from that of the other (as appeared to be the case in *Raffles*), there would be no contract.

2.17   In *Scriven v Hindley* (1913), the claimant was selling bales of hemp and bales of tow at auction. However, he did not make clear which lot was the hemp and which lot was the tow. The defendant, thinking he was bidding for the lot that contained the hemp, actually bid for the tow. It was held that there was no contract for the sale of the tow, because the defendant's apparent intent (to bid for the tow) had been caused by the claimant's carelessness in not making it clear which lot was which. Therefore, because the objective principle did not apply, the court looked at the parties' actual intention. The defendant's intention (to buy the hemp) did not coincide with the claimant's intention (to sell the defendant the tow) so there was no contract.

2.18   Finally, in *Maple Leaf Macro Volatility Master Fund v Rouvroy* (2009), the claimants and defendants signed a termsheet for the claimant to provide funding on specified terms to the defendants. The claimants argued that a contract had come into existence on signature, but the defendants denied this, claiming (among other things) they did not believe that signing the termsheet gave rise to a contract, because they contemplated that it was merely the first step in negotiating a more detailed written agreement. The court accepted that the defendants did not actually intend to enter into the contract on signature, but held that this was irrelevant, because it would have appeared to a reasonable observer that a contract was being concluded.

2.19   The second preliminary point is that a distinction must be drawn between two types of contract: *unilateral* contracts and *bilateral* contracts. The key difference is that only the latter type of contract places obligations upon and grants rights to *both* parties. Say I promise to pay you £100 if you run the London Marathon but make it clear that at no stage would you be under an obligation to do so. You take me up on my offer by running the marathon. What makes this a unilateral contract is that you make no promise so you are under no contractual obligations. You do not promise to run the marathon, so at no stage are you obliged to perform your side of the deal. Similarly, I have no right to have you run the marathon. In contrast, if both sides make promises, there is a bilateral contract. So if I promised to give you £100 if you promised to run the marathon, and you promised to do so, there would be a bilateral contract. You would be under a contractual obligation to run the marathon and I would have a right to have you run the marathon. So to decide whether the contract is a unilateral or a bilateral one, we must enquire whether both parties are promising to do something, or whether only one is doing so.

2.20   Although the offer of a reward for running the London marathon may sound quaint, many significant commercial transactions can be analysed as unilateral contracts, possibly including estate agency contracts (because the estate agent is not bound to find a purchaser but if he does so he will be entitled to commission, as Arden LJ explained in *Wells v Devani* (2016), albeit dissenting on the result). Another example is seen in *Rollerteam Ltd v Riley* (2017), where a family formerly in business together descended into feud, but then agreed by email to settle the feud by the defendants executing deeds of trust over property in the claimant's favour, in return for payment from the claimant. The deeds were executed, but the claimant did not pay. Henderson LJ in the Court of Appeal analysed the arrangement as a unilateral contract: '[the claimant] was in effect saying to [the defendant]: "If you execute the two declarations of trust, I will regard myself as bound to make the payments, and fulfil the other obligations, set out in my email". (The nub of the decision was that the claimant's cheeky attempt to avoid making the payment failed—he had argued that the agreement was void because it fell foul of the statutory requirement that contracts for the disposition of an interest in land are only valid if made by signed writing, but the court held that the statute does not apply to executed unilateral arrangements of this kind.)

Is there an offer?

2.21   As discussed at the start of the chapter, an offer is an indication of one party's willingness to enter into a contract with the party to whom it is addressed, as soon as the latter accepts its terms. It has two key features. First, it indicates that the offeror intends to be legally bound providing that the party to whom the statement is addressed takes certain steps. Second, it contains not only a promise to do something, but also lays down what the offeree must do in return.

2.22   A number of consequences flow from the first feature. One is that, as long as the offeror evinces an intention to be legally bound, it does not matter how many people she makes the offer to. Therefore, a party can make an offer to the whole world if she so desires. In *Carlill v Carbolic Smoke Ball Co* (1893), the defendants were the proprietors of a medical preparation called the 'carbolic smoke ball'. They inserted an advertisement in the newspapers which included the following wording: '£100 reward will be paid by the Carbolic Smoke Ball Company to any person who contracts the increasing epidemic influenza, colds, or any disease caused by taking cold after having used the ball three times daily for two weeks according to the printed directions supplied with each ball. £1,000 is deposited with the Alliance Bank Regent's Street, showing our sincerity in the matter.' The advertisement then went on to describe the efficacious qualities of the smoke ball, stating that one ball would last a family several months and that they cost only ten shillings each. Mrs Carlill, the plaintiff, bought a smoke ball at her local chemists on the faith of this advertisement. She used it as directed three times a day for six weeks, whereupon she was attacked by influenza. She sued the Company for £100. The Company, no doubt because they had a considerable number of other such claims, contested that the advertisement could not give rise to any legal liability on their part.

2.23   One of the arguments made on the Company's behalf was that holding that there was a contract with the claimant would mean that the Company had contracted with everybody in the world, because the advert was addressed to the whole world. This argument was given short shrift by the Court of Appeal:

> It is not a contract made with all the world. There is the fallacy of the argument. It is an offer made to all the world; and why should not an offer be made to all the world

which is to ripen into a contract with anybody who comes forward and performs the condition? (per Bowen LJ)

It was held that a reasonable member of the public reading the advert would believe that the Company intended to be bound by the terms stated in the advert, so the advert was a valid offer.

2.24 A further consequence is that a distinction is drawn between *offers* and *invitations to treat*. Whereas the former demonstrates an intention on the part of the person making the statement to be automatically legally bound if the other party accepts the terms of the statement, the latter does not: it contemplates further negotiations taking place before any contract is formed. In our car example at the start of the chapter, I ask you if you would buy the car for £100. I am clearly indicating my willingness to be legally bound to sell you my car if you agree to the terms of my statement, so I am making an *offer*. Varying the facts, say that instead I tell you 'if you are interested in my car, you can make me an offer for it'. Here, I do not intend to be automatically legally bound if you comply with the terms of my statement, by offering me a price for the car. I envisage further negotiations taking place between us to decide what price the car should be sold for before any contract will be concluded, so my statement is only an *invitation to treat*: I am inviting you to make an offer, not making an offer of my own.

2.25 Let us take an example of this distinction in operation. While negotiating, one party may make a provisional bid or the parties may reach a provisional agreement. However, they do not intend to be legally bound by the terms of the bid or the contents of the agreement and contemplate further negotiations to work out the terms of the final contract. Therefore, they will often make clear that the initial bid or agreement is 'subject to contract' to emphasise clearly that they do not intend to be legally bound at this stage, whether expressly (for example, *Carlton Communications and Granada Media plc v The Football League* (2002)) or implicitly (for example, *Grant v Bragg* (2009)). The effect of 'subject to contract' wording is discussed further at paras **3.17–3.18**.

2.26 Unfortunately, in many situations, it is not clear whether and if so at what stage each party intends to be legally bound. For example, if goods are displayed in a shop window, it may be hard to tell whether the shop is making an offer or just inviting customers to make an offer to buy the goods. This is problematic, because clarity is important in such everyday situations. Therefore, in standard situations like these, the law lays down general rules to help solve the problem. In doing so, it seems that the courts look to factors other than the parties' intent, as was hinted at in the discussion at the start of the chapter.

Display of goods for sale

2.27 The general rule here is that the display only constitutes an invitation to treat, whether it is a display in a shop window (*Timothy v Simpson* (1834)) or on a shelf inside the shop (see next paragraph). Therefore, it is the customer who makes the offer to buy the goods and the shop has a choice whether to accept this offer or not (subject to anti-discrimination legislation). For example, *Pharmaceutical Society of Great Britain v Boots Cash Chemists (Southern) Ltd* (1953) concerned s 18(1)(a)(iii) of the Pharmacy and Poisons Act 1933, which prohibited the sale of poisons except where the sale was effected by or under the supervision of a registered pharmacist. The claimant was the Pharmaceutical Society, which had a duty to take reasonable steps to enforce the Act. The claimant argued that the display of the drug on the shelf in the self-service shop was an offer which was accepted when the purchaser put the drug in his basket, so the sale was carried out without any involvement of the pharmacist, contrary to the Act. The Court of Appeal held that the display was merely an invitation to treat, and it was the prospective purchaser who made the offer by presenting the goods at the cash desk, so the Act was not infringed. A similar approach was taken in the context of a display in a shop window in *Fisher v Bell* (1961).

2.28   Is this general rule correct? A number of reasons have been put forward to justify it. Unger (1953) argues that were the display to constitute an offer, there might be a larger number of customers accepting the offer than the shopkeeper would be able to supply. However, as many have noted, there is an easy solution to this problem: the offer could be construed as only being open while stocks last or imply a term to this effect (see Chapter 7). Second, it is sometimes argued that if a display were an offer, the customer would accept the offer by putting the goods in his basket, so a contract would be made at this point and the customer would not be able to change his mind and put the goods back (see Lord Goddard CJ at first instance in *Boots* and a similar argument by Somervell LJ in the Court of Appeal). However, this is not the case. We could equally say that if the display is an offer, the customer only accepts it when he presents the goods at the cash desk. Indeed, putting the goods in your basket could not be an acceptance because the customer reserves the right to change his mind, so he does not demonstrate an unequivocal intention to accept the offer at this stage.

2.29   A better objection is that holding the display to constitute an offer removes the shop's freedom to decide which of its customers it wants to sell its goods to: as Winfield (1939) commented, 'a shop is a place for bargaining, not for compulsory sales'. However, this view is becoming increasingly out of date, as the law increasingly focuses on the protection of consumers. A consumer would probably be surprised to learn that a shopkeeper was generally not obliged to sell him goods at the marked price (see Atiyah and Smith (2006)). Indeed, if we look closely at the *Boots* decision, its force as a precedent is slightly diminished by the particular context of the case, a statutory prohibition. As Somervell LJ commented, '[i]t is right that I should emphasise, as did the Lord Chief Justice, that these are not dangerous drugs'.

2.30   As a final point, it should be noted that this general rule can be departed from when it is clear from the display that the shop intends to be bound if the customer accepts the terms of the display. For example, say the display read 'Try our new chocolate bar. It's yours as soon as you present it at the cash desk with your 50p.' This would indicate a clear intent to be legally bound as soon as a customer presented the chocolate bar at the checkout with the money.

Advertisements

2.31 The same general rule unsurprisingly applies to advertisements (*Partridge v Crittenden* (1968)). Again, this general rule will be displaced if the advert indicates a willingness to be automatically bound to those who perform the acts stated in the advert. For example, in *Carlill* (the facts of which are set out at para **2.22**), it was held that the advert indicated that the £100 would be paid to those who fulfilled the conditions set out in the advert. One factor that weighed particularly heavily with the Court of Appeal was the fact that the advert said that £1,000 had been deposited with the bank for the purpose of paying those who fulfilled the conditions, indicating the seriousness of their willingness to pay the money.

2.32 *Carlill* was applied in *Bowerman v Association of British Travel Agents Ltd* (1996), where the issue was whether a notice displayed in the offices of members of the Association of British Travel Agents ('ABTA') stating that ABTA would reimburse holiday makers in certain circumstances created a contract between ABTA and people who had booked a holiday with ABTA members. The Court of Appeal held that it did, Hobhouse LJ commenting that the arguments put forward by ABTA 'echo in almost every respect those rejected by the Court of Appeal more than a century ago [in *Carlill*]'. He regarded the wording of the notice as clear and imposing an unqualified obligation on ABTA. Moreover, there is a well-known risk in the travel industry that operators will become insolvent, so that a statement that ABTA would protect holiday makers in such situations would be very important to those booking holidays and choosing the agent or operator through which they should book. Realising this, ABTA had made it a cornerstone of the promotion of their members to emphasise how ABTA would protect holiday makers, and the words 'ABTA promises' were often used by ABTA's president in interviews.

2.33 Similarly, in the well-known decision of the Supreme Court of Minnesota in *Lefkowitz v Great Minneapolis Surplus Stores Inc* (1957), the defendant published the following advert in a newspaper: 'Saturday 9.a.m. sharp, 3 Brand New Fur Coats Worth to $100.00, First Come First Served, $1 each'. It was held that 'the offer by the defendant of the sale of the Lapin fur was clear, definite and explicit, and left nothing open to negotiation' and therefore constituted an offer rather than an invitation to treat.

2.34 Chitty (2016) makes the interesting point that while advertisements of unilateral contracts are commonly held to be offers (as in *Carlill* and *Bowerman*, for example), the courts are less willing to find that an advertisement of a bilateral contract will constitute an offer. Two reasons are offered for this. First, the latter sort of advertisement is often intended to lead to further bargaining. For example, if I advertise my house for sale (an advert to enter into a bilateral contract, a contract of sale), then I probably envisage that there may be negotiation over the price before a contract is entered into. Second, a bilateral contract requires the offeree to promise to do something, so the offeror will naturally wish to assure himself that the offeree is able, financially or otherwise, to perform the contract. If an advert of a bilateral contract were held to be an offer which would automatically create a contract when accepted by the person receiving it, the offeror would not be able to do this, but would be bound regardless.

Rewards

2.35 An advert offering a reward for doing some act, like finding my lost dog, will often be construed as an offer (for example, see *Gibbons v Proctor* (1891)). This situation is discussed further at paras **2.59–2.62**.

Tenders

2.36 The general rule is that if someone invites parties to tender or bid for a particular project, this indicates that he is inviting the parties to make offers for him to consider. Therefore, his statement is generally an invitation to treat, not an offer. In *Spencer v Harding* (1870) the defendants sent out a circular saying that '[w]e are instructed to offer to the wholesale trade for sale by tender the stock in trade of Messrs. G. Eilbeck & Co'. It was held that this was not an offer:

> Here there is a total absence of any words to intimate that the highest bidder is to be the purchaser. It is a mere attempt to ascertain whether an offer can be obtained within such a margin as the sellers are willing to adopt.

However, this general rule will be displaced if it appears that the maker of the statement intended to make an offer. So in *Spencer* itself, the court stated that had the circular gone on to say 'and we undertake to sell to the highest bidder', this would have constituted an offer to sell to the highest bidder, to be accepted by making the highest bid.

2.37 Similarly, in *Harvela Investments Ltd v Royal Trust Co of Canada (CI) Ltd* (1986), D1 invited the claimant and D2 to make confidential bids for some shares and promised to accept the highest bid made in accordance with the terms laid down by D1. The claimant bid $2,175,000, while D2 bid $2,100,000 'or $101,000 in excess of any other bid which you may receive … whichever is the higher'. D1 accepted D2's bid as a bid of $2,276,000 and entered into a contract with them for the sale of the shares. The claimant claimed that D1 were contractually bound to transfer the shares to them and succeeded in the House of Lords. It was held that D1's invitation constituted an offer to enter into a contract for the sale of the shares with the highest bidder. Here, D1's invitation implicitly required the bids to be of a fixed figure, so D2's bid was really only $2,100,000 and it was the claimant who was in fact the highest bidder.

2.38 Finally, sometimes a statement inviting tenders will be construed as an offer with slightly different terms, namely that if a bid is properly submitted in accordance with the terms of the invitation, it is promised that the bid would be considered. So it is an offer just to *consider* bids properly submitted, not an offer to *accept* a bid fulfilling particular conditions.

2.39 These propositions emerge from the case of *Blackpool and Fylde Aero Club Ltd v Blackpool BC* (1990). Blackpool Borough Council ('the Council') invited BFAC and others to submit tenders for a pleasure flight concession from Blackpool airport, BFAC having held the concession since 1975. The invitation stated that the Council 'do not bind themselves to accept all or any part of any tender' and that 'no tender which is received after the last date and time specified shall be admitted for consideration'. The tender deadline was 12 noon on 17 March. BFAC posted their tender at 11 a.m. on that day in the Town Hall post box, which was meant to be cleared each day at noon. However, it was not checked on 17 March and BFAC's tender was dismissed as late. The Court of Appeal held that the Council was in breach of contract. While the Council was under no obligation to accept a particular tender, providing its decision not to do so was bona fide and honest (see *Fairclough Building Ltd v Borough Council of Port Talbot* (1993) for an application of this proposition), the invitation provided impliedly that if BFAC conformed to its terms they were entitled to have their tender considered. The reason for this finding emerges most clearly from the following passage of Bingham LJ:

> where, as here, tenders are solicited from selected parties all of them known to the invitor, and where a local authority's invitation prescribes a clear, orderly and familiar procedure (draft contract conditions available for inspection and plainly not open to negotiation, a prescribed common form of tender, the supply of envelopes designed to preserve the absolute anonymity of tenderers and clearly to identify the tender in question and an absolute deadline) the invitee is in my judgment protected at least to this extent: if he submits a conforming tender before the deadline he is entitled, not as a matter of mere expectation but of contractual right, to be sure that his tender will after the deadline be opened and considered in conjunction with all other conforming tenders or at least that his tender will be considered if others are.

This passage, coupled with Bingham LJ's acceptance that 'contracts are not to be lightly implied', suggests that such an offer will only be implied in limited circumstances. For example, in *Fairclough*, where the invitation in question was held to constitute an offer in the same terms as that in *Blackpool and Fylde*, only a shortlist of six parties were invited to tender for the work, and there was a clearly defined procedure which they had to comply with.

Auctions

2.40   Two types of auction must be distinguished for our purposes: auctions 'with reserve' and auctions 'without reserve'. Where a reserve price is stated, inviting bids to be made constitutes an invitation to treat. The bidders are the ones making offers, and the offer is accepted by the auctioneer bringing down his hammer (*British Car Auctions v Wright* (1972) and Sale of Goods Act 1979, s 57(2)). The auctioneer acts as agent for a vendor, so when the hammer is brought down, a contract (of sale) is made between the highest bidder and the vendor.

2.41   In the latter case, where no reserve price is stated, matters are not so simple. It was suggested *obiter* by Martin B in *Warlow v Harrison* (1859) that it is the auctioneer who makes the offer to sell the goods to the highest bidder, and that this offer is accepted as soon as the highest bid is made. This suggestion proved controversial (see Slade (1952), Gower (1952), and Slade (1953)). However, this approach was taken by the Court of Appeal in *Barry v Davies* (2001) where the auctioneer did not accept the claimant's bid, despite it being the highest. While the decision resolves much of the uncertainty surrounding *Warlow*, it does not deal with the issue of when exactly the offer was made by the auctioneer (because it was not necessary for the court to decide this). There are two possibilities: either it is made when the auction is advertised or it is made when the auctioneer actually puts up the goods for sale at the auction. Either way, the Court of Appeal in *Barry v Davies* controversially held the auctioneer liable in damages for breach of contract (even though he was not the owner of the goods on sale).

Timetables

2.42 The question of when a contract to transport a person is concluded is one to which the law currently gives no clear answer. Some cases suggest that the timetable itself constitutes an offer (*Wilkie v LPTB* (1947)), which is accepted by the passenger's indication that she wishes to travel (for example, by buying the ticket or getting on a London bus). Some cases suggest that matters are different when the journey is booked in advance and that a mere indication by the passenger that she is willing to travel is not always enough to form a contract. For example, *Cockerton v Naviera Aznar SA* (1960) suggests that when a journey is booked, the contract is entered into when the tickets are received by the passengers, Streatfeild J commenting that '[n]obody booking a passage on a ship (or on a railway train) considers that he has a perfected contract merely by paying the passage money. It is the receipt of the ticket in exchange which, in my judgment, clinches the bargain.' It seems from this case that it was the passenger who made the offer by booking the journey. This uncertainty is unfortunate because the time at which the contract is formed may have important consequences for the parties. For example, it may determine whether an exclusion clause formed part of the contract (see further paras **7.30–7.32**).

Other everyday transactions

2.43 The position is also far from clear in respect of many other everyday transactions. For example, is a menu displayed outside a restaurant an invitation to treat or an offer? Chitty (2016) suggests the former interpretation but as yet there do not appear to be any cases directly in point. Such cases will ultimately turn on the court's assessment of the apparent intent of the parties.

2.44 A number of cases have dealt with transactions involving automated machines. For example, in *Thornton v Shoe Lane Parking* (1971), the claimant drove up to the entrance of a garage, and after receiving a ticket from the machine, drove into the garage and parked his car. It was suggested by Lord Denning MR that 'the offer was contained in the notice at the entrance giving the charges for garaging' and '[t]he offer was accepted when Mr Thornton drove up to the entrance and, by the movement of his car, turned the light from red to green, and the ticket was thrust at him'. As he vividly put it:

> The customer pays his money and gets a ticket. He cannot refuse it. He cannot get his money back. He may protest to the machine, even swear at it. But it will remain

unmoved. He is committed beyond recall. He was committed at the very moment when he put his money into the machine. The contract was concluded at that time. It can be translated into offer and acceptance in this way: the offer is made when the proprietor of the machine holds it out as being ready to receive the money. The acceptance takes place when the customer puts his money into the slot.

Similarly, in the case of a vending machine, it would seem that the display of the machine (for example, the machine offers a particular drink for 50p) constitutes an offer. However, there would only seem to be an acceptance once you become unable to get your money back from the machine; only at this moment are you 'committed beyond recall' and do you demonstrate an unequivocal intent to accept.

Communication of offer

2.45   In order for the offer to be effective, English law requires the offer to be communicated to the offeree. This is the flip side of the requirement that the offeree must be aware of the offer in order to accept it, a requirement which will be discussed in detail later.

When will an offer be terminated?

2.46   An offer cannot be accepted once it is validly terminated. There are three ways in which an offer can be terminated: by an act of the offeror, by an act of the offeree or by some other method.

Termination by the offeror

2.47   The offeror can withdraw the offer at any time before it is accepted. Generally, this withdrawal must be brought to the attention of the other party in order to make it effective, so the rule becomes that a withdrawal must generally be communicated to the offeree before the latter accepts it in order to validly withdraw the offer (*Dickinson v Dodds* (1875–6)).

Two contrasting examples can be given. In *Dickinson*, Dodds offered to sell Dickinson his house for £800 on Wednesday 10 June 1874 and promised to keep the offer open until 9 a.m. on the Friday. He withdrew the offer on the Thursday but Dickinson tried to accept the offer at 7 a.m. on the Friday. The Court of Appeal held that the offer had not been accepted by Dickinson because it had been validly withdrawn before he could do so. On the other hand, in *Byrne & Co v Van Tienhoven* (1880), an offer was made on 11 October and accepted on this date. The defendants attempted to withdraw the offer at some later date, probably 20 October (it was not necessary for the court to decide on the exact date). It was held that the attempt to withdraw the offer was ineffective because it had already been accepted.

2.48 Similarly, in the Court of Appeal decision *Grant v Bragg* (2009), having made an offer to buy shares, the buyer's agent told the potential seller that the offer had to be accepted by 4 p.m. on a particular day. The seller purported to accept the offer two days later and the court held that this was too late, so that there was no contract.

2.49 Some have criticised the law here for allowing an offeror to go back on his promise to keep the offer open for a certain amount of time. Indeed, the Law Revision Committee recommended back in 1937 that such a promise should be enforceable by the offeree (Sixth Interim Report, Cmd 5449 (1937); see also Law Commission Working Paper No 60 (1975)). Spence (1999) points out that offerees may rely to their detriment on the promise, for example by incurring expense or legal liability to another, only to find the promise withdrawn before they accept it. Spence suggests that the answer is to apply the doctrine of equitable estoppel (on estoppel generally see para **5.70** onwards) to the situation in order to compensate the offeree. However, it is submitted that the current state of the law here can be defended and the courts have shown little reluctance in applying the principle laid down in *Dickinson* (see, for example, *Scammell v Dicker* (2001)). If it is the act of reliance by the offeree that makes the offeror's promise binding, it will be difficult for the offeror to know if his promise has become binding upon him. Moreover, before relying on the promise, the offeree could protect himself from withdrawal of the offer by making it irrevocable, either by accepting the offer or negotiating a contract to keep it open for a certain period of time. As for the Law Revision Committee's suggestion that such a promise should be binding when made, irrespective of whether there is reliance or not, it is unclear why an exception to the doctrine of consideration (see Chapter 5) should be made in this particular case.

2.50 Two further points require consideration. First, in order to communicate the withdrawal to the offeree, the offeror does not always have to actually make the offeree aware of the withdrawal. For example, if the offer was made to the public, say in a newspaper, it will be validly withdrawn if reasonable steps are taken to bring the withdrawal to the attention of prospective offerees, such as by publishing a retraction in the paper (see the American case of *Shuey v US* (1875)). Similarly, if the offer has been made to a business, and a withdrawal is sent to the business, it will be taken to have been communicated when it would normally have been read (or listened to) in the ordinary course of business (*The Brimnes* (1975)). Therefore, for example, the fact that the staff at the offeree company do not read their e-mails or post at all will not prevent a court holding that the withdrawal has been communicated.

2.51 Second, *Dickinson* suggests that it need not be the offeror who communicates the withdrawal; it is sufficient that the offeree receives the information from someone:

> *Of course it may well be that the one man is bound in some way or other to let the other man know that his mind with regard to the offer has been changed; but in this case, beyond all question, the Plaintiff knew that Dodds was no longer minded to sell the property to him as plainly and clearly as if Dodds had told him (per James LJ).*

The judgment leaves it slightly unclear whether there will *always* be a valid withdrawal where the offeree receives the information from a source other than the offeror or an agent of the offeror. It is submitted that the answer should be in the negative. Allowing a third party to communicate the information places the offeree in a difficult position, because he has to evaluate the reliability of the source. If, for example, the offeree in *Dickinson* had been told by a sometimes unreliable source that the offeror had withdrawn the offer: should he believe him or should he try to accept the offer? Moreover, it is unfair to place the offeree in this position when it is easy for the offeror to inform the offeree of the withdrawal directly or through an agent (as in *Grant v Bragg* (2009)). Indeed, we require such direct communication of the *acceptance* of an offer (see para **2.90**).

2.52 The court in *Dickinson* appeared to believe that the offeree was sure that the information he received about the withdrawal was reliable. It is suggested that, for these reasons, communication by the offeree or his agent should be required in all cases, except where (as in *Dickinson*) the offeror can show that the offeree was informed by a very trustworthy source of the withdrawal and the offeree believed it. Indeed, this is supported by *Cartwright v Hoogstoel* (1911), where the offer was held to be withdrawn because the withdrawal had clearly been brought to the offeree's attention by a trustworthy source, whom the offeree believed.

Rejection by the offeree

2.53 If the offeree rejects the offer, this will terminate it, so the offeree cannot later accept it. Seeking to explore the terms of the offer is one thing, but refusing the offer or making a counter-offer is another (*Grant v Bragg* (2009)).

Other methods of termination

2.54 Two other methods of termination deserve particular attention. First, the offer may be terminated by the passage of time. If the offer is expressed to last only for a set period, it will terminate upon the expiration of this period. If the duration of the offer is not specified, it will terminate after a reasonable time has passed (*Ramsgate Victoria Hotel Co v Montefiore* (1866)). Second, while it was suggested in *Dickinson* that the death of either party should terminate the offer, this is far from clear. It is suggested that death should only terminate an offer if the offer provides for this to happen, such as where the proposed contract involves personal considerations so that it would be inappropriate for a contract to be formed between parties other than the original offeror and offeree (see *Coulthart v Clementson* (1870) and Chitty (2016)). An example would be an offer to paint a portrait of the offeree.

Acceptance

2.55 An acceptance is a clear indication of the offeree's unqualified agreement to the terms of the offer in the manner set out in the offer. A number of preliminary points need to be made.

2.56 First, in determining whether or not an acceptance has been made, we apply the principle of 'objective intention' (see para **2.12**), so we ask whether it would have appeared to a reasonable person in the offeror's shoes that the offeree was accepting the offer.

Second, you can only accept an offer that (on an objective interpretation of the offeror's intention) has been made to you. This requirement will be discussed in greater depth in Chapter 3.

The law reports are full of cases applying these two simple points, a recent example being the Privy Council decision in *Hall v Maritek Bahamas Ltd* (2015).

2.57 Third, the requirement that the acceptance be unqualified means that if the offeree's statement seeks to vary any of the terms of the offer, it generally cannot constitute a valid acceptance. The acceptance must correspond to the terms of the offer. If the offeree's statement seeks to vary the terms of the offer, the offeree will be taken to have rejected the original offer and be making an offer of his own, known as a 'counter-offer'. In *Hyde v Wrench* (1840), for example, W offered to sell his farm to H for £1,000, but H responded that he would give £950. After W had rejected this suggestion, H attempted to accept the original offer of £1,000, but W would not let him. It was held that H's offer to buy for £950 meant that he rejected W's £1,000 offer and made a counter-offer of his own. Accordingly, the £1,000 offer was terminated and could not be accepted at a later date. The principle that a counter-offer terminates the original offer has a sound basis, because it ensures that original offerors know where they stand. For example, in *Hyde*, once W has received the counter-offer, he knows that his original offer can no longer be accepted so he is free to sell the farm to another person. Moreover, it prevents the original offeree holding the original offeror to ransom. If the principle had not applied, H could have made a number of counter-offers of less than £1,000 in the hope that W would agree to one of them, while all the time reserving the right to accept W's initial £1,000 offer.

2.58 Two qualifications must be made to this principle. It is important to note that the offeror will only make a counter-offer if she actually puts forward terms that are different to those in the original offer. So if she merely enquires as to what the terms of the offer are (*Stevenson, Jacques & Co v McLean* (1880)), she will be taken to be exploring what the terms of the original offer are (*Gibson v Manchester CC* (1979)) rather than varying its terms, so no counter-offer will have been made. Further, in some situations, the original offeror, in replying to the counter-offer, might be taken to reaffirm the original offer (see the Canadian decisions in *Livingstone v Evans* (1925) and *Re Cowan & Boyd* (1921)). For example, in *Hyde* Wrench might have responded to Hyde's counter-offer in the following way: 'I am prepared to sell to you for £1,000 but not a penny less.' The effect of this would be to make an offer on the same terms as the original offer.

Must the offeree know of the offer in order to accept it?

2.59 This issue has arisen in a number of cases in which a reward was offered in return for information. While the position is far from clear, it appears that English law requires the offeree to know of the offer in order to validly accept it. So if I offer a reward of £100 to anyone who returns my lost dog, and, without knowing of the offer, you return my dog, you cannot claim the £100. *Gibbons v Proctor* (1891) has often been relied upon in the past to support the proposition that knowledge is not required, but it seems that the offeree in that case did actually know of the offer. Similarly, in the other principal English case on the issue, *Williams v Carwardine* (1833), the offeree knew of the offer.

2.60 Is it correct in principle to require the offeree to know of the offer in order to be able to accept it? Arguably the offeree should not be able to claim that there is a contract if he did not have knowledge of the offer at the time when he did the act said to constitute an acceptance of the offer. He did not intend to accept the offer and therefore had no expectations of being able to claim the money, so why should he be entitled to it? Let us view the situation in terms of the principle of objective interpretation. Can the offeree say that his act or statement constituted an acceptance on the ground that this is how it reasonably appeared to the offeror? The answer is no: as we saw, the purpose of the objective principle is to protect the party to whom a statement is made (here the offeror), not the party who made it. Therefore, we should look at the offeree's subjective intention to determine whether he can claim that he accepted the offer. He did not *actually* intend to accept the offer, so there is no justification for allowing the offeree to claim that there is a contract here.

2.61 However, a number of commentators have argued that in the case of offers to enter into a unilateral contract, such as in the reward cases, the offeree should be able to claim that there is a contract even though they had no knowledge of the offer at the relevant time (for example, Hudson (1968) and Chitty (2016)). Hudson puts forward a number of arguments. First, he argues that 'the offeror will have got whatever he wanted and will merely be called upon to give the return that he proclaimed that he would be prepared to give' so 'it would seem a wholly undeserved benefit to him to free him from legal obligation'. Hudson's first point seems to rest on the assumption that for the offeror to get for free what he was prepared to pay for is a 'wholly undeserved benefit'. This is not necessarily the case.

2.62 Take *Gibbons*: imagine that instead of the claimant providing the information, the perpetrator had confessed or the defendant had happened across the information herself by pure chance. In these circumstances we would be happy to let the defendant have the benefit for free, and would not have regarded it as an undeserved benefit. Secondly, Hudson argues that it would be 'contrary to the offeror's own expectations' to deny the offeree the reward. However, it is unlikely that the offeror gave any thought to whether the offeree should be able to claim the reward if he did not know about it when doing the act in question. Moreover, as argued (para **2.60**), the key point is that the *offeree* had no expectation of getting a reward at the time he carried out the act, so there is no need to protect him.

Hudson further argues that allowing offerees to recover even if they do not know of the offer at the time will encourage, or at least not discourage, those socially valuable acts for which rewards may be expected to be offered. However, it is questionable how many people will be sufficiently aware of the finer details of the law of contract, so it is unlikely that the change in the law advocated by Hudson would have any great effect. Certainly it is not by itself a sufficient justification for changing the law.

2.63 A further issue is whether, in addition to the knowledge requirement, there is an additional requirement that the acceptance must be at least partly motivated or induced by
the offer. As Mitchell and Phillips (2002) have demonstrated, English law does not seem
to recognise this requirement, despite a statement to the contrary in *Lark v Outhwaite*
(1991). In *Williams*, for example, the court remarked that '[i]f the person knows of the
[offer] and does the thing, that is quite enough' (per Littledale J) and that '[w]e cannot
go into the [claimant's] motives' (per Patteson J). Unfortunately, *Williams* was not cited
in *Lark*. It is submitted that there should not be a motive requirement. Apart from the
fact that it is very difficult to ascertain someone's motives, a person can intend to accept
an offer without being motivated by it, as Mitchell and Phillips (2002) point out.

Communication of the acceptance

2.64 In *Brinkibon Ltd v Stahag Stahl und Stahlwarengesellschaft mbH* (1983) Lord Wilberforce
said:

> The general rule, it is hardly necessary to state, is that a contract is formed when accept-
> ance of an offer is communicated by the offeree to the offeror.

While this may seem straightforward, it begs the question of when an acceptance will be
taken to have been 'communicated'. Imagine I leave a message on your answer phone but
you never listen to it: has it been 'communicated' to you and if so, when?

2.65 To answer this question, we must understand why we require an offeree to take steps to
bring an acceptance to the offeror's attention at all. Why is it not enough that I intend in
my own mind to accept the offer? The answer is that we want to give some protection and
certainty to offerors: they need to know when an offer has been accepted so that they know
if they have entered into a contract or not. Therefore, in order to strike a balance between
the interests of the offeror and the offeree, we should require the offeree to take all reasonable steps, using whatever mode of communication is permitted by the offer, to bring the
acceptance to the attention of the offeror. This is the key to understanding the discussion
that follows: the more specific rules that we shall examine are really just ways of giving
effect to this principle. Offerors can increase their protection by stating in their offer that
the acceptance must actually be brought to their attention, but if they do not, the law will
take into account their interests by imposing this requirement upon the offeree. We are
now ready to investigate the specific rules governing particular modes of communication.

Postal acceptances

2.66 If the offeree accepts by post, the general rule is that the offer will be accepted when the
letter is *posted*, not when it reaches the offeror (*Adams v Lindsell* (1818)). This is known
as the 'postal rule'. Whatever the reasons for the emergence of the principle in the first
place (on which see Gardner (1992)), it can be justified on the basis that if both parties

contemplate that the post may be used, on posting the letter the offeree has done all that she can be reasonably expected to do to bring the acceptance to the offeror's attention. Once she puts the letter in the post box, the rest is out of her hands. As we shall see, one of the consequences of the postal rule is that the offer may have been validly accepted even if the letter never reaches the offeror. Some suggest that such consequences make the postal rule unfair and that it should be the responsibility of the offeree to ensure that the letter reaches its destination. However, the offeror controls the terms of the offer so can stipulate that the acceptance must be communicated in a particular manner. If he does not do so, it could be argued that he only has himself to blame.

2.67 The first question is when the rule applies. *Henthorn v Fraser* (1892) provides an answer. In *Henthorn*, the claimant, who lived at Birkenhead, called at the office of a land society in Liverpool, to negotiate for the purchase of some houses belonging to them. The secretary signed and handed to him a note giving him the option of purchase for 14 days at £750. On the next day the secretary posted to the claimant a withdrawal of the offer. This withdrawal was posted between 12 and 1 p.m., and did not reach Birkenhead until after 5 p.m. In the meantime the claimant had, at 3.50 p.m, posted to the secretary an unconditional acceptance of the offer, which was delivered in Liverpool after the society's office had closed, and was opened by the secretary on the following morning. The claimant sought specific performance (see Chapter 17) of the contract, claiming he had accepted the offer before it had been withdrawn. In the Court of Appeal, Lord Herschell laid down the following test for determining when the postal rule should apply:

> Where the circumstances are such that it must have been within the contemplation of the parties that, according to the ordinary usages of mankind, the post might be used as a means of communicating the acceptance of an offer, the acceptance is complete as soon as it is posted.

On the facts, it was held that the rule did apply. The distance between the two parties, one living in Liverpool, the other in Birkenhead, and the fact that the acceptance would be expected to be written, because the subject of the purchase was real estate, meant 'that both parties contemplated that a letter sent by post was a mode by which the acceptance might be communicated' (per Kay LJ).

2.68 *Henthorn* suggests that even though an offer is made orally, where immediate acceptance is not contemplated and the parties live at a distance, the postal rule will apply. However, with the evolution of modern, quicker forms of communication such as e-mail and the telephone, it becomes less likely that the parties will contemplate a postal acceptance because these newer methods of communication will bring the acceptance to the offeror's attention more rapidly.

2.69 Even if the parties contemplate that postal acceptance might be used, the postal rule will not always apply. In *Holwell Securities Ltd v Hughes* (1974), the claimant was granted an option on 19 October 1971 to buy some of the defendant's property. Clause 2 of the agreement stated that the option 'shall be exercisable by notice in writing to the [defendant] at any time within six months from the date hereof'. The claimant posted an attempted acceptance, properly addressed and prepaid, on 14 April 1972 but it was never delivered to the defendant. It was held by the Court of Appeal that the offer had not been validly accepted before it terminated at the end of the six-month period. The court explained that where the offer requires actual communication of the acceptance, the postal rule will not apply, even though it is in the contemplation of the parties that an acceptance might be made by post. Where the offer does not *expressly* require actual communication, the court will be willing to infer such a requirement if applying the postal rule would lead to inconvenient or absurd consequences.

2.70   As Gardner (1992) observes, *Holwell* demonstrates a dislike of the postal rule, Russell LJ referring to 'this artificial concept of communication by the act of posting'. On the facts, it was held that the phrase 'notice in writing to' the defendant meant that the written document had to be communicated or notified to the defendant and was inconsistent with the application of the rule that the mere posting of the document was sufficient. This dislike manifests itself in the willingness of the court to hold that the offer was in-consistent with its application. Therefore, after *Holwell*, it seems that the courts will often be willing to disapply the postal rule. In an age of instantaneous forms of communica-tion, the postal rule is increasingly seen as being out of date.

2.71   Two other issues require attention. First, if the postal acceptance is properly addressed and posted, the postal rule will apply even if the acceptance is delayed in the post or never reaches its destination (*Household Fire Insurance Co Ltd v Grant* (1879)). While this seems hard on the offeror, who may well mistakenly believe that her offer has not been accepted so she is free to contract with others, it may be argued that the offeree has taken all reasonable steps to ensure that the letter reaches the offeror. Against this, it could be said that the offeree should be expected to check that the letter has reached its destination. However, arguably it should be the responsibility of the offeror to enquire as to what has happened to the letter if it does not arrive, as it is she who expects a response to her offer but does not receive it.

2.72   Secondly, if the letter does not reach its destination or is delayed because it is wrongly addressed or not properly posted, the postal rule should not apply (see *LJ Korbetis v Transgrain Shipping BV* (2005) for an example of the former). As he is at fault, the offeree has not done all that he can to communicate his acceptance to the offeror. Moreover, where the acceptance does not reach its destination at all, so that the offeror is unaware of it, to find that a valid contract had nevertheless been formed on posting would in practice give the offeree the wholly unwarranted option of deciding whether or not to reveal the contract to the offeror, which could be particularly valuable where the market had moved against the offeree after postage.

Other methods of communication

2.73   The postal rule does not apply to modern, instantaneous forms of communication (see *Entores Ltd v Miles Far East Corpn* (1955) in the context of telexes). It is commonly said that where the method of communicating the offer is instantaneous, there will not be an acceptance unless and until it is communicated to the offeror. We find the reason for this stance in *Brinkibon* from Lord Fraser in the context of telexes: 'a party (the acceptor) who tries to send a message by telex can generally tell if his message has not been received on the other party's (the offeror's) machine, whereas the offeror, of course, will not know if an unsuccessful attempt has been made to send an acceptance to him'. Generally, a party who unsuccessfully attempts to bring his acceptance to the offeror's attention will know instantly that they have been unsuccessful, so it is reasonable to expect them to try again until they succeed. This tells us that in order to work out whether there is an acceptance, we must again ask whether the offeree has taken all reasonable steps to bring the acceptance to the offeror's attention.

2.74   Let us begin with telephone acceptances. If the offeror and offeree are actually talking on the telephone, the offer will be accepted at the moment that it reasonably appears to the offeree that the offeror has heard and understood the acceptance. So, for example, if the line goes dead in the middle of my acceptance, there will be no acceptance unless I phone him again or inform him of my acceptance in another appropriate way (see Lord Denning in *Entores*).

2.75   However, matters are different if I do not get through to the offeror but reach her answer phone. Here, provided the acceptance is clear, the acceptance will take effect when it would have been reasonable for the offeror to check her answer phone. So if the offeror is a business and I leave a message at 10 p.m. on a Sunday evening, depending on the nature of the business it may be held that the offer was only accepted when business recommenced on Monday morning. While there is no direct authority on this point, the guidance of Lord Wilberforce in *Brinkibon* is apt (quoted with approval by Gatehouse J in *Mondial Shipping and Chartering BV v Astarte Shipping Ltd* (1995)):

> No universal rule can cover all such cases; they must be resolved by reference to the intentions of the parties, by sound business practice and in some cases by a judgement where the risks should lie.

2.76   Turning next to faxes, it is submitted that the acceptance should be valid unless the offeree knows or should know that it has not got through properly (see Chitty (2016)). If the fax has not got through at all, the sender will know this at once, so can reasonably be expected to resend (see *JSC Zestafoni G Nikoladze Ferralloy Plant v Ronly Holdings Ltd* (2004)). The time at which the offer should be taken to have been accepted should be determined in the same way as in our answer phone examples.

2.77   Finally, we should consider e-mails. So much communication is now conducted by e-mail, which the courts treat as any other so-called instantaneous mode of communication. Once again, the acceptance should be valid unless the offeree should realise that the e-mail has failed to be received properly by the offeror. As Hill (2001) notes, if the e-mail is sent to an incorrect address or the receiver's server is not responding, the message will 'bounce back' to the sender, who will receive notification that the message has not been delivered. In such circumstances, there is no prejudice to the offeree—the offer will not have been accepted and the offeree should resend the e-mail. Christopher Clarke J noted in *Bernuth Lines Ltd v High Seas Shipping* (2005), when dealing with a formal notice served on the other party by email, that e-mails are should be treated like other (virtually) instantaneous modes and that the normal qualifications apply:

> That is not to say that clicking on the 'send' icon automatically amounts to good service. The e-mail must, of course, be despatched to what is, in fact, the email address of the intended recipient. It must not be rejected by the system.

Likewise, the acceptance will take effect at the time when the offeror could reasonably have been expected to check her inbox, generally during normal business hours.

2.78 One general point should be made. As in the case of the postal rule, the offeror's fault should not affect whether there is a valid acceptance, and if so, the time at which it takes effect. So if the offeror does not check her inbox (or conceivably her junk folder), or spills coffee on her computer so is unable to receive e-mails, this has no effect (unless perhaps the offeree knew or should have known about these facts). These sentiments are echoed by Lord Denning in *Entores*. Similarly, Gatehouse J commented in an analogous context in *Mondial Shipping* that 'if the telex is sent in ordinary business hours, the receipt is the same as the time of dispatch because it is not open to the charterer to contend that it did not in fact then come to his attention'. More controversially, Coote (1971) argues convincingly for a version of the postal rule where, without fault on the part of the offeree, there is a *gap* between the so-called instantaneous mode of communication leaving the control of the offeree and actually coming to the attention of the offeror (as where the offeror does not listen to her answer phone messages). Far from being anomalous, the postal rule may contain good sense in a so-called instantaneous context, in allocating the risk of the gap to the offeror (who could after all have prescribed a risk free mode of acceptance) rather than the offeree. This point is explored further at para **2.106.**

Unilateral contracts

2.79 If a person makes an offer to enter into a unilateral contract, they waive the requirement that the acceptance be communicated. In *Carlill*, the defendants claimed that there was no contract because the acceptance had not been notified to them. This argument was dismissed on the ground that the defendants had dispensed with the communication requirement. As Bowen LJ commented:

> If I advertise to the world that my dog is lost, and that anybody who brings the dog to a particular place will be paid some money, are all the police or other persons whose business it is to find lost dogs to be expected to sit down and write me a note saying that they have accepted my proposal?

Prescribed modes of acceptance

2.80 It is for the offeror to lay down how his offer is to be accepted. Therefore, if the offeror stipulates that it is to be accepted by a particular method of communication, such as by letter, generally the acceptance can only be communicated in this manner (for example, see *Frank v Knight* (1937)). However, if the method used by the offeree would equally well fulfil the offeror's requirements, then such an acceptance will be valid (*Tinn v Hoffmann* (1873)). For example, say that the offeror made an offer over the phone and told you to telephone her landline to accept because she needed a quick response, but you were in the area and arrived on her doorstep one minute after the offer was made and told her in person, this would surely be acceptable.

Can an offer be accepted by silence?

2.81   As we have seen, the law requires steps to be taken to bring a purported acceptance to the offeror's attention. Therefore, if the offeree decides he has accepted the offer but does nothing to indicate this to anyone, least of all the offeror, this will normally not constitute a valid acceptance.

2.82   However, what if the offeror has said, either expressly or implicitly, that the offeree need not communicate the acceptance at all? In the famous case of *Felthouse v Bindley* (1862), the claimant offered to buy a horse from his nephew for £30 15s and told the nephew that if he heard no more from him, he would consider the horse his at that price. The nephew decided to accept the offer and told the defendant auctioneer, who was going to sell the nephew's horse, that the horse was not to be auctioned. However, the nephew did not tell the claimant that he had decided to accept. Unfortunately, the defendant sold the horse and was sued in the tort of conversion by the claimant. The key issue for our purposes was whether at the date of the auction, the claimant's offer had been accepted, thereby giving him title to sue in conversion. It was held that it had not, the main reason for this conclusion being that the nephew had not communicated his acceptance.

2.83   This general rule that silence will not constitute an acceptance can be justified on two grounds. First, it protects the offeree from accepting offers that they do not intend to accept. Imagine that I received a large amount of offers through my mailbox, each saying something along the lines of 'if I do not hear from you by tomorrow morning, I will take it you to have accepted my offer'. In the absence of the general rule, I would have to go to the trouble of expressly rejecting all these offers in order to stop myself entering into unwanted contracts. So it prevents unwanted contracts being thrust upon me. We see this rationale at work both in *Felthouse* itself, where Wiles J comments that '[i]t is clear that the uncle had no right to impose upon the nephew a sale of his horse for £30 15s. unless he chose to … repudiate the offer', and in the Unsolicited Goods and Services Act 1971, which allows those receiving unsolicited goods to treat them as gifts in certain circumstances. Second, silence is often equivocal, so if an offeree says and does nothing in response to the offer, it is very difficult for the offeror (and court) to tell whether the offeree intended to accept it.

2.84   However, neither of these rationales seems to apply in *Felthouse* itself: the nephew's conduct in telling the auctioneer not to auction the horse shows that he wanted to accept the offer, and the fact that he did not communicate this to the other party should not have mattered because the uncle had waived the need to communicate.

Accordingly, it is arguable that the general rule should not have been applied in *Felthouse* and that the case is wrongly decided: Miller (1972).

2.85   There are other circumstances in which neither of these rationales applies, so a number of exceptions to the rule have been recognised. First, if the offeree does not say anything but his *conduct* clearly indicates to the other party that the offeree intends to accept the offer, then his intent is not equivocal and a contract is not being forced upon him. So in *Nissan UK Ltd v Nissan Motor Manufacturing (UK) Ltd* (1994), the parties were negotiating over the terms on which the latter party ('NMUK') should deliver cars to Nissan UK ('NUK'). The Court of Appeal held that NMUK had accepted NUK's offer by beginning to deliver the cars.

2.86   The second exception is where the silence of the offeree does indicate to the other party an intention to accept the offer even in the absence of any conduct on his part. This will not often be the case, but this exception may apply where, for example, there have been previous dealings between the parties. In *Rust v Abbey Life Insurance Co* (1979), one of the grounds for the Court of Appeal's decision was that the claimant's silence for seven months indicated that she had accepted the property bond which had been allocated to her. Here, the fact that the claimant had started negotiations may have influenced the court because in a sense it was her conduct that led to the offer being made, so there was less danger of an 'unwanted contract' being forced upon her.

2.87   The proposition that silence can in some circumstances constitute acceptance was accepted by the House of Lords in *The Santa Clara* (1996), a case concerned with the analogous issue of whether a repudiation of the contract had been accepted (see para **15.55**):

> Sometimes in the practical world of businessmen an omission to act may be as pregnant with meaning as a positive declaration.

2.88   However, normally silence will be ambiguous, as *Linnett v Halliwells LLP* (2009) illustrates. In that case, an adjudicator nominated to decide a building contract dispute wrote to one of the parties seeking agreement to his terms of engagement. Halliwells did not respond, and it was held that this silence could not amount to affirmative acceptance of the terms.

2.89   Finally, as one of the key purposes of the general rule is to protect the offeree, should an exception be recognised whenever it is the *offeree* who is claiming that they have accepted (and the offeror has indicated that they do not require communication of the acceptance)? On one hand, as silence is usually equivocal, to allow the offeree to do this would mean that they could deny or assert that they had accepted the contract to suit their own convenience (see Miller (1972)), which would place the offeror in a difficult position. Moreover, this exception was doubted in *Fairline Shipping Corpn v Adamson* (1975). However, on the other hand, is the offeror worthy of protection in such circumstances? After all, it is the offeror who has said that silence will suffice to accept the offer.

Who can communicate the acceptance?

2.90   As we have seen (para **2.51**), *Dickinson v Dodds* (1875–6) suggests that the offeror need not personally communicate a withdrawal of an offer, providing that the withdrawal is clearly brought to the other party's attention. One might assume that the law would adopt the same stance in relation to acceptances, namely that it suffices that the acceptance is clearly brought to the offeror's attention and it does not matter how this happens. However, *Powell v Lee* (1908) suggests that '[t]here must be notice of acceptance from the contracting party in some way'; in other words, it appears that only communication by the offeree himself or his duly authorised agent will suffice.

2.91   While this is criticised by Beatson, Burrows, and Cartwright (2016), it is suggested that there may be some sense in it, because it protects the offeree. Imagine you offer to buy my car for £100. I have no intention of parting with it for such a measly sum. However, your best friend tells you (untruthfully) that I have agreed, so you have been clearly told that I have accepted the offer. Remember that there is no requirement that I *actually* intend to accept the offer: on the principle of objective interpretation what matters is how things reasonably appear to the offeror. Unless we have a rule that acceptance must be communicated by the offeree or a duly authorised agent, I will have contracted to sell my car for £100 despite the fact that I have done nothing to indicate that I have accepted the offer. Such a rule also gives the offeror greater certainty: they can know that they will only be bound if the acceptance is communicated by the offeree or his agent.

When is a unilateral offer accepted?

2.92   Imagine I offer you £100 if you will run (and finish) the London marathon. When do you accept this offer? Is it when you start running the marathon or when you cross the finishing line? In general I will not be allowed to revoke the offer after you have started performance. In our example, it would be grossly unfair on you if I were able to retract my offer when you were in sight of the finishing line! There are two different ways that the law can prevent this happening. It could say that the offer is accepted by *commencing* performance. This solution was adopted by Lord Denning, albeit by way of *obiter dicta*, in *Errington v Errington* (1952):

> The father's promise was a unilateral contract—a promise of the house in return for their act of paying the instalments. It could not be revoked by him once the couple entered on performance of the act, but it would cease to bind him if they left it incomplete and unperformed.

So in our marathon example, you would accept my offer by starting the race, but you would not be entitled to the £100 unless and until you finished it.

2.93   The other solution is to say that the offer is only accepted upon complete performance, but that once you start performing, I am under an implied obligation not to revoke my offer. Viscount Cave LC inclined to this view in *Morrison Shipping Co Ltd v The Crown* (1924).

2.94   Both solutions have their problems. The former view has been criticised by Harpum and Lloyd Jones (1979) on the ground that it is difficult to accept that an act of partial performance will necessarily be sufficiently unequivocal in every case to constitute an acceptance. On the other hand, the difficulty with the second solution is that if there is no contract until performance is completed, where does this implied obligation not to revoke come from? It has been suggested by Harpum and Lloyd Jones (1979) that a collateral contract containing this obligation is entered into when performance is started. Although this is a somewhat artificial solution, as the authors admit, it is nonetheless to be preferred. As a matter of general principle, an offer is only accepted when its terms are fully complied with, so if I offer you £100 for running the marathon and finishing it, the main unilateral contract only comes into force when you cross the finishing line.

2.95 This solution seemed to be the one preferred by Longmore LJ in *Soulsbury v Soulsbury* (2008). In that case, an ex-husband paying maintenance promised his ex-wife he would leave her £100,000 in his will instead of continuing to pay her maintenance. Longmore LJ held that '[o]nce the promisee acts on the promise by inhaling the smoke ball, by starting the walk to York or (as here) by not suing for the maintenance to which she was entitled, *the promisor cannot revoke or withdraw the offer*' (emphasis added). Therefore, he appears to have viewed the effect of commencement of performance as being to prevent revocation of the offer, not to constitute its acceptance.

2.96 Finally, notice that where the offer is clearly intended to be revocable even once performance has been commenced, then it can be so revoked (*Luxor (Eastbourne) Ltd v Cooper* (1941)).

Revoking an acceptance

2.97 What happens if the offeree posts an acceptance but later decides that they do not want to accept it? If the situation is one where the postal rule applies (see paras **2.66–2.72**), it would seem that a contract is formed when I post the letter, so it is too late for me to back out. However, what if I manage to get my retraction to the offeror before the offeror receives the letter (for example, by telephoning ahead)? There is no English authority on this point (although Bramwell LJ commented in his dissenting judgment in *Household Fire Insurance Co v Grant* (1879) that the revocation would be effective).

2.98 Some have suggested that the retraction should be effective. Hudson (1966) argues that the purpose of the postal rule is to protect the *offeree*, so it should not be used here to work to his detriment (by preventing his revoking). This is particularly persuasive when we consider that allowing retraction under these circumstances would cause no prejudice to the offeror: he would receive the retraction first and so know that the acceptance that was yet to arrive had been revoked. As argued (see para **2.66**), the postal rule is merely one convenient way to strike a balance between the interests of the offeror and offeree, so where, as here, we can protect the offeree (by allowing him to revoke) without harming the offeror in the process, we should not let the postal rule stand in our way.

2.99 On the other hand, allowing offerees to revoke in this situation allows them to hedge their bets: they can post the acceptance if the offer appears a good one at the time and then retract it if the market turns against them before the acceptance has reached the offeror. Hudson (1966) responds that the offeror can prevent this by expressly stating in the offer that a letter of acceptance cannot be revoked after it has been posted. However, it may be considered unrealistic to expect the offeror to do this. A better response would be to point out that offerees' actions cause no harm to offerors in this fact patter, so why should they not be allowed to hedge their bets in this way?

Contracting in an electronic world

2.100   In coming decades, the rise of artificial intelligence and computerisation will bring big challenges for the law of contract, just as for many other areas of life. Banks and other large commercial organisations are already investing in technology that can produce and analyse contractual documentation automatically; it is only a matter of time before computers can be programmed to 'contract with each other'. How the law should respond is a fascinating theoretical and practical question, beyond the scope of this book. But the law has already had to move with the times, adapting its rules to fit new modes of contracting, now that so many transactions are concluded by e-mail or online, be it booking a holiday, purchasing a book, downloading a music file, or concluding a commercial deal with someone on the other side of the world. Therefore, given that many of the offer and acceptance cases concern older means of communication, such as the post, it is important to consider what rules apply to contracts concluded by electronic media, equipped with our knowledge of the general principles dealt with earlier.

2.101   The first point is that the same basic principles do and should apply: there is no reason why contracts by e-mail or concluded online should be governed by wholly different rules. By and large, the law has developed over the last two decades in keeping with this sentiment—for example legislation now provides that e-signatures are effective where a contract is required to be signed. A good illustration of the sentiment in the common law is *Golden Ocean Group Ltd v Salgaocar Mining Industries Pvt Ltd* (2012), where the court applied orthodox offer and acceptance principles to a series of e-mails making offers and counter-offers (see similarly *TTMI Sarl v Statoil ASA* (2011)). The Court of Appeal in *Golden Ocean* was confident that the application of such principles would typically cause no difficulty, Tomlinson LJ stating that:

> [t]he conclusion of commercial contracts, particularly charterparties, by an exchange of e-mails, once telexes or faxes, in which the terms agreed early on are not repeated verbatim later in the exchanges is entirely commonplace. It causes no difficulty whatever in the parties knowing at exactly what point they have undertaken a binding obligation and upon what terms.

2.102   However, the question of how these basic principles should apply to common electronic contractual situations can give rise to difficult issues (see the first instance judgment in the Singaporean case of *Chwee Kin Keong v Digilandmall.com Pte Ltd* (2004) for a thoughtful analysis of some of the issues set out later).

2.103   First of all, let us think about contracting via a website: does the display of an item for sale on a website constitute an invitation to treat or an offer? We have seen that the general rule is that displaying goods in shops only constitutes an invitation to treat, although there are good reasons for taking a different approach (paras **2.27–2.30**). However, what of a typical website that allows the customer to select the item, enter her payment details, click 'buy', and seemingly conclude the agreement online? In this situation, then (absent the terms and conditions of the site providing to the contrary) it is suggested that it is clear that a contract has been concluded (see Christensen (2001) and Phang (2005)). The natural inference is that a deal has been concluded, as where you get through the checkout at a supermarket and have paid for the goods. In these circumstances you would not expect the seller to be able to pull out, or add new terms to the contract. Naturally, many commercial selling websites wish to avoid this default assumption by creating rules closer to those for shopping in real shops, so as to protect themselves against contractual liability until they are sure the selected item is actually available, by expressly specifying that the contract is *not* formed automatically when the customer clicks 'buy'. In other words, clicking 'buy' is an offer not an acceptance. For example, the Amazon UK website informs customers just about to purchase something, 'When you click the 'Buy now' button, we'll send you an email-message acknowledging receipt of your order. Your contract to purchase an item will not be complete until we send you an e-mail to indicate that the item has been dispatched.'

2.104 When considering the issue of internet contracting, we might also find an analogy with the vending machine example referred to earlier (para **2.44**). Christensen (2001) draws a distinction in this regard between what she terms 'non-interactive sites', which only provide information and require any contact with the seller to be through other means such as confirmation of an order by phone and therefore (she argues) should be governed by the same principles as displays of goods in shops, and 'interactive sites', where the customer can select the item, pay for it, and conclude the agreement on the site. For discussion of other possible distinctions, see Phang (2005).

2.105 Secondly, returning to contracts made by e-mail, one interesting and practically important question that we have already mentioned (para **2.77**) is whether the same acceptance rule should apply to e-mailed acceptance as for postal acceptance, namely that an offer is accepted on sending an e-mail in response, whether or not that e-mail is actually received. According to the pragmatic guidance of Lord Wilberforce in *Brinkibon* (set out at para **2.75**), this should be resolved by reference to the intentions of the parties, by sound business practice, and in some cases by a judgement as to where the risks should lie.

2.106 We have already noted that Coote (1971), writing long before the invention of e-mail, argued that where, without fault on the part of the offeree, there is a *gap* between a so-called instantaneous mode of communication leaving the control of the offeree and actually coming to the attention of the offeror, the offeror should bear the risk of that gap, such that acceptance takes effect as soon as it leaves the control of the offeree. In short, a version of the posting rule. Although the arguments are far from all one-way on the point, it is suggested that Coote's insight should apply equally to e-mail, and that an e-mail response should constitute an acceptance when sent, as long as it is properly addressed, unless the offeree should realise immediately that it has not been received, such as where an immediate bounce-back message is received. However, discovery later on that the e-mail has not got through should be irrelevant, because absent an immediate sign that there is a problem, the offeree should be entitled to proceed on the basis that a contract was concluded immediately on sending the e-mail. After all, a large part of the purpose of contracting by e-mail is to be able to conclude the contract quickly and act upon it. If the offeror has chosen to communicate by e-mail (as opposed to, say, the telephone) and it is clear that the offeror is happy for the offeree to accept by e-mail, then it is submitted that it is the offeror who should be made to bear the risk if something goes wrong with the transmission of the acceptance (whether through hacking or for more benign reasons) where it appears to the offeree that the deal has gone through without a hitch. This also has the advantage of giving certainty as to the time at which the contract is concluded, and avoids entering into the difficult question of when an offeror might be considered to have received the response (see, for example, Al Ibrahim, Ababneh, and Tahart (2007)).

2.107 Finally, throughout this book, we will encounter other legal issues that arise in modern electronic contracting and consider them in context. For example, are terms contained in the small print on a website binding on the party making the contract? Is clicking 'I agree' on a website equivalent to signing the document so as to engage the rule (see paras **3.21–3.27**) that provides that *all* the terms of the contract are incorporated by signature, whether or not they are drawn properly to the attention of the person using the website? On the other hand, if the signature rule is not engaged, what will amount to giving 'reasonable notice' of those terms, often occupying hundreds of webpages, so as to incorporate them into the contract and thus make them binding? Sometimes the customer cannot complete the contract without scrolling down the full terms and conditions, then clicking something like 'I accept' (sometimes known as a 'click-wrap' contract); other websites merely put a link to the terms and conditions but the customer does not have to click on the link to proceed with the contract. These issues are considered in context in Chapters 3 and 7. It is also worth noting legislation that has been passed to protect parties who contract electronically, such as the Electronic Commerce (EC Directive) Regulations 2002, which impose requirements on businesses engaging in e-commerce to, for example, provide information and acknowledge receipt of orders. Those regulations protect anyone dealing electronically, whether a consumer or a business, but we will look in particular at additional legislative protection for consumers, which cover electronic contracting as well as old-fashioned face-to-face transactions (see for example the Consumer Rights Act 2015 discussed in Chapter 8).

Battle of the forms

2.108 In commercial life, one party will often make an offer on a set of standard terms that the party normally trades on. So I might send you a form containing my offer to deliver you some machines for £10,000 and say that if you wish to accept, it must be on my standard terms, which I set out on the form. You send back a response saying '£10,000 sounds good so you have yourself an agreement on my standard terms.' I then write back and say 'I'm ready to perform but only on my standard terms.' This sending back and forth of offers and counter-offers upon each side's standard terms is known as the 'battle of the forms'. At some stage I start delivering the machines. Is there a contract between us? If so, on what terms: my standard terms, your standard terms, or some other terms?

2.109   For many years, the principal case on the subject was *Butler Machine Tool Co Ltd v Ex-cell-O Corpn (England) Ltd* (1979). On 23 May, the claimant sellers offered to deliver a machine tool for £75,535, on the terms set out in the quotation, which included a price escalation clause. The defendant buyers replied on 27 May, giving an order with differences from the sellers' quotation and stating that the order was on the buyers' terms and conditions, which did not include a price escalation clause. The order contained a tear-off slip for the claimant to sign, which stated that the order was to be on the buyers' terms. On 5 June, the sellers returned the completed slip with a covering letter stating that delivery was to be 'in accordance with our revised quotation of May 23'. When the machine came to be delivered, the claimant sought to rely on the price escalation clause. The Court of Appeal unanimously held that he could not, because a contract had been concluded on the buyers' terms.

2.110   What is interesting about the case is the two different approaches taken, by Bridge and Lawton LJJ on one hand, and Lord Denning MR on the other. The first two judges took an orthodox offer and acceptance approach. They looked at the last offer made by either of the parties and asked whether it was accepted by the other party. If it was there would be a contract on the terms set out in the last offer; if it was not, there would be no contract at all. This is known as the 'last shot' approach: he who makes the last offer wins. They held the buyers' reply on 27 May constituted a counter-offer, and that despite the sellers' attempts to reassert their terms in the covering letter on 5 June, they had in fact accepted the buyers' terms by returning the completed tear-off slip. So what appeared to be the last shot, the sellers' letter on 5 June, turned out to have misfired.

2.111   Lord Denning took a more radical route to the same conclusion. He rejected the traditional offer and acceptance analysis. Instead, he distinguished the issue of contract formation from the content of the contract. The first stage was to work out whether there was a contract. A contract would be formed if the parties were agreed on 'all material points': the fact that they might disagree on smaller points did not matter. Only agreement on core issues is required to get the contract up and running. The next stage is to work out what the terms of the contract would be. Lord Denning stated that the terms would sometimes be those of the party who made the last offer, sometimes those of the party who made the first offer, and in yet other cases, a reasonable compromise between the two. In order to decide between these options, 'the documents have to be considered as a whole'. Having done this, Lord Denning decided that the sellers' acknowledgement by tear-off slip on 5 June was the decisive document, so the contract was on the buyers' terms.

2.112   Which approach should be preferred? There are undeniably a number of problems with the 'last shot' approach and it has been subject to criticism. It is arbitrary, in that it focuses just on the last shot fired, rather than the whole course of dealing between the parties. In practice it can be hard to tell what the 'last shot' was (as in *Butler* itself), so it may be difficult for the parties to be confident about whose standard terms prevail. Other critics have pointed out that it does not necessarily reflect the reasonable expectations of both parties; instead, it reflects the expectations of the party who fired the 'last shot'. Sociological studies cited in Morgan (2015) show that parties often paid little attention to standard terms when forming contracts, although the cases on the battle of the forms are normally cases where the parties are focusing on them. Finally, many critics note that the language of 'last shot' espouses the view that the parties are enemies and that negotiating a contract is some sort of battle, arguing that, with the increasing effect of continental notions of 'good faith' on English contract law, such an adversarial approach is out of line.

2.113 These criticisms are powerful and this is a difficult area, reminding us of the artificiality of 'offer and acceptance' analysis and how it sometimes bears little relation to the way parties actually do business. Nonetheless, on balance the 'last shot' approach is preferable, at least in commercial situations, to Lord Denning's more 'holistic' approach. Lord Denning's approach is attractive if you consider the issue from the perspective of litigation, with the judge coming up with a reasonable compromise solution to ascertain the terms of the contract. But it is crucial for the default rules of the law of contract to be clear and predictable in advance, so that litigation is not needed. Although the 'last shot' doctrine can be difficult to apply at the margins, Lord Denning's approach makes it impossible for the parties to tell what their contractual terms are without going to court. Moreover Lord Denning's approach involves the court determining the contents of the contract, rather than the parties. Although we are often willing to impose obligations and bestow rights upon the parties that they have not agreed to, such as the remedial rules about the measure of damages (see Chapter 16), nonetheless a default formation rule that requires that seems commercially unsatisfactory.

2.114 Note that the 'last shot' approach is just a default rule, as can be seen from the Court of Appeal discussion of *Butler* in *Tekdata Interconnections Ltd v Amphenol Ltd* (2009). The court appeared to accept that the traditional approach could be displaced if the documents passing between the parties and their other conduct indicated that the common intention was that some other terms were intended to prevail. However, the judges were keen to emphasise that it will 'always be difficult to displace the traditional analysis', with Longmore LJ requiring a 'clear course of dealing between the parties' to do so, because of the certainty that they felt the traditional approach offered to commercial actors. On the facts, there was not sufficient evidence to show that the traditional approach should be displaced.

2.115 It is suggested that this approach of using the traditional offer and acceptance analysis as a starting point may be a sensible compromise between the two analyses. However, if this approach is to be taken, it is difficult to see why a 'clear course of dealing' should necessarily be required to displace it, because even without such a course of dealing it may be clear from the parties' conduct that they did not intend the 'last shot fired' to govern the relationship between them.

2.116 An interesting question that was dealt with in *Ghsp Inc v Ab Electronic Ltd* (2010) was what happens where both parties make clear in firing their shots that they are not willing to accept the other side's conditions. In that case, both sides had made clear repeatedly that they were not prepared to do so, so the court held that neither side's standard conditions governed. This caused no difficulty in upholding the contract, because the contract was for the sale of goods and therefore the terms implied by the Sale of Goods Act filled the gap. However, the mere fact that a party makes clear to the other that they are unwilling to accept the other's standard terms does not *necessarily* mean that they have avoided those standard terms applying. For example, if they say this initially but then unilaterally start carrying out the contract, then they may, depending on the facts, be taken to have accepted the other side's terms by virtue of their *conduct*.

Contracts that fail to materialise

2.117 A final cautionary note: the rules and principles discussed in this chapter make sense in a perfect world (imagined by lawyers) in which the parties negotiate their deal, reach consensus, make a contract and subsequently perform it. But in the real world, the order of events is often very different—it is surprisingly common for one party to carry out work or supply goods before agreement has been reached on all aspects of the transaction, in the belief that a contract will be concluded, yet in the event this does not happen. Maybe negotiations break down completely, or the parties reach an arrangement of sorts which lacks certainty on key terms (see Chapter 4) and is therefore unenforceable. Can the party who has performed work or provided goods nonetheless claim payment for what has been performed or provided? Some judges look to the law of *restitution* for a solution here, as Goff J did in *British Steel Corpn v Bridge and Engineering Co Ltd* (1984), holding that the defendant benefited from what the claimant did, such that it would be unjustly enriched if it was not required to pay for the benefit. Others prefer to solve the problem with a *contractual* solution, like the Court of Appeal in *Latchin v General Mediterranean Holdings SA* (2003), which emphasised that where someone does preliminary work in the hope that he will be awarded a particular job should a big project go ahead, the fact that the project fails to materialise does not necessarily prevent there being a 'smaller' contract to pay for at least some of the work done by him. Both approaches have advantages and disadvantages, but the debate is beyond the scope of this book.

OVERVIEW

1   Traditionally, we require an offer and acceptance in order to form a contract. An offer is an indication of one party's willingness to enter into a contract with the party to whom it is addressed as soon as the latter accepts its terms, while an acceptance is an agreement to the terms of the offer.

2   However, there is no conceptual reason why a contract must consist of an offer and acceptance. A contract is a legal concept that we invent to help us explain the law; therefore,

we can give it whatever meaning we want. The issue is whether it is helpful to explain a particular situation in terms of contract. So while offer and acceptance is a helpful way of analysing many situations and the presence of offer and acceptance is certainly sufficient to establish a contract (providing the requirements discussed in Chapters 4 and 5 are also fulfilled), it should not be a necessary ingredient of a contract. We should be willing to find that there is a contract even in its absence if it would be an appropriate, helpful interpretation of the situation in question.

3   In order to work out whether a statement amounts to an offer or acceptance, usually we do not look at the intent of the person making the statement; instead, we look at what his intention should have appeared to be to the other party. Words are to be interpreted as they were reasonably understood by the person to whom they were spoken, not as they were understood by the person who spoke them. This is known as the principle of objective intention.

4   A distinction must be drawn between unilateral and bilateral contracts. The key difference is that only the latter type of contract places obligations upon and grants rights to both parties. In a unilateral contract, the offeree makes no promise and so is under no obligation to do anything.

5   An offer indicates that the offeror intends to be legally bound upon acceptance. Providing that the offeror evinces such an intention, it does not matter how many people she makes the offer to, so an offer to the whole world is perfectly acceptable.

6   However, if the offeror's actions suggest that he does not intend to be bound automatically upon acceptance, he has not made an offer, only an invitation to treat, because his actions suggest that further negotiations will need to take place before a contract is concluded and he is legally bound. In many everyday situations, it is unclear whether and if so at what stage each party intends to become legally bound. So in such situations, in the interests of certainty the law seems to lay down general rules to determine when an offer is made. These general rules can be displaced by evidence that the offeror intended something different. The general rule is that the display of goods for sale, advertisements, invitations to tender for a piece of work, and invitations to make a bid at an auction 'with reserve' constitute invitations to treat.

7   An offer can be terminated by an act of the offeror, by an act of the offeree or in some other way:

- The offeror can terminate his offer at any time but must generally communicate this withdrawal to the offeree before the latter accepts the offer. It appears that the offeror need not communicate the withdrawal himself providing that the withdrawal is clearly brought to the offeree's attention by a trustworthy source.

- If the offeree rejects the offer, this will terminate it.

- There are various other ways in which an offer can terminate, such as by lapse of time. The effect of the death of one party upon the offer is unclear.

8   To accept an offer, an offeror must show unqualified agreement to its terms. Therefore, if the offeree's statement seeks to vary any of the terms of the offer, generally it will not

constitute an acceptance. The offeree will be taken to have rejected the offer (thus terminating it) and be making an offer of his own (a 'counter-offer').

9   While the law is not clear on the point, it appears that the offeree must be aware of the offer in order to accept it; however, it is not necessary for the acceptance to be motivated by the offer. Some commentators have attacked the first proposition, but it is sound, particularly in the case of unilateral contracts: the offeree requires no protection in such situations.

10 As a general rule, a contract is only formed when the acceptance is communicated to the offeror. The acceptance will be taken to be 'communicated' when the offeree has taken all reasonable steps, using the prescribed mode of acceptance, to bring the acceptance to the attention of the offeror.

11 In the case of acceptances by post, the general rule is that the offer will be accepted when the letter is posted, not when it reaches the offeror. This rule only applies where the parties contemplated that the acceptance might be posted, so this rule will be less likely to apply with the advent of modern, quicker forms of communication. Even if a postal acceptance is contemplated, the postal rule will not apply where the offer expressly or impliedly requires actual communication of the acceptance.

12 As for more modern types of communication, we must look at the particular situation to determine whether the offeree has taken all reasonable steps to bring the acceptance to the offeror's attention.

13 Acceptance of a unilateral contract need not be communicated because the offeror is taken to have waived this requirement.

14 The general rule is that you cannot accept by silence. While this can be justified on the grounds that it protects the offeree from entering into an unwanted contract and that silence is usually equivocal, these justifications do not always apply so a number of exceptions have developed.

15 If the offeror states that a particular mode of communication must be used to accept the offer, this mode usually must be used to validly accept the offer, unless another mode of communication would equally suit the offeror's purposes.

16 It is unclear whether an offer to enter into a unilateral contract is accepted by the offeree starting to perform or only on the completion of his performance. Either way, unless the offer provides to the contrary, the offer cannot be revoked after the offeree has begun to perform.

17 Another matter that is unclear is whether a postal acceptance can be revoked by the offeree if she communicates her revocation to the offeror before the letter of acceptance reaches her. The better view is that the offeree should be able to do this.

18 Often, one party will make an offer on their standard terms of business and the other party will reply that they are willing to accept but only on the latter's standard terms. The first party might then write back re-asserting that the contract must be on their standard terms. This is known as the 'battle of the forms'. At some stage one party may start to perform the work envisaged by the parties, so two questions arise: is there a contract and if so on what terms?

19 English law seems to apply orthodox offer and acceptance principles to answer these questions. So we should look at the last offer made by either of the parties and ask if it was accepted by the other party. If it was, there will be a contract on the terms of the last offer, and if it was not, there will be no contract at all. This is known as the 'last shot' approach. Although it is not ideal, it is the most satisfactory approach commercially. In any event, it is a default rule that can be displaced in appropriate circumstances.

FURTHER READING

Atiyah 'Contracts, Promises and the Law of Obligations' Chapter 2 in *Essays on Contract* (1986)

Coote 'The Instantaneous Transmission of Acceptances' (1971) 4 NZULR 331

Hill 'Flogging a Dead Horse—The Postal Acceptance Rules and Email' (2001) 17 JCL 151

Hudson 'Retraction of Letters of Acceptance' (1966) 82 LQR 169

Hudson '*Gibbons v Proctor* Revisited' (1968) 84 LQR 503

Morgan *Great Debates in Contract Law* (2015) pp 1–20

Nolan 'Offer and Acceptance in the Electronic Age' Chapter 1 in *Contract Formation and Parties* (2010)

Paterson 'Consumer Contracting in the Age of the Digital Natives' (2011) 27 JCL 152

Phang 'The Frontiers of Contract Law—Contract Formation and Mistake in Cyberspace—The Singaporean Experience' (2005) 17 Singapore Academy of L J 361 (available in the online resources)

Ronan 'Challenged but not Defeated by Technology: Why the Postal Rule Should Apply to Contracts Formed by E-mail' (2006) (available in the online resources)

Spencer 'Signature, Consent and the Rule in *L'Estrange v Graucob*' [1973] 32 CLJ 104

SELF-TEST QUESTIONS

1 Why do we traditionally require an offer and acceptance in order to form a contract? Should we always require this?

2 When does the objective principle not apply?

3 Should I have to be aware of the offer in order to accept it? What stance does English law take on this issue?

4 When do we *not* require an acceptance to be brought to the actual attention of the offeror?

5 Should I be able to revoke a posted acceptance?

6 What approach should we take in 'battle of the forms' situations?

7 Should the display of goods on websites constitute an offer rather than an invitation to treat (absent anything to the contrary in the website's terms and conditions) and, if so, when?

8 When should an offer accepted by e-mail count as a valid acceptance if the e-mail is not received by the offeror?

9 Xavier was about to send his extensive car collection to be sold at auction, but before doing so he sent his uncle Yorick an e-mail offering to sell his vintage Morris Minor for £50,000, knowing that Yorick had always admired it. Yorick replied by first class post, saying 'I will take it, as long as you are able to deliver it to me. If I don't hear anything from you, I will assume we have a deal.' Later the same day, Yorick sent Xavier an e-mail saying, 'Sorry, change of heart, I don't want the car after all.' Unfortunately, because of a problem with Xavier's internet connection, he did not receive Xavier's e-mail, but Yorick's letter was delivered the following morning. Happy to deliver the car to Yorick, Xavier assumed they had a deal and removed it from his collection of cars that were taken away and sold at auction later that day. However, when he contacted Yorick two weeks later to arrange to deliver the car to him, Xavier learnt of Yorick's change of heart; in the meantime, there had been a dramatic fall in the value of vintage Morris Minors. Advise Xavier.

 For hints on how to answer question 9, please see the online resources at **www.oup.com/uk/sullivan8e/**.

3

Offer and acceptance II: three applications of the general principles

SUMMARY

This chapter considers three specific issues that arise from offer and acceptance analysis:

- Intention to create legal relations, exploring presumptions in the domestic, social, and commercial context, and whether there is any need for a separate requirement.
- Signature and the rule in *L'Estrange v Graucob*.
- Unilateral mistake, as to identity and as to the terms of the contract, and the doctrine of non est factum.

3.1 This chapter deals with three particular situations, where the issue seems to be whether there is a valid offer and acceptance but the courts have often chosen not to apply orthodox offer and acceptance principles (in particular, the principle of 'objective intention': see para **2.12**). This has led to various difficulties, but it is arguable that some of these problems can be avoided if orthodox offer and acceptance principles are used.

Intention to create legal relations

3.2 A contract will only be formed if both parties intend their agreement to create legal relations between them, that is, if they intend the agreement to grant legal rights to and impose legal obligations upon each of them, their intent being judged 'objectively' (see *West Bromwich Albion Football Club Ltd v El-Safty* (2006)). Before examining the detail of the doctrine, we need to understand exactly what we mean when we say that there was 'no intention to create legal relations' and how this differs from saying that there was an invitation to treat.

3.3 We have already dealt with invitations to treat and the way in which they differ from legal offers (see para **2.24**). Sometimes, rather than claiming that a statement was only an invitation to treat, a party will allege that there was no intention to create legal relations. These are very similar allegations, because they both allege that the maker of the statement did not intend to be legally bound on acceptance of its terms. The main difference appears to be that a statement tends to be classified as an invitation to treat where the maker of the statement appears to envisage a legally binding arrangement being concluded in the future: he is inviting the other party to make him an offer and negotiate with him. In short, an invitation to treat is a stepping stone to a future contract. For example, if I make an advert to sell my car which is interpreted as an invitation to treat, I appear to envisage entering into a contract of sale at some stage (just not automatically when someone responds to the advert) and I am inviting members of the public to make me an offer.

3.4 On the other hand, we tend to say that there is no intent to create legal relations where the party making the statement does not envisage entering into a legally binding arrangement with the other party at any stage. For example, if a (happily married) couple sit down to carefully decide who should pick up the kids from school on which day, and the husband says that he will do it on Mondays and Tuesdays if his wife does it on the other weekdays, it would not appear to the wife that her husband intended their arrangement to impose legal obligations upon either of them. It is not a situation in which they believe that there will be further negotiations following which they will enter into a legally binding arrangement; they never intend there to be a contract at all.

Ascertaining whether there is an intention to create legal relations

3.5 Often the parties do not think about whether their agreement should have legal consequences or not, and so it is hard to interpret their words and conduct to decide whether, judged objectively, they did have an intention to create legal relations. Therefore, the courts have developed a number of presumptions as to the parties' intent, to help them apply the doctrine:

- If the agreement is concluded in a domestic or social context, it is presumed that the parties did not intend to create legal relations unless there is clear evidence to the contrary (*Balfour v Balfour* (1919) per Atkin LJ).

- If an express agreement is concluded in a commercial context, the onus of demonstrating that there was a lack of intention to create legal relations lies on the party asserting it and it is a heavy one (*Barbudev v Eurocom Cable Management Bulgaria Eood* (2012)), so that strong evidence will be needed to make good such a contention.

- If a party is asking the court to *imply* an agreement in the commercial context, it is for the party alleging the existence of the contract to show that there was an intention to create legal relations (*Baird Textile Holdings Ltd v Marks & Spencer plc* (2002) per Mance LJ; more recently *JD Cleverly Ltd v Family Finance Ltd* (2010) and *James-Bowen v Metropolitan Police Commissioner* (2016)).

- Even if certain terms of economic or other significance to the parties have not been finalised, an objective appraisal of their words and conduct may lead to the conclusion that they did not intend agreement of such terms to be a precondition to a concluded and legally binding agreement (*RTS Flexible Systems Ltd v Molkerei Alois Müller GmbH & Co KG* (2010)).

- There may be agreements that lie somewhere between an obviously commercial transaction and a social exchange. In such circumstances, the onus is on the person claiming that a contract existed to establish an intention to create legal relations, albeit that the onus is less heavy than in the purely social context (*Sadler v Reynolds* (2005)).

3.6 As we shall see, the reasons for adopting a different presumption in the domestic and social context are generally policy reasons: the courts want to limit the role of contract outside the commercial sphere. The doctrine is, in the words of Hedley (1985), a tool 'to keep contract in its place; to keep it in the commercial sphere and out of domestic cases, except where the judges think it has a useful role to play'. It is attractive to the courts to use the doctrine of intention to create legal relations to do this, because it allows them to justify the result that they reach by saying that the parties intended it (see Hepple (1970): 'it enables the courts to cloak policy decisions in the mantle of private contractual autonomy').

Agreements in the domestic context

3.7 The presumption stems from the judgment of Atkin LJ in *Balfour*. In that case, the parties were husband and wife who had moved to Sri Lanka after their marriage. After spending time in England, the husband returned to Sri Lanka but the wife had to stay on, so the husband promised to pay her £30 a month until her return. The couple later fell out and the wife sought to hold the husband to his promise, alleging that a contract had been formed. It was held unanimously by the Court of Appeal that there was no contract. Duke LJ was happy to decide the case on the basis that there was no consideration for the husband's promise (see Chapter 5) and Warrington LJ focused on whether a contract should be implied. Atkin LJ, however, went further and laid down another hurdle for a claimant to surmount, namely that the parties must intend to create legal relations.

3.8 He gave three reasons for his presumption that this requirement would generally not be made out in the domestic context. The most important reason was that it was inappropriate for contract to enter into the domestic sphere because the home is a private place into which the legal system should not intrude. The second was the danger of an explosion in litigation, while the third was that parties do not generally intend domestic agreements to have legal consequences.

3.9 A number of factors seem to guide the courts in determining whether the presumption will be rebutted. First, where one party has performed his side of the agreement and is seeking to hold the other party to their side of the deal, the court will be more likely to find that the presumption is rebutted, because it seems unfair that one party should do something for the other without getting what he was promised in return (see Hedley (1985) and, for example, *Merritt v Merritt* (1970)). Second, where both sides have performed the alleged contract, it will be unrealistic to suggest that there was no intention to be legally bound (*G Percy Trentham Ltd v Archital Luxfer Ltd* (1993)). Third, the more commercial the context, the more likely it is that the presumption will be rebutted (see McKendrick (2003) and, for example, *Snelling v John G Snelling Ltd* (1973)), presumably because the policy reasons that influenced Atkin LJ in *Balfour* have less force in such situations. For similar reasons, the closer the parties are to dealing at arm's length, the more likely the presumption is to be rebutted, so if the relationship was close to breakdown at the time of the agreement, this will point towards rebuttal (again, see *Merritt*, for example).

3.10 The *Balfour* presumption has come under increasing criticism from some quarters. For example, in *Pettitt v Pettitt* (1970), *Balfour* was said to be an extreme example of the presumption and a case which stretched the doctrine to its limits. Freeman (1996) has attacked the privacy argument that formed Atkin LJ's main justification. He argues that the family home is no longer such a private place. For example, husband and wife can now sue each other in tort and a husband can now be found guilty of raping his wife. Moreover, the law now allows those in family relationships a greater freedom to regulate their affairs: for example, parties are now given a greater control over entry into marriage and its terms. The unwillingness in *Balfour* to let the parties regulate their own affairs through contract seems out of line with this trend. Therefore, he suggests that the presumption should be abolished.

3.11 Saprai (2017) has explored the *Balfour* presumption from the perspective of an important theoretical debate in the law of contract, between those who believe contracts are promises (for whom the additional requirement of intention to create legal relations makes no sense) and those who see contracting and promising as distinct (who find support from the additional requirement). Saprai proposes a middle ground, which sees contract as based on promise but with a distinct moral and institutional role: 'The claim is that contracts are promises, not that all promises are contracts'. He therefore defends the requirement of intention to create legal relations, but nonetheless rejects the *Balfour* presumption, exploring and accepting the feminist critique that it:

> creates the risk of unfairness, distributive injustice, and relationships of dependency. Given these effects, that presumption is clearly incompatible with the values of trust, equality and respect that I have argued underpin both promise and contract.

3.12 While these criticisms are powerful, it is suggested that the presumption can still be residually justified. We do want to place some policy restrictions on the ability of parties to contract in this sphere and choose the terms of their agreement: for example, we might not want to allow brother and sister to marry or to let parties divorce by simply agreeing and snapping their fingers. Moreover, it is helpful to have a default rule in circumstances where it is often difficult to tell whether the parties intended to be legally bound. So while there is a good case for making the presumption easier to rebut (and it is hard to disagree with Saprai's criticism of cases such as *Gould v Gould* (1970) where the presumption should have been rebutted but was not), nonetheless it should not be abolished. To the extent that we do want to place some public policy-based restrictions on the ability to make and enforce contracts in the domestic sphere, there should be no objection to using intention to create legal relations as a tool to do this, providing that we acknowledge that we are using policy reasons rather than the parties' intent to determine what presumptions should apply.

Agreements in a social context

3.13   The same presumption applies here as in the domestic context. So, as Atkin LJ explains in *Balfour*, there will be no intention to create legal relations 'where two parties agree to take a walk together, or where there is an offer and an acceptance of hospitality'. Moreover, the same factors should guide the courts in determining whether it has been rebutted as for domestic agreements. In *Wilson v Burnett* (2007) the Court of Appeal rejected the claim of two women that they had a binding agreement with a friend, who won over £100,000 at bingo, that any winnings would be shared three ways: the claimants had come nowhere near to rebutting the presumption with their 'bare-bones account' of casual conversations.

3.14   The same applied in *Blue v Ashley* (2017), the much-publicised dispute between Ashley, the multi-millionaire owner of the Sports Direct group of companies, who was sued for £14 million following a very drunken night out in the pub by the claimant, an acquaintance who alleged Ashley had orally agreed to pay him that vast sum as an incentive to do work aimed at increasing the Sports Direct share price. Leggatt J held that the claimant had clearly not rebutted the presumption that there was no intention to create legal relations, emphasising factors such as the setting, the drunken social nature of the occasion, the jocular tone of the conversation (described as 'banter'), and the commercial implausibility of the alleged deal.

Agreements in the commercial context

3.15   As noted, a distinction was drawn by Mance LJ in the Court of Appeal in *Baird Textiles* between situations where there is 'an express or apparent agreement' and cases where 'an implied contract falls to be inferred from parties' conduct'. It is only in the former case that the presumption that there is an intention to create legal relations arises. In *Baird Textiles* itself, for example, Marks & Spencer regularly acquired garments from Baird over 30 years without ever entering into an express long-term agreement. This indicated that they wanted to retain the flexibility to decide how many garments to buy and when to buy them, and did not want to be tied down by a legal obligation to buy a certain quantity each year. Therefore, the case fell into the latter category (see Mouzas and Furmston (2008) for criticism of the court in *Baird Textiles* for not giving effect to the loose 'umbrella agreement' between the parties and contrasting the position in some other European legal systems). Similarly in *James-Bowen v Metropolitan Police Commissioner* (2016) the Court of Appeal applied *Baird Textiles* and declined to imply a retainer (a contract for legal services between solicitor and client), since as Moore-Bick LJ said:

> In circumstances where the parties could have entered into an express retainer but have not chosen to do so, I think the court should be slow to find that they have entered into such a contract by conduct. In my view it cannot properly do so unless they have

behaved towards each other in a way that can be explained only by the existence of an intention to enter into legal relations of a particular kind. Unless that is so, the court is left uncertain as to their intentions and has no basis on which to impute a contract to them.

3.16 In contrast, where there is an express commercial agreement and so the presumption does apply, it will be hard to rebut, as *Edwards v Skyways Ltd* (1964) makes clear. Often the document embodying the agreement will make sufficiently clear on its own that it was meant to be legally binding, as in *Barbudev v Eurocom Cable Management Bulgaria Eood* (2012). On the other hand, in exceptional circumstances the presumption might be rebutted, for example if the agreement expressly provides that there is no intent to create legal relations (for example, *Rose & Frank Co v JR Crompton & Bros Ltd* (1925)).

3.17 One last point to note is the effect of expressly stating that an agreement is made 'subject to contract'. These words, commonly used in commercial negotiations, are a way of making explicit that the parties do not intend to be legally bound at this stage and that a further agreement will need to be executed in order for a binding contract to be formed. This means that if one side then takes the risk of expending money to put herself in a position to perform the contract that she expects to materialise, she will normally be unable to recover it if no contract is formed (*Regalian Properties Ltd v London Dockland Development Corpn* (1995)). However, if *both* parties carry out the acts that the agreement contemplates them doing, then there is a strong case for saying that the parties' intentions have changed—in other words, they have made an implied binding contract on the terms of their previously 'subject to contract' deal. In *Proforce Recruit Ltd v The Rugby Group Ltd* (2006), the Court of Appeal accepted the judge's finding that an implied contract was formed on this basis (despite reversing his decision to strike out the claim on the basis of the interpretation of the contract, on which see para **7.51**).

3.18 The effect of 'subject to contract' wording was considered by the Supreme Court in *RTS Flexible Systems Ltd v Molkerei Alois Muller GmbH & Co KG* (2010). The claimant began its supply, design, and installation of a production line in one of the defendant's factories before detailed terms had been formally agreed. Negotiations over the terms continued and a draft formal contract was agreed on a 'subject to contract' basis. Unfortunately this contract was never formally executed, but the price had been agreed from early on in the process, the work (that had been going on for months) continued nonetheless, and indeed the parties varied the agreement a month later. The Supreme Court held that, judged objectively, the parties did intend to be bound by the terms of the draft contract (as varied) and had effectively agreed to waive the 'subject to contract' designation.

Certainty and intention to create legal relations

3.19 The greater the degree of precision with which the parties set out their agreement, the more likely that they will be found to have intended to create legal obligations. So returning to *Baird Textiles* once more, Mance LJ decided that 'the fact that there was never any agreement to reach or even to set out the essential principles which might govern any legally binding long-term relationship indicates that neither party can objectively be taken to have intended to make any legally binding commitment of a long-term nature'. But strictly speaking, the requirement of intention to create legal relations is conceptually distinct from the requirement that the terms of the contract must be sufficiently certain (explored in Chapter 4)—sometimes the court finds that there was an intention to create legal relations but that the agreement is nonetheless too uncertain to be enforced.

Signature: the rule in *L'Estrange v Graucob*

3.20 This section deals with situations where an offer is accepted by signing the document. In principle, one would think that acceptance by signature should be treated the same as any other type of acceptance, but this has not proved to be the case. The English courts have held that unless the offeree can make out a defence of fraud, misrepresentation (see Chapter 9), or *non est factum* (see paras **3.57–3.66**), the offeree will be bound by the terms of the document that he has signed.

3.21 The principle that you are generally bound by the terms of a document that you sign has come to be known as the 'rule in *L'Estrange v Graucob*'. While the rule did not actually originate from that case, as Spencer (1973) demonstrates, it is nevertheless worthy of examination. In *L'Estrange v Graucob* (1934), the claimant was persuaded to buy an automatic slot machine by two of the defendant's salesmen. They produced an order form containing in ordinary print the essential terms of the contract, and in small print certain special terms, one of which was 'any express or implied condition, statement, or warranty, statutory or otherwise not stated herein is hereby excluded'. Not only was the clause in small print, it was also printed on brown paper, making it even harder to read. The claimant signed the form without reading it properly. The machine turned out to be defective, so she sued for breach of contract. The defendants replied that she was bound by the special term, so she could not recover. The Divisional Court held that she was bound by the term. The ratio of the case is best summarised by Scrutton LJ:

> When a document containing contractual terms is signed, then, in the absence of fraud, or, I will add, misrepresentation, the party signing it is bound, and it is wholly immaterial whether he has read the document or not.

3.22 On one view, expounded by Spencer (1973), the rule is inconsistent with orthodox offer and acceptance principles. Signing a document is just one way of accepting an offer and the principle of objective interpretation dictates that if it does not reasonably appear to the offeror that you are accepting a particular term by signing a contract, then you should not be taken to accept the term, so the rule in *L'Estrange* seems too absolute. In *L'Estrange* itself, the fact that the clause was in small print and difficult to read arguably meant that it did not reasonably appear to the defendant that Miss L'Estrange was accepting the term in question. Moreover, the term was deliberately made difficult to read by the defendant, so even if it did reasonably appear that Miss L'Estrange was accepting the term, it is arguable she should not be bound, because it was the defendant's fault (in making the offer confusing) that Miss L'Estrange appeared to agree to the term when she did not actually intend to.

3.23 The Ontario Court of Appeal suggested in *Tilden Rent-A-Car Co v Clendenning* (1978) that the rule was too absolute, and chose to distinguish *L'Estrange*. There, the defendant rented a car and signed the contract without reading it. On the back of the contract, in fine and faint print, was a clause seeking to limit the claimant's liability. The court, applying orthodox offer and acceptance principles, held that a signature will only indicate acceptance of a term where it is reasonable for the other party to believe that the offeree really did agree to the term in question. While a court should be reluctant to find that a signature did not indicate acceptance of a particular term (otherwise commercial uncertainty would result), on the facts the term had not been accepted:

> In ordinary commercial practice where there is frequently a sense of formality in the transaction, and where there is a full opportunity for the parties to consider the terms of the proposed contract submitted for signature, it might well be safe to assume that the party who attaches his signature to the contract intends by so doing to acknowledge his acquiescence to its terms, and that the other party entered into the contract upon that belief. This can hardly be said, however, where the contract is entered into in circumstances such as were present in this case.
>
> A transaction, such as this one, is invariably carried out in a hurried, informal manner. The speed with which the transaction is completed is said to be one of the attractive features of the service provided.
>
> The clauses relied on in this case ... are inconsistent with the over-all purpose for which the contract is entered into by the hirer. Under such circumstances, something more should be done by the party submitting the contract for signature than merely handing it over to be signed (per Dubin JA).

3.24 While there are hints of a move away from *L'Estrange* in English law, there has been nothing as bold as *Tilden Rent-A-Car*. In *Lloyds Bank plc v Waterhouse* (1991), Sir Edward Eveleigh suggested that the defendant was not bound by his signature because the bank could not reasonably assume that he had agreed to the terms in question. However, this was only one of the grounds for his decision, and it was not mentioned by the other judges. A different type of limit has been placed upon *L'Estrange* by *Grogan v Robin Meredith Plant Hire* (1996), where it was held that you will not be bound by a document that you have signed if the type of document (here, a time sheet) is not one that 'a reasonable man would expect to contain, relevant contractual conditions'. However, this would have been of no help to Miss L'Estrange, because the order form was certainly the sort of document that a reasonable person would expect to contain contractual terms.

3.25 An alternative view is that the simple, clear-cut rule in *L'Estrange* is very useful commercially, and should be retained for this reason. It gives commercial parties the certainty that if an agreement is signed, it is binding (providing, as we have just seen, that the document is the type that a reasonable person would expect to contain contractual terms). If there are problems with one party being tricked into signing a document or a strong commercial actor taking advantage of a consumer, then these problems can be dealt with by specific doctrines, such as misrepresentation, duress, and unconscionability (see Chapters 9–12), rather than by making inroads into the rule in *L'Estrange*. In particular, statute now offers protection against the type of clause which ensnared Miss L'Estrange, in the shape of the Unfair Contract Terms Act 1977 for non-consumer contracts and the Consumer Rights Act 2015 for consumer contracts (see Chapter 8).

3.26 This approach was adopted in Australia in *Toll (FGCT) Pty Ltd v Alphapharm Pty Ltd* (2004), where the court noted that the fact that each of the parties was a large commercial organisation capable of looking after its own interests made it particularly unattractive to argue that *L'Estrange* did not apply. The suggestion that the clause in question needed to be drawn to the other party's attention (which seems also to have been made in *Tilden*) was firmly rejected and the court offered a further justification for the rule in *L'Estrange*, namely the need for third parties to be able to ascertain from the signed documents what the terms of the contract were. Subsequently the Court of Appeal in *Peekay Intermark Ltd and another v Australia and New Zealand Banking Group Ltd* (2006) took the same view, describing the rule in *L'Estrange v Graucob* as 'an important principle of English law which underpins the whole of commercial life; any erosion of it would have serious repercussions far beyond the business community'.

3.27 The debate has contemporary relevance beyond signatures made by hand, because there are many situations where one accepts electronically in a way that might be regarded as analogous to a signature, such as clicking 'I agree' on a website (see Macdonald (2011)). In a sense, whether the rule in *L'Estrange* should apply to such transactions depends significantly on whether the rule is a good one in its normal sphere of operation. However, there are additional reasons to be cautious about extending it to electronic signatures, not least that the reality of purchasing electronically is that the purchaser does so very quickly, having only seen the standard terms at the point of purchase, and therefore it is important that significant terms are flagged up very clearly. Unsurprisingly, the English courts have shown no support whatsoever for extending the *L'Estrange* principle to an electronic click. Instead, the rules on incorporating written terms into unsigned contracts are being used in this area, which are explored in Chapter 7.

Unilateral mistake

3.28 Often one party will be mistaken as to some matter. For example, if I walk into an antique store and see a nice chair, I might buy it because I think that it is very valuable, but in fact it is a heap of old junk. Where only one party has made a mistake, we say that there has been a 'unilateral' mistake (as opposed to a 'common' mistake: see Chapter 13).

English law is very unsure as to when we should allow a party making such a mistake to say that the mistake has prevented a contract being formed. It allows him to do so in just three different situations, which we shall examine in turn. The first is where a mistake has been made as to the identity of the person that you appear to be contracting with, the second is in the case of a mistake in the terms of the proposed contract, and the third is a mistake as to the very nature of the proposed contract where the mistaken party signs a written contract (this is known as '*non est factum*'). It will be suggested that a great deal of the uncertainty in these first two situations can be resolved by applying orthodox offer and acceptance principles to work out whether a valid contract has been formed, and if so on what terms. As for the third category, it is inconsistent with offer and acceptance principles, and therefore should arguably be discarded.

Unilateral mistake as to identity

3.29 Despite a modern House of Lords decision on the topic, the cases in this area are extremely confused and often seem contradictory (indeed, some of them probably are contradictory!). What follows is an attempt to identify some principles which might help to explain most of the case law. It is submitted that the basic principle is clear: an offer can only be accepted by the person that it is addressed to (see Goodhart (1941)). Therefore, we simply apply the principle of objective interpretation and ask whether it reasonably appeared to the person in question that the offer was addressed to him. A similar principle applies to acceptances.

3.30 A good example of these principles in operation is *Boulton v Jones* (1857). The claimant had just purchased a shop from one Brocklehurst. The defendant used to deal with Brocklehurst and had a set-off against him (ie, a claim against him that could be set against any debt that the defendant might at any time owe him). Believing that it was still Brocklehurst's shop, the defendant sent an order for pipe hose. The claimant simply sent the pipe hose, followed by an invoice, and when the defendant refused to pay, the claimant took legal action. The court held that the defendant was not liable. The claimant could not accept the defendant's offer because it was not addressed to him, it was addressed to Brocklehurst. As Pollock CB commented, '[i]t is a rule of law, that if a person intends to contract with A, B cannot give himself any right under it.' To a reasonable person in the claimant's position, the offer did not appear to be addressed to the claimant. This seems a reasonable conclusion, for the claimant either knew (or should have known) of the set-off and so he should have realised that it was important to the defendant that it was Brocklehurst who fulfilled the order.

3.31 Usually, however, things are not so simple. The traditional scenario is this: fraudster B cons A into entering into a contract with him by pretending to be someone else. The fraudster obtains goods from A, sells them on to C, who has no knowledge of the fraud, and then disappears. We are faced with two innocent parties, A and C, and the issue of which of them should bear the consequences of the fraud. A will argue that he made a mistake as to B's identity. If this makes the A–B contract void ('void' means that the contract never came into existence at all), title to the goods will not have passed to C, so A can recover the goods and C loses out. On the other hand, if the contract is not void, C does get good title to the goods, so it is A who loses out. Both consequences seem unfair on one party!

3.32 Assume for the sake of argument that it is A who has made the offer. Let us apply our orthodox offer and acceptance principles to the situation to work out when A will be able to successfully claim that he did not address his offer to B. The first point to make is that the mere fact that A made a mistake as to some attribute of B is insufficient. The reason for this is that in line with the principle of objective interpretation, we look at matters from a reasonable person in B's shoes to work out the terms of A's offer. So what is relevant is not what A was thinking but how things reasonably appeared to B.

3.33 For example, in *Fletcher v Krell* (1873), Ms Krell entered into a contract with Mr Fletcher to act as a governess for three years (presumably for his children). He was under the mistaken impression that she had never been married, but in fact she had been divorced (she made no misrepresentation about her marital history, simply kept quiet). Strange as it may seem in this day and age, this would have been very important to a person in Mr Fletcher's position, so when he learnt she was a divorcee he refused to honour the contract. Ms Krell brought an action for breach of contract and Mr Fletcher resisted the claim on the ground of mistake. His defence was rejected; Blackburn J held that 'the mere concealment of a material fact, except in cases of policies of insurance, does not avoid a contract'. In other words, something more is needed than a mere mistake on the part of one party as to an attribute of the other.

3.34 What more is required? The answer, it is submitted, is that it must be clear to B that her identity or the fact that she possesses a particular attribute is so important to A that A's offer is only directed to her on condition that B is who she says she is or possesses the attribute in question. The clearest example of this would be A saying 'this offer is only addressed to you if you are indeed the Queen of England'. If B is not the Queen, then from B's perspective, the offer does not appear to be addressed to her. Applying the principle of objective interpretation, we can therefore say that there is no A–B contract.

3.35 Most of the cases on mistake as to identity involve credit transactions, that is, a transaction whereby the purchaser is allowed to pay some or all of the money at a later date. The fraudster claims to be someone else who is creditworthy, and because of this deception, the victim is prepared to offer the goods on credit to him. Therefore, the victim enters into the contract because he mistakenly believes that the fraudster is someone else, and someone else who is creditworthy. The really difficult issue in this area is what effect such a mistake should have. There are two possibilities. The fraudster might merely be making a misrepresentation that he is someone else who is creditworthy. If this is the case, a contract has been formed. The fact that a misrepresentation has been made would normally allow the victim to undo the contract (the contract is said to be 'voidable': see Chapter 9) and get the goods back, but if a third party has innocently bought the goods from the fraudster, the victim will not be able to do this. Alternatively, as explained, the victim's mistake might be so important that he is only making an offer to the fraudster on the condition that the fraudster is who he says he is. Therefore, the fraudster will not be able to validly accept the offer and no contract will be formed, so the victim can get the goods back from anyone who currently has them.

3.36 Different cases have reached different answers to this question. In *Phillips v Brooks Ltd* (1919), a jeweller contracted to sell a ring to a crook that had come into his shop and represented that he was Sir George Bullough. The jeweller had heard of Sir George Bullough and, after checking that he lived at the address given, accepted a cheque for the requisite amount. Horridge J held that the rogue had merely made a misrepresentation, so the contract was voidable, not void. He adopted the following passage from the Massachusetts case of *Edmunds v Merchants' Despatch Transportation Co* (1883):

> the seller ... could not have supposed that he was selling to any other person; his intention was to sell to the person present, and identified by sight and hearing; it does not defeat the sale because the buyer assumed a false name, or practised any other deceit to induce the vendor to sell.

The same result was reached in *Lewis v Averay* (1972), where the rogue pretended to be the then well-known television actor, Richard Green.

3.37 On the other hand, in *Ingram v Little* (1961) and *Lake v Simmons* (1927), the courts took a different approach. In *Ingram*, the three claimants put their car up for sale. A rogue, introducing himself as Mr Hutchinson, offered to buy it. Having agreed a price, the rogue pulled out his cheque book, but the claimant conducting the negotiations told him that cash payment was expected, and so the sale was off. The rogue then claimed to be Mr PGM Hutchinson, a reputable businessman living at an address in Caterham and having business interests in Guildford. The claimants had never heard of this man, so one of them went to the local post office, where she checked the local phone directory and found that there was a person by that name residing at the address given by the rogue. She told the other claimants of her discovery, and so they let the rogue pay by cheque. Of course, the rogue was not who he said he was, his cheque was dishonoured, and he sold the car to an innocent third party, the defendant. The claimant brought an action, alleging that no contract had been formed between the claimant and the rogue, and so the defendant had not acquired good title to the car.

The Court of Appeal held by a majority that no contract had been formed between the claimant and the rogue. Pearce LJ identified two reasons why the rogue should not have interpreted the offer as being made to him. First, once the rogue had pulled out his chequebook and the claimant conducting the negotiations had refused it, the parties 'were concerned with a credit [rather than a cash] sale in which both parties knew that the identity of the purchaser was of the utmost importance'. In other words, the fact that the claimants would have to trust that the cheque did not bounce and that they had made clear their reservations about this form of payment meant that they had made clear to the rogue how important they regarded it that he was who he said he was. Second, the rogue wrote the name and address on the back of the cheque that he had given. Pearce LJ viewed this as 'an additional indication of the importance attached by the parties to the individuality of PGM Hutchinson of Stanstead House'.

3.38   With these two different views in mind, we can examine the most important case on the topic, the House of Lords decision in *Shogun Finance Ltd v Hudson* (2003). A rogue went into a car showroom, fraudulently claiming to be one Mr Patel, and bought a Mitsubishi Shogun via a hire-purchase agreement, which he then sold on to an innocent purchaser, the defendant, before vanishing, leaving most of the purchase price unpaid. The initial deal proceeded in the following way. The dealer produced a copy of Shogun's standard form hire-purchase agreement, onto which Mr Patel's details were entered. The rogue signed the document and produced Mr Patel's driving licence. The dealer relayed these details to Shogun by telephone and faxed them a copy of the draft agreement and driving licence. Shogun made a computer search checking his name and address against the electoral register, whether he had any county court judgments or bankruptcy orders against him, and his credit rating. Finally, Shogun phoned the dealer and told him that the proposal was accepted, so the dealer handed over the car.

3.39   Shogun claimed that it had formed no contract with the rogue. By a majority, the Court of Appeal agreed, and this decision was upheld by a 3–2 majority in the House of Lords. The majority in the House of Lords held that a distinction must be drawn between situations where the parties are dealing 'face to face' and other situations. Where the parties are not dealing face to face, one works out whom the innocent party intended to contract with by construing the terms of the written document(s) in question. If the document clearly identifies the intended other party, this is conclusive and no oral or other extrinsic evidence will be admissible to determine its meaning (applied in *TTMI Sarl v Statoil ASA* (2011)); where the contract does not clearly identify the other party, extrinsic evidence is admissible (*Dumford Trading AG v OAO Atlantrybflot* (2004)). Here, it was held that Shogun and the rogue were not dealing 'face to face', because the rogue only dealt with Shogun by submitting a written document. The document included Mr Patel's name and details, so Shogun intended to contract with him and not the rogue. While technically *obiter* in light of the majority's decision that the parties did not deal face to face, it was agreed that in face-to-face situations, there was a strong presumption that the innocent party intended to contract with the person in front of him (see previous paragraph). Therefore, in the vast majority of face-to-face situations, a valid contract will be formed.

3.40   There are a number of problems with the decision.

- Face-to-face situations should not be treated differently from other situations. As Lords Nicholls and Millett argued, in both cases the legal problem is identical: the innocent party A thinks she is dealing with B but in fact A is dealing with someone else. The presence or absence of writing does not constitute a principled ground of distinction.

- It is too simplistic to say that because the written document included the name and details of Mr Patel, Shogun must be taken to have intended to contract with

Mr Patel and not with the rogue. Shogun thought that the rogue was Mr Patel, so it does not necessarily follow that by referring to Mr Patel, Shogun intended to refer to someone other than the rogue (as Lords Nicholls and Millett explained). Whether this is his apparent intention or not will turn on all the circumstances surrounding the transaction, rather than just the terms of the contract considered in isolation. For example, in *Shogun Finance*, the identity of the customer was of vital importance to Shogun (see para **3.38**), so Shogun did not intend to refer to the rogue in the document; they intended to refer to the creditworthy Mr Patel. On the other hand, if the nature of the transaction had been such that the identity of the customer was of little importance to Shogun, then Shogun would have intended to refer to whichever person they had been dealing with, irrespective of his name or other details.

• Where the parties are dealing face to face, do we need a strong, almost irrebuttable presumption that the innocent party intends to contract with the party that she is actually dealing with? As noted by Dyson LJ in the Court of Appeal in *Shogun Finance*, 'it is important to keep in mind that the face to face principle is no more than an aid to determining … to whom should the offeree reasonably have interpreted the offer as being made?' It is just one piece of evidence, albeit an important one, that goes towards establishing how important the identity of the other party was to the innocent party. It suggests that the victim intended to deal with the person standing in front of him irrespective of who the latter actually was, but does no more than that (see the guidelines set out at paras **3.44–3.46**). Moreover, as Lord Nicholls notes, to start with such a presumption is to favour the innocent third party that has bought from the rogue over the innocent party that sold the goods to him in the first place. Is it right to assume that one innocent party is more deserving than the other?

3.41 In summary, the main difference between the majority and the minority was whether the fraudster had merely misrepresented that he was the creditworthy Mr Patel, or whether the offer was only directed to him on condition that he was the creditworthy Mr Patel. For the minority, Lords Nicholls and Millett, a fraudster who says that he is someone else who is creditworthy is generally just making an ordinary misrepresentation, whether the parties are dealing face to face or in writing:

> *The common law distinguished between a case (1) where a crook fraudulently asserts he is creditworthy and a case (2) where a crook fraudulently asserts he is someone else known to be creditworthy [the 'mistake as to identity situation']. One might suppose there is no difference of substance between these two cases. These are merely two ways a crook may assert a spurious creditworthiness [and so in each case the crook has merely made a misrepresentation] (per Lord Nicholls).*

For the majority, while the fraudster may be making only a misrepresentation in face-to-face situations, where a written document is involved the situation will often be different. When the purported contract is in writing, the victim only intends to contract with the person named or otherwise identified in the written document.

3.42 It is arguable that Lords Nicholls and Millett are correct. Where a rogue fraudulently asserts that he is creditworthy, he has only made a misrepresentation, so why should things be any different where he fraudulently asserts that he is someone else who is creditworthy? As Lord Nicholls commented, '[i]t is little short of absurd that a subsequent purchaser's rights depend on the precise manner in which the crook seeks to persuade the owner of his creditworthiness and permit him to take the goods away with him.'

3.43 On the other hand, there is a difference between the two situations set out in the quote: in the latter case, the rogue is claiming to be someone he is not. In credit transactions such as that in *Shogun Finance*, the identity of the rogue is crucial, because the credit checks are run against the name of the person that the rogue claims to be. As Lord Hobhouse put it, the finance company 'was only willing to do business with a person who had identified himself in the way required by the written document so as to enable it to check before it enters into any contractual or other relationship that he meets its credit requirements' (see also the Court of Appeal's decision). So, the fact that the rogue is making a false assertion about his identity arguably changes things: it makes it easier to say that the offer was only addressed to the rogue on the condition that he was who he claimed to be.

3.44 Looking at the current state of the law in more detail, if we are presented with a set of facts, how are we to work out whether the contract is void or merely voidable? A number of guidelines can be distilled from the case law as it stands after *Shogun Finance*. First, if the parties are dealing 'face to face', there will be a strong presumption that the innocent party intends to contract with the person in front of him (the rogue) rather than the person whom the rogue is pretending to be (see also *Phillips v Brooks Ltd* (1919) and *Lewis v Averay* (1972)). At the very least, this presumption will only be rebutted in rare cases (*Shogun Finance*, per Lord Walker), and two of their Lordships in *Shogun Finance*, Lords Nicholls and Millett, found it hard to envisage a situation in which it could be rebutted. It is difficult to pin down exactly what constitutes a 'face-to-face' transaction. The classic case is where both parties are physically present and the dealings are entirely oral. However, it may well extend to cases where there is a written agreement but the agreement is peripheral to the dealings between the parties (*Shogun Finance*, per Lord Phillips), and agreements made by telephone (*Shogun Finance*, per Lord Walker). On the other hand, if the parties do not deal 'face to face', such as where their dealings are conducted exclusively in writing, this presumption does not apply. Instead, we must construe the written agreement to determine whom the innocent party intended to contract with. If the document specifically identifies this party, this is the end of the matter and oral or other extrinsic evidence will not be admissible to contradict the document on this issue.

3.45 The second guideline is the general nature of the transaction, which will sometimes indicate to the other party that it is essential that he possesses a particular attribute, and that the offer is only addressed to him on the condition that he does. Pearce LJ made the point well in *Ingram*:

> If a man orally commissions a portrait from some unknown artist who had deliberately passed himself off, whether by disguise or merely by verbal cosmetics, as a

famous painter, the impostor could not accept the offer. For though the offer is made to him physically, it is obviously, as he knows, addressed to the famous painter. The mistake in identity on such facts is clear and the nature of the contract makes it obvious that identity was of vital importance to the offeror. At the other end of the scale, if a shopkeeper sells goods in a normal cash transaction to a man who misrepresents himself as being some well-known figure, the transaction will normally be valid. For the shopkeeper was ready to sell goods for cash to the world at large and the particular identity of the purchaser in such a contract was not of sufficient importance to override the physical presence identified by sight and hearing.

Similarly, according to Lord Hobhouse in *Shogun Finance*, the fact that the agreement was a consumer credit agreement where Shogun would not receive most of the money upfront made the identity of the customer crucial (see also Dyson LJ in the Court of Appeal in *Shogun Finance*).

3.46 The third guideline is that if the person who the rogue pretends to be actually exists, and in particular, if this third party is known to the offeror, this will suggest that the offer is not addressed to the rogue. Indeed, this may account for the different results reached in *Cundy v Lindsay* (1878), where the rogue pretended to be a company that actually existed, and *King's Norton Metal Co v Edridge, Merret & Co Ltd* (1897), where this was not the case. It should be noted that this is only a guideline, not a decisive factor (Sellers LJ in *Ingram*).

3.47 Finally, it was sometimes suggested that a distinction should be drawn between a mistake as to identity, which would satisfy this test, and a mistake as to an attribute, which would not. However, this myth was exploded by Glanville Williams (1945) and did not find favour with Lord Denning MR in *Lewis v Averay* (1972):

> *this is a distinction without a difference. A man's very name is one of his attributes. It is also the key to his identity (see also Shogun Finance, per Lord Nicholls).*

3.48 In conclusion, there is general agreement in *Shogun Finance* that the right question to ask in mistaken identity cases is 'To whom is the offer (or acceptance) addressed?'

However, the answer to this question has proved far more elusive. Upon closer inspection, much of the disagreement appears to be over how significant the identity of the purchaser is in a credit transaction. To those who view it as pivotal, particularly where credit checks are carried out, it is easier to say that the offer is only addressed to the rogue on condition that he is who is says he is, while to those who view the rogue's assertion that he is someone else as just another way to deceive the victim into contracting, it follows that the rogue has merely made a misrepresentation.

Unilateral mistake as to the terms of the contract

3.49 If you offer to sell me 100 pears for £10, and I accept because I have misheard you and thought you said 100 bears, what is the position? In other words, what is the effect of my unilateral mistake as to the terms of the offer? To provide an answer, all we need to do is apply orthodox principles of objective interpretation to work out what the terms of the offer are, what the terms of my purported acceptance are, and whether the two coincide (if they do, there will be a contract). In our example, providing you made clear that you were selling pears, then there is an offer for the sale of 100 pears (because that is how it would appear to a reasonable person in my position). To work out whether I have accepted this offer, we need to look at how my words and conduct would appear to a reasonable person in the position of the offeror (ie, you). If you had no reason to know that I had misheard you, and I had simply said 'I accept your offer', then it would reasonably appear to you that there had been an acceptance of your offer, and so there would be a contract for the sale of pears. On the other hand, if I had said to you 'I love bears so I would be delighted to buy the bears from you', then it would appear that I was not accepting the offer to buy pears, so there would be no contract for the sale of pears.

3.50 This example demonstrates that in situations involving a mistake as to terms, the issues are what the terms of the offer are, what the terms of the purported acceptance are, and whether the two coincide to form a contract. In other words, these are standard offer and acceptance problems, because the only issue is how the promises made by each party should have been interpreted by the other. Accordingly, they can be solved by the application of the principle of objective interpretation (see also Chen-Wishart (2009)).

3.51 While the case law seems to be slowly heading towards this realisation, the sticking point is the famous decision in *Smith v Hughes* (1871). Smith was a farmer, who offered to sell some oats to the defendant, a racehorse trainer. The defendant thought the oats were old oats, because trainers as a rule use such oats rather than new ones, and agreed to take the oats. In fact, the oats provided were new oats. The issue was whether the farmer could successfully claim that a contract for the sale of new oats had been formed. The Court of Appeal held that there would be such a contract unless two conditions could be made out:

> If, therefore, in the present case, the plaintiff knew that the defendant, in dealing with him for oats, did so on the assumption that the plaintiff was contracting to sell him old oats, he was aware that the defendant apprehended the contract in a different sense to that in which he meant it, and he is thereby deprived of the right to insist that the defendant shall be bound by that which was only the apparent, and not the real bargain.

In other words, it must first be shown that the defendant made a mistake as to the terms of the offer: that is, he thought he was being *promised* that the oats were old. Second, it must be shown that Smith actually knew of this mistake. The reasoning seems to be this. If Smith knew that the defendant thought old oats were being promised, it would appear to Smith that the defendant was not agreeing to buy new oats. In other words, Smith could not reasonably interpret the defendant's words and conduct as showing an intention to accept an offer to buy new oats. Therefore, there would be no contract for the sale of new oats.

3.52 A comment can be made on each of the conditions laid down in *Smith v Hughes*. With regard to the first condition, it must be shown that the mistake was as to the terms of the offer, not as to some other matter. So the mere fact that the defendant thought that the oats were old would not be enough (this ties in with the fact that there is very rarely a duty of disclosure of material facts in English law—see para **9.2**); he must have believed that he was being *promised* old oats by the claimant. This is a fine distinction but an important one because it helps to determine how the defendant's response should have been interpreted by the claimant. If the defendant actually thought that the proposed contract contained a promise that the oats would be old (and the claimant knew of this belief), then it would appear to the claimant that the defendant was only agreeing to buy old oats: those were the terms on which he was accepting. On the other hand, if the defendant thought only that the oats were old but did not think that the claimant was promising old oats, then the defendant was just hoping that the oats would turn out to be old; he was not making it a term of his acceptance that they had to be old. The following example makes things clearer. Imagine I go to a car boot sale and think I see a Van Gogh painting. The owner offers it to me for £100 and I accept. It turns out not to be a Van Gogh. I have not made a mistake as to the terms of the contract because I did not think that the shop owner was promising that it was a Van Gogh: I merely hoped that it was. This is a matter for me and is not the business of the other party: it does not affect whether I accept his offer or not.

3.53 As regards the second limb, *Smith v Hughes* said that actual knowledge is required. The fact that the claimant should have known the defendant meant to contract for old oats would not be enough. This is the problem with *Smith v Hughes*. The principle of objective interpretation suggests that in order to work out whether the defendant was agreeing to buy old oats, we look at how things ought to have appeared to the claimant. So *Smith v Hughes* is out of line with orthodox rules of offer and acceptance.

3.54 However, subsequent decisions seem to suggest that it might be enough that one party *should have known* of the other's mistake. In other words, they seem to apply orthodox offer and acceptance principles by looking at how each party's words and conduct should have appeared to the other party. For example, in *Hartog v Colin & Shields* (1939) the claim was rejected on the ground that 'the plaintiff could not reasonably have supposed that that offer contained the offeror's real intention'—he was 'snapping up' an offer that contained an obvious error. The objective approach was adopted by the Court of Appeal in *Sherrington v Berwin Leighton Paisner* (2006), holding that no contract was formed when, following an offer made by a firm of solicitors to accept £45,000 in settlement of its fees, the firm wrote a letter containing a typographical error which said 'our present offer to accept the sum of £35,000 remains open', which the claimant promptly purported to accept.

3.55 A similar approach was taken in *Centrovincial Estates plc v Merchant Investors Assurance Co Ltd* (1983) and *OT Africa Line Ltd v Vickers plc* (1996). In *Champion Investments Ltd v Eaitisham Ahmed* (2004) it was explicitly held that 'a contract may be affected by unilateral mistake on the part of one party if the other party ought reasonably to have known of the mistake, even if he did not in fact know of it' (although see the decision of the Singaporean Court of Appeal to the contrary in *Chwee Kin Keong and Others v Digilandmall.com Pte Ltd* (2005)). This has implications for those infamous cases where goods are offered for sale on a website, at an absurdly low price that was included by mistake. Could the website escape liability by arguing that customers ought to have known that the term as to price was incorrect?

3.56 Consistent with approaching the matter as an application of offer and acceptance principles, it only applies where there has been a mistake as to the terms of the contract, rather than a mistake about some other effect. This was confirmed in *Statoil ASA v Louis Dreyfus Energy Services LP ('The Hariette N')* (2008), where the seller made a mistake in its calculations which caused it to enter into a disadvantageous contract. The court held that a mistake about a fact which formed the basis on which one party entered the contract was not sufficient to engage the unilateral mistake jurisdiction, because the mistake had to be as to the terms of the proposed contract, and both parties were clear what those terms were.

Non est factum

3.57 Where a party signing a document has made a fundamental mistake through no fault of his own as to the character or effect of the proposed contract, the contract will be void under the doctrine of *non est factum*. Translating this into offer and acceptance terms, if the offeree makes a fundamental mistake as to the character or effect of the offer, he will not be taken to have accepted the offer.

3.58 The doctrine has two elements. First, the party signing the document must have made a fundamental mistake as to its character or effect (*Saunders v Anglia Building Society* (1971)). Until *Saunders*, a distinction was drawn between mistakes as to the nature of the transaction, which sufficed, and mistakes as to the content of a document, which were insufficient. An example of the former would be if I thought that I was signing an agreement to buy a car, whereas in fact I was agreeing to guarantee your business debts. An example of the latter would be if I thought that I was making a loan to you of £5,000 but in fact I was making a loan to you of £50,000. In such a case, I made no mistake as the nature of the transaction: I thought I was making a loan. In *Saunders*, it was held that this distinction was unsatisfactory and should be replaced with the more flexible test of a fundamental mistake as to character or effect.

3.59 The second requirement is that the party making the mistake must not have done so as a result of his own negligence (*Saunders*). For example, signing a document in blank and leaving it up to another party to fill in the details of what you are agreeing to will prevent you relying on the doctrine (*United Dominions Trust Ltd v Western* (1976), applying the test laid down in *Saunders*). It should be noted that the onus is on the party who signed the document to show that he acted carefully (*Saunders*, applied in *United Dominions*). In practice, this requirement means that the party must show some reason why they completely misunderstood the character of the transaction, such as illness, or a defective education, for example. It is certainly not enough to show that you were too busy or lazy to read through the document!

3.60 Often, the party seeking to rely on *non est factum* will have been misled as to the nature of the transaction by the offeror. In practice, it will be difficult to satisfy the two requirements unless you have been misled, because unless you have asked someone what the document means, you are likely to be considered negligent. However, it is certainly not necessary as a matter of law to show that you have been misled by the *other party to the contract*. Indeed, it is probably not necessary to show that you have been misled *at all* in order to invoke the doctrine. As Lord Wilberforce commented in *Saunders*, 'it is the lack of consent that matters, not the means by which this result was brought about'. Similarly, in the earlier case of *Foster v Mackinnon* (1869), Byles J stated that 'it is invalid not merely on the ground of fraud, where fraud exists, but on the ground that the mind of the signor did not accompany the signature; in other words, that he never intended to sign' (see also *Lloyds Bank plc v Waterhouse* (1993); cf *Hasham v Zenab* (1960)).

3.61 One last point should be made before looking at an example of the operation of the doctrine in practice, which is that the scope of the doctrine is very narrow, as Lord Reid emphasised in *Saunders*, so as 'not to shake the confidence of those who habitually and rightly rely on signatures when there is no obvious reason to doubt their validity' (see also *Norwich and Peterborough Building Society v Steed* (1993)). As Patten LJ put it in *CF Asset Finance Ltd v Okonji* (2014):

> The court's desire to confine the effectiveness of a plea of non est factum to very limited circumstances has undoubtedly been dictated by its legal consequences. To declare the contract a nullity has obviously serious and adverse consequences for third parties who may have relied on the contents of the document such as the claimant in this case.

The doctrine tends to be invoked in two types of situation. First, the offeree may sign as a result of the fraud of a third party (ie, not the offeror). In this situation, it is important to keep the doctrine narrow in order to protect the offeror. Second, the offeree might sign as a result of being misled by the offeror, who then sells the property on to an innocent third party. In this situation, it is important to keep the doctrine within tight limits to protect the third party who would lose out if the offeror–offeree contract is held to be void (because the third party will not acquire good title to the property: see para **3.31**).

3.62 A good example of how the doctrine operates is *Saunders* itself. There, an elderly woman, Mrs Gallie, was prepared to help her nephew raise money by assigning her house to him, which he could then use to raise the money. However, the nephew did not want the house put in his own name, so he arranged for a document to be prepared that would assign the house to his friend and business associate, Mr Lee. The friend was then meant to use the house to raise the money and pay the money to the nephew. The friend asked the woman to sign the document, telling her (untruthfully) that it was a deed of gift of the house to her nephew. The woman had broken her glasses and so could not read the document. It was in fact an assignment of the house to the friend for £3,000. She signed the document but the friend never paid the £3,000. He mortgaged the house to a building society, but defaulted on his instalments (he also failed to pay the nephew) and so the society claimed possession of the house. The woman sought to defend this action on the basis that the contract between her and the friend was void through the operation of the doctrine of *non est factum*.

3.63   The House of Lords held that she could not rely on the doctrine. While the various judgments clarify the law in the area substantially, few of them give many reasons for the decision reached on the facts. A notable exception is Viscount Dilhorne. His analysis seems to suggest that Mrs Gallie failed to make out either of the requirements (see paras **3.58–3.59**). First, there was no fundamental mistake as to the character of the transaction. She thought that she was transferring her property so it could be used to raise money by her nephew and Mr Lee and the transaction did have this effect. The fact that the transaction transferred the property to Mr Lee rather than her nephew was insufficient to make her mistake a fundamental one, because she understood that Lee and her nephew were jointly concerned in a project of raising money on security of the property and so it would not have mattered greatly to her which of the two she was transferring the property to. Second, Viscount Dilhorne also seems to implicitly suggest that Mrs Gallie was negligent: he comments that 'she never asked for the document to be read to her or that it should be explained to her'. However, there may be a difference of opinion between the Lords on this point, for Lord Pearson takes the view that she was not negligent:

> In the present case the plaintiff was not at the material time a person who could read, because on the facts found she had broken her spectacles and could not effectively read without them. In any case her evidence ... shows that she had very little capacity for understanding legal documents and property transactions, and I do not think a reasonable jury would have found that she was negligent.

The Court of Appeal in *CF Asset Finance Ltd v Okonji* (2014) expressed the view, *obiter*, that *non est factum* was not available where the claimant signed a hire agreement in the mistaken view that her signature would just be used for credit checking purposes—this was not a mistake about the fundamental nature of the document, and was a negligent thing to do, particularly since the claimant was a solicitor!

3.64   As a final matter, it is interesting to consider whether the doctrine is justifiable. It is suggested that it is not. As we have seen in our examination of the principle of objective interpretation, generally an offeree should only be able to say that he did not accept an offer where it should have appeared to the offeror that there was no acceptance. The doctrine of *non est factum* is out of line with this requirement, because it does not require the party's mistake to be apparent to the other party. This is unfair, because it means that the offeree's mistake may prevent a contract arising despite the fact that the offeror had no way of knowing that the offeree had made such a mistake.

3.65   The doctrine also seems out of place alongside the normal remedies for fraud and sharp practice. If the other party to the contract deliberately tricks me into a contract or takes advantage of some weakness of mine, the contract will only be *voidable* (see Chapter 9). *Non est factum*, on the other hand, allows me to have a contract declared *void* without needing to show that the other party has done anything wrong: as long as I fulfil the two requirements, I can invoke the doctrine even if I have misled myself as to the nature of the transaction or have been misled by a third party.

3.66 Similarly, *non est factum* places someone who is unable to understand the nature of a document in a far better position than a person who is actually mentally incapable. Excepting situations where the person's property is subject to the control of the court under the Mental Capacity Act 2005, mental incapacity only renders a contract voidable, and it will only have this effect where the other party knows of the incapacity (*Imperial Loan Co v Stone* (1892)).

The doctrine originated from a desire to give special protection to those who were illiterate. 'Not otherwise could an unlearned age be protected' (Fifoot (1949)). However, as this problem has declined, and more subtle and balanced ways of protecting the vulnerable have been developed, *non est factum* has become out of date and out of line with other areas of the law.

OVERVIEW

Intention to create legal relations

1   A contract will only be formed if both parties intend their agreement to create legal relations between them, that is, if they intend the agreement to grant rights to and impose obligations upon each of them, their intent being judged 'objectively' (in the sense discussed at the start of Chapter 2).

2   A finding that there is no intent to create legal relations should be distinguished from a finding that there was an invitation to treat. An invitation to treat means its maker appeared to envisage a legally binding arrangement being entered into at a later date, whereas no intention to create legal relations means that the parties did not envisage entering into a legally binding arrangement at all.

3   Often it is unclear whether the parties had the requisite intent, so the courts have formulated presumptions to help them apply the doctrine:

   •   If the agreement is concluded in a domestic or social context, it is presumed that the parties did not intend to create legal relations unless the contrary can be proved. One of the main reasons originally given for this presumption was that the domestic sphere is a private one which the law should not enter; however, this reasoning is questionable today. The following factors will point towards the presumption being rebutted: the fact that the claimant has performed his side of the deal and is seeking to hold the other party to its side, the fact that the context had commercial elements to it, and the fact that the parties were bargaining at arm's length or close to it.

   •   If an express agreement is concluded in a commercial context, it is presumed that the parties did intend to create legal relations unless there is strong evidence to the contrary, which is sometimes found by expressly labelling the agreement 'subject to contract'.

   •   If it is alleged that an implied agreement has been reached in the commercial context, it is for the party alleging the existence of the contract to show that there was an intention to create legal relations.

4   The greater the precision with which the parties have set out their agreement, the more likely it is that the courts will find that there is intention to create legal relations.

The rule in *L'Estrange v Graucob*

5   Where an offer is accepted by signing a document, the offeree will be bound even if he has not read or understood its contents (unless he can make out a defence of fraud, misrepresentation or *non est factum*). Some argue that this rule is too absolute and out of line with orthodox offer and acceptance principles, because an offeree should only be bound by a term if it reasonably appears to the offeror that the offeree is agreeing to the term, which is not the case where a party clearly has not read or understood a particular term. But on balance the better view is that the simple, clear-cut rule in *L'Estrange* is useful commercially, in that it gives commercial actors the certainty that a signed agreement is binding, while consumers are now protected by statutory regimes.

Unilateral mistake

6   Often one party will be mistaken as to some matter. English law allows the mistaken party to argue that his mistake has prevented a contract being formed on particular terms in three situations.

7   The first is where a mistake has been made as to the identity of the person that you appear to be contracting with. While the cases in this area are confused and contradictory, the basic principle seems to be clear: an offer can only be accepted by a person that it is addressed to. So if the offer, either expressly or impliedly, makes clear that it is only addressed to you on the condition that you are a certain person, then if you are not this person, you cannot accept the offer. It is only in such circumstances that my mistake as to identity will prevent you accepting my offer (an analogous principle applies where the party making the mistake is the offeree). So it is not enough in itself that I make a mistake as to your identity: I must make it clear in my offer that I am only addressing my offer to you on the condition that you possess the attributes in question. We see from all this that 'mistake as to identity' is in fact a mere application of the rules of offer and acceptance.

8   In order to tell whether an offer satisfies this test, a number of factors will provide helpful guidance:

- If the parties are dealing 'face to face', there will be a strong presumption that the offer is being made to the person standing before me. This principle may well apply to some situations where the two parties are not physically present in the same place, such as where they communicate by telephone, for example. When the 'face to face' principle does not apply, the written documents passing between the parties will be interpreted to work out the identity of the intended offeree. If the written document(s) clearly refers to a particular offeree, no oral or other extrinsic evidence will be admissible to suggest that the intended offeree was someone else.

- The nature of the transaction: sometimes this will indicate to the other party that it is essential that he possesses a particular attribute and that the offer is only addressed to him on the condition that he does.

- If the person whom the rogue pretends to be actually exists, and in particular, if the identity of this other person is known to the offeror, this will suggest that the offer is addressed to this third party, not to the rogue.

9   The second type of situation is where one party has made a mistake as to the terms of the proposed contract. The current state of the law seems to be that you will only be able to claim that there is no contract where (1) you have made a mistake as to the terms of the contract, that is, as to what it is that I am promising; and (2) I actually knew of this mistake. The second condition seems unduly restrictive and out of line with the principle of objective interpretation, according to which we should look at how your acts would appear to a reasonable person in my position. The case law seems to be moving in this direction.

10 The last type of situation is where one party has made a fundamental mistake as to the effect of the written document that he is signing. Providing that (1) the party made such a mistake; and (2) this party did not make the mistake as a result of his own negligence (such as being too lazy to read the document), the doctrine of *non est factum* will allow this party to say that he did not accept the offer. While the party seeking to rely on the doctrine will often have been misled as to the nature of the transaction, it is certainly not necessary for him to show that he was misled by the other party and probably not necessary to have been misled at all. While the doctrine is a very narrow one, it is nevertheless suggested that it is inconsistent with orthodox offer and acceptance principles and cannot be justified.

FURTHER READING

Chen-Wishart 'Contractual Mistake, Intention in Formation and Vitiation: the Oxymoron of Smith v Hughes' Chapter 14 in *Exploring Contract Law* (2009) 341

Goodhart 'Mistake as to Identity in the Law of Contract' (1941) 57 LQR 228

Hedley 'Keeping Contract in its Place—*Balfour v Balfour* and the Enforceability of Informal Agreements' (1985) 5(3) OJLS 391

Macdonald 'Incorporation of Standard Terms in Website Contracting' (2011) 27 JCL 198

McLauchlan 'Parol Guidance and Contract Formation' (2005) 121 LQR 9

McMeel 'Interpretation and Mistake in Contract Law' (2006) LMCLQ 49

Phang 'The Frontiers of Contract Law—Contract Formation and Mistake in Cyberspace—The Singaporean Experience' (2005) 17 Singapore Academy of L;1; J 361 (available in the online resources)

Saprai '*Balfour v Balfour* and the Separation of Contract and Promise' (2017) 37 LS 468

SELF-TEST QUESTIONS

1   When will a court hold that there was no intention to create legal relations? How does such a finding differ from saying that there was an invitation to treat?

2   When will my mistake as to the terms of the proposed contract allow me to say that I did not accept an offer? When should it?

3   When will a unilateral mistake as to identity prevent a contract being formed?

4   Why do we have a doctrine of *non est factum*? Can such a doctrine be justified?

5   (a)   Lenny, an antiques dealer, is offering a nineteenth century pewter tankard for sale in his shop for £500. The tankard is worth £150. If it had been made in the sixteenth century, the tankard would be worth £1,500. The tankard is clearly labelled as '19th century'. Meldrew, who is short-sighted and has forgotten his glasses, thinks that the label reads '16th century'. As he approaches the till, Meldrew says to Lenny, 'This is great! I only collect sixteenth-century pewter, you know, and this is such a bargain.' Lenny allows Meldrew to purchase the tankard without correcting him. Advise Meldrew as to his contractual position.

   (b)   Biddy (a retired solicitor) advertised her car for sale in her local church newsletter, specifying that she would only sell to a practising Christian. The advertisement was answered by a man who claimed to be called Revd Dove, who visited Biddy dressed as a vicar and showed her a driving licence in the name of Revd Dove. Reassured, she agreed to sell the car to him, but required him to sign a written memorandum of agreement, having inserted the names 'Biddy' and 'Revd Dove' in the blank boxes headed 'Seller' and 'Purchaser', which also contained a warranty given by the purchaser verifying his identity. The purchaser handed over a cheque and drove off with the car. The cheque was later dishonoured and it transpired that the purchaser was not the real Revd Dove, whose driving licence had been stolen the previous week. The rogue has disappeared, having sold the car to Inez. Advise Biddy.

For hints on how to answer question 5, please see the online resources at **www.oup.com/uk/sullivan8e/**.

4 Certainty

SUMMARY

This chapter deals with the requirement of certainty in contractual formation, considering problem areas such as agreements to agree, agreements to negotiate in good faith and lock out agreements.

4.1 Often parties do not agree on all aspects of their arrangement or set out all parts of their agreement in a clear manner. This causes two problems. First, their failure to do so may indicate that they do not intend to be bound unless and until agreement is reached on the remaining issues or the agreement is set out clearly. We have dealt with this issue already in Chapters 2 and 3, where we noted that unless the parties intend to be legally bound, there will be no contract, so we will only mention this issue in passing at relevant points in this chapter. The second problem is that the parties have left gaps in their agreement, that is, matters on which they have not reached agreement, or they have expressed parts of the agreement in a vague or ambiguous manner. This begs the question of when the courts will be willing to try to fill in the gaps or resolve the ambiguities in the agreement. The courts often have the tools to fill in such holes, for example, by implying terms into the agreement (see Chapter 7), but when should they use these tools to hazard a guess at what the parties intended or would have intended had they thought about the matter in question? In other words, when will an agreement be sufficiently '*certain*' to be a contract? This is the issue we shall focus on in this chapter.

4.2 These two problems are not entirely distinct. The latter may bear upon the former: for example, the fact that the parties have not agreed on all matters may indicate that they did not intend to be legally bound at that point (as was held to be the case in *British Steel Corpn v Cleveland Bridge & Engineering Co Ltd* (1984), for example, on which see para **2.117**). Two examples of the same point are *Dhanani v Crasnianski* (2011) and *Barbudev v Eurocom Cable Management Bulgaria Eood* (2012). As Teare J put it in *Dhanani*, cited with approval at first instance in *Barbudev*:

> the circumstance that an agreement is no more than [an] agreement to negotiate and agree may show objectively that the parties to it cannot objectively have intended it to be legally binding, notwithstanding that it had certain characteristics which otherwise might have evinced an intention to agree, for example, that it was signed by each party.

Similarly, the former may influence the latter: if the court decides that the parties did not intend to be bound, it will not attempt to fill in the gaps in their agreement (as in *Baird Textile Holdings Ltd v Marks & Spencer plc* (2002), for example). Often a party will allege that an agreement fails on both counts (as in *Hillas & Co Ltd v Arcos Ltd* (1932)). On the other hand, if the parties clearly intend to create a legal obligation, the court will try to give it legal effect and only hold it to be void for uncertainty if it is legally or practically impossible to give the agreement any sensible content (*Scammell v Dicker* (2005)). A good example of a case where it was found (by the Court of Appeal) to be impossible to give the agreement sensible content despite the parties intending it to be legally binding is *Barbudev* itself, which we will deal with at para **4.28**.

4.3 Returning to the second issue, when a court has to decide whether an agreement is sufficiently certain to be enforced, it is faced with two competing policy considerations, as Lord Wright famously explained in *Hillas v Arcos*:

> Business men often record the most important agreements in crude and summary fashion; modes of expression sufficient and clear to them in the course of their business may appear to those unfamiliar with the business far from complete or precise. It is accordingly the duty of the court to construe such documents fairly and broadly, without being too astute or subtle in finding defects ... That ..., however, does not mean that the Court is to make a contract for the parties, or to go outside the words they have used, except in so far as there are appropriate implications of law.

On the one hand, the courts want to uphold the expectations of the parties as far as possible, so if the parties intend to be legally bound, the court should do all it can to fill in the holes and resolve ambiguities. As Leggatt J put it in *Astor Management AG v Atalaya Mining plc* (2017) 'The role of the court in a commercial dispute is to give legal effect to what the parties have agreed, not to throw its hands in the air and refuse to do so because the parties have not made its task easy. To hold that a clause is too uncertain to be enforceable is a last resort.' On the other hand, occasionally that 'last resort' is reached, where the agreement is so vague or incomplete that the court would be making a contract for the parties, rather than trying to give effect to the parties' intentions.

4.4 The problem is that it is extremely hard to tell where the line should be drawn, and the courts have found great difficulty in deciding cases near the borderline. Some decisions in the past have taken a rather narrow view of contract and held that there is no contract in such situations, although Leggatt J's quote from the *Astor Management* case exemplifies the more recent shift to a more pragmatic approach that asks whether there is really a practical problem in allowing the agreement to stand as a contract. It is suggested that the courts should be more willing in these borderline cases to hold that there is a contract. Two reasons can be given in support of this proposal. First, to say that there is no contract at all where one party has at least partly performed his side of the agreement causes significant problems, because there is then no obviously satisfactory way to determine whether, and how much, the party should be paid for his performance. Secondly, the narrower notion of contract fails to give proper effect to the shared expectations of the parties. Often they have a number of expectations in common, so to say that there is no contract in such circumstances overlooks these.

General principles

4.5 In deciding whether it would be proper to attempt to fill in the gaps or resolve ambiguities in the parties' agreement, the courts seem to be influenced by a number of factors. A useful discussion can be found in the judgment of Rix LJ in *Mamidoil Jetoil Greek Petroleum Co SA v Okta Crude Oil Refinery AD* (2001). For example, as Rose J noted in *Associated British Ports v Tata Steel UK Ltd* (2017), Rix LJ drew a distinction between those cases where the court is considering whether a contract has been agreed at all between the parties and those where the court is considering whether a particular clause in an otherwise binding agreement is valid. In the former, a phrase such as 'to be agreed' may be fatal because the parties cannot agree to agree. But in the later situation, where a contract has come into existence, even the expression 'to be agreed' in relation to future executory obligations is not necessarily fatal. As Rix LJ explained, the courts will assist the parties to work out their contract 'so as to preserve rather than destroy bargains, on the basis that what can be made certain is itself certain'.

Partly performed agreements

4.6 Where the agreement has been at least partly performed by at least one party, the court will be more willing to find that the contract is sufficiently certain. Many reasons can be given to justify this stance. For example, the fact that at least one of the parties has acted on the agreement by beginning to perform makes it easier to infer that the parties intended to be legally bound by it. Secondly, as Steyn LJ notes in *G Percy Trentham Ltd v Archital Luxfer Ltd* (1993), part performance makes it easier for the courts to fill in the gaps in the agreement, because the performance will shed light on the intentions of the parties in respect of the matters that they did not deal with expressly. As Lord Denning said in *F & G Sykes (Wessex) Ltd v Fine Fare Ltd* (1967), in a commercial agreement, 'the further the parties have gone on with their contract, the more ready are the courts to imply any reasonable term so as to give effect to their intentions ... In this case there is less difficulty than in others because there is an arbitration clause which, liberally construed, is sufficient to resolve any uncertainties that the parties have left.'

4.7 However, it should not be thought that the part or even full performance of an agreement has *always* been enough to persuade the courts that the contract is sufficiently certain. For example, in *British Steel Corpn v Cleveland Bridge & Engineering Co Ltd* (1984) the fact that an agreement to manufacture and deliver steel nodes had been fully performed was insufficient to persuade Goff J that a contract had been formed, because the lack of agreement on a number of fundamental matters indicated that the parties did not intend to be legally bound. Instead, he turned to the law of restitution and ordered the defendant to pay a reasonable sum for the nodes, to prevent the defendant being un-justly enriched at the claimant's expense. *British Steel* was applied by the Court of Appeal in *Whittle Movers Ltd v Hollywood Express Ltd* (2009) but distinguished by the Supreme Court in *RTS Flexible Systems Ltd v Molkerei Alois Muller GmbH & Co KG* (2010).

Previous dealings between the parties

4.8   If the parties have had similar agreements in the past, the gaps in the current arrange-ment may be filled by looking at the terms agreed previously. For example, in *Hillas & Co Ltd v Arcos Ltd* (1932), the claimant contracted to buy a certain quantity of 'softwood goods of fair specification' in 1930, with the option of entering into a contract to buy a certain amount more for delivery in 1931. One of the defendant's arguments was that the words of the option were insufficiently certain. The House of Lords rejected this ar-gument: it was held that the shipping conditions for the 1930 shipment (which had been expressly agreed) could be used to fill in that gap in the 1931 option, and that the goods referred to in the option were the same as those expressly described in relation to the 1930 shipment, namely softwood goods of fair specification.

Standard types of agreement

4.9   If the agreement is of a standard type, such as a contract for the sale of goods, the court will find it easier to fill in the gaps or resolve ambiguities because it will be more fa-miliar with the terms that ordinarily govern such agreements. For example, in *Hillas*, by looking at the custom of the timber trade, the court was able to give the phrase 'fair specification' a sufficiently certain meaning. Indeed, in the sale of goods context, the Sale of Goods Act 1979 will often imply various terms into the agreement, which help to fill any gaps left. For example, if the parties say nothing about what the price should be, a reasonable price will be implied (s 8(2)). If they lay down criteria for calculating the price, this will be perfectly acceptable (s 8(1)). If they agree that the price should be fixed by a third party but the third party is prevented from doing so by the fault of one party, the other can sue for damages (s 9(2)).

4.10 The flip side of this is that if the agreement is unusual or novel in some way, it will be harder for the courts to cure uncertainties in it. For example, in *Scammell & Nephew Ltd v Ouston* (1941), the House of Lords held that the phrase 'on hire purchase terms' was insufficiently certain, so there was no contract. One of the main problems was that the hire-purchase agreement was still fairly novel at the time, so as Viscount Maugham com-mented, 'there was no evidence to suggest that there are any well known "usual terms" in such a contract'. Moreover, as Rose J pointed out in *Associated British Ports v Tata Steel UK Ltd* (2017), there was a further difficulty in *Scammell*:

> the problem did not lie in defining the class of hire purchase agreements or being able to
> decide whether a contract was or was not properly described as a hire purchase agree-

ment. Rather the problem lay in determining which of the many documents undoubt-
edly falling within that class was the one that the parties intended to adopt.

Unlike the detailed, and part-performed, agreement in *Associated British Ports*, the
agreement in *Scammell* 'was inchoate and never got beyond negotiations'.

Long-term contracts

4.11   The longer the period over which the agreement is intended to operate, the more likely
it is that the parties will need, or desire, to leave certain matters to be adjusted as the
contract goes along. The courts will assist the parties to do so wherever possible.

4.12   *Durham Tees Valley Airport Ltd v Bmibaby Ltd* (2010) highlights how far the courts are
willing to go in this regard, where it is clear that the parties intend their agreement to
be binding. Bmibaby agreed to 'operate' two aircraft from the airport for ten years. The
airport would generate money from each flight, but the contract did not set out expressly
the minimum number of flights. In fact Bmibaby only operated one aircraft for a certain
period of time, and then announced a few years into the contract that it would no longer
operate any from the airport. When the airport sued for damages, Bmibaby claimed that
the contract was void for uncertainty, on the basis that Bmibaby could not know in advance how many flights it had to operate in order to comply with its contractual obligation. The Court of Appeal rejected this argument. Interestingly, it held that the test was
not whether the court could determine in advance what the minimum number of flights
was for the rest of the contract, something that it thought was not possible on the facts,
because eventualities like strikes, weather conditions, and terrorism might well affect what
that minimum turned out to be. Instead, the question was whether the court would be
able to determine, on a set of facts which had already occurred, whether Bmibaby had
breached the contract. It was able to do that because the relevant conditions that would
affect what that minimum level was would, by definition, have happened and therefore the
court would be able to take them into account. This is a pragmatic decision, recognising
that the standard of performance required in a long-term contract is likely to be affected
by the conditions that prevail from time to time, and therefore that it is important that
these features should not prevent such an agreement having contractual force.

Machinery/criteria laid down in the agreement

4.13   As we shall see, if there are criteria or machinery laid down in the agreement for determining those matters which have not been dealt with completely, this will often allow the
court to uphold the agreement. For example, the agreement may not lay down a price but
say that it is to be calculated in a particular way. Similarly, if the parties include an arbitration or other type of dispute-resolution clause, this may assist the court in finding the
agreement to be sufficiently certain because it provides a mechanism by which disputes
over the meaning of particular terms can be resolved.

Some thorny issues

4.14 There are a number of situations in which the courts have found particular difficulty in deciding whether the agreement possesses the requisite certainty. As will become apparent, they have often historically been too reluctant to give effect to agreements which the parties intended to be binding. However, in more recent decisions the courts are prepared to look pragmatically at whether there really would be a practical difficulty in allowing the agreement to amount to a contract, and using that as a gauge to judge whether the agreement is sufficiently certain.

An agreement to agree

4.15 Sometimes the parties will reach agreement on some matters, but expressly say that other matters, such as the price for example, are to be agreed at a later date. Often, they will not reach agreement on these latter issues, which causes two problems. The first is that the parties may not intend the agreement to bind them legally until agreement is reached on these outstanding matters. However, as noted at the start of the chapter, this is not a certainty problem; it is a problem relating to the intention to be legally bound. More important for present purposes is that it is often difficult to work out what agreement the parties would have reached on these matters, so it is difficult to fill in the gaps. Even in a sale of goods contract, the Sale of Goods Act cannot be used to imply a term that the buyer must pay a reasonable price, because s 8(2) does not apply where the contract provides that the price is to be agreed by the parties themselves.

4.16 In *May & Butcher Ltd v The King* (1934), the agreement provided for the price to be agreed but the parties were unable to do so. The House of Lords held that this meant that no contract was formed: 'it is not open to them to agree that they will in the future agree upon a matter which is vital to the arrangement between them and has not yet been determined'. However, *May & Butcher* arguably goes too far in suggesting that expressly leaving an important matter to be agreed by the parties at a later date will *always* make an agreement uncertain, because sometimes there may be ways in which the courts can work out or make an educated guess at what the parties would have agreed.

4.17 For this reason, various exceptions have developed to the general rule:

- The agreement may contain criteria for determining the unresolved matters. In *Hillas v Arcos*, the option did not expressly state the price to be paid but provided that it was to be calculated in a particular way by reference to an official price list.

- The agreement may contain a procedure for determining the unresolved matters. For example, it may provide that a particular matter is to be determined by one party, or is to be referred to arbitration (*Queensland Electricity Generating Board v New Hope Collieries Pty Ltd* (1989)). If this machinery fails to work, this may not be fatal because the court may be willing to imply a term (for example, that the price will be a reasonable one: *Sudbrook Trading Estate Ltd v Eggleton* (1983)), particularly where this failure is caused by the fault of the defendant. However, they will not do this where the parties regarded it as essential that the matter would be resolved using the machinery laid down by them, and the parties have not attempted to use the machinery (*Gillatt v Sky Television Ltd* (2000)). Ultimately, as Moore-Bick LJ explained in *Dŵr Cymru Cyfyngedig v Corus UK Ltd* (2007), 'Where many important terms have been left undecided and the contractual machinery for resolving disagreements is incapable of being operated, it may be impossible to avoid the conclusion that the agreement as a whole is unenforceable because the parties have failed to establish objective criteria capable of being applied by the court itself.'

- Where the parties clearly intend the agreement to legally bind them and have acted upon it, the courts may be willing to say that the certainty test is satisfied. In *Foley v Classique Coaches Ltd* (1934), the claimant agreed to sell his petrol station to the defendant on condition that the defendant entered into an agreement to buy petrol exclusively from him, at 'a price to be agreed by the parties from time to time'. The Court of Appeal held that this petrol agreement was sufficiently certain, and that a term should be implied requiring a reasonable price to be paid if the parties failed to agree on the price. There were a number of reasons why the court felt able to distinguish *May & Butcher*. The parties clearly intended the agreement to bind them: it was contained in a stamped document, had been acted upon without problems for three years, and was a condition of the sale of the petrol station. Moreover, there was an arbitration clause to resolve any disputes as to the price. This decision is a sensible one: the prices which the defendant had paid the claimant for the petrol over the three years would allow an arbitrator to make an educated guess at what a reasonable price might be.

An agreement to negotiate

4.18 The parties may agree to negotiate with a view to agreeing a contract. This agreement to negotiate causes a certainty problem, but of a different kind from that previously discussed. It is not a problem in working out what the parties would have agreed; instead it is a problem in judging whether the parties have tried hard enough to reach agreement (see Cohen (1995)). In other words, it is difficult to determine whether a party has made a genuine attempt to negotiate an agreement. This issue arises at a lesser level where the parties contemplate one specific issue being negotiated within an otherwise complete agreement, maybe because negotiating time ran out or to introduce an element of flexibility into a long term contract.

4.19 In *Courtney & Fairbairn Ltd v Tolaini Bros (Hotels) Ltd* (1975), the Court of Appeal held that an agreement to negotiate was too uncertain to be enforced. Lord Denning MR reasoned as follows:

> If the law does not recognise a contract to enter into a contract (when there is a fundamental term yet to be agreed) it seems to me it cannot recognise a contract to negotiate.

The reason is because it is too uncertain to have any binding force. No court could esti-
mate the damages because no one can tell whether the negotiations would be success-
ful or would fall through; or if successful, what the result would be. It seems to me that a
contract to negotiate, like a contract to enter into a contract, is not a contract known to
the law ... I think we must apply the general principle that when there is a fundamental
matter left undecided and to be the subject of negotiation, there is no contract.

4.20   *Courtney* was approved by the House of Lords in *Walford v Miles* (1992). However, there
are a number of problems with its reasoning and its conclusion:

- The analogy drawn with agreements to agree is a dubious one: as explained. First,
  these two types of agreement throw up different problems. Moreover, as we have
  already seen, exceptions had developed to the general rule that an agreement
  to agree was too uncertain, so it was incorrect to lay down an *absolute* rule that
  agreements to negotiate should not be enforced. There will be situations where
  there are criteria (either in the contract or from the surrounding circumstances)
  that can be used to define more precisely the content of the duty to negotiate.

- The argument that it would be impossible to assess damages is unconvincing: the
  claimant has lost the chance to agree a contract and it is well established that a
  court can award damages for loss of a chance by estimating how profitable the
  resultant contract would have been and discounting this amount to take account
  of the fact that agreement might not have been reached even if both sides had negotiated properly (see *Chaplin v Hicks* (1911), for example, discussed in para **16.9**).

4.21   Increasingly the courts are willing to distinguish *Courtney*, particularly where one specific matter is left for negotiation, within an otherwise certain bargain. In *Cable & Wireless
plc v IBM* (2002), a clause in the contract which provided that in the event of a dispute,
the parties should attempt to resolve the dispute through negotiation using an alternative
dispute resolution (ADR) procedure recommended by the Centre for Dispute Resolution,
was held to be sufficiently certain. The identification of a procedure by which they would
negotiate meant that there were sufficient criteria 'for a court to readily ascertain whether
[the obligations to negotiate] have been complied with'. Similarly in *Associated British
Ports v Tata Steel UK* (2017) a licence agreement allowing a steel works to use a tidal
harbour contained a clause providing that, in the event of any major physical or financial
change in circumstances affecting the steel works or the harbour, either party could serve
notice on the other requiring the terms of the licence to be renegotiated, so as to reflect
the change in circumstances. If they failed to agree within six months, the matter would
be referred to an arbitrator, whose decision would be binding. Rose J regarded the clause
as sufficiently certain, noting that this was a case where the parties had part performed a
binding agreement: in such a case 'the court is particularly reluctant to find that a clause
is void for uncertainty'. The judge emphasised that the clause was not open-ended, so an
arbitrator had criteria for determining the matter:

... provided one can posit some changes which would definitely fall within the scope of
the phrase 'major physical or financial change in circumstances' and some changes

which clearly falls outside it, then the phrase is sufficiently certain to be enforceable even though it may be difficult in the abstract to draw the precise divide between changes falling on either side of the line.

An agreement to negotiate in good faith

4.22 Such an agreement is just a particular type of agreement to negotiate, albeit one that carries the additional difficulty of a requirement to act with *good faith*. Therefore, the House of Lords in *Walford v Miles* (1992) applied *Courtney* and held that such an agreement was too uncertain to be enforced.

4.23 In *Walford*, the claimants wished to buy the defendants' business. It was agreed that in return for the claimants providing a letter of comfort from their bankers, the defendants would not negotiate with anyone else. The claimants duly provided the letter but the defendants pulled out of negotiations with the claimants and sold to someone else. The claimants' principal claim was for breach of contract. They alleged two breaches, the first of which was a breach of the agreement not to deal with third parties (the 'lock out' agreement). This issue is discussed in a later section (para **4.35**). What is important for present purposes is that the claimants also alleged that a second term should be implied, requiring the defendants to 'negotiate in good faith' with the claimants. The House of Lords rejected both claims for breach of contract. The principal reason for rejecting the implied term was that it would be too uncertain. Lord Ackner (who gave the only speech) reasoned as follows:

> *... the Court of Appeal appears to have proceeded on the basis that an agreement to negotiate in good faith is synonymous with an agreement to use best endeavours and as the latter is enforceable, so is the former. This [is] ... an unsustainable proposition. The reason why an agreement to negotiate, like an agreement to agree, is unenforceable, is simply because it lacks the necessary certainty. The same does not apply to an agreement to use best endeavours ... How can a court be expected to decide whether, subjectively, a proper reason existed for the termination of negotiations? ... [T]he concept of a duty to carry on negotiations in good faith is inherently repugnant to the adversarial position of the parties when involved in negotiations. Each party to the negotiations is entitled to pursue his (or her) own interest, so long as he avoids making misrepresentations.*

4.24 While *Walford* was perhaps not the best case in which to suggest that a duty to negotiate in good faith was sufficiently certain, because there were few criteria in the agreement or otherwise to help the court to define what such a duty would mean in practice, Lord Ackner's remarks go too far in suggesting that an obligation to negotiate in good faith should *never* be upheld:

- It fails to give effect to the parties' expectations: if the parties intend to create a binding agreement to negotiate, why should the court stand in their way?

- Lord Ackner's argument that giving effect to a duty to negotiate in good faith is 'inherently repugnant to the adversarial position of the parties when involved in negotiations' is, with respect, a dubious one. It is true that the law should be reluctant to impose duties on a party to take the other party's interests into account, such as a duty to negotiate in good faith, because parties should generally be free to act in their own interests. However, as noted by Mason (2000), this does not mean that there should be any objection to the *parties* imposing such duties on themselves by agreement.

- Commercial parties commonly include express obligations to negotiate in good faith in their agreements, and they appear in the 'boilerplate' standard terms and conditions of numerous significant commercial transactions, as well as in important standard form contracts, such as the ISDA (International Swaps and Derivatives Association) Master Agreement. English law has always prided itself on meeting the needs of commercial parties, but in this area the general rule seems out of line and unnecessarily restrictive.

4.25 At the very least, it is suggested that where there are criteria, whether laid down in the agreement or apparent from the surrounding circumstances, that allow the court to flesh out the content of a duty to negotiate in good faith by specifying what such a duty does and does not require of a party, then the agreement should be enforceable. In such a situation, Lord Ackner's argument that such a duty would be unworkable seems to lose its force. As Lord Steyn pointed out extra-judicially (Steyn (1997)), in some circumstances such a duty will be entirely practical and workable, so the enforcement of such a duty should not be dismissed out of hand.

4.26 Lord Steyn's comment applies, as Mason (2000) argues, even more strongly where the contract contains an *express* obligation to negotiate in good faith. The Court of Appeal in *Petromec Inc v Petroleo Brasileiro SA Petrobas* (2005) distinguished *Walford* in a situation where one of the sub-clauses in a complex contract contained an express duty to negotiate. Longmore LJ commented that, unlike *Walford*, where the claimants were seeking to imply an obligation to negotiate in good faith and the alleged contract was simply a contract to negotiate (a 'bare agreement to negotiate' in the words of Lord Ackner), in *Petromec* there was an:

> express obligation which is part of a complex agreement drafted by City of London solicitors ... It would be a strong thing to declare unenforceable a clause into which the parties have deliberately and expressly entered ... To decide that it has 'no legal content' ... would be for the law deliberately to defeat the reasonable expectations of honest men.

More generally, Longmore LJ suggested that while it might sometimes be difficult to tell whether negotiations had been brought to an end in bad faith or not, 'the difficulty of a problem should not be an excuse for the court to withhold relevant assistance from the parties by declaring a blanket unenforceability of the obligation'.

4.27 This willingness to enforce an express obligation to negotiate in good faith mirrors developments in a slightly different context, namely where the parties have agreed to *perform* their agreement, or an aspect of it, in good faith. Such obligations seem generally to be regarded as unobjectionable and are often enforced. So in *CPC Group Ltd v Qatari Real Estate Investment Co* (2010) (the Chelsea Barracks case), Vos J felt able to uphold a clause in a development agreement that required 'utmost good faith' during performance of the contract, as Morgan J had done a few years earlier in *Berkeley Community Villages Ltd v Pullen* (2007). Vos J held that the term required the party to adhere to the spirit of the contract, which was to seek planning consent for the maximum area in the shortest possible time, to observe reasonable commercial standards of fair dealing, to be faithful to the agreed common purpose and to act consistently with the justified expectations of the parties. In *Mid Essex Hospital Services NHS Trust v Compass Group UK and Ireland Ltd* (2013), the Court of Appeal likewise felt able to uphold an express contractual duty to act in good faith in certain respects, interpreting it as a requirement to act honestly in pursuit of the objective in question. Note too that some commentators and judges would go further and seek to *imply* a duty of good faith in contractual performance (see for example Leggatt J's decision in *Yam Seng Pte Ltd v International Trade Corp* (2013), criticised by Carter and Courtney (2016)), an issue we will return to in Chapter 7.

4.28   Nonetheless, there are significant differences between obligations to perform and obligations to negotiate in good faith, and the latter remain more problematic even where express, because they may ultimately require the court to work out what the results of negotiation would have been, rather than merely adjudicate on whether the parties have performed their own bargain. So in *Barbudev v Eurocom Cable Management Bulgaria Eood* (2012), the parties had entered into a complex commercial transaction to transfer Mr Barbudev's business to the defendant, but also signed a side letter expressly requiring the parties to negotiate in good faith an agreement to give Mr Barbudev a 10 per cent stake in the merged business. The Court of Appeal held this side letter was not an enforceable contract, but was no more than an agreement to agree. It was an agreement to offer Mr Barbudev the opportunity to invest, but the terms of any eventual investment agreement remained to be negotiated. All it did was identify the minimum sum of investment and the minimum amount of shares and shareholder debt, which was 'insufficient to create certainty as to the proposed relations between the parties'. Likewise many critical matters, such as when and how Mr Barbudev could be bought out or get out of his investment, were not dealt with; it was therefore not possible or appropriate for the court to fill in all these gaps.

4.29   A similar issue arose in a slightly different way in *Shaker v Vistajet Group Holding SA* (2012). There, the claimant paid a deposit in respect of the purchase of an aircraft from the defendant under the terms of a letter agreed by the two parties. The letter expressly provided that the claimant agreed to proceed in good faith and to use reasonable endeavours to agree the formal sale contract and associated documents. The formal contract could not be agreed, so the claimant sought repayment of the deposit, but the defendant refused, contending that the claimant had not complied with its good faith and reasonable endeavour obligations. Teare J accepted that the intention of the agreement was that the deposit could only be recovered if these obligations had been complied with, but held that the obligations were unenforceable because of the impossibility of 'polic[ing]' them, that is, of working out whether they had been breached or not. It distinguished the *Petromec* decision on the basis that there were objective criteria available in that case to assist the court in determining whether the obligation had been breached. It is respectfully suggested that Teare J may have been too ready to find that the obligations were unenforceable, as this would have allowed the claimant to recover its deposit even if it had acted in bad faith (which on the facts it did not). There are many types of conduct that everyone would agree constitute bad faith, so if the conduct fell into this category, there would be no practical impediment to the court policing the obligation.

An agreement to use 'reasonable endeavours' or 'best endeavours' to reach agreement

4.30 It is very common for commercial agreements to impose an obligation on one of the parties to use 'reasonable endeavours' or 'best endeavours' to achieve a result or do something outside their control, like obtaining planning permission or securing the consent of a landlord to a sublease or assignment. Such clauses are usually unobjectionable and the courts are relatively comfortable with using the context to work out what each formulation requires, how onerous the burden is in terms of financial outlay and commercial risk (see for example *Yewbelle v London Green Developments* (2007)). So in *Jet2.com v Blackpool Airport Ltd* (2012) the Court of Appeal had to consider an obligation on the airport to use its best endeavours to promote Jet2's low cost airline services; the context allowed the court to set out in some detail what the obligation would require of the airport.

4.31 However, an obligation to use reasonable/best endeavours to *reach agreement* is rather different and is really just a type of agreement to negotiate. Lord Ackner in *Walford* described agreements to use best endeavours as enforceable (quoted at para **4.23**), but he almost certainly had in mind the sorts of clauses mentioned in the previous paragraph, rather than obligations to use best endeavours to agree. This was made clear by the Court of Appeal in *Little v Courage Ltd* (1994), where Millett LJ held that '[a]n undertaking to use one's best endeavours to obtain planning permission or an export licence is sufficiently certain and is capable of being enforced: an undertaking to use one's best endeavours to agree, however, is no different from an undertaking to agree, or to negotiate with a view to reaching agreement; all are equally uncertain and incapable of giving rise to an enforceable legal obligation'. Millett LJ's reasoning was applied by the Court of Appeal in *London & Regional Investments Ltd v TBI plc* (2002).

4.32 As with clauses phrased as an obligation to negotiate in good faith, the courts have sometimes been willing to uphold clauses to use reasonable or best endeavours to agree, where they feel able to formulate criteria to judge what such endeavours would involve. In *Queensland Electricity Generating Board v New Hope Collieries Pty Ltd* (1989), the defendant agreed to supply coal to the claimant for 15 years. For the first five-year period, the agreement contained detailed provisions for calculating the price payable. It was provided that for purchases after this period, the provisions for working out the price were to be agreed by the parties. The claimant sought a declaration that this amounted to an agreement to agree and was insufficiently certain. The Privy

Council refused to grant the declaration. It held that the parties were under an implied obligation to use reasonable endeavours to agree on the price provisions beyond the initial five-year period. It felt able to give effect to an agreement to make reasonable endeavours to agree because it was clear that the parties intended the agreement to have binding effect and perhaps most importantly, it felt able to formulate guidelines to judge whether such a duty had been breached, using the terms of the contract and how the contract had operated over the first five-year period.

4.33 However, it is important to be aware of the limits of *Queensland Electricity*: the Privy Council was only willing to uphold the agreement because of these factors. By contrast, in *Phillips Petroleum Co UK Ltd v Enron Europe Ltd* (1997), both Kennedy and Potter LJJ held that the agreement left the parties at liberty to take into account their own financial positions. While neither went so far as to expressly say that the agreement was unenforceable, both felt great unease about allowing the agreement to impose any meaningful duties upon the parties when the court could find no criteria by which to judge if the agreement could be breached. Potter LJ felt that the agreement in question 'utterly fails to reveal any express or implied criteria to be applied'.

4.34 *Dany Lions Ltd v Bristol Cars Ltd* (2014) contains a thoughtful exploration of these points. It concerned a clause in a settlement agreement relating to the restoration of a classic car that required one party to use reasonable endeavours to conclude a contract with a third party to carry out works to the car. The party and third party were unable to come close to agreeing, particularly on price. The judge held that in order to overcome any certainty problems, there needed to be certainty as to what the object of the reasonable endeavours was (what the party had to do), and a yardstick by which to measure the endeavours (could the court work out whether the clause had been complied with?). Where the object was something other than entering into an agreement, like obtaining permission to do something or consent from someone, both requirements would be satisfied. However, where the object was to use reasonable endeavours to enter into an agreement with someone, the second requirement is less likely to be satisfied. This is because unless one can work out what the essential terms of the prospective agreement are meant to be, it is very difficult to judge whether reasonable endeavours have been used or not, and so it becomes too difficult for the court to police the reasonable endeavours clause. On the facts, the clause fell into this trap because it was not possible to work out what the terms of the prospective agreement, such as the price, were meant to be.

Lock out agreements

4.35 A lock out agreement is an agreement that one party (normally the seller) will not negotiate with anyone else. In principle, there would seem no reason *not* to enforce such agreements, because there is little difficulty in telling if the party in question has breached the agreement. However, the current state of the law is that such an agreement will only be valid if it specifies how long the party is not to negotiate with others, but not otherwise (contrast *Walford* and *Pitt v PHH Asset Management Ltd* (1993)).

4.36 As we have seen in our earlier discussion of *Walford*, one of the claims advanced was that the defendants had broken a lock out agreement. The House of Lords held that the fact that the lock out agreement had no express time limit meant it was unenforceable even if a term could be implied that the agreement would last for a reasonable period of time, because 'such a duty, if it existed, would indirectly impose upon the [defendants] a duty to negotiate in good faith [with the claimants]'. There are three problems with this reasoning:

- It is hard to see how a negative obligation, namely not to negotiate with others, indirectly imposes a positive obligation, namely to negotiate with the claimants (O'Neill (1992)).

- The result reached fails to give effect to the parties' intention: if they intend the seller to be bound by the lock out agreement, why should he not be so bound, particularly if there is no difficulty in defining the content of this duty?

- It is unclear what the objection is to implying a term that the agreement last for a reasonable time. Indeed, as Buckley (1993) points out, it was far from impossible to work out what should have constituted a reasonable time on the facts of *Walford*.

OVERVIEW

1   Often parties do not agree on all matters or set out all of their agreement in a clear manner. This causes two problems:

- Their failure to do so may indicate that they do not intend to be bound unless agreement is reached on the remaining issues or the agreement is set out clearly.

- The parties have left gaps and ambiguities in their agreement. Unless the courts are able to fill in these gaps by implying terms and resolving any ambiguous provisions, they will hold that the agreement is too uncertain to be enforced. This is the doctrine of 'certainty'.

2   On one hand, the court must not be too eager to find that a contract is too uncertain because businessmen often record their agreements in a crude and summary fashion. However, a point will be reached where the agreement is so vague or incomplete that the court would be making a contract for the parties, rather than trying to give effect to their intentions.

3   It is arguable that in some cases the courts have been too willing to find that an agreement is insufficiently certain to be enforced. This is unfortunate, for it fails to give proper effect to the expectation of the parties that the agreement would be binding.

4   The courts seem to be influenced by the following considerations in deciding whether an agreement possesses the requisite degree of certainty. If at least one of these factors is present, the court will be reluctant to find that the agreement is unenforceable:

- The agreement has been at least partly performed by at least one of the parties.

- The parties have concluded similar agreements in the past.

- The agreement is of a standard type.

- The agreement lays down criteria or machinery for determining those matters which have not been dealt with fully in the agreement.

5   In a number of situations the courts have found particular difficulty in deciding whether an agreement is sufficiently certain. It is arguable that in such cases, they have sometimes been too reluctant to find that it is.

6   The law is currently as follows:

- The general rule is that an agreement to agree will be insufficiently certain (because it is difficult to work out what the parties would have agreed) but a number of exceptions have developed in situations where the court feels able to determine what agreement the parties would have reached, such as where the agreement contains criteria or machinery for determining the unresolved matters or where the parties have acted upon or partly performed the agreement.

- The general rule is that an agreement to negotiate is insufficiently certain. However, the courts are increasingly recognising that this rule is too absolute and should not be applied where the agreement and surrounding circumstances allow criteria to be formulated that can be used to judge whether the parties have made sufficient efforts to negotiate.

- The general rule is that an agreement to negotiate in good faith is too uncertain to be enforced. The absolute nature of this rule and the reasoning behind it have been heavily criticised; exceptions are beginning to be recognised in the situations outlined in the previous paragraph.

- An agreement to use reasonable or best endeavours to agree should be treated in the same way as an agreement to negotiate; such a clause should not be confused with an obligation to use reasonable or best endeavours to achieve a particular outcome, like securing planning permission, which is much less likely to fall foul of the certainty requirement.

FURTHER READING

Arden 'Coming to Terms with Good Faith' (2013) 30 JCL 199

Carter and Courtney 'Good Faith in Contracts: Is there an Implied Promise to Act Honestly' (2016) 75(3) CLJ 608

Hoskins 'Contractual Obligations to Negotiate in Good Faith: Faithfulness to the Agreed Common Purpose' (2014) 130 LQR 131

Mason 'Contract, Good Faith and Equitable Standards in Fair Dealing' (2000) 116 LQR 66

Mouzas and Furmston 'From Contract to Umbrella Agreement' (2008) 67(1) CLJ 37

O'Neill 'A Key to Lock-Out Agreements' (1992) 108 LQR 405

Peel 'Agreements to Negotiate in Good Faith' Chapter 8 in *Contract Formation and Parties* (2010)

SELF-TEST QUESTIONS

1   What legal problems arise when parties fail to agree on all matters or set out all parts of their agreement in a clear manner?

2   Is English law too willing to hold that a contract is insufficiently certain to enforce?

3   What factors influence a court in deciding whether an agreement is sufficiently certain to be enforced?

4   Should an agreement to negotiate in good faith always be too uncertain to enforce? Are the reasons given in *Walford v Miles* (1992) convincing?

5   Amanda is offering a plot of land for sale for £1 million, which Bridie is interested in buying, but only if it is likely to obtain planning permission for redevelopment. While Bridie makes the necessary planning enquiries, she is keen to prevent other potential buyers purchasing the land, so Amanda and Bridie enter into a written agreement whereby, for an upfront payment of £25,000 by Bridie, Amanda agrees not to negotiate with any other purchaser for 'three months (assuming normal market conditions)'; in addition, in the event of 'a satisfactory response' from the planning authority, Amanda and Bridie agree to use 'reasonable endeavours to agree the sale of the plot for its then market value'. The planning authority takes longer than expected to respond to Bridie's enquiry, but after five months finally indicates that it would be willing to grant planning permission for redevelopment of the plot. Unfortunately, Bridie has now discovered that Amanda sold the plot two weeks after their agreement. Advise Bridie.

 For hints on how to answer question 5, please see the online resources at **www.oup.com/uk/sullivan8e/**.

5 Consideration and estoppel

SUMMARY

This chapter deals with and defends the requirement of 'consideration' for an enforceable contractual obligation, looking at the definition of consideration, when it is required, who must provide it, and stressing the importance of the other party's request. It considers examples of legally insufficient consideration such as past consideration and a pre-existing public duty, concentrating on the two most problematic issues, namely whether performance of (or promise to perform) a pre-existing contractual duty owed to the other party can and should provide consideration for unilateral variation of the other party's contractual promise, and whether payment of (or promise to pay) part of a debt owed can and should provide consideration for the creditor's promise to accept less than the full amount owed. In the latter situation, the harshness of the common law rule is partly softened by the equitable doctrine of promissory estoppel.

5.1 One of the most puzzling aspects of the English law of contract is the requirement (of ancient origin) that, to be binding, a contract must be 'supported by consideration'. It is not enough that an offer made by one party, made seriously and with the intention to create a contract, has been accepted by the other party—without the added magic ingredient of 'consideration' there is no binding, enforceable contract. Many people argue that English law should reform or abolish the requirement of consideration. We will consider this suggestion at the end of this chapter, because proposals for reform can only be understood in the light of the law as it stands. So what is consideration?

5.2 The easiest way to understand consideration is to think of it as the 'price of the promise'—what one contracting party is getting, in return for his promise, from the other. This is subtly different from someone's *motive* for making a promise. You may, for example, promise to give a large sum of money to charity hoping to enjoy the feeling of self-satisfaction you obtain from the gesture. But these motives are not the same as consideration. You are not getting anything from the charity as the price of, or in return for, your promise. It is entirely gratuitous and thus the charity could not sue you if, having made the promise, you changed your mind about paying the money. So on this view, consideration is an essential feature of contracts as *bargains*.

5.3 There is a simple way round the requirement of consideration, frequently adopted in order to make gratuitous promises binding. If a promise is contained in a written document complying with the formal statutory requirements to make a *deed*, that is enough to make the promise enforceable even without any consideration. The statutory requirements for a deed are contained in s 1 of the Law of Property (Miscellaneous Provisions) Act 1989. This states that the document must describe itself as a deed, must be signed by the person making it in the presence of a witness, who must also sign, and must be notionally 'delivered'. However, the vast majority of contractual promises are not made in the form of a deed.

5.4 A commonly cited English definition of consideration is found in *Currie v Misa* (1875): 'either … some right, interest, profit, or benefit accruing to the one party, or some forbearance, detriment, loss, or responsibility, given, suffered, or undertaken by the other' (per Lush J). Students tend to find this definition difficult to follow (principally because it requires confidence in juggling the labels 'promisor' and 'promisee'). It is easier to focus on the definition already mentioned, that consideration is the 'price of the promise', what one contracting party is getting, in return for his promise, from the other.

5.5 Better still, keep in mind some common examples of consideration in practice:

- Simultaneous contract and performance, like sale of goods at a supermarket: you get the goods and provide, by way of consideration, the price in return; the supermarket gets the price and provides, by way of consideration, the goods in return. Contrast this with a gift of goods—the person making the gift gets nothing in return and therefore the gift 'transaction' has no consideration and is not regarded as a binding contract. Of course, the relevance of the distinction between a binding contract and a purely gratuitous exchange is more significant where there is a gap in time between the formation of the contract and the date it is to be performed, as in the next category.

- Bilateral contract made before it is due to be performed, as where A and B make a contract in January for the purchase/supply of grain in August: A's promise to pay the price is made in exchange for B's promise to supply the grain—the law regards A's promise as the consideration for B's and vice versa. So there is a binding contract in January even though nothing is to be physically handed over until August. (Notice there is no external logic to this principle—A's promise is only good consideration for B's because the law regards it as enforceable and therefore of value, and it is only regarded as enforceable because it is supported by consideration. But it is only supported by consideration if B's promise is enforceable and so it goes on *ad infinitum*! Despite this, it is a hugely important commercial principle.)

- Unilateral contract, as where A makes a promise to pay money if B performs a specified act. Here, B provides consideration by doing the specified act—finding A's lost dog or using A's smoke ball. In *Carlill v Carbolic Smoke Ball Co* (1893) (see para **2.22**) the Court of Appeal stuck closely to the benefit/detriment language seen a few years earlier in *Currie v Misa*, holding that Mrs Carlill's use of the smoke ball was of detriment to her and of benefit to the defendants. But this seems to miss the essence of why she had provided consideration, which is that she had done what the defendants had required and fulfilled their specified condition, in return for their promised payment.

When is consideration needed?

5.6 It is very important to bear in mind that consideration is required not just when a contract is formed, but also if the contracting parties wish to vary or discharge their contract by agreement. Much of the controversy about consideration actually concerns its role at this later stage, not as part of a formation process. It might be said that consideration is performing two different functions at the two separate stages. At the formation stage, the concern is to prevent the law's involvement in gratuitous transactions, because they are often informal and because a promisor who gets nothing in return arguably deserves the freedom to change her mind. At the variation stage, consideration is linked with worries about duress (see Chapter 10) and the fear that one party might try and force the other party to agree to alter the contract in a way entirely favourable to him. As we shall see, English law's traditional response to this concern was to insist that to be effective an agreement to vary or discharge a contract had to be supported by consideration, though in some circumstances the requirement has been relaxed if there is no obvious duress present.

5.7 We will deal separately with the basic elements of the *bargain* approach to consideration. If the promisor requested something from the promisee, then that something will count as consideration, no matter how trivial. But the 'something' must be something the promisor is getting in return for this promise—if he was already entitled to it, it will not count.

What counts as consideration?

Request

5.8 Usually this aspect of consideration is utterly straightforward—the contract simply specifies precisely what each party is providing to the other. For example, in a contract of sale, the seller's promise to deliver is consideration for the buyer's promise to pay the price and vice versa. But sometimes it is not so obvious whether something amounts to consideration, and then the courts take refuge in asking, well, was it what the other party *asked* you to provide?

5.9 This requirement is often underplayed, but in fact it is a crucial part of the bargain rationale of consideration. Put simply, if you are asking for something from the other party, that will be the consideration for your promise. It is something of a refinement on the traditional definition of consideration as detriment to the promisee/benefit to the promisor. The courts willingly accept the most trivial things as consideration, even if providing them could not really be said to be a benefit to the promisor or a detriment to the other party (like providing a scrap of paper or a peppercorn, or giving up a claim that had no prospect of success), as long as that is what the promisor requested in return for his promise. As we shall see, the courts' lack of concern with the question of whether the consideration was economically equivalent to the promise makes sense, but only when combined with the request requirement: if that is what the promisor asked for in return, the courts will not interfere.

5.10   Imagine this situation: 'I promise to pay you £100 if you will clean/promise to clean my windows.' Here, the cleaning or promise to clean the windows (as the case may be) is consideration. Contrast: 'I promise to pay you £100' and on hearing this, you clean my windows out of a sense of gratitude. Here, the cleaning of the windows is not consideration, even though the detriment to you and the benefit to me is precisely the same. But the point is, I didn't ask for clean windows.

5.11   Of course, in typical English style, a court might be prepared to imply a request, so as to 'find' consideration in an appropriate case, but only where that was a reasonable way of understanding what was said—a request will not be implied out of nowhere. In *Combe v Combe* (1951) the husband's solicitor wrote to the wife's solicitor, in the course of divorce proceedings, and stated that the husband had agreed to pay her an allowance of £100 per annum. In reliance on this, his ex-wife did not apply to the courts for an order for maintenance, but the husband failed to make any of the promised payments, so some years later she sued him. The Court of Appeal held that the husband's promise was not supported by consideration and was thus unenforceable. The wife had acted in reliance on it by not applying to the court for a maintenance order, but this could not amount to consideration so as to turn an otherwise gratuitous promise into a binding promise. As Denning LJ explained:

> I cannot find ... any request by the husband, express or implied, that the wife should so forebear ... Her forbearance was not intended by him, nor was it done at his request. It was therefore no consideration.

The Court of Appeal went on to hold that the principle of estoppel could not be used to prevent the husband from going back on his promise (see further para **5.87**). It is worth noting that, even without the annual payments from her husband, the wife in *Combe v Combe* actually had a larger income than her husband. Atiyah (1986) suggests that, had their relative incomes been the other way round, the Court of Appeal might have been prepared to 'discover' evidence of a request.

5.12   By way of contrast, conditional gifts are treated differently. If I promise you £100 if you clean/promise to clean my windows, that would almost certainly be interpreted as an offer of £100 supported by consideration, namely the cleaning/promise to clean the windows. But if I promise to pay you £100 if you are unlucky enough to break your leg, I am not asking you to break your leg, and so it is likely that this sort of promise would be interpreted merely as an offer of a gift subject to a condition. In other words, breaking your leg is not consideration for the promise to pay. That is not to say that a 'request' necessarily entails that the promisor *desires* the result. It is not illogical (or particularly unusual) to request something but be indifferent about whether it is received (think of asking the waiter for the bill or the taxman to send you a tax return).

Must 'move from the promisee'

5.13 In order to be valid, consideration must 'move from the promisee', though it need not necessarily 'move to the promisor'. This is closely related to the request requirement and the bargain rationale of consideration. It makes sense for the promisor to request, as the price of his promise, that the other party should benefit some third party, but not to ask the promisee that some third party should do something.

5.14 For example, if A promises to pay B £100 in return for B promising A that he will clean C's windows, A's promise to B is enforceable because B (the promisee) has provided something in return, even though what B is promising benefits C (a third party) rather than A (the promisor). This does not matter: after all, that is what the selfless A asked for in return for her promise and who is to argue with that? In contrast, if A promises to pay B £100 if C cleans her (A's) windows, B provides no consideration in return for A's promised payment and will thus not be able to sue for the money even once C has cleaned A's windows. Of course, if B expressly promised to see to it or procure that C cleans A's windows (or if such a promise could be implied), that promise would *itself* be good consideration for A's promise to pay, but the point is that C's cleaning the windows would not.

5.15 This requirement explains the distinction between motive and consideration. People make promises for all sorts of motives, but their motive for promising is usually some reason internal to them—like the desire to make a profit, to eat the chocolate bar, to benefit their children, or to feel good about making a charitable donation. This is not the same as the consideration for the promise, which must derive from the other party. However, it seems that the promisee need not consciously or subjectively realise that he was providing consideration; it is sufficient, according to the Court of Appeal in *Pitts v Jones* (2007), that judged objectively, this was the effect of what the promisee did. As Smith LJ explained, 'the appellants' cooperation was given in return for the respondent's undertaking … that was good consideration notwithstanding the fact that the appellants did not consciously realise that by signing the documents they were subjecting themselves to a detriment and were giving consideration for the respondent's undertaking'.

5.16 The principle that consideration must move from the promisee is closely related to the doctrine of privity and their coverage often coincides (see Chapter 6 for detail). So a third party who is neither a party to the contract nor provides any consideration is generally scuppered by both requirements. But the two principles are generally thought to be distinct: it is perfectly possible (as the second window cleaning example shows) for someone (B) to be a party—a 'promisee'—but still be unable to enforce the other party's obligations because he did not provide any consideration. Likewise, C cannot sue for the money, even though he *did* provide the consideration, because he is not a party to the contract at all and A's offer to pay was not made to him. So, it is said, privity is about the parties to the contract—who made and who accepted the offer—whereas consideration is about ensuring that the deal is in the form of a bargain.

5.17 In any event, this debate no longer matters very much, because of the provisions of the Contracts (Rights of Third Parties) Act 1999 (see paras **6.62–6.85**). This grants rights of action to a 'third party', who is defined as 'a person who is not a party to the contract'. In its Report recommending the new legislation, the Law Commission explained that the central statutory provision giving a right of action to a third party 'can only be interpreted as also reforming the rule that consideration must move from the promisee'. So even though the 1999 Act does not say so expressly, now if you fall within the terms of the Act as a third party it is irrelevant whether or not you provided consideration.

5.18 What about the opposite problem? The Act does not (by implication from its definition of third party) grant a right of action to someone who *is* a party to the contract but who has *not* provided consideration. This permutation can only really arise where the promisor makes his promise to joint promisees, one of whom does not provide any part of the consideration, a situation considered *obiter* by the High Court of Australia in *Coulls v Bagot's Executor and Trustee Ltd* (1967). Mr Coulls gave a company the right to quarry on his land and the company agreed in return to pay royalties. Mr Coulls authorised the company to pay the royalties to himself and his wife jointly, and Mrs Coulls signed the contract together with her husband. When Mr Coulls died, the High Court of Australia had to decide whether the royalties were payable to his estate or to his wife. The majority decided that Mrs Coulls was not a joint promisee, however, *obiter*, four of the judges suggested that, if Mr and Mrs Coulls *had* made the contract jointly, she could have claimed the royalties even though she had given no consideration herself. As Windeyer J explained:

> The promise is made to them collectively. It must, of course, be supported by consideration, but that does not mean by considerations furnished by them separately. It means a consideration given on behalf of them all, and therefore moving from all of them. In such case the promise of the promisor is not gratuitous; and as between him and the joint promisees, it matters not how they were able to provide the price of his promise to them.

5.19 These dicta in *Coulls* have been criticised by Coote (1978) on the basis that Mrs Coulls could only have been properly categorised as a joint promisee if she was undertaking some joint obligation, not merely as the passive recipient of promises from another. This raises the tricky question of what precisely it means to be a party to a contract. Is it sufficient to be named in the contract as a party and/or to sign it, or must some contractual obligation be undertaken (in which case, there will be no instance of a promisee who does not provide consideration)? Trickier still, how does this work in oral contracts, where for example one party is present when the offer and acceptance are made and indicates his or her assent, without undertaking any obligation? Despite these difficulties, the Law Commission explained that joint promisees had been deliberately left out of the 1999 Act:

> in the confident expectation that the English courts will avoid absurdity by accepting that a joint promisee who has not provided consideration will not be left without a basic right to enforce his contract (ie, would follow dicta in Coulls v Bagot's Executor) (Law Commission Report No 242).

Trivial consideration

5.20   It is sometimes said that consideration need not be 'adequate' as long as it is 'sufficient', but these can be spectacularly confusing labels. What this means is that there is no need for the 'price of the promise' to be the *economic* equivalent of the promise or even anywhere near it, as long as the law regards the consideration as something of *value*. But it will be insufficient if it is of no *legal* value: so it cannot be the price of the promise if it is done and dusted before the promise is made, or if the promisor is already entitled to it.

5.21   It is important to understand why the law does not insist that the consideration should be the 'full' or 'equivalent' economic value of what is being received in exchange. This is because the law of contract is not concerned with whether the parties are getting a good deal. It would be unacceptable if the only contracts that were enforceable were those where the court believed that the full market value of performance had been charged. In any event, on one view this is a meaningless concept anyway. In the absence of some defect in the negotiating process, the buyer must want the goods more than the money he is handing over, and the seller must want that price more than he wants the goods. If you are of full capacity and choose to pay a fortune for an item that most people would prefer to throw away, or to sell off an item at a 'crazy knockdown price', then (unless you have been coerced, pressurised, defrauded, or similar, in which case the contract can be avoided) such a contract should be just as enforceable as any other.

5.22   It follows that consideration need only be something of economic value, no matter how trivial compared with what you are getting in return, as the judge confirmed in *Latimer Management Consultants v Ellingham Investments Ltd* (2005). Of course, the crucial notion of request comes into play again: if you have requested something insignificant in return for your promise, you cannot later complain that the contract should not be enforceable or should be reopened because you did not get a good deal.

5.23   This notion that consideration need not be economically adequate can be seen in a number of cases. For example, in *Chappell & Co Ltd v The Nestlé Co Ltd* (1960) C owned the copyright in a popular song. N, a chocolate manufacturer, offered to supply records containing the song to anyone who sent in 1s 6d plus three chocolate wrappers. The House of Lords had to decide (in the context of a copyright dispute) whether the wrappers formed part of the consideration. The majority decided that they did. For Lord Reid, the significant feature of the case was that N benefited from the extra sales of chocolate and publicity that the offer generated, so the requirement to send in chocolate wrappers was a valuable part of the bargain for N, not a mere administrative matter (for example, sending in a self-addressed envelope):

> It seems to me quite unrealistic to divorce the buying of the chocolate from the supply-ing of the records. It is a perfectly good contract if a person accepts an offer to supply goods if he (a) does something of value to the supplier and (b) pays money: the consid-eration is (a) plus (b).

What really divided the majority and minority in the House of Lords was the fact that N probably threw the individual wrappers away on receipt. For Viscount Simmonds, dissenting, this meant that the wrappers were not part of the consideration but were just a qualifying condition to enable someone to purchase the record for 1s 6d. The majority disagreed, as Lord Somervell explained:

> A contracting party can stipulate for whatever consideration he chooses. A peppercorn does not cease to be good consideration if it is established that the promisee does not like pepper and will throw away the corn.

5.24 Sometimes consideration consists of the promisee doing something that takes absolutely no effort at all or that they might very well have done regardless of the promise. In *Shanklin Pier Ltd v Detel Products Ltd* (1951) S were the owners of a pier, which was undergoing repair work carried out by contractors. S had the right to vary the specifi-cation of work being carried out by the contractors. D were paint manufacturers, who gave S an express warranty that its paint would have a life of from seven to ten years. In return, S required their contractors to buy and use D's paint for the work on the pier. The paint was defective and S sued D under the warranty. McNair J held that S were entitled to recover damages for breach of the express warranty, notwithstanding that the main contract of sale was between D and the contractors, not between D and S. There was no problem with consideration to support this collateral warranty:

> I see no reason why there may not be an enforceable warranty between A and B sup-ported by the consideration that B should cause C to enter into a contract with A or that B should do some other act for the benefit of A.

This was, of course, of absolutely no detriment to S, who were just exercising a right under their own contract to specify which paint they wanted. They might very well have specified D's paint even in the absence of the warranty, but the point was that they were free not to, so making that selection at the request of D was of sufficient value to count as consideration. This case is discussed further at para **6.26**.

5.25 Similar reasoning should have been used in the notorious nineteenth-century case of *White v Bluett* (1853). Bluett owed money to his father on a promissory note. When the father died and his executor reclaimed the money, Bluett pleaded that, before he died, his

father had promised to release Bluett from the promissory note if he stopped complaining about his father's distribution of his property. But his plea failed. Pollock CB said:

> In reality, there was no consideration whatever ... The son had no right to complain, for
> the father might make what distribution of his property he liked; and the son's abstain-
> ing from doing what he had no right to do can be no consideration.

It is quite right in principle to say that abstaining from doing something you have no
right to do is of no value, but quite wrong on these facts: Bluett was at *liberty* to complain.
This is quite different from saying, if you release me from my debt I'll stop trespassing
in your garden or stealing from your house! McKendrick (2003) argues that this case is
better regarded as showing no intention to create legal relations, but recognises that the
court did not use this language; moreover, it is a pretty formal transaction even though
the parties are a father and son. Another explanation is that the court did not believe
the son's self-serving evidence, particularly since the father had retained the promissory
note at the time of his death. The opposite result was reached in the American case of
Hamer v Sidway (1891), where a nephew was promised money if he refrained from a
number of vices (such as smoking and drinking alcohol).

5.26   Agreeing to drop or compromise a legal claim will amount to good consideration, even
where the claim is a hopeless or worthless one, provided the party making the claim
is acting in good faith and believes the claim to be valid. In contrast, where one party
knowingly brings a claim without any foundation (as in *Wade v Simeon* (1846)) their
promise to drop such a claim is no consideration for the other party's promise to pay.
Of course, in either sort of case the party sued gains some 'practical benefit' (see further
at para **5.50**) from being spared the hassle and expense of defending hopeless actions,
but for sensible policy reasons the law only recognises this as consideration where the
claim is brought bona fide: it is a good thing to encourage binding compromises of valid
claims, however hopeless, but a bad thing to encourage people to bring spurious claims
in the hope of extracting a compromise from the other party.

5.27   Moreover, forbearance need not involve legal proceedings, as *R v Attorney General for
England and Wales* (2003) shows. The army's elite SAS regiment was dismayed by the
publication of certain books and films by members of the regiment, giving accounts of
the ill-fated *SAS Bravo Two Zero* patrol captured behind enemy lines in the 1991 Gulf
War. So the Ministry of Defence (MOD) introduced a confidentiality contract to be
signed by all members of the SAS, prohibiting such publications in future. R, a member
of the regiment, was told to sign the contract; if he did not do so he would have been
transferred out of the SAS to another regiment (a course of action usually used as a
disciplinary sanction only). R signed the contract, but later left the army and wrote
his memoirs. The Crown brought proceedings to enforce the contract and R pleaded
various defences (including that he entered into the contract because of duress and/or
undue influence—see Chapters 10 and 11). He also pleaded that the contract was not
supported by any consideration. All his defences were rejected. On consideration, the
Privy Council decided that the MOD's forbearance to exercise its discretion to transfer

R to another regiment was good consideration for R's confidentiality promise. It was irrelevant that, before the confidentiality contracts were introduced, this discretion was never in practice exercised other than for disciplinary purposes—what counted was that the MOD was entitled to exercise it but did not do so.

5.28 This case brings us nicely to the notion that consideration must be legally sufficient. Interestingly, the Privy Council held that the MOD did not provide consideration by *promising* not to transfer R—this would have been an illegitimate fettering of the MOD's public law powers—but by the act of forbearing itself. For legal reasons, some acts or promises that look like good consideration do not count as such. The main reasons are that, as a matter of timing, they were not given in exchange for the relevant promise (the problem of 'past consideration') or that the promisor was already entitled to them.

Examples of legally insufficient consideration

Past consideration

5.29 The basic doctrine can be seen in two nineteenth-century decisions, both of Lord Denman CJ. The first is *Eastwood v Kenyon* (1840), in which a father died and left his entire estate to his young daughter, Sarah. Eastwood, who was the father's executor and acted as Sarah's guardian, borrowed £140 to help pay for Sarah's upbringing. When she came of age, Sarah married Kenyon, who then promised Eastwood he would discharge the debt. However, Kenyon failed to honour his promise, but it was held that there was no consideration for it and it was therefore unenforceable. Lord Denman CJ said:

> ... we find that the consideration for it was past and executed long before ... and the declaration really discloses nothing but a benefit voluntarily conferred by the plaintiff and received by the defendant, with an express promise by the defendant to pay money.

The reasoning is closely tied to the 'bargain' approach to contracts—a contract is an exchange of promises, one in return for the other. Here, Eastwood had performed services to Sarah which could have counted as consideration for Kenyon's promise, but only if performed in return for it. Lord Denman CJ rejected the argument (based on some rather eminent earlier decisions of Lord Mansfield) that Kenyon's promise alone was sufficient, supported by his pre-existing moral obligation to remunerate Eastwood, since this would 'annihilate the need for any consideration at all, inasmuch as the mere fact of giving a promise creates a moral obligation to perform it'.

5.30 The second case was *Roscorla v Thomas* (1842). R bought a horse from T. Subsequently, T gave R an oral warranty that the horse was sound. However, when R later sued alleging breach of this warranty, the court held that it lacked consideration and was unenforceable. The consideration paid for the horse was past and could not support the later warranty (the 'promise must be coextensive with the consideration'). Note that at the time there was no implied promise that the horse was sound (as would now be the case under the Sale of Goods Act 1979—see para **7.71**). Of course, the court's reasoning raises the question of what 'coextensive' means. It is not always easy to tell whether the consideration and the later promise form part and parcel of one transaction though the nub seems to be whether the parties intended, at the time that the original promise was made, that the recipient would give something in return.

5.31   This is at the root of the main common law exception to the past consideration rule; in fact, it is not really an exception, more an explanation of what counts as one coextensive transaction. It is encapsulated in the difficult seventeenth-century language of *Lampleigh v Braithwait* (1615):

> A mere voluntary courtesie will not have a consideration to uphold an assumpsit. But if that courtesie were moved by a suit or request of the party that gives the assumpsit, it will bind, for the promise, though it follows, yet it is not naked, but couples itself with the suit before, and the merits of the party procured by that suit, which is the difference.

This means, if A *asks* B to do something for him and later promises to pay for it or do something in return, A's promise will be enforceable because it is supported by consideration, namely what B did at A's request. So *Eastwood v Kenyon* was not within this *Lampleigh v Braithwait* 'request' exception, because Kenyon did not ask Eastwood to borrow the money or provide the services for Sarah.

5.32   The exception was applied in *Pao On v Lau Yiu Long* (1980), in which Lord Scarman explained:

> An act done before the giving of a promise to make a payment or to confer some other benefit can sometimes be consideration for the promise. The act must have been done at the promisors' request: the parties must have understood that the act was to be remunerated either by a payment or the conferment of some other benefit: and payment, or the conferment of a benefit, must have been legally enforceable had it been promised in advance. All three features are present in this case.

5.33   As well as the *Lampleigh v Braithwait* principle, there are a number of other exceptions to the rule that past consideration is legally insufficient. The most important of these in practice is found in the Bills of Exchange Act 1882 concerning negotiable instruments.

5.34   What is the rationale of the past consideration rule? As ever, it is to avoid putting people into the position of being forced to accept obligations that they have not freely consented to. The fear is moral blackmail: that one party might confer a benefit gratuitously and then later put pressure on the recipient to make a promise to pay for it or enter into some other contractual obligation. This explains the exception: if you requested the benefit in circumstances in which it was clearly intended that it was to be paid for, there is nothing objectionable about enforcing a subsequent contract to pay for it. Likewise the courts are not too strict about chronology, but look at the substance of the transaction. As Phillips J put it in *Marsden v Barclays Bank plc* (2016), quoting Chitty (2016), 'If the giving of the consideration and the making of the promise are substantially one transaction, the exact order in which these events occur is not decisive.'

5.35 The following categories are all variations on the theme of whether it counts as good consideration to do, or promise to do, something that you are already obliged to do.

Pre-existing public duty

5.36 If you are under a public duty to do something, in other words a duty that is enforceable by the general law irrespective of contract, then the performance of this duty (or a promise to perform it) will not count as good consideration to support another person's promise. This makes sense according to the bargain theory of consideration, since the promisor is obtaining nothing of value *as a result of* his promise. It should, of course, be noted that that proposition could be reversed but be equally valid as a matter of logic, the same logic that deems bilateral promises to be good consideration for each other: if the law said that the performance of the promisor's public duty, or a promise to perform it, *was* good consideration, then the promisor *would* be getting something of value, namely the personal, contractual right to enforce the public duty. The reason for the rule is not, then, one of formal legal reasoning but one of policy: to discourage those with public duties from demanding contractual payments or other benefits in return for performing their duties.

5.37 The traditional authority for this rule is *Collins v Godefroy* (1831), where Collins received a subpoena requiring him to appear as a witness for Godefroy at a trial. Godefroy promised to remunerate Collins for attending, but this promise was held to be without consideration, since a subpoenaed witness was under a public duty to attend without payment. The result in this case has subsequently been reversed by statute, but the principle remains valid.

5.38 Where, however, the promisee does *more* than his public duty requires, this will amount to good consideration. The problem is that it is not always easy to define the precise content of the public duty or to work out whether or not the promisee has exceeded what it requires. This issue has tended to arise in two distinct areas, the performance of statutory functions by the emergency services and the performance of familial duties to support spouses or children. In *Glasbrook Bros Ltd v Glamorgan County Council* (1925) a colliery owner requested the police to provide a police garrison as protection during a strike, which he promised to pay for. The majority of the House of Lords held that the police provided 'special services' beyond the duty imposed on them by the general law, so the colliery owner's promise to pay was binding. The minority on the other hand, nervous of the implications of allowing the police to charge the public to protect them, thought that the police had merely done their public duty in the circumstances. Today the principle in *Glasbrook* is enshrined in s 25(1) of the Police Act 1996, considered by the Court of

Appeal in *West Yorkshire Police Authority v Reading Festival Ltd* (2006) and *Leeds United FC Ltd v Chief Constable of West Yorkshire Police* (2013).

5.39   The public duty concept is particularly malleable where familial obligations are concerned. Here the concern is not so much about extortion by public officials but about the delicacy of imposing legal obligations in the domestic setting. So in *Ward v Byham* (1956) a father promised to pay £1 per week to the mother of his illegitimate child, in return for her ensuring that the child was well looked after and happy. The majority of the Court of Appeal held that, by ensuring that the child was well and happy, the mother was going beyond the bare minimum level of care required by the general (presumably criminal) law and thus provided consideration for the father's promise. Denning LJ, more radical as usual, thought that the mother was merely doing what the law required but that this was no barrier to enforcing the father's promise, saying:

> I have always thought that a promise to perform an existing duty, or the performance of it, should be regarded as good consideration, because it is a benefit to the person to whom it is given.

5.40   The same difference of opinion emerged in *Williams v Williams* (1957) in which a husband promised to pay a weekly sum to his wife, who had deserted him, in consideration for her promise to support and maintain herself and not to sue the husband. For Denning LJ the promise was enforceable even though the wife was merely promising to do what, being in desertion, she was already bound to do. The majority of the Court of Appeal found good consideration in the wife's promise to maintain herself, on the basis that she might have returned to her husband at any time, whereupon her right to be maintained by him would have resurrected. The majority's solution invokes a somewhat fictitious extra obligation—though no more so than, for example, the MOD's forbearance to transfer the soldier in *R v Attorney General for England and Wales* (see para 5.27)—in order to maintain the formal integrity of the rules of consideration. Denning LJ is being more honest in his interpretation of the facts but still wants the husband's/father's promise to be enforceable, so he must do away with the rule of consideration itself. What these cases really show is that the 1950s rules governing financial support on matrimonial break-up needed reforming, which is of course what has since happened!

Pre-existing contractual obligation owed to a third party

5.41   Suppose A is already under a contractual obligation in a contract with B to do something: can performing or promising to perform that contractual obligation amount to consideration to support a promise made by C? You might think that there would be very little difference, so far as consideration is concerned, between a public duty owed under the general law (see the earlier section 'Pre-existing public duty') and a contractual duty owed to a third party. But in fact, the law takes the opposite view. So a promise to perform a pre-existing obligation already owed to a third party, and actual performance of such a third party obligation, can both count as good consideration.

5.42   In *Shadwell v Shadwell* (1860) S was engaged to be married (a contractually binding commitment at the time). S's uncle wrote to him, saying that he was delighted to hear of his impending marriage and promising to pay him £150 a year, to assist S in getting started as a chancery barrister. S got married but later alleged that his uncle had failed to honour this promise and sued for the arrears. The uncle pleaded that his promise was not supported by consideration, but (by a majority) the court disagreed, finding consideration in S's performance of his contractual obligation to marry his fiancée. Erle CJ found detriment to S, in that he might have acted in reliance on the promise and induced his fiancée to do the same, thereby incurring 'pecuniary liabilities resulting in embarrassments' if the income had been withheld. He also held that the promise was an inducement to the marriage and that the uncle, as a near relative, would derive some intangible benefit from seeing his nephew get married.

5.43   How does this case differ from an unenforceable conditional gift? The majority construed the uncle's letter as an implicit *request* to the nephew to get married (having held that the uncle intended it as an inducement to marriage) on the basis that this was a reasonable objective interpretation of the words used. But request and inducement are not quite the same thing. The letter would surely have been just as much of an inducement to the nephew to go ahead with his marriage, even if his uncle had not mentioned the marriage at all but had merely promised an annual sum. So it seems to have been the finding that the uncle *intended* to induce the marriage that clinched the case in the nephew's favour.

5.44   Why does English law regard a promise made by A to C that A will perform a contractual obligation already owed to B as good consideration? One explanation is that, by 'repeating' the contractual obligation, A is burdened by being exposed to the possibility of being sued by an extra person, namely the new promisor (C), as well as the original third party (B), while C obtains the corresponding benefit of a right against A. As the Privy Council put it in *The Eurymedon* (1975):

> An agreement to do an act which the promisor is under an existing obligation to a third party to do, may quite well amount to valid consideration ... the promisee obtains the benefit of a direct obligation.

But of course this is circular logic: A is only subject to an additional burden if C can *enforce* A's promise, but C can only enforce the promise if it is supported by consideration. Likewise A's actual *performance* of an obligation owed to B is regarded as good consideration for C's promise, because A has curtailed his freedom of action by performing the obligation which he might otherwise have breached. But again it would be just as logical (and perhaps more consistent with the treatment of public duties) to say that this performance is of no detriment to A, because A is doing no more than he is already obliged to do.

5.45   In truth, performing or promising to perform a contractual duty owed to a third party is allowed as consideration simply because there are no reasons of policy why it should not be. There is no risk of extortion of money for the performance of public duties, nor is there any concern about economic duress. Duress (as we will see) is one of the main problems about allowing the performance of or a promise to perform a contractual obligation owed to the other contracting party to count as consideration for a new contract or, more commonly, a unilateral variation of the original one. It is easy to see the potential for extortion in a two-party situation, where one party can threaten the other by saying, 'Vary the contract in my favour or else I will not honour my side of the contract.' But this is less of a risk in a three-party situation: the other contracting party will rarely be remotely bothered about a threat to breach a contract with a third party.

What, however, is the position if no third party is involved—can performing or promising to do what you are already contractually bound to the other contracting party to do count as good consideration?

Pre-existing contractual obligation owed to the other party

5.46 The basic rule has traditionally been that it is *not* good consideration to do or promise to do what you are already contractually bound to the other contracting party to do. This is because doing what you are already bound to do is no legal detriment (you can already be sued to enforce the original promise) and equally it is of no legal benefit to the other party to receive performance that they are already entitled to receive. In an interesting illustration of this point, the Court of Appeal in *Robinson v Lane* (2010) pointed out that a vendor of land is normally entitled to retain the deposit if the purchaser declines to complete the contract, so if the vendor promises instead to return the deposit, this is gratuitous and the purchaser generally provides no consideration for this promise even if he 'forebears' to press for its return. However, on the unusual facts of *Robinson*, the original contract was oral and therefore void; this meant that the purchaser *was* entitled to the return of his 'deposit' and thus his forbearance from pressing for its return provided consideration for additional promises by the vendor.

5.47 This reminds us that consideration is traditionally required, not just for the formation of a new contract, but also for the variation or discharge of an existing one by agreement, if such agreement is itself to be contractually effective. Where a contract is varied by altering the obligations on both sides, there is no problem. Imagine we have a contract in which you promise to deliver goods on 1 April and I promise to pay £100 for them. If we agree to vary the contract so that I agree to pay £10 extra for the goods, my promise will be supported by consideration, as long as we agree to alter your obligation in some way as well, for example by promising to bring forward the delivery date, alter the specification of the goods or change the place of delivery. There is consideration on both sides, so the variation is binding and enforceable. The problem lies with unilateral variations, where there is no corresponding alteration in the other party's obligation.

5.48 The classic authority on this question is *Stilk v Myrick* (1809). S was a sailor, who contracted to sail on a voyage to the Baltic and back again for wages of £5 per month. During the voyage, two other sailors deserted, so M (the ship's captain) agreed that if the rest of the crew worked the ship back to England, he would divide the wages of the deserters between them. On arrival in England, M did not pay so S sued, but the court held that M was not obliged to pay the extra sum representing S's share of the deserters' wages, only his original wage. The reasoning in *Stilk v Myrick* is difficult to pinpoint, because two law reporters gave two rather different accounts of Lord Ellenborough's judgment. Espinasse reports Lord Ellenborough as deciding the case on the grounds of 'just and proper policy', namely the policy of discouraging sailors (and indeed any contracting parties) from threatening not to perform the contract unless they are paid more than the contractual sum. Campbell's report, on the other hand, emphasises that S provided no consideration for M's promise of extra remuneration, because S was obliged under his original contract to sail the ship back 'under all the emergencies of the voyage'. Campbell reported Lord Ellenborough as saying that 'the desertion of a part of the crew is to be considered an emergency of the voyage as much as their death; and those who remain are bound by the terms of their original contract to exert themselves to the utmost to bring the ship in safety to her destined port'. This can be contrasted with *Hartley v Ponsonby* (1857), in which so many sailors deserted that those remaining were no longer obliged to continue with the voyage (in modern theory, the contract was frustrated), rendering their promise to do so good consideration for the captain's promise of more money.

5.49   For many years Campbell's version of the case was favoured and Espinasse mocked as an unreliable law reporter. The 'consideration' approach met the concern about duress at a time when the courts had not formally adopted economic duress as a vitiating factor and indeed, rendered the need for such a development less pressing. There is, after all, no need to worry about trying to identify which variations were extorted and which were not, if there is a blanket rule saying that there is simply no consideration. Of course, this approach meant that some genuine renegotiations will be rendered unenforceable, but that was regarded as a price worth paying to prevent extortion.

5.50   This position is open to criticism. After all, as long as there is no extortion, the parties (assuming them to be rational) will presumably have agreed to vary their contract for sound commercial reasons, which should arguably be respected by enforcing the variation despite the technical lack of consideration. For example, there was no evidence of extortion by the sailors in *Stilk v Myrick*—the ship was in port, not on the high seas, when the promise was made, so the captain could presumably have engaged replacements for the deserters without undue difficulty. Having decided not to do so, why should he not be obliged to pay his existing crew what he promised? In any event, there may very well be a *practical* detriment to the promisor in going ahead and doing what he had promised to do, rather than taking the option of breaching the contract and paying damages, even if it is not regarded as a legal detriment. Likewise there will certainly be a *practical* benefit to the promisee in receiving the promised performance without having to take proceedings for breach of contract, where the remedy obtained would generally only be an award of damages, not specific enforcement. Claiming damages brings the responsibility on the promisee to mitigate his loss (with the hassle and expense of seeking substitute performance), and an award of damages is unlikely to reflect everything that would be obtained by performance, because of the restrictive rules of contractual remoteness of damage (see generally Chapter 16).

5.51 Moreover English law now has a developing doctrine of economic duress (see Chapter 10). As a result of this and the objections to *Stilk v Myrick* mentioned already, the courts are now prepared to try and distinguish between cases of duress and genuine renegotiations, refusing to enforce the former but enforcing the latter by treating the practical benefit from obtaining the promised performance as sufficient consideration.

5.52 In the leading case *Williams v Roffey Bros & Nicholls* (1990), Roffey, a building firm ('the builders'), had a building contract to refurbish 27 flats and subcontracted the carpentry work to Williams ('the carpenter') for a price of £20,000. After finishing work on nine of the flats, the carpenter got into financial difficulties because his contract price was too low and because he failed to supervise his workmen adequately. The builders were concerned that they would be liable under a penalty clause in the main building contract if the carpenter did not finish the remaining 18 flats on time, so promised to pay him an extra £10,300 (at the approximate rate of £575 on each completed flat). The carpenter completed eight more flats but the builders paid him only £1,500 extra. The carpenter then abandoned work on the job, so the builders were obliged to engage other carpenters to finish the work and incurred liability under the penalty clause. The carpenter sued, claiming the balance of the extra sum promised. The builders argued that he had provided no consideration for this additional promise, but the Court of Appeal disagreed. They held that there *was* consideration for the additional promise and awarded damages of £3,500, representing the balance of the extra money promised for the eight completed flats plus a proportion of the outstanding instalment of the original contract price, less the £1,500 already paid and certain other minor deductions.

Russell LJ's judgment was relatively orthodox. He found that the additional promise was not an entirely unilateral variation, in that the parties had replaced 'what had hitherto been a haphazard method of payment by a more formalised scheme involving the payment of a specified sum on completion of each flat'. But Glidewell and Purchas LJJ were more radical. They reinterpreted *Stilk v Myrick* as a case where the only reason for the result was the fear of duress, holding that now English law has a sophisticated doctrine of duress, and can deal with it when it is present, there is no longer any reason not to enforce genuine renegotiations. So they held that, in genuine renegotiations, the *practical benefit* derived by the promisor from performance of the promisee's contractual obligations should be regarded as good consideration. As Glidewell LJ put it:

> The present state of the law on this subject can be expressed in the following propositions: (i) if A has entered into a contract with B to do work for, or supply goods or services to, B in return for payment by B; and (ii) at some stage before A has completely performed his obligations under the contract B has reason to doubt whether A will, or will be able to, complete his side of the bargain; and (iii) B thereupon promises A an additional payment in return for A's promise to perform his contractual obligations on time; and (iv) as a result of giving his promise, B obtains in practice a benefit, or obviates

a disbenefit; and (v) B's promise is not given as a result of duress or fraud on the part of A; then (vi) the benefit to B is capable of being consideration for B's promise, so that the promise will be legally binding.

5.53 Many commentators praised this result, if not all of the court's reasoning: see for example Birks (1990), Halson (1990), and Chen-Wishart (1995). It is said to recognise commercial reality, to separate genuine renegotiations from examples of duress and to move English law away from an absurd requirement of consideration in contractual variations. Variations that are unilateral in substance have always been enforceable as long as they are bilateral in form, so if the court can point to a tiny, meaningless detrimental variation in the promisee's obligations, that will suffice. *Roffey*, it is said, is just being honest about this and recognising that all genuine variations should be enforced.

5.54 However, the decision is not altogether satisfactory. There are a number of problems with it, on the particular facts and more generally. On the facts of *Roffey* itself the following problems should be considered:

- The carpenter got more than he was originally promised for doing less than he promised to do, given that he downed tools before finishing the flats. The builders still had to engage replacement subcontractors and still incurred liability under the penalty clause: so did they actually gain any practical benefit from what happened?

- Glidewell LJ's explanation of the law is puzzling. It is easy to see how *performance* of one's contractual obligations can be of practical benefit to the other party (who thereby avoids litigation, mitigation, the penalty clause, etc), but Glidewell LJ refers as well to a *promise* to perform existing contractual obligations. How can it be good consideration to repeat a promise but not perform it—surely this can lead to an infinite cycle? And what of performance in part, or defective performance?

- The decision about whether there is duress or not is not entirely straightforward. The case law on duress is in a formative stage in England, with much uncertainty about when a threat to breach a contract suffices as an illegitimate threat (see paras **10.11–10.17**). In *Roffey*, what convinced the court that there was no duress seems to be that it was the builders' idea to offer more money to the carpenter. But it is not difficult to give someone the hint that, if they don't agree to pay more, you won't be able to perform, until eventually it occurs to them to offer more money. It is certainly clear from the case law on economic duress that implied or veiled threats are sufficient: Hobhouse J said as much in *The Alev* (1989)—is this so very different from the situation in *Roffey*? This matter is discussed further by O'Sullivan (1996).

5.55 Furthermore, there are several more general problems with the decision:

- Fear of duress might not be the only reason for the rule in *Stilk v Myrick*: it may also operate to encourage parties to price their contracts properly in advance. As O'Sullivan (1996) points out: 'Why should any contractor bother to estimate his price accurately or supervise his staff, now that the law is willing to treat his difficulties in performing his contractual obligations as a sufficient "reason" for enforcing a subsequent promise to pay him more than the contract price?'

- Those who criticise a consideration requirement in this context point out that many contracts, rather than embodying a one-off transaction, are in fact long-term relational arrangements, which must be allowed to develop with the parties' relationship over time. In such cases, the requirement of consideration for each variation is unrealistic and, it is said, should be modified to meet commercial reality. One response is to say that, if properly drafted, such relational contracts can contain their own mechanism for alteration over time (like a rent review clause in a long commercial lease). But more fundamentally, of course, the point is that *Roffey* was not such a contract anyway—it was a one-off job for a price.

- Commercial parties need certainty. Supporters of the *Roffey* approach say that it is nonsense that a contractual variation is enforceable if the other side's obligations are altered in a trivial way, but not otherwise. But that is at least a fairly straightforward way of making the variation work, allowing for clear legal advice at the time and thus avoiding litigation later.

- Finally, it should be noted that those who advocate the abolition of consideration for contractual variation do not necessarily agree with the approach in *Roffey* that practical benefit *suffices* for consideration. For example, the New Zealand Court of Appeal has since gone further and decided that contractual variations, once relied on, do not need consideration at all (see *Antons Trawling Co Ltd v Smith* (2003), noted by Coote (2004)).

5.56 *Roffey* is not without its judicial critics. In *South Caribbean Trading Ltd v Trafigura Beheever BV* (2004) Colman J said, 'But for the fact that *Roffey* was a decision of the Court of Appeal, I would not have followed it. That decision is inconsistent with the long-standing rule that consideration must move from the promisee.' As a first instance judge Colman J was, of course, bound by the decision, although his acknowledgement of this was prefaced by the pointed remark, 'seeing that *Roffey* has not yet been held by the House of Lords to be wrongly decided … '. Nonetheless, English law, for now at least, holds that performance of (or even a promise to perform) an existing obligation can amount to good consideration for the other party's promise to vary their obligation, generally (as in *Roffey*) by increasing the contract price. Can the same reasoning be applied to what looks at first glance very similar: an agreement to accept less than the full amount of a debt owed?

Part payment of a debt

5.57 Where a debtor owes money to a creditor, consideration is required if the debtor's obligation to repay the debt is varied in any way. So, for example, if the debtor agrees to pay an instalment of the debt earlier than the due date and the creditor agrees in return to give the debtor more time to pay the balance or to reduce the total amount owed, there is consideration on both sides and the variation is contractually binding. The difficulty, once again, comes with unilateral variations, in particular where the creditor agrees to accept part only of the debt and let the debtor off paying the rest. Is this concession binding on the creditor or not?

5.58   This problem appears on the surface to be the mirror image of the *Roffey* situation, concerning a promise to accept less money than is already owed, rather than a promise to pay more for goods or services that the promisor is already contractually entitled to receive. The language used to express the two issues is different, with the cases of part payment of debts asking whether there has been 'accord and satisfaction' instead of a contractually binding variation, but this is not particularly significant because this phrase simply means agreement to discharge a debt obligation ('accord') that is supported by consideration ('satisfaction'). Yet, in fact the symmetry is a little misleading. The substantive difference is that the existing duty in *Roffey* is a duty to provide *services*, whereas the existing duty in a debt case is an obligation to *pay money*. But it is still instructive to compare the two situations and the law's response to them.

5.59   Just like the traditional approach in *Stilk v Myrick*, the general rule has always been that the mere payment of a smaller sum in satisfaction of a larger debt is not good consideration and does not discharge the debtor's obligation to pay the balance of the debt. As Lord Coke famously explained in *Pinnel's Case* (1602):

> That payment of a lesser sum on the day in satisfaction of a greater, cannot be any satisfaction for the whole, because it appears to the judges, that by no possibility a lesser sum can be satisfaction to the plaintiff for a greater sum.

5.60   This was applied by the House of Lords in *Foakes v Beer* (1884). Dr Foakes owed Mrs Beer just over £2,090, so she obtained judgment against him for this amount. The full amount of this judgment debt was due immediately and interest was payable until it was fully paid. Dr Foakes asked for time to pay so the parties entered into an agreement, in which he agreed to pay £500 immediately and the balance of the debt by half-yearly instalments. In return Mrs Beer agreed not to take proceedings to enforce the debt or to claim the interest on it. Dr Foakes repaid the £2,090 in full in accordance with the agreement, but Mrs Beer then sought to recover the interest on it. The House of Lords held that there was no consideration for Mrs Beer's promise not to sue for the interest, since Dr Foakes was doing no more than he was already obliged to do in repaying the debt. *Pinnel's Case* had been accepted as part of the law of England for many years and would be applied. The members of the House of Lords were not particularly enthusiastic about the principle they were applying. Earl Selborne LC thought it would be 'an improvement in our law' if a release of part of a debt were to be binding even though not made by deed, but nonetheless felt unable to distinguish *Pinnel's Case*. Lord Blackburn was even more troubled by the result, tantalisingly hinting that he had prepared a dissenting speech but decided against delivering it:

> What principally weighs with me in thinking that Lord Coke made a mistake of fact is my conviction that all men of business, whether merchants or tradesmen, do every

day recognise and act on the ground that prompt payment of a part of their demand may be more beneficial to them than it would be to insist on their rights and enforce payment of the whole. Even where the debtor is perfectly solvent, and sure to pay at last, this often is so. Where the credit of the debtor is doubtful it must be more so. I had persuaded myself that there was no such long-continued action on this dictum as to render it improper in this House to reconsider the question. I had written my reasons for so thinking; but as they were not satisfactory to the other noble and learned Lords who heard the case, I do not now repeat them nor persist in them.

So, as their Lordships in *Foakes v Beer* recognised, acceptance of part of a debt can be of just as much 'practical benefit' to the creditor as the practical benefit to a promisor of obtaining contractual performance in a *Roffey* situation. But the courts have refused to extend the *Roffey* reasoning to this analogous problem.

5.61   In *Re Selectmove Ltd* (1995), a case in which a company was alleging that it had made an agreement with the Inland Revenue to pay income tax arrears by instalments, the Court of Appeal held that no such agreement had been reached but that, even if it had been, it was unsupported by consideration. The court considered that it was bound to apply *Foakes v Beer* and that this was unaffected by the decision in *Roffey*:

> *When a creditor and a debtor who are at arm's length reach agreement on the payment of the debt by instalments to accommodate the debtor, the creditor will no doubt always see a practical benefit to himself in so doing. In the absence of authority there would be much to be said for the enforceability of such a contract. But that was a matter expressly considered in Foakes v Beer yet held not to constitute good consideration in law. Foakes v Beer was not even referred to in Williams v Roffey and it is in my judgement impossible, consistent with the doctrine of precedent, for this court to extend the principle of the Williams' case to any circumstance governed by the principle in Foakes v Beer. If that extension is to be granted, it must be by the House of Lords or, perhaps even more appropriately, by Parliament after consideration by the Law Commission.*

So as a matter of precedent, only the Supreme Court or Parliament can get rid of *Foakes v Beer*. In fact, the Law Reform Committee recommended as long ago as 1937 that the rule in *Foakes v Beer* should be abolished, but this recommendation was never implemented.

5.62   The Supreme Court may soon get the opportunity to consider *Foakes v Beer*, because a controversial recent decision of the Court of Appeal, *MWB Business Exchange Centres Ltd v Rock Advertising Ltd* (2016) is (at the time of writing) on appeal to the Supreme Court. The Court of Appeal decision is considered by O'Sullivan (2017a). Rock occupied office premises in London managed by MWB. In August, Rock decided to expand its business, and entered into a written licence agreement with MWB for larger premises, for a term of 12 months beginning on 1 November. Rock's expanded business did not prosper, and by late February it had already incurred licence fee arrears of over £12,000. Rock's managing director had a conversation with MWB's credit controller, Miss Evans, on her mobile phone, in which she agreed to re-schedule the licence fee payments for the rest of the term: Rock would pay less than the originally agreed amount for the first few months, but after that would pay more, clearing the arrears by the end of the year. The trial judge held that this Miss Evans had authority to bind MWB. Pursuant to the oral variation, Rock immediately paid the first revised instalment. Two days later, Miss Evans sent an e-mail informing Rock that her finance director was 'not happy to allow you to accumulate any more debt on the account' and rejected the revised payment schedule. Shortly afterwards, MWB exercised its contractual right to exclude Rock from the premises for being in arrears, then gave notice terminating the licence agreement and sued for unpaid arrears. The trial judge gave judgment for MWB and Rock appealed to the Court of Appeal, which unanimously allowed its appeal. (There was another issue in *MWB* that will not be considered here, namely that the written licence agreement required any variation to be made in writing—see para 1.9 and O'Sullivan (2017a) for discussion of this point.)

5.63   MWB relied on the rule in *Foakes v Beer*, as interpreted in *Selectmove*, arguing that the variation lacked consideration, but the Court of Appeal purported to *distinguish* those authorities, reinterpreting them as cases in which the only benefit to the creditor was the prompt receipt of part payment, and confining their ratios accordingly. In contrast, the court held that where a creditor gains an additional commercial advantage from such part payment, this falls outside *Foakes'* ratio and is governed instead by *Williams v Roffey* reasoning. In other words, such additional practical benefit was regarded as good consideration for the creditor's promise. On the facts, the additional practical benefit was, in the words of the trial judge, the commercial advantage of 'retaining an existing tenant, even if a questionable payer, in the hope of perhaps recovering its arrears rather than getting rid of them, probably saying goodbye to the arrears and allowing the property to stand empty for some time at further loss to themselves'.

5.64   What should we make of the importation of *Williams v Roffey* reasoning here? Many commentators will welcome it; after all, there is certainly much that seems absurd about the *Foakes v Beer* rule. We saw in the earlier section on 'Pre-existing contractual obligation owed to the other party' that one of the criticisms of the rule in *Stilk v Myrick* was that the slightest detrimental variation in the promisee's position could be seized upon as consideration, even when in substance the variation was unilateral. A similar position applies to discharge of debts. *Pinnel's Case* made it clear that if the debtor's obligation was varied in some respect *other than* a reduction in the amount to be paid, this variation could be sufficient consideration. This might be payment on a date earlier than the due date for payment, or payment in a different place or currency. Likewise, if the creditor accepts payment of part of the debt from a third party, in discharge of the whole, this is a binding accord and satisfaction. So in *Hirachand Punamchand v Temple* (1911) a creditor accepted and cashed a cheque in settlement of the debt from the debtor's father, for part of the amount the son owed, and this was held to discharge the balance of the debt.

5.65   Lord Coke further explained in *Pinnel's Case* that:

> the gift of a horse, hawk or robe etc in satisfaction is good, for it shall be intended that
> a horse, hawk or robe etc might be more beneficial to the plaintiff than the money, in

respect of some circumstance, or otherwise the plaintiff would not have accepted it in satisfaction.

Of course this looks absurd. It is hard to explain why, if a creditor accepts even a token item like a peppercorn in settlement of a debt of £1,000, this will discharge the debt, whereas accepting £900 in settlement will not and the creditor will be free to sue for the £100 balance. Arden LJ in *MWB* regarded Lord Coke's 'horse, hawk or robe' qualification as 'no different in principle from the conferral of a benefit or advantage' and thus as authority for the proposition that additional commercial benefit acts as consideration, so as to distinguish *Foakes*. But the basic rule may not be quite as crazy as it first appears.

5.66 First, bear in mind that the creditor cannot be forced to accept this sort of variation in performance, which will only count as accord and satisfaction if done at the *request* of the creditor. As O'Sullivan (2017a) argues, the *MWB* reasoning is problematic because the trial judgment revealed no evidence of any such request with regard to the 'additional commercial benefit'. Indeed, the only objective evidence pointed strongly the other way: if MWB regarded 'retaining the existing tenant' as commercially beneficial to it, why would it exercise its right to exclude Rock from the premises and terminate the licence? More fundamentally, where the only benefit to the creditor is 'less money', it is hard to challenge the creditor's decision without calling into question the premise that the law is not concerned with ensuring economic equivalence. If the creditor chooses to value a hawk more than £1,000, that is up to her. It is hard to apply the same reasoning to the creditor's decision to accept £900 in place of £1,000, because money (being currency) cannot really be valued other than at its face value. Of course, the creditor is choosing £900 now because she regards that as of more benefit than a right to claim £1,000. But if the £1,000 is not yet due, immediate accelerated receipt of £900 will be good consideration. If on the other hand the £1,000 is already due, an action for its recovery will yield £1,000 plus costs and interest: there is no risk to that entitlement (unlike the situation in *Roffey*) from either the process of converting loss into damages or the requirement of mitigation.

5.67 Where the creditor accepts less than the full debt because of fear of the debtor's *insolvency*, of course it makes commercial sense for the creditor to accept £900 now, but then if the debtor duly becomes insolvent the creditor's notional right to claim the £100 balance is of academic interest only. The significant question is what should happen where, against the odds, the debtor staves off insolvency.

5.68 Secondly, the fear of duress is relevant again. In *D&C Builders v Rees* (1966) D&C, a small building company, had done building work for Rees. Rees owed D&C over £400 for the work, but did not pay despite repeated requests for payment, leaving D&C in dire financial straits. Mrs Rees offered a cheque for £300 in full settlement and D&C had no choice but to accept it on that basis, but later brought an action for the balance. The Court of Appeal held that *Foakes v Beer* applied: the purported settlement was not binding, being unsupported by consideration, and so did not prevent D&C suing for the balance. It made no difference that the debtor offered a cheque instead of cash and the creditor accepted it. This was not like a different mode of payment as discussed in

Pinnel's Case, although Winn LJ did hint that it might be different if a creditor *requests* a cheque instead of cash.

5.69 Thirdly, there is the fundamental question of who deserves protection. There is a difference between the position of a debtor who has acted in reliance on the release of part of a debt, and a debtor who has not. Where, for example, the creditor finds herself short of money having agreed to release part of the debt, and the debtor has not relied in any way on the release, it seems appropriate to allow the creditor to reclaim the balance. Where there has been no reliance by the debtor, why should the debtor not pay what he owes in full? As will be seen, the law makes this distinction and offers some form of protection to a debtor who has acted in reliance on the creditor's release of part of the debt, using the principle of promissory estoppel. (As we will see, promissory estoppel usually acts as a 'softener' to the harshness of the rule in *Foakes v Beer*, yet in *MWB* things were the other way around. As Kitchen LJ said, Rock did not deserve an estoppel defence, because it 'could be restored to the position it was in before the further agreement was made and it could not say that it had suffered any prejudice by relying upon it', so it is perhaps surprising that the court regarded the merits as requiring *Foakes* to be distinguished and consideration found.)

Estoppel

Generally

5.70 Estoppel is a principle of law that is difficult to define or place. Essentially, it embodies the general principle that if you say or do something and another person takes you at your word or at face value, and relies on what you have said or done, you cannot later change your mind or resile from your position—you will be prevented or 'estopped' from doing so. A good colloquial equivalent, in soap opera language, is: 'You said X so you can't now *turn round and say Y*.' There are a number of different branches of estoppel (one of the hot questions in legal scholarship at the moment is the extent to which these various branches can be unified into one global formulation), but each shares the underlying role of restricting one person's freedom to 'go back on' a belief or assumption he induced in another person.

5.71 For example, *proprietary estoppel* allows the court to give a remedy in the relatively common situation where a landowner encourages a claimant to believe that he has or will be given an interest of some kind in the landowner's land, either actively by making an assurance to that effect or passively by acquiescing in the claimant's mistaken belief. If the claimant acts to his detriment in reliance on this state of affairs, such that it would be unconscionable for the landowner to act inconsistently with it, the court will give effect to the estoppel and give the claimant an appropriate remedy. Such a remedy might even involve enforcing the claimant's expectation by ordering the landowner to grant to the claimant the relevant interest in land, despite the absence both of any consideration and of the appropriate formalities for a trust, a will, or a gift of land, as in the House of Lords decision in *Thorner v Major* (2009).

5.72   Another important form of estoppel in practice is *estoppel by convention*. Unlike proprietary estoppel, which involves one party inducing a belief in the other, estoppel by convention arises where the parties to a transaction have both, for whatever reason, proceeded on a common but mistaken assumption that a given state of facts is true. Having proceeded on that basis, they will be estopped from later challenging the assumed state of facts if it would be unconscionable to do so (see *Amalgamated Investment & Property Co Ltd v Texas Commerce International Bank Ltd* (1982) and *Blindley Heath Investments Ltd v Bass* (2015)).

5.73   Both these forms of estoppel clearly have very little to do with the *Foakes v Beer* problem of discharge of part of a debt. In the nineteenth century, the debtor in the case of *Jordan v Money* (1854) attempted to plead another form of estoppel, known as *estoppel by representation*, to prevent a creditor going back on an assurance that she would not claim the balance of a debt, but the attempt failed, because this form of estoppel required a representation of present fact, not a statement of intention as to the future (in other words, a promise would not do). In *Jordan v Money*, the unfortunately named Mr Money owed a debt to C and gave him a written bond to cover it. On C's death, his executrix Mrs Jordan frequently told Money that she would never enforce the bond. In reliance on these assurances, Money got married and then sought a declaration from the court that the debt had been abandoned. The House of Lords held that the debt was still enforceable—Money's plea of estoppel by representation failed because Mrs Jordan had made statements as to her future intentions, but no representation of fact. Money was obliged to put his case this way, because he had even less chance of persuading the court that Mrs Jordan's promise not to sue on the bond was binding, since it had not been made in writing, essential for its formal validity.

5.74   So *Jordan v Money* appeared for some time to rule out estoppel as a device to help debtors in the *Foakes v Beer* situation. However, during the second half of the twentieth century the courts (led by Lord Denning) managed to find and adopt another branch of estoppel for use when one contracting party *promised* the other that he would not insist on his strict legal rights in the contract, the so-called principle of *promissory estoppel*.

Promissory estoppel

5.75   The process began when Denning J (as he then was) heard the case of *Central London Properties v High Trees House Ltd* (1947). In 1937, Central London Properties (the landlord) granted a long lease of a block of flats in London to High Trees at an annual rent of £2,500. When the Second World War broke out, High Trees had trouble letting out all the flats in the block and so the landlord agreed in 1940 to reduce the annual rent to £1,250. By the end of the war, the flats were fully let and the landlord's receiver (the landlord having gone bust) brought proceedings to claim the balance of the full rent for the last two quarters of 1945. Denning J held that the balance *was* payable, but only because the landlord's concessionary reduction in the rent had been expressed just to cover the war years. If the receiver had been trying to claim the balance for the war years, such a claim would have failed, because Denning J regarded the landlord's concession as effective despite the absence of any consideration.

5.76   Denning J observed that equitable developments had not stood still since *Jordan v Money*, suggesting that the time had come to recognise that a promise made with the intention to be bound should be enforced, regardless of the absence of consideration. For Denning J, these developments went beyond 'estoppel' (which label he did not want to adopt precisely because *High Trees* involved a promise) and constituted a full-blown assault on the need for consideration:

> The logical consequence, no doubt, is that a promise to accept a smaller sum in discharge of a larger sum, if acted upon, is binding notwithstanding the absence of consideration: and if the fusion of law and equity leads to this result, so much the better.

5.77   Denning J was here referring in particular to the case of *Hughes v Metropolitan Railway* (1877). There, a landlord served a notice on his tenants to carry out certain repairs to the leased property within six months. (The lease provided that the tenants were responsible for repairs to the property and that the landlord was entitled to terminate ('forfeit') the lease if the repairs were not performed in accordance with the notice.) The tenants replied saying that they would carry out the repairs, but wondered whether the landlord might be interested in buying out their leasehold interest and suggested that the repairs might be deferred pending any negotiations. The landlord entered into negotiations and, while these were going on, the tenants deferred the repairs. After negotiations broke down, the tenants began the repairs but they were not completed within the initial six-month period, whereupon the landlord attempted to forfeit the lease. The House of Lords held that he could not do so, but was obliged to allow six months from the breaking down of negotiations. As Lord Cairns LC explained:

> if parties who have entered into definite and distinct terms involving certain legal results—certain penalties or legal forfeiture—afterwards by their own act or with their own consent enter upon a course of negotiation which has the effect of leading one of the parties to suppose that the strict rights arising under the contract will not be enforced, or will be kept in suspense, or held in abeyance, the person who might otherwise have enforced those rights will not be allowed to enforce them where it would be inequitable having regard to the dealings which have thus taken place between the parties.

Notice that the issue in *Hughes* was rather different from the problem of part payment of debts, which may explain why Lord Blackburn did not think *Hughes* a relevant precedent when deciding *Foakes* just seven years later, despite having been one of the Lords in *Hughes*. Nonetheless, for Denning J in *High Trees*, *Hughes* was authority for a radical new approach to the problem of unilateral variations, which, even if unsupported by consideration, could be treated as binding if acted upon and if it would be inequitable if they were withdrawn.

5.78   *High Trees* is in many ways a weak precedent. The case is so influential and well known that students often forget that it was a first instance decision, which was (remarkably) delivered unreserved, and that all the discussion about the binding nature of the promise to reduce the rent during the war years was strictly *obiter* (described by Arden LJ in *Collier v P&MJ Wright (Holdings) Ltd* (2007) as Denning J's 'brilliant *obiter dictum*'). Yet, despite these weaknesses in the precedent, *High Trees* has undoubtedly been followed ever since (if in a slightly narrower form than Denning J had in mind) and is the source of what is now called *promissory estoppel*. A number of elements are required to establish promissory estoppel (in what follows the parties will be called 'creditor' and 'debtor' for convenience, but don't forget that promissory estoppel has a wider role to play than in just the *Foakes v Beer* situation).

5.79   First, there must be a clear and unambiguous *promise or representation* that the creditor will not insist on his strict legal rights, satisfying an equivalent test of certainty as is required for contractual obligations (see *Baird Textiles v Marks & Spencer plc* (2002) discussed at paras **3.15–3.18**, and *BMIC Limited v Chinnakannan Sivasankaran, Siva Limited* (2014)). This requirement is not surprising—it is unacceptable to deprive a party of a legal right unless, judged objectively, this was the only plausible interpretation of his words or conduct. More important is the requirement that the promise must relate to *existing* legal rights, a significant limitation because it means there must be an existing legal relationship between the parties. Promissory estoppel cannot take the place of consideration when a contract is being *formed* for the first time between the parties, only (as in the *Foakes v Beer* problem) when existing contractual rights are being *varied*. Denning J did not emphasise this restriction in *High Trees* (although, of course, the landlord's representation there was as to existing legal rights—the right to claim the full rent) but it has been applied ever since. Brennan J regarded this restriction as 'illogical' in *Walton Stores v Maher* (see para **5.94**): 'If a promise by A not to enforce an existing right against B is to confer an equitable right on B to compel fulfilment of the promise, why should B be denied the same protection in similar circumstances if the promise is intended to create in B a new legal right against A?'

5.80   Second, the debtor must have *relied* on the promise or representation. Fundamentally, in order to count as reliance, it must be shown that the debtor acted differently from the way in which he would have acted had the representation not been made, as the Privy Council emphasised in *Prince Jefri Bolkiah v State of Brunei Darussalam* (2007). But beyond this, reliance is a slippery concept, which could mean anything from altering one's conduct solely because of the promise, to merely trusting that the creditor meant what he said. In some forms of estoppel, *detrimental* action in reliance is required but (despite some authority to the contrary) the test in promissory estoppel does not seem to be so strict. If it were, promissory estoppel would very rarely be useful (after all, debtors who are let off the balance of their debt usually spend it on something beneficial). Most cases require that the debtor 'acts differently' or 'alters his position' (see for example *Ajayi v RT Briscoe (Nigeria)*

Ltd (1964)), but even this is not uncontroversial. For, as Goff J pointed out in *The Post Chaser*, the tenant in *High Trees* did nothing *active* in reliance on the landlord's concession, but merely 'conducted his affairs on the basis that he would only have to pay rent at the lower rate', presumably by not going to extraordinary lengths to attempt to let the flats.

5.81   Writing extra-judicially, Lord Denning (1952) drew a distinction between *promises* not to insist on strict legal rights, which in his view bind once the other party acts on them as in *High Trees*, and *conduct*, which leads the other party to believe strict rights will not be insisted on, for which detrimental reliance is necessary. This distinction has not been expressly accepted in subsequent case law, but some support for it can be found in the decision of the Court of Appeal in *Collier v P&MJ Wright (Holdings) Ltd* (2007). Here, three partners were jointly liable to the creditor on a judgment debt, which meant each was liable for the whole debt. Two of the partners disappeared, but the third partner, Collier, alleged that the creditor had agreed to accept one-third of the outstanding sum from him in settlement, which he paid. The court held that Collier had no real prospect of successfully arguing that he had entered into a binding contract with the creditor, but allowed a defence of promissory estoppel to proceed to trial, despite the fact that the only arguable reliance was that Collier paid his one-third share of the debt in full, as he was already obliged to do. This decision is surprising, but can be understood in context: first, the court merely refused to strike out the issue of reliance and allowed it to proceed to trial, where it might very well be unsuccessful; second, the court may have been influenced by the burdensome nature of joint partnership liability, particularly when all but one of the partners defaults and disappears.

5.82   We have already seen (in para **5.63**) that consideration was found in *MWB Business Exchange Centres Ltd v Rock Advertising Ltd* (2017), but obiter the Court of Appeal also dealt with Rock's plea of promissory estoppel, but rejected it. Rock had relied on *Collier* as expressing a general rule that part payment counts as sufficient reliance, but Kitchen LJ rejected this argument (and the plea of promissory estoppel on the facts—see para **5.69**), making clear that the position was much more context specific:

> All will depend upon the circumstances. It follows that I do not for my part think that it can be said, consistently with the authorities, including, in particular, the decisions of the House of Lords in Foakes v Beer and this court in In re Selectmove, that in every case where a creditor agrees to accept payment of a debt by instalments, and the debtor acts upon that agreement by paying one of the instalments, and the creditor accepts that instalment, then it will necessarily be inequitable for the creditor later to go back upon the agreement and insist on payment of the balance. Again, all will depend upon the circumstances.

Overall, perhaps it is better to regard reliance, not as a wholly separate requirement in its own right, but merely as the most common reason for the next requirement, that is, why it would be inequitable for the promisor to act inconsistently with or resile from the promise.

5.83   Thirdly, the creditor is estopped from going back on or acting inconsistently with what he promised, where it would be *inequitable* to do so. So unlike a concession supported by consideration, which is binding immediately without further enquiry into the situations of the creditor and debtor, someone who makes a gratuitous concession will only be estopped from withdrawing it if (and to the extent that) it would be inequitable, unconscionable, or unfair to do so. This element of judicial discretion and flexibility is the essence of promissory estoppel, separating those cases where the debtor does and does not deserve protection. For example, it was *not* inequitable for the creditors to claim the balance of the debt in *D&C Builders v Rees* (see para **5.68**), because the debtor's wife had coerced them into settling for less than the full amount of the debt. This reminds us why *MWB* is controversial, because it arguably inverts the usual balance of who does and does not deserve protection, finding consideration in circumstances where it was not inequitable for MWB to withdraw its disputed oral concession two days after making it.

Although the elements needed to establish promissory estoppel are tolerably clear, a number of puzzles about its scope and operation remain.

Suspensory or extinctive?

5.84 First, does promissory estoppel extinguish the creditor's rights or merely suspend them until revived by notice? The most common view in cases and commentary is that promissory estoppel is merely suspensory. After all, the landlord in *Hughes* was allowed to reactivate the six months' repair period by giving the tenant the appropriate notice. Moreover, the House of Lords took the same view in *Tool Metal Manufacturing Co v Tungsten Electric Co* (1955), the first case on promissory estoppel to reach the House of Lords after *High Trees*. Here, TM granted TECO a licence in 1937 to deal with hard metal alloys which they had patented. The licence agreement provided for TECO to pay 'compensation' to TM in any month if they sold more than a stated quantity of the alloys. When the war broke out, TM agreed to forgo the contractual compensation and none was paid after the end of 1939. In 1944 negotiations for a new agreement broke down and, in an action brought the following year by TECO for breach of the licence agreement, TM counterclaimed that compensation was again payable from 1945 onwards (as in *High Trees*, no claim was made for the war years). The Court of Appeal held that TM could withdraw the concession not to claim the compensation by giving reasonable notice to TECO. In a subsequent action, the House of Lords confirmed that the serving of the counterclaim was itself sufficient notice to restart TECO's obligation to make compensation payments (in fact, from 1947 onwards).

5.85 Of course, this case only decided that the right to claim *future* periodic payments could be resumed, since TM's concession could be withdrawn on the serving of reasonable notice and that, on expiry of the notice, TECO's obligation to pay compensation restarted. But, like the landlord in *High Trees*, TM did not attempt to resurrect its right to claim compensation for past periods and so the House of Lords did not need to rule on whether it would have been permitted to do so. Denning J in *High Trees* was certainly of the view that the landlord would not have been entitled to claim the balance of the rent from the war years—the landlord's rights were, in that respect at least, extinguished.

Although Denning J did not adopt the language of estoppel but regarded the landlord's promise as straightforwardly 'binding', his approach to this question is entirely sensible. Otherwise, a creditor would be entitled to give 'retrospective' notice to reclaim the balance of past instalments, which would empty promissory estoppel of all its scope to prevent inequitable conduct. In other words, promissory estoppel can be part-extinctive, part-suspensory.

5.86   This was certainly the view expressed in *JT Sydenham & Co v Enichem Elastomers Ltd* (1989). Here, the judge decided that an independent surveyor, who was responsible for the rent review on a commercial lease, misinterpreted the provisions of the lease and thus set the rent too low. However, the landlord could not claim the excess on those rental instalments that had already been paid by the tenant at the erroneous reviewed rate. The same view was expressed by the Court of Appeal in *Collier v P&MJ Wright (Holdings) Ltd* (2007), although Longmore LJ made an important observation linking the potential for promissory estoppel to extinguish creditors' rights with the 'inequitable' requirement discussed at para 5.83, noting that 'it is perhaps all the more important that agreements that are said to forego a creditor's rights on a permanent basis should not be too benevolently construed'. Kitchen LJ approved the *Collier* approach in *MWB*, rooting the issue in the 'inequitable' requirement. He explained that promissory estoppel is often suspensory only, but that in some circumstances:

> It may be the case that it would be inequitable to allow the promisor to go back upon his promise without giving reasonable notice, as in the Tool Metal case; or it may be that it would be inequitable to allow the promisor to go back on his promise at all with the result that the right is extinguished.

Sword or shield?

5.87   The tenants in *Hughes* and *High Trees* were both *defending* claims against them by pleading that their respective landlords were estopped. But is promissory estoppel confined to this defensive role (as a 'shield not a sword') or might it be used as a cause of action in an appropriate case? Denning J in *High Trees* suggested that promissory estoppel could found a cause of action, to render a promise enforceable even though it was unsupported by consideration, but later recanted in *Combe v Combe* (1951), explaining that the *High Trees* principle:

> does not create new causes of action where none existed before. It only prevents a party from insisting upon his strict legal rights, when it would be unjust to allow him to enforce them, having regard to the dealings which have taken place between the parties? ... That is I think its true function. It may be part of a cause of action, but not a cause of action in itself.

5.88   This represents the current orthodoxy in English law (see *Baird Textiles v Marks & Spencer* (2002)). This is why there was no possibility of the carpenter in *Williams v Roffey* relying on estoppel to claim the extra payments he had been promised. This is important when making sense of why the Court of Appeal in *Roffey* perceived the need to relax the 'existing contractual duty' consideration rule. Some have argued that it would be better and more consistent to come clean and recognise that there really was no consideration in *Roffey*, and that a form of estoppel would be a more limited but more appropriate solution. It has also been noted by Chen-Wishart (1995) that the remedy in *Roffey* did not reflect the court's reasoning that there was consideration, but is more consistent with estoppel reasoning. This is an interesting suggestion, though once again the facts of *Roffey* do not quite fit the estoppel principle either. It does not appear particularly 'inequitable' for the builder to go back on his promise to pay extra, given that the carpenter did not fully perform his existing contractual obligation and the builder did not obtain the practical benefit of avoiding the penalty clause in the head contract.

5.89 In any event, it is important not to simplify the position unduly by thinking purely in terms of swords and shields (language described as 'misleading' by Judge LJ). As Halson (1999) points out, there are a number of intermediate possibilities between the entirely unproblematic use of promissory estoppel to defend a claim and, at the other end of the spectrum, the use of promissory estoppel to create a new cause of action and enable an otherwise gratuitous promise to be enforced. For example, the court in *Robertson v Ministry of Pensions* (1949) allowed promissory estoppel to assist a plaintiff claiming a statutory right to a military disablement pension to establish just one of the necessary elements of his cause of action, namely that his injury was attributable to his war service. And in *Hearn v Younger* (2002) Etherton J indicated that, in theory, estoppel could be used as part of a cause of action by pension beneficiaries:

> to enlarge [their] pre-existing rights or rather to prevent the Trustees (and the Company) from relying upon the strict legal meaning and effect of the Trust Deed (emphasis added).

5.90 In a similar vein, but more controversial, is *Shah v Shah* (2001), where the Court of Appeal held that the defendant was estopped from pleading that a deed (promising money to the claimant) was void for non-compliance with statutory formalities, so the claimant's claim succeeded. Most of the discussion in the case concerned the legislative intent behind the statutory formality requirements for deeds (so, for example, the court indicated that estoppel could not be used to 'cure' a more fundamental defect in a deed such as the absence of a signature by the donor). Moreover, *Shah* was not a case of promissory estoppel but rather estoppel by representation, the defendant having led the claimant to believe, erroneously, that a witness had signed in his presence. But it is an interesting precedent to set alongside the *Combe v Combe* view of promissory estoppel: why are the courts happy for claimants to use estoppel to avoid a statutory requirement of form but not a requirement of consideration? Some would argue that it seems the wrong way round.

5.91 Those who argue that promissory estoppel should have a role in creating a new cause of action point out that its cousin *proprietary estoppel* can support a cause of action: indeed, Lord Scott suggested in *Yeoman's Row Management Ltd v Cobbe* (2008) that proprietary estoppel is in fact a mere sub-species of promissory estoppel, although this view was not shared by his fellow Law Lords and was doubted by Lord Walker in *Thorner v Major* (2009). What is more, proprietary estoppel can even be used to enforce expectations in the absence of a binding contractual obligation, as in *Crabb v Arun District Council* (1975), *Gillett v Holt* (2000), and *Thorner v Major* (2009). Notice that in these cases the successful plea of proprietary estoppel had the effect of enforcing the expectation generated by the landowner's assurances, even though the 'arrangement' between the parties was not contractual. After all, the proprietary estoppel claimant does not generally act to his detriment at the *request* of the landowner, so his detriment is not the 'price of the promise' (see the exchange of views on *Crabb v Arun District Council* between Atiyah (1976) and Millett (1976)). So should the scope of promissory estoppel be enlarged in the same way, to allow it to create a cause of action and support enforceable non-contractual expectations? Such a development would carry a number of problems.

5.92 First, the use of proprietary estoppel to enforce expectations is itself quite controversial, not least because it often involves enforcing rights purportedly created with neither the appropriate formalities nor consideration. Plus, it is important to bear in mind that proprietary estoppel does not *invariably* generate an enforceable expectation, but that such a remedy is within the range of options open to the court when tailoring an equitable solution. Sometimes the appropriate solution will merely be reversal of the claimant's unjust enrichment (perhaps where the claimant has spent money improving the owner's property) or recompense of reliance losses. As the Court of Appeal clarified in *Jennings v Rice* (2002), it all depends on what would be the most 'proportionate' way of achieving justice, with the court exercising its discretion to balance the claimant's expectation and the detriment he incurred. For a recent example of this discretionary process, in a bitter family dispute, see *Davies v Davies* (2016).

5.93 This shows the danger of pushing the analogy between promissory and proprietary estoppel too far, and of Lord Scott's attempt to align the two concepts. Remedial discretion of this kind is acceptable in the limited context of landowners who renege on informal assurances that others will have interests in their land, given the strict requirements of form in land transactions. But it would be an unworkable mechanism for resolving more generally whether promises are binding. To allow judicial discretion about the appropriate remedy for reliance on a gratuitous promise, based on the justice of the case and all the circumstances, would surely be unacceptably uncertain.

5.94 On the other hand, uncertainty would not necessarily result if, in an appropriate case, the courts allowed promissory estoppel to operate as a cause of action and to protect the claimant's expectations. The law has already developed in this way in some American jurisdictions and in Australia where, in *Waltons Stores (Interstate) Ltd v Maher* (1987), Mr and Mrs Maher (M) owned a building, which Waltons (W) wished to lease. While the parties' solicitors were negotiating the terms of the draft lease, M (to the knowledge of W) began demolishing the existing building with a view to replacing it with a new building in accordance with W's specifications. W began to have second thoughts and instructed its solicitor to 'go slow' in the negotiations. Eventually, W told M that it did not wish to proceed with the lease, by which time the new building was almost half built. The High Court of Australia held that, although no formal contract had been executed by the parties, W was estopped from denying that they were bound by an agreement to take a lease and was obliged to pay damages to M.

5.95 The members of the High Court did not adopt identical reasoning. Deane and Gaudrom JJ held that M had assumed that a binding lease had *already* been made (in other words, a mistake of existing fact, not a thwarted expectation that an agreement would be made) and that W was estopped from pointing out that all the appropriate formalities for a lease had not been observed when sued by M. This solution, which resembles the reasoning in the later English case of *Shah v Shah*, avoids tackling the question of whether promissory estoppel can be used to create an entirely new cause of action, but it has problems of its own. It does not really match the facts of the case—M were presumably advised throughout by their solicitors that, until exchange of the two signed parts of the lease, there was neither legally binding lease nor agreement for one—and seems to assume without explanation that defects in form are a less 'serious' impediment than the absence of consideration. The remaining members of the High Court proceeded on the basis that W had led M to believe that it would enter into the lease and that it would be unconscionable for it to renege later—this estoppel sufficed, instead of consideration, to create an agreement which W had breached. However, Brennan J treated this as a mode of protecting M's detrimental reliance, while only Mason and Wilson JJ regarded it as a substitute for consideration in creating and enforcing contractual expectations.

5.96 What are we to make of *Waltons Stores*? It is hard to disagree with the observations of the members of the High Court that it is illogical to draw a rigid line around proprietary estoppel cases, and say that only there can enforceable expectations be created by estoppel. After all, the facts of *Waltons Stores* are tantalisingly close to, but just miss, a proprietary estoppel model. In *Waltons Stores*, the claimant acted to its detriment on the understanding that the defendant wanted an interest in the claimant's property, as opposed to the classic proprietary estoppel pattern of the claimant acting to its detriment on the understanding that the claimant would obtain an interest in the defendant's property. On the other hand, it is important to look at the facts of the case in context. W's behaviour was clearly unethical, but we should be wary of creating a whole new cause of action in response to sympathy. After all, M were not vulnerable little old ladies—they were negotiating for a major commercial transaction and were legally advised. Do we really need to protect commercial parties who take the risk of doing expensive work during negotiations, without ensuring either that a formal contract is in place or, at the very least, that they obtain a binding side-letter (a kind of mini-contract) from the other party to protect their position? It is instructive to compare the attitude of the court in the *Regalian Properties* case (see para **3.17**) to parties who incur expenditure during 'subject to contract' negotiations. Perhaps the more appropriate solution in *Waltons Stores* would have been for M to sue their solicitors in negligence.

Conclusion: does English law need a requirement of consideration?

5.97 The requirement in English law of consideration for the formation and variation of a contract is almost universally vilified. For example, Atiyah (1986) argues that, historically, judges simply looked for the 'considerations', meaning reasons, why a contract should or should not be enforced, and that the law should return to this more flexible position, objecting to the notion of a formal 'doctrine' of consideration. Even Fried (2015), in his seminal defence of the classical bargain model of contract, regards the requirement of consideration as internally inconsistent and random in its operation, allowing some freely made, rational promises to be enforced but not others.

5.98 These criticisms are obviously very powerful. But is the practical operation of the requirement of consideration really as objectionable as its critics suggest? After all, most people would agree that the law should not regulate and enforce *every* promise that is ever made. Some sort of filter is required, to remove inappropriate promises from the purview of the courts: at present English law chooses to filter out gratuitous promises (on the basis that such promises are more likely to be informal and tend to be non-commercial, and that a promisor who gets nothing in return should not have his freedom to change his mind curtailed). If the requirement of consideration were to be abolished, a replacement filter would be needed.

5.99 There are three plausible alternative candidates. First, a requirement of *form* might be introduced, so that, for example, only promises made in writing were enforceable. But this would be unworkable in modern society, where many thousands of oral transactions are made every day. Second, more emphasis could be given to the requirement that the promisor *intended to create legal relations*. This is a much more realistic alternative, reflecting the position in many civilian jurisdictions that even a gratuitous promise is enforceable if it was made seriously with the intention of attracting legal effect. It has the advantage of flexibility, allowing a court to explore whether a particular promise was seriously made and whether on the facts it should or should not be enforced. But with flexibility comes uncertainty: the parties could not be certain until the matter was litigated whether or not their particular promise was enforceable. Of course, rules might grow up to encourage certainty, whereby a promisor might be *deemed* to have intended to create legal relations in certain circumstances—but the chances are those rules would not be so very different from the rules of consideration. A third possibility is to choose *reliance* as the relevant filter and to allow any promise to be enforced, but only once it has been relied on by the promisee. For all its apparent fairness, this approach has significant disadvantages. It would make it almost impossible for promisors to order their affairs safe in the knowledge that their promise either was or was not enforceable, since enforceability would not 'kick in' until some time after the promise was made, when the other party relied on it for the first time. Promisors would be obliged to keep track of the actions of the other party—not a very attractive prospect commercially. Furthermore, 'reliance' is a slippery concept (as we have seen in our discussion of estoppel): it is hard to imagine first instance courts reaching and applying a consistent, generally acceptable definition of reliance.

5.100 In fact the problems inherent in a system based on consideration do not seem so significant when compared with the task of finding a workable alternative filter. And consideration does have a fundamental advantage, often overlooked by academic critics. Those critics tend to focus on reported cases, involving (by definition) the resolution of contractual disputes by the courts, where it can of course seem bizarre that the result turns on the status of a chocolate wrapper or a peppercorn, or whether the promisee's pre-existing duty was owed to the promisor or a third party. But this focus on litigation ignores the main function of the law of contract, which is to provide a clear set of rules that can be understood and employed by those involved in making contracts work *without* recourse to litigation, for example by allowing legal advice to be given at the time a contract is made as to whether it is likely to be enforceable or not. A requirement of consideration makes a lot more sense when the average contract is being drafted than it does on the unusual facts of the reported case law about consideration. We must be aware of looking at the law of contract from the wrong end of the telescope!

OVERVIEW

1   Consideration is required for the formation of an enforceable contract (assuming the contract is not contained in a deed). Consideration is sometimes defined in terms of benefit to the promisor or detriment to the promisee, but it is easier to think of consideration as 'the price of the promise'.

2   To count as consideration, the act or promise must have been requested by the promisor, though in some circumstances the courts will imply a request. An offer of a gift subject to a condition is treated differently, because the promisor is not requesting fulfilment of the condition.

3   Consideration must move from the promisee, though need not move to the promisor. If A promises B that, if B does something for C, A will pay B, B provides consideration for A's promise. But if A promises B that, if C does something for A, A will pay B, B provides no consideration for A's promise (unless B is promising to see to it that C does something for A). This is closely related to the rules of privity, but is usually treated as a separate requirement. A joint promisee can enforce a promisor's promise without providing independent consideration for it.

4   The requirement of consideration is not about checking that the parties are getting good value for money or the economic equivalent in return for their own performance. It follows that consideration may be of trivial value, as long as this is what the promisor requested. However, consideration must be legally sufficient.

5   Since consideration must be given in return for the promise, consideration given in the past is not sufficient to support a subsequent promise. However, there are a number of exceptions

to the prohibition on past consideration. Some are statutory; at common law, an exception is recognised where A asks B to do something for him, B does it and A later promises something in return. In such a situation, B's previous performance will count as consideration.

6   Performance of or promise to perform a public duty does not count as legally sufficient consideration, because the promisor is not obtaining anything above what he was already entitled to. But where the promisee does more than his public duty requires, this can count as valid consideration. Likewise if the promisee owes a pre-existing contractual obligation to a third party, performance of or a promise to perform this obligation can be consideration for the promisor's promise.

7   However, traditionally, where the promisee was merely promising to perform or performing an existing contractual obligation owed to the promisor, this did not count as consideration. Since English law requires consideration for the variation or discharge of a contract, this rule meant that a one-sided variation of a contract was unenforceable. Nowadays, the courts are more concerned with preventing one party extorting a variation of the contract by duress (usually, threatening not to perform), so where there is no duress, the court will regard the promisor's practical benefit derived from the promisee's performance of or promise to perform his existing obligations as good consideration for a variation in the promisor's obligations (usually a promise to pay more than the agreed contract price). While many commentators welcome the flexibility of this development, others regard it as problematic.

8   The practical benefit relaxation of consideration does not extend to a creditor's promise to accept less than the full amount of a debt in satisfaction of the whole, so at common law the balance of the debt remains due (although the Court of Appeal has recently controversially applied a version of the practical benefit relaxation where part payment brings some 'additional commercial advantage'). However, the rigours of this rule are tempered by the doctrine of promissory estoppel. Estoppel means that, having led another person to think or believe X and to act accordingly, you may be prevented from going back on or denying X.

9   Therefore a creditor who has led the debtor to believe that he will accept less than the full amount of the debt may be estopped from claiming the balance, if the debtor has acted in reliance in some way and if it would be inequitable for the creditor to go back to the original position. Promissory estoppel cases generally involve ongoing periodic obligations to pay money by instalments, where a concession to accept less than the full amount can be withdrawn by notice as to future instalments. Although other forms of estoppel (such as proprietary estoppel) can operate in different ways, in England promissory estoppel does not give rise to enforceable expectations.

FURTHER READING

Atiyah 'Consideration: A Restatement' Chapter 8 in *Essays on Contract* (1986)

Chen-Wishart 'Consideration: Practical Benefit and the Emperor's New Clothes' Chapter 5 in *Good Faith and Fault in Contract Law* (1995)

Halson 'The Offensive Limits of Promissory Estoppel' [1999] LMCLQ 257

Morgan *Great Debates in Contract Law* (2015) pp 46–57

O'Sullivan 'In Defence of *Foakes v Beer*' [1996] CLJ 219

O'Sullivan 'Unconsidered Modifications' (2017) 133 LQR 191

Waddams 'Principle in Contract Law: The Doctrine of Consideration' Chapter 3 in *Exploring Contract Law* (2009)

SELF-TEST QUESTIONS

1   Why does consideration depend on a request by the promisor?

2   Should the requirement of consideration be abandoned for agreements to vary or discharge contracts?

3   Should promises to accept part of a debt in satisfaction of the whole be enforceable, if the creditor has derived a practical benefit in return?

4   What is meant by 'estoppel'?

5   Is any useful purpose served by a requirement of consideration in the twenty-first century?

6   On 1 June 2016 Brian obtained a judgment against Fred for £20,000. Fred, being short of money, asked for time to pay. On 2 June 2016 Brian agreed that if Fred would pay £5,000 at once and the remaining £15,000 in five half-yearly instalments of £3,000 (commencing on 1 December 2016 and ending on 1 December 2018) he would take no steps to enforce the judgment or claim interest. (By statute, interest runs on judgment debts from the date of the judgment.) After paying the £5,000 and the first instalment, Fred inherited a fortune on 1 January 2017. Brian wishes to know whether he may: (a) enforce the outstanding portion of the judgment debt forthwith; and (b) recover interest on the sum unpaid between 1 June 2016 and the present. Advise him.

   For hints on how to answer question 6, please see the online resources at **www.oup.com/uk/sullivan8e/**.

6 Privity

SUMMARY

This chapter explores the controversial question of whether third parties can and should acquire enforceable rights purportedly given to them in contracts to which they were not party (there is hardly ever any question of third parties being subjected to obligations). At common law, third parties were prevented by the doctrine of privity from enforcing promises made for their benefit, although the common law did recognise a number of exceptions, some giving rights to the third party directly, others allowing the promisee to enforce the contract for the benefit of the third party (though there is some confusion as to whether the promisee is recovering damages for his own or the third party's loss). A statutory exception to privity now exists, the Contracts (Rights of Third Parties) Act 1999, although only if the third party falls within the structure and requirements of the Act, so the common law exceptions remain important.

Note: in this chapter, 'A' and 'B' will be used to denote the parties to the contract and 'C' will be used to denote the third party.

6.1 The doctrine of privity dictates that a person who is not a party to the contract cannot be granted contractual rights by the contract or be placed under contractual obligations by it.

6.2 The doctrine has two limbs. First, only the parties to a contract have *rights* under it; third parties do not. Therefore a third party cannot invoke the terms of the contract against a party to the contract. So if A and B agree that in return for A giving B her sports car, B will build an extension to the mansion of A's brother, C, C cannot claim damages from B if B fails to perform his side of the deal properly. Of the two limbs, it is this limb that will receive the greater attention in this chapter.

6.3 Second, a contract cannot place contractual *obligations* upon a third party. Therefore, a party to a contract cannot invoke its terms *against* a third party. So for example, if A and B agree that in return for A doing some work, C (a third party) will pay A £1 million, C cannot be forced to pay the money.

6.4 As we shall see, there are a number of problems with the first limb, which have led to the development of methods to circumvent it at common law and the creation of statutory exceptions. Indeed, the mounting pressure for reform of the first limb has culminated in legislation, the Contracts (Rights of Third Parties) Act 1999, which creates a large exception to it. In contrast, the second limb causes less injustice, so while a small number of exceptions have developed, no large-scale exception exists and the limb is unaffected by the Act. Accordingly, discussion of this limb is postponed until the end of the chapter.

Why should we normally allow only parties to a contract to have rights under it?

6.5 Four main reasons can be put forward to justify this general rule. First, it is sometimes argued that a third party should not have rights under a contract because he is not a party to the contract. However, this argument is circular—a third party cannot sue because he is a third party—and leaves the real issue unanswered: why shouldn't third parties be allowed to sue?

6.6 Second, some of the earlier cases on the subject suggested that the reason for the general rule is that the third party has provided no consideration. However, the promisee has already provided consideration; is it not asking a bit much to require two sets of consideration to be provided for the promisee? Moreover, the promisee is often allowed to assign all his rights under the contract to a third party, so we are happy to let the third party sue under the contract without providing consideration in some circumstances. Finally, as we have seen in Chapter 5, the doctrine of consideration is being eroded in a number of ways.

6.7 Third, a more promising reason is that neither party under the contract has made any promises to the third party. For example, A and B agree that B will pay C £100 if A builds B a shed and that C should have rights to enforce the contract. B is not promising C that he will pay him £100; he is promising A that he will pay C £100. Therefore, some argue that B's duty to pay the £100 is a duty owed only to A, not to C (see Smith (1997a) and Kincaid (2000)), and so only A, and not C, should have rights against B under the contract. Put simply, their argument is that only a promisee should be able to enforce the contract because the promisor has undertaken obligations towards the promisee and no one else. This argument helps to explain why we have the general rule against allowing a third party to acquire rights under contracts: it is up to the contracting parties to determine to whom they should owe contractual obligations. However, one of the problems with this argument is that it will sometimes ignore the intention of the contracting parties. Take the same example: both A and B explicitly agree that C should have rights under the contract, despite the fact that no promise is being made to him. This shows that where the parties *intend* to allow a third party to enforce the contract, the third party should be allowed to do so. So we need to carve out an exception to the general rule in situations where the parties intend the third party to acquire rights under the contract. As we shall see later, the Contracts (Rights of Third Parties) Act 1999 has performed this task.

6.8   The fourth main argument is that if we give the third party rights under the contract, we may have to restrict the right of the contracting parties to vary the contract in some situations (because this might affect the third party's rights). This has some merit: it is necessary to reconcile the contracting parties' freedom to vary their contract with the third party's reasonable expectations. However, giving the third party *no* rights at all under the contract is an unfair solution, because it completely ignores any expectations that the third party may have of being able to enforce the contract.

6.9   The discussion has brought out a number of important points. It has shown that there are two reasons why, as a general rule, a third party cannot sue on a contract. The first is that he has not provided consideration. However, this is not a strong justification for the existence of the rule. More important is the fact that generally, contracting parties do not *intend* third parties to be able to enforce the contract. So if I contract to build you an extension for £500, we do not intend the entire world to be able to enforce the contract. This second reason tells us that the general rule is not merely an aspect of the doctrine of consideration. The main reason for the general rule is not the absence of consideration flowing from the third party, but the intentions of the contracting parties. Therefore, even if we had no doctrine of consideration, there would still be strong reasons for having the general rule. Equally importantly, it tells us that in those situations where the contracting parties do intend the third party to have rights under the contract, the third party should be granted such rights. Therefore, a large exception to the general rule is required. This has been recognised in the Act, discussed later.

Cases establishing that a third party cannot acquire rights under a contract

6.10   While the first limb of the privity rule has been a feature of English law for many hundreds of years, there were cases in the seventeenth, eighteenth, and early nineteenth centuries in particular that, perhaps influenced by continental developments, seemed to suggest the contrary. It was with this backdrop that the general rule was affirmed in the two famous cases of *Tweddle v Atkinson* (1861) and *Dunlop Pneumatic Tyre Co Ltd v Selfridge & Co Ltd* (1915).

6.11   In *Tweddle*, A and B were the father and father-in-law of C. In return for A's promise to pay C £200, B agreed to pay C £100. Their agreement explicitly provided that C should be able to sue on the contract. A failed to pay the money, and thereupon died, so C sued his estate for the £200. The Court of Queen's Bench held that his claim must fail. As Wightman J stated, 'it is now established that no stranger to the consideration can take advantage of a contract, although made for his benefit'. Therefore, the decision suggests that the general rule was based on nothing more than the fact that C had not provided consideration.

6.12   In *Dunlop*, the existence of the general rule was confirmed, and the rule applied. Of particular interest are the words of Viscount Haldane LC:

> My Lords, in the law of England certain principles are fundamental. One is that only a person who is a party to a contract can sue on it. Our law knows nothing of a jus quaesitum tertio [a third party right of action] arising by way of contract ... A second principle is that if a person with whom a contract not under seal has been made is to be able to enforce it consideration must have been given by him to the promisor or to some other person at the promisor's request.

In other words, as suggested, the reason for the first limb of the privity rule is not the failure of C to provide consideration. While Viscount Haldane does not explain what the basis of the rule is, he clearly distinguishes the rule from the doctrine of consideration.

6.13   In these examples, C is trying to sue A on the contract between A and B but is prevented from doing so by the general rule. Does this rule also apply where C is seeking to rely on an *exclusion clause* from the A–B contract, intended for his benefit, to protect himself from a non-contractual action brought against him by A? In other words, we have seen that the rule prevents C using the contract as a sword; does it also prevent him using it as a shield?

6.14   Despite the fact that there seems to be a stronger case for allowing C to invoke the contract in the latter case, it was confirmed by the House of Lords in *Scruttons Ltd v Midland Silicones Ltd* (1962) that the general rule prevents C relying on an exclusion clause in the main contract. In *Scruttons*, a drum of silicone had been shipped on B's vessel to be delivered to A. Under the contract between A and B, the liability of 'the carrier' was limited to $500. The drum was damaged by the negligence of C, a firm of stevedores who had contracted with B to unload the ship and deliver the drum to A. A sued C in tort. One of C's defences was that he should be entitled to rely on the clause limiting liability in the A–B contract. It was held that he could not, because he was not a party to the A–B contract.

Problems caused by the rule

6.15   As has already been intimated (see paras **6.5-6.9**), there are a number of problems with the rule that a third party cannot acquire rights under a contract. These are helpfully summarised in Part III of Law Commission Report No 242 and in an article by Burrows (1996), the Law Commissioner responsible for the Act.

6.16   First, as mentioned (see para **6.7**), it thwarts the intention of A and B where they both intend to give C a right to enforce the contract.

6.17   Secondly, it is arguable that in situations where the contract suggests that the intention of A and B is to give C rights under the contract, C has a reasonable expectation of having a legal right to enforce the contract. These expectations are ignored by the rule. However, there are those who question why C's expectation of gaining rights under the contract is reasonable (for example, Smith (1997a)). Similarly, Stevens (2004) remarks that '[i]t may be queried how deserving of sympathy a party who relies upon a promise made to someone else is'.

6.18 Thirdly, it creates a lacuna in the law, because where a contract intended to benefit C is breached by A, it is often C rather than B who suffers the loss. C has suffered the loss but has no right to sue on the contract, while B has the right to sue on the contract but has suffered no loss. The consequence of this is that A is not held to account for his breach of contract. The courts have on occasion attempted to use tort law to fill this gap, as in *White v Jones* (1995).

6.19 Fourthly, the rule sometimes causes practical difficulties. For example, it means that a life insurance policy taken out for the benefit of a cohabitee will not be enforceable by the cohabitee.

6.20 Finally, the injustice of applying the rule in certain situations has led to an increasing number of exceptions being developed, both judge-made and statutory, whose scope is often uncertain. Moreover, the common law exceptions are often complex and artificial.

Having hinted at the exceptions to the general rule, let us examine them in greater depth. For further discussion of the exceptions, the reader is referred to the excellent account of the Law Commission in Law Com No 242, Part II.

Judge-made exceptions

6.21 The non-statutory exceptions can be conveniently divided into two categories: those that give C himself rights against a party to the contract and those that instead allow the promisee B rights to enforce the contract in a manner that will benefit C.

Exceptions giving C rights against a party to the contract

The trust of a promise

6.22 The first way to circumvent the rule is to find that B holds his contractual rights against A on trust for C. Such a device is known as a 'trust of a promise', the promise in question being A's promise to do some act beneficial to C. The trustee, B, should use the contractual rights for the benefit of C, for example, by suing A if A breaches the contract. B can recover for the loss suffered by C (*Lloyd's v Harper* (1880)) and C will be entitled to the benefit of any damages recovered. If B refuses to sue, C can sue himself, joining B as defendant (*Vandepitte v Preferred Accident Insurance Corpn of New York* (1933)) unless A waives this requirement.

6.23 However, there are two pitfalls for those seeking to rely on this exception. First, it appears that only contractual rights to have money paid or property transferred can be held on trust. Attempts to extend it to other contractual rights, such as the benefit of an exclusion clause, have failed: see, for example, *Southern Water Authority v Carey* (1985).

6.24 Secondly, and perhaps more importantly, the courts are reluctant to infer an intention to create a trust in the absence of express words. There was a time when the courts were willing to infer such an intent just from the intention to benefit a third party (see *Lloyd's v Harper* and *Les Affréteurs Réunis SA v Leopold Walford (London) Ltd* (1919)), but despite the exhortations of Corbin (1930), the courts soon took a stricter line, requiring a clear indication of an intent to create a trust (*Vandepitte* and *Re Schebsman* (1944)) and not merely a gift. So, for example, it will generally be necessary to show that the intention to benefit the third party is *irrevocable* (*Re Sinclair's Life Policy* (1938)). In other words, it must generally be shown that A and B were not reserving the right to change their minds and alter the contract at a later date. This is no easy task.

Establishing an A–C contract

6.25 The second way to avoid the rule is to establish that a contract exists between A and C, which will of course give C contractual rights against A. This is known as a 'collateral contract'. Strictly speaking, this is not an exception to the rule, because C is a party to the A–C contract. However, the fact that the courts have in some circumstances been particularly willing to find an A–C contract to avoid the harsh consequences of the rule means that it can be conveniently dealt with as one.

6.26 A good example of the principle in operation is *Shanklin Pier Ltd v Detel Products Ltd* (1951) already discussed at para **5.24**. Similarly, in *Wells (Merstham) Ltd v Buckland Sand & Silica Co Ltd* (1965), A, a firm of sand merchants, promised C, chrysanthemum growers, that the sand was of a particular composition (suitable for growing chrysanthemums). In reliance on this, C persuaded B, a firm who often dealt with A, to buy some sand from A for C's use. So as a result of A's promise, C persuaded B to contract with A. The sand was not of the specified composition so C sued A. The court, applying *Shanklin Pier*, held that there was a collateral contract between A and C: in return for A's promise, C had caused B to enter into a contract with A. In other words, it seems that the collateral contract will usually be a unilateral contract: A will promise that something is the case in return for C carrying out an *act,* but C is under no obligation to carry out the act. While the main hurdle to establishing a collateral contract is demonstrating an offer and acceptance, consideration and so forth, the cases suggest that the courts are relatively generous to C in this respect (in addition, see *Charnock v Liverpool Corpn* (1968) where the court was extremely willing to find that there was consideration).

6.27 A particular form of collateral contract has been developed in the context of carriage of goods to allow C to take the benefit of an exclusion clause in the A–B contract. While *Scruttons* confirmed that the first limb of the privity rule covers exclusion clauses, Lord

Reid suggested that had the following conditions been satisfied, C might have been able to establish a contract between A and C (recall that in *Scruttons*, C, the stevedore, was attempting to rely upon a clause limiting liability in the contract between A, the consignee and B, the carrier):

> *I can see a possibility of success of the agency argument if (first) the bill of lading makes it clear that the stevedore is intended to be protected by the provisions in it which limit liability, (second) the bill of lading makes it clear that the carrier, in addition to contracting for these provisions on his own behalf, is also contracting as agent for the stevedore that these provisions should apply to the stevedore, (third) the carrier has authority from the stevedore to do that, or perhaps later ratification by the stevedore would suffice, and (four) that any difficulties about consideration moving from the stevedore were overcome.*

In response to Lord Reid's suggestions, the 'Himalaya clause' was devised in the carriage of goods context, which states that all exemption clauses and other clauses reducing liability that apply to the carrier's liability shall also protect his servants and agents (Treitel (2002)). Such a clause seems to clearly satisfy the first two of Lord Reid's requirements, but what of the other two? This issue was addressed by the Privy Council in *The Eurymedon* (1976).

6.28 In *The Eurymedon*, a contract for the shipment of a drilling machine contained a clause discharging B, the carrier, from all liability for loss or damage unless suit was brought within one year, and a Himalaya clause stating that the same immunity extended to B's servants or agents. B was a wholly owned subsidiary of C, a stevedore company. Due to C's negligence in unloading the machine, the machine was damaged, so A, the consignee (the other party to the shipping contract), sued C in tort. However, the action was brought after the one-year time limit had elapsed. C claimed the protection of the time limit clause, and it was held that he could do so, on the basis of Lord Reid's remarks. It was held that B had authority to contract on C's behalf and that the Himalaya clause showed that C was intended to be protected by the clause laying down the one-year time limit. Therefore, the first three of Lord Reid's requirements were satisfied. As to the fourth, it was held that C had provided consideration for A's promise by unloading the goods and delivering them (even though C had already contracted with B to perform the same act—see paras **5.44-5.45**).

6.29 The Privy Council analysed the formation of the A–C contract in the following way. They said that the combined effect of the clause limiting liability and the Himalaya clause in the A–B contract was that A was making an offer to enter into a unilateral contract with anyone that unloaded the goods (note that it was later suggested in *The Mahkutai* (1996) that the A–C contract was in fact a bilateral one). The offer would be that 'if you unload the ship, A promises that your liability will be limited in the way set out in the A–B contract'. By unloading the goods, C accepted A's offer and so the A–C contract was formed, allowing C to take advantage of the time limit clause.

6.30 While the decision has been repeatedly followed, it has been criticised for its artificiality. For example, the Law Commission comments that *The Eurymedon* 'effectively rewrites the Himalaya clause, which was an agreement between the shipper and the carrier and from which it is difficult to detect an offer of a unilateral contract made by the shipper to the stevedore' (Law Com No 242 (1996)). Indeed, the need to stretch traditional contract notions to accommodate *The Eurymedon* was noted in the case itself by Lord Wilberforce, who commented that the need to take a 'practical approach' in such cases often came 'at the cost of forcing the facts to fit uneasily into the marked slots of offer, acceptance and consideration'.

6.31   The main difficulty for those seeking to use *The Eurymedon* to found a contractual claim is the reluctance of the courts to apply the decision outside the carriage of goods context. In *Southern Water Authority v Carey* (1985), a case concerning construction, the judge was reluctant to apply it because of its perceived artificiality. Indeed, those who have sought to rely on the case outside the carriage of goods context have generally failed: *Kendall v Morgan* (1980), a case concerning employment law, being a good example. However, there have since been hints of a wider approach. First, in *The Mahkutai*, Lord Goff attempted to discourage the drawing of 'fine distinctions' in applying *The Eurymedon*. Second, in *Borkan General Trading Ltd v Monsoon Shipping Ltd* (2003) (the facts of which occurred before the Act came into force), *The Eurymedon* was applied by the Court of Appeal outside the carriage of goods context. A owned an oil tanker and wished to berth at B's terminal in order to load a cargo of crude oil. A contracted with B for the latter to supply tugs to help the tanker berth. The tanker collided with a tug owned by C.

6.32   It was held, applying *The Eurymedon*, that C could rely on the terms of the A–B contract. Applying the broad approach advocated by Lord Goff in *The Mahkutai*, Clarke LJ commented that 'if, as here, the contract expressly provides that it is made for the benefit of another person, that seems to me to be a strong pointer to the conclusion that the contract was made on behalf of that person, especially if, as is the case under English law (absent a trust), such a person would not be entitled to the benefit of the contract unless the contract was made on his behalf'.

Assumption of risk by A

6.33   In some circumstances outside the carriage of goods context, the courts may sometimes allow C to rely on a clause in the A–B contract stating that A is to bear a particular risk in order to prevent A establishing that C owes a duty of care in tort to A. In other words, sometimes a clear indication in the A–B contract that the risk of a certain event occurring is to be borne by A alone will stop A successfully suing C in tort by preventing C owing a duty of care to A. Therefore, a similar result is achieved in the collateral contract situations discussed.

6.34   The circumstances in which a clause in the A–B contract will have this effect are far from clear. This exception stems from the following comment of Lord Roskill in *Junior Books Ltd v Veitchi Co Ltd* (1983) (discussed at para **6.38**):

> *During the argument it was asked what the position would be in a case where there was a relevant exclusion clause in the main contract. My Lords, that question does not arise for decision in the instant appeal, but in principle I would venture the view that such a clause according to the manner in which it was worded might in some circumstances limit the duty of care just as in the Hedley Byrne case (1964) the plaintiffs were ultimately defeated by the defendants' disclaimer of responsibility.*

Although the ratio of *Junior Books* no longer represents an accurate view of the duty of care in tort, this dictum has been applied in *Southern Water Authority v Carey* (1985). B agreed to construct sewage works for A. Clause 30(vi) of their contract stated that, subject to certain conditions, neither B nor the subcontractors C would be liable in contract or tort to A. A brought a negligence action against C, and one of C's defences was that liability in tort was excluded by clause 30(vi) (C's attempt to establish a collateral contract failed). Lord Roskill's words were applied, the judge holding that the clause clearly indicated that A had accepted the risk of such damage occurring, so no duty of care arose in tort:

> *As [A] did so choose to limit the scope of the sub-contractors' liability, I see no reason why such limitation should not be honoured.*

6.35   Similarly, in *Norwich City Council v Harvey* (1989), B contracted with A to build an extension to A's swimming pool complex, and subcontracted some of the roofing work to C. Both the A–B and B–C contracts provided that A should bear the risk of damage by fire. A sued C in negligence for setting fire to the complex while carrying out the work. It was held by the Court of Appeal that C owed A no duty of care because all the parties had contracted on the basis that A alone would bear the risk of such damage:

> *In the instant case it is clear that as between the employer and the main contractor the former accepted the risk of damage by fire to its premises arising out of and in the course of the building works. Further, although there was no privity between the employer and the sub-contractor, it is equally clear from the documents passing between the main contractors and the sub-contractors to which I have already referred that the sub-contractors contracted on a like basis.*

It should be noted that these cases are far from uncontroversial, particularly the extension of the exception in *Harvey* to cases of physical damage (Hopkins (1990)), and the Law Commission labelled the use of this technique to avoid the privity rule 'rather artificial' (Law Com No 242).

Tort

6.36   The tort of negligence will sometimes be able to provide C with a direct right of action against A, albeit not, of course, a contractual one. Two particularly striking examples of tort being used to circumvent the privity rule are *White v Jones* (1995) and *Junior Books Ltd v Veitchi Ltd* (1983).

6.37 In *White*, B, the father, cut C, his daughters, out of the estate after a family dispute. After making up with them, B wished to change the will to include £9,000 legacies to them. However, due to the negligence of A, the solicitor contracted by B to carry out this task, the will remained unchanged at the time of B's death. C sued A in negligence. By 3–2, the House of Lords allowed C to recover damages. It was held that the need to do practical justice required a duty of care to be recognised in such a situation. Otherwise, there would be nobody able to hold A to account for his negligence, as Lord Goff pointed out:

> In the forefront stands the extraordinary fact that, if such a duty is not recognised, the only persons who might have a valid claim (ie, the testator and his estate) have suffered no loss, and the only person who has suffered a loss (ie, the disappointed beneficiary) has no claim ... It can therefore be said that, if the solicitor owes no duty to the intended beneficiaries, there is a lacuna in the law which needs to be filled. This I regard as being a point of cardinal importance in the present case.

Indeed, we have already commented earlier that this is one of the main problems caused by the first limb of the privity rule (see para **6.18**). An interesting issue is whether the lacuna pointed out by Lord Goff still exists after *Alfred McAlpine Construction Ltd v Panatown Ltd* (2000) (discussed at paras **6.55–6.61**). The reasoning of some of the judges in *Panatown* suggests that if *White* were to be decided today, it might be held that B has suffered a loss for which he (or rather his estate) is able to recover by virtue of not getting what he bargained for.

6.38 In *Junior Books* A contracted with B to have a factory constructed. A nominated C to lay the floor, so B entered into a subcontract with C. A sued C in negligence, alleging that C's workmanship was seriously defective. The House of Lords held that there was sufficient proximity of relationship to give rise to a duty of care owed by C to A, and so A's claim succeeded. There are two main disadvantages for a claimant seeking to use this exception. First, it will not always be easy to establish a duty of care. By way of illustration, subsequent cases have taken an extremely restrictive view of the scope of *Junior Books*: for example, *D & F Estates Ltd v Church Commissioners for England* (1989) describes its facts as 'unique' (almost certainly a polite way of saying that the case is wrong!). Secondly, the claimant will of course have to show that the defendant was negligent.

Agency

6.39 An agent, B, has the power to conclude a contract between his principal, C, and a third party, A. In this way C can acquire rights under contracts made by B with A. Strictly, this is not an exception to the privity rule because the contract is between A and C: B is acting on C's behalf and normally drops out of the picture. However, it is possible for B to conclude a contract on C's behalf even though B has not told A that he is acting as an agent for C. In such a situation C may acquire contractual rights against A, despite the fact that A never intended to contract with C. This is known as the 'undisclosed principal' doctrine.

Assignment

6.40   Generally, B may assign his contractual rights against A to C without A's consent. Therefore, this constitutes a very good way of getting around the first limb of the privity rule. There are, however, two disadvantages in using this doctrine to give C contractual rights against A. First, not all types of contractual rights can be assigned. Where there is a personal element to the contract, that is, where it is of particular importance to A that the other party to the contract is B, assignment will be prohibited: *Farrow v Wilson* (1869). Second, the assignee C takes B's contractual rights subject to any defences which A had against B and any defects in B's title: C can be in no better position than B (*Crouch v Crédit Foncier of England* (1873)).

Covenants concerning land

6.41   Certain covenants relating to freehold or leasehold land run with the land so as to benefit or place a burden on third parties who acquire the land (for more detail, see Megarry and Wade (2012)).

Exceptions giving B rights to enforce the contract in a manner beneficial to C

6.42   The principal reason why C wants a contract between A and B to be enforced is because it would be beneficial to him. Therefore, even if C does not have direct rights of enforcement by virtue of the exceptions to the first limb of the privity rule, C may still be able to obtain the benefit if B is able to enforce the contract in some way.

Specific remedies

6.43   The first way in which B may be able to enforce the A–B contract is by obtaining an order that A perform his contractual obligations. The remedy that B requires to do this depends on whether the obligations in question are 'positive' obligations, that is, obligations to do something, or 'negative' obligations, that is, obligations not to do something.

6.44   If B is trying to enforce a positive obligation, then he will seek an order for specific performance or bring an action for an agreed sum (see Chapter 17). A good example of the former remedy being successfully invoked to the benefit of C, a third party, is *Beswick v Beswick* (1968). B transferred his business to his nephew A in return for A's promise to pay £5 a week to B's widow, C, after B's death. A made one payment of £5 but failed to pay anything further. C sought an order for specific performance. She made her claim in two capacities, first as B's widow C (a third party to the contract) and, second, as administratrix of his estate (for this purpose she stepped into B's shoes and held the same rights as he did). The House of Lords held that, as administratrix, she should be granted specific performance (they therefore found it unnecessary to express a concluded view on her claim in her personal capacity, but inclined to the view that such a claim would fail). Their Lordships regarded specific performance as the appropriate remedy, giving a number of reasons. These were that B would only have been able to recover nominal damages, that even if an action for damages could be brought, in order to enforce a continuing obligation it would be necessary to bring a series of actions as each payment fell due, that C had received the benefit of the business, and that A could have obtained specific performance if it had been B who had defaulted.

6.45 A third party C who wishes B to obtain an order for specific performance in order to benefit C faces two potential problems. First, B might not be willing to go to the trouble of suing; this was obviously not a problem in *Beswick*, where B and C were the same person, but may be where there is no link between them. Second, specific performance is a discretionary remedy, only available in exceptional circumstances (see para **17.46**). Having said that, the courts sometimes treat 'avoiding a privity problem' as an exceptional reason to grant specific performance. In *Latin American Investments Ltd v Maroil Trading Inc* (2017), Teare J declined to rule out specific performance of A's obligation to pay money to C, the joint venture company of which B was a shareholder, on the basis that 'the promisee should be able to obtain specific performance in favour of a third party wherever that is the most appropriate method of enforcing the contract'.

6.46 If the obligation in question is a negative obligation, such as where A promises B that he will not compete with C, B may generally seek an injunction to stop A breaching the contract (see paras **17.50-17.54**). However, where the negative obligation is an obligation not to sue C, and A has already breached this obligation by commencing proceedings against C, the appropriate remedy for B to seek is not an injunction but to ask that the proceedings against C be stayed, or even that A's action be dismissed by the court. While *Gore v Van der Lann* (1967) suggests that B can only obtain such a remedy where A's breach exposes B to legal liability to C, this was not required in *Snelling v John G Snelling Ltd* (1973).

Damages in respect of C's loss

6.47 As a general rule, B can only sue A for damages in respect of B's own losses. But in some situations where C appears to suffer loss as a result of A's breach of contract but has no right to sue A in contract, B may exceptionally be able to recover damages in respect of C's loss. One such exception applies in domestic or social situations, where B makes a contractual booking on behalf of himself and others, but where it would not be plausible to expect those others to appoint B their agent (as would happen in a commercial setting). So in *Jackson v Horizon Holidays Ltd* (1975) the Court of Appeal awarded damages for a disastrous family holiday to the father who made the holiday contract, to cover his own and his family's losses (this case is discussed further at para **16.36**). Lord Denning in *Jackson* was pretty dismissive of the privity doctrine in general, but the House of Lords in *Woodar Investment Development Ltd v Wimpey Construction (UK) Ltd* (1980) later approved the result in its specific context, though not Lord Denning's more general reasoning. Lord Wilberforce treated it as an example of a specific exception:

> I am not prepared to dissent from the actual decision in that case. It may be supported either as a broad decision on the measure of damages (per James LJ) or possibly as an example of a type of contract, examples of which are persons contracting for family holidays, ordering meals in restaurants for a party, hiring a taxi for a group, calling for special treatment. ... there are many situations of daily life which do not fit neatly into conceptual analysis, but which require some flexibility in the law of contract. Jackson's case may well be one.

6.48 In the commercial context, the courts have also devised an exception to avoid a lacuna, where no one would otherwise be able to obtain damages for the loss: C appears to have suffered the loss but cannot sue on the contract, while B can sue on the contract but appears to have suffered no loss of his own. Therefore, unless B can recover damages, there would be a gap in the law, a 'legal black hole', because no one would be able to hold A to account for his breach. The scope and rationale of this exception are highly controversial. Some view the loss as B's, while others regard the loss as C's and see B as suing on C's behalf. Moreover, both views give rise to the question of whether B will have to hand over any damages recovered to C. It was suggested by Lord Millett in *Alfred McAlpine Construction Ltd v Panatown Ltd* (2000) that this is the only true common law exception, in the commercial context, to the rule that B can only recover damages in respect of his own loss. However, Unberath (2003) has argued persuasively that this is not the case: there are pockets of cases from many areas of law, among them bailment, insurance, and agency, where B can recover for what is in substance C's loss.

6.49 In any event, the best-known exception, and the one that Lord Millett considered to be the only true exception, is the '*Albazero* principle'. In *The Albazero* (1977), B chartered a ship from its owner A to carry some crude oil from Venezuela. The ship sank and the cargo was lost. On the day before the ship sank, ownership of the oil had passed to the buyer, C. So it appeared that the loss had been suffered by C, not B. C had a contractual right against A under the bill of lading. However, C failed to bring a claim within the relevant time limit for doing so, so his claim became time barred. B sued A for breach of contract but his claim failed in the House of Lords. Lord Diplock, drawing on the earlier decision of the House in *Dunlop v Lambert* (1839) and other cases from the field of mercantile law, explained when the exception would apply:

> The only way in which I find it possible to rationalise the rule in Dunlop v Lambert so that it may fit into the pattern of the English law is to treat it as an application of the principle, accepted also in relation to policies of insurance upon goods, that in a commercial contract concerning goods where it is in the contemplation of the parties that the proprietary interests in the goods may be transferred from one owner to another after the contract has been entered into and before the breach which causes loss or damage to the goods, an original party to the contract, if such be the intention of them

> both, is to be treated in law as having entered into the contract for the benefit of all persons who have or may acquire an interest in the goods before they are lost or damaged, and is entitled to recover by way of damages for breach of contract the actual loss sustained by those for whose benefit the contract is entered into.

6.50 Three elements are necessary: that there is a commercial contract concerning goods, that A and B contemplate that the proprietary interests in the goods may be transferred by B after the contract has been entered but before the breach occurs, and that A and B intend that B should be able to recover damages for C. It was held that while the first two elements were made out on the facts, A and B did not have such an intention because C had a direct right of action against A (albeit one that had become time barred). While the reasoning was based on the intention of A and B, it has since been recognised in *Panatown* (see paras **6.55–6.61**) that this is artificial. The better explanation is that where C has suffered the loss but has no rights of action, B will be allowed to recover damages for C's loss to allow someone to hold A to account and to avoid C's loss disappearing down a 'legal black hole'. However, where C has direct contractual rights against A, he can sue for the loss that he has suffered, so there is no need to let B recover damages on C's behalf.

6.51 The *Albazero* principle has subsequently been transplanted to the building context by three interesting and extremely controversial cases. The first of these is *St Martins Property Corpn Ltd v Sir Robert McAlpine Ltd* (1994). B contracted with A for the latter to build a development in Hammersmith but A breached the contract. Before the breach in question occurred, B transferred its proprietary interest in the development to C (B also attempted to assign its contractual rights against A to C, but this assignment was held to be invalid). B and C were both wholly owned subsidiaries of another company. C paid for another contractor to carry out remedial work. B sued and it was held by the House of Lords that it could recover damages for C's loss. While it was noted that *The Albazero* only provided an exception in the context of carriage of goods by sea, it was held that the logic behind the exception was equally applicable outside that context:

> ... the present case falls within the rationale of the exceptions to the general rule that a plaintiff can only recover damages for his own loss. The contract was for a large development of property which, to the knowledge of both Corporation and McAlpine, was going to be occupied, and possibly purchased, by third parties and not by Corporation itself. Therefore it could be foreseen that damage caused by a breach would cause loss to a later owner and not merely to the original contracting party, Corporation (per Lord Browne-Wilkinson).

Therefore, in effect the *Albazero* principle was transplanted into the context of building contracts. On the facts, B had transferred the property to C before the breach and C did not have a direct contractual right of action against A, so B could recover damages for C's loss (see Figure 6.1).

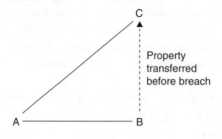

Figure 6.1 *St Martins*

6.52 However, Lord Griffiths decided the case on a much wider basis. He controversially suggested that B had suffered a loss and so was recovering for his *own* loss. This treats B (on one interpretation) as suffering a loss merely because he did not get what he bargained for; in other words, the breach *itself* is a loss to B. So while B suffered no financial loss, he had still suffered a loss for which he could recover damages.

6.53 Therefore, in situations where C suffers financial loss and B appears to suffer none, there are two ways of explaining why B can sometimes recover damages. The first is that sometimes B will be able to recover damages for *C's loss* (the 'narrow ground' approach), while the second suggests that B is recovering for his *own* loss (the 'broad ground' approach).

6.54 In the next case, the *St Martins/Albazero* principle was extended slightly, although the case for allowing recovery is arguably even stronger. In *Darlington BC v Wiltshier Northern Ltd* (1995), the land was never owned by B (a merchant bank who provided the funding for C): it was always owned by C. So unlike *St Martins* and *The Albazero*, there was no transfer of the property from B to C. B entered into a contract with A for the latter to build a recreational centre on C's land. The reason why B and not C entered into the contract with A was the need to avoid government restrictions on local authority borrowing (C was a local council). In breach of contract, the work was defective and B assigned its contractual rights to C (so C became entitled to whatever contractual rights B had) (see Figure 6.2).

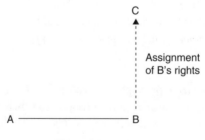

Figure 6.2 *Darlington*

The issue for the Court of Appeal to decide was whether B would have been entitled to substantial damages despite the land being C's. It was held that he was: only a limited extension of the *St Martins/Albazero* principle was necessary because it was eminently foreseeable to A and B that a breach of contract by A would cause loss to C. While Steyn LJ expressed support for Lord Griffiths' 'broad ground' approach, the other two judges did not.

6.55 The last and most important case is *Alfred McAlpine Construction Ltd v Panatown Ltd* (2000). As in *Darlington*, B never owned the land. B contracted with A for the latter to construct an office building and car park in Cambridge, on C's land. B was chosen to enter the contract rather than C for tax reasons: both B and C were members of the same group of companies. The key difference from *Darlington* is that C had *also* entered in a contract directly with A, requiring A to use reasonable care and skill in the construction of the building (a duty of care deed) (see Figure 6.3). The building was defective, so B sued. By a 3–2 majority (Lords Goff and Millett dissenting), the House of Lords held that B could *not* recover substantial damages due to the presence of an A–C contract.

6.56 *Panatown* establishes two things. First, by a 3–2 majority, it was held that where C has a direct contractual right against A, B will usually be able to recover only nominal damages (ie, nothing!) from A. For Lords Clyde and Jauncey, the reason for this was that it was C who had suffered the loss ('the narrow ground'), so where C could protect himself, B should not be able to sue on C's behalf. Lord Browne-Wilkinson thought that had there been no A–C contract, B would have suffered loss ('the broad ground'), but that the presence of the A–C contract removed this loss. Further, B will be restricted to nominal damages even if the A–C contract does not impose quite such stringent obligations on A as the A–B contract (in *Panatown* itself, for example, the A–C contract only imposed a duty on A to take reasonable care, while the A–B contract placed a more demanding duty on A). This latter proposition has been criticised. It means that A cannot be held to the more stringent duties imposed by the A–B contract: he can only be held to the less demanding fault-based duties of the A–C contract. In other words, some of his contractual duties under the A–B contract disappear into a 'legal black hole' because he cannot be held to them.

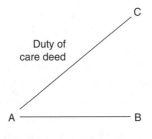

Figure 6.3 *Panatown*

6.57 It appears that the courts will distinguish the situation where C's right against A arises other than pursuant to contract, for example under statute. In *Catlin Estates Ltd v Carter Jonas* (2005), it was suggested (albeit *obiter*) that where C's right of action in respect of a defectively constructed building arose under the Defective Premises Act 1972, and not on the 'same conditions' as the A–B contract, B's claim would not be barred.

6.58 Second, if there is no A–C contract covering similar ground to the A–B contract, then B will be able to recover substantial damages in the event that A breaches the A–B contract, because B and not C has suffered a loss. In other words, the 'broad ground' view was adopted here, Lord Browne-Wilkinson joining Lords Goff and Millett to form a majority on this point. While it is justifiable to allow B to recover damages in such circumstances, it is submitted that there are grave problems with taking the 'broad ground' view that B is recovering for his own loss, not C's.

6.59 There are a number of problems caused by taking the broad ground view in this three-party context (see Unberath (2003)):

- The broad ground, as its name suggests, expands what is normally meant by loss for the purpose of recovering damages, by suggesting that the breach of contract is *itself* a loss. However, there is no need to take a broader concept of loss in these three-party situations. The problem in these situations is not that B has suffered a loss which English law was failing to recognise until the broad ground came along; it is that C has suffered a clear financial loss but may have no contractual rights of his own.

- If B had been allowed to recover, he would have been able to recover consequential losses, such as loss of profit caused by delay in finishing the work to a proper standard. However, such losses are clearly C's losses: it is C who suffers this loss of profit. So it is difficult to see how such losses could justifiably be recovered on the broad ground view, which only allows B to recover for his own loss (see *Rolls-Royce Power Engineering plc v Ricardo Consulting Engineers Ltd* (2003)).

- It is artificial to suggest that B has suffered any meaningful loss just by not getting what he bargained for.

The practical reality is that it is C who has suffered the loss: it is he who is left with the defective building, for example.

- The logical consequence of the broad ground view is that B can pocket the money he recovers. On that view, he has recovered for his own loss so should be under no duty to use the damages recovered for C's benefit. It is notable in *Panatown* how uneasy all the Lords who supported the broad ground view felt about this consequence, for they all found ways to redirect the damages recovered to C. For example, Lord Goff said that if C allows B to contract for A to do work on C's land, it is implicit in this B–C arrangement that if A does the work defectively and B recovers damages, B will use the damages to have the defects remedied if this is possible. Lord Millett had the same idea, and also said that if it is C who funds B's side of the A–B contract, any damages recovered by B will be held on trust for C. So despite holding that the loss suffered was B's, the supporters of the broad ground felt compelled to let C have the benefit of the money, which suggests that at some level they felt that it was C who had really suffered the loss.

6.60 The initial indications are that when confronted with the practical consequences and difficulties of the broad ground view, courts may be reluctant to apply this approach outside the building contract context of *Panatown* itself. For example, in *Rolls-Royce Power Engineering plc* (2003), the judge refused to apply the broad ground view to a contract for the provision of services in respect of the development of an engine. That said, in a subsequent case considering the application of *Panatown* in the building contract context, *Mirant Asia-Pacific Construction (Hong Kong) Ltd v Ove Arup and Partners International Ltd* (2007), the court appeared to accept the broad ground view without hesitation.

6.61 In summary, C faces a number of difficulties if he attempts to get B to recover damages on his behalf. First, he has to persuade B to go to the trouble of suing. While B may be willing to sue where he is linked to C in some way (as in *Panatown*, where B and C were members of the same group of companies), outside this context B is likely to be reluctant to do so. Second, if the discussion has highlighted anything, it is that the scope of the exception is far from certain! Third, even if B recovers, it is not clear that he will always be obliged to hand the money over to C. While Lords Goff and Millett found some ways to redirect the money to C (see para **6.59**), it is not certain that these methods will always be available. Finally, if C has direct contractual rights against A (sometimes even contractual rights that are inferior to those that B has against A), B will be unable to recover more than nominal damages in respect of C's loss.

Statutory exceptions: the Contracts (Rights of Third Parties) Act 1999

6.62 By 1999, Parliament had introduced a number of piecemeal statutory exceptions to the first limb of the privity rule. However, as a result of the problems discussed earlier in the chapter, a more general exception was felt necessary, and so the Contracts (Rights of Third Parties) Act 1999 was passed.

6.63 The Act creates a large exception to the first limb of the privity principle by allowing C rights under contracts in certain circumstances, namely where A and B intend to give C such rights. It is equally important to understand what the Act does NOT do:

- It does not *abolish* the first limb of the rule: it only allows certain third parties to sue.
- It does not make C a party to the contract. Rather C is treated in some ways (although not all) as if he were a party (see s 1(5)).

- It does not remove the rights of B and C that exist outside the statute (see ss 4 and 7(1) of the Act), so we must still look at other possible routes to recovery, particularly where the Act does not cover the situation at hand or where other remedies may be more advantageous (see paras **6.22–6.41**).

- It does not affect the second limb of the privity rule that *obligations* can generally not be imposed on third parties, so the case law on this is still as relevant as ever.

6.64 A helpful way to examine the provisions of the Act in more detail is to go through the various hurdles that a third party must overcome in order to obtain a right of action under the Act. It is suggested that the Act should be commended, although there are a number of small problems with it. Moreover, it is important not to over-emphasise the impact that the Act has made in practice, because it is true that many contracting parties do *not* want third parties to be able to enforce their contracts, and therefore many expressly contract out of the Act (Morgan (2015)). It may be for this reason that there have not been many cases on the Act outside the shipping context, where such contracting-out seems to be less widespread, although the courts are increasingly facing arguments based on the Act in other contexts (see recently *Royal Bank of Scotland plc v McCarthy* (2015) and *Cavanagh v Secretary of State for Work and Pensions* (2016)).

Is the contract of a type covered by the Act?

6.65 The Act generally only applies to contracts entered into after 11 May 2000 (s 10(2)). It applies to all types of contracts except those mentioned in s 6 (so for example bills of exchange, promissory notes, partnership agreements, some aspects of contracts of employment, and contracts of carriage of goods by sea are outside the Act).

Is the s 1 test satisfied?

6.66 The s 1 test has three components, which must all be satisfied in order for C to have the right to enforce the contract.

6.67 The *first component* is that C must establish that A and B intended him to be able to enforce the contract. There are two ways that C can do this. The easier way is to show that the contract expressly provides that C can enforce the term of the contract in question (s 1(1)(a)), for example by stating that 'C is to be allowed to enforce this term of the contract'. The harder way to do this is to show that despite not expressly providing that C should be able to enforce the term, A and B nevertheless intended him to be able to do so. C is aided in his task by s 1(1)(b), which provides that if the term 'purports to confer a benefit' on C, this will give rise to a rebuttable presumption that they intended C to have the right to enforce the term. However, this presumption will be rebutted if on a proper construction of the contract it appears that A and B did not intend C to be able to enforce the term (s 1(2)).

6.68 Two key questions arise. First, when will a term 'purport to confer a benefit' on C? Second, when will the rebuttable presumption laid down in s 1(1)(b) be rebutted? The first question has generated great debate among commentators. The Law Commission was unable to give comprehensive guidance on when this test would be made out in its Report that led to the Act. Instead, it gave examples of when the test would and would not be satisfied, in order to demonstrate how the test might apply. It spent most time on a particular example of a situation where the test would *not* be satisfied. It suggested that the test would not have allowed the claimants in *White v Jones* (see para **6.37** for the facts) to claim under the Act against the negligent solicitor, because '[t]he solicitor's express or implied promise to use reasonable care [in drawing up the will] is not one by which the solicitor is to confer a benefit on the third party. Rather it is one by which the solicitor is to enable the client [the testator] to confer a benefit on the third parties [the intended legatees]' (Law Com No 242). While the distinction has been criticised as an extremely difficult one to draw, it is tentatively suggested that it is valid. Imagine that the solicitor had properly drawn up the will in *White*. The testator does not have to sign it; the choice is his. If he does not sign it, no benefit is conferred on the legatees named in the will. So it is the testator, not the solicitor, who actually confers the benefit on the third parties: it is he who decides who should get his money. Therefore, the testator–solicitor contract is indeed a contract to enable the client to confer a benefit on third parties; the contract itself does not confer such a benefit.

6.69 Several other ways of applying the test have been suggested. Burrows (1996) suggests that the test will only be satisfied where the contract is designed to benefit the third party 'directly'. Unberath (2003) suggests that the key issue is whether the parties intended C to have the right to 'primary performance', that is, not only the right to damages, but also the right to actual performance of the contract. However, it will often be extremely difficult to discern whether the parties intended this: they often simply will not think about this issue at all. Moreover, this distinction appears to be out of line with the purpose of s 1(1)(b): the s 1(1)(b) test seems to focus on whether the parties intended to *benefit* C, not on whether they intended him to have primary rights of enforcement.

6.70 The test was considered at first instance in *Prudential Assurance Co Ltd v Ayres* (2007), where Lindsay J held that it was sufficient that 'on a true construction of the term … its sense has the *effect* of conferring a benefit on the third party' (emphasis added), and that there was no requirement that the benefit on the third party be the predominant purpose or intent behind the term or that the third party be the only person benefited by it. On appeal, the decision in favour of the third party was reversed because the Court of Appeal took a different view on the construction of the relevant contract, so no question arose as to the operation of the Act.

6.71 The point was considered again at first instance in *Dolphin Maritime & Aviation Services Ltd v Sveriges Angfartygs Assurans Forening* (2009). Some underwriters engaged Dolphin to seek to recover compensation in respect of a lost cargo that the underwriters had paid out on, following the grounding of a ship called the *New Flame* in Gibraltar. Dolphin's standard terms provided for a commission based on any recovery obtained from the owners of the *New Flame*. Dolphin negotiated on the underwriters' behalf a letter of undertaking with contractual force from the owners that provided (among other things) that if a settlement was agreed, the sums payable under it would be paid in the first instance to Dolphin. However, the underwriters then concluded a settlement agreement themselves with the owner and the owners paid the underwriters direct. Dolphin claimed that this term of the letter of undertaking purported to confer a benefit on it for the purposes of s 1(1)(b), so that it could sue the owners for breaching the letter of undertaking by paying the underwriters direct, rather than paying Dolphin and thereby allowing Dolphin to deduct its commission.

6.72　The court held that the reference in s 1(1)(b) to purporting to 'confer' a benefit connoted that the language used by the parties showed that one of the purposes of their bargain (rather than one of its incidental effects if performed) was to benefit the third party. If A agrees with B to pay B by making a payment to a specified account of B at C's bank, the contract is not purporting to confer a benefit on C for the purposes of the Act, because paying the money to C is merely the agreed way to benefit B. Similarly, here, the letter was just setting out how the owners' obligations to the underwriters would be discharged, and transferring the money to Dolphin in the first instance was the agreed method of benefiting the underwriters, rather than a means of benefiting Dolphin in its own right. This approach is sensible: a contract may have the effect of benefiting many people, but the class that should be able to enforce it should be limited to those whom the contract is there to benefit. This reasoning was applied in *Royal Bank of Scotland v McCarthy* (2015), where Picken J emphasised that the focus must be 'not on benefit in a general sense, but on whether the 'term' itself 'purports to confer a benefit on' [the third party]'.

6.73　As to the issue of when the s 1(1)(b) presumption has been rebutted, Burrows (1996), the Law Commissioner responsible for the Act, has suggested that the presumption is a 'strong one' which will not normally be rebutted unless there is an express term in the contract inconsistent with C having such rights, or A, B, and C have entered into a chain of contracts which gives C a contractual right against another party for a breach of A's obligations. Therefore, the presumption will not be rebutted if the contract is neutral as to whether C should be able to enforce the term (*Nisshin Shipping Co Ltd v Cleaves & Co Ltd* (2003)). And as *Cavanagh v Secretary of State for Work and Pensions* (2016) emphasises, 'whether a contract does express a mutual intention that the third party should not be able to enforce the benefit conferred on him, or is neutral on that point, is a question of construction having regard to all the relevant circumstances'. This still allows A and B easily to exclude the application of the Act if they so desire, for example by including a clause to the effect that 'C has no right to enforce any term of this contract, whether under the Contracts (Rights of Third Parties) Act 1999 or otherwise'. In practice, it is quite common for the Act to be expressly excluded—see for example such a clause in the 'after the event' insurance policy in *Harlequin Property (SVG) Ltd and another v Wilkins Kennedy (a firm)* (2015). It has been held that the mere fact that there is a chain of contracts between A, B, and C will not necessarily mean that the presumption is rebutted (*Laemthong International Lines Co Ltd v Abdullah Mohammed Fahem & Co* (2005), applied in *Far East Chartering Ltd v Great Eastern Shipping Company Ltd* (2012)). While the Law Commission envisaged a chain of *construction* contracts (as in *Junior Books Ltd v Veitchi & Co Ltd*, discussed at para **6.38**) rebutting the presumption, the same need not be the case for other types of contract.

6.74   The *second component* is that C be expressly identified in the contract by name, as a member of a class or as answering a particular description (s 1(3)). It is not necessary that C be in existence at the time that the A–B contract is entered into. However, the requirement that the identification of C be *express* will be strictly applied, so that if there is not a specific mention of a name, class, or particular description, one cannot be implied, or apparently even arrived at, by a process of construction (see *Themis Avraamides v Colwill* (2006)).

6.75   The *third component* is that C's right to enforcement is subject to any other relevant terms of the contract (s 1(4)). For example, if there is a time limitation clause saying that B and C must bring any contractual claim within two years, this will bind C as much as it will B.

6.76   If these three components are present, C has a 'provisional' right to enforce the term in question. He will be entitled to any remedy that would have been available to him had he been a party to the contract (s 1(5)). So in the case of a contract between A and B where A is to build a house on C's land but breaches the contract in some way, C will be able to sue A for damages if he fulfils the three requirements in s 1. His claim for damages or whatever other relief he seeks will be subject to the same principles as if he were a party (for these principles, see Chapters 16–18). This right to enforce the term in question extends to exclusion clauses (s 1(6)). So if A sues C in tort and there is an exclusion clause in the A–B contract, C can claim the protection of the exclusion clause providing the s 1 requirements are made out. Therefore, much of the unfairness caused by the decision in *Scruttons Ltd v Midland Silicones Ltd* (1962) (see para **6.14**) has been removed.

6.77   Why then, have we described C's right as a 'provisional' right? The answer is that, as we shall see later, C's rights can be removed by A and B unless and until C takes one of the further steps specified in s 2(1), such as communicating his acceptance of the term to A. So even if the s 1 requirements are made out, C's rights of enforcement do not 'crystallise' and become irrevocable until C does something further and until that point he will be vulnerable to having these rights removed.

Can C's rights be removed or have they 'crystallised'?

6.78   If A and B are trying to remove C's rights, by agreeing to vary the contract, for example, then we must turn to s 2 of the Act. C's rights will have crystallised, so A and B will be unable to do this without C's consent, providing that at least one of the following three conditions is made out (s 2(1)):

- C has communicated his assent to the term to A.

- C has relied on the term and A is aware of this.

- C has relied on the term and this was reasonably foreseeable to A.

Note that C's reliance need not be detrimental (Law Com No 242); that is, C need not be worse off as a result of relying on the term. Moreover, trivial reliance suffices.

6.79   However, C's protection under s 2(1) is weakened in two ways. First, if there is an express term in the contract saying that A and B can remove C's right without his consent, this term will be effective even if one of the conditions set out earlier is made out (s 2(3)). Second, even if one of those conditions is made out, the court may nevertheless grant A and B permission to remove C's rights in a number of circumstances, which are set out in s 2(4) and (5).

6.80   There are a number of problems with s 2. First, s 2(1) states that A and B cannot '*by agreement*' remove C's rights if one of the three conditions is made out. As Andrews (2001) points out, at first glance this would seem to allow B unilaterally to release A from his contractual obligations, because C's rights would not be removed 'by agreement'. It is to be hoped that the phrase 'by agreement' is given a broad interpretation here, for otherwise C's protection would be much decreased. Second, problems arise from the requirement that C rely on the term in two of the conditions set out in s 2(1). It is unclear whether C will be held to have relied on the term where he is not fully aware of what the term says, or whether reliance before the contract is entered into will suffice. More fundamentally, it is unclear why, as a matter of principle, reliance should be required at all, even as an alternative to communicating acceptance. As we have seen (at para **6.17**), one of the reasons for the Act was that C's reasonable expectations were not being given effect (see also Law Com No 242). However, if the Act aims to protect C's reasonable expectations, why should it not be enough that C is aware of the contract? As Smith (1997a) comments, 'if the third party's expectations were reasonable, then they remain reasonable, and ought to be protected, whether or not the third party relies on the contract' (see also Adams, Beyleveld, and Brownsword (1997)).

Has B already made a claim against A for breach of contract?

6.81   If B has already made a claim for damages from A for breach of contract, this may prevent C recovering damages. The idea here is that A should not be liable twice over in respect of the same loss. Section 5 provides that if B has already recovered damages from A for C's loss or for expense sustained by B in making good C's loss, then any amount that C recovers in a claim against A will have to be reduced to take account of the amount that B has already recovered.

6.82   As Andrews (2001) notes, if B fails in his action against A, s 5 does not stop C suing in a second action and succeeding in his claim. This may result in inconsistent judgments: the court may hold in the action brought by B that A's work was not defective and did not breach the A–B contract, whereas the court in the action brought by C may hold that A's work was defective and that he did breach the A–B contract. This is of course undesirable, and so it is suggested that the Act should have required that B and C always be joined as parties to the proceedings (whether the action is brought by B alone or C alone) unless impracticable or uneconomic, to avoid this happening, as Andrews

(2001) had previously suggested. Currently, the court only has a *discretion* to join (Civil Procedure Rules, r 19.2(2)).

Does A have a defence to C's claim?

6.83 As has been noted, the Act treats C for some purposes as if he were a party to the contract. Therefore, if C brings a claim against A under the Act, A is allowed to rely on all the defences that would have been available had the action been brought by the other party to the contract, B (s 3(2)–(4)), providing that the defence arises from or in connection with the contract and is relevant to the term. So if A would be able to raise the defence of undue influence against B, for example, A can also raise this defence against C. Indeed, in one respect, C is placed in a better position than B would have been in: for A to rely on a defence against C, it must arise from or in connection with the contract (unless there is an express term to the contrary: s 3(3)).

6.84 However, in one important respect, C is placed in a worse position than B. If A seeks to rely on an exclusion clause in response to C's claim, C cannot use s 2(2) of the Unfair Contract Terms Act 1977 (on which see para **8.38**) to attempt to strike down the clause (s 7(2) of the Act). C can use the other provisions of the 1977 Act, just not s 2(2). The Law Commission's justification for this stance is as follows:

> Our test of enforceability rests on effecting the intention of the contracting parties to confer legal rights on the third party. To apply UCTA 1977—much of which is concerned to protect consumers irrespective of the true construction of the contract—to claims by third parties would cut across that essential basis of our reform (Law Com No 242).

This stance has been criticised, Adams, Beyleveld, and Brownsword (1997) pointing out 'where UCTA strikes down a contractual provision as unreasonable, this usually signifies that the provision has not been freely agreed—in which case it would be a distortion to treat such a provision as representing the contractors' intentions'. It also seems peculiar to allow C to have the protection of some provisions of UCTA, like s 2(1), but not s 2(2).

6.85 As a final point, it is interesting to note that the Act does not allow A to invoke against C any defences that B would have had against C. This can lead to unfortunate consequences, as Stevens (2004) shows: for example, if C induces B to enter into a contract with A for his benefit through a misrepresentation, duress, or undue influence (see Chapters 9–11), and A subsequently breaches the contract, there seems no way to stop C enforcing the contract against A by an action for damages.

The fate of the judge-made exceptions after the Act

6.86 While the Act will reduce the need for the judge-made exceptions to the first limb of the privity rule, many of them will still be extremely useful.

Exceptions giving C rights against a contracting party

6.87   The Law Commission emphasised that it did not intend the Act to hamper the judicial development of third party rights. Indeed, it envisages possible *further* judicial development of such rights (Law Com No 242). This is reflected in s 7(1) of the Act, which states that the Act does not affect any right or remedy of a third party that is available outside the Act. The following comments can be made on some of the exceptions discussed earlier in the chapter.

Trusts of a promise

6.88   Trusts of a promise will continue to be important because they offer C a number of advantages over the Act. In particular, C's rights cannot be extinguished or varied, unlike under the Act, which allows this to happen in certain circumstances (s 2). Moreover, unlike under the statute (see s 3(2)), C's action against A is not subject to the defences that A could invoke against B. Indeed, in *Nisshin Shipping Co Ltd v Cleaves & Co Ltd* (2003) Colman J suggested that the Act would not restrict the operation of the doctrine.

Collateral contracts

6.89   There will be less pressure on the courts after the Act to find collateral contracts to avoid the first limb of the privity rule. In particular, 'Himalaya clauses' will generally satisfy the test in s 1(1) and (2) of the Act, allowing C to rely on such clauses under the Act. However, Treitel (2002) suspects that C may still prefer to try to establish a collateral contract between himself and A in some circumstances, because C's 'rights under the Act are … subject to its provisions … while Himalaya clauses are not'. So for example, C's rights cannot be removed without his consent under a collateral contract.

It is hard to predict what attitude the courts will take to collateral contracts after the Act and there is as yet no caselaw on the point. On one hand, they may still be willing to find them, on the basis of s 7(1) and the comments in the Law Commission Report. On the other, the courts may be reluctant to outflank the Act by finding collateral contracts, particularly as this is often a somewhat artificial exercise and was criticised as such by the Law Commission.

Assumption of risk by A

6.90   In most of the cases where this exception has been applied, there has been a chain of contracts between A, B, and C (an A–B contract and a B–C contract). It seems that the Act will generally not allow C contractual rights under the A–B contract, because the presumption under s 1(1)(b) will be rebutted under s 1(2) (see para 6.73 and Law Com No 242). Therefore, this exception will remain useful after the Act. However, the Law Commission described the exception as 'controversial' and 'rather artificial', so there must be a lingering suspicion that the courts will now be more reluctant to apply the exception after the Act.

Tort

6.91 This exception will still be important because it catches some situations that fall outside the Act, such as *White v Jones*-type situations (see para **6.37**).

Assignment

6.92 This will continue to be extremely important because it can be used to give C rights under the contract without A intending this to happen. (For a discussion of assignment, see *Offer-Hoar v Larkstore Ltd (Technotrade Ltd Pt 20 defendant)* (2006).) As the Law Commission noted, '[t]he practical importance of assignment is considerable; the whole industry of debt collection and credit factoring depends upon it'.

Exceptions giving the promisee rights to enforce the contract in a manner beneficial to C

6.93 Again, the Law Commission emphasised that it did not intend the Act to hamper judicial development of the promisee's rights and even envisaged the possibility of further judicial development of such rights. This is reflected in s 4, which provides that the Act is not to affect the promisee's rights outside the statute.

Specific remedies

6.94 The Law Commission was of the view that C would now have a right under the Act to get specific performance in *Beswick v Beswick* (1968) (see para **6.44**). This suggests that the need to use this exception will be reduced. However, sometimes the contract will not satisfy the s 1 test, so there is still a use for this exception. Moreover, Treitel (2002) questions whether it is clear that C would have rights of enforcement under the Act in *Beswick*. In practice, specific relief is still pleaded in three party situations (see *Latin American Investments Ltd v Maroil Trading Inc* (2017) discussed in para **6.45**).

Damages in respect of C's loss

6.95 This exception will retain its utility even after the Act. The Law Commission (Law Com No 242) acknowledged that the Act often would not give C rights of enforcement in situations falling under this exception:

> [o]n the facts of Linden Gardens [a case heard together with St Martins] itself, there would be no question of the third party having a right of enforcement under our pro-

posed reform. The property in question had been sold to the third party after the con-
tract for work on the property had been entered into and there was a clause in the works
contract barring assignment of the rights under it. The recognition in that case that the
promisee could have recovered damages based on the third party's loss will be as im-
portant after the implementation of our proposed reform as it is under the present law.

It is also arguable that the Act would not have given C rights of enforcement in *Darlington*
or *Panatown*: in both these cases C employed B as an intermediary to avoid C becoming
a party to the main contract, so it seems unlikely that C was intended to have rights of
enforcement under the A–B contract.

6.96   The stance of the Law Commission suggests that there is scope for this common law
exception to be generalised further. However, Andrews (2001) urges caution, suggesting
that it would be odd if the courts found it possible to carve out doctrines benefiting C in
parallel to the statutory scheme and that such a result would be untidy, even chaotic. It is
suggested that despite this objection, the development of the exception should continue,
because it is based on a firm foundation: that without such an exception, C suffers loss
but cannot sue, while B can sue but can only recover nominal damages.

The imposition of contractual obligations on third parties

6.97   The second limb of the privity rule rests on the rationale that contractual obligations
are created by consent, so a person should not be subject to a contractual obligation
that he has not consented to. As mentioned (para **6.63**), the Act does not alter this
general rule or create an exception to it. However, there are a number of situations in
which we are happy to place obligations on people who are not parties to the contract.
Two situations deserve brief mention.

Contracts concerning property

6.98   In *The Pioneer Container* (1994), the House of Lords held, following *Morris v CW Martin
& Sons Ltd* (1966), that a sub-bailee (A) can protect himself from being sued by C (the
bailor) by relying on a term in A's contract with B (the bailee), providing that C has expressly or impliedly consented to the goods being sub-bailed on the terms of the A–B
contract or had ostensibly authorised this. In effect, this means that C may sometimes
be bound by a provision of a contract to which he is not a party. This exception is in
keeping with the rationale behind the general rule of not imposing burdens on third parties because it is based on C's consent (see para **6.3**). The Court of Appeal suggested in
Sandeman Coprimar SA v Transitos y Transportes Integrales SL (2003) that more general
contractual principles may be at work here, via the collateral contract device, opening

up the possibility of collateral contract reasoning being used to extend the boundaries of this doctrine beyond the sub-bailment context.

Tortious interference with contractual rights

6.99 Interfering with A's contractual rights may lead to C being liable in tort. Therefore, the A–B contract can lead to the imposition of obligations upon C, albeit of the tortious rather than the contractual variety. The definition and elements of the relevant torts (intentionally inducing breach of contract and causing loss by unlawful means) were clarified by the House of Lords in *OBG Ltd v Allan* (2007).

OVERVIEW

1   The doctrine of privity has two limbs. First, only the parties to a contract have rights under it; third parties do not. Therefore a third party cannot invoke the terms of the contract against a party to the contract.

2   Second, a contract cannot place contractual obligations upon a third party. Therefore, a party to a contract cannot invoke its terms against a third party.

3   There are a number of problems with the first limb, which have led to the development of methods to circumvent the first limb at common law and the creation of statutory exceptions. Indeed, mounting pressure for reform of the first limb culminated in a new piece of legislation, the Contracts (Rights of Third Parties) Act 1999, which creates a large exception to the first limb.

4   The best justification for the general rule is that it is up to the contracting parties to determine to whom they should owe contractual obligations. Generally, contracting parties do not intend third parties to be able to enforce the contract.

5   However, there are difficulties with the general rule, most notably that sometimes contracting parties do intend a third party to be able to enforce the contract, so the general rule fails to uphold the intentions of the contracting parties.

6   As a result of the unfairness caused in certain circumstances by the first limb, a number of exceptions sprang up both at common law and by statute. Some of these exceptions allow the third party rights against one of the parties to the contract. These exceptions include:

   - trusts of a promise;

   - finding a collateral contract between the third party and one of the parties to the main contract;

   - bringing a negligence claim in tort against a contracting party;

   - using agency to make the third party a party to the main contract; and

   - assigning the rights under the contract to the third party.

Others allow the promisee to enforce the contract in a manner beneficial to the third party:

- obtaining a court order that the other party to the contract perform his contractual obligations;
- recovering damages for loss suffered by the third party as a result of the breach of contract.

7   However, many of these exceptions are uncertain in scope, controversial, and somewhat artificial. For this reason, and by reason of the injustice caused by the first limb, the Contracts (Rights of Third Parties) Act 1999 was passed to create a large exception to the general rule by allowing the third party to enforce the contract under certain circumstances.

8   To obtain a right to enforce the contract under the Act, the third party must satisfy three requirements (s 1):

- The parties must have intended the third party to enforce the contract. This can be established by showing that the contract expressly provides that the third party should have such a right. Alternatively, if the term 'purports to confer a benefit' on the third party is used, it will be presumed that the parties intended to grant rights of enforcement to the third party. However, this presumption will be rebutted if on a proper construction of the contract, it appears that the parties did not intend the third party to be able to enforce the contract.
- The third party must be expressly identified in the contract by name, as a member of a class or as answering a particular description.
- The third party's rights of enforcement will be subject to any other relevant terms of the contract.

9   If these requirements are satisfied, the third party will have a provisional right to be able to enforce the term(s) of the contract, be it a clause requiring the party to do something or be it a clause exempting the third party from liability. He will be entitled to any remedy that would have been available to him had he been a party to the contract (for example, damages for breach of contract).

10 However, the parties to the contract will be able to remove these rights of the third party without his consent unless and until the third party's rights have crystallised, which will happen once the third party:

- communicates his assent to the term to the promisor; or
- relies on the term (and the promisor is aware of this); or
- relies on the term (and this was reasonably foreseeable to the promisor).

11 If one or more of these conditions is fulfilled, the third party's consent will generally be required if his rights are to be removed (although the court can sometimes give permission to dispense with this consent requirement).

12 If the third party sues a party to the contract, the party will be able to rely on all the defences that would have been available to him had the action been brought by the other

party to the contract, providing that the defence arises from or in connection with the contract and is relevant to the term.

13   While the Act will reduce the need for the judge-made exceptions to the first limb of the privity rule, many of them will still be extremely useful. The Act and the Law Commission Report preceding it both make clear that the Act is not intended to hamper the development of these exceptions (see ss 4 and 7(1) of the Act).

14   The second limb of the privity rule is far less controversial, because it is based on the sound premise that parties should not be placed under contractual obligations without their consent. Accordingly, the second limb causes less injustice, so while a small number of exceptions have developed, no large scale exception exists and the limb is unaffected by the Act.

15   Nevertheless, a few exceptions have been developed, principally in relation to contracts concerning property. In addition, the third party may be liable in tort if he deliberately induces a breach of a contract to which he is not a party.

FURTHER READING

Andrews 'Strangers to Justice No Longer: The Reversal of the Privity Rule under the Contracts (Rights of Third Parties) Act 1999' [2001] CLJ 353

Beale 'A Review of the Contracts (Rights of Third Parties) Act 1999' Chapter 11 in *Contract Formation and Parties* (2010)

Burrows 'Reforming Privity of Contract: Law Commission Report no 242' [1996] LMCLQ 467

Burrows 'No Damages for a Third Party's Loss' (2001) 1 Univ of Oxford Commonwealth LJ 107

Furmston and Tolhurst *Privity of Contract* (2015) Chapter 2

Morgan *'Great Debates in Contract'* (2015) Chapter 10

Smith 'Contracts for the Benefit of Third Parties: In Defence of the Third Party Rule' (1997a) 17 OJLS 643

Stevens 'The Contracts (Rights of Third Parties) Act 1999' (2004) 120 LQR 292

Unberath *Transferred Loss* (2003), particularly Chapters 2, 7, and 8

SELF-TEST QUESTIONS

1   Why should we only allow parties to a contract to acquire rights under it?

2   What problems are caused by only allowing parties to a contract to acquire rights under it?

3   When does the law allow you to recover damages for a loss suffered by another party? When, if ever, should you be able to do so?

4   What common law exceptions are there to the rule that only parties to a contract can acquire rights under it? What effect do you think the Contracts (Rights of Third Parties) Act 1999 will have on these exceptions?

5   What exceptions are there to the rule that a contract cannot impose obligations on a third party?

6   Apricot plc contracted with Broadbrush Ltd, a building company, for the construction of an office block on land owned by Apricot, for a contract price of £2 million. At the time the contract was made, Apricot was planning to transfer the land to a subsidiary company for tax reasons and so a recital was included in the contract, explaining that the contract was being made for the benefit of any subsequent owner of the land within Apricot's corporate group. Two months after the contract was made, Apricot set up a new subsidiary company, Cherry Ltd, the land was transferred to it and notice of the transfer was given to Broadbrush. As a gesture of goodwill, Broadbrush then executed a deed in favour of Cherry, promising to take reasonable care to perform its obligations under the building contract. The work was completed and paid for, but it quickly became clear that the building did not comply with the detailed health and safety specifications in the contract in a number of important respects and, as a result, Cherry was unable to find tenants willing to take leases of office space in the building. Advise Apricot and Cherry.

 For hints on how to answer question 6, please see the online resources at **www.oup.com/uk/sullivan8e/**.

7 Terms of the contract I

SUMMARY

This chapter considers a number of issues to do with the terms of the contract:

- Distinguishing between terms and mere representations: how to draw the distinction, and why does the distinction matter in practice.

- Incorporation of express terms: contrasting signed contracts (incorporation by signature) and unsigned contracts, where incorporation is generally by reasonable notice.

- Interpretation of written contracts: considering the modern contextual approach to contractual interpretation.

- Implied terms: some terms are implied by statute; others are implied by the courts. Of the common law variety, some are implied to reflect trade custom, others are implied 'in fact' to give effect to the parties' presumed intentions or 'at law' into a defined category of contract for broader policy reasons.

7.1 Having determined that the parties have reached a binding agreement, it is now time to consider the *content* of the agreement. This chapter is concerned with general questions about what the terms of a contract are, that is, the promises undertaken by each party which have legal effect once there is a valid contract. As we saw in Chapter 1, the law attaches considerable significance to contractual obligations and so it is vital to be able to work out what will count as a contractual term and how it will be construed. We also need to consider why, and the circumstances in which, terms might be *implied* into contracts.

Distinguishing between terms and mere representations

7.2 Here, we are considering statements made by one of the contracting parties about the contractual subject matter, commonly assurances that it possesses a certain quality or attribute. The tense is important—this is about the present, not the future. We are not concerned here with the common sorts of contractual term in which one of the contracting parties promises what they will or will not do.

7.3   The parties say lots of things in the run up to forming a contract and at the time a contract is made. Some of those statements are obviously terms of the contract. If, for example, one of the parties signs a contractual document containing the statement, 'I hereby promise that this car/business/house is in good condition', there is no difficulty at all in telling that the statement is a term of the contract (although there may be difficulty in deciding what is meant by 'good condition'). At the other end of the scale, some statements are obviously not terms of the contract. A car salesman might say, 'This car goes like a rocket', but it would be hard to persuade a court that he had made a promise to that effect. But between those extremes, it can be difficult to tell.

7.4   Why does it matter? After all, as we shall see in Chapter 9, legal consequences may arise if the defendant made a false statement (misrepresentation), even if it was not one of the terms of the contract. The reason is that the claimant has a greater level of legal protection if the statement *is* a term of the contract, because the defendant actually promised (or, if you prefer, is deemed to have promised) that the state of affairs is true. So if it turns out not to be true, (1) the defendant will be liable for breach of the term even if she is not at fault, and (2) the claimant will be entitled to the contractual, expectation measure of damages, which (as we will see in Chapter 16) will put him into the position he would have been in if the statement had been true. But if the defendant's statement is a mere misrepresentation which induced the claimant to contract, (1) the claimant can only recover damages where the defendant was at fault, and (2) then only by reference to the less favourable tort measure (see Chapter 9). More to the point, before the mid-1960s (with the decision in *Hedley Byrne v Heller* (1964) and the enactment of the Misrepresentation Act 1967) the claimant could not recover any damages at all unless the defendant had been fraudulent. This should be borne in mind when reading cases from before the mid-1960s, where the only way for a court to award damages in the absence of fraud was by finding that the statement was a term of the contract. So how do we decide whether the statement made is a term or not?

Test depends on the parties' intention, judged objectively

7.5   A good starting point is a dictum of Lord Moulton in *Heilbut, Symons & Co v Buckleton* (1913) that a statement will be a term of the contract 'provided it appears on the evidence to be so intended'. But, as ever in the law of contract, it is not the subjective intention of the parties which counts; intention is judged objectively and 'can only be deduced from the totality of the evidence'. In *Heilbut*, a rubber company was being launched and promoted by D, well-known rubber merchants. P said to D 'I understand that you are bringing out a rubber company', to which D replied 'We are.' P then asked if the company was 'alright' and D replied 'We are bringing it out.' P responded 'That's good enough for me' and invested in it. In fact, the company was so far from 'alright' that what P had invested in could not really be described as a rubber company at all. The House of Lords held that, looking at all the circumstances of the parties' exchanges, judged *objectively*, D had no intention of warranting either that the company was a rubber company or that it was a good investment.

Factors commonly taken into account

7.6 Although according to *Heilbut* 'all the circumstances' can be taken into account, a number of issues have arisen regularly in the cases and they provide a helpful structure when considering the question.

Timing of statement

7.7 Lightman J in *Inntrepreneur Pub Co v East Crown Ltd* (2000) drew attention to two relevant timing issues. He made the straightforward point that the lapse of time between the statement and the making of the formal contract will be significant: 'The longer the interval, the greater the presumption must be that the parties did not intend the statement to have contractual effect in relation to a subsequent deal.' He also observed that a further:

> important consideration will be whether the statement is followed by further negotiations and a written contract not containing any term corresponding to the statement. In such a case, it will be harder to infer that the statement was intended to have contractual effect, because the prima facie assumption will be that the written contract includes all the terms the parties wanted to be binding between them.

Importance of statement

7.8 Perhaps fairly obviously, the more important the statement is to the contracting parties (particularly the party to whom it is addressed), the more likely it is to be considered a term. In *Bannerman v White* (1861), the statement was about the most important aspect of the subject matter so far as the plaintiff was concerned (without the assurance, he would not have contracted at all) and was thus found to be a term. An assurance about a very trivial aspect of the contractual subject matter is more likely to be a mere representation. (As we will see in Chapter 9, a really trivial representation might not influence the claimant's decision to enter the contract at all and thus will not trigger the remedies for misrepresentation, even if false.)

Relative positions of the parties

7.9 Roughly speaking, where an expert makes a statement to an amateur, the statement is more likely to be a term of the contract, whereas if an amateur makes a statement to an expert, the statement is more likely to be a mere representation. (Of course this test is no help where, as in many cases, the parties' expertise is equal.) In *Oscar Chess Ltd v Williams* (1957), D, a member of the public, sold his second-hand Morris car to car dealers in part exchange for a new car and described it as a '1948 Morris' because that is what it said in the log book. In fact it was a 1939 model and consequently worth much less. By the time the dealers realised, it was too late for them to rescind the purchase on the basis of misrepresentation (see Chapter 9), so their only possible remedy was to sue D for damages if they could establish that he had promised ('warranted') the age of the car. The Court of Appeal held D's intention, judged objectively, was not to make such a promise. As an amateur, it was highly unlikely that he would have intended to make such a promise, especially to a car dealer.

7.10 The opposite result was reached in *Dick Bentley Productions Ltd v Harold Smith (Motors) Ltd* (1965), where car dealers sold a Bentley car to the claimant saying that it had only done 20,000 miles when in fact it had done 100,000 miles. This time, the statement was a term of the contract: 'Here we have a dealer … who was in a position to know or at least find out the history of the car.'

7.11 The preceding cases are very obvious examples of weight being given to this factor, but sometimes its influence is more subtle. In *Esso Petroleum v Mardon* (1976), Esso owned a petrol station and was negotiating with Mardon to grant him a tenancy of it. Esso told Mardon that the estimated throughput of the petrol station was 200,000 gallons a year. This used to be correct, but Esso had overlooked that the local planning authority had recently insisted that the petrol pumps must be moved to the back of site, obscuring them from the road and reducing passing trade. The throughput estimate should therefore have been revised downwards. Mardon took the tenancy, but lost money and gave up the business. Esso brought proceedings to repossess the petrol station and Mardon counterclaimed for damages, arguing that Esso was liable for breach of warranty and/or negligent misrepresentation (notice that, unlike the previous two examples, damages for negligent misrepresentation were available by the date of this case). The problem with both limbs of Mardon's counterclaim was that Esso's statement appeared to be a mere statement of *opinion*, not suitable to be the subject matter of a contractual promise or an operative representation. But the Court of Appeal held that, because of Esso's relative expertise compared with Mardon, they must be deemed to have *warranted* that the forecast was made with reasonable care and skill.

7.12 Two things are worth noticing about this case. First, the court's decision that Esso's statement about throughput was a contractual term is surprising, because it added nothing to the conclusion that Mardon could recover damages for negligent misrepresentation. In other words, since the term was merely a promise that Esso had taken reasonable care, if Esso had *not* been at fault, they would not have been in breach of contract either. Likewise, the measure of damages was the same on either analysis. As Lord Denning explained:

> Mr Mardon is not to be compensated here for 'loss of bargain'. He was given no bargain that the throughput would amount to 200,000 gallons a year. He is only to be compensated for having been induced to enter a contract which turned out to be disastrous for him.

Second, *Esso* is a good illustration of the objective version of intention at work here. Such a warranty was not what Esso intended to give, judged subjectively, but is what it is *taken* to have intended.

External verification

7.13 If the defendant encouraged the claimant to rely on his assurance without seeking external verification of its accuracy, this will readily persuade the court that the statement was a term of the contract (see *Schawel v Reade* (1913)). Where, on the other hand, the defendant encourages external verification, this will suggest that, judged objectively, the parties intended the opposite. In *Ecay v Godfrey* (1947), E bought a boat from G for £750. The boat was in an appalling condition, incapable of sea voyages, and E resold her for only £45. He claimed damages, alleging that G had warranted that she was in good condition. Lord Goddard's judgment used most colourful prose, describing the boat as 'on its last legs' and 'in a pretty dicky condition'. He also described E as a 'babe in the wood', whereas G was undoubtedly a boat expert, which might suggest that G's statements were terms. But the judge reached the opposite conclusion, first since on the facts he doubted that G had actually given the unequivocal assurances alleged and, second, even if he had, he had also asked E whether he was planning to have a survey. The judge reasoned it would have been inconsistent for G to recommend a survey if he was intending to warrant that the boat was in good condition.

Collateral contracts

7.14 Occasionally the court might find that, although a statement is not part of the main contract, it is nonetheless a term of a separate, collateral contract. Usually, this reasoning is used quite instrumentally, in order to avoid troublesome difficulties with the simpler conclusion that the statement is incorporated into the main contract. Such difficulties include a requirement of form with which the statement does not comply (for example contracts for the sale of land must be in writing), the problem of privity (see para **6.25**), or the so-called 'parol evidence rule' (see para **7.40**). It is a popular technique—after all, all three of those examples are technical limitations which prevent the courts giving full effect to parties' intentions and are unpopular with the courts as a result. On the other hand, where the evidence is that commercial parties had ample opportunity to contract but deliberately chose not to, the courts are reluctant to supplement their contractual arrangements by implying a collateral warranty (as in *Fuji Seal Europe Ltd v Catalytic Combustion Corpn* (2005) where the claimant contracted with a subsidiary of the defendant but did not obtain a guarantee from the defendant).

7.15 Where it is adopted, the collateral contract device can be quite powerful: usually the statement which ends up as a collateral contract will merely add to the terms of the main contract, but occasionally it might even *contradict* them. In *City & Westminster Properties Ltd v Mudd* (1959) an oral assurance was given on behalf of a landlord when renewing the lease of a shop that, although the lease said the premises were not to be used for sleeping, the landlord would not object if the tenant slept on the premises. Nine years later, the landlords sought to forfeit the lease for breach of this covenant in the lease. The court held that there was a clear oral promise that the landlords would not forfeit the lease if the tenant slept on the premises. As it was oral, it could not simply be incorporated as a term of the lease, but this did not stop it forming a collateral contract. Notice the interrelation here with promissory estoppel (see paras **5.75–5.96**). The judge said this was not a case of *High Trees*-style promissory estoppel, but rather of a contractually binding promise made to the tenant. The key difference is that the problem which promissory estoppel solves is normally the absence of consideration for the promisor's promise not to insist on his strict legal rights. But here there was consideration (allegedly), namely the tenant entering into the lease which he would not otherwise have done. Unlike the tenant's detrimental reliance in *High Trees*, here the landlord was actually asking the tenant to enter into the lease and his doing so was the 'price' of the collateral contract.

7.16   Of course, the court will only give contractual effect to a separate oral or written promise if the court thinks this is what the parties intended, judged objectively. In *Business Environment Bow Lane Ltd v Deanwater Estates Ltd* (2007) a tenant sought to rely on a letter from the landlord, given at an early stage of negotiations, as a collateral contract, citing *Mudd* as authority. The Court of Appeal did not agree, emphasising that there was over a month of further negotiation after the letter was sent, during which the tenant continued to regard it as important to press the landlord, ultimately unsuccessfully, for an amendment to the draft lease. As May LJ said, 'That letter said what it said, but things moved on and the agreed outcome was that which was contained in the lease. There is in these circumstances no room for a collateral agreement ... preventing the landlord from relying on the terms of the lease.'

7.17   Sometimes the main written contract will contain an 'entire agreement clause' in which the parties acknowledge that all their contractual terms are contained in this contract and nowhere else (see further para **9.85**). The effect of an entire agreement clause is to rule out arguments about collateral contracts—as Lightman J put it in *Inntrepreneur Pub Co v East Crown Ltd* (2000), 'to preclude a party to a written agreement from thrashing through the undergrowth and finding some (chance) remark or statement (often long forgotten or difficult to recall or explain) on which to found a claim ... to the existence of a collateral warranty.' The certainty such a clause brings to a commercial transaction is obvious, but there may be cases in which the intentions of the parties are thwarted by giving conclusive effect to an entire agreement clause, an issue discussed by McLauchlan (2012). Perhaps this should not concern us, since if a commercial contract is caught by s 3(2)(b) of the Unfair Contract Terms Act 1977 the clause will be subject to a requirement of reasonableness, while such a clause in any consumer contract will be subject to the test of fairness in s 62 of the Consumer Rights Act 2015 (both regimes are covered in Chapter 8).

Incorporation of express terms

Introduction

7.18   We are concerned here with how terms come to be incorporated into a contract; in practice this means a contract made on the standard terms of one of the parties, rather than a unique contract negotiated by the parties. Two introductory points should be borne in mind. First, although the rules to be discussed are applicable to all contractual terms, the cases usually involve the question of whether very one-sided terms such as exclusion or limitation clauses have been incorporated into the contract. This is because, before the enactment of the Unfair Contract Terms Act 1977, one of the devices developed by the courts for regulating the use of exclusion clauses was a series of rather artificial rules making it relatively difficult for a contracting party to incorporate such terms into its contract in the first place. Since 1977, the need for artificially restrictive common law rules has diminished, but the principle that a disputed term must have been incorporated into the contract remains as valid as ever (seen particularly in the 'battle of the forms' cases discussed in Chapter 2).

7.19   Second, there is (in theory anyway) an important distinction between contracts that have been *signed* and those that have not. If one party has signed a contractual document, then the basic rule, subject to exceptions, is that he or she is straightforwardly bound by the terms contained in that document; in all other cases, terms will only be incorporated if the party relying on them has taken reasonable steps to bring the terms to the other party's notice.

Signed contracts—incorporation by signature

7.20   We have already seen (in paras **3.20-3.27**) the strictness of the law's approach to incorporation of contractual terms by signature, as exemplified in the decision in *L'Estrange v Graucob*, although, as has been discussed, this seemingly rigid rule is subject to a number of exceptions (such as where the signed document is not 'contractual' in nature) and does not fit neatly with the objective offer and acceptance approach to agreement. So why is the *L'Estrange* principle, 'You signed it, you're bound by it', so influential in English law?

7.21   One reason is that it is extremely beneficial from the perspective of commercial certainty. If signature alone is sufficient, then no elaborate steps are needed to draw terms to the other party's attention and there is very little scope for argument later about whether enough was done to incorporate the terms. This attitude reflects the classic freedom of contract position: if a sane adult signs a document then, provided he was not misled or forced to do so, he is *deemed* to agree to everything in it, even if he did not read it or agree to its contents in a meaningful sense. After all, he need not have signed it at all. This was the attitude of the great commercial judge Scrutton LJ in *L'Estrange* itself. But the rigid application of the *L'Estrange* rule is not without its critics. For example, Lord Devlin in *McCutcheon v David MacBrayne* (1964) regarded the elevation of the party's signature to crucial status as most artificial:

> If it were possible for your Lordships to escape from the world of make-believe which the law has created into the real world in which transactions of this sort are actually done, the answer would be short and simple. It should make no difference whatever. This sort of document is not meant to be read, still less to be understood. Its signature is in truth about as significant as a handshake that marks the formal conclusion of the bargain.

7.22   Another influential opponent of the *L'Estrange* principle was Lord Denning, who acted as counsel for the hire purchase company in the case but always felt uneasy about his client's victory. He did not regard the commercial certainty justification as compelling, given the inequality of bargaining power between the parties which meant that Miss L'Estrange was in no position to decide whether or not to agree to the terms. Indeed, much of his judicial career years after *L'Estrange* were devoted to developing doctrines (most now overruled) that would have reversed the result in the case!

7.23   Now, with legislative controls on unfair terms, both views can be accommodated, since the battle for protection of weaker contracting parties has shifted away from the common law rules on incorporation of terms. Commercial certainty remains the default position, so if you sign a contractual document, you are prima facie bound by all the terms included in it, but with legislation in place to relieve deserving parties from any risk of abuse. As will be seen in Chapter 8, if the facts of *L'Estrange v Graucob* arose today, Miss L'Estrange would be able to challenge the exemption clause in her contract by invoking the Unfair Contract Terms Act 1977 (or the Consumer Rights Act 2015 if she was making the contract to hire the cigarette machine not for the purposes of her business, which seems unlikely).

Unsigned contracts–incorporation by notice

7.24   Where the contract is not embodied in a signed document, a term will be incorporated only where reasonable steps are taken by one party to bring it to the other's notice. The first thing to realise is that this is an *objective test*: it is about whether one party has taken reasonable steps to bring the terms to the other party's attention, not whether the other party has actually spotted, read or understood them.

7.25   In *Thompson v London Midland & Southern Railway Co* (1930) Mrs Thompson, an old lady who could not read, bought a railway ticket from the railway company for 2s 7d. The ticket contained the words, 'issued subject to the conditions and regulations in the company's timetables and notices and other bills'. As a result of the negligence of an employee of the company, she was injured when alighting from the train and sued for damages, but the company relied on an exclusion clause contained on page 552 of its timetable, of which Mrs Thompson was wholly unaware. The Court of Appeal held that this was irrelevant, since what counts is whether reasonable notice has been given of the conditions. Lawrence LJ said:

> The facts of the case are simple. On the ticket ... there was a statement in plain terms that it was issued subject to conditions which would be found on the back, and on the back there is a plain statement indicating where those conditions were to be found. In those circumstances (the notice on the ticket not being tricky or illusory) it seems to me that there is no room for any evidence that the company had not done all that was reasonably necessary as a matter of ordinary practice to call attention to the conditions upon which the ticket was issued.

So the focus was on whether the *company* had acted reasonably and the court concluded that it had, heavily influenced by the social conditions of the time, which meant that it would have been impossible to run a railway with cheap tickets without reliance on exclusion clauses. Today, the opposite result would be reached, because such an exclusion clause would be absolutely prohibited under the Unfair Contract Terms Act 1977 and the Consumer Rights Act 2015 (see Chapter 8), but the principle of objectivity it embodies remains entirely relevant today.

7.26 The court takes into account all the circumstances prevailing when the contract was made to determine whether reasonable steps to give notice of terms have been taken, of which the following are the most significant:

Is there a 'prior course of dealing' between the parties?

7.27 The contract in issue might not be an isolated transaction—the parties might have had lots of dealings in the past. Sometimes, if they have always contracted on certain terms in the past, it will not matter that those terms have not been expressly mentioned or pointed out on this occasion. They can be incorporated on the basis of a course of dealing between the parties.

However, two conditions apply. First, the course of conduct must be *consistent*—if not, there is no reason to assume that the conditions were included this time, since they might just as well not be. In *McCutcheon v David MacBrayne Ltd* (1964) Lord Pearce explained, 'where the conduct is not consistent, there is no reason why it should still produce an invariable contractual result'. Second, the course of conduct must be *regular* (*Hollier v Rambler Motors (AMC) Ltd* (1972)), meaning that these terms were used often enough that the parties must have intended (judged objectively, as ever) to transact on that basis.

Usual conditions in a particular business

7.28 A similar approach is sometimes taken where the parties to the contract are both in the same business. For example, in *British Crane Hire v Ipswich Plant Hire* (1974) both parties were in business hiring cranes and both had standard terms and conditions based on the same trade association standard form. The defendants had hired cranes from the claimants in the past and knew the claimants' terms and conditions, but on this occasion the defendants needed to hire a crane urgently and so the claimants supplied it immediately, before the contractual paperwork was dealt with. As Lord Denning said:

> In view of the relationship between the parties ... the plaintiffs were entitled to conclude that the defendants were accepting [the crane] on the terms of the plaintiff's own printed conditions—which would follow in a day or two. It is just as if the plaintiffs had said: 'We will supply it on our usual conditions' and the defendants had said 'Of course, that is quite understood'.

7.29 The defendant in *Scheps v Fine Art Logistic Ltd* (2007) tried, unsuccessfully, to rely on the principle in *British Crane Hire*. The claimant had purchased a piece of modern art called *Hole and Vessel II* (a sculpture made of polystyrene, cement, earth, acrylic, and pigment) for $35,000 and contracted with the defendant to transport and store the sculpture.

Unfortunately, it was apparently mistaken for rubbish by a member of the defendant's staff and disposed of in a skip! The claimant sued the defendant for damages based on the sculpture's value at the date of trial of £600,000; the defendant claimed that, by a term in its contractual conditions, its liability for loss of the sculpture was limited to £587.13. The defendant had not provided the claimant with a copy of its contractual terms, nor even mentioned them when contracting, but it argued that because the claimant had been involved in art transactions in the past, he should be deemed to have contracted on the basis of the defendant's terms as in *British Crane Hire*. This argument was given very short shrift by Teare J, who pointed out that the two cases were entirely different: 'The claimant was a private customer of the defendant's. There was nothing about the status in which the claimant dealt with the defendant which might have led the defendant to believe that the claimant was dealing with the defendant on the basis of the defendant's terms and conditions.' Accordingly, the limitation clause was not incorporated into the contract, since the defendant had taken no steps whatever to bring it to the claimant's notice.

Most cases are not quite this straightforward. Where there is no prior course of dealing between the parties and they are not in the same business, the most significant factors to consider are as follows.

Timing

7.30　Terms can only be introduced before or at the time the contract is made. Thereafter, no amount of notice will do the trick, as it is simply too late to add terms to the contract. As has been seen in Chapter 2, it is not always easy to determine precisely at what point the contract was made. In *Olley v Marlborough Court* (1949) Mr and Mrs Olley reserved a room in a hotel, paid in advance, and booked in at reception on arrival. Displayed in their hotel room was a notice exempting the hotel from liability for lost or stolen articles. Later some jewellery, furs, and a hat box were stolen from their room. The Court of Appeal held that the contract was made when Mr and Mrs Olley booked in at reception (by which time no mention had been made of an exemption clause), so it was simply too late for the hotel to incorporate such a term thereafter, however prominently the notice might have been displayed in the room.

7.31　*Olley* is a quaint old case, but it illustrates a very real, contemporary commercial issue. Today it is extremely common for contractual dealings to be initiated by telephone or on the internet, with delivery or performance accompanied at a later stage by the contractor's set of standard terms and conditions. Where, as is common, those conditions are not referred to at the initial order stage, what is their status? It is obviously vital to know at what point the parties' contract was formed. If the contract was made over the telephone or internet, *Olley* shows that it is too late to add terms later, but if the contract was not made until the date of performance this leaves an unsatisfactory lack of contractual protection for the customer if performance is delayed or cancelled.

7.32　A more sophisticated solution is to consider whether later terms might operate as an offer to *vary* the terms of the initial contract, although the courts will take some convincing that this represents what the parties intended. In *Jayaar Impex Ltd v Toaken Group Ltd* (1996) a contract was made over the telephone. Later the sellers sent their contract form, which contained a reference to a set of standard terms issued by a trade association. The form contained the words, 'Important—please sign and date this form' but the buyers did not do so. The goods were unsatisfactory, so the buyers sued, but the sellers tried to rely on two of the trade association's standard terms. The sellers could, of course, only rely on these terms if they had been incorporated into the oral contract or had varied it. Rix J had no difficulty in holding that they were of no effect. They were not incorporated into the original oral contract, because they had not been mentioned until after it was made. Nor had the sellers' written form operated to vary the oral contract, because the buyers had not agreed to such a variation. Indeed, the buyers did not sign and return it precisely because it did not represent what they had agreed. Rix J stressed that such a variation will not be lightly inferred, especially where (as here) it would involve worsening the other party's position from that agreed in the original contract. So the sellers' later terms were of no effect.

What sort of document is it?

7.33 In *Thompson*, the court held that terms found in a railway timetable and referred to in a railway ticket had been incorporated into the contract. However, nowadays we tend to say that if terms are contained in the sort of document in which a reasonable person would not expect to find contractual terms, this is unlikely to count as reasonable steps to bring the terms to the notice of the other contracting party. So in *Chapelton v Barry UDC* (1940) there was a notice on a beach saying that anyone wishing to hire a deckchair should get a ticket from the attendant, but it said nothing about exclusion of liability. C hired two deckchairs from the attendant, paid 2d per chair and was given two tickets, which he did not even glance at. In fact, the tickets contained the phrase 'The council will not be liable for any accident or damage arising out of the hire of the chair.' C was injured when the deckchair collapsed, so D tried to rely on the exclusion clause on the ticket. But the Court of Appeal held that the ticket was a mere receipt for the money he had paid. The relevant conditions of hire were those contained in the notice, which made no mention of exclusion of liability. The reasonable person would not expect to find contractual terms contained in mere receipts of this kind.

How onerous is the term?

7.34 The degree of notice required to count as reasonable depends on the content of the term and, in general, the more onerous it is, the greater the steps that will be needed to draw it to the other party's attention. Before the enactment of the Unfair Contract Terms Act 1977, the courts (spearheaded by Lord Denning) used this principle to mitigate the effect of particularly unreasonable terms, in a way which came close to saying that some very onerous clauses must actually be drawn to the other party's attention. So in *J Spurling Ltd v Bradshaw* (1956) Lord Denning said:

> *the more unreasonable the clause, the greater the notice which must be given of it. Some clauses which I have seen would need to be printed in red ink on the face of*

the document with a red hand pointing to them before the notice could be held to be sufficient.

7.35 This was an incredibly useful way of removing the impact of onerous exclusion clauses, by making it almost impossible to incorporate them into the contract. Since the Unfair Contract Terms Act 1977 (as amended by the Consumer Rights Act 2015), it might be thought that there is little need for a special rule to incorporate onerous or unusual clauses, but the courts still have recourse to it in exceptional cases. For example, in *Interfoto Picture Library Ltd v Stiletto Visual Programmes Ltd* (1989) Stiletto telephoned Interfoto enquiring about borrowing photographic transparencies; there was no prior course of dealing between them. Interfoto duly sent 47 photographic transparencies, which arrived with a delivery note containing terms and conditions: one was that if the transparencies were kept for more than 14 days, a daily fee of £5 per transparency was payable. Stiletto phoned back accepting Interfoto's offer, but did not notice the term and returned the transparencies after one month, for which Interfoto charged them over £3,700. The Court of Appeal held that a term charging the daily fee had not been incorporated into the contract. It was onerous and unusual, so it should have been specifically drawn to Stiletto's attention. Instead, Interfoto were only entitled to a reasonable fee for Stiletto's use of the transparencies. (The Court of Appeal also expressed surprise that Stiletto did not plead that the term amounted to an unenforceable penalty clause, on which see paras **17.22–17.38**.)

7.36 This result is interesting. After all, the parties were both businesses and the clause was not of a type that is regulated under the Unfair Contract Terms Act, so one might have expected the court to adopt the 'harsh but certain' commercial approach to Stiletto's predicament, namely 'bad luck that you did not bother to read the contents of the delivery note'. However the Court of Appeal regarded the rules on incorporation of onerous terms as having a role beyond the protection of consumers. Bingham LJ noted that, unlike civilian systems, English law does not adopt a general notion of good faith in contractual dealings, but instead has a number of piecemeal devices to ensure fair dealing between contracting parties, of which the requirement of sufficient notice of onerous terms is one. Yet this fair dealing approach conflicts with another desirable objective, the need for certainty and predictability in commercial dealings. Hobhouse LJ made this point in his dissenting judgment in *AEG (UK) Ltd v Logic Resource Ltd* (1996), stressing that *Interfoto* should be regarded as exceptional:

> *... it is necessary to consider the type of clause, and only if it is a type of clause which it is not to be expected will be found in the printed conditions referred to then to go on to the question of its incorporation ... it is desirable as a matter of principle to keep what was said in the Interfoto case within its proper bounds. A wide range of clauses are commonly incorporated into contracts by general words. If it is to be the policy of English law that in every case those clauses are to be gone through with, in effect, a toothcomb to see whether they were entirely usual and entirely desirable in the particular contract, then one is completely distorting the contractual relationship between the parties and the ordinary mechanisms of making contracts. It will introduce uncertainty into the law.*

Although Hobhouse LJ was in the minority on this point, it is suggested that his view is sensible (on the facts of *AEG*, the majority's reliance on the *Interfoto* principle of incorporation was unnecessary, since the court unanimously held that the relevant clause was ineffective under the Unfair Contract Terms Act) and consistent with the reasoning in *Interfoto* itself, in which Bingham LJ stressed the exceptional, disproportionate effect of the daily fee provision.

7.37 The Court of Appeal endorsed this view of *Interfoto* in *O'Brien v Mirror Group Newspapers Ltd* (2001), concluding (albeit with some reluctance) that the rules of the *Daily Mirror* 'scratchcard' game had been incorporated into the contract with a player of the game. An error by the newspaper meant that over a thousand players, including Mr O'Brien, appeared to have won the £50,000 jackpot. The newspaper invoked one of its rules, which provided that in the event of more than one winner, the newspaper would draw lots to determine who received the prize. The rules had not been printed in the newspaper that day, but the existence of a set of rules was mentioned. Mr O'Brien argued that the rule depriving him of his prize was unusual and onerous, but the Court of Appeal reluctantly disagreed and held that the newspaper *had* done enough to incorporate the rules into its contract with him. Such a clause was not 'unusual' in the newspaper industry, nor was it exceptionally onerous, since it did not:

> ... *impose any extra burden upon the claimant, unlike the clause in* Interfoto. *It does not seek to absolve the defendant from liability for personal injuries negligently caused ... It merely deprives the claimant of a windfall for which he has done very little in return.*

7.38 So the current position is a slightly uneasy compromise between the certainty of the objective reasonable notice regime, but with a stricter level of notice demanded where a clause is exceptionally onerous or unusual, such that it would be contrary to a notion of fair dealing not to draw the offending clause specifically to the other party's attention. It does not seem to matter whether the clause is also regulated by statute, or whether the affected party is a consumer or a business. Finally, as will be seen (para **8.58**) the Consumer Rights Act 2015 includes provisions with similar effect to the common law rules relating to incorporation, that terms in consumer contracts defining the subject matter or affecting the price will not be operative unless they are 'prominent'.

7.39 Finally, we should consider how terms should be regarded as incorporated in electronic contracting, in particular via a website, where the customer typically clicks 'I agree' to form the contract. On the assumption that this does not equate with signing a contract (and the courts have shown no appetite for extending *L'Estrange v Graucob* to this situation), the question will turn on reasonable notice. But what will amount to giving 'reasonable notice' of those terms, often occupying hundreds of webpages, so as to incorporate them into the contract and thus make them binding? Sometimes the customer cannot complete the contract without scrolling down the full terms and conditions, then clicking something like 'I accept' (known in digital licensing terminology as a 'click-wrap' contract); other websites merely put a link to the terms and conditions but the customer does not have to click on the link to proceed with the contract. The latter is unlikely to be effective, as the Law Commission Report leading to the Consumer Rights Act 2015 made clear, since there is no mechanism to indicate acceptance of the terms. A court is more likely to find that the click-wrap method constituted reasonable notice, and thus the terms were incorporated, although if it is a consumer contract there are additional statutory protections against unfair terms (see paras **8.52–8.78**), which will take into account whether there was any real opportunity for the consumer to become acquainted with the term, in determining fairness or unfairness.

Parol evidence rule

7.40 Where there is a written contract, the question sometimes arises whether evidence can be given to show that the parties agreed to additional terms, which were not contained in the written document. Traditionally, the rule was that where the parties have reduced their contract to writing it was not permissible to adduce 'parol' (ie, oral) evidence to add to, vary, or contradict the written instrument (the same applied to other pieces of writing, like earlier drafts). This supposed general rule is now subject to so many exceptions (for example, oral evidence can be introduced to show a custom, to imply a term, to prove fraud, or to provide evidence of consideration) that it rarely operates. Lord Mance in *Prince Jefri Bolkiah v State of Brunei Darussalam* (2007) noted that one of the parties had 'rightly conceded that the trouble with the parol evidence rule ... is one is liable to go round in a circle with [it]. If the court finds that ... all the terms of an agreement have not been reduced to the written document, of course the court is going to let in evidence of other terms.' Indeed, Law Commission Report No 154 (1986) concluded that today the so-called rule is really a statement of the obvious: where the parties intended all the terms of the contract to be in the written document, they cannot bring evidence of other terms, but where the parties did not intend the document to represent the whole agreement, outside evidence is admissible.

Interpretation of written contracts

Traditional approach

7.41 The court's task, when interpreting a written contract, is to find the intention of the parties, judged objectively (see *Reardon Smith Line Ltd v Yngvar Hansen Tangen* (1976)). Traditionally, judges approached this task by focusing entirely on the language used in the contractual document (assisted by various legal 'canons of construction'), attempting to discern its meaning without considering the background to the contract or any other 'external' matters. This literal, legalistic, approach had the benefit of clarity and predictability (different judges are more likely to reach consistent results if they are merely construing words by reference to well-known legal rules), but was also somewhat artificial to construe a document without taking into account the commercial context in which it was drawn up.

7.42 In an important decision, the House of Lords in *Prenn v Simmonds* (1971) moved away from the traditional approach, allowing some limited consideration of the commercial background when construing ambiguous words in a contract. As Lord Wilberforce put it:

> *The time has long passed when agreements, even those under seal, were isolated from the matrix of facts in which they were set and interpreted purely on internal linguistic consideration.*

Lord Wilberforce's concept of the 'factual matrix' is now invariably regarded as relevant when construing written contracts, though as will be seen there is some tension between the contemporary trend towards ever greater use of contextual commercial material to decide the meaning of the contract and the opposing view, defended by Staughton (1999), that the literal approach should prevail unless there are very good, precisely defined reasons for looking outside the text.

Modern approach

7.43 Lord Hoffmann has been the most staunch advocate of Lord Wilberforce's 'factual matrix' approach, and built on it when setting out five new principles for interpreting written contractual terms in *Investors Compensation Scheme Ltd v West Bromwich Building Society* (1998), which can be summarised as follows:

7.44 *Principle 1*: objectivity—ascertaining the meaning of the contract as it would appear to a reasonable person in the position of the parties—remains the central tenet.

7.45 *Principle 2*: Lord Hoffmann redefined the 'factual matrix', saying that it includes 'absolutely anything which would have affected the way in which the language of the document would have been understood by a reasonable man'.

Staughton LJ (writing extra-judicially) (1999) has pointed out that the phrase 'factual matrix' is inherently unhelpful, because 'counsel have wildly different ideas as to what a matrix is and what it includes', preferring a restrictive concept of 'surrounding circumstances which the parties must have had in mind' to assist in applying the objective test of intention. Moreover, he observes that Lord Hoffmann's version of the admissible background is far wider than anything previously adopted: 'It is hard to imagine a ruling more calculated to perpetuate the vast cost of commercial litigation … the proliferation of inadmissible material with the label 'matrix' [is] a huge waste of money, and of time as well' (he made similar criticisms in his judgment in *Scottish Power plc v Britoil* (1997)). Lord Hoffmann subsequently explained his reference to 'absolutely anything' in *Bank of Credit and Commerce International SA (in liquidation) v Ali (No 1)* (2001) as follows:

> *I did not think it necessary to emphasise that I meant anything which a reasonable man would have regarded as relevant. I was merely saying that there is no conceptual limit to what can be regarded as background.*

With respect, this does not really answer the criticisms, which are not that *irrelevant* material will be brought in as evidence, but that there is now no obvious limit on what an ingenious counsel will be able to argue is relevant (although it should be possible for counsel's enthusiasm to be kept in check by the civil procedure rules about time management and wasted costs).

7.46 Calnan (2017), who is rare amongst academic commentators in also being hugely experienced at drafting and negotiating commercial contracts, suggests a helpful compromise. In Calnan's view, the admissible factual matrix ought to be confined to three matters—the identity of the parties, the nature and purpose of the contract, and the market in which the transaction took place. These limited contextual factors will be easily available to the parties themselves, and accessible to third parties who might subsequently gain an interest in the contract. This is a very sensible compromise between a return to absolute literalism and the unmanageable torrent of contextual material that judges now have to contend with whenever a point of interpretation is pleaded.

7.47 *Principle 3*: 'the law excludes from the admissible background the previous negotiations of the parties and their declarations of subjective intent'.

It may seem surprising that, having declared in his second proposition that 'absolutely anything' is admissible to determine the meaning intended by the parties, Lord Hoffmann should make an exception for 'the previous negotiations of the parties'. The reason for the exclusion (according to Lord Wilberforce in *Prenn v Simmonds*) is said to be that it is only the final bargain that must be construed, so evidence of the parties' shifting positions in negotiation and discarded drafts are irrelevant and unhelpful. Others (such as Lord Nicholls (2005)) take a different view and argue that, because such negotiations are *usually* unhelpful, that does not justify a rule automatically excluding them, on rare occasions when they might be helpful.

7.48 Nonetheless this exception has been reaffirmed by the House of Lords in *Chartbrook Ltd v Persimmon Homes Ltd* (2009). The case was Lord Hoffmann's last appearance in the House of Lords so it is fitting that his speech considered and defended the *West Bromwich* approach to contractual construction. It involved a development agreement, whereby the owners of land in London granted the developers a licence to redevelop the site into commercial units and residential flats (in accordance with planning permission to be obtained by the developers). The price to be paid to the owners in respect of the flats was to be calculated by reference to an agreed minimum amount per square foot, *plus* an additional profit element if a flat sold for more than a specified figure. However, the clause in the contract setting out this additional profit formula was ambiguous and very badly drafted. The owners' interpretation was commercially highly implausible (it would have given them an element of additional profit even if market prices had fallen) but represented the more natural meaning of the words and syntax in the clause; the developers' interpretation, on the other hand, made more sense commercially and was a common method of calculating consideration in a development agreement known as 'overage', but was not a natural reading of the relevant clause.

7.49 The House of Lords unanimously adopted the developers' interpretation, by looking at the language of the contract as a whole, in its commercial context. This meant that there was, strictly, no need to reconsider the question of whether evidence of the parties' prior negotiations should be admissible. However, *obiter* Lord Hoffmann was not convinced that the exclusionary principle should be abandoned, noting that:

> *Whereas statements of surrounding circumstances are, by definition, objective facts, which will usually be uncontroversial, statements in the course of the pre-contractual negotiations will be drenched in subjectivity and may, if oral, be very much in dispute.*

However, this is not entirely satisfactory. Their Lordships *did* have the pre-contractual evidence before them, because the developers had also brought a claim for rectification (on which see paras **13.72–13.104**), and as Baroness Hale said:

> *I have to confess that I would not have found it quite so easy to reach this conclusion [favouring the developers' interpretation] had we not been made aware of the agreement which the parties had reached on this aspect of their bargain during the negotiations which led to the formal contract. On any objective view, that made the matter crystal clear.*

It is interesting to speculate about whether their Lordships would still have opted for the developers' interpretation if the prior negotiations had revealed unequivocally that, unlikely though it might be commercially, the owners' interpretation was correct. If not, then some would argue—why not openly admit that prior negotiations can (exceptionally) be admitted when helpful?

7.50 The exclusion of pre-contractual negotiations has been the subject of influential criticism, in particular by Lord Nicholls (2005). It is a pity that the House of Lords in *Chartbrook* did not address all of Lord Nicholls' arguments, particularly the inconsistency that prior negotiations *are* admissible to prove whether a contract has been formed in the first place, so that a judge who, with the aid of the prior negotiations evidence, has concluded that a contract exists, must immediately banish from his mind those prior negotiations when interpreting that contract. On the other hand, it would be possible to formulate an exception to allow admissibility in such cases only; most commercial interpretation disputes involve detailed written agreements, where there is no issue about the existence of a contract. In the latter sort of case, maybe it is sensible to adopt the limits to the admissible factual matrix suggested by Calnan (2017) (para **7.46**), and concentrate on finding the objective interpretation of what the parties intended by their final executed contract, without recourse to pre-contractual negotiations which Lord Hoffmann described as 'drenched in subjectivity'.

7.51 Exceptions already exist allowing evidence of the pre-contractual negotiations to be admitted for certain purposes as part of the process of construction (not just in an action for rectification), so it is not easy to delineate when such evidence will and will not be admissible. For example, in *Proforce Recruit Ltd v The Rugby Group Ltd* (2006) the Court of Appeal allowed a claim to proceed to trial concerning the meaning of the words 'preferred supplier status' in a contract, even though the claimant's interpretation of the phrase was based on what had been said by the parties before making the contract: such evidence was permissible to illuminate and identify the meaning of the undefined, unusual phrase in the contract. This is known as the 'private dictionary exception'. However, when the case eventually got to trial in *Proforce Recruit Ltd v The Rugby Group Ltd* (2007), Cresswell J held that there was no agreed meaning of the phrase in the pre-contractual negotiations and found for the defendant. In doing so, he was not enthusiastic about the exception admitting evidence of the pre-contractual negotiations to show that the parties negotiated on an agreed basis that words bore a particular meaning:

> Where the agreement is silent as to the meaning of the words in question, and those words have been used in a particular sense in correspondence preceding the agreement (which forms part of the factual matrix), it would be surprising if commercial parties intended to contract on the basis of some other meaning, without saying so in the contract. The exception under consideration should not be allowed to become a means, regularly adopted by litigants, of attempting to circumvent the fundamental principle that generally the law excludes from the admissible background the previous negotiations of the parties and their declarations of subjective intent.

7.52 The *Proforce* case was not mentioned in any of the speeches in *Chartbrook*, but their Lordships did cast doubt on an earlier decision, *The Karen Oltmann* (1976), in which the 'private dictionary' exception was used to admit evidence of the parties' prior negotiations. According to Lord Hoffmann, the case did not in fact involve a private dictionary, but merely 'a choice between two perfectly conventional meanings of the word "after" in a particular context' which therefore did not justify admitting the pre-contractual negotiations.

7.53 A further exception to the inadmissibility of pre-contractual negotiations was recognised in *Oceanbulk Shipping & Trading SA v TMT Asia Ltd* (2010), namely that they are admissible to establish that a particular fact was known to the parties when they entered the contract (see Davies (2011)). The Supreme Court applied this exception in *Oceanbulk* despite the fact that the negotiations concerned were conducted 'without prejudice'. Lord Phillips emphasised that evidence of facts within the parties' common knowledge is admissible as an exception, but the general exclusionary principle remains firm. But, as Lord Clarke acknowledged, it may not be easy to distinguish between the two. Indeed as Flaux J in *Excelsior Group Productions Ltd v Yorkshire Television Ltd* (2009) observed, the dividing line between admissibility and inadmissibility regarding pre-contractual negotiations is 'so fine it almost vanishes'.

7.54 The next two principles can conveniently be taken together.

Principle 4: concerns the difference between the meaning which a document would convey to a reasonable man and the meaning of its words: 'The meaning of words is a matter of dictionaries and grammars; the meaning of the document is what the parties using those words against the relevant background would reasonably have been understood to mean.'

Principle 5: concerns what to do when something has gone wrong with the language. Despite the common sense proposition that we do not easily accept that people have made linguistic mistakes, particularly in formal documents, nonetheless 'if one would nevertheless conclude from the background that something must have gone wrong with the language, the law does not require judges to attribute to the parties an intention which they plainly could not have had.'

7.55 The fourth and fifth propositions, controversially, also demonstrate a willingness to override the words which the parties chose to use in their contract. The traditional approach required the language chosen by the parties to be given its 'natural and ordinary' meaning, but was not entirely blind to the consequences of possible interpretations, with the courts stressing that the more unreasonable the consequences the less likely it is that the parties can have intended it. Lord Hoffmann's approach seems to give the courts more latitude to resolve 'linguistic mistakes' to give a commercially acceptable solution, even where the contract as drafted is not ambiguous and the consequences of the literal interpretation not obviously absurd. Lord Hoffmann cited in support a dictum of Lord Diplock from *The Antaios* (1985) who said, 'if detailed semantic and syntactical analysis of words in a commercial contract is going to lead to a conclusion that flouts business common sense, it must be made to yield to business common sense', whilst acknowledging that the courts must not stray over the line from construction into the forbidden territory of rewriting the parties' bargain.

7.56 Whilst all judges would accept that there is a crucial line between construing and rewriting a contract, they do not concur on where that line is located in particular cases. As ever, this reflects the tension between the desire for commercial certainty versus a desire to produce a just resolution to the dispute, particularly difficult when the parties have made a professionally drafted contract the language of which does not seem to make sense. The difference in emphasis can be seen by contrasting Lord Hoffmann's speech in *Charter Reinsurance Co Ltd v Fagan* (1997) with Staughton LJ in the Court of Appeal in the same case. Lord Hoffmann's willingness to interpret the words 'the sum actually paid' in a reinsurance policy as covering a sum 'payable but not yet paid', because of the common sense commercial context, arguably falls foul of Andrews' (2017) vivid warning that commercial common sense 'should not become a promiscuous pretext for rewriting the text in the name of abstract "improvement" of the contract'.

7.57 Two cases can be used to illustrate the fine line between construing and rewriting a contract, and different judicial attitudes to what is permissible. *Pink Floyd Music Ltd v EMI Records Ltd* (2010) concerned the interpretation of the licence agreement between EMI and Pink Floyd's service company (PFM), granting EMI licence to sell and distribute Pink Floyd's music. PFM were seeking a declaration that a particular clause (clause 4.13) caught online sales and digital downloads, whereas EMI argued that its language was clearly confined to old-fashioned 'Albums', 'Records', and 'Single records'. By a majority, the Court of Appeal agreed with PFM, despite finding EMI's argument (based on the defined terms in the contract) 'telling'.

7.58 The majority were convinced that, judged objectively, the commercial purpose of clause 4.13 was to 'preserve the artistic integrity of the albums' and thus it must be interpreted so as to apply to online distribution as well as more old-fashioned methods. The majority were able to dispense with EMI's 'telling' argument that the words chosen in the drafting of clause 4.13 did not cover online distribution, because they managed to find ambiguity in the clause (somewhat artificially), when read against other clauses and the definitions which were not very tightly drafted. Neuberger LJ said:

> In all these circumstances, I have reached the conclusion that clause 4.13 ... is not by any means a clearly drafted provision, whose effect is unambiguous as a matter of language, and that it is therefore quite permissible, indeed positively appropriate, to invoke commercial common sense to assist on the issue of clarifying a rather opaque provision. I also consider that the commercial common sense which PFM invokes for the purpose of interpreting clause 4.13 is simple and uncontroversial.

Carnwarth LJ, dissenting, was much more cautious about rewriting the contract and did not accept that 'commercial common sense' was quite so uncontroversial or obvious:

> I accept that, with hindsight, it seems surprising that a distinction would have been drawn for this purpose between physical and on-line sales. However, that is far from saying that it would have been arbitrary or irrational for the parties to have made an agreement on that basis in 1999. On this part of the case, we are not asked to consider evidence outside the terms of the contract itself as to the factual matrix. We have no evidence, therefore, as to the precise commercial significance to either party of a restriction on 'uncoupling'. It is impossible, and in any event impermissible, to try to recreate the thinking of either party in the negotiations.

7.59 Carnwarth LJ's caution is to be welcomed, in the absence of evidence of the commercial reality at the time the contract was made. After all, as Lord Neuberger has said writing extra-judicially (Neuberger (2014)):

> judges should be diffident about pontificating about the commercial realities of any particular interpretation ... [It] does not seem obvious that a judge, who is normally fairly remote from business matters, would be particularly good at identifying the commercial common sense of any conclusion, let alone what a reasonable person might regard as commercially sensible.

7.60 *Rainy Sky SA and others v Kookmin Bank* (2011) is a further excellent illustration of different judicial attitudes to the permissible level of re-writing on the basis of 'commercial common sense', where the Supreme Court took the opposite view from the majority of the Court of Appeal. The claimants were the buyers under six identical shipbuilding contracts made with a shipbuilder, who was a customer of the defendant bank. Each contract obliged the shipbuilder to provide 'on demand advance payment bonds', which were issued by the defendant bank, to guarantee refunds of pre-delivery instalments in certain events named in the contract, including in the event of the shipbuilder's insolvency. However, the list of events included in the bonds themselves as triggering a refund of the pre-delivery instalments did not include the shipbuilder's insolvency and the surrounding wording was ambiguous.

The shipbuilder became insolvent, so the claimants sought refunds of the instalments paid thus far from the defendant bank under the bonds, but the defendant refused to pay. The claimants issued proceedings, arguing that the bonds should be interpreted so as to match the shipbuilding contracts and include insolvency events. The defendant argued that the words of the bonds were clear and could not therefore be rewritten.

7.61 The Court of Appeal, by a majority, agreed with the defendant and applied the literal words of the bonds. According to Patten LJ:

> This is not a case in which the construction contended for would produce an absurd or irrational result in the sense described in the cases I have referred to and merely to say that no credible commercial reason has been advanced for the limited scope of the bond does, in my view, put us in real danger of substituting our own judgment of the commerciality of the transaction for that of those who were actually party to it.

7.62 The Supreme Court, however, unanimously allowed the claimants' appeal in *Rainy Sky* and took the view that Patten LJ's approach was wrong. As Lord Clarke said, 'It is not in my judgment necessary to conclude that, unless the most natural meaning of the words produces a result so extreme as to suggest that it was unintended, the court must give effect to that meaning.' Instead, wherever the wording used by the parties has more than one possible meaning, 'the court is entitled to prefer the construction which is consistent with business common sense and to reject the other', as the Supreme Court did on the facts of *Rainy Sky* itself. Although this is a more interventionist approach than that of the majority in the Court of Appeal, it is still not as radical as Lord Hoffmann envisaged in *West Bromwich*, since the Supreme Court stressed that where the parties have used *unambiguous* language, the court must apply it, even if the result is commercially implausible.

7.63 Of course, the official position was always that unambiguous language must be respected (hence Neuberger LJ's emphasis in the *Pink Floyd* case on the ambiguity of clause 4.13) but, since *Rainy Sky*, the courts have been much less willing to find artificial ambiguity and have increasingly resisted pressure to 'rewrite' agreements under the guise of 'construing' them, despite the fact that it is commonplace for ingenious counsel to plead and argue that this should happen. This new mood of restraint, deferring as it does to the parties' original, professionally-drafted, contractual language, promotes certainty in commercial transactions and is to be welcomed. As Moore-Bick LJ said in *Procter & Gamble v Svenska Cellulosa Aktiebolaget* (2012):

> the starting point must be the words the parties have used to express their intention and in the case of a carefully drafted agreement of the present kind the court must take care not to fall into the trap of re-writing the contract in order to produce what it considers to be a more reasonable meaning.

7.64 This more cautious approach is exemplified in Gloster LJ's restrictive phraseology in *Amlin Corporate Member Ltd and others v Oriental Assurance Corporation* (2014): 'the court is reluctant to introduce words not used in the actual contractual provisions as part of the construction exercise, unless the court is satisfied that the words selected by the parties are commercially nonsensical and it is clear that the parties intended some other purpose.' (See also Arden LJ in *Scottish Widows Fund and Life Assurance Society v BGC International* (2012)). Likewise in *Ardagh Group SA v Pillar Property Group Ltd* (2013), a case concerning a share sale agreement which ended up having adverse tax consequences for the purchaser, the purchaser asked the court to 'construe' the agreement in a manner that would dramatically improve its financial outcome, to the detriment (of course) of the vendor's. The Court of Appeal unanimously declined, pointing out that the express words of the agreement were unambiguous and thus must be applied as drafted. As Underhill LJ pithily explained:

> All that has happened is that the Agreement failed to provide for the circumstances created by the particular arrangement which [the purchaser] made (or, rather, chose to make) with [the Revenue] ... But that is not a licence for departing from the straightforward meaning of the words used: parties not uncommonly make contracts which work out expensively for them in particular situations for which they have failed to provide. This is a very long way from the sort of case considered in Chartbrook.

7.65 The Supreme Court decision in *Arnold v Britton* (2015) shows how far the courts have moved away from the emphasising 'commercial common sense' to justify interventionist 're-writing by construction' in recent years. The case concerned terms in a number of leases of chalets on a leisure park. Although the leases were each said to have matching provisions, in fact some of the leases contained terms explicitly requiring the service charge payments to increase annually on a steep compound basis, while others had much less onerous provisions. The lessor sought a declaration that the onerous service charge provisions should be given their natural meaning and enforced, whilst the tenants argued that the lessor's construction produced an absurdly high rate of service charge that defied commercial common sense, and thus should not be accepted. Nonetheless the Supreme Court supported the lessor's literal construction, which was clear and unambiguous, even though it produced what many would regard as an 'unfair' outcome for the tenants: it is not the role of the courts, in construing contracts, to give relief from harsh terms. Lord Neuberger distilled seven principles from the cases, all of them cautious about being unduly interventionist in contractual construction, including pointing out the dangers of prioritising commercial common sense over the language the parties had chosen, which should prevail other than in the most exceptional situations, and that common sense should in any event not be invoked retrospectively to rewrite what subsequently turned out to be a bad bargain. As he explained:

> while commercial common sense is a very important factor to take into account when interpreting a contract, a court should be very slow to reject the natural meaning of a provision as correct simply because it appears to be a very imprudent term for one of the

parties to have agreed, even ignoring the benefit of wisdom of hindsight. The purpose of interpretation is to identify what the parties have agreed, not what the court thinks that they should have agreed. Experience shows that it is by no means unknown for people to enter into arrangements which are ill-advised, even ignoring the benefit of wisdom of hindsight, and it is not the function of a court when interpreting an agreement to relieve a party from the consequences of his imprudence or poor advice. Accordingly, when interpreting a contract a judge should avoid re-writing it in an attempt to assist an unwise party or to penalise an astute party.

7.66 *Arnold v Britten* suggests we may now have reached a stable compromise, between the very literalist approach of the past and the very interventionist contextual approach ushered in by *West Bromwich*. Lord Hodge certainly thought so in the most recent Supreme Court decision on interpretation, *Wood v Capita Insurance Services Ltd* (2017), which interpreted the wording in an indemnity 'arising out of claims or complaints registered with' various authorities as only being triggered when a claim or complain was actually made. It is very hard to quibble with this interpretation of unambiguous words, but the appellant argued unsuccessfully that this interpretation gave too much weight to the literal words of the agreement and insufficient to the factual matrix, criticising the Supreme Court in *Arnold v Britten* as 'rowing back' from *Rainy Sky*. But for Lord Hodge, this talk of rowing back, of literal v. contextual interpretation, misses the point, because they are not actually in conflict. Interpretation in a *unitary exercise* involving:

> *an iterative process by which each suggested interpretation is checked against the provisions of the contract and its commercial consequences are investigated ....once one has read the language in dispute and the relevant parts of the contract that provide its context, it does not matter whether the more detailed analysis commences with the factual background and the implications of rival constructions or a close examination of the relevant language in the contract, so long as the court balances the indications given by each.*

> *Textualism and contextualism are not conflicting paradigms in a battle for exclusive occupation of the field of contractual interpretation. Rather, the lawyer and the judge, when interpreting any contract, can use them as tools to ascertain the objective meaning of the language which the parties have chosen to express their agreement. The extent to which each tool will assist the court in its task will vary according to the circumstances of the particular agreement or agreements.*

7.67 A final point is worth considering—as can be seen in all the cases just discussed, wherever it is alleged that 'something has gone wrong with the language', it is clear that the distinction between interpretation and rectification is no longer a sharp one. Rectification (see paras **13.72-13.104**) is an equitable remedy that is traditionally used where a written contractual document does not accurately record what the parties 'actually' agreed and is rectified to bring it into line with that agreement. Even taking account of the more overtly cautious approach taken by the courts since *Rainy Sky*, the modern approach to contractual construction since *West Bromwich* has undoubtedly come closer to a broader based examination of what the parties really *meant* by the words they used, rather than what the words they used mean, potentially swallowing up much of the role of rectification.

7.68   Buxton LJ, writing extra-judicially (Buxton (2010)), argues that the present 'uneasy parallel' between the two actions is illogical (since evidence of prior negotiations is inadmissible for interpretation but admissible for rectification), concluding: 'Rectification should in future occupy the whole of the field when it is necessary to correct errors in the formal expression of a contractual consensus.' Certainly, if that is not to happen and interpretation continues to perform a 'rewriting' function closer to the traditional role of rectification, it would be helpful for the courts to consider this shift in emphasis explicitly. For example, the extremely strict tests for rectification (see paras **13.72–13.104**), traditionally justified because the courts recognise that rectification involves rewriting the contract for the parties, are absent in construction actions. Further, rectification is operative only from the date of the court's order, whereas a decision on construction is, by definition, a decision about what the contract has always meant, with corresponding implications for third parties who might have relied on the contract or taken some form of interest in it. For these reasons, as well as the inconsistency in the admissibility of evidence of pre-contractual negotiations and the desirability of being transparent about whether the parties' contract is being judicially rewritten, the current confusion over whether a contract is being 'construed' or 'rectified' is unwelcome. Such issues should be considered openly, not hidden by a broad process of construction. As Davies (2016) concludes, rectification 'is better placed to limit interference with formally agreed written documents—upon which commercial parties should rightly be encouraged to place great weight—and protect third party interests.' It is a great pity, therefore, that the Supreme Court in *Rainy Sky* did not mention rectification at all, despite effectively 'rewriting' the bonds.

Implied terms

7.69   It is extremely common for terms to be *implied* into a contract, sometimes as a result of statute, other times by the courts. It might be thought that it is quite a bold and controversial step for a *court* to insert a term into a contract that the parties did not expressly agree to—after all, it is important for reasons of commercial certainty that the parties can tell what their contractual obligations are without too great a risk of extra terms being added later. This section will explore the circumstances in which contractual terms will be implied and how the process can be justified.

7.70   When a simple oral contract is made, the parties commonly say very little about their obligations beyond the basic subject matter and price. Even in a detailed written contract, it is difficult for the parties to specify an entirely comprehensive regime. If a court is later called upon to resolve a dispute about some aspect of performance not expressly covered by the contract, its approach is *not* to ask what a reasonable way of resolving the dispute would be (or to 'remake the bargain'). It is restricted (in theory anyway) to implying terms *deemed* to have been in the bargain all along. Imagine I phone up a taxi firm and book a taxi for the next morning, to take me to the airport; it is unlikely that anything will have been said about the firm's obligations. But that barest of bargains will be supplemented by a number of implied terms. Statute will imply an obligation on the firm's driver to drive with reasonable care and skill, while the courts would almost certainly conclude, for example, that the driver was in breach of an implied term if he drove at only 10 miles per hour or via the craziest, most indirect route imaginable.

Terms implied by statute

7.71   In practice, statutory implied terms are extremely significant. Statutes frequently imply terms into all contracts of a specified type and this is an efficient way of regulating the terms of important types of contracts and providing protection for specified classes of contractors who might not be in a position to negotiate equivalent protections for themselves. We have already encountered some of the provisions of the Sale of Goods Act 1979 (see para **4.9**), as amended by the Consumer Rights Act 2015 for consumer transactions, which imply important terms about, for example, the quality of the goods, into contracts for the sale of goods made in the course of the seller's business. Equivalent provisions in the Supply of Goods and Services Act 1982 (also amended by the Consumer Rights Act 2015) imply similar terms into, for example, contracts of hire purchase; the same statutes imply the important term into contracts for the provision of business services that the supplier will carry out those services with reasonable care and skill. There are numerous other examples in all sorts of areas, like the Landlord and Tenant Act 1985, which implies landlord's covenants into leases of houses at a low rent that the house is and will be kept fit for human habitation. Many statutory implied terms cannot be ousted even by the contrary agreement of the parties.

Terms implied at common law

7.72   Two general restrictions apply to all forms of common law implied terms. First, any implied term must be sufficiently certain, that is to say, a court will refuse to imply a term which would be insufficiently certain to be enforced had it been an express term (see Chapter 4). It follows from this, as *Wells v Devani* (2016) makes clear, that it is not legitimate, under the guise of implying terms, to make a contract for the parties: 'it is wrong in principle to turn an incomplete bargain into a legally binding contract by adding expressly agreed terms and implied terms together'. Secondly, a term will not be implied where it would be inconsistent with the express terms of the contract. This was described by Lord Neuberger in *Marks & Spencer plc v BNP Paribas Securities Services Trust Co (Jersey) Ltd* (2015) (discussed in detail in paras **7.80-7.86**) as a 'cardinal rule'. For example, in *Holding and Management (Solitaire) Ltd v Ideal Homes North West Ltd* (2004) the court had no hesitation in rejecting a lessee's argument that terms should be implied into a long residential lease, which would have conflicted with its 'clear', 'un-equivocal', and 'unambiguous' express terms.

7.73 Before exploring the tests for common law implied terms, it is worth pausing to notice how useful the device of implying terms can be, when the courts wish to impose some restrictions on unfettered freedom of contract, with great practical and commercial significance. Two topical examples will be briefly mentioned. The first is the use of implied terms to control the exercise of contractual discretion. Many commercial contracts give one party the power to make discretionary decisions or judgments. On the face of the contract, that discretion is absolute, but in several cases, culminating in the Supreme Court decision *Braganza v BP Shipping Ltd* (2015), the courts have been willing to imply a term that the discretion must be exercised in good faith and must not be exercised arbitrarily, capriciously, or irrationally. This includes a specific invocation of good faith, but occasionally judges have been willing to go much further and imply a *general* promise to act in good faith in commercial dealings, for example the obiter suggestion of Leggatt J in *Yam Seng Pte Ltd v International Trade Corp Ltd* (2013). His dictum has proved very controversial, not least because it is a first instance judgment that effectively reverses the default rule in the English law of contract that the parties do not owe each other a general obligation of good faith. This default rule sounds unjustifiable, until you reflect on how it would detract from commercial certainty and that there are numerous individual doctrines that bring in an obligation of good faith in specific situations (see further paras **4.25, 7.36,** and **12.5**). Indeed, the ratio of the decision in *Yam Seng* was the implication of specific terms involving good faith, so the proposed general term was redundant (for a detailed critique, see Carter and Courtney (2016)). For our purposes, these recent developments show how implied terms are central to the common law method of regulating contractual dealings.

7.74 Leaving these topical controversies to one side, we should now consider terms implied by the courts in detail. Common law implied terms can be divided into three categories:

Terms to give effect to trade custom

7.75 Terms may be implied into a contract on the basis of an established usage of a particular market or a particular trade, on the basis that the parties did not bother to spell out in their contract a term which both would have understood as self-evidently regulating their bargain. So, for a term to be implied on this basis, the alleged custom must be certain, notorious (in other words extremely well known in the particular market) and reasonable, all of which were satisfied in *Hutton v Warren* (1836). Terms implied on the basis of trade custom *are* based on the deemed intentions of the parties when contracting, so will not be implied where it would contradict the express terms of the contract (see *Palgrave Brown & Son Ltd v Owners of SS Turid* (1922), where the House of Lords refused to imply a term because the custom was 'absolutely inconsistent' with the express terms).

7.76 In *Garratt v Mirror Group Newspapers Ltd* (2011) the Court of Appeal was prepared to apply the 'certain, notorious and reasonable' test to imply a term based on established practice within a single commercial organisation, rather than a trade or industry, although the same conclusion was also reached by the usual tests for implying a term in fact based on the intentions of the parties.

Terms implied 'in fact' where necessary to give effect to the parties' presumed intentions

7.77 These are terms implied by the courts into *individual* contracts. The focus is on establishing the *presumed intentions* of the parties, judged objectively as ever, by looking at the words used in the contract and the surrounding circumstances. In other words, terms are implied in fact on the basis of what the parties *must have* intended. Because of the emphasis on the presumed intentions of the parties, the court is less likely to imply a term in fact when the contract is detailed, because it is more likely to contain a comprehensive reflection of what the parties intended. More importantly, terms in fact can only be implied where it is *strictly necessary*. However, this principle of 'necessity' is somewhat vague (necessary for what?) and consequently is not always applied in the same way. Indeed, there are a number of different formulations of the 'necessity' test. The Privy Council suggested in *Attorney General of Belize v Belize Telecom Ltd* (2009) that the different formulations are just helpful ways of answering one underlying question of objective contractual interpretation, namely whether the proposed implied term 'would spell out in express words what the instrument, read against the relevant background, would reasonably be understood to mean'. Lord Hoffmann said that the various tests should be regarded as 'a collection of different ways in which judges have tried to express the central idea that the proposed implied term must spell out what the contract actually means, or in which they have explained why they did not think that it did so'. The Supreme Court in *Marks & Spencer* (2015) did not accept that implication of terms involved the same process as construing the express words of a contract (although recognised that both processes were closely related and part of the search for the objective intention of the parties), and thought the traditional formulations continued to be useful in ascertaining when it would be necessary to imply a term.

7.78 The first, the 'business efficacy' test, was adopted in *The Moorcock* (1889), in which Bowen LJ gave the following guidance on the test for implication of terms in fact:

> ... the law is raising an implication from the presumed intention of the parties with the object of giving to the transaction such efficacy as both parties must have intended that at all events it should have. In business transactions such as this, what the law desires to effect by the implication is to give such business efficacy to the transaction as must have been intended at all events by both parties ...

May LJ in *Ilyssia Cia Naviera SA v Bamaodah, The Elli 2* (1985) expressed the test in more modern terms, stating that terms will be implied where necessary 'in order to give business reality to a transaction and to create enforceable obligations between parties who are dealing with one another in circumstances in which one would expect that business reality and those enforceable obligations to exist', and this was applied by the

Court of Appeal in *Stack v Ajar-Tec Ltd* (2015) to imply a term into a contract between the promoters of a company that the director would be paid for his work.

7.79 This 'business efficacy' approach is, deliberately, very restrictive: a term will only be implied if the contract simply would not work without it, from the point of view of the parties' respective commercial positions. Lord Salmond in *Liverpool City Council v Irwin* (1977) phrased it that a term will not be implied unless, without the suggested term, the contract would be 'futile, inefficacious and absurd' or, as Lord Sumption put it in *Marks & Spencer*, would lack 'commercial or practical coherence'.

7.80 In *Marks & Spencer* the defendants were the landlords and the claimant was the tenant of office premises in central London, pursuant to a complex, detailed commercial lease. Basic annual rent of over £1.23m was payable in three-monthly instalments, in advance, in March, June, September, and December. The leasehold term was expressed to last until February 2018, but the lease contained a 'break clause' giving the tenant the option to terminate the lease early, on 24 January 2012. To exercise the break, the tenant had to give the landlord six months' prior written notice, which would only have effect if on the break date there were no arrears of rent; the tenant also had to pay a premium of £919,800. In July 2011 the tenant served a break notice to terminate the lease; as required, it paid its quarterly advance rent on 25 December 2011 and, just before the break date, also paid the premium, so the lease duly expired on 24 January 2012. The tenant later claimed a *refund* of an apportioned part of its advance rent payment, in respect of the period 24 January to 25 March. As there was no express provision in the lease obliging the landlords to pay this apportioned sum, the tenant sought to persuade the court to imply such a term.

7.81 The tenant had some formidable commercial arguments up its sleeve as to why such an implied term would be eminently reasonable, but the Supreme Court emphasised that reasonableness is not the test. The lease was not remotely absurd or unworkable without such a term, so its implication failed the 'business efficacy' test of necessity. As Sir Thomas Bingham MR cautioned in *Philips Electronique Grand Public SA v British Sky Broadcasting Ltd* (1995) 'the court comes to the task of implication with the benefit of hindsight, and it is tempting for the court then to fashion a term which will reflect the merits of the situation as they then appear. Tempting, but wrong.' We will discuss *Marks & Spencer* further in para **7.86.**

7.82 There is a second formulation of the test for implying terms in fact, the 'officious bystander test', which is summed up in Mackinnon LJ's judgment in *Shirlaw v Southern Foundries Ltd* (1939):

> *Prima facie that which in any contract is left to be implied and need not be expressed is something so obvious that it goes without saying; so that, if, while the parties were making their bargain, an officious bystander were to suggest some express provision for it in their agreement, they would testily suppress him with a common, 'Oh, of course!' ...*

This second test is vivid, but somewhat unhelpful, in that it is not clear whether both have to be satisfied, whether it is an alternative to 'business efficacy' or just a practical way of testing it. Lord Neuberger's view in *Marks & Spencer* was that 'business necessity and obviousness can be alternatives in the sense that only one of them need to be satisfied' and this does seem to have been the stance of the courts over the years (though for criticism see Kennedy (2016)). For example, the Court of Appeal in *R Griggs Group v Evans* (2005) implied a term on the 'officious bystander' basis into a logo design contract, holding that it 'goes without saying' that copyright in the logo (for Doc Martens footwear) vested in the Doc Martens company and not the freelance artist who designed it. Notice that the role of this hypothetical officious bystander is not to be the arbiter of *whether* a particular term should be included—it is merely to raise the issue and thus bring to light what the parties understood their contract to mean, even though they had not explicitly spelt it out. (Interestingly, Lord Clarke appears, whether by accident or design, to have enhanced and altered the role of the officious bystander in *Aberdeen City Council v Stewart Milne Group Ltd* (2011), by saying 'If the officious bystander had been asked whether such a term should be implied, he or she would have said "of course".')

7.83   The 'officious bystander' formulation emphasises the parties' presumed intentions at the time of contracting. It is not sufficient for the term to reflect the intentions of only one of the parties—*both* must testily suppress the interfering bystander (see *Spring v National Amalgamated Stevedores and Dockers Society* (1956) where the proposed implied term did not represent the presumed intention of *both* parties, because at the time of contracting the worker would have had no idea what the proposed term was about). But, as Lord Hoffmann made clear in *Attorney General of Belize* it does not prevent the implication of a term into a complicated contract that the meaning of the proposed term was not immediately obvious, so that 'the actual parties might have said to the officious bystander "Could you please explain that again?"'. Nor is it sufficient, as *Dear v Jackson* (2013) makes clear, that if the officious bystander had raised with the parties the absence of the relevant term, this 'would have brought the negotiations to a swift halt'.

7.84   What is the principle lying behind these various tests? As we have seen, Lord Hoffmann's speech in *Attorney General of Belize* set out to demonstrate that the process of implying terms in fact is merely part of the process of contractual construction (on which see paras **7.43-7.68**), of determining the objective intention of the parties and thus what the contract would reasonably be understood to mean, a proposition he regarded as supported by logic 'since the court has no power to alter what the instrument means' as well as by authority. The nub of his view was 'There is only one question: is that what the instrument, read as a whole against the relevant background, would reasonably be understood to mean?' Although Lord Hoffmann's suggested approach was an elegant one and many welcomed it (see Hooley (2014)), others were less certain that interpreting the express words on the page involves the same process as 'reading between the lines' to fill the gaps left by the parties. Earlier authorities treated the two tasks as fundamentally different: in *Philips Electronique* Sir Thomas Bingham MR regarded the task of implying terms as distinct from the task of construing a contract, the former being more intrusive and thus needing stricter constraints. And there are problems of principle too. Of course silence can convey meaning, but where the parties have simply not thought in advance about what should happen, where the risk should lie, in the event of a particular eventuality, it is a little unreal to regard the courts as interpreting the bargain, when a term is later implied, although of course the term implied must be consistent with and fit into the scheme of the express words of the contract, duly interpreted.

7.85 Despite this somewhat unorthodox view of the principle underlying the implication of terms in fact, it is clear on careful reading that Lord Hoffmann was not advocating any practical change in the approach to implying such terms. The problem was not what he actually said, but rather the risk that it might have been misinterpreted: his emphasis on the objectively 'reasonable' interpretation is easy to mistake as a call for the strict test of 'necessity' for implication to be replaced with an unacceptably lax test whereby a term would implied it if would be reasonable. The courts since have been at pains to minimise this risk of interpretation. Immediately after *Attorney General of Belize*, in *Mediterranean Salvage & Towage Ltd v Seamar Trading & Commerce Inc* (2009), the Court of Appeal went out of its way to emphasise that the test for implication of terms had not been watered down. Here, charterers had chartered a ship on a voyage charter and nominated a berth for the ship to load in Lebanon, but the ship's hull was damaged during loading by a hidden underwater projection. The contract made no mention of any obligation on the charterers to ensure that they nominated a safe berth (so prima facie the loss would lie where it fell, with the owners), but the owners argued that such a term should be implied. The Court of Appeal unanimously declined to imply such a term, Lord Clarke MR noting that although Lord Hoffmann's analysis emphasised 'that the process of implication is part of the process of construction of the contract, he is not in any way resiling from the often stated proposition that it must be necessary to imply the proposed term. It is never sufficient that it should be reasonable.' Moreover in *Dear v Jackson* (2013) the Court of Appeal was cautious about the 'construction' approach to implying terms to reflect commercial common sense, pointing out that 'the implication of the terms proposed would involve an impermissible re-writing of the parties' contract or, in other words, would subject them merely to one notion of "what might have been the most sensible solution to the parties' conundrum". That is not a proper basis for implying terms into the Agreement.'

7.86 Subsequently, the Supreme Court has rejected Lord Hoffmann's approach in *Marks & Spencer*, with the majority politely concluding that his 'observations should henceforth be treated as a characteristically inspired discussion rather than authoritative guidance on the law of implied terms.' For Lord Neuberger, Lord Hoffmann's approach 'could obscure the fact that construing the words used and implying additional words are different processes governed by different rules.' And this matters for a reason of logic:

> Until one has decided what the parties have expressly agreed, it is difficult to see how one can set about deciding whether a term should be implied and if so what term ... Further, given that it is a cardinal rule that no term can be implied into a contract if it contradicts an express term, it would seem logically to follow that, until the express

terms of a contract have been construed, it is, at least normally, not sensibly possible to decide whether a further term should be implied.

7.87   The point was explained further by Lord Hodge in *Trump International Golf Club Ltd v Scottish Ministers (Scotland)* (2015):

> *Interpretation is not the same as the implication of terms. Interpretation of the words of a document is the precursor of implication. It forms the context in which the law may have to imply terms into a document, where the court concludes from its interpretation of the words used in the document that it must have been intended that the document would have a certain effect, although the words to give it that effect are absent.*

So it is now tolerably clear that implication of terms is not the same process as interpreting the contract. This raises a number of further questions, such as whether pre-contractual negotiations are admissible for the purpose of implying a term in fact, an issue raised by O'Sullivan (2016a). More fundamentally, is it possible to make such a binary division between the two?

7.88   After all, many cases of interpretation involve the courts making sense of the drafting by reading words into the contract that were not expressly included in it—think of the *Rainy Sky* case. Perhaps this is qualitatively different from implying a new, discrete term (meaning a wholly new promise) that was absent from the original drafting. Yet some judges emphasise that there is a continuum between those sorts of cases; others, like Lord Hodge in *Trump International*, distinguish between 'implying words' and 'implying terms'. It is noteworthy that, when invited to qualify the express exclusion wording in an insurance policy by adding words to it, the Supreme Court in *Impact Funding Solutions Ltd v AIG Europe Insurance Ltd* (2016) declined, citing interpretation principles *and* that the test for implication of terms was not satisfied (see further para **8.34**). All this suggests that *Marks & Spencer* may not be the last word on the inter-relation between interpretation and implication of terms in fact.

Terms implied 'at law' into a defined category of contract

7.89   Here, the issue is whether a term should be implied into *all* contracts of a particular type, unless it is specifically excluded by the terms of the contract. So, for example, when an employment contract between A and B comes before the court, the issue is not whether a term should be implied just into the A–B contract, but whether it should be implied into all contracts of the same type, that is, as an incident of *all* employment contracts (or at least all employment contracts of the same variety as the one before the court). As Lord Denning explained in *Shell UK Ltd v Lostock Garage Ltd* (1976), 'these obligations are not founded on the intentions of the parties, actual or presumed, but on more general considerations'.

7.90   Peden (2001) identifies a number of such general, 'policy' considerations that have influenced the implication of a term in law, which reflect concerns as to how the implied term will sit with the existing law and affect the parties' relationship, as well as wider issues of fairness and society. For example, in *Liverpool City Council v Irwin* (1977) the House of Lords held that a term should be implied at law into leases of council blocks of flats that the landlord covenanted to take reasonable care to keep the common parts of the block in reasonable condition, although such a term would not have satisfied the strict test for implication in fact. This conclusion recognised that the council was best placed to undertake responsibility for the common parts, compared with the individual council tenants, and that it would be fair to require it to do so.

7.91   Similarly, in *Scally v Southern Health and Social Services Board* (1991) an amendment to the Health Services Pension Regulations gave health authority employees a very advantageous right to purchase extra pension entitlement, but the right had to be exercised within 12 months. The authority neglected to publicise the new Regulation or to inform its employees about it, so Dr Scally lost the opportunity to take advantage of the right. He alleged that there was an implied term in his contract of employment that the authority would take reasonable steps to bring such rights to his attention. The House of Lords agreed, but stressed that such a term could not be implied on the business efficacy/officious bystander test:

> A clear distinction is drawn between the search for an implied term necessary to give business efficacy to a particular contract and the search, based on wider considerations, for a term which the law will imply as a necessary incident of a definable category of contractual relationship.

Those wider considerations were essentially reasons of fairness—to protect employees with valuable rights which were useless unless they knew about them, but which they could not be expected to know about unless brought to their attention by their employer. However the decision in *Scally* was very restrictive as to the sort of contract into which such a term would be implied: not contracts of employment generally, but contracts of employment negotiated between employers and a representative body containing a particular term conferring on the employee, acting as required to obtain the benefit, a valuable right contingent, of which he could not be expected to be aware unless the term was brought to his attention. The Court of Appeal in *Crossley v Faithful & Gould Ltd* (2004) subsequently emphasised that the decision in *Scally* does not support a broader implied obligation on employers to take care of employees' financial well-being, a term which would be unfair and unduly onerous for employers.

7.92   Two general points are worth bearing in mind. First, it might be thought that a rough approximation of the courts' approach in these cases is that a term will be implied in law if it is *reasonable*, but the courts have repeatedly stressed that reasonableness alone is *not* the guiding principle: see, for example, Lord Wilberforce in *Liverpool City Council v Irwin*, and Steyn LJ in *The Star Texas* (1993). Indeed, although the basis of implied terms in law is not the same as for implied terms in fact, the current orthodoxy is that, like implied terms in fact, a term will only be implied in law where it is 'necessary': see Lord Bridge in *Scally*. However, given that the courts approach the two sorts of case very differently, with the adoption of an overtly policy-driven approach to implied terms in law, it is confusing that the same language is used for both categories and it would be preferable for the two tests to be phrased differently. Dyson LJ expressed disquiet with the use of the label 'necessary' in the context of terms implied in law in *Crossley*, describing it as 'protean' and 'elusive'.

7.93 Secondly, implied terms in law are inherently more difficult to justify than implied terms in fact, which are simply meant to make the contract better reflect the parties' true agreement. Implied terms in law are not justified by reference to the parties' intentions, but this does not necessarily mean that it is wrong to imply terms in this way. For example, we will see in Chapter 16 that the law imposes obligations on the parties that they have not expressly agreed to following a breach of contract (such as the duty to pay damages), so it is not a fatal objection that implied terms in law are not the reflection of what the parties agreed. But it does mean we should scrutinise the court's quasi-legislative role in these cases with particular care.

Can the distinction between terms implied in fact and terms implied in law be maintained?

7.94 Phang (1993) has suggested that the distinction between the two categories is flawed. He points to the House of Lords' decision in *Scally* as illustrating his point. Terms implied in law are implied into all contracts of a particular type unless specifically excluded, so the first task for the court in deciding whether to imply such a term is to ask what type of contract is before it. In *Scally*, the court defined the type of contract before it in a very precise way, as we have seen.

7.95 Phang (1993) comments that 'by focusing exclusively on the specific fact situation of the case at hand, Lord Bridge has, with respect, wholly done away with whatever semblance of generality the concept of a contract "of a defined type" had in the first place'. However, there may be good reasons for the court to be cautious and define the type of contract in a specific way. As Peden (2001) notes, 'in today's complex society, there is a vast difference between different contracts of a similar general type. For example, the nature of the employment contract of a secretary to a self-employed businesswoman cannot be assimilated with that of a worker in a factory employing several thousand.' But defining the type of contract in such a specific way means that few contracts will be of 'this type', which in turn means that the term is only going to be implied as a necessary incident of a small number of contracts. Since the distinction between terms implied in law and terms implied in fact is meant to be that the latter are only implied into a single contract, as terms are implied in law into fewer contracts the distinction between the two categories becomes ever more fragile.

7.96 Does this mean that implied terms in law should be abandoned altogether? After all, the courts are really only equipped to resolve questions as between the individual parties to litigation, not to decide what terms should be implied into all contracts of a particular type, a legislative-type role arguably best left to Parliament. On the other hand, Peden (2001) (cited with approval in *Crossley*) sees implied terms in law as a useful judicial technique for regulating and ensuring fairness within particular categories of relationship, although recognising that 'it would be appropriate for courts to be more open about the policy issues with which they are wrestling'. It is suggested that the implication of terms in law can be an efficient way given the pressures on parliamentary time, of fleshing out the incidents of (generally) non-commercial contractual relationships, where the parties protected by such implied terms cannot be expected to negotiate such protections for themselves—the development in *Malik v BCCI SA* (1998) of the implied term of mutual trust and confidence in employment contracts is a good illustration.

7.97 Finally, do not overlook that the implication of a term is not the end of the story. In many of the cases discussed earlier (including *Liverpool City Council v Irwin*), having decided that a term was to be implied, the court went on to decide that it had not been *breached*.

OVERVIEW

1 Where one party makes a statement about some aspect of the contractual subject matter, this might be a term of the contract or a mere representation. The distinction matters if the term turns out to be false, because the measure of damages if the statement is a term will put the other party into the position as if the statement had been true, but if it is a mere representation will only restore the other party to the pre-contract position.

2 The classification is based on an objective interpretation of the contract. The courts take into account factors such as the timing and importance of the statement, the relative position of the parties, and whether external verification was encouraged or discouraged.

3 Much of the case law on how terms are incorporated into contracts dates from before legislative controls on unfair terms and should be seen as part of the judicial way of tackling such terms, but it is nonetheless still important. If a contract is signed, the party's signature is usually deemed sufficient to incorporate all the terms in the document. If a contract is not signed but one party is seeking to rely on standard terms and conditions, the question is whether that party took reasonable steps to bring those terms to the other party's attention (not whether the other party read or understood them). Relevant factors include whether there was a prior course of dealing between the parties, timing in relation to the formation of the contract, whether the document was of a contractual type, and whether the term was exceptionally onerous and unusual (in which case a stricter approach to incorporation is taken).

4 When construing what the terms of a written contract mean, the courts were at one time required to focus almost exclusively on the literal words the parties had used. Now, the courts adopt a more purposive approach, seeking to understand the words in the commercial context in which they were used. The modern approach makes the courts more willing to

depart from the strict meaning of the contractual words and look for assistance in outside material and evidence. All relevant background can be used to aid construction, except that there is a controversial exception excluding evidence of the parties' pre-contractual negotiations to construe the final contract. Arguably, this modern approach blurs the distinction between construing and rectifying written contracts, although recently the courts have begun to reaffirm a more traditional, cautious view that unambiguous wording cannot be rewritten under the guise of commercial interpretation.

5   Terms can be implied into contracts in a number of situations. Many statutes add terms to particular types of contract, regardless of the intention of the parties. Indeed many statutory implied terms cannot be ousted by the contrary agreement of the parties. The courts also imply terms, although never if this would conflict with the express terms of the contract. Sometimes this is done to give effect to trade custom, but of more significance are the other two categories of terms implied by the courts.

6   The first is that a term will be implied 'in fact' into just the specific contract before the court, to give effect to the presumed common intention of the parties. The test is a strict one of necessity, though there are various formulations to decide whether the term is necessary in practice (implication and interpretation share a common role, namely to ascertain the parties' intentions, judged objectively, but the suggestion that the two processes are the same has been rejected by the Supreme Court). Second, terms will be implied more generally 'in law' as part of the incidents of a particular category of contract, on more nebulous policy grounds. The distinction between terms implied in law and in fact is not entirely clear-cut and the almost legislative role of the courts in implying terms in law is somewhat controversial.

FURTHER READING

Andrews 'Interpretation of Contracts and "Commercial Common Sense"' (2017) 76 CLJ 36

Buxton 'Construction and Rectification after Chartbrook' (2010) 69 CLJ 253

Davies 'The Meaning of Commercial Contracts' in Davies and Pila (eds) The Jurisprudence of Lord Hoffmann (2015)

Davies 'Rectification versus Interpretation' (2016) 75 CLJ 62

Leggatt 'Making Sense of Contracts: the Rational Choice Theory' (2015) 131 LQR 454

McCaughran 'Implied Terms: the Journey of the Man on the Clapham Omnibus' (2011) CLJ 607

Morgan Great Debates in Contract Law (2015) Chapter 4

Nicholls 'My Kingdom for a Horse: The Meaning of Words' (2005) 121 LQR 577

O'Sullivan 'Silence is Golden: Implied Terms in the Supreme Court' (2016) 75 CLJ 199

Peden 'Policy Concerns Behind Implication of Terms in Law' (2001) 117 LQR 459

Staughton 'How Do the Courts Interpret Commercial Contracts?' (1999) 58 CLJ 303

SELF-TEST QUESTIONS

1   Why does the categorisation of a statement as either a term of the contract or a mere representation matter?

2   What is the difference between a term implied 'in fact' and 'in law'?

3   How do the courts decide whether a term has been incorporated into (a) signed, and (b) an unsigned contract?

4   Why can a court consider some background matters but not others when construing the meaning of a written contract?

5   Gerald's Gardens Ltd (GG) is a small garden landscaping business owned and run by Gerald. GG is commissioned to do a landscaping job that requires a lot of earth to be moved, so must hire a digger from Hodulike Ltd, a tool-hire company with which GG has an account and has dealt before. Gerald visits Hodulike's showroom and selects a suitable digger, which is then reserved on the computer by Hodulike's receptionist for hire by GG for three days from the following Monday, for a price of £800. No terms and conditions are drawn to Gerald's attention, but on the wall of the showroom there is a large notice displaying Hodulike's 'Standard conditions of hire', some of which are printed in red, which Gerald does not see. The following Monday the digger is delivered to GG's premises and Gerald signs a receipt, which has a copy of Hodulike's standard conditions of hire printed on the back. That night, the digger is stolen from GG's premises and cannot be traced. Gerald has just been told that one of the terms of the standard conditions of hire is as follows: 'Hirer must insure equipment for full value' and that Hodulike are demanding £20,000 as the replacement cost of the digger. Gerald is furious, since he is adamant that he did not agree to this clause. Advise GG.

 For hints on how to answer question 5, please see the online resources at **www.oup.com/uk/sullivan8e/**.

8

Terms of the contract II: common law and statutory controls on unfair terms

SUMMARY

This chapter deals with the law's response to exemption clauses and other unfair terms. The common law traditionally regulated such terms by strict rules of construction: these rules are less significant today, though still relevant. Nowadays there are also statutory controls. The Unfair Contract Terms Act 1977 prohibits some types of exemption clause altogether and subjects others to a requirement of reasonableness, though it now catches only non-consumer contracts. More significantly, the Consumer Rights Act 2015 imposes a test of fairness on all terms in consumer contracts, other than the 'core terms' of price and main subject matter.

8.1 We have already encountered a number of cases involving 'exemption' or 'exclusion' clauses, in which one party purports to exclude or limit his liability to the other party for failure to perform or defective performance. Students tend to regard such clauses as necessarily a 'bad thing', but the reality is more complex. Contractual dealings between business parties would be extremely difficult without exclusion and limitation clauses, because they enable one party's liability to be capped at a level that makes it viable for him to contract at all or at a realistic price, while making clear the extent of the risk that the other party is undertaking (enabling him to protect himself in other ways, such as by taking out insurance). Even where consumers are involved, exclusion clauses are not unwelcome per se. For example, the economy end of the package holiday industry makes extensive use of exclusion clauses to provide a pared down, but correspondingly cheaper, level of contractual protections (though see para **8.72**).

8.2 However, particularly where consumers are involved, there is a risk that exclusion clauses will be used in a manner which exploits the inferior bargaining position of the other party in a wholly unreasonable way. Part of the concern is that such clauses tend to be tucked into the small print of standard form contracts and not drawn to the other party's attention; also, more substantively, that they can cut down the contractor's liability to such an extent that the consumer's contractual expectations are rendered worthless, leaving him with no meaningful redress. Initially, the courts developed a number of doctrines to meet these concerns; in 1977, Parliament intervened and passed the Unfair Contract Terms Act ('UCTA') to regulate exclusion clauses in certain areas (now confined to non-consumer contracts and notices); finally, we now have a more general consumer protection regime for controlling unfair terms, the Consumer Rights Act 2015 ('CRA').

8.3   These legislative developments have greatly reduced the significance of the common law rules, but they are still relevant. Some contracts are not caught by the legislative regimes (though it can plausibly be argued that the legislation catches all contracts deserving of protection, such that the common law need not worry about those, invariably commercial, contracts falling outside). More importantly, the courts still *begin* with the common law rules, before moving on to consider whether the legislation applies, so you must do the same.

8.4   A final word of warning: do not overlook, before considering whether an exclusion clause is effective, that it is essential as a matter of logic (and good technique) to consider first whether the defendant *would have been liable* in the absence of the exclusion clause. Sometimes this is straightforward, as where the contractor negligently causes personal injury or property damage (so that he would ordinarily be liable in tort) or where he breaches an express term of the contract. But commonly, you will need to consider whether the contractor is in breach of an *implied term*—after all, exclusion clauses are usually found in standard forms drafted by the contractor, which may very well spell out very little about the contractor's obligations. Only when you have discussed whether the contractor would have been liable in the *absence* of the exclusion clause, is it meaningful to go on and consider the impact of the clause itself.

8.5   We have already considered the rules of incorporation of terms, which (at least before 1977) were an important common law device for controlling exclusion clauses (see paras **7.18-7.39**): if the clause was not incorporated into the contract, there was no way it could exclude liability. Assuming then that the relevant clause has been incorporated into the contract, the other significant common law control was a series of strict legal rules of *construction* of exclusion clauses. If the court could conclude that the clause, when properly interpreted, did not *cover* the contractor's liability, then the clause was ineffective to exclude that liability.

Common law principles of construction/interpretation

8.6   In Chapter 7, we saw that the modern approach to construing written contracts is to move away from a literal interpretation of the words used, aided by legalistic rules of construction, towards an examination of the commercial context and background to discover what the parties meant to say. In *West Bromwich* Lord Hoffmann said, 'Almost all the old intellectual baggage of "legal" interpretation has been discarded', by which he meant to include the traditional common law rules for construing exclusion clauses (although as Lord Phillips said wryly in *The Tychy (No 2)* (2001) 'a little intellectual hand luggage is no bad thing when construing a contract'). So the current status of these rules is not entirely certain. It is true that, before UCTA, the rules were frequently invoked to justify extremely artificial interpretations of exclusion clauses in order to protect the other party, by deciding that the clause did not cover the contractor's liability when on the natural meaning of the words it plainly did. Lord Hoffmann may simply have been intending to point out that, since UCTA, the courts no longer have any need for this sort of artificial approach to construction and have, as you will see, rejected it. However, to say that courts no longer *distort* the rules of construction is not quite the same as saying that the rules have been discarded altogether. It seems that the courts are not taking Lord Hoffmann's *obiter* remark quite this far; they simply do not need to have recourse to the traditional common law rules to resolve problems of interpretation as often as before, because the contextual approach to interpretation can be used to resolve many of those problems. The following rules should therefore be viewed with caution, in that light.

Ambiguous clauses are construed *'contra proferentem'*

8.7 This principle (which applies generally, though most commonly to exclusion clauses) means that the clause is construed against the interests of the person seeking to rely on it, so any ambiguity is resolved in favour of the person who would otherwise be bound by it. Before UCTA, the courts managed to find ambiguity where none really existed and construed the clause, most artificially, so that it did not cover the contractor's liability. For example, in *Webster v Higgin* (1948), a sale contract contained what looked like a very thorough exclusion clause which said 'no warranty, condition, description or representation … is given or implied', but the court still managed to find ambiguity in the use of the present tense, concluding that the clause did not catch oral warranties given *before* the contract was made. The Court of Appeal in *KG Bominflot Bunkergesellschaft v Petroplus Marketing AG* (2010) took a similar approach, despite *West Bromwich*'s more flexible, contextual approach to contractual construction. The case involved a contract for the sale of a cargo of gasoil, which contained the following clause: 'There are no guarantees, warranties or representations, express or implied' about the merchantability or fitness for purpose of the gasoil. Although the court expressed sympathy with the argument that, taking the modern contextual approach to construction, it was clear that this clause was intended to catch the implied conditions in the Sale of Goods Act, nonetheless there has been a judicial consensus for many years that the word 'conditions' should be used in order to exclude them and it is important to preserve certainty of this kind in commercial law. Nonetheless, this is merely the almost-invariable result of applying a strong presumption, not a rigid rule of law, according to Cooke J in *Air Transworld Ltd v Bombardier Inc* (2012) concerning an aircraft purchase agreement. Here the words used were explicit and unambiguous (providing that the purchaser's statutory rights and remedies were replaced by the terms in the agreement), and thus susceptible to only one meaning—that the Sale of Goods Act implied conditions were excluded.

8.8 The *contra proferentem* principle is still used today—for example it was applied by the Court of Appeal to construe an ambiguous clause in an insurance contract in favour of the insured in *Pratt v Aigaion* (2008)—though only where there is genuine ambiguity in the wording of a clause and not as an excuse for reading the words in an artificial way. Since *West Bromwich*, the courts are more likely to be able to choose between possible alternatives by a consideration of the 'factual matrix' and thus to conclude that there is no ambiguity requiring the *contra proferentem* rule in the first place. As the Court of Appeal said in *Direct Travel v McGeown* (2003): 'Too early recourse to the *contra proferentem* rule runs the danger of "creating" ambiguity where there is none.' The courts certainly do not look kindly on sophisticated commercial parties, who were professionally advised when the contract was drafted, invoking the *contra proferentem* principle in an effort to escape a clear allocation of risk by means of an exclusion clause. One such unsuccessful attempt was *Transocean Drilling UK Ltd v Providence Resources plc* (2016), where a negotiated clause excluded liability for certain types of consequential loss. Moore-Bick LJ pointed out the parties' equality of bargaining position and the importance of freedom of contract, stating that the *contra proferentem* principle does not, 'provide sufficient justification for overriding the parties' intention where that has been clearly expressed'. Likewise invoking the *contra proferentem* rule could not 'rescue' the commercial claimants in *Persimmon Homes Ltd v Ove Arup & Partners Ltd* (2016), since the meaning of the clause was clear and unambiguous.

8.9 Nonetheless the principle has intuitive appeal and the courts continue to insist that if a contractor wishes to cut down or exclude what would otherwise be his liability under a contract, he must use clear, explicit words (see *William Hare Ltd v Shepherd* (2010) where Waller LJ cited Lord Bingham in *Dairy Containers Ltd v Tasman Orient Line CV* (2004) that 'if a party otherwise liable is to exclude or limit his liability … he must do so in clear words; unclear words do not suffice; any ambiguity or lack of clarity must be resolved against that party'). The Court of Appeal in *The Hut Group Lt v Nobahar-Cookson* (2016) preferred to explain the principle, not as a mechanistic one applicable wherever there is ambiguity, but as part of the broader search for what the parties must be taken to have intended:

> Ambiguity in an exclusion clause may have to be resolved by a narrow construction because an exclusion clause cuts down or detracts from the ambit of some important obligation in a contract, or a remedy conferred by the general law such as (in the present case) an obligation to give effect to a contractual warranty by paying compensation for breach of it. The parties are not lightly to be taken to have intended to cut down the remedies which the law provides for breach of important contractual obligations without using clear words having that effect.

8.10 Notice finally that, although *contra proferentem* is a common law rule, an equivalent principle is embodied in s 69(1) of the CRA that 'if a term in a consumer contract, or a consumer notice, could have different meanings, the meaning that is most favourable to the consumer is to prevail' (see para **8.66**).

Exclusion of liability for fundamental breach?

8.11 As has been mentioned already (para **7.34**) Lord Denning MR was the principal player in judicial efforts to control the unfair use of exclusion clauses. During the 1960s and 1970s, he 'discovered' and systematically applied a supposed rule that it was impossible, as a matter of law, to exclude liability for fundamental breach. There were a number of problems with this. First, 'fundamental breach' was not a precise term of art (it did not, for example, mean the same as breach of a condition or serious breach of an innominate term). Second, although Lord Denning's motivation was to protect consumers, the doctrine was not so restricted and when applied to commercial transactions negotiated at arm's length, it was liable to upset perfectly fair bargains for the reasonable allocation of contractual risks.

8.12 Following the enactment of UCTA, there was no longer any justification for Lord Denning's doctrine and it was roundly rejected by the House of Lords in *Photo Production Ltd v Securicor Transport Ltd* (1980), who concluded that there is no rule of law that liability for fundamental breach can never be excluded. In its place, we have a common sense principle of construction that, the more serious the breach, the clearer the words needed to exclude it, but if sufficiently clear words are used, the courts will give effect to them (safe in the knowledge that legislation will now protect deserving parties from unreasonable exclusion clauses).

8.13 In *Photo Production*, a security guard, employed by S to guard PP's factory, lit some boxes to warm his hands; the fire got out of control and burnt the factory down. PP sued S (as his employer), but S pointed to an exclusion clause in its contract, which provided that S was 'under no circumstances' to be liable for the acts of their own employees, unless S as employer could 'by the exercise of due diligence' have prevented it. In other words, S was trying to exclude vicarious liability for acts of its employees and was only accepting responsibility if it was 'personally' at fault, such as by hiring someone with a record of arson. PP retorted that the clause was an attempt to exclude liability for a fundamental breach (ie, burning down the factory instead of guarding it) and as such ineffective. The House of Lords disagreed and applied the clause literally, exempting S from liability, since there is no rule of law that liability for fundamental breach can never be excluded. Here, despite the seriousness of the breach, clear enough words had been used to exclude S's vicarious liability.

8.14 A number of points can be made about this case. First, its overruling of the 'fundamental breach' line of cases is uncontroversial but its conclusion that, on the facts, the words of the clause were clear enough to exclude liability, deserves some explanation. Lord Wilberforce stressed that the parties were in equal bargaining positions, that S was making a very modest charge (about 25 pence a visit) and that PP was better placed to insure the factory against fire damage. The contract was a fair commercial exchange in a competitive market and the court should not interfere with it—PP got the contractual protection it paid for. This is not obviously relevant to the question of whether the *words* used were clear enough, but is best seen as a backlash against Lord Denning's doctrine with its potential to unsettle too many commercial bargains. As Lord Toulson said in *Impact Funding Solutions Ltd v AIG Europe Insurance Ltd* (2016), *Photo Production* 'is authority that business people capable of looking after their own affairs should be free between themselves to apportion risks as they choose'.

8.15 Secondly, it is worth noting that the facts of *Photo Production* occurred before UCTA came into force, but the House of Lords' decision was afterwards. If the facts had occurred slightly later, S would have been obliged to demonstrate that the clause was reasonable under UCTA and, indeed, the House of Lords' reasoning was more obviously relevant to this issue (see Adams and Brownsword (1988)). Third, since *Photo Production,* the courts have not invariably adopted quite such a robust attitude towards exclusion clauses even in commercial contracts, and occasionally still decide that clear enough words have not been used to exclude particularly serious breaches (see for example *The Chanda* (1989)). In particular, the courts remain reluctant to accept a construction which leaves the contractor promising nothing and with no meaningful obligations. For example, in *Tor Line v Alltrans Group (The TFL Prosperity)* (1984) the House of Lords held that a clause in a charterparty of a ferry, which purported to exclude the shipowner's liability for 'damage whatsoever and howsoever caused', did not cover *financial* loss suffered by the charterers because of the shipowner's breach of a warranty concerning the size of the ferry. To construe 'damage' this broadly would mean, as Lord Roskill pointed out, that:

> the charter virtually ceases to be a contract ... and becomes no more than a statement of intent by the owners, in return for which the charterers are obliged to pay large sums by way of hire.

In other words, the contract has to impose some obligations on both sides. If, read literally, the exemption clause essentially empties one side's obligations of all effect, rendering the party's apparent obligation no more than a statement of intent, the courts will reject that interpretation and will aim to find a narrower one (see also Flaux J in *Astrazeneca UK Ltd v Albemarle International Corporation* (2011) applying Lord Roskill's dictum). The reasoning and result in *Photo Production* were consistent with this since, as Lord Diplock pointed out, in *Photo Production* there was, even on a literal construction of the clause, *some* obligation on S: they could not supply a guard they ought reasonably to have known was an arsonist.

Attempts to exclude liability for negligence

8.16 Contractual liability is usually 'strict', in the sense that the contracting party is undertaking to do something not just to take reasonable care in doing it, and so it is usually this 'strict liability' which the party relying on an exemption clause is trying to exclude. The courts are traditionally hostile to attempts to go further and exclude liability for negligence, and are reluctant to construe exclusion clauses to cover negligence, unless very clear words have been used. Guidelines can be found in the Privy Council decision in *Canada Steamship Lines Ltd v The King* (1952), which concerned an exclusion clause in a lease, which did not mention negligence explicitly, but merely said that the tenant 'shall not have any claim … for damage to goods' in the warehouse. The Privy Council held that this clause did not cover liability for *negligent* damage to goods on the premises. After all, it would have been easy to insert a reference to negligence in the clause, so its absence strongly suggested that the parties had not intended negligence liability to be excluded. In the course of its opinion, the Privy Council laid out three guidelines, which can be summarised as follows:

8.17 *First guideline*: if the clause expressly refers to negligence (or a synonym, such as 'liability for breach of a duty of care'), this presents no particular difficulty and the courts will give effect to the clause. For example, in *Monarch Airlines v London Luton Airport Ltd* (1998), a plane was damaged during take-off by defective paving on the airport runway. The airline sued and the airport sought to rely on a clause in its contract with the airline excluding liability:

> for any loss or damage to the aircraft … occurring while the aircraft is in the course of taking off … arising or resulting … from any act, omission, neglect or default on the part of the airport company or its servants or agents unless done with intent to cause damage or recklessly and with knowledge that damage would probably result.

The court held that these words made it perfectly clear that the airport was only accepting liability for damage caused intentionally or recklessly and that the words 'neglect or default' meant precisely the same as negligence. So the clause excluded any liability for the negligence of the airport or its employees, as a matter of construction. (The court went on to consider whether the clause was reasonable under UCTA—see para **8.47**.)

8.18 *Second and third guidelines*: if negligence is not expressly referred to, the court considers whether the ordinary meaning of the words is wide enough to cover negligence *but*, crucially, if the contractor could be liable on some other basis as well as negligence, the clause will be interpreted so as not to exclude liability for negligence. For example, where a contractor is liable strictly *and* in negligence, the presumption is that the negligence liability is not being excluded (see *The Emmanuel C* (1983) where a clause exempting a shipowner from 'errors of navigation' was held not to cover negligent errors). In some cases, the second and third guidelines can pull in opposite directions, since drafting a clause wide enough to cover negligence risks catching some other form of liability as well, thereby ousting negligence from the ambit of the clause. This is unsatisfactory, although the dilemma can be avoided by the draftsman by using the word 'negligence' or equivalent, thus falling within the first guideline.

8.19 If on the other hand the words could only conceivably cover negligence (because the contractor is only liable to take reasonable care), logic would suggest that the clause *must* exclude liability for negligence (otherwise it would be meaningless) and this logical construction has occasionally been adopted (see for example *Alderslade v Hendon Laundry* (1945)). However, in practice, the courts have tended to resist this powerful argument and to insist that clear words must be used to exclude liability in negligence even where there is no other sort of liability potentially covered by the clause. One explanation is that, particularly in cases before UCTA, the courts preferred to be illogical than unfair.

8.20 For example, in *Olley v Marlborough Court Ltd* (1949) (see para **7.30**) the Court of Appeal did not stop at their conclusion that the notice exempting the hotel from liability for theft of customers' belongings was not incorporated in the contract, but went on to consider whether, if it had been incorporated, it would have exempted the hotel for a theft caused by its negligence. The Court of Appeal pondered whether the hotel would have been under strict liability as a common innkeeper, but even if not, held that the notice would not have exempted it from liability. As Lord Denning said:

> Ample content can be given to the notice by construing it as a warning that the hotel is not liable in the absence of negligence ... It is unnecessary to go further and to construe the notice as a contractual exemption of the hotel company from their common law liability in negligence.

8.21 Similar reasoning was used in *Hollier v Rambler Motors* (1972), where a clause said that a garage was 'not responsible for damage caused by fire to customers' cars on the premises'. In fact, the garage would not be liable in the first place for damaging customers' cars unless it was negligent, so logic would suggest that the clause can only have been referring to negligence liability. But the court disagreed, pointing out that a non-lawyer might *think* there was liability without negligence, and interpreted the clause as a mere 'statement of fact in the nature of a warning' that there was no strict liability for fire.

8.22 Of course, both *Olley* and *Hollier* pre-date UCTA (as amended by the CRA). Today, attempts to exclude liability in negligence for damage to or loss of property must pass the statutory tests of reasonableness (for non-consumer contracts) and fairness (for consumer contracts), so there is far less incentive for the courts to strain the construction of clauses and notices to prevent them covering negligence. The House of Lords made the same point in *HIH Casualty and General Insurance Ltd v Chase Manhattan Bank* (2004), emphasising that post-UCTA and *West Bromwich* the *Canada Steamship* guidelines should not be applied mechanistically. As Lord Hoffmann explained:

> The question, as it seems to me, is whether the language used by the parties, construed in the context of the whole instrument and against the admissible background, leads to the conclusion that they must have thought it went without saying that the words, although literally wide enough to cover negligence, did not do so.

8.23 This flexibility in interpreting clauses excluding liability for negligence is to be welcomed, since it subjects such clauses to the same contextual approach to construction used for all other contractual terms. Indeed in *MIR Steel UK Ltd v Morris* (2012) the Court of Appeal took a further step away from reliance on *Canada Steamship*, in accepting that an exclusion clause, properly construed, excluded any liability the defendants might have under the *intentional* economic torts, despite those torts not being expressly mentioned.

The facts were exceptional—the defendants were administrators from whom the claimant had bought the assets of a business, in full knowledge of a dispute about ownership of some of those assets and thus of the risk of potential tortious liability, so the whole point of the relevant clause was to protect the administrators against attempts by the claimant to pass that risk back to them. Nonetheless, the court's attitude to *Canada Steamship* was instructive—nowadays the guidelines are no more than a starting point and 'do not provide an automatic solution to any particular case'. Likewise in *Greenwich Millenium Village Ltd v Essex Services Group plc* (2014) Jackson LJ emphasised that the *Canada Steamship* guidelines are ultimately based upon the presumed intention of the parties and so, in applying them 'the court must have regard to the commercial context of the contract under consideration', concluding that, for clear commercial reasons, the correct interpretation of an indemnity clause in a complex building contract was that it covered negligent breaches.

Legislative controls on unfair terms

8.24 The enactment of UCTA was the single most significant event in the English law of contract in the twentieth century. Although earlier legislation had allowed the courts to invalidate exclusion clauses in very specific situations, UCTA was the first general regime giving judges the power to interfere with certain terms of a contract because they are substantively unreasonable. Some parts of UCTA were designed to protect consumers, but other provisions extended to some business transactions. Then, some years after UCTA was enacted, the European Community issued a Directive (93/13/EEC) on Unfair Terms in Consumer Contracts ('the Directive'), part of its commitment to a free market and intended to harmonise the domestic rules relating to unfair terms in consumer contracts in different legal systems in the Community.

8.25 The UK faced two main problems in implementing the Directive. First, its provisions overlapped with UCTA, but were in some respects significantly different (wider in some places, narrower in others). Secondly, the Directive used concepts not generally found in English contract law ('good faith' in particular) and was drafted in an unfamiliar style (general and aspirational, not in precise statutory words). Ducking these difficulties, Parliament decided to reproduce the wording of the Directive as a Statutory Instrument, the first in 1994, later replaced with the Unfair Terms in Consumer Contracts Regulations 1999, leaving UCTA in place as well. The two parallel, overlapping regimes coexisted rather awkwardly, a situation that was unsatisfactory in principle and confusing in practice. Following a Law Commission Report in 2005 *Unfair Terms in Contracts* (Law Com No 292), and a further consultation paper in 2013 *Unfair Terms in Consumer Contracts: Advice to the Department for Business, Innovation and Skills*, there has been a major legislative reform of this area, in the form of the enactment of the CRA, which came into force on 1 October 2015. The CRA replaced the Unfair Terms in Consumer Contracts Regulations 1999 (which have been repealed) and significantly amended UCTA.

8.26   Although it may appear complicated at first glance, the new regime is actually significantly simpler than what went before, because it is based on a clear-cut, logical division. The CRA deals exclusively with *consumer* contracts, while UCTA now covers only *non-consumer* contracts. This means that the logical and essential first step in dealing with any question of this kind is to determine which piece of legislation governs it, which means deciding whether you are dealing with a consumer situation or a non-consumer situation (happily, the two Acts adopt identical definitions).

8.27   According to s 61 of the CRA, a 'consumer contract' is defined in s 61(1) as a 'contract between a trader and a consumer'. In turn, 'trader' and 'consumer' are defined in s 2 of the CRA as follows:

> *(2) "Trader" means a person acting for purposes relating to that person's trade, business, craft or profession, whether acting personally or through another person acting in the trader's name or on the trader's behalf.*
>
> *(3) "Consumer" means an individual acting for purposes that are wholly or mainly outside that individual's trade, business, craft or profession.*
>
> *(4) A trader claiming that an individual was not acting for purposes wholly or mainly outside the individual's trade, business, craft or profession must prove it.*

8.28   The first thing to notice about this definition is that it concerns both parties—there must be a trader (acting for purposes *relating to* his trade, business, craft, or profession) on one side, and a consumer (acting for purposes *wholly or mainly outside* his trade, business, craft, or profession) on the other side. In the 'trader' definition, what does 'relating to' mean? It seems likely that this meaning extends beyond transactions which are an 'integral' or 'regular' part of the trader's trade, business, craft, or profession (as the test used to be in UCTA, see *R & B Custom Brokers v United Dominions Trust* (1988)), so as to catch transactions that are incidental to (but still connected with) the trade, business, craft, or profession. This would enhance consumer protection and reflect the interpretation of the phrase 'in the course of a business' from the Sale of Goods Act in cases such as *Stevenson v Rogers* (1999), where the sale by a fisherman of his fishing boat was held to be a sale 'in the course of his business' even though the sale of boats was incidental to his business, not his main or regular trade: it was after all a sale by a businessman of his one business asset. So nowadays, the same transaction would almost certainly be treated as the fisherman acting for purposes 'relating to' his business under the CRA definition.

8.29   So far as the definition of a 'consumer' is concerned, it is vital to remember that only an 'individual'—ie, a human being—can count as a consumer. So any contract made by a *company*, even if it is a tiny, one-man-band company with no bargaining strength contracting in a field it knows nothing about, nonetheless counts as a non-consumer contract falling under UCTA, not the greater protection of the CRA. The Law Commission's 2005 Report had proposed an intermediate category of protection for very small businesses, but this was subsequently abandoned. Secondly, notice that to count as a consumer, the individual needs to be acting for purposes that are wholly or *mainly* outside his or her trade, business, craft or profession, so the CRA may in appropriate cases protect someone who entered into a contract for a mixture of business and personal reasons.

Once you have decided whether you are dealing with a consumer or a non-consumer contract, you can proceed to apply the right statute.

Non-consumer contracts: the Unfair Contract Terms Act 1977

Introductory points

8.30   The drafting of UCTA is not entirely straightforward, but certain basic points can be made about its scheme. First, its name is misleading, being both too broad and too narrow. It is too broad, because UCTA does not deal with *all* 'unfair contract terms' in non-consumer contracts, only terms which exclude or limit liability (subject to anti-avoidance provisions, discussed at para 8.31). It is also too narrow, because it is not confined to exclusion and limitation provisions in *contracts*, but covers attempts to exclude or limit non-contractual liability as well, such as notices excluding or restricting tort liability for negligence. Secondly, several important sorts of contracts are outside the ambit of UCTA altogether. These are listed in Sch 1, and include insurance contracts, contracts for the sale of land, contracts dealing with intellectual property and in shares; likewise international supply contracts (defined in s 26 and considered in *Air Transworld Ltd v Bombardier Inc* (2012)) and trustee exemption clauses in trust deeds (see *Baker v JE Clark & Co* (2006)) are not within the scope of UCTA. Thirdly, the principal sections only apply to attempts to exclude or limit 'business liability', which is defined in s 1(3) as 'liability arising from things done in the course of a business or from the occupation of premises used for business purposes of the occupier' (the upshot is that *neither* statutory regime offers any protection in wholly non-business transactions, as where a consumer contracts with another consumer).

8.31   Fourthly, there are 'anti-avoidance provisions' contained in s 13(1). If UCTA only caught clauses expressly worded to exclude or limit liability, it would be an easy matter for a draftsman to reach the same substantive result using a different form of words and thus avoid the effect of the Act. So s 13(1) provides that, to the extent UCTA prevents exclusion of liability, it also prevents (a) making liability or its enforcement subject to onerous conditions (for example, providing that the claimant must give notice of a claim within 24 hours); (b) excluding or restricting any right or remedy (for example, providing that no damages shall be payable for breach of a particular provision); or (c) excluding or restricting rules of evidence or procedure. It goes on to add, 'and (to that extent) sections 2, 6 and 7 also prevent excluding or restricting liability by reference to terms and notices which exclude or restrict the relevant obligation or duty'.

8.32 This subsection has been interpreted extremely broadly. In *Stewart Gill Ltd v Horatio Myer & Co Ltd* (1992) Gill (the Company) contracted to supply an overhead conveyor system to Myer (the Customer). Payment was to be made in stages, with the final 10 per cent payable on completion of the work. Myer withheld the final 10 per cent because it alleged defects in the work, so Gill sued for the final stage, relying on a (very common) term in the contract, which provided that:

> The Customer shall not be entitled to withhold any payment ... by reason of any payment, credit, set off, counterclaim, allegation of incorrect or defective goods, or for any other reason whatsoever ...

However, the Court of Appeal held that, although in form not an exclusion clause, this term fell within s 13(1), in particular part (b), because it excluded a right or remedy (the right to set off) which the customer would otherwise have had. Moreover, the clause was unreasonable, not necessarily on the particular facts but because of its potential to catch all instances in which a customer might justifiably be entitled to exercise a right of set-off (see paras **8.45–8.51** on how reasonableness is tested).

8.33 A clause restricting the right of set-off is common and useful in business transactions, but its use is now likely to be challenged as unreasonable. This decision has far-reaching implications. For example, a clause providing for payment in advance might now be interpreted as excluding the purchaser's usual 'remedy' of not paying until goods are received and thus will be caught by UCTA.

8.34 It is also worth noticing the final part of s 13(1), which states that ss 2, 6, and 7 also prevent excluding or restricting liability by reference to terms and notices which exclude or restrict the relevant obligation or duty. It is usual to think of exclusion clauses and notices as defensive; in other words, they operate as a defence to exclude a liability which would otherwise exist. But what about clauses or notices that purport to prevent a duty existing, and thus liability arising, in the first place? The final part of s 13(1) suggests that they would be covered by UCTA as well (a view endorsed by Lord Jauncey in *Smith v Eric S Bush* (1989)). However, it is unclear how widely these words should be interpreted. *Smith* involved an attempt by a surveyor engaged by the mortgagee to disclaim any duty of care in tort to the purchaser (see further para **8.47**), but could a surveyor, for example, restrict the extent of his duty to his client by stating, 'I will not be checking the roof or the wiring', without engaging UCTA? It seems unlikely that Parliament intended UCTA to apply here. In the Supreme Court case of *Impact Funding Solutions Ltd v AIG Europe Ltd* (2016), which did not directly concern UCTA but which concerned the interpretation of wording excluding certain situations from the coverage of an insurance policy, Lord Toulson noted the Law Commission's view in the report preceding UCTA: 'If a decorator agrees to paint the outside woodwork of a house except the garage doors, no-one can seriously regard the words of exception as anything but a convenient way of defining the obligation'. Nonetheless there does remain some ambiguity at the heart of the legislation, though notice that, in any event, the facts of *Smith* involved a consumer transaction, which would nowadays be outside the UCTA regime and caught by the CRA.

8.35 Finally, the basic map of UCTA is that most sorts of terms are ineffective *unless* the person seeking to rely on the term proves it is *reasonable*, but one sort of term is objectionable for public policy reasons and is therefore rendered *automatically* ineffective.

Clauses excluding liability for negligently causing death or personal injury–automatically ineffective

8.36 UCTA provides that one important category of liability can *never* be excluded, namely liability in negligence for causing death or personal injury (s 2(1) of UCTA), and indeed precisely the same applies under the CRA. Many of the common law cases on the incorporation and construction of terms (such as *Thompson* (see para **7.25**) and *Chapelton* (see para **7.33**)) would today be decided differently as a result. This prohibition applies equally to claims in tort (so that, where UCTA applies, it is no longer possible to rely on a notice excluding liability for breach of the Occupiers' Liability Act 1957 causing death or personal injury) as well as for breach of contractual terms.

Clauses subject to a requirement of reasonableness

Which clauses are subject to this requirement?

8.37 UCTA imposes a test of reasonableness on a number of clauses, of which the three most significant will be considered (although notice that the same test is applied by s 3 of the Misrepresentation Act 1967 to clauses purporting to exclude liability for misrepresentation, on which see para **9.80**).

8.38 First, s 2(2) subjects clauses which exclude liability in negligence for other sorts of losses apart from death or personal injury (in other words for property damage and pure economic loss) to a requirement of reasonableness. Secondly, clauses which exclude liability for selling or otherwise supplying defective goods or services to non-consumers are also, by ss 6 and 7, only effective insofar as they are reasonable.

8.39 The third category to consider is that, where one party makes a contract on the other party's *written standard terms of business,* then any clause purporting to exclude or restrict *liability for breach of contract* is subject to the test of reasonableness (s 3 of UCTA). So even where the party subject to the term is a large corporation, somewhat surprisingly it obtains the benefit of UCTA if it deals on the other party's written standard terms of business.

8.40 For this reason, the courts have tended to be quite demanding about what it means to deal on the other party's 'written standard terms of business'. In *British Fermentation Products v Compair Reavell* (1999) a contract between two commercial parties was made subject to the 'Institute of Mechanical Engineers Model Form of Contract General Conditions'. The court held that these terms, though plainly written and standard, were not the *defendants'* written standard terms of business, since the defendants did not 'invariably or usually use the model form'. Likewise in *Keen v Commerzbank AG* (2006) the Court of

Appeal rejected the argument that terms as to the payment of discretionary bonuses in a bank employee's contract of employment represented the bank's written standard *terms of business*—the employers' business was banking and provisions as to the payment of remuneration to employees were not the standard terms of the business of banking.

8.41 Another issue is what degree of individual negotiation can there be before the agreement cannot be regarded as being on the other party's written standard terms. In *Watford Electronics Ltd v Sanderson CFL Ltd* (2001) the claimant ordered from the defendant a software system, to enable it to control its accounts and run its mail order business. Three contracts were executed, based on the defendant's standard terms and conditions, but each slightly tailored to the particular transaction. In particular, the parties negotiated an addendum to each of the three contracts, but the judge considered that the contracts were essentially still made on the defendant's written standard terms, because the addenda were 'immaterial', 'vague', 'narrow and insubstantial'. Accordingly, UCTA applied and exclusion clauses in the contracts were subject to the reasonableness test under UCTA (see further para **8.51**). But this is likely to be rare—more commonly, one party in a commercial transaction will begin negotiations by tabling a model form of some kind as a starting point, which will then be the subject of negotiations. *African Export-Import Bank v Shebah Exploration and Production Company Ltd* (2017) involved a sophisticated syndicated loan facility agreement (where the lender is a syndicate of several banks) and associated guarantees. The Court of Appeal had no doubt that, although agreement was based on the form of syndicated facility agreement, recommended by the Loan Market Association (LMA) as a starting point for negotiation, there had in fact been 'detailed negotiations … which render it impossible to say that either the LMA model form was, or the terms ultimately agreed were, the claimants' standard terms of business.' So the borrowers/guarantors could not invoke the protection of UCTA against the banks. Nonetheless Longmore LJ left the door ajar for UCTA to apply in an appropriate case, saying obiter that he:

> [did] not find it necessary to engage with [the banks'] submission that a contract based on an LMA form can never be made on standard business terms because there is always a need for adoption and amendment. I suspect that the submission goes too far; if a lender habitually used a particular LMA form and refused to countenance any amendment, it would be difficult to say that the deal was not done on that lender's standard business terms. But a final decision on that question does not have to be made in this case and can safely be left for another day.

Overall, it appears to be a question of fact and degree whether the contractual terms count as a defendant's 'written standard terms of business'—the greater the degree of negotiation, the less likely they are to count as such.

8.42 Despite these clarifications, the application of the UCTA reasonableness test to any non-consumer contract is inherently controversial. Consumer protection is a legitimate justification for judicial intervention in contractual terms, but that function is now entirely served by the CRA. Section 3 of UCTA embodies the dubious assumption that dealing on standard forms is inherently a matter of concern, even between commercial parties. Any interference with terms in contracts between commercial parties will be at the expense of certainty and predictability in commercial transactions, particularly where the interference is based on an impressionistic matter such as 'reasonableness'. As will be seen, many judges are reluctant to conclude that exclusion and limitation clauses in commercial contracts are unreasonable, but there remains the destabilising risk of more interventionist decisions (described by Adams and Brownsword (1988) as 'maverick') in the commercial context.

8.43 Finally on s 3, notice that specific anti-avoidance provisions are contained in s 3(2)(b). This provides that a contractor cannot 'get round' the reasonableness requirement by drafting a clause which, instead of excluding liability, has the same effect by defining his obligation so as to entitle him to 'render a contractual performance substantially different from that which was reasonably expected of him' or 'no performance at all'.

8.44 Like s 13(1), the anti-avoidance provision in s 3(2)(b) is potentially very far-reaching, if it is interpreted as catching any contractual right to substitute one sort of performance for another. For example, in *Timeload Ltd v British Telecommunications plc* (1995) the Court of Appeal tentatively suggested that a clause entitling British Telecom to terminate a customer's telephone service without reason on giving notice might be caught by s 3(2)(b), as one which 'purports to permit partial or different performance from that which the customer expected'. However, *Timeload* was distinguished in *Nash v Paragon Finance plc* (2001), where the Court of Appeal decided that s 13(1) does not cover a term in a mortgage contract permitting the lender to vary the rate of interest payable by the borrower. As Dyson LJ explained, 'The contract term must be one which has an effect (indeed a substantial effect) on the contractual performance reasonably expected of the party who relies on the term. The key word is "performance". By fixing the borrower's rate of interest, the lender is not altering its own performance obligation. Notice that *Nash* involved a consumer transaction, so would nowadays be outside UCTA and covered by the CRA instead. Nonetheless, the scope of s 3(2)(b) remains uncertain. For example, in *AXA Sun Life Services plc v Campbell Martin Ltd* (2011) Stanley Burton LJ made the commercially significant suggestion that, in appropriate circumstances, an entire agreement clause (on which see para **7.17**), which as a matter of construction is effective to exclude collateral contracts and warranties, might purport to entitle a contracting party to 'render a contractual performance substantially different from that which was reasonably expected of him' and thus fall to be tested for reasonableness under UCTA. This is because one party's 'reasonable expectations' of the other party's performance might be shaped and affected by the very collateral contracts and warranties that are ruled out by the entire agreement clause.

How is 'reasonableness' tested?

8.45 The reasonableness test is set out in s 11(1), which provides that a term 'shall be a fair and reasonable one to be included having regard to the circumstances which were, or ought reasonably to have been, known to the parties when the contract was made'. Three preliminary points can be made. First, the test is applied without the benefit of hindsight so what counts is whether it was reasonable to have included the term at the time the contract was made: the circumstances giving rise to liability are irrelevant. This can be harsh, as we saw in *Stewart Gill Ltd v Horatio Myer & Co Ltd* (see para **8.32**) where the court decided that the clause was unreasonable because of its *potential* effect in circumstances very different from those in the actual dispute between the parties. Second, the courts cannot rewrite a clause to make it reasonable and this was interpreted in the *Stewart Gill* case as precluding severance of unreasonable words in a clause. Third, the burden of proof is on the person seeking to rely on the contract term or notice to demonstrate that it is reasonable.

8.46 Section 11(1) is not intended to be precise or comprehensive, so as to allow trial judges considerable flexibility in determining the reasonableness of a term (a decision with which appellate courts rarely interfere, although see *Regus (UK) Ltd v Epcot Solutions Ltd* (2008) for an example of the Court of Appeal reversing the judge's finding of unreasonableness because it construed the relevant clause differently). There are some indications in UCTA as to how the courts should approach the reasonableness enquiry in specific situations (in particular guidelines contained in Sch 2, supposedly confined to questions of reasonableness in ss 6 and 7, but given more general application by the courts). In addition, a number of other factors not mentioned expressly in the statute crop up regularly in decisions on reasonableness. Relevant factors include (a) the relative strength of the parties' bargaining positions; (b) the availability of insurance against the excluded liability; (c) whether the claimant knew or ought to have known about the term; (d) whether the term is clearly worded; (e) whether the term is standard or unusual within the relevant market; (f) the defendant's remaining obligations within the contract; (g) whether liability would, in the absence of the clause, be disproportionate; and (h) whether liability is excluded altogether or merely limited.

8.47 Sometimes all the relevant factors in a case will point clearly in one direction. For example, in *Smith v Eric S Bush* (1989) (a case that would now be outside UCTA and caught by the CRA) a surveyor, instructed by a mortgagee to value a residential property, tried to exclude the *Hedley Byrne* duty of care to the potential purchaser by means of a disclaimer in his valuation report, but the House of Lords unanimously held that such a disclaimer (caught by s 2(2) of UCTA) was unreasonable. Relevant considerations included the fact that surveyors knew that purchasers of modest residential properties commonly relied on mortgage valuation reports (and indeed paid for them); that surveyors were only required to exercise reasonable care and skill in the relatively simple task of valuing a residential property; that purchasers had no effective bargaining power to object to the disclaimer; and that surveyors could easily obtain liability insurance at a modest cost, which cost could be passed on, and thus the risk spread, to all potential purchasers. In contrast, in *Monarch Airlines v London Luton Airport Ltd* (1998) (see para **8.17**) the clause excluding the airport's negligence liability for damage to planes on takeoff was held to be reasonable, principally because the airline knew about the clause and accepted it without complaint, its meaning was clear and (most importantly) both parties had made their insurance arrangements on the basis that the airport was not liable for negligent damage.

8.48 Often, however, the courts must balance conflicting factors and reach an impressionistic decision as to the reasonableness of the term. A striking example is *George Mitchell (Chesterhall) Ltd v Finney Lock Seeds Ltd* (1983). The defendants were seed merchants who agreed to supply the farmers with 30lb of winter cabbage seeds, for just over £200. The contract contained a clause limiting the defendants' liability to the price of the seed. The seed supplied was of a different and inferior variety, so the crop failed and the farmers claimed damages of over £60,000. The House of Lords held that, on balance, the clause limiting the seed merchants' liability to £200 was unreasonable and ineffective, even though some factors pointed in the defendants' favour. For example, the seed was very cheap relative to the magnitude of the damages claimed, the clause did not exclude liability altogether, and the farmers knew about the clause, which was clearly worded. But other factors tipped the balance. First, the parties were not of equal bargaining strength and there had been no negotiation about the clause. Second, the clause was standard in the industry but, crucially, seed merchants generally rarely invoked it and, more particularly, the defendants had offered to negotiate the farmers' claims without enforcing the limitation. This was seen as a tacit acknowledgement in the trade, and by the defendants in particular, that it was an unreasonable provision. This second factor has been criticised as giving too much weight to informal concessions made by the defendants. Interestingly, this case concerned the *transitional* statutory provision before UCTA came into force, in which the test was whether it was fair and reasonable to allow *reliance* on the clause. Now, under the UCTA framework, the test is whether the clause was a fair and reasonable one to be included in the contract, which should in theory make the parties' post-breach conduct irrelevant.

8.49 It seems likely that any clause caught by UCTA nowadays (being, by definition, a clause in a non-consumer contract) has little prospect of being found to be unreasonable unless the balance of the parties' relationship is, in substance, closer to the usual consumer situation (for example where there was great disparity in economic weight and bargaining strength, such as a tiny 'one man band' business contracting with a huge corporation). Otherwise this conclusion will be relatively rare. As Tuckey LJ stressed in *Granville Oil & Chemicals Ltd v Davis Turner* (2003), he was unenthusiastic about the intrusion of a statutory reasonableness test 'into contracts between commercial parties of equal bargaining strength, who should generally be considered capable of being able to make contracts of their choosing and expect to be bound by their terms'. The Court of Appeal in *Goodlife Foods Ltd v Hall Fire Protection Ltd* (2017) stressed exactly the same point, upholding the clause as a 'perfectly sensible allocation of the risk of loss and damage as between two commercial concerns of broadly equal size and bargaining power'.

8.50 Even where, as in *Röhlig (UK) Ltd v Rock Unique Ltd* (2011), the party resisting the clause was a much smaller company than the party relying on it, the Court of Appeal nonetheless held that the clause (taken from the industry's standard trading conditions) was reasonable:

> *The relative sizes in corporate terms of the parties to the contract is unlikely to be a significant factor in cases of this kind where a small but commercially experienced*

organisation contracts to obtain services of a kind that are available from a large number of competing suppliers.

8.51 Precisely the same reluctance to interfere with commercial bargains was evident in *Watford Electronics Ltd v Sanderson CFL Ltd* (2001) (see para **8.41**), involving the sale by S of a computer software system to W, a personal computer mail order business. Two clauses were in issue: one excluding liability for indirect or consequential loss, whether or not arising from negligence, and another limiting liability in any event to the contract sum (just over £100,000). W was not happy with the system and eventually replaced it, claiming damages of over £5.5 million. The Court of Appeal regarded both clauses as reasonable, when viewed in the context of the other, individually negotiated, obligations in the contracts, which made the deal struck by the parties look a lot more balanced. The court was also influenced by the fact that W's *own* standard terms and conditions, used when they supplied computers to their customers, contained equivalent exclusion and limitation clauses. Overall, it was not impressed by W, a large company thoroughly familiar with the computer industry, attempting to rewrite the deal it had negotiated and claim damages of more than 50 times the contract price. This was not what UCTA was designed to achieve. As Chadwick LJ put it:

> *Where experienced businessmen representing substantial companies of equal bargaining power negotiate an agreement, they may be taken to have had regard to the matters known to them. They should, in my view, be taken to be the best judge of the commercial fairness of the agreement which they have made, including the fairness of each of the terms of that agreement ... Unless satisfied that one party has, in effect, taken unfair advantage of the other—or that a term is so unreasonable that it cannot properly have been understood or considered—the court should not interfere.*

Overall, authorities where a term in a non-consumer transaction has been held to be unreasonable under s 3 are few and far between—from now on, remember that such a finding should and will be exceptionally rare.

Consumer contracts: the Consumer Rights Act 2015

Historical background and implementation

8.52 As part of its commitment to a free market, the European Community issued a Directive (93/13/EEC) on Unfair Terms in Consumer Contracts ('the Directive'), intended to harmonise the domestic rules relating to unfair terms in consumer contracts in different legal systems in the Community. As Collins (1994) explains, without such harmonisation, consumers cannot be sure what they are getting for their money in another jurisdiction and will be deterred from contracting there: 'A holiday-maker in Athens should compare not only the price of a new camera or piece of jewellery, but also the mandatory warranties given by the retailer in Greece, as opposed to the home state.' So the idea is that, if every jurisdiction has equivalent controls on warranties and other subsidiary contractual provisions, consumers will be more likely to trade throughout the Community. Paradoxically, the Directive also recognises that when consumers shop, their focus tends to be exclusively on 'price' and 'product', and they do not tend to realise that an apparently cheaper product comes with a less favourable set of contractual terms and conditions than a more expensive but similar product. To counter this problem of 'unfair surprise', the Directive ensures that consumers must now be offered a minimum level of contractual protection. This latter justification has less to do with promoting a free market and more to do with the second objective of ensuring that, in each domestic market, consumers' interests are protected.

8.53   As has been seen earlier (para **8.25**) Parliament initially implemented the Directive by simply enacting its provisions in the form of a Statutory Instrument, the Unfair Terms in Consumer Contracts Regulations (the Regulations), which overlapped with and sat uneasily alongside UCTA, creating a regime for the protection of consumers that was complex, inaccessible and unpredictable. Finally in a major legislative reform in 2015, the Regulations were repealed, UCTA was amended and the CRA was passed, a harmonised statute that now contains all the statutory provisions regulating unfair terms in consumer contracts. Notice that terms and notices excluding liability in negligence to consumers are now also governed by the CRA, but the regime remains the same as it was under UCTA: under s 65 a term or notice purporting to exclude negligence liability for death and personal injury is automatically ineffective. For a very useful study of the detailed provisions of the CRA, considering case law of the Court of Justice of the European Union (CJEU) that has interpreted equivalent provisions in the Directive and the potential impact of Brexit on developing jurisprudence, see Giliker (2017).

Scope and effect of the CRA

Contracts covered

8.54   The CRA is not subject to the same restrictions as UCTA as to what sort of contracts are covered. For example, insurance contracts are caught by the CRA as are some contracts concerning interests in land, such as mortgage contracts, since the mortgagor is providing a service to a consumer (though contracts for the sale of land itself are not). Contracts of employment and apprenticeship, which are heavily regulated elsewhere, are exempt.

Unfair terms

8.55   Section 62(1) provides: 'An unfair term of a consumer contract is not binding on the consumer.' So what is an 'unfair term'? The key provision is s 62(4): 'A term is unfair if, contrary to the requirement of good faith, it causes a significant imbalance in the parties' rights and obligations arising under the contract to the detriment of the consumer'. We will look in more detail at the meaning of 'good faith' in paras **8.73–8.78**. Section 62(5) explains whether a term is fair is to be determined '(a) taking into account the nature of the subject matter of the contract, and (b) by reference to all of the circumstances existing when the term was agreed and to all of the other terms of the contract'. Unlike the previous Regulations, the CRA applies whether a term is in standard form or individually negotiated by the parties, a significant improvement in consumer protection in theory (though in practice less so, since very few consumer contracts are genuinely individually negotiated).

The CRA also prohibits the use of unfair consumer notices—such as non-contractual statements put on the trader's website or displayed in a shop—the fairness of which is tested in exactly the same way as for terms (see s 62(6) and (7)).

8.56   Guidance on the sorts of terms that may be regarded as unfair is found in an 'indicative and non-exhaustive list' of potentially unfair terms in Schedule 2. It is sometimes called a 'grey list' not a 'blacklist', because a term appearing on the list is not necessarily unfair in a given contract, while other terms not appearing on the list might also be unfair. The terms on the grey list nicely illustrate the 'significant imbalance' aspect of the definition of unfair terms. Examples include:

> 4 A term which has the object or effect of permitting the trader to retain sums paid by the consumer where the consumer decides not to conclude or perform the contract, without providing for the consumer to receive compensation of an equivalent amount from the trader where the trader is the party cancelling the contract; ...

> 8 A term which has the object or effect of enabling the trader to terminate a contract of indeterminate duration without reasonable notice except where there are serious grounds for doing so; ...

> 18 A term which has the object or effect of obliging the consumer to fulfill all the consumer's obligations where the trader does not perform the trader's obligations.

8.57   As all the examples on the grey list show, for a term to be unfair, the imbalance it creates between the parties must be 'significant'. In *West v Ian Finlay & Associates* (2014) (which involved the identical language from the now-repealed Regulations) a wealthy professional couple, Mr and Mrs West, contracted with an architect for the refurbishment of their home. The contract contained a 'net contribution clause' (NCC) which had the effect of ousting the usual common law rule of joint and several liability, by providing that an architect's liability was to be limited to a reasonable amount in relation to the defaults of other contractors. The work was done badly—the fault of both the builder and the architect—but the builder had gone bust. This meant the Wests wished to claim all their losses from the architect, but this was prevented by the NCC. The Wests therefore alleged that the NCC was unfair, but the Court of Appeal disagreed, holding that although the NCC created an imbalance between the parties, it was not a *significant* imbalance. Reasons given included the prevalence of the usage of the NCC in standard forms supplied by the architect's professional body, the fact that the clause would be regarded as not unusual in a commercial contract, and the fact that the contract was made before the builder was chosen and it was the Wests who would be taking the final decision, knowing that that builder's financial stability was a matter of importance. Moreover the requirement of good faith had not been breached (see para **8.55**). This is a surprisingly hard-nosed decision, arguably unduly swayed by the fact that the consumers were actually sophisticated, professional people—but is this material to the level of imbalance created by a contractual term?

8.58 Finally, the CRA has a role to play in protecting consumers contracting electronically on websites, in addition to the rules of reasonable notice for incorporation of unsigned terms (on which see para **7.25**). The 'grey list' of illustrative unfair terms includes, 'A term which has the object or effect of irrevocably binding the consumer to terms with which the consumer has had no real opportunity of becoming acquainted before the conclusion of the contract'. The judge in *Spreadex Ltd v Cochrane* (2012) had no hesitation in concluding that the manner in which terms were purportedly incorporated into a Customer Agreement for spread betting reinforced his conclusion that a particular term was unfair:

> the potential customer was told that four documents, including the Customer Agreement, could be viewed elsewhere on-line by clicking "View". Many, one might suspect most, would have passed up on that invitation and proceeded directly to click on "Agree", even though it was suggested that they should do so only when they had read and understood the documents. Even if, exceptionally, the Defendant in fact chose to look at the documents, he would have been faced in the Customer Agreement alone with 49 pages containing the same number of closely printed and complex paragraphs. It would have come close to a miracle if he had read the second sentence of Cl 10(3), let alone appreciated its purport or implications, and it would have been quite irrational for the Claimant to assume that he had. (In most cases, the limited time spent on the on-line application would in any event probably preclude any serious perusal of the documents.)

Core terms excluded from the assessment of fairness (as long as transparent and prominent)

8.59 Section 64(1) provides that a term of a consumer contract may not be assessed for fairness to the extent that '(a) it specifies the main subject matter of the contract, or (b) the assessment is of the appropriateness of the price payable under the contract by comparison with the goods, digital content or services supplied under it'. These two sorts of terms are commonly called the 'core terms', a useful label but not one actually used in the legislation.

8.60 Importantly, s 64(2) goes on to say that a core term is excluded from an assessment of fairness 'only if it is transparent and prominent'. Section 64(3) says a term is transparent 'if it is expressed in plain and intelligible language and (in the case of a written term) is legible'. Section 64(4) says a term is prominent 'if it is brought to the consumer's attention in such a way that an average consumer would be aware of the term.' 'Transparency' is required for all terms (para **8.66**), but 'prominence' is mentioned only at this point, as a precondition on the exclusion of assessment of the core terms. The prominence requirement is similar to the common law rules on incorporation for onerous or unusual terms (para **7.34**) and, like its common law equivalent, stops short of saying the trader must ensure the actual consumer read and subjectively understood the term, which would be an almost impossible burden to fulfil. Nonetheless, the new requirement adds meaningfully to consumer protection—a trader can no longer tuck a term into the small print which deals with the contractual subject matter or part of the price calculation, but which the average consumer would not have spotted or taken the trouble to read.

8.61   Some advocates of greater consumer rights regret the exclusion of these core terms, arguing that a consumer ought to be free to prove, for example, that a particular product was too expensive and the price was thus 'unfair' in itself. But they are excluded for good reasons of principle. First, the 'unfair surprise' justification for intervention (see para **8.52**) does not apply to the price or the main subject matter, which are the two matters consumers do take notice of when contracting. Second, from a freedom of contract standpoint, it would be unacceptable for sellers and suppliers if consumers were allowed to undo bargains freely entered into, on the ground that they later regretted their original willingness to pay a given price for a given product. It might be thought that there are simply two opposing views here: those who value freedom of contract versus those who advocate greater consumer protection, but it is not quite this simple. There will come a point where more substantive regulation of contract terms begins to interfere with *competition* and *choice*, contrary to the interests of consumers. So the Directive and the CRA embody a compromise, by regulating subsidiary terms but leaving the market free to regulate price and product. After all, as Smith (1994a) points out, it is not unfair 'to advertise a pencil for sale at the non-negotiable price of £1000. It is simply bad business.' Nonetheless, despite the principled justifications for the exclusion of the core terms, in practice matters are not quite so clear cut. After all, as the Law Commission pointed out (in its 2013 paper *Unfair Terms in Consumer Contracts: Advice to the Department for Business, Innovation and Skills*, the paper which led to the enactment of the CRA): 'In a world of price comparison websites, there is increasing pressure on traders to advertise low headline prices, whilst earning their profits through other charges.' It is to be hoped that the CRA's requirement that core terms are only excluded from fairness assessment if they are transparent and prominent will help protect consumers from this sort of tactic.

8.62   There is as yet no UK case law on the meaning of the core terms provision in the CRA, but it is instructive to look briefly at how the relevant wording in its predecessor, the Unfair Terms in Consumer Contracts Regulations, was construed by the courts. Notice that the wording of the now repealed Regulations was somewhat different from the wording of s 64: the old wording in reg 6(2) said that 'the unfairness of a term shall not relate to the adequacy of the price or remuneration, as against the goods or services supplied'. In *Director General of Fair Trading v First National Bank plc* (2002), the House of Lords emphasised that, if the protective effect of the legislation is not to be emasculated completely, the core terms provisions must be restrictively interpreted.

After all, in a broad sense, all contractual terms are in some way related to the price or subject matter of the contract. According to the House of Lords, there is an important distinction between the terms 'which express the substance of the bargain', and those which are merely 'incidental' or 'subsidiary'. The term in dispute merely prescribed the consequences of a borrower's default and was 'plainly' a subsidiary term. It was thus assessable for fairness, though duly held to be fair.

8.63 The issue was again explored by the courts in *Office of Fair Trading v Abbey National plc and others* (2009). The question was whether various bank charges levied by a number of High Street banks when a customer's account goes into unarranged overdraft fell within the relevant regulation, or whether they were outside it, in which case they could be assessed for fairness. Both Andrew Smith J at first instance and the Court of Appeal thought that reg 6(2) must be restrictively interpreted, to give effect to the purpose of the Directive and avoid undermining its effect, holding that the various charges were ancillary provisions and did not form part of the essential bargain at the time a customer took out his current account.

8.64 The Supreme Court, however, unanimously allowed the banks' appeal, controversially adopting a notably broader interpretation of reg 6(2). The court held that, unlike the term in *First National Bank* which was correctly regarded as a default provision, the bank charges fell within reg 6(2). They formed part of a 'package of consideration', in return for the 'package of banking services' supplied to current account customers, in the same way as the interest charged on overdrawn accounts and the benefit to the bank of accounts in credit where little or no interest is paid. Members of the Supreme Court expressed sympathy with bank customers who felt that the charges were very unfair and should be subject to assessment by the courts (Lord Mance in argument described the banks as engaged in a 'reverse Robin Hood exercise'), but hinted that Parliament should consider legislation to regulate the level of bank charges for unauthorised overdrafts.

8.65 The crucial question now is whether the *Abbey National* case would have been decided differently if the revised wording of the CRA had been in force at the time (to recap, the test is now that a term may not be assessed for fairness if the assessment is of the 'appropriateness of the price payable under the contract by comparison with the goods, digital content or services supplied under it'). Certainly, the complexity of the Supreme Court's decision in *Abbey National* was one of the principal catalysts for reform, leading to the enactment of the CRA. On one view, the result would be the same under the CRA—after all, the Supreme Court held it had to look at the bank charges in their context as part of the bank's remuneration for providing a package of banking services to current account customers, which it could be argued is effectively an assessment of the appropriateness of the bank charge term for what the customer gets in return. But the Law Commission's 2013 Consultation Paper took the view that the language of the CRA means that 'it is only the *amount* of the price which is excluded from review. Other aspects of price terms, such as timing, may be assessed for fairness' which suggests that *Abbey National* would be decided differently today, since the gist of the complaint was not the amount of the charges per se. In any event the question may not matter unduly, because of the further important change in the CRA: as we have seen, banks must also now ensure that any such term is both 'transparent and prominent', or else it will be subject to fairness assessment anyway. One of the main accusations of unfairness levelled against the bank charges was that they were hidden away in the small print of a banking contract and certainly never drawn to customers' attention. As the Law Commission 2013 Consultation Paper explained: 'The emphasis on prominence, however, offers a practical way of distinguishing between a headline price and other charges. It also emphasises that whether a term is exempt is within the control of the trader.' Overall, Giliker (2017) explains that the aim of s 64 is not 'to overturn the *Abbey National* case, but to render its application as a precedent more straightforward ... to restate the [core terms] exemption in more "user-friendly" language, making clear that other aspects of the price other than the amount, for example timing of payment, can be assessed for fairness'.

Requirement for 'transparency'

8.66 In addition to the new requirement that a core term will only be excluded from assessment for fairness if it is transparent and prominent, there is also a freestanding requirement in s 68 that all written terms in consumer contracts and written consumer notices must be transparent, again defined as 'in plain and intelligible language and ... legible'. Section 69(1) adds a further rule (echoing the *contra proferentem* principle of construction discussed in para **8.7**) that '[i]f a term in a consumer contract, or a consumer notice, could have different meanings, the meaning that is most favourable to the consumer is to prevail'.

8.67 The requirement of 'plain, intelligible language' appeared in the now-repealed Regulations (though without the word 'and' separating the two adjectives), but the additional requirement that the term be 'legible' is new. The drafting of the CRA (and its predecessor Regulations) mirrors the Directive in that it does not spell out whether the requirement of plain, intelligible language (and now legibility) is part and parcel of the 'fairness' enquiry or a separate requirement. It reads like a separate requirement (and after all, there is no obvious connection between convoluted language and a significant imbalance in the parties' rights and obligations), but if so there is no explicit sanction for breach of it. The Law Commission's 2013 Consultation Paper explained:

> [The Directive] does not spell out the consequences of failing to make a term transparent. We do not think that non-transparent terms are automatically unfair, though it is an important factor to consider. ... We recommend that the legislation should clarify that enforcement bodies may use their powers ... against terms which are not transparent.

So it seems that the public bodies with regulatory powers under the CRA (see para **8.72**) can enforce the transparency requirement per se, and that a lack of transparency will also impact on the broader question of fairness of a term, though will not be conclusive.

8.68 A further difficulty is what 'plain [and] intelligible language' actually means. It would be hard to draft a consumer finance or insurance contract colloquially without using legal language and, as Lord Wilberforce explained in a different context in *Ailsa Craig Fishing Co Ltd v Malvern Fishing Co Ltd* (1983), a clause may need to be intricate in order to be clear. Section 69 contemplates resolving doubts about interpretation in favour of the consumer, but it could be argued that ambiguity is more likely to be avoided by detailed, technical drafting than by plain, intelligible language. On the other hand, as Andrew Smith J pointed out in the *Abbey National* case, the typical consumer 'does not need an education in the full complexities of banking systems, and [the plain, intelligible language requirement does] not, in my judgment, require a supplier such as the banks to provide it'. The judge posed the question 'whether the contractual terms put forward by the seller and supplier are sufficiently clear to enable the typical consumer to have a proper understanding of them for sensible and practical purposes' and decided that (with minor exceptions) the various provisions imposing bank charges for unarranged overdrafts were indeed in plain intelligible language, a conclusion which was not challenged on appeal. (For a further exploration of the meaning of 'plain, intelligible language' under the now-repealed Regulations, see *Bankers Insurance Co Ltd v South* (2003).)

8.69 The transparency requirement under the CRA is subtly different from the language used in the now-repealed Regulations, because it adds the wholly new requirement of legibility (as well as separating 'plain, intelligible language' into 'plain *and* intelligible language'). Legibility will cover stylistic matters such as font style and size, location, and layout of the term. It will be interesting to see what the English courts and regulators make of the new rules.

Effect of unfair term on rest of the contract

8.70 Under s 67, if a term of a consumer contract is not binding on the consumer, 'the contract continues, so far as practicable, to have effect in every other respect'. It is not entirely clear what happens in the unlikely event that it is not practicable for the contract to continue without the term. English law has a number of possible responses, including rescission *ab initio,* frustration, and prospective-only termination as if for repudiatory breach, but the CRA leaves the question open.

Enforcement

8.71 Two important features distinguish the CRA from UCTA. First, s 71(2) provides that the court must consider whether a term is fair even if none of the parties to the proceedings has raised that issue or indicated that it intends to raise it. This is an unfamiliar notion to common law judges and reflects a model of civil procedure more familiar in civilian systems, but was included to comply with decisions of the CJEU. It remains to be seen how often this is invoked in practice, particularly since there is a qualification in s 71(3) that the requirement 'does not apply unless the court considers that it has before it sufficient legal and factual material to enable it to consider the fairness of the term'.

8.72 In practice a much more significant difference between UCTA and the CRA is that the provisions of the CRA are not *just* enforceable in private litigation. Important powers are also given in s 70 to the Competition and Markets Authority (the CMA) and other public organisations such as the Consumers' Association to police and regulate the use of unfair terms in consumer contracts. For example, the CMA's predecessor body, the Office of Fair Trading, regularly required holiday tour operators to modify unfair terms and conditions and published authoritative 'Guidance on Unfair Terms in Package Holiday Contracts' (March 2004, OFT 668); moreover, the two highest profile unfair terms cases to reach the courts under the now-repealed Regulations were challenges of this kind, namely the *First National Bank* and *Abbey National* cases. These public regulatory powers are far more likely to change practice in particular sectors than private law challenges by individual consumers.

Meaning and implications of the 'good faith' requirement

8.73 To recap, a term is unfair under s 62(4) if 'contrary to the requirement of good faith, it causes a significant imbalance in the parties' rights and obligations arising under the contract to the detriment of the consumer'. It is clear from the grey list in Sch 2 that 'significant imbalance' is the defining feature of the sorts of terms likely to be regarded as unfair, and that 'significant imbalance' refers to the substantive rights and obligations of the parties (as opposed to negotiating imbalance or inequality). So what does 'good faith' add to the definition? Two possible answers need to be distinguished. It could be argued that the good faith requirement is just meant to tackle *procedural unfairness*. This refers to the way that the contract is formed: for example, whether the seller or supplier *dealt* in good faith with the consumer, ensuring that the consumer knew about the term in question when he entered into the contract. This approach led to terms in the Joint Contracts Tribunal (JCT) standard form building contract being held unfair (under the now-repealed Regulations) in *Munkenbeck & Marshall v Harold* (2005). A similar procedural focus led to the opposite conclusion in *Bryen & Langley v Boston* (2005) because it was the *consumer* who had insisted on the JCT form, which made his argument that the contractors lacked good faith in incorporating those terms as 'repugnant to common sense'. More recently the Court of Appeal in *West v Ian Finlay & Associates* (2014) (para **8.57**) also adopted a mainly procedural approach to good faith, focusing on the conduct of the parties' dealings—the key factor once again was that the Wests were sophisticated people, so although in an ideal world the defendant would have expressly drawn the NCC to their attention and explained its meaning, 'we do not think that factor alone is enough to cause the NCC to fall foul of the fairness requirement'.

However, the prevailing view is now that, like 'significant imbalance', the good faith requirement also looks at the substantive contents of the contract, in addition to the way it was formed, and that it adds something extra to the 'significant imbalance' enquiry.

8.74 For example Collins (1994) sees the good faith requirement as importing 'social market considerations' into the unfairness enquiry. He argues that the reference to 'significant imbalance' means that the contract must be good value for money for the consumer, but that the 'contrary to good faith' requirement is separate. Collins' explanation is that 'good faith' requires the goods or services supplied under the contract to be of at least a certain minimum quality that consumers reasonably expect. It is not enough that the goods or services be fair value for money. A contract supplying very poor quality goods at a very low price with virtually no contractual protections for the consumer would be fair value for money, but might not satisfy the good faith requirement, because consumers reasonably expect that goods are of a certain quality, irrespective of how cheap they are. This interpretation is strengthened by recital 16 of the preamble to the Directive, which says that good faith requires the seller/supplier to take into account the 'legitimate interests' of the consumer: rather than act in an entirely self-interested way, he must have regard to the consumer's reasonable expectations. In practice, the courts have yet to adopt social market reasoning of this kind explicitly, but that is not to say that it does not represent the rationale for the good faith requirement.

8.75 *Director of Fair Trading v First National Bank* helps to clarify matters slightly and, on balance, supports the view that the good faith requirement is predominantly a substantive one. Lord Millett seems to view good faith as being concerned with substantive matters, asking: 'if [the term] were drawn to his attention the consumer would be likely to be surprised by it'. In other words, he is looking at the reasonable expectations held by the consumer as regards the contract. He is not looking at *whether* the term was drawn to the consumer's attention, so his focus is not on procedural fairness. Lord Steyn seems to take a similar view, commenting that 'any purely procedural or even predominantly procedural interpretation of the requirement of good faith must be rejected'. Lord Bingham, giving the leading judgment, appears to treat good faith as imposing both procedural and substantive requirements (which accords with the view of Beale (1995)), stressing that it requires 'fair and open dealing', openness being concerned with how the contract was formed and fairness dealing with the contents of the contract. So at the very least, the decision supports the proposition that the good faith requirement deals, at least partly, with substantive issues.

8.76 This interpretation now seems beyond doubt, since the Supreme Court in *ParkingEye Ltd v Beavis* (2015) declined to hold that a term in a car parking contract was unfair (see also para **17.29** for the other aspect of the case, concerning the penalty clause jurisdiction). The car park was free for a two-hour maximum stay, but a charge of £85 was imposed for overstaying, as Mr Beavis did for a further hour. The Supreme Court by a majority held that any imbalance between the parties did not arise 'contrary to the requirement of good faith'. The court unanimously adopted the test laid down by the CJEU in the 'leading case' of *Aziz v Caixa d'Estalvis de Catalunya* (2013) that asks whether the reasonable consumer in the position of the specific consumer would have agreed to the term in individual contract negotiations. This undeniably involves substantive questions about the term itself, as well as procedural questions about the parties' dealings. The majority answered the *Aziz* question in the affirmative, emphasising that the charge was clear, simple, and prominently displayed, and that the car park company had a legitimate interest in enforcing a two-hour limit, to allow as many customers as possible to make use of the free parking. Lord Toulson adopted the identical test but alone took a different view on the facts, pointing out in a powerful dissent that, 'By most people's standards £85 is a substantial sum of money … by way of comparison … the basic state pension is £115 per week.' He was also swayed by the fact that there may be numerous unforeseen reasons why motorists might be a minute or two late, through no fault of their own, yet the full charge would apply, and that there was no exemption for disabled drivers. Whether one prefers the majority or the dissenting analysis of the facts, there is no doubt that all members of the court were evaluating both substantive and procedural issues to determine whether the term was 'contrary to the requirement of good faith'.

8.77 As we saw in Chapter 1, English law differs from European systems in not recognising a general substantive principle of good faith between contracting parties. When the Directive was first implemented into English law, some commentators suggested that the requirement of good faith in the context of unfair terms might lead to the principle being recognised in the law of contract generally (see for example, MacMillan (2002)). With hindsight, there seems little hint of good faith spilling over into other contexts; certainly MacMillan's prediction that 'revolutionary changes will occur in the common law of contract', has not come to pass. Moreover, caution must be exercised in borrowing a principle from the consumer protection context and allowing it to expand into a general principle, catching purely commercial situations. As Brownsword (2006) points out, certain commercial situations can only function in an adversarial environment, such as the 'ruthlessly competitive' financial derivatives market (though this would not necessarily be a problem if parties were free to contract out of an underlying good faith regime). In addition, good faith is a slippery concept, impossible to define and inherently subjective, which does not fit comfortably with the certainty needed in commercial transactions.

8.78 Finally, the recognition of a general principle of good faith in English law would not necessarily have a major impact on the law in practice. In the view of Hedley (2001c):

> most of what continentals call 'good faith' is there [in English law] right enough, though called something different. It is the terminology, not the law, that differs … It is not obvious, therefore, that overt recognition [of a general principle of good faith in English law] is a matter of very high importance.

So for example, the Canadian Supreme Court decided in *Bhasin v Hrynew* (2014) that, unlike English law, the Canadian law of contract is subject to a 'general organising principle of good faith'. Although the language is revolutionary, the result (that the parties 'must not lie or otherwise knowingly mislead each other about matters directly linked to the performance of the contract') is one that could and would have been reached easily in English law in the tort of deceit and by the implication of specific terms (see further paras **7.69–7.97**).

OVERVIEW

1   At common law, exclusion and limitation clauses were subject to strict rules of construction. Sometimes the courts bent the rules of construction to produce a 'fair result', though they have no need to do so since UCTA introduced statutory controls on exclusion clauses. But this does not necessarily mean that these rules of construction have been discarded completely.

2   The common law rules of construction include a presumption that ambiguity is construed against the interests of the party seeking to rely on the clause; the recognition that very clear words are needed to exclude liability for serious breaches of contract (as ever when one party is arguing for a very unlikely or unreasonable interpretation); and guidelines to help determine whether a particular clause does or does not exclude liability for negligence.

3   Parliament has recently amended the statutory regimes providing protection against unfair terms. Non-consumer contracts are now regulated by UCTA, while consumer contracts are governed by the CRA. UCTA covers contractual exclusion and limitation clauses and non-contractual exclusion and limitation notices, insofar as they purport to exclude or limit business liability. It contains anti-avoidance provisions to prevent clever drafting of clauses which technically are not worded to exclude liability but which have substantively the same effect. One sort of purported exclusion is automatically invalidated by UCTA, namely exclusions of negligence liability for causing death or personal injury (exactly the same applies to the consumer regime under the CRA).

4   Other parts of UCTA provide that certain exclusions are only valid insofar as they satisfy the requirement of reasonableness and it is for the party seeking to rely on the exclusion to establish reasonableness. For example, UCTA imposes a test of reasonableness on clauses seeking to exclude liability for breach of contract, where the party subject to the term was dealing as a consumer or on the other party's written standard terms of business. There are no rigid rules for testing reasonableness, but a number of factors are commonly taken into account. The courts are very unwilling to intervene and label a clause as unreasonable where the contract was made between two businesses and, as UCTA no longer catches consumer transactions, it is likely that findings of unreasonableness will be very rare from now on.

5   Consumer contracts and notices are now governed by the CRA, which implements an EC Directive. Any term, whether standard form or individually negotiated, in a consumer contract can be challenged as an 'unfair term' (guidance is found in a Schedule) apart from the 'core terms' as to price and product, which generally cannot be assessed for fairness as long as they are transparent and prominent. More generally, terms in consumer contracts are required to be transparent, which means in plain and intelligible language, and legible. As well as allowing a private challenge by an aggrieved consumer, the CRA gives powers to public bodies, in particular the CMA, to police and stamp out the use of unfair terms. The CRA contains a 'good faith' requirement, as part of the definition of fairness. Good faith is not usually regarded as a general principle of the English law of contract, although the courts are more than familiar with handling good faith requirements in other contexts.

FURTHER READING

Adams and Brownsword 'The Unfair Contract Terms Act: A Decade of Discretion' (1988) 104 LQR 94

Beale and Goriely 'An Unfairly Complex Law' (2005) NLJ 318

Bright 'Winning the Battle against Unfair Terms' (2000) 20 LS 331

Collins 'Good Faith in European Contract Law' (1994) OJLS 229

Davies 'Bank Charges in the Supreme Court' (2010) CLJ 21

Giliker 'The Consumer Rights Act 2015—a Bastion of European Consumer Rights?' (2017) 37 LS 78

See explanatory notes on the Consumer Rights Act 2015 at: http://www.legislation.gov.uk/ukpga/2015/15/notes/division/3

SELF-TEST QUESTIONS

1 How has the courts' approach to construing exemption clauses changed since UCTA was passed?

2 Do you think section 3 of UCTA should be repealed?

3 Why are the core terms as to the main subject matter and the adequacy of the price excluded from assessment for fairness?

4 What does the 'good faith' requirement add to the definition of an unfair term in the Consumer Rights Act?

5 Smith sells a machine to Thomas, stipulating that if anything proves to be wrong with the machine, his liability is to be limited to repairing or replacing it, but is not to extend to consequential damage; and also providing that Thomas must inform Smith within 48 hours if he has any complaint about the machine. Soon after the machine has been installed, it catches fire because of an electrical fault, burning Thomas' hands severely and destroying the building in which Thomas has installed it. As a result of his injuries, Thomas does not notify Smith of the incident until 72 hours later. In what way are the legal rules likely to differ if (a) neither party; (b) both parties; (c) Smith but not Thomas, made the contract in the course of a business? Would your advice differ if Thomas was a limited company not a human being?

 For hints on how to answer question 5, please see the online resources at
http://www.oup.com/uk/sullivan8e/.

9 Misrepresentation and non-disclosure

SUMMARY

This chapter covers pre-contractual misrepresentation, a vitiating factor. It deals with the definition and requirements for an actionable misrepresentation, contrasting the treatment of non-disclosure, and the test of causation/reliance. It then considers the remedies for misrepresentation:

- rescission, how it operates and the circumstances in which it will be barred;
- damages, including damages for fraud and under the Misrepresentation Act 1967; and
- exclusion of liability for misrepresentation.

What counts as an actionable misrepresentation?

9.1 Contracting parties frequently make all sorts of statements, both before and at the time a contract is made, and such statements are not all treated in the same way. We have already looked at how to tell whether such a statement is a term of the contract or not (see Chapter 7). Even if the statement is *not* incorporated as a term, it may nonetheless have been very influential in persuading the other party to enter into the contract. What if this sort of statement (generally called a representation) turns out not to be true—in other words, it turns out to be a *mis*representation? The misrepresenting party (or 'misrepresentor') is plainly not in breach of contract, but this does not mean that the other party (the 'misrepresentee') is without any remedy. Rescission is commonly available for misrepresentation and, in certain circumstances, damages might be available, in addition or as an alternative to rescission.

Silence: misrepresentation or non-disclosure?

9.2 English law draws a fundamental distinction between misrepresentation (which gives rise to liability) and non-disclosure (which generally does not). If you buy my house, I have no obligation to tell you that it is subsiding, even if I know full well that it is. As Cockburn CJ explained it in *Smith v Hughes* (1871) (see para **3.51**), such a case may well be one 'in which a man of tender conscience or high honour would be unwilling to take advantage of the ignorance' of the purchaser, but nonetheless 'there can be no doubt that the contract … would be binding'. If, by contrast, I tell you that the house is in good condition, I will be liable for misrepresentation (and the contract can be rescinded) even if my statement was made entirely innocently. (The purchaser of a subsiding house is not well protected in English law. There is no 'real property' equivalent of the Sale of Goods Act incorporating into the contract an implied term that the house is in satisfactory condition, and it is most unusual for the vendor to give an express promise of this kind.) This explains why conveyancing solicitors acting for purchasers ask vendors lots of detailed questions about the property, called 'preliminary enquiries', to minimise the risk that the vendor will leave unsaid some vital piece of information about the property. But, of course, the vendor need only answer the question asked. In *Sykes v Rose* (2004) the vendor answered 'No' to the question, 'Is there any other information that you think the buyer may have a right to know?' without disclosing that a gruesome murder had been committed in the house several years before. This was held not to amount to a misrepresentation, since the vendor honestly believed that the buyer had no 'right' to be told.

Contracts uberrimae fidei

9.3   There is a very limited, exceptional group of contracts that can be avoided by one party if the other party has not disclosed material matters known to him. These are known as contracts '*uberrimae fidei*', or contracts of the utmost good faith of which the best known example is a contract of insurance (other contracts, such as guarantee contracts, contracts made between parties in a fiduciary relationship such as trustee and beneficiary, and contracts to subscribe for shares, have analogous but slightly more limited disclosure obligations). So when making a contract of insurance, the insured is obliged to disclose material circumstances and, if he does not do so, the insurer is entitled to avoid the contract (of course, both parties are under a duty of disclosure to each other, but in practice it is non-disclosure by the insured that is significant). The House of Lords in *Pan Atlantic Insurance Co v Pine Top Insurance Co Ltd* (1994) explained that 'materiality' has a broad meaning here. A circumstance will be material if it would influence the decision of a prudent insurer to enter the policy or the terms on which it would contract even if it would not have been decisive, in the sense that a prudent insurer would have declined the policy had it been disclosed (although there must also be some inducement or causal connection between the non-disclosure and the making of the contract of insurance). This broad test of materiality is extremely favourable to insurers. It covers factual information not obviously connected with the particular risk insured (so non-disclosure of a conviction for robbery might be held material to a fire insurance policy) and also matters of opinion and 'intelligence'.

9.4   The breadth of the materiality test in insurance contracts reminds us of why English law does not generally hold contracting parties liable for non-disclosure. In general, parties in arm's length commercial negotiations are entitled to keep their own counsel and need not lose the tactical advantage of intelligence or research by giving up their information to the other side. It is only where the parties' relationship is not commercial (as with fiduciaries) or where one party has exclusive access to salient information (as in insurance contracts) that the law requires active disclosure. However, English law recognises that non-disclosure and misrepresentation sometimes shade into one another. Even where ordinary contracts not *uberrimae fidei* are concerned, a party who remains silent might in certain circumstances be treated as making an implied representation. These cases do not strictly involve liability for non-disclosure, but are examples of silence combining with other statements or circumstances to create a misrepresentation.

Representation later falsified

9.5 If a statement is true when made but is later falsified by a subsequent event, the maker of the original statement must disclose the new position and will be liable if he keeps silent without doing so. In *With v O'Flanagan* (1936) the vendor of a medical practice told the potential purchaser in January that the practice was worth £2,000 a year. This was true at the time, but thereafter the vendor became ill, so the income of the practice had fallen dramatically by the time the contract for sale was entered into in May. The Court of Appeal held that the vendor should have disclosed the change in circumstances and the contract was set aside. (*With v O'Flanagan* was distinguished by the Court of Appeal in *IFE Fund SA v Goldman Sachs International* (2007), but on the specific basis that the terms of the contract made it clear that the defendant did not make any initial representation of fact and so cannot have been under any continuing obligation to disclose new information.)

9.6 There is even authority to suggest that the 'continuing representation' principle applies where the representor accurately states his *intention* at the outset, then subsequently (but before contracting) changes his mind without informing the other party. This is justifiable on the basis that, at the time of contracting, there is a continuing, and false, representation of fact as to the state of the representor's mind (see para **9.17**). The 'continuing representation' analysis is also useful where the representation is false from the outset but where, for example, the eventual contracting party is a company not yet in existence at the time the representation was made to its promoter (and where the representor knew that the company was to be set up as the vehicle for making the contract)—see *Cramaso LLP v Ogilvie-Grant* (2014).

Telling only half the truth

9.7 Where the representor tells the literal truth, this may nonetheless be misleading in the light of other salient matters which the representor has left out. So in *Notts Patent Brick and Tile Co v Butler* (1886) a purchaser of land was told by the vendor's solicitor that he was not aware of any restrictive covenants. This statement was literally true, but only because the solicitor had omitted to read any of the relevant title documents that would have disclosed the covenants. It therefore amounted to a misrepresentation that he had checked properly for restrictive covenants, made on behalf of the vendor.

Conduct as misrepresentation

9.8 Misrepresentations usually take the form of words, but sometimes conduct or gestures can 'make a statement' that amounts to an actionable misrepresentation. Where simple gestures are concerned, this is fairly obvious, such as where a contracting party, in response to a question, puts his thumb up rather than expressly answering 'yes' or where, as Lord Campbell explained in *Walters v Morgan* (1861), he gives 'a nod or a wink, or a shake of the head or a smile'. But representations by conduct may be subtler than this.

9.9 This is illustrated by *Spice Girls Ltd v Aprilia World Service BV* (2002). In May 1998 the Spice Girls' service company entered into a contract with A under which the pop group (then consisting of five members) agreed to promote a new scooter and A agreed to sponsor the Spice Girls' international tours. In the pre-contract negotiations, the five girls undertook photo shoots and their images were included in promotional material and on the scooters. Throughout this time, all members of the group knew that 'Ginger Spice' wished to leave the group and, two weeks after the contract was signed, she did so, rendering useless the marketing of the scooters that had already been prepared. The Court of Appeal held that the Spice Girls' conduct before the contract, such as supplying logos and images and participating in photocalls, combined with express assurances about their commitment to the project, amounted to an implied representation that the service company:

> did not know and had no reasonable grounds to believe at or before the time of entry into the agreement that any of the Spice Girls had an existing declared intention to leave the group.

A had relied on this representation by conduct, and was therefore entitled to damages.

Misrepresentation must be of fact

9.10 Only a misrepresentation of fact will give rise to liability. Other sorts of statements, such as exaggerated, flippant comments not intended to be taken seriously (known as 'mere puffs'), statements of opinion, or statements of future intention, will not generally be actionable. The position with regard to misrepresentations of law will be considered separately (see para **9.18**).

Mere puffs?

9.11 Contracting parties are expected to realise that exaggerated sales hype or vague boasts about the subject matter of a contract are not intended to be and should not be relied upon. Such statements do not give rise to liability, even if they are unjustified. But if, judging the matter objectively, the court thinks that the statement was intended to be taken seriously, it will not be dismissed as a mere puff even if it is somewhat extravagant (of which a well-known example is the unsuccessful plea to that effect by the Carbolic Smoke Ball Company). The distinction is not always easy to draw. For example, in *Fordy* *v Harwood* (1999) the Court of Appeal disagreed with the judge at first instance as to whether the description of a sports car as 'absolutely mint' was a mere puff or an actionable misrepresentation.

Statement of fact or statement of opinion?

9.12 As a general rule, a statement of opinion or belief is not the same as a statement of fact, so a statement of opinion which turns out to have been unjustified will not give rise to liability for misrepresentation. In *Bisset v Wilkinson* (1927) W purchased some land in New Zealand from B, to be used for sheep farming. During negotiations, B stated that if the land was worked properly, he estimated it would 'carry two thousand sheep'. In fact, its true capacity turned out to be somewhat less. As W knew, the land had never before been used for sheep farming, either by B or by anyone else. The Privy Council agreed with the trial judge that, in these circumstances, W was 'not justified in regarding anything said by the plaintiff as to the carrying capacity as being anything more than an expression of his opinion on the subject'. Thus he had no right to rescind the contract.

9.13 However, the distinction between fact and opinion is not a clear-cut one. (Indeed some judges regard it, as Bridge LJ put it in *Cremdean Properties Ltd v Nash* (1977), as 'a distinction without a difference … I cannot see why one should not be making a misrepresentation when giving information or when stating one's opinion or belief'.) Think for a moment about statements like 'This car has been constructed to an extremely high standard' (*Fordy v Harwood* (1999)) or, 'The estimated profits for the current year are £750,000' (*Thomas Witter Ltd v TBP Industries Ltd* (1996)): both could legitimately be categorised either as facts or opinions. It is worth bearing in mind that in *Bisset v Wilkinson* the forecast was treated as a statement of opinion principally because B was in no better position than W to predict the sheep capacity of the land. The same applied in *Kyle Bay (t/a Astons Nightclub) v Underwriters Subscribing under Policy No 019157/08/01* (2007), in which the Court of Appeal held that an inaccurate statement about the interpretation of the policy, made by the insurer's loss adjuster to the insured's loss assessor, was merely a 'contention not a representation', since 'the statement was as to the meaning of a policy to an agent of the claimant who had relevant professional qualifications and experience, and who had, or at least would reasonably have been taken to have, a copy of the policy'.

9.14 But if the maker of a statement has special knowledge or expertise relative to the other party (which is, after all, likely to be the more common fact pattern), the courts tend to treat what appears to be an opinion as nonetheless actionable as a misrepresentation. This mirrors the approach taken in cases like *Esso Petroleum Co Ltd v Mardon* (1976) (see paras **7.11–7.12**) to deciding whether a statement is a term of the contract. So a statement of opinion is commonly interpreted as carrying the implication that there are facts to support it. As Bowen LJ said in *Smith v Land and House Property Corpn* (1884), 'if the facts are not equally known to both sides, then a statement of opinion by one who knows the facts best involves very often a statement of material fact, for he impliedly states that he knows facts which justify his opinion'.

9.15   Finally, what do the courts make of statements of fact which are expressly qualified by reference to the maker's belief or opinion? So if I sell you a painting, stating merely 'I believe this is by Constable' rather than, 'This is by Constable', have I managed to turn a representation of fact into one of opinion? Of course, if I do not believe that the painting is by Constable, I have misrepresented a separate fact, not the provenance of the painting, but what my opinion is. And even where my opinion is honestly held, the court is likely to treat me as having made a representation that I had reasonable grounds for holding that opinion. So, for example, where I am in a better position than the other party to check the facts to back up my opinion, but did not do so, I am liable for misrepresentation. This was the result in *Brown v Raphael* (1958), where the court concluded that a purchaser of an interest in a trust fund 'was entitled to expect that the [vendor's] opinion or belief was expressed on reasonable grounds'.

9.16   Overall, though (as in the *Bisset v Wilkinson* sort of case), amateurs are more likely to get away with qualifying facts as opinions. In *Hummingbird Motors Ltd v Hobbs* (1986) an innocent but inaccurate statement about the mileage of a second-hand car, which the seller qualified as correct 'to the best of my knowledge and belief' was held not to be a misrepresentation: his statement 'was an accurate representation of his knowledge and belief'.

Statements of fact distinguished from statements as to the future?

9.17   A statement of a party's future intention is not a statement of fact and is of no effect as a misrepresentation. Of course, if the maker of the statement *promises* that he will act upon or otherwise honour that future intention, it will be enforceable as a term of the contract. In *British Airways Board v Taylor* (1976) Lord Wilberforce neatly summarised this as the difference between 'a promise as to future action, which may be broken or kept, and a statement of existing fact, which may be true or false'. However, a statement of future intention, or expectation, as to the future, can implicitly contain a statement of fact. As the Court of Appeal put it in *Spice Girls Ltd v Aprilia World Service BV* (2002), 'though the representation must be one of fact, representations as to the future or of opinion frequently contain implied representations with regard to the present or to the knowledge of the representor'. For example, if the maker of the statement did not genuinely hold the intention or belief at the time of making it, he will have misrepresented a fact, namely the state of his mind. As Bowen LJ graphically explained in *Edgington v Fitzmaurice* (1885):

> There must be a misstatement of existing fact: but the state of a man's mind is as much a fact as the state of his digestion. It is true that it is very difficult to prove what the state of a man's mind at a particular time is, but if it can be ascertained it is as much a fact as anything else.

Where, however, the belief is genuinely held, it does not matter that it was unreasonable. In *Royal Bank of Scotland v Chandra* (2011) a husband gave his wife, in good faith, an 'over-optimistic assessment' of the financial prospects of his business project; it was held that this did not amount to an actionable misrepresentation.

Representations of law

9.18 It used to be well established that a misrepresentation of law was not actionable, giving neither a right to rescind nor an action for damages (although a number of borderline cases, like statements about a person's legal rights or about foreign law, were regarded as statements of fact). However, in *Kleinwort Benson Ltd v Lincoln City Council* (1998) the House of Lords held for the first time that money paid as a result of a *mistake of law* could be reclaimed by the mistaken party. Once a spontaneous mistake of law became actionable, it was no longer possible to justify retaining a rule that misrepresentations as to the law do not give rise to liability (after all, a misrepresentation induces a mistake in the representee) and in *Pankhania v London Borough of Hackney* (2004) the court held that the rule is no longer good law.

The impact on the misrepresentee

9.19 It has often been said that a misrepresentation must satisfy two distinct requirements in order to be actionable, namely that it was a material misrepresentation and that it induced or caused the representee to enter the contract (a similar twofold test applies to actionable non-disclosure—see para **9.3**). The difference is that materiality is an objective question, dealing with the significance the representation would have had to a hypothetical, reasonable person, whereas causation concerns the impact the representation had on the actual representee (although the language of the cases can be misleading, with 'material' sometimes used as an abbreviation for 'material to the representee'). However, despite numerous references to these as two distinct requirements in older case law and in textbooks, the better view is that objective materiality should not be regarded as a separate requirement, and indeed it is rare to find separate consideration of the two requirements in modern cases. Instead the focus tends to be on whether the representation *caused* the representee to enter the contract.

9.20 This is unsurprising. In the vast majority of cases, the representee does not differ very markedly from the 'hypothetical reasonable person', so that the materiality of the representation can be taken as read, once it has been shown that the representation caused the representee to contract. So materiality will only be a live question in cases where the representee is claiming that he relied on a representation that most people would have regarded as trivial or immaterial. In such cases, the court will of course scrutinise very carefully the representee's assertion that the representation mattered to him. But there may well be a feasible explanation for the representee's unusual reaction—perhaps the representee had a particular, idiosyncratic interest in one minor aspect of the contractual subject matter—which convinces the court of the causal impact of the representation. If so, it is unlikely that the court would dismiss the claim on the grounds that the representation would have been immaterial to the average person.

9.21 This interpretation accords with the position where a contractual term, specified by the individual contractor, is of no significance to the average person (the arbiter of market value). The other party, when in breach of such a term, cannot be heard to say that, since the difference in market value between performance and breach is minimal only nominal damages are payable (see the discussion in Chapter 16 of *Ruxley Electronics & Construction Ltd v Forsyth* (1996)). The law respects the individual preferences of a contracting party, but protects the other party by only holding them liable in respect of preferences about which they knew or ought to have known.

9.22 One way to reconcile the two apparent requirements of materiality and causation is that where the representation was material in that it would have influenced a reasonable person, this raises an inference that it caused the representee to enter the contract, which the other party may then rebut. Jessel MR said as much in *Redgrave v Hurd* (1881), a case of rescission for innocent misrepresentation, and the same has been held to apply to actions for deceit, both for rescission and for damages (see *Smith v Chadwick* (1884), approved in *Barton v County NatWest Ltd* (1999)) and occasionally in claims for damages for non-fraudulent misrepresentation (see, for example, *Street v Coombes* (2005)). The Supreme Court said in *Hayward v Zurich Insurance Co plc* (2016) that, in a case of fraud, this burden is difficult for a fraudster to rebut; Lord Clarke quoted with approval a rhetorical question asked by Lord Chelmsford LC in *Smith v Kay* (1859), 'can it be permitted to a party who has practised a deception, with a view to a particular end, which has been attained by it, to speculate upon what might have been the result if there had been a full communication of the truth?' In any event, whichever party has the burden of proof, it is important to establish precisely what level of causation is required for a claim based on misrepresentation.

Causation in fact–reliance

9.23 The relevant causal test for misrepresentation is sometimes referred to as a requirement that the representation 'induced' the representee to enter the contract. This usage is not ideal, since 'induced' has the connotation that the representee's entry into the contract was somehow desired by the representor. This is appropriate in cases of fraudulent misrepresentation and the tort of deceit (where the cause of action requires such intention—see for example *Ludsin Overseas Ltd v Eco3 Capital Ltd* (2013) and para 9.53), but in all other cases there is no need to demonstrate anything about the attitude of the representor or that the representation was 'calculated' to make the representee act in a certain way. For this reason, it is better to regard the causation requirement as one of 'reliance' by the representee (a linguistic distinction approved by Hobhouse LJ in *Downs v Chappell* (1996)). Also, bear in mind that the correct counterfactual for judging reliance will normally be to ask what the representee would have done had *no representation been made*, rather than what he would have done had he been *told the truth*, but occasionally the courts explore both issues—see *Raiffeisen Zentralbank Österreich AG v Royal Bank of Scotland* (2010).

9.24 The basic rule, then, is that the representee must have relied on the representation, so where the representation did not influence the representee at all, there can be no remedy.

For example if, as in *Hunt v Optima (Cambridge) Ltd* (2014), the representation did not come to the representee's attention until *after* the contract was made, or if the representee knew that the representation was not true, there was no reliance. But many cases are not so straightforward. Very often, one contracting party makes a number of statements to the other party prior to contracting. One may be false, others true, and it is the combined effect of all the statements that together persuades the representee to contract. Moreover, the representee's decision whether to contract, and on what terms, will be influenced not only by these representations but also by numerous other factors, such as outside information and his own priorities and attitudes.

9.25 The law compromises by requiring that the misrepresentation need not be the claimant's sole or main inducement to enter into the contract, provided it formed *a* reason why he did so. As Stephenson LJ said in *JEB Fasteners v Marks Bloom & Co* (1983), 'as long as a misrepresentation plays a real and substantial part, though not by itself a decisive part, in inducing the plaintiff to act, it is a cause of his loss and he relies on it, no matter how strong or how many are the other matters which play their part in inducing him to act'. In *Edgington v Fitzmaurice* (1885) (discussed in para **9.17**) Edgington lent money to a company in reliance on the false statement by the directors of the company in its prospectus, but also because of his own mistaken belief that he would have a charge on the company's assets. He admitted that, but for his mistaken belief, he would not have lent, but nonetheless was entitled to damages for deceit, since but for the false statement in the prospectus he would not have proceeded either. As Christopher Clarke J said in *Raiffeisen Zentralbank Österreich AG v Royal Bank of Scotland* (2010), 'the representation must play a causative part in inducing the contract and … that involves "but for" causation'.

9.26 However, where the misrepresentation made no difference at all to the representee, in that he would have acted in precisely the same way and contracted on precisely the same terms even if the misrepresentation had not been made, there is no possibility either of rescission or damages. Or, as Lord Toulson graphically put it in *Hayward v Zurich Insurance Co plc* (2016), 'A misrepresentation which has no impact on the mind of the representee is no more harmful than an arrow which misses the target'. This is illustrated by *JEB Fasteners v Marks Bloom & Co* (1983). JEB were negotiating the take-over of a manufacturing company. The company's audited accounts, drawn up by the defendant accountants, contained substantial inaccuracies. JEB read the accounts, suspected that they were erroneous in a number of respects, but proceeded with the take-over anyway because they wished to acquire the services of its two directors. JEB sued the defendants for negligence, but the Court of Appeal agreed with the judge's finding that they did not rely on the accounts and thus there was no causal connection between the defendant's negligence and the loss incurred on the take-over. Sir Sebag Shaw said:

> while the content of the accounts was observed and considered by [JEB], it did not in any material degree affect their judgement in deciding whether to take-over [the company].

Put another way, as Donaldson LJ explained in the *JEB Fasteners* case, a decision to contract might be supported by:

> subsidiary factors which support or encourage the taking of the decision. If these latter assumptions are falsified in the event, whether individually or collectively, this will be a cause for disappointment to the decision-taker, but will not affect the essential validity of his decision in the sense that if the truth had been known or suspected before the decision was taken, the same decision would still have been made.

9.27 It may be plausible to regard the representee as having 'relied', in a very weak sense, on matters of this kind, but as a causal link it is generally insufficient in English law. It should be said that, in some cases of fraudulent misrepresentation, claimants have succeeded by showing this weak level of reliance, where for example the fraudulent material misrepresentation merely made the representee 'persevere in a decision already made' (see *Barton v County Nat West Ltd* (1999)), but such decisions are difficult to justify on principle, other than as examples of more generous treatment for claimants in fraud cases: this is how they were explained in *Raiffeisen Zentralbank Österreich AG v Royal Bank of Scotland* (2010). The Supreme Court's discussion in *Hayward v Zurich Insurance Co plc* (2016) of the causal issue in deceit cases made no mention of this little pocket of cases.

9.28 The intermediate position, where the representee would nonetheless have entered a contract with the representor if the representation had not been made, but *on different terms*, is one which is very rarely examined by the English courts. Such a level of reliance is clearly sufficient, for both rescission and, where appropriate, an action for damages. The Court of Appeal in *Huyton SA v Distribuidora Internacional de Productos Agricolas SA* (2004) regarded the critical question as 'whether if [the misrepresentee] had known the true position they would have concluded the [agreement] on the same terms, and whether if not the difference in terms was of materiality'. As we will see, *Hayward v Zurich Insurance Co plc* (2016) falls into this category.

9.29 The usual reason why a claimant relies on a representation, or is induced to contract because of that representation, is because the claimant believes the representation, but the Supreme Court has recently made clear that belief in the truth of the representation is not a separate requirement. In *Hayward v Zurich Insurance Company plc* (2016) a man suffered an injury at work, for which his employer was responsible. Zurich, the employer's liability insurer, entered into an agreement to pay over £134,000 in full and final settlement of the employee's damages claim, even though it strongly suspected (but had been unable to prove) that he had exaggerated the extent of his injury. Two years later, neighbours of the man came forward with clear evidence that he had indeed grossly exaggerated the extent of his injury. So Zurich applied to rescind the settlement agreement and claimed damages, on the basis of the employee's fraudulent misrepresentations. The claim succeeded at first instance, but the Court of Appeal found in the employee's favour, on the basis that Zurich entered into the agreement with its 'eyes open', knowingly taking the risk that the statements might not be true, and thus did not rely on their truth. The Supreme Court unanimously allowed Zurich's appeal, holding that if a claimant is induced to enter into the particular contract by the representation, there is no additional requirement that the claimant must have believed its truth. On the exceptional facts, Zurich could not categorically prove that the statements were false and so reluctantly opted to settle, concerned that a court might believe the employee's statements. The degree of difference in the figures demonstrates that Zurich was indeed influenced by the fraud—the settlement agreement was for more than £134,000, but the judge decided that the employee was only entitled to damages of £14,720. As Lord Clarke said, 'There can be no doubt on the judge's findings of fact that, if Zurich had known the true position as to Mr Hayward's state of recovery, it would not have offered anything like as much as it in fact offered and settled for.'

9.30 This leaves the knotty problem of whether a representee who had an opportunity to discover the truth, but did not take it, can be said to have relied on the representation. The traditional rule is that, certainly in a claim for rescission (whether for fraudulent or non-fraudulent misrepresentation), the representee who neglects such an opportunity can nonetheless rescind.

In *Redgrave v Hurd* (1881) H agreed to buy R's solicitor's practice in reliance on H's misrepresentations about the turnover of the business. H could have discovered the true position by reading some paperwork provided by R, but did not do so. On discovering that the business was practically worthless, H sought to rescind the agreement (pleaded as a counterclaim in R's action for specific performance) and H succeeded in the Court of Appeal. Jessel MR held:

> Nothing can be plainer, I take it, on the authorities in equity that the effect of false representation is not got rid of on the ground that the person to whom it was made has been guilty of negligence ... It is not sufficient, therefore, to say that the purchaser had the opportunity of investigating the real state of the case, but did not avail himself of that opportunity.

This principle has been frequently applied, but a couple of qualifications should be made to it.

9.31 First, in *Redgrave v Hurd* the representor was better informed than the representee and thus better placed to provide accurate information, so it was appropriate that the risk that the representee would take the representor at his word and not check the accuracy of the information should fall on the representor. The same applied in *Street v Coombes* (2005), where C 'naively' agreed to buy S's business, trusting S's false assurances that the business was solvent, but was not thereby prevented from rescinding. But where the balance between the parties is the other way round, the opposite conclusion may be appropriate. So where the representor was wholly innocent and the representee was better placed to acquire accurate information or confirmation, but failed to take reasonable steps to do so, the court might well conclude that the representee did not rely on the initial representation but took the risk of its accuracy.

9.32 Second, *Redgrave v Hurd* involved a rescission claim, but it is now possible to recover *damages* for negligent misrepresentation, both in tort and (where the representation was made by the other contracting party only) under the Misrepresentation Act 1967 (see paras **9.62-9.71**). Tort liability under the *Hedley Byrne* principle depends in part on the reasonableness of the representee's reliance. Although the focus in cases of tortious negligent misstatement is on whether a duty of care was owed by the representor, and rather different considerations apply to representations made by a contracting party, it is possible that the same reasoning would be adopted in a claim for damages under the Act. Moreover, in a negligent misstatement claim in tort, damages can be reduced to take into account the representee's *contributory negligence*, and it was held in *Gran Gelato v Richcliff* (1992) that a reduction for contributory negligence can also be made for a claim under the Misrepresentation Act, at least where the facts attract concurrent liability in tort and under the Act (although see para **9.67**).

9.33   A related problem arose in *Peekay Intermark v Australia and New Zealand Banking Group* (2006), in which P, an investor, bought bonds from a merchant bank, having been misled by 'fundamental misrepresentations' about the bonds in the bank's marketing literature and by one of its officials, and later claimed damages. The problem was that the contract document described the bonds accurately, but P had just signed and returned the contract without reading it. The bank argued that the accurate description in the contract document 'over-rode' the earlier misrepresentations. The judge at first instance disagreed with the bank and awarded damages to P, holding that the issue was one of reliance and that the representations were still operative when P initialled the contract. However, the bank appealed successfully to the Court of Appeal, where the court approached the law in the same way but adopted a significantly different view of the facts. According to Moore-Bick LJ, the misrepresentations provided P with a 'rough and ready' description of the bonds only. The contractual terms:

> *were the first and only opportunity he was given to satisfy himself that the nature of the investment and the terms relating to it were consistent with the broad description [the bank's official] had given him and that it was satisfactory. He may not have been expecting the documents to contain any nasty surprises, but only by reading them could he satisfy himself that the product was what he had been led to expect ... [P] was induced to sign the documents and enter into the contract not by what [the bank's official] had told him, but by his own assumption that the investment product to which they related corresponded to the description he had previously been given.*

Interestingly, contributory negligence was not pleaded either at first instance or on appeal. Arguably, a reduced award of damages to P might have been a more appropriate solution than the 'all-or-nothing' stances of the judge and the Court of Appeal.

Remedies for misrepresentation: rescission

9.34   The principal remedy for misrepresentation is rescission. In some circumstances, it may also be possible to recover damages, either as well as or instead of rescinding the contract. It makes sense to consider rescission first, not least because rescission is potentially available whatever the misrepresentor's state of mind was (in other words, for fraudulent, negligent, and innocent misrepresentation), whereas the availability and measure of damages is affected by the representor's level of fault.

What is rescission?

9.35 A person who enters into a contract in reliance on a misrepresentation may elect to rescind, or 'undo', the contract. As Millett LJ explained in *Bristol & West Building Society v Mothew* (1998), 'Misrepresentation makes a transaction voidable not void. It gives the representee the right to elect whether to rescind or affirm the transaction. The representor cannot anticipate his decision. Unless and until the representee elects to rescind the representor remains fully bound.' Rescission involves, so far as possible, restoring the parties to the pre-contract position, or as it is sometimes expressed, restoring the '*status quo ante*'. This means that 'executory' obligations under the contract (ie, obligations that have yet to be performed) no longer have to be performed and, crucially, any parts of the contract that have already been performed ('executed' obligations) are 'undone'. Putting it metaphorically, rescission means unravelling the contract *ab initio*—setting it back to the beginning. So any property transferred pursuant to the contract is returned. In a simple case in which, for example, I buy a painting from you in reliance on your false representation that it was painted by Constable, rescission will involve me returning the painting to you and you returning the price to me. There are two fundamental things to bear in mind about rescission, before going any further.

9.36 The first is that rescission differs significantly from the process which occurs when an innocent party elects to terminate a contract for repudiatory breach by the other party (discussed in detail in Chapter 17). Where a contract is terminated for breach, that termination is prospective only—the parties are released from outstanding primary obligations under the contract, but there is no attempt to undo any parts of the contract that have already been performed. This distinction was not always strictly observed, but the House of Lords clarified the position in *Johnson v Agnew* (1980). As Lord Wilberforce explained, termination for breach is sometimes referred to as 'rescission', but this is a source of confusion, as the two processes are distinct:

> ... this so-called 'rescission' is quite different from rescission ab initio, such as may arise for example in cases of mistake, fraud or lack of consent. In those cases, the contract is treated in law as never having come into existence ... In the case of an accepted repudiatory breach the contract has come into existence but has been put an end to or discharged. Whatever contrary indications may be disinterred from old authorities, it is now quite clear, under the general law of contract, that acceptance of a repudiatory breach does not bring about 'rescission ab initio'.

Alas, despite this clarification of the different concepts, many judges and commentators persist in describing the process of termination for breach as 'rescission'. This temptation should be resolutely resisted!

9.37 The second fundamental issue is the question of how rescission actually occurs. It is often said that rescission is a self-help remedy, which means that the innocent party's own act or election is itself enough to rescind the contract (in *Street v Coombes* (2005) discussed at para **9.31**, C successfully rescinded by means of a letter from his solicitor to S). This notion seems to have two aspects. The first is that it is theoretically possible to rescind a contract merely by giving notice to the other party (or in some exceptional cases, without notice to the other party as long as reasonable steps to disaffirm the contract are taken—for example, in *Car and Universal Finance Co Ltd v Caldwell* (1965) informing the police and Automobile Association that a contract to sell a car to a fraudster had been rescinded). There is no formal requirement to obtain a court order, although of course in practice recourse to court proceedings may be necessary, for example where the other party disputes the ground of rescission or refuses to return property transferred under the contract, but in theory the operative act of rescission remains that of the innocent party. This leads to the second aspect of rescission as a self-help remedy, namely that even where a court order of rescission is obtained, the order is said to be 'back-dated' to the date of the party's own act of rescission.

9.38 Both aspects are problematic (see O'Sullivan (2000)) in circumstances where the contract has been executed and property has been transferred pursuant to it: in particular, what is the status of title to that property in the period between the representee electing to rescind and a later court order either confirming the rescission (or even deciding that it was not justified)? Moreover, historically it was only at common law that rescission was regarded as a self-help remedy—for our purposes, this means only where fraudulent misrepresentation was concerned, since this was the only sort of misrepresentation that was actionable at common law. In equity, on the other hand, rescission was definitely a judicial remedy only, and it was only in equity that relief could be obtained for non-fraudulent misrepresentation. So for both historical reasons and reasons of principle, it might be better to do away with the notion of rescission as a self-help remedy, at the very least for misrepresentations that were not made fraudulently.

When rescission is unavailable

9.39 In certain circumstances, the misrepresentee loses the right to rescind the contract—in technical language, rescission is said to be *barred*. First, a contract cannot be rescinded if the misrepresentee does something unequivocal, intending to *affirm* the contract after discovering the truth. Affirmation can involve expressly communicating to the representor that the contract is affirmed, or acting in a way that is inconsistent with a desire to set aside the contract. But it will not be inferred lightly: for example, in *Street v Coombes* (2005) the purchaser's actions in trying to keep the business going, having discovered its true, disastrous financial position, came nowhere near to evincing an intention to affirm the contract.

9.40 Second, it is sometimes suggested that if the misrepresentee delays too long before rescinding, this will bar the claim. Of course, delay after discovering the truth is closely analogous to affirmation, but it is not entirely clear whether delay operates merely as *evidence* of affirmation or is a distinct bar in its own right. The relevant question is whether lapse of time alone operates as a bar, even if the misrepresentee seeks rescission immediately on discovering the truth. There are several authorities which suggest not, such as the fraud case of *Clough v London and North Western Railway* (1871), on the basis that a representee cannot be blamed merely because it takes an inherently long time for the falsity of a representation to come to light, as long as he acts promptly as soon as it does.

9.41 One well known case, however, suggests the opposite. In *Leaf v International Galleries* (1950) L bought a painting from IG in 1944, in reliance on their innocent representation that it had been painted by Constable. L only discovered the truth five years later when he tried to sell the painting through Christies auctioneers and attempted to rescind immediately. The Court of Appeal held it was too late to do so—he had not acted within a reasonable time. For Lord Denning, 'it behoves the purchaser either to verify or, as the case may be, to disprove the representation within a reasonable time, or else stand or fall by it'.

9.42 *Leaf* involved a wholly innocent misrepresentation, where some indulgence to the representor can be expected. Perhaps it is only in such cases that Lord Denning's view should prevail over conflicting considerations of fairness to the representee. Recently the Court of Appeal in *Salt v Stratstone Specialist Ltd* (2015) has pointed out that *Leaf* is out of date—it reflected the principle that the misrepresentation regime should not give greater protection to a purchaser than if the statement had been incorporated as a term of the contract, and at the time the Sale of Goods Act provided that a purchaser would be deemed to have accepted the goods if he did not reject them within a reasonable time. Since then, amendments to the Sale of Goods Act, and the enactment of the Misrepresentation Act, cast doubt on the reasoning and conclusion in *Leaf*, therefore the court in *Salt*, although unable to overrule the earlier Court of Appeal decision, doubted that lapse of time alone should generally bar rescission.

9.43 Third, intervening third party rights bar rescission. Once a third party has gained an interest in property that was the subject of the contract, it is too late for the representee to rescind (this is why it is critical for the owner of goods, who sells them in reliance on a fraudulent misrepresentation, to rescind the contract *before* the fraudster sells the goods to an innocent third party). The third party must have acquired his interest in good faith, for value and without notice of the defect in the initial contract. A similar principle prevents rescission of a contract to acquire shares once steps have been commenced to wind up the company, since thereafter rescission would prejudice third parties, namely the company's creditors (for example, *Oakes v Turquand* (1867)). However, as Nahan (1997) has pointed out, the need to protect third parties should not rule out altogether a personal remedy as between misrepresentor and misrepresentee. Her solution would be the financial equivalent of rescission (see para **11.38**) since 'even as a matter of policy there is no reason why a defendant should not have a personal duty to return the value of the asset'.

9.44 Fourth, the impossibility of restoring the *status quo ante* bars rescission. In a simple case, such as the sale of the painting discussed at para **9.15**, it is easy to restore the parties to the precise pre-contract position, by returning the painting and the price, respectively. However, many cases are more complicated. Rescission cannot literally turn the clock back, so what happens where subsequent events or the passage of time mean that it is not possible to put the parties back to precisely the position in which they started?

9.45   Where it is genuinely impossible to achieve the necessary taking and giving back (in other words, to make *restitutio in integrum*) then rescission is barred. As is sometimes said, 'You cannot both eat your cake and return your cake.' In *Thomas Witter Ltd v TBP Industries Ltd* (1996) TW purchased a carpet business from TBP, relying on negligent misrepresentations made by TBP in the management accounts about financial matters. TW later sought rescission, but by the time of the trial they had made numerous changes to the structure, organisation, and personnel of the business, with new pension schemes and new mortgages in place. The judge declined to order rescission, since it 'is not available where it is not possible to restore the parties to their position before the contract', though awarded damages instead (see para **9.75**).

9.46   However, the requirement of restoring the *status quo* is not a rigid, inflexible one and where the court can ensure that the parties are substantially restored to the pre-contract position, this will suffice. As Lord Blackburn explained in *Erlanger v New Sombrero Phosphate Co* (1878), the court can 'take account of profits, and make allowance for deterioration. And I think the practice has always been for a Court of Equity to give this relief whenever, by the exercise of its powers, it can do what is practically just, though it cannot restore the parties precisely to the state they were in before.' So where a financial adjustment between the parties can help to achieve such practical justice, the court will make an appropriate order. This might, for example, reflect the fact that the subject matter of the contract has been improved at the representee's expense or conversely that the representee has obtained a valuable service from performance of the contract, for which he should pay a reasonable sum. It is all a matter of flexibility and doing what is just: for example, in an appropriate case rescission might still be allowed where the value of the subject matter has deteriorated since the contract, with no need for any financial adjustment either (see *Adam v Newbigging and Townend* (1888)). For example, in *Salt v Stratstone Specialist Ltd* (2015) the defendant sold a Cadillac car to the claimant in 2007 for £21,895, describing it as 'brand new'. In fact, the defendant had owned the car since 2005 (though never registered itself as owner), it had been repaired several times, and had been involved in a collision. When the claimant sought rescission in 2008, the defendant tried to argue that it was impossible to restore the parties to their pre-contract position, because in the meantime the car had been registered, had depreciated in value, and been used and enjoyed by the claimant. But the Court of Appeal rejected all these arguments and ordered rescission—the return of the car and the full purchase price. Registration was a mere paper formality that changed nothing of substance, while the 'absence of evidence about depreciation or the value of the use of the car should not operate to the disadvantage of the representee who should never have been put in the position of having a troublesome old car rather than a brand new one'.

9.47 Finally, the House of Lords has suggested that the courts might be prepared to be more flexible than has previously been envisaged in finding ways round the fact that *restitutio in integrum* is literally impossible. In *Smith New Court Securities Ltd v Scrimgeour Vickers (Asset Management) Ltd* (1997) Smith purchased shares in a public company, Ferranti plc, as a result of Scrimgeour's fraudulent misrepresentations. The share price subsequently plummeted because of an unrelated fraud and Smith sold their shares at a loss. They then sought rescission of the purchase transaction or, in the alternative, damages for deceit. In the Court of Appeal, the claim for rescission was rejected on the basis that Smith, having sold the shares, could no longer restore them to Scrimgeour, and Smith did not pursue the rescission claim, appealing to the House of Lords only on the measure of damages for deceit. But in the House of Lords, Lord Browne-Wilkinson expressed the view, *obiter*, that rescission was more flexible than this:

> If the current law in fact provides (as the Court of Appeal thought) that there is no right to rescind the contract for the sale of quoted shares once the specified shares purchased have been sold, the law will need to be closely looked at hereafter. Since in such a case other, identical shares can be purchased on the market, the defrauded purchaser can offer substantial restitutio in integrum which is normally sufficient.

This is a most sensible observation. After all, when a contract of sale is rescinded, the law does not require the seller to return precisely the same notes and coins as he received from the purchaser, since money is currency and one note or coin is as good as any other of the same denomination. The same should apply to shares quoted on the stock market, which closely resemble currency: the seller should not be able to object that the shares being returned do not bear the same serial number as the ones he sold, when in every other respect they are exactly the same. Alternatively, the pecuniary equivalent of rescission can be ordered in such a case (discussed further at para **11.38**).

Rescission where the misrepresentation was not made by party to the contract

9.48 Normally, rescission is only available where the misrepresentation was made by the other party to the contract. So if X makes a misrepresentation to Y which causes Y to contract with Z, Y is generally confined to a claim against X for damages in tort (either for deceit or negligent misstatement) and the contract with Z cannot be challenged. Indeed, to be consistent with the rules on unilateral mistake (see the discussion of *Smith v Hughes* (1871) at para **3.51**), this general position should prevail even where the other contracting party—Z in our example—knows of the misrepresentation (so long as the misrepresentation is not as to the *terms* of the proposed Y–Z contract). Since a contracting party can generally keep quiet, even though he knows that the other party has made a mistake, the same should apply even though the mistake was induced by a third party's misrepresentation.

9.49 However, in one limited context, the law allows a contract to be rescinded because of a misrepresentation as to terms made by a third party, where the other party to the contract has mere *constructive* notice of that misrepresentation. This is pursuant to the House of Lords decision in *Barclays Bank plc v O'Brien* (1994), which concerned a wife who entered into a charge (the same would apply to an unsecured guarantee) with a bank guaranteeing her husband's business debts, as a result of her husband's misrepresentation as to the terms of the security. It was held that the surety wife can obtain rescission of the charge or guarantee if the bank has actual or constructive notice of the misrepresentation. This principle, refined by the House of Lords in *Royal Bank of Scotland v Etridge (No 2)* (2001), is usually pleaded in the context of undue influence (and is discussed in detail in Chapter 11), but it should not be forgotten that it applies equally to misrepresentations made in the same context (and indeed in *O'Brien* itself the only successful plea was one of misrepresentation). This regime has not been without its critics, who point out that, for example, although there is a heightened risk of *undue influence* where the relationships between surety and debtor are 'emotional', justifying a stricter regime of constructive notice for third party creditors, there is not necessarily a heightened risk of *misrepresentation*. In the House of Lords appeal in the Scots case of *Smith v Bank of Scotland* (1997) Lord Jauncey said:

> ... while I can follow the policy reasons for clothing a creditor with constructive knowledge of the risk of undue influence by a husband in the special circumstances of a cautionary [ie, security] obligation, I have the greatest difficulty in seeing why such constructive notice should extend to misrepresentation. There has so far as I am aware never been any suggestion in the law of Scotland that any particular class of persons is more likely to misrepresent in relation to a contract than any other. (See also O'Sullivan (1998).)

9.50 Despite Lord Jauncey's unease, the *O'Brien* regime is well established for misrepresentation as well as undue influence, although there is one problematic issue peculiar to misrepresentation. That is the question of whether, if the misrepresentation was as to the terms of the transaction, rescission must be total or whether it can be ordered on terms that the surety should at least be liable for the terms as they had been represented to be.

9.51 The English courts have consistently refused to allow 'partial rescission' of this kind. In *TSB Bank plc v Camfield* (1995) Mrs C was induced to stand surety for her husband's business debts and to execute a joint mortgage over the matrimonial home, because of her husband's innocent misrepresentation that liability was limited to a maximum of £15,000 when in fact it was unlimited. The bank was fixed with constructive notice of the misrepresentation, but argued that Mrs C should only be entitled to rescission on terms that she acknowledged that the security was valid as to £15,000. The Court of Appeal disagreed, deciding that it had no jurisdiction to order rescission on terms of this kind—rescission is an all or nothing process. *Camfield* has been followed at first instance in *Molestina v Ponton* (2002).

Interestingly, the Australian courts reached the opposite conclusion in *Vasdasz v Pioneer Concrete (SA) Pty Ltd* (1995), allowing rescission in part, but leaving the guarantee in place on the terms as they were represented to be. On balance, the Australian approach is to be preferred: there seems no reason to allow Mrs C to escape from her obligations altogether when she was by her own admission willing to guarantee £15,000. It is true that, in cases of rescission for misrepresentation involving just two parties, no enquiry is usually made into what different terms the misrepresentee would have agreed to had the misrepresentation been *true*, but then in most cases that would be mere speculation. The unusual feature of the facts of *Camfield* is that it is possible to know precisely what Mrs C would have done had the misrepresentation been true, because, unusually, the misrepresentation was as to the *terms* of the transaction. Relief should therefore be on this basis, particularly since it is being ordered as against a party with mere constructive notice of the misrepresentation, and not the less deserving misrepresentor.

9.52   Meikle (2003) agrees, concluding that the remedy of partial rescission should in principle be available 'where the party ordinarily entitled to rescind has, despite the vitiating defect, evidenced an unvitiated intention to enter into a contract on terms differing from those in the contract objectively concluded'. He notes, however, that the results in *Camfield* and *Vasdasz* were the wrong way round, because the misrepresentation in *Vasdasz* was made *fraudulently* and wrongdoers like fraudsters should not be entitled to the advantage of partial rescission. Otherwise fraudsters would have nothing to lose from misrepresenting the terms of a guarantee, knowing that the only risk was of partial, not full rescission.

Remedies for misrepresentation: damages

Fraudulent misrepresentations

9.53   Where a misrepresentation was made fraudulently, the innocent party may elect not to rescind the contract but to claim damages for the tort of deceit instead. Damages are also available for fraudulent *non-disclosure* in cases of contracts *uberrimae fidei*, whereas for non-fraudulent non-disclosure the claimant's only remedy is rescission (confirmed by the Court of Appeal in *Conlon v Simms* (2006) concerning a solicitors' partnership agreement where one of the partners fraudulently failed to disclose dishonest conduct that ultimately led to him being struck off by the Solicitors' Disciplinary Tribunal). To establish fraud, it must be shown that 'a false representation has been made (1) knowingly, or (2) without belief in its truth, or (3) recklessly, careless whether it be true or false'—*Derry v Peek* (1889). Despite the reference to carelessness in this definition, mere negligence is insufficient for fraud. A more modern exposition of the requirements for deceit was set out by Jackson LJ in *Ludsin Overseas Ltd v Eco3 Capital Ltd* (2013):

   (i)   *The Defendant makes a false representation to the Claimant.*
   (ii) *The Defendant knows that the representation is false, alternatively he is reckless as to whether it is true or false.*
   (iii) *The Defendant intends that the Claimant should act in reliance on it.*
   (iv) *The Claimant does act in reliance on the representation and in consequence suffers loss.*

9.54 The measure of damages for deceit is more generous than the equivalent measure for the tort of negligence. First, the representee can recover for all losses caused directly by, and which he would not have incurred but for, the deceit, even if they were not reasonably foreseeable. So in *Smith New Court Securities Ltd v Scrimgeour Vickers (Asset Management) Ltd* (1997) (see para **9.47**) Smith, who purchased the shares for 82 pence when their true value at the time was 78 pence, were able to recover their total loss when they eventually sold the shares for only 44 pence. This was despite the fact that the further fall in the share price was caused by a separate, unforeseeable fraud, entirely unrelated to Scrimgeour's. Similarly in *Nationwide Building Society v (1) Dunlop Haywards Ltd and (2) Cobbetts (a firm)* (2009) a building society recovered damages against the first defendant, a valuer who fraudulently overvalued property on which the society lent and lost considerable sums, but many of which represented unforeseeable heads of loss. For example, in response to the fraud the society made a provision of £10 million in its accounts, triggering widespread adverse publicity which led a credit rating agency to downgrade its view of the society from 'stable' to 'negative'—this in turn caused the withdrawal of retail deposits and the loss of further mortgage business valued at £7.5 million. All these losses were recoverable in the deceit action against the first defendant, but not against the second defendant, solicitors who had merely been negligent.

9.55 *Smith New Court Securities* was also applied by the Court of Appeal in *Parabola Investments Ltd v Browallia Cal Ltd* (2010), deciding that there was no principled reason why the date of discovery of the fraud should be taken as the cut-off point that terminated the claimant's damages, when loss of investment opportunity continued thereafter. The Court of Appeal returned to this issue in the deceit case of *OMV Petrom SA v Glencore International AG* (2016), where the claimant's loss actually decreased rather than increased after the fraud but before it came to light, deciding that the 'purpose of the flexibility of approach about the valuation date to which Lord Browne-Wilkinson [in *Smith New Court Securities*] referred was to ensure that the person duped should not suffer an injustice by failing to recover full compensation in the type of circumstances to which he referred. There is no need to adopt such an approach in order to relieve the fraudster from the general rule as to damages.' For a powerful critique of this treatment of the date of assessment, which the authors regard as out of step with general principles of mitigation, see Summers and Kramer (2017).

9.56 Second, in negligence it is also necessary to establish that the claimant's losses fell within the scope of the misrepresentation by checking whether they would have been suffered if the misrepresentation had been true (see the speech of Lord Hoffmann in *South Australia Asset Management Corpn v York Montague Ltd* (1996)). There is no equivalent qualification in deceit.

9.57 Third, there is no reduction in deceit for the claimant's own contributory negligence (*Standard Chartered Bank v Pakistan National Shipping Corpn (No 4)* (2002)), although, as with all damages claims, the claimant will be required to mitigate his loss once he discovers, or has reasonable grounds to discover, the fraud, so that any extra losses incurred thereafter will not generally be the responsibility of the defendant.

9.58   Although generous to the claimant, the measure of damages for fraud is nonetheless not the same as the expectation measure (discussed in detail in Chapter 16), since the fraud-ster did not promise the truth of the representations made. So the claimant will not be put into the position he would have been in had the representation been true, only the position he would have been in had the representation (which caused him to contract) not been made.

9.59   Sometimes this distinction can be a hard one to draw, particularly where the fraud in-duced the claimant to purchase a loss-making business, thereby forgoing the opportun-ity to acquire some other, potentially profitable business. It has been held that the profits which the claimant lost the opportunity to make on an alternative business are recover-able (though not the profits which the claimant thought he would make on the business actually purchased). In *East v Maurer* (1991) E purchased one of M's two hairdressing salons for £20,000 in reliance on M's deliberate false assertion that he intended to stop working at his other salon in the same town. As a result of the unexpected competition from M, E's business was unsuccessful and she eventually sold it for £7,500. The Court of Appeal held the trial judge was wrong to award damages for loss of profits that E would have made if M's statement had been true. However, the judge should instead have as-sessed, 'the kind of profits which she might have expected to make in another hairdress-ing business bought for the same sum'.

9.60   Marks (1992) is critical of the reasoning in *East v Maurer*, arguing that the decision 'may well overcompensate the plaintiff by considering as certain that which was merely pos-sible' (compare damages for loss of a chance, discussed in para **16.9**). Marks also points out that the court assumed a hypothetical third party contract essentially identical to the one made with M, even though there was no evidence that any other suitable hairdress-ing business was available, so that the contractual measure of damages was adopted in all but name. Nonetheless, the *East v Maurer* approach was followed by the Court of Appeal in *Clef Aquitaine v Laporte Materials (Barrow) Ltd* (2000).

Non-fraudulent misrepresentations

9.61   Until the 1960s, the only possibility of obtaining damages for a misrepresentation that had not been incorporated as a term of the contract was to discharge the onerous bur-den of proving that it was made fraudulently. However, two developments in the 1960s changed that. First, the House of Lords in *Hedley Byrne v Heller* (1964) decided for the first time that a duty of care in tort might be owed in respect of negligent misrepresen-tations causing pure economic loss. Then, shortly afterwards, Parliament enacted the Misrepresentation Act 1967, which also provides for damages, in certain circumstances, for non-fraudulent misrepresentations. The scope of the Misrepresentation Act is nar-rower than the *Hedley Byrne* duty of care, since it deals only with representations made by a party *with whom the representee then contracts*. (This is why the Act is of no rele-vance on, for example, facts like those of *Hedley Byrne* itself, where the claimant relied on the defendant's negligent misrepresentations to contract with a third party.) In contrast, under *Hedley Byrne*, there need not be a contract between representor and representee, only some form of a 'special relationship' or 'voluntary assumption of responsibility'. However, as will be seen, the Misrepresentation Act is more generous to claimants than the damages regime under *Hedley Byrne* in two significant respects.

Misrepresentation Act 1967

9.62 There are two provisions for damages under the Misrepresentation Act, contained in s 2(1) and s 2(2), which should be considered separately.

Section 2(1)–damages where the representor did not have reasonable grounds to believe that the representation was true

9.63 The Act states:

> *2 (1) Where a person has entered into a contract after a misrepresentation has been made to him by another party thereto and as a result thereof he has suffered loss, then, if the person making the misrepresentation would be liable to damages in respect thereof if the representation had been made fraudulently, that person shall be so liable notwithstanding that the misrepresentation was not made fraudulently, unless he proves that he had reasonable grounds to believe and did believe up to the time the contract was made that the facts represented were true.*

9.64 It is worth bearing in mind that s 2(1) can sustain a claim for damages either instead of, *or* in addition to, rescission of the contract. In a simple case, rescission will fully restore the misrepresentee to the pre-contract position: if you give back the painting that I said was by Constable and I give back the price you paid, you have no further losses to worry about. Sometimes, however, rescission will not suffice, because the misrepresentation has caused *consequential* losses. For example, reliance on a representation that a car was roadworthy might cause the misrepresentee to suffer personal injury: returning the car and obtaining a refund of the price will not compensate for that sort of loss. So s 2(1) is useful whether or not rescission is also obtained.

9.65 The drafting of this subsection is not as straightforward as it might be! It is often said that it provides for damages for negligent misrepresentations, but although that is the essence of the subsection, it is not an entirely accurate description. There are two respects in which, because of its convoluted drafting, liability under s 2(1) differs subtly from straightforward negligence liability, both in the representee's favour.

9.66 First, consider the burden of proof. In an ordinary negligence action, it is for the claimant to prove that the defendant was acting negligently (which, in the *Hedley Byrne* context, means proving that the misrepresentation was made negligently). However, the burden of proof is reversed in s 2(1)—the misrepresentor is liable unless he can prove that he had reasonable grounds to believe and did believe that the representation was true. In other words, he is liable unless he disproves negligence. Notice too that those reasonable grounds must exist up until the time the contract was made, so the burden under s 2(1) is quite an onerous one for the misrepresentor.

9.67 Second, s 2(1) does *not* say simply that a representor shall be liable in damages for a negligent misrepresentation. Instead it says that *if* the representor *would have been* liable if he had made the representation fraudulently, he shall be *so liable* even though he was not fraudulent. The section is probably drafted in this way because, at the time, liability in damages for negligent misrepresentations was a novel and revolutionary idea, whereas every common lawyer was familiar with the concept of damages for fraud: see Brown and Chandler (1992). This is sometimes called the 'fiction of fraud', and that little word 'so' in the phrase 'so liable' has led some courts to interpret the section to mean that the representor should be treated as if he actually was a fraudster. It is not clear whether every facet of the tort of deceit applies to s 2(1)—for example, it seems wrong in principle to disallow the defence of contributory negligence in claims under s 2(1) simply because it is not a defence to deceit (see *Gran Gelato v Richcliff* (1992) and para **9.32**).

9.68 Crucially, however, the more generous foreseeability rules for deceit have been held to apply to s 2(1). The leading case is *Royscot Trust Ltd v Rogerson* (1991). Under hire purchase arrangements, RT, a finance company, bought a car from a car dealer and simultaneously hired the car to the customer. RT's policy was to require a 20 per cent deposit from the customer immediately and leave 80 per cent outstanding, payable as hire instalments. However, the dealer exaggerated the purchase price of the car and because of this misrepresentation, the balance paid by RT exceeded 80 per cent of the true purchase price. RT would not have entered the arrangement if it had known the true position, since the customer was not providing the required deposit. Later the customer defaulted after paying some of the hire charge instalments, dishonestly disposing of the car. So RT sued the dealer for damages under s 2(1), claiming the difference between the total amount it had paid out and the hire instalments received from the customer. The Court of Appeal held that the measure of damages under s 2(1) is the same as for the tort of deceit, because of the 'clear wording' of the subsection. Therefore:

> *the finance company is entitled to recover from the dealer all the losses which it suffered as a result of entering into the agreements with the dealer and the customer, even if those losses were unforeseeable ...*

9.69 Authoritative though it is, this decision should not be taken entirely at face value. First, RT's losses *were* held on the facts to be reasonably foreseeable, so it did not much matter that the Court of Appeal opted to apply the fraud rules rather than the negligence equivalent. Second, the hidden agenda is almost certainly that the Court of Appeal smelt a rat in the dealer's conduct—maybe the dealer deliberately exaggerated the price of the car to relieve the customer from having to find the full 20 per cent deposit? There are several reasons why claimants shy away from alleging fraud, even in an obvious case, sometimes because the requirements of the tort of deceit are difficult to prove or because defendants' indemnity insurance policies often do not cover fraud. So if the Court of Appeal suspected fraud, it would not have found it too painful to apply the fraud measure on the facts of *Royscot* itself. But, of course, in many cases, the s 2(1) defendant is not a fraud-ster—he may not even be negligent, merely unable to discharge the burden of disproving negligence—so in general the fiction of fraud derived from *Royscot* is difficult to justify and has inspired a lot of judicial and academic criticism (see Hooley (1991)).

9.70 This was certainly the view of the House of Lords in *Smith New Court* (1997) (see para **9.54**). There, the House justified the generous measure awarded against actual fraudsters on moral grounds. As Lord Steyn said, 'as between the fraudster and the innocent party, moral considerations militate in favour of requiring the fraudster to bear the risk of mis-fortunes caused directly by his fraud'. This makes it particularly difficult to justify the s 2(1) fiction of fraud and, *obiter*, Lord Steyn doubted whether the 'rather loose wording of the statute compels the court to treat a person who was morally innocent as if he was guilty of fraud'. This sounds like a broad hint that *Royscot* would not survive a direct challenge in the Supreme Court!

9.71 In the meantime, first instance courts have expressed their unease with the fiction of fraud in different ways. In *Pankhania v Hackney LBC* (2004), the judge pointed out that, even in cases of fraud, the claimant must still mitigate his loss and damages should be as-sessed accordingly. And in *Avon Insurance plc v Swire Fraser Ltd* (2000), Rix J was mind-ful of the draconian measure of damages under *Royscot* (a Court of Appeal decision) and so erred on the side of finding that the relevant statements were not *mis*representations at all but were 'substantially correct'. In his words, 'since this is the law that binds me, it ought in my view to follow that, where there is room for an exercise of judgment, a misrepresentation should not be too easily found'. Judicial creativity of this kind would not be necessary if *Royscot* were to be overruled, as Rix J went on to observe. If this hap-pened and the tortious 'scope of the duty' approach was introduced under s 2(1), then there would be 'nothing to be said against adopting a more closely focused approach to the proof of misrepresentation'.

Section 2(2)—court's discretion to award damages in lieu of rescission where equitable to do so

9.72 The Act states:

> 2 (2) Where a person has entered into a contract after a misrepresentation has been made to him otherwise than fraudulently, and he would be entitled, by reason of the misrepresentation, to rescind the contract, if it is claimed in any proceedings arising out of the contract, that the contract ought to be or has been rescinded the court or arbi-trator may declare the contract subsisting and award damages in lieu of rescission, if of opinion that it would be equitable to do so, having regard to the nature of the misrep-resentation and the loss that would be caused by it if the contract were upheld, as well as to the loss that rescission would cause to the other party.

9.73 Section 2(2) differs from s 2(1) in a number of respects. As we have seen, a misrepresen-tee can make a claim for damages under s 2(1) either as well as, or instead of, rescinding the contract, and such damages are available as of right as long as the conditions in s 2(1) are met. In contrast, a claimant cannot directly claim damages under s 2(2). Instead, where the claimant asks for rescission for non-fraudulent misrepresentation, the court has a discretion under s 2(2) to award damages instead, where it would be equitable to do so. The court must weigh up the nature and seriousness of the misrepresentation, whether damages would adequately protect the misrepresentee if the contract were to be upheld, and the effect rescission would have on the misrepresentor. In *UCB Corporate Services v Thomason* (2005), the Court of Appeal had to decide whether to rescind a waiver agreement under which a bank agreed not to enforce a guarantee against the debtor T (a Conservative MP) in return for some immediate repayments. The court was scathing about T's non-fraudulent but misleading statements as to his financial position (described as 'lamentable' and a 'sorry tale of prevarication and half truth'), but nonetheless declined to rescind: the bank was not really any worse off than it would have been if it had not entered the waiver agreement, since without the agreement T would have simply gone bankrupt, giving the bank little chance of recovering its money. This meant that leaving the waiver agreement in place did not have a particularly adverse effect on the bank, whereas rescinding it would have led to T's bankruptcy.

9.74 There is, however, one puzzle at the heart of this section, which is the meaning of 'in lieu of rescission'. The judge only has a discretion under s 2(2) to award damages 'in lieu of rescission', meaning instead of or in place of rescission. Does this mean that rescission must still be potentially available as a remedy when the discretion is exercised, or can discretionary damages be awarded even though rescission has become barred (see paras **9.39-9.47**) by the date of the judgment? As a matter of common sense, it might be thought that there is little point to this discretion unless it can be exercised in situations where rescission is no longer available, since that is the very time that the victim of an entirely innocent misrepresentation would otherwise be left with no remedy at all. However, this interpretation is difficult to square with the language of the section: after all, it presupposes a representee who 'would be entitled, by reason of the misrepresentation, to rescind the contract' and requires the court to have regard to the impact that rescission would have on the representor.

9.75 Over the years trial judges have adopted different approaches to this difficult question. For example, in *Thomas Witter Ltd v TBP Industries Ltd* (1996) (see para **9.45**), having decided that rescission of the contract of sale of the carpet business was barred (because it was no longer possible to restore the business in the pre-contract state), Jacob J went on to consider whether it was still open to him to award damages under s 2(2). He decided (*obiter*) that the discretion was still available, despite rescission being barred, for reasons of fairness to the representee and relying on statements in Hansard when the Misrepresentation Act was originally debated. The opposite conclusion was reached, also at first instance, in *Government of Zanzibar v British Aerospace (Lancaster House) Ltd* (2000) where the judge decided that, since rescission was barred, he had no discretion to award damages in lieu: damages under s 2(2) are 'an alternative to an order for rescission or the upholding of a prior rescission by the representee if that has occurred'. He relied primarily on the wording of the Act and on other references in Hansard (contradicting the statement relied on by Jacob J in *Thomas Witter*) and in the Report of the Law Reform Committee, which led to the Misrepresentation Act.

9.76   The dispute now appears to have been resolved, at least at Court of Appeal level, by the decision in *Salt v Stratstone Specialist Ltd* (2015), which favoured the *Government of Zanzibar* conclusion. As Longmore LJ put it:

> But the words 'in lieu of rescission' must, in my view, carry with them the implication that rescission is available (or was available at the time the contract was rescinded). If it is not (or was not available in law) ... rescission is not available and damages cannot be said to be awarded 'in lieu of rescission'.

9.77   Damages under s 2(2) are calculated to compensate the representee for the fact that the contract is not being rescinded. So in many cases this will not be as great as the amount of damages awarded under s 2(1), where all the consequential losses resulting from having relied on the misrepresentation and entered into the contract are recoverable on the fraud measure. Section 2(3) contemplates this, stating that damages can be awarded under s 2(2) as well as s 2(1), but that any award under s 2(2) shall be taken into account in assessing damages under s 2(1).

9.78   The Court of Appeal has given some guidance on the damages to be awarded under s 2(2) in *William Sindall plc v Cambridgeshire County Council* (1994). S, a building company, agreed to buy land for development purposes from the Council, for £5 million. The property market later slumped and the land declined in value to £2 million. It transpired that there was a foul sewer running under the site and S saw a potential way out of its disastrous investment (even though the sewer could be, and eventually was, re-routed at a cost of just £18,000). It sought rescission of the contract, on the grounds of the Council's representation that it was not aware of any rights affecting the property, or alternatively for common mistake (see Chapter 13), but both grounds failed. The Court of Appeal decided that there had been *no* actionable misrepresentation, but *obiter* indicated that, even if there had been, it would nonetheless have exercised its discretion to award damages in lieu under s 2(2). This was because the misrepresentation related to something of relatively minor importance, costing only £18,000 to put right, whereas rescission would mean that the Council would have to return the £5 million purchase price plus about £3 million in interest, in exchange for land now worth less than £2 million. Moreover, S's loss could be made good by an award of damages: Hoffmann LJ indicated that the appropriate measure would have been the £18,000 cost of diverting the sewer plus a small amount for the consequent delay to the development.

Hoffmann LJ reached this conclusion by explaining first that:

> section 2(1) is concerned with the damage flowing from having entered into the contract, while section 2(2) is concerned with damage caused by the property not being what it was represented to be.

He also stressed that:

> *damages under section 2(2) should never exceed the sum which would have been awarded if the representation had been a warranty.*

9.79 Of course *William Sindall* was an appropriate case for damages in lieu of rescission, because rescission would have made the Council bear the burden of the market slump, when it was entirely appropriate that this should be borne by S. After all, the collapse in value of the property was nothing to do with the presence of the sewer. In other words, S had made a bad bargain anyway, regardless of any misrepresentation about the sewer. For this reason, a certain amount of caution is needed in treating Hoffmann LJ's words as if they are generally applicable to s 2(2) cases. The problem is that 'damage caused by the property not being what it was represented to be' sounds very much like the *contractual* expectation measure for breach of warranty ('put the claimant into the position they would have been in if the warranty had been true'—discussed in detail in Chapter 16), and indeed Evans LJ recognises as much in his judgment in *William Sindall*. In a bad bargain case like *William Sindall*, this will be less than the tort measure, because putting the claimant into the position they would have been in had the warranty been true *enforces* the contract, and therefore retains all the other reasons why the bargain was a bad one (such as an unrelated market fall). But in the majority of cases, the expectation measure will exceed the tort measure (even the generous s 2(1) version), because the bargain would usually have been a good one but for the misrepresentation.

Exclusion of liability for misrepresentation

Section 3 Misrepresentation Act

9.80 At common law, it has never been possible for reasons of public policy to exclude liability for one's own fraudulent misrepresentation and this remains the position today—see *Pearson v Dublin Corpn* (1907), applied in the *Government of Zanzibar* case (2000) (see para **9.75**). On the other hand, it may be possible by very clear words to exclude liability for the fraud of one's agent, a point left open by the House of Lords in *HIH Casualty and General Insurance Ltd v Chase Manhattan Bank* (2003). Clauses excluding liability for other forms of misrepresentation, although valid at common law, are now subject to the statutory requirement of reasonableness. Section 3(1) of the Misrepresentation Act 1967 (as amended by s 8(1) of the Unfair Contract Terms Act 1977 and the Consumer Rights Act 2015) provides as follows:

> *3 (1) If a contract contains a term which would exclude or restrict—*
>
> (a) *any liability to which a party to a contract may be subject by reason of any misrepresentation made by him before the contract was made; or*
> (b) *any remedy available to another party to the contract by reason of such misrepresentation;*

that term shall be of no effect except in so far as it satisfies the requirement of reason-
ableness as stated in section 11(1) of the Unfair Contract Terms Act 1977; and it is for
those claiming that the term satisfies that requirement to show that it does.

9.81 Note that this section no longer applies to a term in a *consumer* contract, but clauses purporting to exclude liability for misrepresentation in consumer contracts are caught by the
general provision invalidating unfair terms in s 62 of the CRA, on which see para **8.55**.
Notice as well that s 3 does not explicitly state whether it applies to all contracts, or only to
those contracts which are subject to the jurisdiction of UCTA (see para **8.30**). In *Trident*
Turboprop (Dublin) Ltd v First Flight Couriers Ltd (2009) the Court of Appeal had to decide this very issue, as it was faced with a clause purporting to exclude liability for misrepresentation contained in an international supply contract falling within s 26 of UCTA and
thus itself exempt from the reasonableness regime. The court decided that the boundaries
of UCTA should apply equally to s 3 of the Misrepresentation Act, to reflect the policy of
Parliament to exclude international supply contracts from this type of statutory control
and to avoid creating an anomaly between clauses excluding liability for misrepresentation
and for breach of contract. Nothing was said in the case about whether s 3 catches other
types of contract excluded from part of UCTA by Sch 1, and it is noteworthy that contracts
for the sale of land, though also excluded from UCTA, are regularly regarded as within
the jurisdiction of s 3 (see for example *Schyde Investments Ltd v Cleaver* (2011) discussed
at para **9.92**). On balance *Trident* should perhaps be treated merely as a decision about
international supply contracts and the meaning of s 26.

9.82 As with all exclusion clauses, it is important to check first whether the clause has been
incorporated into the contract (see paras **7.18-7.39**). Assuming that it has been, the second issue to consider is whether the clause as drafted does in fact seek to exclude or restrict liability for misrepresentation: if not, s 3 does not apply to it. A good example is the
oddly named case *Taberna Europe CDO II plc v Selskabet AF 1.September 2008* (2017) in
which the claimant, an investment company, tried to argue that a clause excluding liability for misrepresentation should be construed *contra proferentem* (see para **8.7**), but the
Court of Appeal disagreed: the clause was not ambiguous and was effective as a matter
of drafting to exclude liability for misrepresentation. Finally, if it does have that effect,
the question of whether it is caught by a statutory protective regime and, if so, whether
it satisfies the relevant statutory test of reasonableness/fairness must be considered. We
will explore drafting issue and the statutory regimes in a little more detail.

Does the wording of the clause exclude or restrict liability for misrepresentation?

9.83 In *Thomas Witter* (see para **9.45**), the judge explained, 'if a clause is to have the effect of
excluding or reducing remedies for damaging untrue statements then the party seek-
ing that protection cannot be mealy-mouthed in his clause. He must bring it home that
he is limiting his liability for falsehoods he may have told.' Of course, some clauses, like
those simply stating 'Liability for any pre-contractual misrepresentations is excluded',

are clearly worded and are straightforwardly caught by s 3. But what of clauses, for example, that deem that no representation was made in the first place or that neither party placed any reliance on any such representation?

9.84 Whilst the courts do not generally allow skilful drafting to defeat the protection that Parliament intended to confer in s 3 (and now s 62 of the CRA), in exceptional cases clear wording will succeed in achieving an equivalent result. In *Overbrooke Estates Ltd v Glencombe Properties Ltd* (1974) property was sold at auction and the contract of sale stated, 'The vendors do not make or give and neither the auctioneers nor any person in the employment of the auctioneers has any authority to make or give any representation or warranty in relation to these premises.' The purchasers alleged that the auctioneer had made a misrepresentation, but Brightman J held that even if he had, the clause in the sale contract prevented the vendors being liable for it. Section 3 was not triggered, since it was not designed to catch clauses whereby a principal genuinely sought 'publicly to limit the otherwise ostensible authority of his agent'.

9.85 Of more commercial significance today is the so-called 'entire agreement' clause, in which the parties acknowledge that the written contract contains their entire agreement. As we saw in para **7.17**, if this is the extent of the wording, then the clause merely operates to prevent arguments about the existence of *collateral warranties* (see *Inntrepreneur Pub Co (GL) v East Crown Ltd* (2000)) and does not catch misrepresentation liability at all. The Court of Appeal in *AXA Sun Life Services plc v Campbell Martin Ltd* (2011) reached the same conclusion, where the relevant entire agreement clause was less straightforward than the one in *Inntrepreneur* because the word 'representations' was included. The relevant wording was, 'this Agreement shall supersede any prior promises, agreements, representations, undertakings or implications whether made orally or in writing between you and us relating to the subject matter of this Agreement.' Despite this, the Court of Appeal held that, properly construed, the clause did not exclude liability for misrepresentation. The crucial difficulty was the word 'supersede'. As Rix LJ said:

> the exclusion of liability for misrepresentation has to be clearly stated. It can be done by clauses which state the parties' agreement that there have been no representations made; or that there has been no reliance on any representations; or by an express exclusion of liability for misrepresentation. However, save in such contexts, and particularly where the word 'representations' takes its place alongside other words expressive of contractual obligation, talk of the parties' contract superseding such prior agreement will not by itself absolve a party of misrepresentation where its ingredients can be proved.

9.86 As a simple entire agreement clause does not operate to exclude liability for misrepresentation, it is not caught by s 3 of the Misrepresentation Act. As the court held in *McGrath v Shah* (1987), s 3 'is not apt to cover a contractual provision which seeks to define where the contractual terms are actually to be found', although as we have seen in para **7.17**, an entire agreement clause might be caught by s 3(2)(b) of UCTA, if the contract was made on the defendant's 'standard written terms of business' and is likely to be regarded as an unfair term under the CRA if the claimant is a consumer.

9.87   However, as Rix LJ pointed out in the *AXA* case, there is a variant of the entire agreement clause which is an effective way of excluding liability for misrepresentation—that is for the parties to acknowledge in the contract either that no representations have been *made* or that they have not *relied* on any representations; after some judicial hesitation initially, such clauses are now undoubtedly effective as a matter of common law. This was made clear in *Peekay Intermark Ltd v Australia & New Zealand Banking Group Ltd* (2006) (see para **9.33**) and in *JP Morgan Chase Bank v Springwell Navigation Corpn* (2010), in which the Court of Appeal said:

> If A and B enter into a contract then, unless there is some principle of law or statute to the contrary, they are entitled to agree what they like ... there is no legal principle that states that parties cannot agree to assume that a certain state of affairs is the case at the time the contract is concluded or has been so in the past, even if that is not the case, so that the contract is made upon the basis that the present or past facts are as stated and agreed by the parties.

9.88   This sort of clause operates by giving rise to a form of estoppel, sometimes known as 'contractual estoppel'. For a detailed discussion of the origins and implications of this analysis, see Braithwaite (2016). The idea is that if the parties assert in their agreement that, for example, no representations were made or that they have not relied on any representations, they cannot later assert in litigation to the contrary, so they are unable to establish the essential elements of the misrepresentation cause of action. At common law, the courts are willing to give effect to this estoppel: as Aikens LJ said in *Springwell*, the relevant terms 'mean that Springwell is contractually estopped from contending that there were any actionable representations'. Notice, however, that this is an unusual form of estoppel, established without the usual requirements of reliance or of it being inequitable to go back on what was said. Where the representee is a consumer and the representor a large commercial entity, this sort of clause can be very prejudicial indeed to the consumer, particularly since the consumer may find themselves estopped even where there was no meaningful reliance by that commercial entity on the consumer's assertion, which was merely tucked in the boilerplate. Such clauses are definitely subject to the general regime for protection against unfair terms discussed in para **8.55**. On the other hand, contractual estoppel is undeniably useful in contracts involving well-advised commercial parties, who wish to be able to worry just about statements incorporated as terms of the contract. Whether such clauses are caught by s 3 has been the subject of differences of judicial opinion.

9.89   In *Watford Electronics Ltd v Sanderson CFL Ltd* (2001) (discussed in para **8.51**) the Court of Appeal held that because the effect of such wording was that the purchaser was estopped from asserting that it had relied on any misrepresentations not incorporated in the contract, the clause did *not* fall within s 3. As Chadwick LJ explained:

> Liability in damages under the Misrepresentation Act 1967 can arise only where the party who has suffered the damage has relied upon the representation. Where both parties to the contract have acknowledged, in the document itself, that they have not

relied upon any pre-contract representation, it would be bizarre (unless compelled to do so by the words which they have used) to attribute to them an intention to exclude a liability which they must have thought could never arise.

This reasoning takes a very formalistic view of the ambit of s 3 although, as Peel (2001) notes, s 3 does *not* contain anti-avoidance wording to catch clauses which prevent misrepresentation liability arising in the first place, unlike the equivalent drafting of UCTA (see para **8.34**).

9.90   Since *Watford*, however, the courts have proved much more inclined to look at the *substance* and recognise that these contractual estoppel clauses do have the practical effect of excluding liability for misrepresentation, thereby bringing them within the ambit of s 3. As Bridge LJ said in *Cremdean Properties Ltd v Nash* (1977), if a contract contains a 'form of words the intended and actual effect of which was to exclude or restrict liability … I would not have thought that the courts would have been ready to allow such ingenuity in forms of language to defeat the plain purpose at which s 3 is aimed'. In *Peart Stevenson Associates Ltd v Holland* (2008), Judge Richard Seymour QC *obiter* favoured Bridge LJ's approach in *Cremdean*, noting that it was not cited to the Court of Appeal in *Watford Electronics*. (On the facts of *Peart*, the misrepresentations were made fraudulently and as we have seen liability for fraud cannot be excluded as a matter of public policy.) Overall, the better view is to recognise that such clauses do fall within s 3, on the basis explained by Christopher Clarke J in *Raiffeisen Zentralbank Österreich AG v The Royal Bank of Scotland plc* (2010) (cited by the Court of Appeal in *Springwell*):

> *to tell the man in the street that the car you are selling him is perfect and then agree that the basis of your contract is that no representations have been made or relied on, may be nothing more than an attempt retrospectively to alter the character and effect of what has gone before and in substance be an attempt to exclude or restrict liability.*

(Of course, the precise facts of this example would probably constitute a consumer contract and thus no longer be within the jurisdiction of s 3, but instead caught by the CRA.)

Is the clause reasonable?

9.91   Where a clause, properly construed, does purport to exclude or restrict liability for misrepresentation and thus falls within s 3, the remaining question is whether the misrepresentor can demonstrate that the clause was reasonable. The same factors are taken into account here as with other exclusion clauses judged for reasonableness under UCTA (dealt with in paras **8.45–8.51**): see for example *Lloyd v Browning* (2013).

9.92   As ever, the same sort of clause can be either reasonable or unreasonable, depending on its context. Of course, an exclusion clause in a consumer contract is most likely to attract a finding of unreasonableness, and such clauses are no longer within the jurisdiction of s 3 but caught by the CRA. But even non-consumer situations can be imagined, such as where the proprietor of a small business purchases highly technical goods for the business, wholly outside his area of expertise, only because of reassurances and technical information about the goods provided by the retailer, in response to the purchaser's oral enquiries. If the information was false, but the small print of the contract contained a clause excluding liability for misrepresentation, it will be difficult for the retailer to justify the clause as reasonable: the parties' bargaining positions were unequal, the purchaser was not legally represented and the clause was not specifically drawn to his attention. For example, in *Schyde Investments Ltd v Cleaver* (2011) the Court of Appeal declined to interfere with the trial judge's conclusion that condition 7.1.3 of the standard conditions of sale (the set of standard terms and conditions used in residential conveyancing), which substantially restricts a buyer's right to rescind for misrepresentation, was unreasonable in the circumstances (even though both parties *were* legally represented). However, as Longmore LJ reminded us, 'the question is not whether the clause is, in general, a reasonable clause. The question is whether it was a reasonable clause in the contract made between this vendor and this purchaser at the time when the contract was made.'

9.93 On the other hand, imagine long and complex negotiations for the sale of a business, where both parties are represented by solicitors, during which the vendor provides lots of information about the business. In such a case, it makes perfect sense for both sides if an exclusion clause is included in the ultimate written contract and such a clause will almost inevitably be regarded as reasonable. The purchasers' solicitors can see to it that any significant pieces of information are warranted by the vendors in the contract, while the vendors can concentrate on making sure that those warranties are true, safe in the knowledge that other things they might have said in the course of negotiations will not come back to haunt them. Commercial parties dealing at arm's length and with professional advisers should not need the protection of the statutory reasonableness test. In *Springwell* the claimant trying to plead unreasonableness was a 'sophisticated investor in emerging market investments who was conscious of the risks of this type of investment' and so the Court of Appeal saw no reason to depart from the judge's conclusion that the clause was reasonable.

OVERVIEW

1   Where one party makes a false statement of fact that influences the other party into entering the contract, the contract is voidable and, in some cases, damages for misrepresentation may also be available in addition to or instead of rescinding the contract.

2   English law does not treat contractual non-disclosure in the same way, other than in exceptional contractual situations (contracts *uberrimae fidei*) that require disclosure of anything material. However, failing to correct a statement that is true when made but later falsified, telling only half the truth and giving a false impression by conduct may count as a misrepresentation.

3   To be actionable, a misrepresentation must be of fact, not a 'mere puff' or a statement of opinion, though the distinction between fact and opinion is not a clear one. A statement of future intention is not actionable, though a misrepresentation of law probably is.

4   A misrepresentation must satisfy a subjective test of causation and possibly also an objective requirement of materiality (though this may simply be an evidential aspect of proving subjective causation). The causal test is whether the misrepresentee relied on the misrepresentation in entering the contract, though the misrepresentation need not be the only or decisive cause. Relief will be possible even where, if the misrepresentation had not been made, the misrepresentee would still have contracted with the misrepresentor but on different terms and also where the misrepresentee had the opportunity to discover the truth but did not take it.

5   Rescission is the principal remedy for misrepresentation, which involves setting the contract aside and restoring the parties to the pre-contractual position (the *status quo ante*). Rescission is sometimes said to be both a self-help and a judicial remedy, but there are good historical and practical reasons not to adopt a self-help analysis, at least where the representation was not made fraudulently.

6   Rescission is said to be barred where the innocent party affirms the contract or, possibly, delays too long before rescinding, where third parties have acquired rights in the subject matter of the contract or where it is no longer possible to restore the parties to the pre-contract position, though there is some flexibility if substantial restitution can be achieved.

7   In certain situations (principally involving guarantee contracts), the misrepresentee (the surety) might be able to rescind the contract with the creditor, even though the misrepresentation was made by a third party (the debtor), as long as the creditor had actual or constructive notice of the misrepresentation. This jurisdiction is more naturally suited to cases of undue influence, but the courts tend to treat the two vitiating factors similarly in this context. Regrettably the English courts have declined to award 'partial rescission' even where the misrepresentation was as to the terms of the transaction, such that there is clear evidence of the misrepresentee's unvitiated intention.

8   Damages can be claimed at common law for fraudulent misrepresentation (the tort of deceit). Although negligent misrepresentation is now commonly actionable in tort, where the misrepresentation leads to a contract between misrepresentor and misrepresentee there is a statutory regime for damages under the Misrepresentation Act 1967 that is more favourable to the misrepresentee than a negligence action. The misrepresentee has the advantage of a reversed burden of proving negligence and a generous measure of damages linked to the measure for fraud. In addition, for non-fraudulent misrepresentations, the statute gives the court a discretion to award damages in lieu of rescission, though it is unclear whether this discretion can be exercised if rescission is barred.

9   Any clause in a non-consumer contract that, properly construed, has the effect of excluding or restrict liability for misrepresentation is subject to the UCTA requirement of reasonableness; similarly, such a clause in a consumer contract is subject to the CRA requirement of fairness.

FURTHER READING

Atiyah and Treitel 'Misrepresentation Act 1967' (1967) 30 MLR 369

Brown and Chandler 'Deceit, Damages and the Misrepresentation Act 1967, s 2(1)' [1992] LMCLQ 40

Hooley 'Damages and the Misrepresentation Act 1967' (1991) 107 LQR 547

Meikle 'Partial Rescission—Removing the Restitution from a Contractual Doctrine' (2003) JCL 40

O'Sullivan 'Rescission as a Self-Help Remedy: A Critical Analysis' [2000] CLJ 509

Peel 'Reasonable Exemption Clauses' (2001) 117 LQR 545

Trukhtanov 'Misrepresentation: Acknowledgment of Non-Reliance as a Defence' (2009) 125 LQR 648

SELF-TEST QUESTIONS

1   Should English law recognise a general duty of pre-contractual disclosure?

2   What is the relationship between the reliance and materiality requirements for actionable misrepresentation?

3   When is rescission unavailable for misrepresentation?

4   What are the differences between liability under s 2(1) of the Misrepresentation Act and tort liability for negligent misstatement at common law?

5   Should damages be available under s 2(2) of the Misrepresentation Act if rescission is barred?

6   Rook sold Gull for £50,000 a business which he told Gull was 'worth £75,000'. At Gull's request, Rook wrote on the back of the written contract 'I guarantee the business to be worth at least £75,000'. The contract contained a clause which said 'the purchaser acknowledges that he has not relied on any pre-contractual statements or representations about the value of the business'. Rook thought that the business was indeed worth £75,000, though he made little effort to check the facts. In fact, although the turnover of the business has been around £75,000, the business has for some years made a net loss of £5,000 a year. Gull has been running the business for three months now and calculates that it will take him about five years and considerable extra expense to make the business profitable, but he would rather do that than rescind the contract if he can be adequately compensated for his loss. Advise Gull.

 For hints on how to answer question 6, please see the online resources at **www.oup.com/uk/sullivan8e/**.

10 Duress

SUMMARY

This chapter deals with contracts induced by duress, a vitiating factor. It considers duress to the person and duress to goods, then concentrates on the most important category, economic duress and its various requirements, as well as the question of whether a threat to do a lawful act can constitute actionable duress.

Introductory points

10.1 Duress involves one party coercing or pressurising the other party into making a contract. But it is not easy to define precisely what sorts of pressure will count as duress. At one end of the spectrum, a contract signed at gunpoint is undoubtedly vitiated by duress. At the other, a contract entered into under pressure of circumstances (like the social 'pressure' to purchase a new car to impress the neighbours) is undoubtedly valid. Somewhere in between is the boundary of actionable duress. The most important feature of duress is that it generally involves pressure applied by means of an *illegitimate threat*, although occasionally a threat to do something lawful made in bad faith will suffice (see paras **10.29-10.35**). An *express* threat is not necessary: the law is subtle enough to recognise that a threat can be implicit (such as where a robber twirls a gun menacingly while asking for money, without expressly threatening his victim that he will use it). The Court of Appeal in *B & S Contracts and Designs Ltd v Victor Green Publications Ltd* (1984) treated a 'veiled threat' to breach a contract as sufficient for economic duress. Moreover, a threat that is carried into effect may equally establish duress—a contract signed after a beating is just as tainted by duress as a contract signed under threat of a beating.

10.2 Notice that some cases involve one party seeking to set aside or resist enforcement of a contract (or contractual variation) entered into as a result of duress; others involve a restitutionary action to recover money paid under duress. The courts do not seem to draw any real distinction between the two sorts of claim—the elements of duress are the same in both. And the justification for relief is the same too, which is that the victim's consent to enter the transaction was vitiated by the wrongful pressure to which he was subjected.

It is also clear that, just as for misrepresentation and other vitiating factors, rescission of a contract for duress will be subject to the usual bars to rescission (see *Halpern v Halpern (No 2)* (2007)). In contrast with misrepresentation, there is at present no independent remedy of damages for duress (though sometimes the conduct amounting to duress will give rise to separate tortious liability), so if rescission is barred the victim is without a remedy. In *Ruttle Plant Ltd v Secretary of State for the Environment and Rural Affairs* (2008) Ramsey J noted that, 'there are good arguments for the existence of a remedy in damages for duress'.

Duress to the person

10.3 A threat of violence, known as duress to the person, is the most obvious form of duress and was for some time the only form for which relief was given at common law. There are really only two controversial issues regarding duress to the person, namely what the relevant test of causation is and whether the resulting transaction is void or voidable. The Privy Council considered both issues in the extraordinary case of *Barton v Armstrong* (1976). A was the chairman of a company and B was its managing director. A made death threats against B to persuade B to buy out A's shareholding in the company, but ironically B wished to do this anyway because he thought (wrongly, as things turned out) that this was a commercially desirable course of action. So B executed a deed purchasing A's shares, but later regretted the transaction and sought to undo the transaction. A argued that B would have executed the deed even if there had been no threats; his threats were not a 'but for' cause and thus there should be no relief. The Privy Council disagreed. As Lord Cross explained:

> ... if A's threats were 'a' reason for B's executing the deed he is entitled to relief even though he might well have entered into the contract if A had uttered no threats to induce him to do so.

10.4 Notice how unusual the facts of *Barton v Armstrong* were. In the vast majority of cases of threatened violence, there will be no doubt whatsoever that the threat was the overwhelming cause of the resulting transaction. But, as *Barton v Armstrong* demonstrates, it seems wholly right that the defendant should not benefit just because, by sheer coincidence, some other factors served to reinforce his threats of violence. As we will see, this relaxation of the test of causation is only made for the benefit of victims of duress to the person and is analogous to the position for fraudulent misrepresentation (see para **9.27** onwards). In less serious forms of wrongdoing, in particular economic duress, a strict test of factual causation applies.

10.5 The other notable feature of *Barton v Armstrong* is that the Privy Council decided that the deed executed by B was *void*, not merely voidable (an issue which made little difference on the facts, but which is critical if the subject matter of the contract has been sold on to a third party). Some commentators have criticised this as being inconsistent with other forms of duress (particularly economic duress), which render transactions voidable only, but this criticism smacks of over-generalisation. It is perfectly understandable that the more serious form of duress should have a greater vitiating effect on transactions and it seems right in principle that if you hand over your goods at gunpoint, the legal effect should be the same as if the goods had been stolen from you.

Duress to goods

10.6 Historically duress to the person was the only form of duress recognised as deserving of legal redress, but this changed in 1731 in *Astley v Reynolds* when a pawnbroker who refused to release the claimant's goods until the claimant paid far more than the agreed interest rate was held liable to repay the excess. The pawnbroker tried to argue that the claimant was not really compelled to make the payment because he had an alternative course of action open to him, namely suing in the tort of trover for the return of his goods, but the court was not convinced:

> We think also that this is a payment by compulsion. The plaintiff might have such an immediate want of his goods that an action in trover would not do his business.

It was later established that the same reasoning applies to contracts (and not just payments) executed because of duress of goods. Once the common law recognised that the unlawful seizure or detention of the claimant's goods (or a threat to do the same) might amount to illegitimate compulsion, at least where the alternative of resisting and suing in tort for the return of the goods was not realistic, it became hard to justify drawing the line at duress of goods. After all, *economic* pressures will often have much the same impact on the claimant. If I threaten to breach our contract unless you pay or promise to pay me more than the contract price, you could in theory resist and sue me for damages (if I breach as I have threatened), but in practice this may be unrealistic if you need performance immediately. English law eventually recognised that economic duress might vitiate a contract in *The Siboen and The Sibotre* (1976), although the claim failed on the facts.

Economic duress

10.7 It is now well established that certain forms of economic pressure can count as duress. Some cases involve threats to induce third parties to breach their contracts with the claimant, usually in the context of industrial disputes. The best known derive from the campaign by a maritime union to improve the terms and conditions of sailors working on ships flying 'flags of convenience', by persuading dockworkers to 'black' such ships by refusing to load or unload them, explored by the House of Lords in *The Universe Sentinel*

(1983) and *The Evia Luck* (1992). For the purposes of this chapter, we will focus on the simpler form of economic duress, in which one party threatens to breach an existing contract *with the other party*, unless the other party acts in a particular way (usually paying or promising to pay more than the contract price, or entering into a new contract).

10.8 As we have seen in Chapter 5, English law traditionally had no need of a principle of economic duress when deciding the validity of a contractual variation, because only variations supported by consideration were enforceable in any event. This helped to weed out variations induced by unfair pressure, but was a blunt way of doing so. Since *Williams v Roffey Bros & Nicholls (Contractors) Ltd* (1991), in effect even a unilateral variation is enforceable unless it was made as a result of economic duress, so economic duress has assumed greater importance by replacing consideration as the limiting principle in such cases. Notice the 'other side of the coin' when considering the relationship between economic duress and consideration: the *presence* of consideration is not fatal to a finding of economic duress. So it is possible for the court to decide that a contract or contractual variation is voidable for economic duress, even though there *was* some consideration for it. Overall, this means that it is now crucial to be able to identify the necessary elements of economic duress.

10.9 This is no easy matter, because this area is bedevilled with problems of terminology. To impose some order on the cases, there seem to be three distinct requirements for economic duress:

    step 1: illegitimate pressure or threat;

    step 2: which (subjectively) caused the victim to act as he did; and

    step 3: which (objectively) would have caused a reasonable person in the victim's position to act in the same way (ie, there was no realistic alternative course of action).

10.10 This division is logical, because step 1 says something about the sort of pressure or threat, whereas steps 2 and 3 concern the victim's reaction to it. But beware that the cases often adopt slightly different terminology and commonly say, 'the threat was not illegitimate' to express an *overall conclusion* about whether there is actionable economic duress. For example, Dyson J in *DSND Subsea Ltd v Petroleum Geo-services ASA* (2000) (who repeats the same analysis in *Carillon Construction Ltd v Felix (UK) Ltd* (2000)) appears to adopt a similar threefold analysis, stating that:

> *The ingredients of actionable duress are that there must be pressure (a) whose practical effect is that there is compulsion on, or a lack of practical choice for, the victim, (b) which is illegitimate, and (c) which is a significant cause inducing the claimant to enter into the contract.*

However, he goes on to expand on the meaning of illegitimate pressure as follows:

> *In determining whether there has been illegitimate pressure, the court takes into account a range of factors. These include whether there has been an actual or threatened breach*

of contract; whether the person allegedly exerting the pressure has acted in good or bad faith; whether the victim had any realistic alternative but to submit to the pressure; whether the victim protested at the time; and whether he affirmed and sought to rely on the contract ... Illegitimate pressure must be distinguished from the rough and tumble of the pressures of normal commercial bargaining.

In other words, when considering whether there has been 'illegitimate pressure', Dyson J is asking questions relevant to *all three* of our (and his) steps, not just questions relating to our step 1. This is confusing and, for the sake of clarity, it is preferable to organise those factors to make clear which relate to the pressure or threat and which relate to the victim's reaction to it.

(Step 1) Illegitimacy of the threat

10.11 This requirement is all about what sort of threat was made. The most important point is that the threat must be to do something illegitimate and so, for our purposes, requires a threat to *breach* an existing contract. This is very different from a threat to do something that the defendant is entitled to do, which as a general rule will *not* amount to an illegitimate threat (although see paras **10.29-10.35**). In *Huyton SA v Peter Cremer & Co* (1998) the purchaser of a consignment of wheat, which had been duly delivered by the seller, refused to pay for it unless the seller presented shipping documents in proper form and agreed not to arbitrate over disputed 'demurrage' charges. Mance J held that the purchaser was not contractually obliged to pay the price unless and until it received proper shipping documents from the seller, and so its threat not to pay was *not* illegitimate and, accordingly, the seller's agreement not to arbitrate had not been procured by economic duress.

10.12 The more difficult question is whether or not a threat to breach a contract is *automatically* illegitimate, leaving just the second and third steps to determine whether there is actionable duress. The courts generally say that a threat to breach a contract is *not* automatically illegitimate. For example, Kerr J in *The Siboen and The Sibotre* rejected as 'much too wide' counsel's submission to this effect and (as Kerr LJ) said much the same thing in *B & S Contracts and Design Ltd v Victor Green Publishing Ltd* (1984), remarking that 'a threat to breach a contract ... can, but by no means always will, constitute duress'. However, the *context* of remarks of this kind is usually that the court wishes to exclude threats which were not causative of the victim's subsequent action, or where the victim had alternative courses of action and so objectively should not be treated as having been coerced. In other words, the court has in mind factors better regarded as nothing to do with step 1, the legitimacy of the threat, but concerned with our steps 2 and 3.

10.13 On the other hand, it is noteworthy that, generally, cases in English law in which the victim has succeeded in pleading economic duress have involved not just a threat to breach the contract, but additional *bad conduct* by the other party in making the threat. A good example is *Atlas Express Ltd v Kafco* (1989). K was a small basket weaving firm, which received a large order to supply basketware to Woolworths. K made a contract with A, a large haulage company, to deliver the baskets at a rate of £1.10 per basket. In fact, A's manager had made an error when calculating the rate (through no fault of K) and had overestimated the number of baskets that would fit into each lorry. (A's unilateral mistake had no impact on the validity of the contract so the contract rate stood at £1.10 per basket: see paras **3.52**.) So A tried to 'renegotiate' the deal by threatening that, unless K agreed to double the rate, no further deliveries would be made. It would have been almost impossible for K to have found another haulier in time to honour their contract with Woolworths, business which they could not afford to lose, so they reluctantly agreed to the price increase. Tucker J held that K's agreement to the alteration was procured through economic duress. Although he did not accept that every threat to breach a contract was illegitimate per se, he was content to accept that this threat was, primarily because of the *manner* in which A exerted the pressure. The threat was made by A's driver, at the last possible opportunity, knowing that the Woolworths contract was essential for K's economic survival.

10.14   This suggests that a threat to breach a contract will only count as 'illegitimate' where the party making the threat was in *bad faith*, a proposition that attracts some commentators. For example, Birks (1990) argues that bad faith should be a prerequisite to recovery, so that a threatened breach of contract made to exploit the other party's difficult position would be illegitimate, whereas a threatened breach made with a view to solving financial or other difficulties of the threatening party would not. Burrows (2010) takes the view that a threat should not be considered illegitimate if 'the threatener is merely seeking to correct what was always a clearly bad bargain'. *DSND Subsea Ltd v Petroleum Geo-services ASA* (2000) supports the view that, for a threatened breach of contract to count as illegitimate, it must have been made in 'bad faith'. DSND and PGS had a complex contractual arrangement in connection with the development of an oilfield in the North Sea. Technical disputes arose and DSND informed PGS that it was ceasing its part of the work, until aspects of the insurance arrangements for the work were clarified. PGS then reached agreement with DSND on the disputed issues. Dyson J dismissed PGS' claim of economic duress, even though DSND had threatened to breach the contract. One reason was that DSND had been 'entirely justified' in wanting to resolve the dispute, particularly the insurance position. The threat was not, in the circumstances, illegitimate, since it was 'reasonable behaviour by a contractor acting bona fide in a very difficult situation'.

10.15   However, *DSND*'s suggestion that a threat to breach a contract will only be illegitimate if made in bad faith is not universally accepted. Bigwood (2001) comments that:

> To suggest ... that it may not be illegitimate for D to breach or propose to breach his contract with P (in support of D's demands) if D is acting 'reasonably' and 'bona fide in a very difficult situation' is effectively to suggest that P's rights are somehow destructible by D unilaterally and without compensation if D is acting from the right commercial motives.

Mance J in *Huyton SA v Peter Cremer & Co* is also doubtful, noting that it is 'difficult to accept that illegitimate pressure applied by a party who believes bona fide in his case could never give grounds for relief against an apparent compromise'. The issue did not matter in the *DSND* case, because the other requirements for relief were not satisfied either, but in some cases it might be critical.

10.16   It is suggested that a threat to breach a contract should always count as an illegitimate threat, leaving the causal requirements (steps 2 and 3) to filter out inappropriate pleas of duress, because this accords with English law's strict approach to frustration of contracts. For example, a dramatic rise in prices may make it very difficult for a contractor to honour his contractual obligations, but this alone does not relieve him of them. For the law to say that, in those circumstances if the contractor in good faith persuades the other party to pay more than the contract rate by threatening to breach the contract, the other party can get no relief (even if he agrees purely because of the threatened breach of contract, having no realistic alternative), would come close to allowing one party to relax the frustration rule by threatening to breach the contract. The law should not bend over backwards to assist a threatener who is trying to escape the consequences of his own bad bargain, contrary to the suggestion of Burrows (2010).

10.17   Some commentators, like Halson (1991), regard English law's strict frustration regime (see Chapter 14) as a *good* reason to enforce contractual renegotiations in these circumstances (and so find that there has *not* been duress), at least where the contractor is unable to perform because of an unforeseen change in circumstances beyond his control (such as dramatic price rises). But this seems to reward contractors who bid too low and undermines the function of contracts in allocating in advance who will bear the risk of such unforeseen changes in circumstances. Smith (1997) meets the point by distinguishing between a threat and a warning, arguing that a contractor who *warns* that he is about to breach the contract for reasons beyond his control is not applying illegitimate pressure and should be treated differently from a contractor who *threatens* to breach for reasons within his control, though goes on to suggest (see para **10.28**) that the other party's lack of genuine consent when faced with a 'warning' of this kind should, in certain circumstances, be a separate reason for vitiating the contract. It is suggested that a distinction between threats and warnings in this context is complex and unreal, since in many cases, no clear line can be drawn between reasons outside and within a party's control (like a contractor who feels the effect of external price rises because he has not priced his job or controlled his costs sensibly).

(Step 2) Factual causation—did the threat cause the victim to act as he did?

10.18   Unlike duress to the person, relief will only be given for economic duress if the threat or pressure was the main and overwhelming reason why the victim agreed to act or acted as he did: as Mance J in *Huyton SA v Peter Cremer & Co* said:

> The illegitimate pressure must have been such as actually caused the making of the agreement, in the sense that it would not otherwise have been made either at all or, at least, in the terms in which it was made. In that sense, the pressure must have been decisive or clinching.

In other words, this is the 'but for' test (in contrast to the more favourable test applied for the benefit of the victim of duress to the person, discussed in paras **10.3–10.4**). But factual causation will not be established if the victim was only persuaded to contract because of the combined effect of the illegitimate threat and other reasons. In *Huyton*, Mance J concluded that the buyer's refusal to pay for the goods was not an illegitimate threat (see para **10.11**), but went on to decide that, if it had been illegitimate, it was in any event *not* the decisive cause of the seller's agreement to give up its right to arbitrate. A number of other issues combined to persuade the seller to reach the agreement, such as its misconception that the buyer was untrustworthy and its realisation that there was a risk that its own interpretation of its contractual rights might turn out to be wrong.

10.19 Traditionally, this factual causation test was phrased as a requirement that the victim's 'will' must have been 'coerced' or 'overborne'. This language was adopted by Kerr J in *The Siboen and The Sibotre*, and approved by the Privy Council in *Pao On v Lau Yiu Long* (1980), in which Lord Scarman said that economic duress:

> must amount to a coercion of will which vitiates consent. It must be shown that the payment made or the contract entered into was not a voluntary act.

Today, the language of 'coercion of will' is unpopular. For example, Atiyah (1982) argues that it is inappropriate: 'the victim of duress does normally know what he is doing, does choose to submit, and does intend to do so—indeed the more extreme the pressure, the more real is the consent of the victim.' This criticism is somewhat unfair: the concern of the law of contract is with voluntariness not intention, so it makes sense to say that a victim of duress deserves relief because he did not have a *free* choice, whilst recognising that he entered the contract intentionally (see Tiplady (1983)). Although the language of 'coercion of will' is still used from time to time (see *Dawson v Bell* (2016)), the courts tend now to ask instead whether the threats or pressure induced or caused the victim to enter into the contract (see Lord Goff in *The Evia Luck*), but have recognised that the difference between the old and new approach is only terminological. In particular, the factors that were used to determine whether the victim's 'will' was 'coerced' are precisely the same as the factors used to determine causation today.

10.20 Those factors were identified by the Privy Council in *Pao On*, a case involving contracts for the acquisition of shares. The basic issue was that, having contracted to sell shares to a public listed company controlled by D, the claimants realised that one aspect of their deal was very disadvantageous and so 'persuaded' D to replace a very unwise 'buy-back' contract with a more balanced 'price guarantee' contract. D agreed, but later regretted its decision (when the share price slumped) and sought to avoid liability under the price guarantee, alleging that there was no consideration for it (see Chapter 5) and that it was procured by economic duress. The Privy Council rejected the plea of economic duress, holding that D's will had not been coerced. Lord Scarman emphasised four relevant factors:

1. whether the victim did or did not protest;
2. whether he did or did not have an alternative course open to him such as an adequate legal remedy;

3. whether he was independently advised; and

4. whether after entering into the contract he took steps to avoid it.

On the facts, the crucial feature was that D was in a strong position to resist the claimants' pressure, since (unusually) it had available to it the powerful alternative remedy of seeking specific performance of its original buy-back agreement and only agreed to replace it with the price guarantee because it was worried about the effect the dispute would have on its commercial reputation as a public company. Moreover, it had been advised that it need not accommodate the claimants' demands, but had done so without protest at the time.

10.21 In *Pao On*, these four factors were said to be aspects of the factual causation enquiry (our step 2), but on reflection, matters are not quite this simple. First, the factors are definitely not of equal weight. By far the most important is undoubtedly (2), the adequacy of other alternative courses of action, including other legal remedies, open to the victim, which is invariably the decisive factor in the cases. So in *Atlas v Kafco* (see para **10.13**) the judge emphasised that K had no real alternative but to submit to A's demand, because the alternative course of resisting and suing A for damages for breach of contract would not have allowed K to honour its contract with Woolworths. But, second, this factor makes most sense as part of an objective test of causation (our step 3)—it really tells us whether it was *reasonable* for the victim to have resisted the pressure. For this reason, the courts are beginning to recognise that there is a strong objective element involved in the causal test for economic duress.

(Step 3) Objective causation—would a reasonable person have acted as the victim did?

10.22 In *Huyton*, Mance J advocated an objective approach to causation for economic duress, in addition to asking whether the 'but for' test was satisfied, explaining that:

> ... relief must, I think, depend on the Court's assessment of the qualitative impact of the illegitimate pressure, objectively assessed ... relief may not be appropriate, if an innocent party decides, as a matter of choice, not to pursue an alternative remedy which any and possibly some other reasonable persons in his circumstances would have pursued.

So for Mance J, the most important of the *Pao On* factors is an *objective* question. Where the courts say that the victim had no 'real' choice, they are better understood as meaning that the victim had no 'reasonable' choice and thus the reasonable person would have acted in the same way. This certainly accords with the reasoning (if not the terminology) in cases where economic duress has been established, such as the decision in *Borrelli v Ting* (2010) in which the Privy Council used a graphic metaphor to illustrate the claimant liquidators' objective lack of reasonable choice: 'Put colloquially Ting had the Liquidators over a barrel.'

10.23 A good example is *B & S Contracts and Design Ltd v Victor Green Publishing Ltd* (1984). VG was putting on an exhibition at Olympia and B & S contracted to erect stands for VG at a contract price of just over £11,000. Shortly before the exhibition,

B & S (faced with an industrial dispute with its workers) threatened that it would cancel the contract (purportedly under an express *force majeure* clause) unless VG agreed to pay an additional £4,500 on top of the contract price, to meet the workers' demands. VG agreed, since it had no realistic choice in the circumstances with the exhibition imminent, and B & S erected the stands as promised. When B & S sued for the extra £4,500, VG counterclaimed, alleging that its promise had been procured by economic duress. The Court of Appeal held that B & S could not have relied on the *force majeure* clause to cancel the contract and so its threat to cancel was illegitimate. Moreover, the economic consequences for VG if the stands had not been erected would have been disastrous. As Kerr LJ put it, an illegitimate threat will constitute economic duress:

> if the consequences of a refusal would be serious and immediate so that there is no reasonable alternative open, such as by legal redress, obtaining an injunction etc.

10.24 In *Adam Opel GmbH v Mitras Automotive UK Ltd* (2007) the claimant told the defendant, a company with a contract to supply vehicle parts for the manufacture of vans by the claimant, that it would be changing to a new supplier in six months' time. In response, the defendant threatened to stop the supply of parts with immediate effect (a breach of contract) unless the claimant paid it over £400,000. The claimant reluctantly paid the money, to keep production of the vans going, but later reclaimed the amount on the basis that it was procured by the defendant's duress. The judge allowed the claim, even though the claimant had seriously contemplated seeking an injunction to prevent the defendant from breaching the contract:

> Given [the claimant's] legitimate concern to ensure security of supply, I do not in these circumstances consider that the injunction route was an alternative adequate to nullify the pressure created by [the defendant's] threat.

Controversies

10.25 We have seen that the availability of alternative remedies, the most important of the *Pao On* factors, is best understood as relating to objective causation. So how should the other, subsidiary factors be classified?

- Factor (a), the question of whether the victim *protested* at the time, is concerned with a subjective test of factual causation. If the victim did not protest at the time, it is a strong indication that she was happy to enter the contract anyway (although caution is needed, since it may indicate the opposite, that she realised that to protest would be pointless or make matters worse).

- Factor (c), whether the victim received independent advice, combines subjective and objective reasoning. If the victim is advised that he does have realistic alternative courses open to him, but decides to enter the contract anyway, a court is unlikely to find that it was the threat or pressure that caused him to

enter the contract or that a reasonable person would have done so in the circumstances. However, in some cases independent advice will be totally irrelevant. If the victim is advised that there are no realistic alternative remedies (as
the victims in the *Atlas* or *B & S* cases would presumably have been told, had
they sought advice), this reinforces rather than undermines a conclusion of economic duress.

- Factor (d), *steps taken to avoid the contract*, can be explained as part of subjective causation (since a victim who is happy with the contract will find it hard
  to convince the court that she only entered into it because of illegitimate pressure). But a better interpretation is that it establishes a *defence*, namely that the
  victim has *affirmed* the contract and will thus be barred from rescinding it
  (see para **9.39**). This approach was taken in *The Atlantic Baron* (1979), where
  Mocatta J held that a shipyard's demand for a price increase on a shipbuilding
  contract *did* amount to economic duress, but the fact that the purchaser paid
  the instalments without protest for several years amounted to an 'affirmation of
  the variation of the terms of the original contract'.

10.26 Two important theoretical issues remain. The first is to ask whether an objective approach to causation can be justified, in addition to a subjective test. Of course, in
most cases the two approaches will be identical because the victim will have acted in
precisely the same way that a reasonable person would have done. So the issue only
really matters when the victim *did* act solely because of the threat, but the reasonable person would have resisted. One answer is to say that an objective approach is
merely an evidential tool, to enable the court to decide whether to *believe* the victim's
assertion that it entered the contract solely because of the illegitimate threat (such
that step 3 is merely an aspect of step 2). This reflects the way the courts use the 'materiality' requirement in cases of misrepresentation (see para **9.22**). However, Mance
J gives a reason in *Huyton* for an additional, self-standing, objective requirement. He
explains:

> ... the application of a simple 'but for' test of subjective causation in conjunction with
> a requirement of actual or threatened breach of duty could lead too readily to relief
> being granted. It would not, for example, cater for the obvious possibility that, al-
> though the innocent party would never have acted as he did, but for the illegitimate
> pressure, he nevertheless had a real choice and could, if he had wished, equally well
> have resisted the pressure and, for example, pursued alternative legal redress.

10.27 It is interesting to contrast this attitude to duress as a vitiating factor with the law's
treatment of undue influence. In undue influence cases, the 'victim' is not denied relief
merely because, objectively, a reasonable person in the same position would not have
succumbed to the influence—there is simply no enquiry of this kind. In many undue influence cases (like *Credit Lyonnais Bank Nederland NV v Burch* (1996) discussed at para
11.17) the transaction set aside is one that no reasonable person would have entered
into. This is, presumably, because duress and undue influence vitiate the consent of the
victim in different ways. Undue influence operates at an unconscious level, making the

victim willing to enter into a disadvantageous transaction, whereas the victim of duress knows that she is entering the transaction unwillingly, but does so (through 'gritted teeth') because there is no realistic alternative. So it makes no sense to require victims of undue influence to show that they acted in an objectively rational way, when the undue influence affected their ability to do just that.

10.28 Second, Smith (1997) argues that most duress actually involves *two* justifications for relief—wrongdoing by the threatening party *and* vitiated consent on the part of the victim—but that each justification alone should be *sufficient* for relief. His suggestion is that, in the absence of an illegitimate threat or other wrongdoing by one party, the other party should nonetheless be able to escape from a contract *merely* because he had no real choice about entering into it (giving the example of the captain of a sinking ship who enters into an onerous contract with a rescue vessel because he has no other option). However, as Smith acknowledges, this argument does not square with other areas of the law such as the objective approach to agreement, whereby an offeror is entitled to assume that the offeree is accepting it if he appears to be accepting it, whatever the offeree's subjective intention might be (see Chapter 2), and the rules on mental incapacity, which do not allow one party to escape from the contract on the basis of his own incapacity unless the other party was aware of it (see Chapter W1). It also sits uneasily with the rules on unconscionability (discussed in Chapter 12), that disadvantageous terms alone are not sufficient to invalidate a contract unless imposed because of reprehensible behaviour by one party in exploiting the other's weakness. Smith's approach does, however, give insights into the remaining category of duress, the so-called cases of 'lawful act duress'.

'Lawful act duress'

10.29 We have seen that duress requires an illegitimate threat, which almost invariably means a threat to do something unlawful (commit a crime or a tort) or otherwise wrongful (such as breach a contract). But occasionally, a threat to do something *lawful* might itself be illegitimate. The most obvious examples involve blackmail, where a threat to do something lawful is coupled with an improper demand for money. Here, although the threat is to do something lawful, like publishing a true report in a newspaper (and may even be to do something laudable, like providing information about a criminal offence to the police), it is nonetheless an illegitimate threat if it is made with the motive of extorting money. As Atkinson J said in *Norreys v Zeffert* (1939), just because 'a person may have a legal right to do something which will injure another is not sufficient justification for the demand of money as the price of not doing it'.

10.30 Although most such cases involve the criminal offence of blackmail, this would appear not to be essential for relief from a contract entered into as a result. The term 'lawful act duress' is sometimes coined to catch these rare examples of an improper threat to do something lawful, although for some commentators this label is self-contradictory. The most significant issue today is whether a threat *not to contract* can ever ground relief on this basis. The answer seems to be that the courts have not ruled it out, but would require exceptional circumstances before such relief will be given.

10.31 In *CTN Cash and Carry Ltd v Gallagher Ltd* (1994) CTN ran a warehouse 'cash and carry business'. G, a large corporation with the sole right to distribute well-known brands of cigarettes in the UK, regularly sold cigarettes to CTN. CTN relied heavily on credit from G, but (crucially) G had no contractual obligation to sell to CTN, nor to give such credit. G sold a consignment of cigarettes to CTN, but by mistake delivered them to the wrong warehouse. G agreed to collect and redeliver them but, in the meantime, the cigarettes were stolen. G believed that CTN was obliged to pay for the cigarettes so sent an invoice for their price (£17,000) and made it clear that it would not grant any discretionary credit in the future unless CTN paid. CTN did not believe they were obliged to pay, but did so because of G's threat not to grant any more credit: they regarded paying as 'the lesser of two evils'. CTN later reclaimed the price, on the ground that G's threat not to sell to it on credit in the future amounted to economic duress.

10.32 The Court of Appeal held that, on the facts, G's threat did *not* amount to economic duress. As Steyn LJ observed, G was in law entitled to refuse to enter into any future contracts with CTN for any reason or no reason at all, and did so 'in order to obtain payment of a sum which they bona fide considered due to them'. Interestingly, the Court of Appeal stopped short of saying that a threat not to contract can *never* amount to economic duress, but merely declined to extend the category to the case itself. For Steyn LJ:

> ... an extension capable of covering the present case, involving lawful act duress in a commercial context in pursuit of a bona fide claim, would be a radical one with far-reaching implications.

Sir Donald Nicholls VC agreed, also stressing that it was G's good faith when it made the demand and its reasonable belief at the time that it was entitled to be paid for the cigarettes that defeated CTN's plea of economic duress. (Sir Donald Nicholls VC nonetheless expressed unease at the outcome because, somewhat bizarrely, G conceded at trial that CTN was not obliged to pay for the cigarettes, but nonetheless refused to repay the price.)

10.33 Of course, the Court of Appeal's refusal in *CTN Cash and Carry* to rule out a potential extension of duress to 'bad faith' threats not to contract must be seen in context. That case involved parties in an *existing* contractual relationship, where one party made a threat not to contract again in the future as part of a dispute about whether the price was due under that existing contract. Likewise in *Progress Bulk Carriers Ltd v Tube City IMS* (2012) Cooke J considered CTN and held that, exceptionally, a shipowner's bad conduct in demanding a waiver of rights, though not itself unlawful, could amount to illegitimate pressure on the charterer's when seen in the context of the shipowner's earlier repudiatory breach:

> *the pressure created by the Owners in their demand for a waiver of rights by the Charterers has to be seen both in the light of their repudiatory breach and in the light of their subsequent conduct, including their deliberate refusal to comply with the assurances they had previously given about providing a substitute vessel and paying full compensation in respect of that breach. Their refusal to supply the substitute vessel to meet the Charterers' needs, in circumstances which they had created by their breach and their subsequent misleading activity, unless the Charterers waived their rights, could readily be found by the Arbitrators to amount to 'illegitimate pressure'.*

10.34 The more fundamental question is whether a 'bad faith' threat not to contract in the first place could ever suffice. On the one hand, we are free to decide whether or not to make a contract, so it should follow that there is nothing wrong with *threatening* not to contract, even in bad faith. On the other hand, many people regard English law as unethical in this regard, often citing the fact that the unpleasant practice of 'gazumping' during negotiations for the sale of land is perfectly lawful. An 'agreement' to buy land is not binding until signed written contracts have been exchanged, but before then the potential purchaser will already have spent a lot of time, effort, and money on searches and surveys, plus he will have found a potential purchaser for his current house. Knowing this, the seller may threaten to pull out of the sale just before contracts are exchanged, unless the purchaser agrees to pay more than the provisionally agreed price. (Of course, sellers tend to behave like this at a time when the property market is buoyant: where the market is slow, purchasers have the upper hand and sometimes threaten to pull out of the purchase before contracts are exchanged unless the price is dropped, sometimes called 'gazundering'!) If the purchaser succumbs and agrees to pay the increased price, the resulting bargain is currently perfectly enforceable.

10.35 Should the category of 'lawful act duress' be extended to negotiating tactics of this kind? The answer is probably not. For a start, the threat will fail the relevant causal tests. In most 'gazumping' cases, the purchaser has a genuine choice whether to pull out of or proceed with the transaction, and even where the purchaser truly has no choice (for example, if he has already exchanged contracts to sell his existing house and has run out of money to pay any more search or mortgage valuation fees), objective causation is missing because the *reasonable purchaser* would have realised that the negotiations were 'subject to contract' and that the seller was free to withdraw its offer at any time. Moreover, to condemn a threat not to contract in the first place as illegitimate would mark an unacceptable inroad into freedom of contract. This conclusion is, of course, based on English law's refusal to recognise that parties owe duties to each other in pre-contractual negotiations. If the underlying legal framework were to change, the duress conclusion might follow suit, but for now the courts are instinctively opposed to such a move. So in *Bank of India v Riat* (2014) the judge gave short shrift to an argument that a bank had applied illegitimate pressure when it demanded a personal guarantee from the director/shareholder of a family business before it would lend money to the business: 'There was no concluded agreement and the Bank was free to walk away from the negotiations as was Mr Riat also free to walk away.'

OVERVIEW

1 Duress involves improper pressure or coercion, usually taking the form of a threat to do something illegitimate, which induces the victim to contract and thus vitiates the victim's consent. Some cases involve the victim setting aside or resisting enforcement of the resulting contract or contractual variation; others involve actions to recover money paid under duress.

2 Duress to the person is straightforward. The victim of violence or threats of violence gets the benefit of a generous causation test and any contract will be rendered void, whereas lesser forms of duress merely render transactions voidable. Where a contract is made or money paid because one party wrongfully refuses to release the other's goods, duress to goods will be established.

3 English law now recognises economic duress, for example a threat to breach a contract, as potentially actionable. The cases do not adopt consistent terminology, though there is a fair degree of consensus about the factors that are relevant. A threefold division is helpful.

4 First, is the threat illegitimate? There is some support for the proposition that a threat to breach a contract is only illegitimate if made in bad faith, but the better view is that all such threats should count as illegitimate. Second, the illegitimate threat must have caused the victim to contract, judged subjectively. Third, on an objective test, the victim must have had no reasonable alternative course open to him. Other relevant, though less significant, factors are whether the victim protested, whether he received independent advice and his subsequent efforts to avoid or affirm the contract. An objective test of causation is justified in addition to a subjective test, but there is no justification for relief merely based on the victim's vitiated consent without the additional element of an illegitimate threat by the other party.

5 The courts have not entirely ruled out extending the inelegantly labelled category of 'lawful act' duress to cover threats not to contract, at least if made in bad faith.

FURTHER READING

Bigwood 'Economic Duress by Threatened Breach of Contract' (2001) 117 LQR 376

Birks 'The Travails of Duress' [1990] LMCLQ 342

Morgan *Great Debates in Contract Law* (2015) pp 194–205

Smith 'Contracting under Pressure: A Theory of Duress' [1997] CLJ 343

SELF-TEST QUESTIONS

1   What is the relationship between duress and consideration?

2   Should a threat to breach a contract invariably count as an illegitimate threat for the purposes of establishing economic duress?

3   In establishing economic duress, why is it so important to ask whether the victim had a reasonable alternative course of action open to him?

4   Why is a threat not to contract treated differently from a threat to breach a contract?

5   Edmund made a contract with Wecanvas Ltd, a small company, for the hire of a luxury white marquee for his daughter's wedding reception, which was to take place in the garden of the family home. The contract price was £6,000, of which Edmund paid a deposit of £2,000 on contracting; the balance of £4,000 was due two days before the wedding. Three days before the wedding, the managing director of Wecanvas telephoned Edmund, saying 'I am so sorry sir, I have realised that we misquoted your job: the contract price should have been £9,000. In normal circumstances I'd overlook the error, but times are very hard so I must warn you that I am going to have to ask you for £7,000 before we commence installation tomorrow.' Edmund was furious and phoned round all the other marquee hire companies in the area; all were fully booked apart from Chavtent Ltd, which had only one marquee available made of sparkly cerise pink fabric, which Edmund regarded as a wholly unacceptable alternative. He contacted his brother, a city solicitor, who told him that he would not be able to get a court order forcing Wecanvas to honour the original price and erect the marquee, but said, 'Why not pay the extra £3,000 now, you can easily afford it, then sue to get it back on grounds of duress when the wedding is over?' So Edmund paid the £7,000, the wedding was a great success, but he now seeks to reclaim the £3,000. Advise him.

For hints on how to answer question 5, please see the online resources at
www.oup.com/uk/sullivan8e/.

11 Undue influence

SUMMARY

This chapter covers undue influence, a vitiating factor. It considers how undue influence is proved, either by actual evidence or, more commonly, by means of a rebuttable presumption based on a relationship of trust and confidence coupled with a transaction that calls for an explanation. The remedy of rescission for undue influence is explored and whether damages are or should be available. Undue influence is commonly pleaded in a three-party debtor/creditor/surety situation, where relief is available against a third party creditor only if it has notice of the undue influence which it has not taken reasonable steps to avoid.

Introductory points

11.1 Undue influence, like misrepresentation and economic duress, renders a contract voidable: so one party can seek to rescind or 'set aside' the contract (either as claimant or by way of a defence) if it was executed as a result of the other party's undue influence. Undue influence is commonly also pleaded as a ground of restitution to reclaim a gift, but the test is essentially the same whether or not there is a contract in place. (This should be contrasted with the regime for setting aside dispositions in wills on the basis that the testator had been subject to undue influence, where the rules are different and undue influence slightly more difficult to establish.)

11.2 Undue influence is difficult to define—indeed, the courts have remarked that it would be a mistake to try and do so, content to give examples of its common features. As Lord Clyde noted in *Royal Bank of Scotland v Etridge (No 2)* (2001) ('*Etridge*'), 'It is something which can more easily be recognised when found than exhaustively analysed in the abstract.' Essentially, undue influence requires a relationship between the parties, generally one of trust and confidence or vulnerability and dependency, which pre-dated the contract or gift between them and which one party exploits for his own advantage. It is, of course, only within a relationship that there is any possibility of influence: this makes undue influence significantly different from duress. Occasionally the two come close, as in *Drew v Daniel* (2005) where a dominant 'forceful' family member coerced a vulnerable elderly relative, but the presence of the pre-existing relationship nonetheless marks the situation as one of undue influence. A stranger can assert pressure or make threats, but cannot benefit from the altogether subtler exercise of influence, which can make undue influence more invidious.

11.3 Undue influence cases reveal the difficulty of striking the right balance between protecting the vulnerable from exploitation, without unduly patronising them or restricting their freedom to be generous. For example, a common scenario involves an elderly person making gifts before his or her death to someone who had been caring for them, which are challenged after the elderly person's death by his or her relatives: it is by no means easy to adjudicate on the merits of the relatives' challenge. A related concern is the need for security in receipts—the more willing the courts are to undo transactions, the less secure recipients can be that they will be entitled to keep what they have received. This is seen where a family member, commonly a wife, guarantees her husband's business debts to a bank, which may or may not have been procured by the husband's undue influence. The courts must find the right balance between protecting vulnerable spouses from victimisation within their marriage without discouraging creditors from being willing to finance small businesses on the security of the matrimonial home.

11.4 Para **11.3** shows that undue influence can arise in a simple two-party case, where A unduly influences B to contract with A, and in more complex three-party cases, such as those involving a surety/wife, debtor/husband, and creditor/bank. Here, where A unduly influences B to contract with C, the question of whether the transaction can be set aside as against C depends on two distinct issues. These are, first, has there been undue influence between A and B and, if so, is the third party C 'tainted' by the undue influence by having notice of it? Beware: confusion can arise when these two issues are not kept distinct.

Actual and presumed undue influence

11.5 There is often no concrete evidence of undue influence, which frequently occurs subtly within a relationship of trust, without documents or dispassionate witnesses. Wise to this risk, the courts began to give relief on the basis that evidence of undue influence could be *presumed* on the facts unless there was evidence to the contrary to rebut the presumption. The presumption arose from a relationship between the parties coupled with a suspicious transaction, unless rebutted by evidence that the presumptively influenced party had nonetheless entered into the transaction with full and informed consent.

11.6 Over time, litigants and judges started to treat actual and presumed undue influence as if they were two distinct vitiating factors (often called 'Class 1' and 'Class 2' undue influence). This meant in turn that judges felt able to reject a plea of actual undue influence whilst finding, with no sense of inconsistency, that presumed undue influence had arisen and not been rebutted. Commentators also began to regard actual and undue influence as distinctly different grounds of relief. For example, Birks and Chin (1995) argued that actual undue influence, being a species of improper pressure, was 'defendant-sided' and based on the defendant's wrongdoing, while presumed undue influence was 'claimant-sided', justified on the basis of the claimant's impaired consent. This is not entirely surprising, since the circumstances in which undue influence would be presumed came to be stripped of any connotations of wrongdoing, with the courts stressing that the terms of the transaction had to be 'disadvantageous' rather than 'suspicious'.

11.7 This sharp division of actual and presumed undue influence as two separate vitiating factors is no longer arguable. The House of Lords in *Etridge* emphatically reminded us that there is only one relevant ground of relief, 'undue influence', the 'presumption' meaning no more than that, as an evidential matter, actual undue influence might be inferred if certain elements are present, as Lord Clyde explained:

> *At the end of the day, after trial, there will either be proof of undue influence or that proof will fail, and it will be found that there was no undue influence. In the former case, whatever the relationship of the parties and however the influence was exerted, there will be found to have been an actual case of undue influence. In the latter there will be none.*

With this in mind, the case law can now be examined.

Cases where presumption unnecessary: actual evidence of undue influence

11.8 Actual evidence of the exploitation of influence by one party is rare (after all, why go to the trouble of adducing actual evidence when you could rely on the presumption?). A modern example in which there was compelling evidence of actual undue influence (although the wife's plea failed for other reasons) was *BCCI v Aboody* (1990). Mrs A, who understood nothing of business matters and was culturally entirely subservient to her husband, executed an all monies charge to secure her husband's business. She had been receiving advice from an independent solicitor about the implications of signing the charge when her husband burst into the room, interrupting the solicitor and shouting at his wife to sign, a scene which reduced Mrs A to tears.

11.9 In *Drew v Daniel* (2005) a 'forceful' and 'insensitive' man bullied his elderly aunt into retiring as trustee of a family trust without the opportunity of seeking legal advice, thereby taking advantage of her naivety in business matters. Although there was no evidence of overt acts of coercion, there was evidence of a forceful personality exploiting his vulnerable aunt to an unacceptable extent, persuading her to execute the deed against her free will. The Court of Appeal confirmed that the trial judge had applied *Etridge* correctly in finding actual undue influence.

11.10 Notice that in both these cases there was a relationship between the parties—it is difficult to see how influence (as opposed to duress) can be exerted in the absence of a relationship—so it is not surprising that the presumption mirrors the facts that give rise to actual undue influence. Of course, just because the parties are in a relationship where one has the 'upper hand' over the other does not necessarily mean that the facts will reveal undue influence. In *Prince Jefri Bolkiah v State of Brunei Darussalam* (2007), the claimant reached a settlement agreement with his brother, the Sultan of Brunei, following allegations that the claimant had misappropriated state funds, but later sought to rescind it for (inter alia) undue influence. The Privy Council rejected the allegations of undue influence as 'obviously false', noting that the claimant, who was advised by top city lawyers in the negotiation of the settlement agreement, certainly 'did not have a knee-jerk reaction to obey all commands or comply with all expressed wishes of the Sultan'.

Cases where presumption used: to infer evidence of undue influence

11.11 As has been said, undue influence can be presumed where there is (1) a relationship of trust and confidence between the parties, combined with (2) a suspicious transaction, unless (3) rebutted by evidence that the alleged victim entered into the transaction on the basis of full and informed consent. We will consider each limb in turn.

Relationship

11.12 The relationships attracting the presumption of undue influence are generally organised into two categories, which before *Etridge* were commonly described as 'Class 2A' and 'Class 2B'.

11.13 The first (once called Class 2A) is a closed list of certain standard relationships that will *always* be held to be relationships of trust and confidence, the main examples being doctor and patient; solicitor and client; religious adviser and follower (though interestingly, not husband and wife). So in *Wright v Carter* (1903) the plaintiff executed a deed of trust whereby the whole of his property (present and future) was held on trust for his two children and his solicitor in equal shares! The court had no hesitation in finding that a presumption of undue influence arose and had not been rebutted by the solicitor. In *Markham v Karsten* (2007) the judge held that the relationship of solicitor and client attracts the presumption even where the two parties were also cohabiting, since 'the influence which is presumed to exist between solicitor and client may be strengthened if they are also in a marriage or domestic partner relationship'.

11.14 In *Allcard v Skinner* (1887) Miss Allcard, a wealthy young woman, joined a convent. She bound herself to observe the rules of the order, including poverty, which required members to give up all their property; seclusion, which prevented members seeking outside advice without permission; and obedience, which told members to regard the voice of the Mother Superior as the voice of God. Miss Allcard transferred large sums of money and stocks to the Mother Superior, but later left the order and sought to set the gifts aside. The Court of Appeal held that the presumption of undue influence arose.

11.15 In *Etridge*, Lord Nicholls described relationships falling into this first category as raising an *irrebuttable* presumption, but this probably means no more than that these relationships invariably involve influence (and so count as relationships of trust and confidence), but it may or may not give rise to a presumption of *undue* influence, depending on whether there is a suspicious transaction as well. It is crucial to remember that a relationship of trust and confidence is not on its own sufficient to give rise to a presumption of undue influence.

11.16 Second, any other kind of relationship can suffice if on the facts it is one of trust and confidence, or vulnerability and dependence (formerly described as Class 2B). All sorts of relationships have fallen into this category. For example, in *O'Sullivan v Management Agency & Music Ltd* (1985) the relationship between a young pop star and his manager was sufficient. In *Re Craig* (1971) an 84-year-old widower employed a housekeeper companion, and in the next six years until his death made gifts to her worth almost £30,000, reducing the total value of his estate by about 75 per cent. The judge held that their relationship was one of trust and confidence and (coupled with the suspicious transaction) attracted the presumption of undue influence. The same conclusion was reached in *Leeder v Stevens* (2005), where a divorced lady placed trust and confidence in the new man in her life; in *Watson v Huber* (2005), where a widow left all financial matters to her step-sister, whom she (unwisely) 'trusted implicitly'; and in *Abbey National Bank plc v Stringer* (2006), where a vulnerable widow who could not read and whose spoken English was very poor relied entirely on her beloved only son in business matters.

11.17 Perhaps the most extraordinary example of a relationship giving rise to the presumption of undue influence, in what is normally an exclusively commercial situation, is found in *Credit Lyonnais Bank Nederland NV v Burch* (1996). Helen Burch worked as a secretary for a company run by a middle-aged man, Mr Pelosi. Over the years she had got to know Pelosi well, babysitting for his children and visiting his family in Italy, but there was no sexual relationship between them. The company got into financial difficulties, so Pelosi asked Burch to execute an unlimited all-monies charge over her modest flat in favour of the bank and, inexplicably, she agreed. The Court of Appeal had no hesitation in holding that there was a presumption of undue influence in the relationship, setting aside the charge with the words 'this transaction cannot possibly stand'. (For a subsequent first instance example of a business relationship attracting the presumption of undue influence, see *Trustees of Beardsley Theobalds Retirement Benefit Scheme v Yardley* (2011).)

Suspicious transaction

11.18 The original test was defined in *Allcard v Skinner* as follows:

> *The mere existence of such influence is not enough in such a case ... but if the gift is so large as not to be reasonably accounted for on the ground of friendship, relationship, charity or other ordinary motives on which ordinary men act, the burden is on the donee to support the gift.*

11.19   Later cases subtly changed the way this requirement was described, shifting to the language of a 'manifestly disadvantageous transaction': see, for example, Lord Scarman in *National Westminster Bank v Morgan* (1985). But there were problems with this way of expressing the requirement. First, what did 'manifestly' mean in this context? The Court of Appeal in *Aboody* explained that the 'overall disadvantageous nature of a transaction cannot be said to be manifest, if it only emerges after a fine and close evaluation of its various beneficial and detrimental features'. Yet sometimes the level of disadvantage was not as 'screamingly' obvious as this, but was still sufficient to attract the presumption (see, for example, *Mahoney v Purnell* (1996) discussed at para **11.36**), rendering the word 'manifest' somewhat superfluous.

11.20   A more significant problem was how the stereotypical case of a wife giving a guarantee or mortgaging the matrimonial home to secure the debts of her husband's business should be dealt with. In a narrow sense such a transaction is plainly disadvantageous to the wife, yet in the ordinary course there is nothing suspicious about such a transaction and there may be very good reasons for the wife to enter into it, because the family finances are linked to the fate of the husband's business. The House of Lords recognised these difficulties in *Etridge* and disapproved of the language of manifest disadvantage, which had given rise to 'misunderstanding' and 'ambiguity', preferring to return to the original formulation from *Allcard v Skinner*. The Court of Appeal in *Smith v Cooper* (2010) confirmed that the House of Lords in *Etridge* used the phrase 'a transaction which calls for explanation' as shorthand for the formula in *Allcard v Skinner*.

11.21   The return to a test of whether the transaction 'calls for an explanation' because it cannot 'be reasonably accounted for' in the circumstances is very welcome, as it captures the sense that, within families, some transactions look financially one-sided, but overall are unobjectionable. In *Turkey v Awadh* (2005) a father helped his daughter and son-in-law by paying off the amount due on their mortgage-loan, in return for the transfer of the house to him. Although the daughter and son-in-law reposed considerable trust and confidence in her father, particularly in financial matters, the Court of Appeal agreed with the trial judge that, looked at in the familial context, the transaction 'curious as it might otherwise seem, was explicable by the ordinary motives of people in the position of [the parties]' and so the deed transferring the house was not set aside for undue influence. In contrast, the mother in *Abbey National Bank plc v Stringer* mortgaged her home, her only asset, as security for her son's business venture, having received no explanation of the document she was signing. The judge entirely rejected the claimant's submission that the transaction was 'no more than that which is readily explicable as a mother's generosity to her son'. The Court of Appeal in *Hart v Burbidge* (2014) emphasised that, when deciding if a transaction called for an explanation, it should be judged, not in isolation, but in its context at the time, and not with the benefit of hindsight.

11.22   Some commentators have argued that the presence of a relationship alone should be enough to raise the rebuttable presumption of undue influence. For example, Oldham (1995) notes that for duress and misrepresentation, 'the fairness or unfairness of the terms of the contract is irrelevant'. However, this is not a valid criticism. Transactions within a relationship are not wrongful in themselves; it is only the combination of a relationship and a suspicious transaction that justifies a presumption of wrongdoing.

11.23 Put another way, it is the unusual terms of the transaction that should set the 'alarm bells' ringing for the defendant, and thus provide the justification for requiring him to see to it that the claimant is acting voluntarily or surrender the benefits of the transaction (O'Sullivan (1998)). It is because undue influence operates in the context of a relationship that an evidential presumption is so useful—there is after all no need for a notion of presumed duress or presumed misrepresentation—but also why it is so vital not to trigger the presumption unless the transaction itself should have alerted the defendant to the risk of the claimant's lack of voluntariness. Their Lordships took this view in *Etridge*, regarding the 'suspicious transaction' requirement as a necessary limitation:

> It would be absurd for the law to presume that every gift by a child to a parent, or every transaction between a client and his solicitor or between a patient and his doctor, was brought about by undue influence unless the contrary is affirmatively proved. Such a presumption would be too far reaching. The law would be out of touch with everyday life if the presumption were to apply to every Christmas or birthday gift by a child to a parent, or an agreement whereby a client or patient agrees to be responsible for the reasonable fees of his legal or medical adviser. The law would be rightly open to ridicule, for transactions such as these are unexceptionable. They do not suggest that something may be amiss. So something more is needed before the law reverses the burden of proof, something which calls for an explanation (per Lord Nicholls).

This 'alarm bells' explanation also explains the apparent inconsistency, noted by Lord Browne-Wilkinson in *CIBC Mortgages v Pitt* (1994) (see para **11.49**), that dealings between fiduciaries and those to whom they owe fiduciary duties (such as solicitors with their clients) are vulnerable even if they were not in any way suspicious, and of course some of the 'Class 2A' relationships are also fiduciary. The fact of fiduciary status provides its own 'alarm bells' for the fiduciary, who ought to know in any event of the risks of entering into such transactions. The balance between protecting the claimant and preserving the security of transactions for the defendant is consequently rather different.

Rebutting the presumption

11.24 If the presumption arises, it can be rebutted by proof that undue influence was not in fact operating, because the claimant entered the transaction or made the gift 'only after full, free and informed thought about it' (per Evershed MR in *Zamet v Hyman* (1961)). Or, as Cotton LJ explained in *Allcard v Skinner*, the presumption is rebutted by proof that the transaction or gift:

> ... was the spontaneous act of the donor acting under circumstances which enabled him to exercise an independent will and which justifies the court in holding that the gift was the result of the free exercise of the donor's will.

It is insufficient for the recipient to show that the donor understood the implications of making the gift or making the contract. Instead, it must be shown that it was a product of the donor's own free will. After all, someone may fully understand the mechanics and implications of a transaction, yet still act under the influence of another. Moreover, *Goodchild v Bradbury* (2007) shows that it is plainly insufficient to rebut the presumption for a vulnerable donor to give evidence that he had not felt pressured by the recipient.

11.25 The most obvious (but not the only) way in which this can be established is by proving that the donor received independent legal advice. As Lord Hailsham said in the Privy Council in *Inche Noriah v Shaik Allie Bin Amar* (1929), the presumption is generally rebutted by showing:

> that the gift was made after the nature and effect of the transaction had been fully explained to the donor by some independent and qualified person so completely as to satisfy the court that the donor was acting independently of any influence of the donee and with the full appreciation of what he was doing.

This is quite a strict test—for example, the elderly donor in *Goodchild v Bradbury* (2007) spent a few minutes alone with a solicitor, but this was insufficient to ensure that there was no operative undue influence. The Privy Council in *Inche Noriah* went on to decide that the legal advice given to the donor, although independent and in good faith, was not sufficient to rebut the presumption because the solicitor did not disclose the material facts (namely that the gift being made by the elderly appellant represented virtually the whole of her estate). As Nourse LJ explained in *Hammond v Osborn* (2002), 'It can hardly be suggested that a donor would act spontaneously under circumstances which enabled him freely to exercise an independent will if he was not fully informed of the nature of the gift but also of its effect.' Likewise in *Smith v Cooper* (2010), a mentally fragile woman, Miss Cooper, transferred a 50 per cent beneficial interest in her home to her new partner who 'ran her finances'; a relationship and a transaction which triggered the presumption of undue influence. The same solicitor acted for both parties and offered no independent advice to Miss Cooper. The Court of Appeal held that there was no evidence that she had 'entered into the transaction of her own free will, independently of, and not in any way as a result of' her partner's influence, so the presumption was not rebutted and the transaction was set aside.

11.26 Importantly, the ease with which the presumption of undue influence can be rebutted will vary from case to case. Lord Scott commented in *Etridge* that the weight of the presumption will depend on the particular nature of the relationship and the impugned transaction, and that the strength of the evidence required to rebut the presumption will depend on the weight of the presumption itself. At one end of the spectrum, in an extreme case like *Allcard*, where the transaction was particularly disadvantageous and the influence profound, even independent legal advice may not have sufficed. At the other end of the spectrum, independent legal advice may be unnecessary.

11.27   The most striking example of the latter, where the donor insisted on proceeding without legal advice, is the colourful though very exceptional case of *Re Brocklehurst* (1978). Sir Philip Brocklehurst, an eccentric aristocrat, was helped in his old age by a local garage proprietor, John Roberts, who did odd jobs for Sir Philip and kept him company. Their relationship was not on equal terms: Roberts was subservient and 'knew his place'. Sir Philip gave Roberts a very valuable long lease of all the shooting rights over his estate (which reduced the estate's value considerably), insisting on doing so and refusing to countenance any suggestion that he should obtain independent advice. After Sir Philip's death, his (distant) relatives applied to have the lease set aside. The majority of the Court of Appeal (with a very strong dissent by Lord Denning MR) held that the nature of the parties' relationship was not such as to attract the presumption of undue influence, but (*obiter*) if it did, the presumption would nonetheless be rebutted, despite the absence of independent advice, by the clear evidence that Sir Philip had been acting independently and of his own free will. As Lawton LJ put it, the autocratic Sir Philip told Roberts 'what to do and he did what he was told', so Roberts 'was not imposing his will on Sir Philip'.

11.28   We should be wary of too readily applying *Brocklehurst*, because its facts were exceptional, not least because (unusually in such cases) there was a great wealth of evidence about Sir Philip's motives and the extent to which he was influenced. It is extremely hard to find another case in which the presumption has been rebutted in the absence of independent legal advice, though in *R v Attorney General for England and Wales* (2003) (discussed at para **5.27**) the Privy Council remarked that the absence of independent legal advice need not be fatal, depending on the circumstances. The confidentiality contract entered into by the SAS soldier was a simple one and he understood its terms. The most that an independent legal adviser could be expected to tell him would be to reflect on the matter, but he probably would have proceeded in any event. Moreover, the contract probably did not trigger a presumption of undue influence in the first place, despite the soldier's 'relationship' with his commanding officers, because it was readily explicable and not suspicious.

Basis and status of presumed undue influence since *Etridge*

11.29   The House of Lords in *Etridge* made a number of observations and criticisms of the prevailing treatment of presumed undue influence, so it is important to take stock and consider the current status of the presumptions. First, although the House criticised the division of cases of undue influence into actual (Class 1) and presumed (Class 2), the effect of this criticism was *not* to abolish the presumption of undue influence. Lord Nicholls (whose speech represents the ratio of the case) specifically retains it, so claimants can still rely on it, and indeed have done so successfully in cases since *Etridge* such as *Hammond v Osborn* (2002), *Niersmans v Pesticcio* (2004), *Watson v Huber* (2005), and *Goodchild v Bradbury* (2007). The thrust of the criticism was terminological, to show that even when the claimant relies on a presumption, he is still trying to establish undue influence. Adducing 'actual' evidence of undue influence and relying on the presumption are just two different routes to establishing the same thing, namely undue influence. The same applies to the further criticisms of the subdivision of presumed undue influence into two sub-classes.

11.30 However, the changes are not entirely terminological. The downgrading of presumed undue influence, especially Class 2B, suggests that claimants will not necessarily succeed if they show the two elements of the presumption, but will need to convince the court more generally that, overall, undue influence existed. Phang and Tjio (2002) view the decision in this way, arguing that there is now little if any difference between Class 1 and Class 2B cases and this is supported by the reasoning and conclusion in *Drew v Daniel* (2005). If so, this poses potential problems for legal advisers. We have already noted (in para **11.2**) that it is difficult to define undue influence or to explain what it is. The presumptions traditionally mean that the claimant and his lawyers need not worry about such difficult questions: as long as they could show the elements of the presumption, they are home and dry. The challenge post-*Etridge* is to ensure that the presumptions are not too rigid but merely assist with evidence of undue influence, without downgrading them so far that undue influence is established entirely by 'looking at the question in the round'.

11.31 The other continued source of occasional confusion is whether undue influence invariably involves wrongdoing. There is no doubt that, properly understood, it does. Lord Nicholls repeatedly describes undue influence as a 'wrong' in *Etridge*, saying for example:

> Typically this occurs when one person places trust in another to look after his affairs and interests, and the latter betrays this trust by preferring his own interests. He abuses the influence he has acquired.

Subsequently, in *Goodchild v Bradbury* (2007) the Court of Appeal accepted that the reasoning in *Etridge* means that undue influence has 'a connotation of impropriety'. Likewise for Norris J in *Davies v AIB Group (UK) plc* (2012), undue influence involves 'wrongdoing' and the law 'does not protect against folly, but against victimisation'.

11.32 This is not to say that dishonesty or conscious wrongdoing is required for undue influence. As Silber J said in *Hackett v Crown Prosecution Service* (2011), 'it is not an ingredient of undue influence that the wrongdoer cheated the victim'. This is demonstrated by the fact that the court in *Allcard* was keen to stress the Mother Superior's moral probity and that 'no suggestion of impropriety could be made against her', but nonetheless a finding of undue influence was made:

> The court interferes, not on the ground that any wrongful act has in fact been committed by the donee, but on the ground of public policy, and to prevent the relations which existed between the parties and the influence arising therefrom being abused.

11.33 Unfortunately, this dictum is still occasionally cited as authority that the presumption of undue influence has *nothing* to do with wrongdoing. For example, Nourse LJ in *Hammond* regards it is a 'continuing misconception' that presumed undue influence involves wrong-doing. But, as *Etridge* makes clear, the true position seems to be that it *is* wrongful per se to prefer your own interests where someone has placed trust and confidence in you, without seeing to it that he or she was acting freely and voluntarily. So undue influence can be presumed even if no obvious misconduct is involved, as the Court of Appeal emphasised in *Macklin v Dowsett* (2004). A helpful analogy can be drawn with the law on fiduciaries. We say someone is a fiduciary where there is a particularly strong relationship of trust and confidence, and impose correspondingly stringent duties of loyalty to prevent abuse. Undue influence deals with relationships where it would not be appropriate to impose full-scale fiduciary status, but where nonetheless analogous, though somewhat weaker, protection is called for. So although the defendant's *conduct* need not be overtly wrongful in a case where the presumption is successfully relied on (although it often is), he has nonetheless failed to prove that he did not 'betray or abuse' the trust and confidence reposed in him. As Bigwood (1996) demonstrates, relief for undue influence has (like economic duress) both 'claimant-sided' and 'defendant-sided' elements.

Remedies

Rescission

11.34 The orthodox view is that rescission is the only remedy for undue influence: there is certainly no statutory regime equivalent to the Misrepresentation Act providing for damages for undue influence. Rescission will be barred by the same bars already discussed in Chapter 9 on Misrepresentation: delay, affirmation, intervening third party rights, and the impossibility of restoring the parties to the *status quo ante*.

11.35 So, for example, the final result in *Allcard v Skinner* was that Miss Allcard had delayed too long after leaving the order (and thus becoming free of the Mother Superior's influence) before seeking rescission and it was therefore held to be barred on the basis both of delay and affirmation. In fact, the crucial issue is affirmation—she did not act promptly to disaffirm the gifts once freed from the undue influence and was thus treated as having confirmed them. (A similar finding was made by the Court of Appeal in *Samuel v Wardlow* (2007), where the pop star Seal unsuccessfully attempted to set aside a management agreement with his former manager.) The mere passage of time will not bar rescission if the donor is still subject to the influence, as was made clear in *Mutual Finance Ltd v John Wetton & Sons Ltd* (1937) (interestingly, a rare case in which a *company* succeeded in pleading that it was subject to undue influence).

Any prospect of damages?

11.36 Of course the bars to rescission are more of a problem for the claimant in undue influence cases than in cases of misrepresentation, because of the absence of an obvious alternative damages remedy. As a result, the courts are becoming more flexible and granting a form of relief where, strictly, rescission is barred because, for example, it is impossible to restore the *status quo* by making *restitutio in integrum*. A good example of this trend is *Mahoney v Purnell* (1996). May J first determined that the sale by the elderly Mr Mahoney of his shares in his hotel business was made under the presumed undue influence of his son-in-law, and that the presumption had not been rebutted, then turned to the question of Mr Mahoney's remedy. It was obvious that the parties could not be restored to their former positions, as the son-in-law had sold the hotel business and wound up the company, but May J held that (to do 'practical justice') Mr Mahoney should receive 'equitable compensation', equivalent to the value of what he surrendered, giving credit for the value of what he received. The problem is that equitable compensation is a well-recognised remedy for breach of trust and breach of fiduciary duty but not for undue influence, so May J was obliged to *deem* the parties' relationship to be a fiduciary one: 'The relationship which existed in this case between Mr Mahoney and Mr Purnell from which undue influence is presumed is based upon trust and may be described as fiduciary.'

11.37 Some commentators (see Birks (1997)) have pointed out that there was no need for May J to strain the already problematic definition of a fiduciary relationship to fit these facts. Instead, he could have achieved the same result by awarding the *financial equivalent* of rescission, a *gain-based* pecuniary award, which focuses on removing the benefit received by the person exerting the undue influence (rather than compensating for the loss suffered by the victim, as equitable compensation does). This way, rescission will no longer need to be barred by the impossibility of restoring the *status quo ante* or the intervention of third party rights, since if the defendant is unable to restore precisely the property that passed as a result of undue influence, he will simply be ordered to pay its financial equivalent instead.

11.38 An alternative view of *Mahoney v Purnell* is offered by Ho (2000), who argues that May J was correct to describe the sum awarded as *compensation* for undue influence (and could justifiably have done so without categorising the parties' relationship as 'fiduciary'). Ho explains that undue influence is a species of equitable wrongdoing (see para **11.31**), for which a loss-based compensatory remedy should be (and historically would have been) available in lieu of rescission, at least in cases where the defendant's conduct was not entirely innocent. Indeed, as Cane (1996) points out, it is principally for historical reasons, not reasons of principle, that undue influence (like many other forms of 'equitable wrongdoing') is not in appropriate cases treated as a tort. This is a good point: after all, undue influence is often as culpable as negligent misrepresentation, which is commonly actionable as a tort in its own right.

Rescission on terms

11.39 Another important, and less controversial, way in which rescission can be tailored to provide appropriate relief, fair to both parties, is for the court to attach terms to their order for rescission (using the valuable equitable device of 'taking accounts'). A good example is *O'Sullivan v Management Agency & Music Ltd* (1985). A pop star successfully alleged that when he was a young, unknown singer, he had entered into management contracts as a result of the presumed undue influence of his management company, which had not been rebutted. Rescission of these contracts was difficult, because they were contracts for the provision of services and had been completely executed by the time of the proceedings. Undeterred, the court ordered the defendants to account for the profits made from the contracts, but allowed them to retain some remuneration for their work, though at a reasonable level, not at the excessive contractual rate. This is actually a fairly straightforward example of rescission granted subject to a requirement that the innocent party make counter restitution of benefits received. The jurisdiction to grant rescission on terms has occasionally been used in more controversial circumstances.

11.40 For example, in *Cheese v Thomas* (1994) C, aged 85 and T, his great-nephew, purchased a house for £83,000, with a view to living in it together. C contributed £43,000 in cash generated from the sale of his previous home, while T borrowed the remaining £40,000 from a mortgagee, secured by a mortgage on the house (which was in T's sole name). T defaulted on the mortgage and C asked for his money back. Eventually the house was sold and raised only £55,000. C alleged that he entered into the transaction under the presumed undue influence of T and the court agreed. Their relationship was one of trust and confidence, while the transaction was 'manifestly disadvantageous': C had given up his own home and a large chunk of capital in return for a 'seriously insecure' right tying him to this particular house (probably best described as a contractual licence). However, when it turned to the appropriate remedy, the court did not order T to pay back C's £43,000 in full. Instead, it held that the loss on the sale of the property, caused by the fall in the property market, should be shared by the parties in proportion to their initial contributions to the purchase price. The transaction was in the nature of a 'de facto joint venture' so it would be 'practically just' for the parties to share the fall in the house's value. So C was only entitled to approximately £28,000.

11.41 This result is problematic for a number of reasons. First, the result seems meaningless, since T could almost certainly not have afforded to pay C even the lesser sum of £28,000: the house had been sold by the mortgagee, exercising its power of sale, who was entitled to be repaid its £40,000 secured loan *first* out of the £55,000 proceeds of sale, leaving only £15,000 in the pot. T, who had defaulted on the mortgage repayments, was unlikely to be able to afford to pay C anything more than that. (It should be stressed that, unlike the common three-party cases that will be considered at para 11.43 onwards, there was no question of the mortgage itself being set aside on the grounds of undue influence.) Second, as Dixon (1994) has pointed out, the judgment is internally inconsistent: C is treated as a mere contractual licensee when determining manifest disadvantage, but a beneficial owner of the house (obliged to bear his proportion of the property's fall in value) at the remedial stage. Third, the court's reasoning was based squarely on the fact that T was 'innocent', not a wrongdoer, who had not been found to have exerted *actual* undue influence, so it was not appropriate for him to bear the entire burden of the house's fall in value. This reasoning cannot survive the *Etridge* clarification that actual and presumed undue influence are not two distinct vitiating factors, but that the presumption is merely an evidential device permitting a finding of undue influence.

11.42   Finally, remember that at para **9.51** we considered the problem of *partial rescission*, where a contract can in certain circumstances be set aside as to part only where there is clear evidence of the claimant's unvitiated intent. Commonly this will occur where the defendant misrepresented the terms of the transaction, so that it is possible to be certain that the claimant was at the very least willing to contract on those terms. In contrast, it is conceptually impossible to conceive of a case of undue influence operating only on part of the claimant's will and so the notion of partial rescission should have no role to play in undue influence cases.

Undue influence in three-party cases

11.43   Thus far we have concentrated on the simple two-party case in which A unduly influences B into contracting with (or making a gift to) A, but many cases actually involve three parties. The most common fact pattern is where A unduly influences B into contracting with C, although occasionally, a three-party case reaches the courts which does not strictly involve setting aside a transaction as against the third party. A good example is the first instance case of *Hackett v Crown Prosecution Service* (2011). Here an elderly, deaf and dumb, illiterate woman who reposed trust and confidence in her son, transferred her house to him for no consideration and without any independent advice. Subsequently the Crown Prosecution Service sought to enforce a confiscation order against the son's property, including the house. The mother alleged that the son had procured the transfer to her by undue influence, an allegation which the son (unsurprisingly) did not dispute. The Crown Prosecution Service, on the other hand, did dispute the existence of undue influence, but were unsuccessful.

11.44   Much more commonly, however, three-party cases involve an attempt to set aside a transaction between B and C on the grounds of A's undue influence. Generally they involve (to adopt the common, stereotypical parties) a husband (A) unduly influencing his wife (B) to enter into a surety contract (a guarantee or mortgage) with a creditor (C) (usually a bank) to guarantee the debts of the husband's business: can the surety wife set aside the contract with the creditor bank? The seminal House of Lords decision in *Barclays Bank v O'Brien* (1994) established that this depends on whether the creditor has *notice* (actual or constructive) of the husband's undue influence. (It should be noted that many of the relevant cases involve allegations of misrepresentation as well as undue influence and indeed in *O'Brien* itself the wife's plea of undue influence failed, but her plea of misrepresentation succeeded.)

11.45   A useful threefold approach for tackling three-party cases of this kind is as follows:

> *'Stage 1': Is undue influence (or some other vitiating factor such as misrepresentation) established as between A and B? This first question is approached in exactly the same*

way as in the two-party cases already discussed, without any consideration of the role of the third party C. If, on the application of the normal rules, undue influence is estab-lished/presumed to have been established between A and B, then: 'Stage 2': Does the third party C have notice, actual or constructive, of the undue influence? If yes, then: 'Stage 3': The third party C will be 'bound' by the undue influence unless it has taken reasonable steps to avoid it.

11.46 We have already considered how to resolve the first stage. So far as the second and third stages are concerned, the House of Lords in *Etridge* has done a lot to clarify when a third party creditor will have notice of undue influence and, if so, what 'reasonable steps' it must take to avoid having the transaction set aside:

'Stage 2': notice

11.47 It will be rare for a creditor to have *actual* notice of undue influence, so the question of *con-structive notice* is much more significant in practice. In *O'Brien* Lord Browne-Wilkinson said that the creditor:

> ... will take subject to the wife's equity to set aside the transaction if the circumstances are such as to put the creditor on inquiry as to the circumstances in which she agreed to stand surety.

He went on to explain that in a surety case:

> ... in my judgement, a creditor is put on inquiry when a wife offers to stand surety for her husband's debts by the combination of two factors: (a) the transaction is not on its face to the financial advantage of the wife; and (b) there is a substantial risk in transactions of that kind that, in procuring the wife to act as surety, the husband has committed a legal or equitable wrong that entitles the wife to set aside the transaction.

Lord Nicholls in *Etridge* clarified that these are not two rigid conditions which must be proved to establish constructive notice, but are instead a 'broad explanation of the reasons why a creditor is put on inquiry when a wife stands surety for her husband's debts'.

11.48 Bear in mind that the concept of *notice* is being used in a different sense from its more familiar role of determining priority between successive proprietary rights, such as whether a purchaser takes subject to or free from existing interests or restrictions on the seller's title (although occasionally undue influence cases involve third party purchasers and the more familiar use of notice in that context, such as *Goodchild v Bradbury* (2007)). In an *O'Brien* case, there is no right existing prior to the transaction with the creditor C, despite attempts in some cases (notably the decision of Roch LJ in *Banco Exterior Internacional SA v Thomas* (1997)) to force the facts into this pattern by imagining a prior 'transaction' between A and B. Likewise, there is traditionally no way of avoiding notice of a prior right by taking steps to cure the taint of the prior transaction, whereas under *O'Brien*, a creditor fixed with prima facie notice (Stage 2) can nonetheless avoid being 'tainted' by taking certain reasonable steps (Stage 3). This is not a problem. As Lord Scott explained in *Etridge*, *O'Brien* involves 'contractual questions, not questions relating to competing property interests'. The terminology of notice is simply being used in an analogous context.

11.49 The constructive notice test in Stage 2 *resembles* the test for raising the presumption of undue influence at Stage 1, *but* the two issues must be kept distinct. In Stage 2, the issue is constructive notice so the focus is on how the transaction *appeared* to the creditor, hence the reference to whether what is on the *face* of the transaction is to the financial advantage of the surety wife. For example, in *CIBC Mortgages v Pitt* (1994) Ingrid Pitt (once a famous horror-film actress) established that she had been subject to the actual undue influence of her husband when mortgaging her home to fund his grossly speculative share transactions (Stage 1). However, the mortgagee did not have constructive notice of this undue influence (Stage 2), because Mr Pitt had falsely stated on his loan application form that he wished to borrow the money, not for share speculation but to purchase a holiday home for himself and his wife, so the transaction appeared 'on its face' perfectly unobjectionable.

11.50 Although both Lord Browne-Wilkinson's formulation in *O'Brien* and the clarification of it in *Etridge* refer to the parties as 'husband' and 'wife', it should not be thought that the principle is confined to married couples. It also applies to unmarried couples, heterosexual and homosexual, where the creditor is aware of the relationship (and has been applied in other circumstances, such as to the employer/employee relationship in *Credit Lyonnais Bank Nederland NV v Burch* (1996), where a relationship giving rise to undue influence could be inferred from the very nature of the transaction itself). Indeed, in *Etridge* Lord Nicholls suggested (*obiter*) that *O'Brien* should be given much more general application:

> ... the reality of life is that relationships in which undue influence can be exercised are infinitely various ... These considerations point forcibly to the conclusion that there is no rational cut-off point, with certain types of relationship being susceptible to the O'Brien principle and not others. Further if a bank is not to be required to evaluate the extent to which its customer has influence over a proposed guarantor, the only practical way forward is to regard banks as 'put on inquiry' in every case where the relationship between the surety and the debtor is non-commercial.

11.51 This means that, as the judge in *HSBC Bank plc v Brown* (2015) observed, the third stage is now readily activated: '[A]lthough not a hair trigger, there is little resistance built into the firing mechanism'. It might at first sight appear that this will dramatically and unacceptably increase the number of transactions liable to be set aside as against creditor banks on the basis of undue influence, but this fear is in fact unfounded. Remember that the court only reaches the 'Stage 2' issue of notice to the creditor *if* undue influence is established as between creditor and debtor at 'Stage 1'. *Etridge*, very sensibly, makes it *more* difficult for a surety to rely on a presumption in order to establish undue influence (see, for example, para **11.23**) so that fewer transactions will get past Stage 1 and actually be set aside, but balances this by *increasing* the sorts of cases in which banks must guard against the risk of undue influence via the Stage 3 'reasonable steps' regime (now considerably improved—see para **11.56**). The point is that it is impossible for a bank to tell whether a surety transaction is objectionable or not simply by looking at it, so to be on the safe side it must trigger the reasonable steps regime, which (as will be seen) now goes a long way towards reducing the possibility that undue influence is present. But unless undue influence is established as between surety 'wife' and debtor 'husband', the transaction will be unimpeachable as against the creditor bank.

'Stage 3': reasonable steps

11.52 In *O'Brien*, Lord Browne-Wilkinson explained that the creditor bank must take certain 'reasonable steps' to avoid being fixed with constructive notice:

> ... in my judgment the creditor, in order to avoid being fixed with constructive notice, can reasonably be expected to take steps to bring home to the wife the risk she is running by standing as surety and to advise her to take independent advice.

In particular, he suggested that, thereafter, banks should hold a private meeting with the surety wife:

> ... a creditor will have satisfied these requirements if it insists that the wife attend a private meeting (in the absence of the husband) with a representative of the creditor at which she is told of the extent of her liability as surety, warned of the risk she is running and urged to take independent advice.

(Lord Browne-Wilkinson went on to suggest that more may be required if the creditor *knows* of facts which make the presence of wrongdoing not just possible but probable.)

11.53 However, after *O'Brien*, it soon became obvious that banks were not keen to adopt this 'private meeting' suggestion. Many were not traditional high-street banks with premises in which such meetings could be held, while others feared that they would come under direct obligations to the wife, or even be presumed to have unduly influenced her themselves, if they had any direct contact with her. Instead, banks took a different route and *required* the wife to obtain independent legal advice from a solicitor, insisting on a certificate to this effect from the relevant solicitor, as a condition of lending.

11.54 This in turn gave rise to a host of litigation, concerning the circumstances in which, and extent to which, banks could rely on such certification to avoid being saddled with constructive notice. Two issues tended to dominate the case law: the adequacy and independence of the advice. First, the advice given to the surety wife was often wholly inadequate or, indeed, non-existent. The courts tended to say, relying on *Bank of Baroda v Shah* (1988), that as long as the solicitor certified that he had advised the wife in the form required by the bank, the bank was free to rely on that certification and assume that the wife had received proper advice (if not, her remedy was to be in negligence against the solicitor, not to set aside the transaction as against the bank). Moreover, banks were not required to provide any basic financial information about the transaction to sureties (although the general law relating to sureties required that 'exceptional features' of a transaction must be disclosed). Second, the courts were content for the wife to be advised by a solicitor who was acting for *all* the other parties in the transaction. This was in sharp contrast both with the stringent rules on independent advice to rebut the presumption of undue influence at 'Stage 1', and with judicial reluctance in other contexts to allow even different departments of the same firm of solicitors to act for parties with conflicting interests.

11.55 In general, the pre-*Etridge* law could be summarised by saying that, with limited exceptions, reliance on the *appearance* that a solicitor had advised the wife counted as 'reasonable steps' and operated to prevent saddling the bank with constructive notice. This position was most unsatisfactory and attracted criticism, in particular, from two senior Chancery judges, Lords Hobhouse and Millett (see Hobhouse LJ's dissent in *Banco Exterior Internacional SA v Mann* (1995) and in *Royal Bank of Scotland v Etridge (No 1)* (1997), and Millett (1998)). Lord Hobhouse summarised his views in *Etridge*:

> The crux of this situation is that the bank requests the solicitor to give a certificate which the bank then treats as conclusive evidence that it has no notice of any undue influence which has occurred. But the wife may have no knowledge that this certificate is to be given and will not have authorised the solicitor to give it and, what is more, the solicitor will deny that he is under any obligation to the wife (or the bank) to satisfy himself that the wife is entering into the obligations freely and in knowledge of the true facts. The law has, in order to accommodate the commercial lenders, adopted a fiction which nullifies the equitable principle and deprives vulnerable members of the public of the protection which equity gives them.

11.56 Happily, the House of Lords in *Etridge* addressed most of these concerns and since then, the reasonable steps regime should be much more meaningful (for an unusual but dramatic example of a bank's failure to comply with the reasonable steps regime and thus rendering a legal charge unenforceable, see *HSBC Bank plc v Brown* (2015)). There is now a 'core minimum content of legal advice' which must actually be given by the solicitor to the surety wife. Input is now required from the bank as well, to ensure that the solicitor advising the surety wife can give informed advice, in the knowledge of the nature and details of the transaction. The only respect in which the House of Lords did not improve the reasonable steps regime was with regard to the independence of the wife's solicitor. Their Lordships decided that it would be impractical to introduce a rule that the same solicitor may not act for surety and other parties (though with the other new safeguards, this should be less significant). They concluded that the advantages of having a solicitor acting solely for the wife would not justify the additional expense this would involve, particularly since in the vast majority of cases there will be nothing suspicious about the transaction and the couple would be acting harmoniously, with no need or desire to pay the bill of another solicitor.

OVERVIEW

1   Undue influence is difficult to define, but involves a subtler form of exploitation than duress, usually in the context of a relationship of trust and confidence or dependence and vulnerability. Like duress, undue influence is a form of wrongdoing that vitiates the victim's consent to the transaction, though (unlike duress) the victim is generally unconscious of such vitiation.

2   Traditionally, undue influence cases were divided into cases of actual undue influence and presumed undue influence. The courts no longer favour such language, because it tends to mask the fact that there is really only one vitiating factor, undue influence. The presumptions are merely evidential devices to assist in a finding of whether or not there was undue influence.

3   Evidence of undue influence can, it seems, still be presumed from a combination of a relationship between the parties and a suspicious transaction that calls for an explanation, though the presumption will be rebutted if it is shown that the victim was nonetheless free of any influence and exercising an independent will. The precise status of these evidential presumptions is not entirely clear at present: if they are downgraded too far, it will become difficult for lawyers to give advice to clients as to their prospects of mounting a successful plea of undue influence.

4   A contract made as a result of undue influence can be rescinded. Unlike misrepresentation, there is no tortious or statutory jurisdiction to award damages for undue influence, so if rescission is barred the victim may be left without a remedy altogether (although the courts may have the jurisdiction to award equitable compensation or the financial equivalent of rescission). Rescission may be awarded subject to terms.

5   Undue influence is commonly pleaded in a three-party situation, where, for example, a wife gives a guarantee to a bank to secure the business debts of her husband's company (though the rules are not restricted to cases involving married couples). In such a case, the guarantee contract with the bank may be rescinded if the bank had notice of the undue influence. The best approach is to ask, first, whether there was undue influence between debtor and surety; if so, ask, second, whether the creditor had notice of the undue influence; if so, ask, third, whether the creditor took reasonable steps to remove the risk of undue influence. The courts have clarified what will be required in future to count as 'reasonable steps'.

FURTHER READING

Bigwood 'Undue Influence: Impaired Consent or Wicked Exploitation' (1996) OJLS 503

Birks and Chin 'On the Nature of Undue Influence' Chapter 3 in *Good Faith and Fault in Contract Law* (1995)

O'Sullivan 'Undue Influence and Misrepresentation after *O'Brien*: Making Security Secure' Chapter 3 in *Restitution and Banking Law* (1998)

Phang and Tjio 'The Uncertain Boundaries of Undue Influence' [2002] LMCLQ 231

SELF-TEST QUESTIONS

1   Why do we have evidential presumptions of undue influence, but not of duress or mis-representation?

2   Should damages be available for undue influence?

3   Why should a bank ever be permitted to enforce a guarantee given as a result of undue influence?

4   Does the law strike the right balance between protecting the vulnerable and unduly re-stricting their freedom to be generous?

5   Jasper, a millionaire drug addict, has been attending intensive one-to-one drugs coun-selling with Kringe for the past nine months and has finally managed to kick his habit. Jasper believes that Kringe has transformed his life and so, overwhelmed by gratitude, tells Kringe that he wishes to renounce his fortune and give it all to Kringe. Kringe suggests in response that Jasper should keep some of his fortune for himself, but that he might like to invest £1 million in a private drug rehabilitation clinic that Kringe is setting up and might also consider guaranteeing Kringe's borrowing for the venture. Jasper readily agrees. Kringe also suggests that Jasper should take legal advice, but Jasper refuses, saying that this would spoil the pure feeling of goodness the gesture has given him, describing it as a 'bigger high than any drugs'. Jasper pays the money to Kringe and enters into a guarantee with Loot Bank plc of Kringe's indebtedness. Two years later, Kringe has run off with one of his clients from the private clinic, and is no longer keeping up repayments on the loan to Loot Bank. Jasper, who now bitterly regrets his involvement with Kringe, seeks your advice as to whether he has any claim against Kringe and whether Loot Bank can enforce the guarantee against him.

 For hints on how to answer question 5, please see the online resources at **www.oup.com/uk/sullivan8e/.**

12

Unconscionable bargains

SUMMARY

This chapter deals with unconscionable bargains and the circumstances in which unconscionability will operate as a vitiating factor, both in two- and three-party cases.

12.1 As we saw in Chapter 1, the law of contract is traditionally concerned only with matters of procedural unfairness, such as misrepresentation, undue influence, and duress, and (outside statute) generally has no independent jurisdiction to ensure the substantive fairness of a contract (for the one common law exception see paras **17.22-17.38**). But it is impossible to keep the two notions entirely separate: for example, we have seen that the 'suspicious' terms of a contract help to provide evidence that undue influence has been asserted. There is certainly a ragbag assortment of cases in which the courts appear to allow a claimant to avoid the contract on the basis that its *terms* are unconscionable, but in fact the concern is still with procedural unfairness, namely whether the other party *exploited* the claimant's weakness in obtaining the contract.

12.2 We need to be a little careful about the label 'unconscionability', which is used in a number of different ways in the law of contract. Sometimes it is merely one of the elements of a separate legal principle (like the 'inequitable' requirement for estoppel). On other occasions, the courts use unconscionability as an overarching principle, a more general explanation of *why* relief is given in cases of undue influence and duress (this usage is gaining in popularity in Australia). English courts generally have a more specific, but limited, notion in mind when talking about relief for 'unconscionability' and 'unconscionable bargains'.

Historical background

12.3 The court's jurisdiction to give relief in cases of 'unconscionable bargains' has a distinguished historical pedigree, from two distinct lines of equitable cases. First, the Courts of Equity were willing to protect 'expectant heirs' who sold away their future rights to receive an inheritance in exchange for a derisory sum, as in *Earl of Aylesford v Morris*

(1873), and *Fry v Lane* (1888), where Kay J reviewed the expectant heir cases, concluding that they represented a general principle:

> *that where a purchase is made from a poor and ignorant man at a considerable under-value, the vendor having no independent advice, the Court of Equity will set aside the transaction.*

12.4 Similar concerns are evident in another well-established line of equitable cases, allowing relief against oppressive mortgage transactions, such as *Knightsbridge Estates Trust v Byrne* (1940) and *Cityland & Property (Holdings) Ltd v Dabrah* (1968). As the court explained in *Multiservice Bookbinding Ltd v Marden* (1979), intervention is not justified because the terms are unreasonable, but only where the conduct of the mortgagee in imposing such terms was 'morally reprehensible'.

12.5 The courts today have taken these historical strands and, while retaining their defining features, have recognised a more general jurisdiction to give relief against unconscionable bargains. Blair J in *Strydom v Vendside Ltd* (2009) has summarised the jurisdiction as follows:

> *... before the court will consider setting a contract aside as an unconscionable bargain, one party has to have been disadvantaged in some relevant way as regards the other party, that other party must have exploited that disadvantage in some morally culpable manner, and the resulting transaction must be overreaching and oppressive. No single one of these factors is sufficient—all three elements must be proved, otherwise the enforceability of contracts is undermined.*

Requirements for relief from unconscionable bargains

Weakness/disability of party seeking relief

12.6 What lay behind the equitable jurisdictions already discussed was the significantly weak position of the party seeking relief. For some time, the courts retained the *Fry v Lane* language that the claimant had to be 'poor and ignorant', straining facts to fit that label, as Megarry J did in *Cresswell v Potter* (1978). The modern test is now more general, requiring a 'significant bargaining weakness' on the part of the claimant in the particular transaction. The High Court of Australia in *Commercial Bank of Australia v Amadio* (1983) expressed it as a jurisdiction to set transactions aside 'whenever one party by reason of some condition or circumstance is placed at a special disadvantage *vis-à-vis* another and unfair or unconscientious advantage is then taken of the opportunity thereby created'. Good examples include *Ayres v Hazelgrove* (1982), where an 82-year-old woman sold her valuable paintings to a door-to-door dealer for a derisory sum, and the earlier Australian decision in *Blomley v Ryan* (1956). Here relief was granted to the defendant, a

78-year-old alcoholic (described as 'sodden with rum'), who had sold his property at an undervalue to purchasers who knew about and exploited his intoxication by bringing a bottle of rum with them to the negotiations.

12.7 That is not to say that mere inequality of bargaining strength will suffice for this element of the test. To qualify, it seems the party must be under some significant *personal* disadvantage, rather than simply being in an economically inferior position as against the other party. In other words, it should be possible to identify a party who has sufficient 'weakness' within this element by looking just at them, without knowing anything about the bargaining position of the other party.

Unconscionable behaviour of the stronger party in exploiting the other's weakness

12.8 This second requirement is the gist of the jurisdiction to give relief for unconscionable bargains. Where the stronger party has not behaved unconscionably in seeking to *exploit* the other party's weakness, there can be no question of relief, however one-sided or unreasonable the bargain may be. In a sense, the label 'unconscionable bargains' is a little too condensed—it would be better (if somewhat clumsy) to refer to 'unconscionably-obtained bargains'.

12.9 This can be illustrated by contrasting two Privy Council cases. In *Hart v O'Connor* (1985) the vendor, an elderly farmer, held farm land on trust for the benefit of himself and his siblings, and had for many years farmed the land in partnership with two of his brothers. When they were too old to continue farming successfully, the vendor (without consulting his brothers) sold the land to the defendant (on terms that the vendor and his brothers had the right to continue residing in their houses on the land during their lifetimes). One of the brothers sought to set the transaction aside on the basis that it was an unconscionable bargain. He *conceded* that the defendant had acted with complete innocence throughout, arguing that relief should be available for objectively unfair transactions without the need for proof of unconscionable conduct by the stronger party. The Privy Council disagreed and refused to set the transaction aside. As Lord Brightman explained:

> There was no equitable fraud, no victimisation, no taking advantage, no overreaching or other description of unconscionable doings which might have justified the intervention of equity. ...

12.10 This can be contrasted with *Boustany v Pigott* (1993). Miss P was an elderly lady who leased one of her properties for five years in 1976 to Mrs B and her husband. Miss P was becoming 'quite slow' because of senile dementia and so in 1977 her cousin took over responsibility for the management of her properties. In 1980, while the cousin was away on business, Mrs B invited Miss P to tea to meet a bishop and lavished attention and flattery on her. Mrs B then took Miss P to the office of Mrs B's solicitor, where she produced a new draft ten-year lease of the property to replace the existing lease (which still had a year to run). The terms of the new lease were extremely favourable to Mrs B and the solicitor 'forcibly' pointed this out, while Mrs B said nothing. Miss P insisted on signing. Later Miss P's cousin sought to have the lease set aside. The Privy Council agreed, concluding that:

> Mrs B must have taken advantage of Miss P before, during and after the interview with [the solicitor] and with full knowledge before the 1980 lease was settled that her conduct was unconscionable.

12.11   The Privy Council explained in *Hart v O'Connor* that it is not necessary to show *active* exploitation of the weaker party's weakness—passively omitting to act properly can do too, since victimisation 'can consist either of the active extortion of a benefit or the passive acceptance of a benefit in unconscionable circumstances'. But nonetheless relief will not be given unless the stronger party knew of the other's weakness and, judged subjectively, acted wrongfully. Some Commonwealth authorities have suggested that a purely objective approach will suffice, but the English approach, exemplified in the *Boustany v Pigott* references to morally reprehensible behaviour, evidently does not allow relief where the stronger party had no conscious intention to exploit the other's weakness. As Bamforth (1995) points out, insistence on subjective exploitation reduces the risk of excessive intervention in transactions, although the difference in practice is unlikely to be great, because courts will be reluctant to believe that the stronger party did not know of and was not exploiting the other's weakness, if in the circumstances that weakness would have been apparent to a reasonable person.

Terms of the transaction

12.12   It is not surprising that the cases in which a party seeks relief for an unconscionable bargain tend to involve manifestly unfair, disadvantageous terms—parties tend not to regret or seek to undo good deals. Disadvantageous terms alone will not suffice to ground relief without the other two crucial requirements, but is it a *requirement* of relief that the terms should be disadvantageous, or are disadvantageous terms merely an *evidential device* by which the court can infer that one party has exploited the other's weakness?

12.13   Despite the dictum of Blair J in *Strydom v Vendside Ltd* (2009) (see para **12.6**) it seems the balance of authority suggests a merely evidentiary role. This was certainly the approach in *Nichols v Jessop*, where Cooke P explained that 'a gross disparity of consideration, if it ought to have been evident to the purchaser, may be one factor in deciding whether in all the circumstances of a particular case he has made an unconscionable bargain'. *Boustany v Pigott* (1993) hints at the opposite approach, with its references in the first two submissions to the 'objectionable' and 'unreasonable' terms of the bargain not being *sufficient* for relief, suggesting by implication that such terms are *necessary* for relief. But in *Boustany* the terms of the transaction were principally relevant as facts from which the court was able to infer unconscionable conduct by Mrs B (who declined to give evidence), while in other authorities the evidentiary approach is explicitly adopted. For example, in *Blomley v Ryan* (see para **12.14**) the court suggested that inadequacy of consideration is an 'important' element in the unconscionable bargain jurisdiction, but that it was not 'essential in all cases that the party at a disadvantage should suffer loss or detriment by the bargain'.

12.14 So where there is little concrete evidence of wrongful exploitation by the stronger party, the focus of the court will be on the terms of the transaction, requiring a high degree of unfairness to infer impropriety. But where there is freestanding evidence of wrong-doing, the court will give relief even where the terms are not particularly objectionable. In *Blomley v Ryan*, the intoxicated defendant contracted to sell his property for £25,000 when the market price was £33,000. Although the undervalue was not particularly stark, the court nonetheless set aside the contract because of the purchasers' deliberate exploitation, when negotiating, of the defendant's fondness for rum.

Absence of adequate independent advice?

12.15 It seems that, rather like the role which independent advice plays in rebutting the presumption of undue influence, the absence of adequate independent advice is not a *requirement* for relief from unconscionable bargains, but is merely *evidence* of the weakness of the claimant's position (as in *Cresswell v Potter*) and/or the extent to which the stronger party acted unconscionably (as in *Ayres v Hazelgrove*, where the defendant knew that the senile, elderly plaintiff was selling valuable family pictures without consulting anyone). This approach explains the result in *Boustany v Pigott*, where despite the presence of 'forcible advice' given to Miss P against entering the transaction, Mrs B knew that Miss P was unable to and did not take any notice of the advice, and thus could not rely on it to counter the evidence of Miss P's weakness or her own exploitative behaviour.

12.16 Conversely, if the weaker party *was* adequately and independently advised, it will be difficult to establish the other requirements for relief. Even where the advice was inadequate, if there was no reason for the other party to suspect this then they will be unlikely to be held to have acted unconscionably. In *Hart v O'Connor*, the defendant had always dealt with the vendor via their respective solicitors, and, as the Privy Council put it, 'had no means of knowing or cause to suspect that the vendor was not in receipt of the most full and careful advice'.

Unconscionable bargains and third parties

12.17 We have seen (in paras **11.47–11.51**) that the courts use *notice* principles to determine whether a transaction obtained by undue influence or misrepresentation can be set aside as against a third party. It is rare to find the unconscionable bargain jurisdiction pleaded in a three-party situation, but in theory the same notice principles should apply equally to it. After all, Lord Browne-Wilkinson did not confine his discussion in *Barclays Bank plc v O'Brien* (1994) to particular vitiating factors.

12.18 Unconscionability was discussed in addition to undue influence in *Credit Lyonnais Bank Nederland NV v Burch* (1996) (see para **11.17**). The Court of Appeal decided that the charge should be set aside as against the bank on the basis that it had constructive notice of undue influence, but two members of the court suggested that the unconscionable bargain jurisdiction would also ground relief on the facts. Unfortunately, these dicta are not consistent as to whether this was based on the *bank's* unconscionable conduct or, alternatively, because the bank had constructive notice of the *employer's* unconscionable conduct.

12.19 Nourse LJ favoured the former interpretation, indicating that the terms of the charge alone were sufficient to make it 'very well arguable that Burch could, *directly as against the Bank*, have had the legal charge set aside as an unconscionable bargain' and regarding the unlimited past, present and future indebtedness guaranteed under the terms of the mortgage as 'the truly astonishing feature of this case'. With respect, Nourse LJ's approach elevates the unreasonable terms of the transaction to the sole test for relief, and ignores the other requirements altogether. In particular, there was nothing in the bank's conduct close to the 'morally reprehensible' behaviour required under *Boustany v Pigott*. Commenting on Nourse LJ's dictum, Hooley and O'Sullivan (1997) observed:

> ... typical O'Brien instances of failure to take reasonable steps to avoid notice of another's undue influence and, a fortiori, cases in which the complaint is the use of an unnecessarily wide standard form ... should not be sufficient to count as unconscionable conduct. This would strip the requirement of all meaning, and come perilously close to justifying intervention on the grounds of harsh terms and unequal bargaining power alone. ...

12.20 Millett LJ's approach was different. He did not suggest that there was any direct unconscionability as between the bank and Burch, but noted that the bank obtained the guarantee as a result the unconscionable conduct of Burch's employer. In his view, the *O'Brien* third party notice regime applies as much to unconscionability as to undue influence:

> In either case it is necessary to show that the conscience of the party who seeks to uphold the transaction was affected by notice, actual or constructive, of the impropriety by which it was obtained by the intermediary and in either case the court may in a proper case infer the presence of the impropriety from the terms of the transaction itself.

Millett LJ's approach is entirely satisfactory in theory, although it is not altogether clear that it added anything on the facts of *Burch* itself. After all, the only 'weakness' afflicting Burch was the effect of her employer's undue influence.

12.21 The treatment of unconscionable bargains in *Burch* was considered in *Portman Building Society v Dusangh* (2000). D, an elderly immigrant with very poor English, mortgaged his home to a building society, to enable his son (who guaranteed the mortgage repayments) to purchase a business. The business failed, the son went bankrupt and the building society sought to repossess D's house. D defended on the normal *O'Brien* ground that the building society had notice of his son's undue influence and misrepresentation, but this failed and was not pursued. In the Court of Appeal, D argued that the charge should be set aside directly as against the building society on the basis of its own unconscionable conduct, but Simon Brown LJ rejected this argument:

> *... To my mind none of the essential touchstones of an unconscionable bargain are to be found in this case ... The building society did not act in a morally reprehensible manner. The transaction, although improvident, was not overreaching and oppressive. In short, the conscience of the court is not shocked.*

12.22   Ward LJ agreed with Simon Brown LJ that there was no direct unconscionability by the building society. But he also explored the alternative third party analysis, agreeing with Millett LJ in *Burch* that the *O'Brien* notice principles apply equally to cases of unconscionable conduct, though found that the plea failed on the facts. The son was not guilty of unconscionable behaviour, since 'no conscientious advantage has been taken of the father's illiteracy, his lack of business acumen or his paternal generosity'. The case was sad, but 'moral outrage' was absent.

Conceptual questions

12.23   For some commentators, there is an important conceptual connection between undue influence and unconscionable bargains, such that both vitiating factors (and the *O'Brien* third party regime) should be seen as examples of a broader jurisdiction to give relief for unconscionability (see, for example, Capper (1998) and Phang and Tjio (2002) discussing *Etridge* in this context). However, it is difficult to see the practical advantage of such a proposal: the differences between the two vitiating factors are as important as the similarities and it is important not to over-generalise for reasons of conceptual elegance. After all, it is possible to rip someone off without being in a relationship of trust and confidence with them. Defendants in unconscionability cases (as opposed to undue influence cases) are liable simply because they have knowingly exploited a very weak victim, not because they were disloyal and preferred their own interests to those of the victim. Lawyers need to be able to advise clients on the clearly defined and internally coherent categories of relief, a goal not served by calls for greater levels of conceptual generalisation.

12.24   In the 1970s Lord Denning MR did attempt to unify the principles of unconscionability, undue influence and indeed duress as examples of a more general jurisdiction to give relief on the basis of 'inequality of bargaining power' between the parties, culminating in his judgment in *Lloyds Bank v Bundy* (1974). This approach proved very problematic, until the House of Lords in *National Westminster Bank plc v Morgan* (1985) expressly disapproved of inequality of bargaining power as a general principle justifying relief.

12.25 Some commentators are more receptive than the courts to the suggestion that the courts should exercise control over substantively 'unfair' contracts obtained by a party in a dominant bargaining position. On balance, however, it is suggested that the courts are right to restrict their role to scrutinising contractual formation for procedural defects such as misrepresentation, undue influence, duress, and unconscionability. Inevitably, considerations of inequality of bargaining power and substantive unfairness will inform these procedural decisions, but they should not be grounds of relief in their own right, for two main reasons. First, any jurisdiction to undo or interfere with contracts must be clearly defined and delineated, or else transactional certainty would be reduced to an unacceptable extent.

12.26 Secondly, inequality of bargaining power is often not a simple concept. For example, a consumer may have very little choice about the terms offered by a particular package holiday company, but within the package holiday market there are lots of companies frantically competing for the consumer's business, while the consumer retains the ultimate choice of whether to contract at all. In the absence of abusive behaviour by the stronger party which is already caught by common law controls, inequality of bargaining power per se is only really objectionable in a monopoly situation, but it is far better to regulate monopolies by public law controls on competition than by private law contractual remedies.

OVERVIEW

1   In limited cases, a contract may be avoided because one party acted unconscionably by exploiting the weakness of the other party. This is not a loose, wishy-washy principle, but a specific vitiating factor with well-established requirements, derived from the traditional concern of the Courts of Equity to protect vulnerable contractors such as young expectant heirs and mortgagors.

2   The elements in the modern case law on unconscionable bargains are, first, that the party seeking relief must have some significant weakness or disability, such that they were in a materially disadvantageous bargaining position as against the other party. Secondly, the stronger party must have acted badly in knowingly exploiting this weakness. Conscious wrongdoing, active or passive, is required: mere constructive notice of the weakness will not ground relief. Thirdly, it is sometimes said that the terms of the transaction must be substantively unfair, though this may not be essential, rather just evidence from which wrongful exploitation is commonly inferred. Likewise the presence or absence of independent legal advice, is not conclusive, merely evidence of the victim's weakness and the stronger party's wrongful exploitation.

3   Where a three-party case is involved, the same tests of actual or constructive notice as are used for cases of undue influence and misrepresentation will determine whether the transaction can be avoided. English law has no wider jurisdiction to set aside bargains because of inequality of bargaining power or, outside statute, substantively unfair terms. This is for good reason, to prevent uncertainty and because strict control over specific procedural defects should be all that is needed to ensure 'fair' dealing.

FURTHER READING

Bamforth 'Unconscionability as a Vitiating Factor' [1995] LMCLQ 538

Capper 'The Unconscionable Bargain in the Common Law World' (2010) 126 LQR 403

Thal 'The Inequality of Bargaining Power: The Problem of Defining Contractual Unfairness' (1988) OJLS 17

SELF-TEST QUESTIONS

1   Is English law's insistence on morally reprehensible conduct as an essential element for relief for unconscionability too restrictive?

2   Should contracts be voidable on the basis of either (a) inequality of bargaining power, or (b) substantively unfair terms?

3   Sly called at the home of Ted, a wealthy elderly man in the early stages of senile dementia, asking whether Ted needed any jobs to be done around the house. Ted was impressed with Sly's polite, deferential manner and immediately told Sly he wanted him to decorate the exterior of the house. Sly suggested a grossly extravagant figure for the work, imagining that Ted would negotiate a much lower price, but to Sly's delight Ted agreed at once. When Sly had completed half of the decorating, Ted's daughter Ursula arrived to visit her father and was appalled to discover the exorbitant price Ted had agreed to pay. She told Sly to leave at once and that he would not be paid a penny. Discuss.

For hints on how to answer question 3, please see the online resources at **www.oup.com/uk/sullivan8e/**.

13

Common mistake and rectification

SUMMARY

This chapter deals with the law's response to contracts entered into when the parties shared a common mistake, for example as to the existence of some important quality of the subject matter, considering whether the case law is better explained by an 'implied terms' approach or by the separate common law rule currently favoured by the courts, and whether there is any role for an equitable regime. It also covers the related remedy of rectification, available where a written document does not properly reflect the parties' underlying agreement.

13.1 One of the most intractable problems in the English law of contract is what to do when a good contract is apparently made—with offer and acceptance coinciding perfectly—but where both parties share a mistaken assumption about their contract. For example, both may think that the subject matter of the contract is in existence when it is not, or that the subject matter has some quality or characteristic that it does not actually have. Of course, in such a case, when the true position comes to light, both parties may be happy to 'walk away' and the law need not get involved, but more often than not one party is happy with the true position but the other is not, and a dispute arises. The key issue is: which of the parties, if either of them, should bear the risk of their assumption's turning out to be false? How we distribute this risk forms the subject matter of this chapter.

13.2 We have seen already that English law is generally pretty strict about enforcing the apparent terms of a contract where one party is mistaken, even where the other party actually knows of that mistake (see para 3.28). Although this represents a completely different conceptual problem, it is worth bearing in mind here since it sets the tone for any regime as to common mistake: after all, where both parties shared the mistake and were entirely '*ad idem*' there is arguably even less of a pressing case for disrupting the apparent bargain.

13.3 Take the following example: imagine that we are negotiating for the sale of my bicycle. The cycle is being stored in my garage. You agree to buy it for £100. Unfortunately, unbeknown to both of us, my garage was struck by lightning half an hour before the contract was made and the bicycle has been completely destroyed. Who should bear the risk of the bicycle being destroyed? There are several possible conclusions. We might place the risk on the seller. I might be taken to have promised that the cycle existed at the time of the contract, so I will be liable in damages for breach of contract. Alternatively, we might place the risk on the purchaser. You might be taken to have promised that you would pay even if the cycle were destroyed before the contract was entered into (unlikely but possible), so you would have to pay the £100 even though the cycle has been destroyed. Finally, we might place the risk on neither party. We might conclude that the contract was not to come into effect unless the cycle was in existence at the time of the agreement (a 'condition precedent'), so I will not be liable in damages and you will not have to pay me the price.

13.4 Another analogous problem is when events change after the contract is formed, so that the parties' assumptions about their contract are *subsequently* falsified: in such a case the contract might be discharged by frustration (see Chapter 14). Such situations are extremely similar to the situations covered by common mistake: they both deal with situations where the parties' joint assumption turns out to be incorrect. Let us return to our bicycle example but change the facts slightly. In scenario 1, let us say that the cycle is destroyed one minute before the contract was concluded. In scenario 2, it is destroyed one minute after the contract was made. The first scenario raises common mistake issues, the second issues of frustration. Bearing in mind how narrow and in a sense arbitrary the line between the two scenarios is, it is unsurprising that we should want to deal with the two situations in a very similar way. Indeed, the Court of Appeal in *Great Peace Shipping Ltd v Tsavliris Salvage (International) Ltd* (2002) emphasised the similarities between common mistake and frustration. The law requires a significant, radical change in order to frustrate the contract and this also has an impact on the law's attitude when, in contrast, the parties are mistaken as to some feature *at the time of contracting*. It makes sense to be less generous about giving relief when the parties have made a mistake that could, by definition, have been avoided at the time of contracting, than when relieving parties of the effects of a subsequent, unexpected turn of events.

13.5 This area of law is complicated further by apparent differences in the approaches adopted historically at common law and in equity. Although it may seem cumbersome, it makes sense to consider the common law position first, then turn to whether equity might give relief in a wider category of cases, since if a contract is void at common law there is no scope or need to invoke any further remedies. However, as will be seen, it is by no means clear that there is any wider 'equitable regime', despite firm assurances in some cases to this effect.

The chapter will be divided into two main parts: we shall first deal with common mistake in general, and then go on to look at rectification, a remedy that is available for a particular type of mistake in the context of contracts that are recorded in written documents.

Common mistake at law

13.6 There are undoubtedly a number of cases which seem to decide that certain sorts of common mistake render contracts *void* at common law (in fact, a 'void contract' is a contradiction in terms, since the adjective 'void' means that there never was a good contract) and this is the stance adopted by most textbook writers on the law of contract.

13.7 However, there are actually two schools of thought about such cases. The first (which we can term the 'doctrine of mistake' approach) asserts that, as a matter of law, certain sorts of common mistake inevitably render a contract void: that where the contract has not distributed the risk of the parties' common assumptions being false, there is a legal 'doctrine' of common mistake that has the effect of rendering such a contract void in certain circumstances. This is the currently favoured judicial view (see, for example, the Court of Appeal in *Great Peace Shipping Ltd v Tsavliris Salvage (International) Ltd* (2002)). The second school of thought (the 'construction approach' or 'implied terms approach') argues that the effect of common mistake is ascertained by construing and interpreting the contract, implying terms in the normal way (see paras **7.72–7.97**) and that 'voidness' will *only* be the appropriate solution if, unusually, this is what the contract says should happen. This approach denies that there is any room for an independent doctrine of mistake. As we will see, both approaches have their difficulties, but overall the construction approach is preferable in principle and provides a better explanation of the result in the majority of the decided cases.

The currently favoured test

13.8 The most recent articulation of the conditions necessary for the application of common mistake at law is by the Court of Appeal in *Great Peace*. Drawing upon the test for frustration, the Court of Appeal proceeded as follows:

> [T]he following elements must be present if common mistake is to avoid a contract: (i) there must be a common assumption as to the existence of a state of affairs; (ii) there must be no warranty by either party that that state of affairs exists; (iii) the non-existence of the state of affairs must not be attributable to the fault of either party; (iv) the non-existence of the state of affairs must render performance of the contract impossible; (v) the state of affairs may be the existence, or a vital attribute, of the consideration to be provided or circumstances which must subsist if performance of the contractual adventure is to be possible.

13.9 In short, for common mistake at law to operate, both parties must make a false assumption (it does not matter whether this mistake is one of fact or law: *Brennan v Bolt Burdon* (2004)). We must then ask if the risk of the assumption being false has been placed on either party by the terms of the contract, be they express terms or implied terms, or has been positively placed by the contract on *neither* party (in which case the correctness of the assumption will be a condition precedent to the contract coming into effect). The reason, as the Court of Appeal pithily explained in *SAW (SW) 2010 Ltd v Wilson* (2017), is that 'a party cannot rely upon a common mistake as the escape route from a transaction if it has itself warranted the truth of the common assumption'. Only if there is no allocation of risk in the contract can common mistake at law operate. This should be stressed: we must first construe the contract to determine whether it distributes the risk, and it almost invariably will. A good example of this test in operation is *Standard Chartered Bank v Banque Marocaine du Commerce Exterieur* (2006). D agreed to meet a $4 million loan repayment by Parmalat to C in the event of Parmalat's default. Parmalat defaulted and C sought to enforce the agreement. D argued that the contract with C was void for common mistake, because they had both assumed that Parmalat would use the loaned funds for its normal business purposes, whereas D contended that the money had in fact been used for fraudulent purposes. It was held that the risk of the money being used in this way had been firmly allocated to D under the C–D agreement: the very purpose of the agreement was so that C could safely rely on being repaid the $4 million.

13.10 Assuming that the contract does *not* distribute the risk of the assumption being false, the next question is whether the falsity of the assumption has made it impossible to perform the contract. Finally, neither party must be at fault. The requirement that the mistake be so serious as to render performance of the contract 'impossible' is controversial and will be examined further in what follows.

Mistakes which render performance of the contract impossible

13.11 It is worth starting our discussion with the extreme cases of really serious common mistake, for which there is the most pressing justification for the doctrine of mistake approach. Surely, it might be argued, where (unbeknown to both parties) the subject matter of the contract does not exist, the contract must be void. Likewise, if a seller purports to sell something to a buyer which (unbeknown to both of them) already belongs to the buyer. In such cases, it is impossible to perform the contract, so condition (iv) of the *Great Peace* test is made out.

13.12 In *Couturier v Hastie* (1856), a quantity of corn was sold whilst on board ship. Unbeknown to the parties, by the time the contract was made the corn had deteriorated so much that it had been lawfully disposed of by the ship's master to someone else. The seller brought an action for the price and the question was whether the purchaser was bound to pay it. The seller tried to argue that the purchaser took the risks of deterioration in the cargo and was thus bound to pay, but both the Court of Exchequer Chamber and the House of Lords disagreed—the purchaser was not bound to pay the price.

13.13 *Couturier* can be interpreted as supporting a rule of law that renders a contract automatically void because of common mistake as to the existence of the subject matter (and this was the view adopted by the draughtsmen of the original Sale of Goods Act 1893—see para **13.16**), but it is clear that it should not be read in that way. As Atiyah (1957) points out, all the argument in the case turned on how the contract should be construed: whether the purchaser had 'bought the adventure' and thereby taken the risk of the non-existence of the corn, or whether the contract was, as the court held, 'for the sale of a cargo supposed to exist, and to be capable of transfer'. Lord Cranworth made this absolutely explicit, stating that 'the whole question turns upon the construction of the contract'. As in our bicycle example (see para **13.3**), there were three possible constructions: that the purchaser had promised to pay even if the corn did not exist, that the seller had promised that the corn existed, or that the agreement was not to come into effect unless the corn was in existence. The court rejected the first construction, and so held that the purchaser was not liable to pay. Accordingly, it was unnecessary to go on to decide between the second and third constructions and thereby express a view on whether there was any contract in existence at all. The lesson to be drawn from this is that while such serious mistakes will *often* result in the contract being void, this will not be the case if the contract is construed as placing the risk on one of the parties. It is a matter of construction.

13.14 Similarly, in many of the other cases of extreme common mistake, such as *Strickland v Turner* (1852), *Gompertz v Bartlett* (1853), and *Gurney v Womersley* (1854), it was unnecessary to decide whether the contract had come into existence or not (see Fleming (1952)). The construction approach was also used in *Galloway v Galloway* (1914).

13.15 The advantages of the construction approach are exemplified by the Australian decision in *McRae v Commonwealth Disposals Commission* (1951). The Commonwealth Disposals Commission ('CDC') purported to sell a wrecked oil tanker 'lying on Jourmand Reef' to McRae. At considerable expense, McRae launched a salvage expedition, but in fact there was no such tanker in existence. Strange though it seems, the case proceeded on the basis that both parties were mistaken as to the existence of the tanker. McRae claimed damages on a reliance basis (see para 16.29), whilst the CDC resisted on the basis that the contract must be void. The High Court of Australia regarded *Couturier* as turning entirely on the construction of the contract and held that, in this case, there was a valid contract, which included a promise by the CDC that there was a tanker in the position specified, and that the CDC was liable to pay damages for breach of that promise. In the alternative, if the court was wrong in its view that *Couturier* established no doctrine of mistake but merely turned on contractual construction, nonetheless such doctrine would have no application here since the mistake was induced by the CDC's own culpable conduct.

13.16 This is an entirely sensible decision, but unfortunately it would not be straightforward to apply it to our bicycle example. The reason is that the draughtsmen of the original Sale of Goods Act 1893 thought that *Couturier* had established an absolute rule of law that contracts for the sale of goods which no longer exist at the time of contracting must be void, and incorporated a provision to that effect in the legislation. This remains in force and is now s 6 of the Sale of Goods Act 1979, which provides:

> Where there is a contract for the sale of specific goods, and the goods without the know-
> ledge of the seller have perished at the time when the contract is made, the contract is void.

13.17 This provision would not apply on facts like those of *McRae*, since the tanker did not perish (never having existed at all), but it would seem to force the conclusion in our bicycle example that the contract was void and damages unavailable. Moreover, unlike other provisions in the Sale of Goods Act that create a mere presumption, rebuttable by evidence that the parties agreed something different, this section appears to be an irrebuttable rule (despite the attempts of Atiyah (1957) to argue to the contrary).

13.18 One solution for the disappointed purchaser in our bicycle example would be to sue for damages for misrepresentation, rather than sue on the purported contract in any way, but the measure of damages would be for reliance losses only, not the purchaser's lost expectation. If such a remedy had been available in Australia in 1951 it would have served McRae's purpose, since McRae was only claiming reliance losses (see para **16.31**), but it is no substitute for full expectation damages for breach of an express or implied promise that the goods are in existence. A second solution might be to argue that s 6 does not prevent there being a separate, valid collateral contract containing a promise that the goods exist. But this solution is cumbersome and artificial: it would be much better to acknowledge that s 6 should be repealed.

13.19 So it seems that, apart from where the solution is forced on us by statute, even in extreme cases of common mistake there is no need for an automatic doctrine which insists that a purported contract must be void. It is far better to examine the contractual terms and surrounding circumstances, so as to establish whether the parties dealt with the risk of a possible common mistake. The same should surely be even clearer where the parties' mistake is less extreme and merely as to the quality of the contractual subject matter.

Common mistakes as to quality

13.20 Some cases suggest that where the parties share a misapprehension about the quality or value of the contractual subject matter the contract might be rendered automatically void. However, there must be real doubt as to whether this is so.

13.21 For example, in *Harrison & Jones Ltd v Bunten & Lancaster Ltd* (1953), Bunten sold Harrison '200 bales of Calcutta kapok, "Sree" brand'. On delivery, Harrison found that the commodity supplied was unsuitable for its purposes, and sought to reject it. It transpired that both parties erroneously believed that 'Sree' brand kapok was pure kapok, when in fact 'Sree' brand was a mixture of kapok and bush cotton. The court held that Bunten had made no misrepresentation or warranty, and that goods answering the contractual description had been delivered. Therefore:

> the parties are bound by their contract, and there is no room for the doctrine that the contract can be treated as a nullity on the ground of mutual mistake, even though the mistake from the point of view of the purchaser may turn out to be of a fundamental character.

13.22 In other words, if the seller made no representations and gave no warranty as to the quality of the goods, this is generally very good evidence that the parties intended the contract to be valid if the buyer's assumptions about quality turn out to be false. And it makes no difference that the seller might have shared those mistaken assumptions. Of course, in other cases, the appropriate interpretation of what the parties agreed might be that the contract was entirely dependent on the mistaken assumption, so that if that assumption was false there should be no valid contract. For example, in *Griffith v*

Brymer (1903), Griffith agreed to rent a room in Brymer's house in order to watch the Coronation procession of King Edward VII. Unbeknown to either party, at the time of contracting the procession had already been cancelled because the King needed an operation for appendicitis. Griffith sued for the return of the price and succeeded. The judge held that the agreement was void because it 'was made on the supposition by both parties that nothing had happened which made performance impossible'.

The difficulty with treating all the cases on common mistake as turning purely on contractual interpretation is that there is a problematic decision of the House of Lords which contains suggestions that where the parties are under an 'essential mistake', the contract must automatically be void.

13.23 In the case in question, *Bell v Lever Brothers Ltd* (1932), Lever employed Bell as its chairman under a service agreement. Following a company reorganisation, Lever entered into a compensation agreement with Bell, whereby Bell's service agreement was terminated and Lever agreed to pay him £30,000 as compensation for his loss of office. It later transpired that Bell had committed serious breaches of his service agreement, which would have entitled Lever to terminate it without payment. Lever sought repayment of the compensation. Its allegations of fraud against Bell were rejected, so the case proceeded on the basis that Bell had forgotten about his breaches of contract and that therefore both sides entered into the compensation agreement mistaken as to the status of the original service agreement. By a majority of 3–2, the House of Lords held that this common mistake did not invalidate the compensation agreement.

13.24 The difficulty with this case is not the result, which seems perfectly correct—any other conclusion on common mistake would have undermined the other aspect of their Lordships' decision, namely that Bell owed no duty of disclosure to Lever to reveal his breaches. The difficulty lies in Lord Atkin's speech, which is most commonly cited and which seems to set out a test rendering a contract void if the parties' mistake is as to the 'essence' of the contract:

> Mistake as to quality ... will not affect assent unless it is the mistake of both parties, and is as to the existence of some quality which makes the thing without the quality essentially different from the thing with the quality.

Applying this test to the facts, Lord Atkin held that the mistake was not significant enough and the compensation agreement was valid.

13.25 Lord Atkin went on to give a number of examples in which the mistake as to quality would not be sufficiently 'essential'. He gave as one of the examples the sale of a horse which both parties believed to be sound: in the absence of a warranty or misrepresentation, the buyer could not complain if it later turned out that the horse was in bad condition. A sound horse is not 'essentially different' from an unsound horse. Similarly, if there is a contract for the sale of a painting that both parties believe to be by an old master but is in fact a copy, the buyer cannot complain unless the seller promises or represents that it is the work of the old master. Therefore, he intended his test only to be satisfied in rare circumstances.

13.26   This 'essential quality' test has caused confusion ever since. Since it is difficult to think of a more 'essential' mistake than one which, over 70 years ago, cost £30,000, and one where the subject matter was in fact worth nothing, some commentators argue that, on Lord Atkin's test, the opposite result should have been reached on the facts. Employing similar reasoning, others suggest that on the basis of Lord Atkin's comments, a mistake as to quality will *never* be enough to make a contract void (Smith (1994)).

13.27   Treitel (2015) has tried to rationalise Lord Atkin's approach by confining it to mistakes as to the essential quality by which the subject matter of the contract is *defined* or *identified*. Only in such cases, Treitel suggests, will a common mistake as to quality render a contract void. Some support for this interpretation is found in *Nicholson and Venn v Smith Marriott* (1947), where the contract was tentatively held void on the ground that 'a Georgian relic … is an "essentially different" thing from a Carolean relic'.

13.28   However, this case is not very satisfactory. The judge did not seem to appreciate that his comments about the contract being void were inconsistent with his primary finding that the sellers were liable for breach of contract. And secondly, the way the parties choose to identify their subject matter is somewhat random. Possibly the most puzzling aspect is that, if there really is a rule of law rendering contracts automatically void if the parties' mistake as to quality renders the subject matter 'essentially different', one would expect to find some subsequent cases in which this was the ratio. But such authorities are almost impossible to find.

13.29   One that comes close is *Associated Japanese Bank v Crédit du Nord SA* (1988). Bennett, a fraudster, entered into a sale and leaseback transaction, whereby he sold four machines to the plaintiff bank AJB and the bank leased the machines back to him. In fact, the machines did not exist and Bennett disappeared with the proceeds of sale. CDN had guaranteed Bennett's leaseback obligations, so AJB sued CDN to enforce the guarantee. Steyn J held that, as a matter of construction, the guarantee was subject to an 'express condition precedent that there was a lease in respect of four existing machines' or, at the very least, that such a condition should be implied. (For another example of the implication of a condition, rendering it unnecessary for the court to consider principles of common mistake, see *Graves v Graves* (2007).) Therefore the guarantee had not come into force and CDN could not be liable under it. But Steyn J went on to say that, if the contract had been silent on the issue, the *Bell* test of common mistake would have applied and the contract would have been void. 'For both parties the guarantee of obligations under a lease with non-existent machines was essentially different from a guarantee of a lease with four machines which both parties at the time of the contract believed to exist.'

13.30   This endorsement of the 'essentially different' test in *Bell* is not entirely compelling. First, it is *obiter* and in any event only a first instance decision. Secondly, it seems strange to make a bargain that the parties by definition did not make: surely if 'voidness' is not what the guarantee provided for, either expressly or impliedly, this conclusion should not readily be imposed by the law. But the main difficulty is the assumption by Steyn J that the *Bell* voidness test is separate from the question of contractual construction. Moreover the contractual construction reasoning is by far the more natural interpretation of what the parties must have agreed, judged objectively—think about the tests for implying terms (in Chapter 7) and it becomes obvious that the contract lacks business efficacy (i.e. is commercially nonsensical) without the implied term.

13.31 A recent first instance authority that does indeed appear to apply *Bell* as its ratio, holding the contract void for fundamental common mistake, is *British Red Cross v Werry* (2017). Here, a man died without apparently leaving a will, which meant that his unmarried partner inherited nothing and his estate passed to others. The partner brought a statutory claim for support from the estate, pursuant to the Inheritance (Provision for Family and Dependants) Act 1975; this claim was settled and the settlement embodied in a consent agreement. Some time later, a valid will made by the man was discovered! The judge applied *Bell* and held that the settlement agreement was therefore void for fundamental common mistake: the parties had contracted on the common assumption that there was no valid will, when the true position was essentially different. The result is no doubt correct, but it would have been much more natural to construe the settlement agreement as subject to an implied condition that a valid will did not exist—that is undeniably what the parties *intended*, judged objectively, at the time they contracted and meets all the relevant tests for the implication of terms in fact.

13.32 The most radical re-examination of the subject at appellate level is the decision of the Court of Appeal in *Great Peace Shipping Ltd v Tsavliris Salvage (International) Ltd* (2002). A ship, the *Cape Providence*, suffered serious structural damage in the Indian Ocean and T was commissioned to salvage her. T contacted an information service to enquire about ships near enough to the *Cape Providence* to assist with the salvage and was told that the *Great Peace* was only 35 miles away. T therefore chartered the *Great Peace* from its owners for five days, seeking no warranty or further information from the owners as to its position. In fact, unbeknown to both parties, the *Great Peace* was 410 miles away from the *Cape Providence*. On discovering this, T cancelled the charter and refused to pay anything, so the owners of the *Great Peace* sued for five days' hire. T defended by alleging that the charter contract was either void at common law or, alternatively, voidable in equity, for common mistake.

13.33 At first instance, Toulson J applied the construction approach. He held that while there was an implied condition precedent that the *Great Peace* was close enough to provide the specified service, this condition was satisfied, so the contract was valid. The Court of Appeal came to the same conclusion, but through the application of the doctrine of mistake approach. While both courts made important remarks regarding the existence of a doctrine of common mistake at equity, we are not concerned with this part of the decision for the time being. Importantly for present purposes, the Court of Appeal criticised Lord Atkin's test in *Bell* as being based on weak authority.

13.34 The Court of Appeal put forward a different test of their own, suggesting that (providing there is no express or implied term to the contrary), the common mistake would only be serious enough to render the contract void if:

> it transpires that one or both of the parties have agreed to do something which it is impossible to perform (emphasis added).

13.35 There are two problems with this test. It is unclear how the *Court of Appeal* can simply dismiss part of the ratio of the *House of Lords* decision in *Bell* and replace it with a new test. Moreover, the Court of Appeal does not seem to have taken its own new test literally. On the facts, it was held that the issue was whether 'the distance between the two vessels was so great as to confound that assumption and to render the contractual adventure impossible of performance'. The Court of Appeal found that it was not, because the *Great Peace* could have arrived in time to provide several days of escort services. However, it is hard to see why the contract would have been 'impossible' to perform even if the *Great Peace* was too far away to reach the *Cape Providence* in the allotted time. The contract was simply for the charter of the ship for a minimum of five days. The claimants made no promise as to the position of the *Great Peace* (see Toulson J's judgment) so they were under no obligation to ensure that it reached the *Cape Providence* in time. Therefore, it is unclear whether a mistake as to quality can ever render a contract void: the test of the Court of Appeal suggests not, but its application of the test might suggest otherwise.

13.36 The 'impossibility' test has since received a mixed welcome from the Court of Appeal in *Brennan v Bolt Burdon (a firm)* (2004). While Maurice Kay LJ applied it literally, Sedley LJ expressed doubts as to whether the test should be applied in all contexts, in particular to common mistakes of *law*. Indeed, in *Kyle Bay Ltd v Underwriters subscribing under Policy No 019057/08/01* (2007), the Court of Appeal held that as Steyn J's 'essentially and radically different test' in *Associated Japanese Bank* (see para **13.29**) was approved in *Great Peace*, the Court of Appeal in *Great Peace* must have considered that the impossibility test amounted to much the same thing as the *Associated Japanese Bank/Bell* test. *Kyle Bay* concerned an attempt by the insured to set aside a compromise of an insurance claim on the basis that both parties had made a mistake as to the nature of the insurance policy in question, resulting in the insured receiving 33 per cent less than he should have done. The Court refused the claim on the basis that the difference was not radical or essential, because it did not go to the validity of the policy, and a 33 per cent difference, while a significant and even substantial one, was not an essential or radical difference.

13.37 Finally, in *Apvodedo NV v Collins* (2008), Henderson J suggested that the correct test might be not whether the incorrect assumption rendered performance impossible, but whether it rendered performance *in accordance with the common assumption* impossible. This must be correct, otherwise even the extreme facts of *British Red Cross v Werry* (2017) (para **13.31**) would not meet the test, since it was perfectly *possible* for the settlement agreement to be enforced and the estate distributed in accordance with its terms.

The relevance of fault

13.38   It is relatively clear that a person will be barred from relying on common mistake where he is at 'fault' (from *Great Peace*, although note the doubts expressed as to the relevance of fault in *West Sussex Properties Ltd v Chichester DC* (2000)). Far less clear is what we mean by 'fault' here. At least three subtly different tests have been put forward.

13.39   In *McRae*, it was held that 'a party cannot rely on mutual mistake where the mistake consists of a belief which is, on the one hand, entertained by him without any reasonable ground, and, on the other hand, deliberately induced by him in the mind of the other party'. This test consists of two requirements: that the party seeking to rely on common mistake held a mistaken belief which it was unreasonable for him to hold, and that he deliberately caused the other party to hold the same belief. It is not necessary that the former *knows* that his belief is incorrect. Imagine that in our bicycle example (see para **13.3**), I saw flames pouring out of my garage just before I contracted, but I thought the bike was fine and told you that this was the case. The *McRae* test might well prevent me from invoking common mistake.

13.40   In *Associated Japanese Bank (International) Ltd v Crédit du Nord SA* (1989), Steyn J held that a party cannot rely on common mistake where 'the mistake consists of a belief which is entertained by him without any reasonable grounds for such belief'. This test is identical to the first limb of the *McRae* test, but suggests that the second limb of the *McRae* test is unnecessary. Third, and most recently, the Court of Appeal in *Great Peace*, drawing on the test laid down in the context of frustration in *Hobson v Pattenden* (1903), held that a party cannot rely on common mistake if 'the non-existence of the state of affairs' (not the mistake itself) is 'attributable to the fault of either party'.

13.41   It is suggested that the *McRae* test is to be preferred. The *Great Peace* test suffers from a number of problems. First, it states that the fault of *either* party prevents common mistake being relied upon. It is unclear why one party should be barred from relying on common mistake by the fault of the other party. Second, the Court of Appeal in *Great Peace* suggests that its test is 'exemplified' by the decision in *McRae* and discusses the latter in some depth. However, as we have seen, the *McRae* test differs significantly from the test set out in *Great Peace*. Therefore, it is unclear which of the two tests the Court of Appeal intended to lay down. Finally, taken at face value, the *Great Peace* test allows a claimant to rely on common mistake even if it is her negligent misrepresentation that has caused the other party to labour under the mistake in question (because the misrepresentation only caused the mistaken belief, not the non-existence of the state of affairs).

13.42   One final point can be made. As we have seen, the focus of the 'doctrine of mistake' approach is on the seriousness of the mistake. Using this approach, it is hard to see why fault should be relevant. On the other hand, if we take the implied term approach, it is easy to see why fault is relevant: it would affect whether a term should be implied, and the content of such a term.

A better approach?

13.43   Having pointed out a number of problems with recognising a doctrine of common mistake, let us examine the alternative: the 'construction approach', also known as the 'implied terms approach'. In *Bell v Lever Bros*, Lord Atkin went on to offer what he described as an 'alternative mode of expressing the result in a mutual mistake case'. This was a more orthodox approach based on the interpretation of the contract: does it expressly or impliedly provide that the contract is to be void unless a particular assumption proves true? Not surprisingly, such a term will generally only be implied where it is *necessary* to make sense of the contract (see para **7.77**) and this explains Lord Atkin's insistence on the mistake being as to something 'fundamental' or 'a foundation to its existence'. Likewise, all Lord Thankerton's reasoning in *Bell* is based on the appropriate interpretation of the contract.

13.44   It is not surprising to find the bulk of the reasoning in *Bell* based on the construction of the contract. After all, at the time the case was decided the courts rationalised the analogous principle of frustration of contracts in the same way, as being based on implied terms in the contract, and Lord Atkin was anxious to find a common approach to the two issues.

13.45   The main problem for the construction theory has been what to do when the parties simply have not even begun to think about how a particular risk should be allocated. Often, parties simply do not think about what would happen if the subject matter of the contract does not exist anymore, or if the painting that is thought to be a Van Gogh turns out to be a cheap imitation. The common accusation levelled against the construction approach is that it cannot deal with such situations. It is said that it would be fictitious to imply terms in such a situation because the parties simply do not have any intention one way or the other about it, so it is fictitious to impute an intention to them. In such circumstances, it is said, a doctrine of mistake is necessary. This was why the Court of Appeal rejected the construction approach in *Great Peace*.

13.46   However, this criticism proceeds on the assumption that terms can only properly be implied into contracts if it would reflect the parties' implied agreement. This assumption is incorrect for two reasons. First, terms can be implied in fact even if the parties have not specifically adverted their minds to the matter in question (see paras **7.77–7.88**; Lord Steyn in *Equitable Life v Hyman* (2002)). Second, even if a term in fact cannot be implied on the particular facts, we are quite happy to imply terms *in law* even though they do not reflect the parties' intentions (see paras **7.89–7.93**).

13.47   So in situations where the parties have simply not begun to think about how the risk in question should be distributed, we should first ask whether a term can be implied in fact. If it cannot, it is suggested that the way forward is to draw on the concept of terms implied *in law*. Such terms are implied into all contracts of a certain type because of the nature of the contract, unless this would be inconsistent with the intentions of the parties. Such terms do not reflect the intentions of the parties; this is the role of terms implied in fact. Instead, their role is to provide *default rules* for standard situations, to fill in gaps where the parties have not thought about something. The courts draw on many policy reasons to determine what these default rules should be. Now there are many standard situations where issues of 'common mistake' arise: where the goods have perished, where they never existed, where the seller doesn't have title, etc. In each of these situations, a term should be implied in law unless it would be inconsistent with the parties' intentions. Sometimes this implied term will place the risk on the seller, sometimes on the buyer and sometimes it will be an implied condition precedent, so the contract will be void.

13.48 Take, for example, a situation where the goods that form the subject matter of the contract do not exist. Both Smith (1994) and Atiyah (1957) suggest that generally, the seller promises that the goods do exist, so this should be the default rule. The risk is placed on the seller; if the goods do not exist, he is in breach of the contract. On the other hand, if the contract shows that it is the buyer who is taking a chance the goods exist, that is, the contract places the risk on her, the default rule will not be implied (it has been displaced by the intentions of the parties).

13.49 To take another example, in contracts for the sale of land, the familiar *caveat emptor* ('buyer beware') principle means that the buyer takes the risk of any adverse matters (like unknown easements or structural defects) which are not the subject either of a warranty or representation by the seller: the contract is invariably construed in that way even if it is actually silent on the point. So a purchaser will be highly unlikely to establish that a defect in a property, which was unknown to both parties, should render the contract void: that would be totally inconsistent with the way the general law allocates the risk of such mistakes in contracts for the sale of land.

13.50 Support for this 'implied terms in law' approach can be found in the judgment of Toulson J at first instance in *Great Peace*. He seems to suggest that all we need do is construe the contract and imply terms in fact or in law as required.

> At common law, the effect of a mistake must depend on the proper construction of the contract, which in almost every case will leave certain things unstated. Its proper interpretation will depend, therefore, on a combination of the particular words used and the general principles appertaining to contracts of the relevant kind, e.g. sale of goods. In *William Sindall plc v Cambridgeshire County Council* Hoffmann LJ emphasised that it is the unspoken as well as the spoken terms of a contract that affect where the risk lies *(emphasis added)*.

Similarly, Hoffmann LJ seems to take this approach in *William Sindall Plc v Cambridgeshire CC* (1994) (see also para **9.78**) when he discusses *Associated Japanese Bank*.

13.51 Indeed, it appears that even the Court of Appeal in *Great Peace* recognised that terms may be implied in law. In discussing the need to construe a contract before applying the doctrine of mistake, they noted that 'In *William Sindall Plc v Cambridgeshire CC* (1994)

Hoffmann LJ commented that such allocation of risk can come about by rules of general law applicable to contract, such as "*caveat emptor*" in the law of sale of goods.' These comments of the Court of Appeal are surprising in light of their rejection of the implied terms theory. If implied terms in law can be used to distribute the risk where the parties have not thought about the matter, what need is there for an independent doctrine of mistake to do the job?

13.52 Therefore, the construction approach can deal with situations where the parties have not distributed the risk themselves equally well as a doctrine of mistake. In light of this, does it matter which approach we take? It does for the following reasons:

- There is no *need* for a doctrine of mistake, the ambit of which is far from certain, when orthodox principles of construction and implication of terms can deal with the issue.

- If, as noted, implied terms at law can be used to distribute the risk in question where the parties simply have not thought about the matter, what room *can* there be for an independent doctrine of mistake with the same role?

- As we have seen from the discussion, the construction approach better explains many of the cases than does the application of a doctrine of mistake.

- The construction approach better accommodates the relevance of fault. Fault is clearly relevant to whether a term should be implied but it is not so clear why it has a place in a doctrine of mistake that is predominantly focused on the seriousness of the mistake.

- Use of a doctrine of mistake has led to an awkward categorisation of different types of mistake: mistakes as to the existence of the subject matter, mistakes as to the ownership of the property forming the subject matter, mistakes as to quality, mistakes as to substance, and so forth. As we have seen, this rigid categorisation has caused as many problems as it has solved. A more sensitive approach based on the construction of the contract and implication of terms is called for.

Rescission in equity for common mistake?

13.53 We have seen that, at common law, the courts generally approach common mistake by asking what the contract (backed up by the general law) provides. The contract might occasionally be subject to an express or implied provision (as in *Couturier v Hastie* and *Associated Japanese Bank*) that it only comes into force if the parties' mutual assumption proves to be correct, so that the contract is void where the parties are mistaken, but this is an unusual result. But is there a separate equitable jurisdiction to give relief for common mistake if the contract is valid at common law? Put another way, is it possible to rescind or avoid a contract for common mistake even if it is not void *ab initio* at common law? The distinction matters, because rescission can be granted on terms and because it will not be granted where third parties would be prejudiced. For a historical account of the development of the law, supporting an equitable doctrine of mistake, see MacMillan (2010).

13.54 In the leading case of *Solle v Butcher* (1949), B acquired a flat, did some structural alterations to it and then leased it, together with a garage, to S (a surveyor). The flat without the garage had previously been leased to a different tenant at an annual rent of £140. The parties discussed whether the new lease was affected by statutory rent restrictions requiring that the old rent be charged unless notice was served, and concluded that it was not, hence B let the flat to S at the market rate of £250 per annum without serving the appropriate notice. S later commenced proceedings, alleging that £140 was the maximum rent lawfully chargeable and seeking to recover the amount overpaid. The judge found that the flat should have been subject to the original controlled rent and that the lease had been entered into under a mutual mistake of fact. In the Court of Appeal, Denning LJ held that, although not void, the lease was voidable in equity because of the parties' fundamental mistake. Rescission would be granted on terms as to an appropriate new rent and the payment by the tenant of a reasonable sum for use and occupation of the property. Jenkins LJ dissented, holding that the parties had merely made a mistake of law, which was not a good ground for rescission.

13.55 Denning LJ took the view that there was no common law doctrine rendering contracts void for common mistake, but that the appropriate approach was to ask whether the contract should be rescinded in equity. Rescission is available not just for misrepresentation, but also 'if the parties were under a common misapprehension either as to facts or as to their relative and respective rights, provided that the misapprehension was fundamental and that the party seeking to set it aside was not himself at fault'. Denning LJ went on to suggest that had this equitable principle and not just the common law been considered in *Bell v Lever Bros*, 'the result might have been different'.

13.56 *Solle v Butcher* has been applied occasionally since, for example in *Grist v Bailey* (1967). B contracted to sell a property to G for £850, which both parties believed was occupied by a statutory tenant. In fact this was not the case, and the true value of the property with vacant possession was about £2,250. B therefore refused to complete the sale at £850, alleging common mistake. Goff J observed that, under the 'essentially different' test from *Bell v Lever Bros*, the contract was perfectly valid. However, he regarded himself as bound by *Solle v Butcher* and ordered rescission of the contract on the basis that the parties' mistake as to the value of the property was 'fundamental'.

13.57 *Grist v Bailey* illustrates a number of the problems which *Solle v Butcher* generates. First, there is its relation with *Bell*: it seems strange that, if there is a separate equitable jurisdiction allowing relief for common mistake, it was not mentioned by the House of Lords in *Bell*. Second, as discussed, Lord Atkin gave a number of examples in *Bell* of situations where a contract should not be unravelled on the ground of mistake: for example, where there is an agreement for the sale of a painting which is thought (but not warranted) to be by an old master, but turns out to be a copy. It is hard to see the distinction between the examples given by Lord Atkin and the situations in which relief was given in *Solle* and *Grist* (see the comments of Toulson J at first instance in *Great Peace*). Third, Goff J clearly thought that the test for a 'fundamental' mistake was easier to satisfy than the *Bell* test, but this leaves the meaning of 'fundamental' shrouded in confusion. If all it means is 'a mistake without which the transaction would not have proceeded' or 'a mistake which makes a significant difference in value', it would disrupt far too many transactions and undermine the strict common law approach entirely.

13.58 Moreover, the result in *Grist* seems wrong on principle—the vendor merely made a bad bargain, by failing to realise the true value of her property, so why should she be able to escape from it? *Solle v Butcher* is a different and more unusual factual situation, since the party who lost out by the mistake was the tenant S, and equally unusually, was the party with greater expertise who, arguably, made innocent misrepresentations as to the rent-controlled status of B's flat at the time the contract was made. Yet the result comes close to allowing S to plead his *own* misrepresentations to allow him to escape from the contract.

13.59 The Court of Appeal in the *Great Peace* case concluded that *Solle* should be disapproved on the grounds that it cannot be reconciled with the earlier decision in *Bell*. The facts of *Great Peace* have been set out earlier in the chapter (see para **13.32**). Having reviewed the case law at great length, the Court of Appeal held that *Solle* simply could not stand with *Bell*. Moreover, *Solle* was objectionable on policy grounds, because it seemed to give relief merely on the ground that a party had entered into an extremely bad bargain. Indeed, the cases in which it had been considered merely emphasised the confusion which it had caused.

13.60 On balance, it is suggested that the disapproval of *Solle* in *Great Peace* should be applauded. There are a number of reasons why there should not be a category of 'mistake in equity'. First, if we prefer the implied terms approach to a doctrine of mistake at common law (see paras **13.43–13.52**), there is no room for a separate concept of mistake at equity. Once we have worked out what all the terms of the contract are, by interpreting the express terms and implying terms in fact and law where appropriate, and given effect to these terms, this should be the end of the matter. Once the risk of the event occurring has been distributed by an express term, implied term in fact, or implied term in law, this risk allocation should not be upset by any doctrine of 'mistake in equity'. If the terms of the contract suggest that the contract remains valid despite the 'common mistake', the courts should not be able to unwind such a contract by the use of 'mistake in equity'.

13.61 Secondly, even for those who think that there should be a doctrine of mistake and that the doctrine of mistake at common law is too narrow, the answer is to widen its scope, rather than to invent a new category of mistake in equity (see both Toulson J and the Court of Appeal in *Great Peace*).

13.62 Thirdly, the broad potential scope of mistake in equity, and the lack of clarity over its boundaries, undermines the certainty of transactions. This is, of course, undesirable, particularly in the commercial sphere.

13.63   Fourthly, despite being intended to be easier to satisfy, the test used for mistake in equity is phrased in very similar terms to the test used at common law in relation to common mistake as to quality. This can only cause confusion.

13.64   Fifthly, *Solle* proceeded on the basis that the House of Lords in *Bell* had overlooked or failed to consider the possibility of mistake in equity. This is implausible: the Lords in *Bell* simply did not believe that relief was justified in situations not covered by mistake at common law. And the cases which Denning LJ relied on in *Solle* in support of his assertion that there was an equitable jurisdiction to undo mistakes provided little authority for the proposition (see Slade (1954)).

13.65   Sixthly, by broadening the situations in which relief was given, mistake in equity allowed contracts to be undone in situations where Lord Atkin had suggested in *Bell* that they should not be undone (see Toulson J in *Great Peace*). For example, as Smith (1994) points out, in economic terms, the mistake in *Bell*, for which relief was not given, seems more serious than the mistake in *Solle*, where relief was given. In economic terms, the difference in *Solle* was between £250 per annum and £140 per annum, compared with £30,000 and nothing in *Bell*.

13.66   Finally, mistake in equity allowed the contract to be set aside *on terms*: for example, in *Solle*, the tenant was given the option of having a new lease at the higher rent of £250 per annum. This is a more far-reaching remedy than holding the contract to be void, because it allows the court positively to write a new contract for the parties (Hilliard (2002)). Accordingly, we should show caution in making such a powerful remedy available to the courts, particularly where neither party is guilty of any wrongdoing.

13.67   Nonetheless some commentators have criticised *Great Peace*'s treatment of mistake in equity and some jurisdictions, like Canada, have chosen not to adopt it (*Miller Paving Ltd v B Gottardo Construction Ltd* (2007); see more generally Capper (2009)). It is submitted that on closer examination, none of these criticisms provides a good reason to retain the category of mistake in equity.

13.68   Midwinter (2003b) argues that as a matter of precedent, the Court of Appeal (or Toulson J at first instance) in *Great Peace* was bound by *Solle*. It is not open to the Court of Appeal, he argues, to declare that a Court of Appeal decision, in this case *Solle*, is bad law because of its inconsistency with an earlier House of Lords decision, in this case *Bell*. Even if this argument is correct (and it should be noted that the Court of Appeal in *Great Peace* considered this issue), it does not mean that we should recognise a category of mistake at equity: it just means that the appropriate tribunal to overrule *Solle* is the Supreme Court.

13.69   Hare (2003), while broadly welcoming *Great Peace*, argues that abolishing mistake in equity 'reduces the protection afforded to innocent third parties'. His argument is based on the idea that if a third party receives property that is the subject matter of a *void* contract, he receives no protection, whereas if he receives property that is the subject matter of a *voidable* contract, he is protected: for example, the contract may not be rescinded. However, this overlooks that, before *Great Peace* a party could say that the contract was void on the ground of common mistake at law in certain circumstances. *Great Peace* would only reduce the protection of third parties if it *broadened* the circumstances in which a contract would be void for common mistake at law. The case certainly does not do that. As we have seen, if anything it slightly reduces the ambit of common mistake at law.

13.70 Hare (2003) also points out that 'a court no longer has any of the remedial flexibility afforded by the equitable doctrine, but is limited to declaring the contract void and ordering the restitution of any benefits conferred' (see more recently Capper (2009)). The solution he puts forward is to bring in legislation to allow such flexibility. However, before *Great Peace*, the better view is that the court only had such remedial flexibility where the party seeking to get out of the contract was relying on common mistake in equity rather than common mistake at law. If he relied on the latter doctrine, the contract was either void or not. Therefore, the main situation in which the doctrine of common mistake in equity gave the court such remedial flexibility was in cases where the mistake was insufficiently serious to make the contract void for common mistake at law. If, as argued, we do not want to give relief *at all* for such less serious mistakes, we do not want to give the courts any remedial flexibility in such situations: we want such contracts to be perfectly valid. Therefore, the court in *Great Peace* was correct to abolish the category of common mistake in equity.

Broadening common mistake more radically?

13.71 In a thought-provoking article, Tettenborn has suggested that the law on common mistake needs to be altered more radically (Tettenborn (2011)). He views the purpose of contracts as being to allow people to allocate the risk of particular contingencies, that is, as insurance against uncertainties, both existing and in the future. Therefore, if it turns out the parties are mistaken about something they were *not* contracting in order to guard against, the law should give relief for such a mistake. This broad approach would be tempered in a number of ways, such as by limiting the doctrines to contracts that have not yet been performed. However the purpose of contracts is normally more than just to guard against particular contingencies. I pay to download a music file from the internet because I want to listen to the music; I buy a house because I want to make my home there. Therefore, I contract because I want the other party's performance, and there are a range of reasons why I might want it, of which the desire to guard against contingencies is only one. Therefore, the mere fact that I was not contracting to guard against a particular contingency is insufficient to justify undoing the contract for mistake: parties often have many other important reasons for contracting and the law should be extremely reluctant to upset such bargains.

Rectification

13.72 Rectification is the rewriting of a written document where one or both parties are mistaken as to its terms. In other words, rectification deals with mistakes in written documents. For the purposes of this book, we are only concerned with situations where this written document is a contract. Traditionally, rectification is available where the parties reached an oral agreement, but its terms were incorrectly recorded in the final written document. This is *rectification for common mistake*.

13.73 However, rectification may also be available where only one party is mistaken as to the terms of the written document and the other is seeking to take advantage of this fact. This is *rectification for unilateral mistake*.

13.74 Rectification is a potent remedy because it allows the courts to rewrite the contract. As we have seen in Chapter 1, it is generally for the parties to determine the contents of the contract, so why should the court be able to interfere in this way? The answer is straightforward in the case of common mistake: both parties intended the terms of the contract to be different to those set out in the written document, so rectification is necessary to give effect to the parties' intentions. However, this reasoning cannot be used to justify rectification for unilateral mistake, where the written document in its original form does accord with the intention of one party, and so rectification does not give effect to this party's intentions. Therefore, rectification for unilateral mistake is in fact very different from the superficially similar doctrine of rectification for common mistake, with a very different rationale, and so we shall deal with the two separately.

13.75 The other important contrast to draw is the difference of the impact on third parties of correcting mistakes by rectification as opposed to correcting them by construction (the latter method having been dealt with at paras **7.54–7.68**). As Lewison LJ pointed out in *Cherry Tree Investments Ltd v Landmain Ltd* (2012), rectification is far more sensitive to the third party's position. A third party who has acquired rights in the subject matter of the contract is not affected by rectification if he has given value and has no notice of the problem (because the court will not exercise its discretion to grant rectification in a way that prejudices him), whereas this is not necessarily the case if the matter is cured by construction because the court simply reads the contract as if it did not contain the error from the outset, and there is no discretion to protect the third party in this way. Therefore, this should make us reluctant to push the construction principles discussed at paras **7.54–7.68** too far in correcting apparent mistakes in contracts.

Rectification for common mistake

13.76 The various conditions which must be satisfied before rectification for common mistake is possible were helpfully summarised by Mustill J in *The Olympic Pride* (1980) (see also Peter Gibson LJ in *Swainland Builders Ltd v Freehold Properties Ltd* (2002)). They were considered by Lord Hoffmann in his last case as a Law Lord, *Chartbrook Ltd v Persimmon Homes Ltd* (2009), which we examine in more detail in para **13.85** (see also paras **7.48-7.49**). Dealing with each condition in turn:

13.77 Condition 1—mistake in recording agreed terms in document:

> *The remedy of rectification is available only for the putting right of a mistake in the terms of a document which purports to record a previous transaction. It is not an appropriate remedy where the mistake relates to the transaction itself rather than the document which purports to record it.*

In other words, the mistake must relate to the manner in which the oral agreement is recorded in writing, and not to any other matter. This can be illustrated by contrasting the following two cases.

13.78 In *Craddock Bros v Hunt* (1923), a vendor was selling two plots of land at auction. C successfully bid for one plot and H for the other. However, when the subsequent written contracts and conveyances were prepared, a yard forming part of the plot bought by C was erroneously excluded from C's documents and included in H's. The Court of Appeal held that both contracts (and the conveyances giving effect to them) could be rectified to correct the errors.

13.79 In contrast, in *Frederick E Rose (London) Ltd v William H Pim Jnr & Co Ltd* (1953), Rose, a firm of London merchants, were asked by an English firm based in Egypt to supply 'Moroccan horsebeans described here as feveroles'. Rose did not know what feveroles were and consulted Pim, who replied (after investigating the issue) that feveroles meant just horsebeans. On that basis, Pim entered into a written contract with Rose to supply 'horsebeans' and Rose contracted in similar terms with its Egyptian purchasers. Once the beans were delivered to Egypt and paid for, the Egyptian purchasers complained that the goods supplied were not feveroles but were in fact 'feves', a larger (and less valuable) sort of horsebean. The Egyptian purchasers claimed damages from Rose, who in turn sought to have its contract with Pim rectified to read, not 'horsebeans', but 'horsebeans described in Egypt as feveroles'. The Court of Appeal unanimously refused rectification. As Denning LJ explained:

> *There was no doubt an erroneous assumption underlying the contract—an assumption for which it might have been set aside on the grounds of misrepresentation or mistake— but that is very different from an erroneous expression of the contract, such as to give rise to rectification.*

13.80 Rose had no prospect of obtaining rescission of the contract with Pim, either for mistake or misrepresentation, as the beans had been accepted and paid for by the Egyptian buyers, hence Rose's claim for rectification. If the facts occurred today, Rose might be able to claim damages for misrepresentation under the Misrepresentation Act 1967.

13.81 The next two conditions will be considered together:

Condition 2—common mistake:

> [A] mistake common to both parties, being the belief that the document accurately records the transaction.

Condition 3—prior concluded agreement or common intention required:

> The prior transaction may consist either of a concluded agreement or of a continuing common intention. In the latter event, the intention must be objectively manifested ... [and] in terms which the court can ascertain. It is the words and acts of the parties demonstrating their common intention, not the inward thoughts of the parties, that matter.

13.82 Often in rectification cases there is a concluded oral contract between the parties, but it must be put into writing in order to be legally enforceable (for example, if it is a contract to dispose of an interest in land). But the remedy is also available where the parties' prior understanding did not strictly amount to a concluded contract, as long as there was a *common intention* as to what the ultimate terms of the contract were to be (*Joscelyne v Nissen* (1970)). While the requisite 'continuance of accord of intention may be the more difficult to establish if a complete antecedent contract could not be shown', this should not be ruled out as a matter of law. Otherwise 'if the all-important terms of an agreement were set out in correspondence with clarity, but expressly "subject to contract", and the contract by a slip of the copyist unnoticed by either party, departed from what had been agreed, there could be no rectification'. The common intention must continue up to the execution of the written instrument (see *KPMG LLP v Network Rail Infrastructure Ltd* (2007)), so where the parties' intention has changed significantly before execution of the written contract, rectification will be unavailable, although in *Milton Keynes Borough Council v Viridor (Community Recycling MK) Ltd* (2017) Coulson J said that 'minor tweaks and changes' to the deal between the prior agreement and the final instrument did not preclude rectification.

13.83 While these conditions appear straightforward, the question of what precisely one must show in order to demonstrate a 'common intention' for these purposes is a matter of some controversy. The controversy centres around whether the parties' common intention is judged subjectively or objectively. It was held in *Joscelyne* that there must be some outward expression of this accord, and the same approach was taken in *The Olympic Pride* (condition 3). The rationale given for this in *The Olympic Pride* and a number of the earlier cases, including *Rose v Pim* (para **13.79**), is that the common intention must be made out using ordinary principles of objective interpretation, so that one must demonstrate such intention from communications between the parties rather than relying on their *subjective* intentions.

13.84 In *Munt v Beasley* (2006) the Court of Appeal took a different view as to the relevance of an outward expression of accord, holding that it is merely a factor that helps to show a continuing common intention, not a strict legal requirement. *Munt* appears to suggest (this being the obvious basis for its view as to the relevance of an outward expression of accord) that it is sufficient to show that the parties had a shared *subjective* intention as to what the contract would and did provide, whether or not they communicated this to each other, and whether or not an objective bystander would glean this from the documents exchanged between them. Moreover some years earlier, a subjective version of common intention was explicitly endorsed by the majority of the Court of Appeal in *Britoil Plc v Hunt Overseas Oil Inc* (1994) (with Hoffmann LJ in dissent).

13.85 However, in *Chartbrook Ltd v Persimmon Homes Ltd* (2009), Lord Hoffmann favoured an approach based on *objective* intention. While his views were *obiter* (because the issue was resolved by interpreting the contract—see para **7.48**) and he did not refer to *Munt* (which was cited to him) he subjected the case law to a detailed analysis and was supported by all four other Law Lords. His reasoning was that where the parties' continuing common intention comes from a prior concluded contract (see para **13.81**), one necessarily has to interpret the prior contract in an objective manner in the ordinary way, so the position should be no different where the parties' continuing common intention falls short of a prior concluded contract. Therefore, it was necessary to show that an objective observer would have thought that the parties shared a continuing common intention that the contract meant something other than it did. This accords with the view that Christopher Clarke J had taken a year earlier in *PT Berlian Laju Tanker v Nuse Shipping* (2008), where the comments in *Munt* were treated as *obiter* and not going as far as indicating that subjective intention sufficed. *Britoil* was dismissed by Lord Hoffmann, somewhat surprisingly, as providing 'no support to the view that a party must be mistaken as to whether the document reflects what he subjectively believes the agreement to have been'.

13.86 There are two questions here. First, should a shared *subjective* intention suffice for rectification? While Lord Hoffmann's reasoning is powerful, it is respectfully suggested that his conclusion may be overly restrictive in this respect. Recall the discussion of the ordinary objective principle of contractual interpretation in Chapter 2 (paras **2.12–2.18**). The justification for interpreting a party's intention in an objective manner (rather than going directly to their actual intention) is primarily for the protection of the counter-party to the contract, to allow him to treat the first party's *apparent* intention as being his actual intention. However, it is difficult to see that this rationale applies in a case where *both* parties intend the contract to mean something other than it does.

13.87 There are two possible reasons (in addition to those articulated by Lord Hoffmann himself) why one might want to take his approach and stick to the objective principle of interpretation in these circumstances. First, if party A intends the contract to mean something other than the contract actually provides, and B shares this intention, allowing party B to seek rectification without requiring B to show that A should have known that B shared A's intention might be thought to place A in a difficult position. Prior to B seeking rectification, A will not know whether or not the contract is liable to be rectified or whether A should proceed on the objective reading of the contract. However, apart from the fact that it is difficult to have too much sympathy for a party such as A that wishes to place a construction on the contract that he never intended it to have, in practice A is highly likely to know or suspect through pre-contractual communications what B intends and vice versa. Second, allowing rectification without an outward manifestation of the parties' intention makes it difficult for a third party to know whether rectification is a possibility and therefore know what the contract will ultimately turn out to mean. However, third parties are adequately protected by the bona fide purchaser defence to rectification.

13.88 The second question is if a common *subjective* intention should suffice for rectification, should a common *objective* intention also suffice, that is, be an alternative means of obtaining rectification (as suggested by McLauchlan (2008))? It is submitted that it is not clear that as a matter of principle it should suffice to show that an *objective observer* would have thought that the parties intended the contract to mean something different from what it actually provided (at least in the absence of a prior concluded contract), without needing to show that both parties *actually* had this intention. If party A intends that a contract should mean one thing, and objectively construed the contract does have this meaning, it is quite harsh on A to allow the contract to be rectified to mean something else merely because this is the objective interpretation of the *pre*-contractual communications, particularly if party B shared A's intention so that rectification would produce a contract that neither of them *actually* intended. Pre-contractual communications do not amount to an enforceable contract. Therefore, why should they be construed in an objective manner? Moreover, the counter-party has the opportunity to read the final contract to see what it means, and if he did so, would see that it did not accord with his intention. Put another way, the concluded document is surely the best evidence of what the parties objectively agreed. The High Court of Australia in *Simic v New South Wales Land and Housing Corporation* (2016), noted by Davies (2017) has adopted this view, deciding that Lord Hoffmann's obiter comments in *Chartbrook* do not represent the law in Australia, which was regarded as a departure from traditional equitable principles that focus on the parties' actual intentions. As Davies (2017) puts it, 'It is difficult to see why an earlier objective accord should trump a later, formal agreement unless the written instrument fails to reflect the parties' actual intentions'.

13.89 Following on from this, allowing objective common intention to count (at least outside cases where there are prior concluded contracts) blurs the line between *common* mistake rectification (the subject of this section) and *unilateral* mistake rectification (the subject of the section beginning at para **13.95**), because it means that common mistake rectification does not in fact require a common mistake, merely that a reasonable bystander would consider the parties to have been mistaken (see also Häcker (2008)).

13.90 The strongest case for allowing an objective approach is where (as in *Chartbrook*) the pre-contractual communications suggest that it is intended that the contract between A and B should mean one thing, and B is reasonably led to believe that the contract will provide for this, but in fact the contract provides for something else (and this something else accords with A's actual intention so there is no common subjective intention at the time of the contract): see Smith (2007). However, if the contract provides what

A thinks it is meant to mean, A hasn't deliberately taken advantage of B's misreading of the contract and all B has to rely upon is a pre-contractual communication not intended to have binding force. Rectification for unilateral mistake (paras **13.95–13.104**) requires that where only party that has actually made a mistake as to what the terms of the final contract mean, the other party must have known of this or suspected this if rectification is to be available. Given that the law has deliberately set the bar this high in relation to unilateral mistake, it is not clear why a party should be able to circumvent this by alleging that it is a case of common mistake on the basis that the parties are (on the basis of their objective intentions) both mistaken.

13.91 Similar reservations about *Chartbrook* have been voiced by Toulson LJ in the Court of Appeal in the troubling case of *Daventry DC v Daventry and District Housing Ltd* (2012). Here, the claimant local housing authority sold its housing stock and housing department staff to the defendant. The pension fund for those staff had a deficit of £2.4 million. One issue concerned who should bear responsibility for that deficit. In early discussions, the parties agreed that the defendant would meet the deficit, but at a late stage in negotiations a clause was inserted into the draft contract by the defendant that the claimant should retain its pension scheme liabilities. The claimant did not raise an objection, because (despite professional legal advice) it did not appreciate that the change had been made. The court held by a 2–1 majority (Etherton LJ dissenting) that the claimant should be able to rectify the contract, because on an objective construction of the 'prior accord' reached in the early negotiations, the defendant should have known that the claimant did not intend to agree to bear the deficit.

13.92 All of the judges agreed that the *obiter* approach of Lord Hoffmann in *Chartbrook* should be taken to represent the law, but while Etherton LJ put forward a number of well-reasoned arguments in favour of the objective approach, Toulson LJ considered that there was a serious question-mark over whether it was correct. On the facts, the majority decision that the objective construction of the early negotiations was that the defendant had agreed to bear the deficit was extremely surprising, because the draft contract later sent by the defendant provided clearly and explicitly to the contrary. The consequence of the majority view is to undermine the protection afforded to the primacy of the final, agreed, written terms of a contract—a significant problem for commercial transactions. Perhaps the conduct of the defendant influenced the decision, Toulson LJ in particular considering that the defendant's negotiator had been 'disingenuous' in inserting the clause without flagging it up to the claimant. But even *if* this view of the severity of the defendant's conduct was correct (and it is suggested that it may have been slightly harsh) it would have been better to rest the decision on rectification for *unilateral* mistake, which is dealt with later in the chapter, both Toulson LJ and Lord Neuberger MR being of the view that had it not been for the objective approach in *Chartbrook*, this would have been a more satisfactory way of deciding the case. If the test for rectification for unilateral mistake was not satisfied, then the claim should have failed.

13.93 Adopting a different test for rectification for *common* mistake to that advocated in *Chartbrook* would not have helped justify the result in *Daventry*, because, while the defendant might not have acted impeccably, its intention was that the deficit be borne by the claimant, so applying a subjective test of intention for the purposes of rectification for common mistake would not entitle the claimant to relief. Rectification for unilateral mistake would have been a better way to reflect sharp conduct by the defendant, so there was no need for the majority to squeeze the facts into a rectification for common mistake cause of action, but it is suggested that the defendant's actions fell well short of the level of bad conduct needed to justify rectification for unilateral mistake (see Davies (2012)).

13.94 Turning finally to the standard of proof for rectification, *Joscelyne v Nissen* also illustrates that, for sensible practical reasons, the courts are strict about requiring 'convincing proof' of the relevant mistake before allowing rectification. Otherwise, as Mustill J explained in *The Olympic Pride*, 'certainty and ready enforceability would be hindered by constant attempts to cloud the issue by reference to pre-contractual negotiations'. Rectification allows the court positively to rewrite the contract to accord better with the parties' true intentions; in this sense, it is more potent a remedy than merely striking down a contract (Hilliard (2002)). Accordingly, its application must be more jealously guarded, although as we have seen at para **7.67** the modern approach to contractual construction is arguably straying into a territory formerly occupied exclusively by rectification. For a convincing critique of this development and defence of rectification as the proper process for correcting errors in contracts, see Davies (2016).

Rectification for unilateral mistake

13.95 Where there is genuine disagreement as to what the underlying deal is, then rectification has no role to play at all. For example, where a written agreement states 'X' and one party genuinely believes that this represents what the parties agreed, but the other party believes that the parties in fact agreed or intended 'Y', it would be wholly inappropriate to rectify the document to read 'Y'.

13.96 This point is well illustrated by *Riverlate Properties Ltd v Paul* (1975). R granted a 99-year lease of a maisonette to P. The lease provided that R, as landlord, should bear the cost of structural repairs and this was P's understanding of the position. However, R had intended to make P responsible for half the cost of structural repairs and applied for rectification of the lease to this effect. The Court of Appeal refused, holding that there is nothing in either principle or authority 'which requires a person who has acquired a leasehold interest on terms on which he intended to obtain it, and who thought when he obtained it that the lessor intended him to obtain it on those terms, either to lose the leasehold interest, or, if he wish to keep it, to submit to keep it only on the terms which the lessor meant to impose but did not'. Likewise, R's claim to rescind the lease was rejected as totally without foundation.

13.97 So rectification cannot be used as a way round the usual objective interpretation of contracts. If the document says 'X', and one party reasonably believes that this is what was really agreed, then the document will not be rectified. However, rectification may be available where the defendant knows that the written contract does not reflect the underlying deal agreed by the parties and, for example, does not draw this to the attention of the other party—as Buckley LJ put it in *Thomas Bates & Son v Wyndham's (Lingerie) Ltd* (1981), 'the conduct must be such as to affect the conscience of the party who has suppressed the fact that he has recognised the presence of a mistake'.

13.98 This was the case in *Templiss Properties Ltd v Hyams* (1999). T agreed to lease to H a sports shop and gymnasium, at a rent of £12,000 per annum exclusive of business rates. However, the lease as executed erroneously described the rent as £12,000 'inclusive of business rates'. T sought rectification, but H resisted on the alternative grounds either that the deal was indeed for rent inclusive of business rates, or, if not, that he did not know of the error in the executed lease. The judge rejected both arguments and ordered rectification, holding that H knew that the draft lease did not reflect what had been agreed, 'but took advantage of the error'.

13.99 However, it is sometimes suggested that actual knowledge may not be strictly necessary. In *Commission for the New Towns v Cooper (GB) Ltd* (1995), the Court of Appeal held that suspicion and 'turning a blind eye' were sufficient. It is, however, worth bearing in mind that the court held that Cooper had 'put up a smokescreen' and deliberately omitted to draw the Commission's attention to the issue of the option. Rectification would not have been available if Cooper had, for example, merely been negligent in not spotting the Commission's erroneous understanding of the terms of the contract. It is sometimes said that 'sharp practice' or 'unconscionability' is required (for example, *Well Barn Shoot Ltd v Shackleton* (2003)). In *George Wimpey (UK) Ltd v VI Components Ltd* (2005), W's claim for rectification failed, since it 'failed to provide convincing evidence that VIC shut its eyes to the obvious or wilfully and recklessly failed to do what an honest and reasonable person would have done in the circumstances'. This can be contrasted with the successful claim for rectification in *QR Sciences Ltd v BTG International Ltd* (2005), in which BTG's negotiator deliberately misled QR about the meaning of a clause, such that it would be 'unconscionable' to allow BTG to rely on the clause.

13.100 There was a suggestion by Toulson LJ in *Daventry* (para 13.91) that a preferable test might be whether the defendant *should* have known of the claimant's mistake, without the need to show anything more than that, but it is submitted that this should be rejected. As explained at paras 13.74, rectification for unilateral mistake is imposing on the defendant a contract he did not intend to make, and we should rightly be reluctant to do this.

13.101 Two final points must be made. First, while the issue is far from clear, it appears that, unlike in the case of common mistake, rectification for unilateral mistake does not require the party seeking rectification to show that there was a prior agreement or common intention as to the term in question (see Buckley LJ in *Thomas Bates & Son v Wyndham's (Lingerie) Ltd* (1981)). For example, this requirement does not appear in the general formulations of the doctrine in *Commission for the New Towns, Well Barn Shoot* or in Buckley LJ's speech in *Thomas Bates*. Therefore, it seems to suffice that (1) one party is mistaken as to a term of the agreement; (2) the other party knows of this mistake or suspects it has been made; (3) this latter party acts badly in some way, whether by preventing the mistaken party from discovering its mistake, making a misrepresentation as to the terms of the written document or doing something else. This highlights just how different a creature rectification for unilateral mistake is from its common mistake brother.

13.102   More fundamentally, allowing rectification for unilateral mistake in any circum-stances is inherently controversial. Lightman J in *Rowallan Group Ltd v Edgehill Portfolio No 1 Ltd* (2007) explained that, 'the remedy of rectification for unilateral mistake is a drastic remedy, for it has the result of imposing on the defendant ... a contract that he did not, and did not intend to, make'. As we have seen, a party la-bouring under a unilateral mistake can get out of the contract where the mistake is as to the terms of the contract and the other party knows (or perhaps should have known) of the mistake (see paras 3.49-3.56). However, it is one thing to allow a party to get out of a contract where he has made a mistake as to its terms, quite another to hold the non-mistaken party to a contract she did not intend to make (as rectification for unilateral mistake does). Indeed, the former doctrine is best viewed as being an example of orthodox offer and acceptance principles.

13.103   One way to meet this objection is to say that rectification for unilateral mistake is based on estoppel (*Thomas Bates* per Eveleigh LJ; see paras 5.70-5.74 for the meaning of 'es-toppel'). For example, where the non-mistaken party draws up a version of the written contract that differs from the common accord of the parties, she may be representing that the written contract is in the same terms as the accord and so can be held to her word by estoppel. However, the doctrine of rectification for unilateral mistake, as cur-rently formulated, appears to extend beyond situations where the non-mistaken party can be said to have made such a representation (see *Thomas Bates* per Buckley LJ; *Agip SpA v Navigazione Alta Italia SpA* (1984) per Slade LJ). Moreover, it is increasingly suggested that in addition to these conditions, the mistake 'must be one calculated to benefit' the non-mistaken party or to be detrimental to the mistaken party—this ori-ginated in Buckley LJ's statement of principles in *Thomas Bates*, and has been applied for example in *George Wimpey UK Ltd v VI Construction Ltd* (2005) and *Milton Keynes Borough Council v Viridor (Community Recycling MK) Ltd* (2017). The former require-ment certainly has no place in estoppel.

13.104   McLauchlan (2008) has put forward an alternative suggestion, namely that rectification for unilateral mistake just allows a claimant to enforce the contract that he *did* make. His reasoning is that the principle of objective interpretation of contracts (see paras 2.12-2.18) means that if party A gives counter-party B the impression during pre-contractual nego-tiations that the contract will mean one thing, then A's intention should be interpreted objectively and he should be held to his intention. However, it is submitted that this sug-gestion is wrong, for two reasons. First, the principles of objective interpretation of con-tracts do not apply to pre-contractual conduct that precedes the formal offer and accept-ance, because such pre-contractual conduct does not form part of the contract. Misleading statements and silences in the pre-contractual context are dealt with by the doctrines of misrepresentation and estoppel instead. Second, if the principle of objective interpretation really did apply to pre-contractual conduct rather than just to formal offer and acceptance, so as to hold A to his pre-contractual statements, then there would be no need for any doctrine of rectification for unilateral mistake at all: normal objective interpretation principles would be doing all the work.

OVERVIEW

1   Issues of common mistake arise where both parties share a mistaken assumption about their contract. For example, if you contract to buy my bicycle, when it has been destroyed half an hour before we contract, we may both mistakenly assume that the cycle is still in existence. The law is generally very reluctant to let a party get out of a bargain where the other party is not at fault, so common mistake will rarely allow a party to do this.

2   This situation must be distinguished from a situation where circumstances change *after* the contract is made: the latter situation raises issues of frustration, not common mistake. However, the two issues are closely linked, and are dealt with in similar ways.

3   There have traditionally been two versions of common mistake: common mistake at common law, and common mistake in equity. The former is narrower than the latter, so we only go on to consider if the latter applies once we have determined that the former does not. Second, the former makes a contract void, while the latter (if it exists at all) only makes the contract voidable.

Common mistake at law

4   The most recent version of the test (from the *Great Peace* case) suggests that four requirements must be satisfied in order to make the contract void:

- the parties must both mistakenly believe that a state of affairs exists (for example, the bicycle is still in existence);

- there must be no warranty by either party that the state of affairs exists;

- the non-existence of the state of affairs must render performance of the contract impossible; and

- the non-existence of the state of affairs must not be attributable to the fault of either party.

5   In short, for common mistake at common law to operate, both parties must make an assumption. We must then ask if the risk of the assumption being false has been placed on either party by the terms of the contract, be they express terms or implied terms. Only if the answer is in the negative, can common mistake at common law operate. This should be stressed: we must first construe the contract to see whether it distributes the risk in question. The doctrine of mistake can only apply where it has not. Next, if the assumption is false, this must make it impossible to perform the contract. Lastly, neither party must be at fault.

6   The penultimate requirement, that performance must be rendered impossible, requires further examination. If the mistake is as to the existence of the subject matter of the contract or the parties mistakenly think that the property belongs to the seller when in fact it has always belonged to the purchaser, then performance of the contract is impossible and the last requirement is made out.

7   Things are more complicated if the mistake is only as to the quality or value of the subject matter of the contract. So for example, I may contract to sell a painting to you, both of us believing to it be a Van Gogh when in fact it is just a cheap imitation. Originally, it was held that such a mistake would only be serious enough to make the contract void if it was 'as to the existence of some quality which makes the thing without the quality essentially different from the thing with the quality', a test which was intended to be very difficult to satisfy. However, this test seems to have been narrowed even further by *Great Peace*, which suggests that the mistake must be such as to make performance of the contract 'impossible'. Therefore, mistakes as to quality will rarely, if ever, satisfy this requirement.

8   Some have suggested that there is no need for a doctrine of common mistake at all. They argue that all that is necessary is to interpret the terms of the contract, implying terms in fact or in law as appropriate, and see what the contract says about distributing the risk. While this seems the better approach, it has been rejected by the Court of Appeal in *Great Peace*.

Common mistake in equity

9   *Solle v Butcher* (1949) suggested that if the parties share a 'fundamental' mistake, the contract will be voidable in equity. This test was meant to be easier to satisfy than that for common mistake at law.

10 There was great controversy over whether there should be a separate category of common mistake in equity, and the lack of clarity over its boundaries sat very uneasily with the approach of common mistake at common law to hold parties to their contracts in all but exceptional circumstances. The Court of Appeal held in *Great Peace* that *Solle* is wrong and that there is no room for a separate doctrine of equitable common mistake.

Rectification

11 Rectification is the rewriting of a written document where one or both parties are mistaken as to its terms. There are two varieties, rectification for common mistake and unilateral mistake.

12 In the first category, there is an error when a deal reached orally is set out in writing, and both parties mistakenly believe that the document accurately records the oral deal. There are traditionally four main requirements for the doctrine to operate:

- the mistake must relate to the manner in which the oral agreement is recorded in writing and not to any other matter;
- both parties must mistakenly believe that the document accurately records the oral agreement;

- before the written contract, there must be an oral agreement and it will not matter if it did not strictly amount to a concluded contract, providing that there was a common intention as to what the ultimate terms of the written contract would be; and

- there must be convincing proof of the mistake.

13 However, Lord Hoffmann in *Chartbrook Ltd v Persimmon Homes Ltd* (2009) controversially suggested, *obiter*, that it was necessary and sufficient to show that the written contract departed from the parties' *objective* intention.

14 The second category, rectification for unilateral mistake, is equally controversial because the written document in its original form does accord with one party's intentions, so rectification does not give effect to this party's intentions. The requirements appear to be as follows:

- a mistake by one party as to the terms of the written contract;

- the other party knows of this mistake or suspects that it has been made; and

- the latter party acts badly or unconscionably in some way, for example by diverting the mistaken party's attention from the mistake (and thereby preventing him discovering his error) or by making a misrepresentation as to the terms of the written contract.

FURTHER READING

Atiyah '*Couturier v Hastie* and the Sale of Non-Existent Goods' (1957) 73 LQR 340

Buxton 'Construction' and Rectification after *Chartbrook*' [2010] CLJP 253

Capper 'Common Mistake in Contract Law' (2009) Singapore J Legal Stud 457

Davies 'Rectifying the Course of Rectification' (2012) 75(3) MLR 387

Davies 'Rectification versus Interpretation' [2016] CLJ 62

Fleming 'Common Mistake' (1952) 15 MLR 229

Häcker 'Mistakes in the Execution of Documents: Recent Cases on Rectification and Related Doctrines' (2008) 19 KLJ 293

Macmillan *Mistakes in Contract Law* (2010) Chapter 10

McLauchlan 'The 'Drastic' Remedy of Rectification for Unilateral Mistake' (2008) 124 LQR 608

McLauchlan '*Chartbrook Ltd v Persimmon Homes Ltd*: Commonsense Principles of Interpretation and Rectification?' (2009) 125 LQR 8

McLauchlan 'Refining Rectification' (2014) 130 LQR 83

Morgan *Great Debates in Contract Law* (2015) pp 183–92

Patten 'Does the Law Need to be Rectified? *Chartbrook* Revisited', Chancery Bar Association 2013 Annual Lecture, available at http://www.chba.org.uk/for-members/library/annual-lectures/does-the-law-need-to-be-rectified-chartbrook-revisited

Ruddell 'Common Intention and Rectification for Common Mistake' [2014] LMCLQ 48

Smith 'Contracts—Mistake, Frustration and Implied Terms' (1994) 110 LQR 400

Smith 'Rectification of Contracts for Common Mistake, *Joscelyne v Nissen* and Subjective States of Mind' (2007) 123 LQR 116

Tettenborn 'Agreements, Common Mistake and the Purpose of Contract' (2011) 27 JCL 91

SELF-TEST QUESTIONS

1   When will a contract be void for common mistake at common law?

2   Should there be an independent doctrine of common mistake at all? Does it really matter what the answer to this question is?

3   Is there a doctrine of common mistake in equity? Should there be?

4   What is rectification and when can it be successfully invoked?

5   Doolittle plans a summer holiday cruise for himself and his paying guests. On 1 April he contracts to hire from Sinbad the pleasure ship *The Venus* for the months of June and July, paying a deposit of £5,000. On 1 May, having spent £10,000 on preparation for the voyage, he learns that the ship is not going to be available. An alternative vessel cannot be found in time, and the project has to be abandoned. Doolittle loses the £12,000 profit that he expected to make. Advise him, on the following assumptions:

   (a)   unknown to the parties when they make their contract on 1 April, *The Venus* had been wrecked on a reef the week previously;

   (b)   *The Venus* never existed.

 For hints on how to answer question 5, please see the online resources at **www.oup.com/uk/sullivan8e/.**

14 Frustration

SUMMARY

This chapter covers the doctrine of frustration, applicable where performance of a contract becomes impossible or 'radically different' after it was made. Frustration is exceptionally rare, because it only applies where the parties have not made provision for, and thus allocated the risk of, the changed circumstances in their contract. The chapter explores the theoretical basis for the doctrine (giving examples of potential frustrating events), the issue of 'self-induced frustration', and the remedies following frustration in the Law Reform (Frustrated Contracts) Act 1943.

14.1　This chapter seeks to explain what attitude the law takes when matters change, often unexpectedly, *after* the contract has been concluded. In such a situation, one party may attempt to invoke the doctrine of frustration to argue that the contract should be brought to an end because of the change in circumstances. As in the case of common mistake, English law is very reluctant to let a person escape from a contract where the other person is not in breach and not otherwise at fault. As Bingham LJ explained in *J Lauritzen AS v Wijsmuller BV (The Super Servant Two)* (1990): 'Since the effect of frustration is to kill the contract and discharge the parties from further liability under it, the doctrine is not to be lightly invoked, must be kept within very narrow limits and ought not to be extended.'

14.2　Indeed, at one stage of its development, English law *never* allowed contracting parties to escape from a contract by reason of a change of circumstances after the time of contracting (*Paradine v Jane* (1646)).

14.3　This attitude was not unfair where only one party had made an assumption that subsequent events showed to be false. Often this is the case. For example, I may agree to sell a top-of-the-range television to you for £500 because I believe that I can get hold of one for £250 from my friend Carlton who works on a market stall. However, shortly afterwards Carlton's market stall and all his televisions are destroyed in a heavy storm, and I have to buy one from someone else for £700. This is not your concern, so I should not be able to escape the bargain. The risk should be placed firmly on me.

14.4   Imagine, however, that *both* of us make an assumption that subsequent events prove to be false. For example, I get you to do some renovations to my house: both of us implicitly assume that the house will still be in existence when the time comes for the work to be done. If the house is struck by lightning the day after the contract is signed (but before you are due to start work), there seems a stronger case here for saying that we should not be bound by the contract, that it should be discharged. In other words, the risk should not be placed on either of us.

14.5   Accordingly, the doctrine of frustration was developed, to allow a contract to be brought to an end where the parties both make an important assumption when contracting that is later shown to be incorrect. As was discussed in the last chapter, this doctrine deals with similar situations to common mistake. The key difference is that for common mistake to apply, the parties must be mistaken as to some feature *at the time of contracting*, whereas for frustration to apply, the parties' joint assumption must be shown to be false by events occurring *after* the contract has been entered into. It was suggested in *Great Peace Shipping Ltd v Tsavliris Salvage (International) Ltd* (2002) that this distinction should make us slightly less reluctant to invoke the doctrine of frustration than common mistake.

The current test for frustration

14.6   The currently favoured test for ascertaining whether the contract is frustrated is that laid down by the House of Lords in *Davis Contractors Ltd v Fareham UDC* (1956):

> [F]rustration occurs whenever the law recognises that without default of either party a contractual obligation has become incapable of being performed because the circumstances in which performance is called for would render it a thing radically different from that which was undertaken by the contract ... There must be ... such a change in the significance of the obligation that the thing undertaken would, if performed, be a different thing from that contracted for.

One very important rider needs to be added to this test, namely that frustration can only operate where the contract does not deal properly or at all with what will happen on the occurrence of the alleged frustrating event (for example, see *Joseph Constantine SS Line Ltd v Imperial Smelting Corpn Ltd* (1942) and *Great Peace*).

14.7   Therefore, the test has three elements: there must be a radical change in the obligation, the contract must not distribute the risk of the event occurring, and the occurrence of the event must not be due to either party. The second stage requires some explanation. If the contract resolves what should happen on the occurrence of such an event, either by an express term or an implied term, then that is generally the end of the matter: the contract itself dictates what happens and there is no room for the doctrine of frustration to operate. Accordingly, if the contract itself contains a mechanism (even a rudimentary or fairly incomplete one) for dealing with certain changes in circumstances, the contract will be taken to contemplate such changes and not be frustrated by reason of them (see, for example, *Ogilvy & Mather Ltd v Silverado Blue Ltd* (2007)).

14.8 This explains in part why frustration cases are increasingly rare. Commercial contracting parties almost invariably make provision in their contract for what is to happen in the event of unexpected eventualities, thereby ousting the rules of frustration. The most common method for doing so is the *force majeure* clause, which provides a comprehensive list of events and problems, and provides a contractual regime for dealing with them (maybe a right of cancellation, suspension, changes in price, etc). This has a number of advantages for the parties: it provides certainty about what the impact of the specified events will be, it enables the parties to allocate the risk of events which would not count as frustrating events at common law and also to make provision for a more flexible remedial regime than that which applies on frustration. Some commentators even suggest that we do not need a doctrine of frustration, that parties should be required to look after themselves by inserting a *force majeure* clause if they want protection from unexpected events (see the discussion of the relevant viewpoints in Morgan (2015)). However, while it is important that the doctrine is not applied too readily, it would be overly harsh to abolish it altogether, to cover eventualities not provided for in the contract, but which falsify both parties' assumptions in an important respect. Nonetheless the moral is, we must carefully construe the terms of the contract first when faced with a situation where frustration is potentially applicable and only if the contract does not make provision for the event can we go on and consider frustration. (One exception, where public policy insists on frustration even if the parties have made provision in their contract, applies to contracts that would involve trading with the enemy during wartime, but this is very much the exception that proves the rule.)

14.9 As in the case of common mistake (see throughout Chapter 13), there is debate as to whether it is necessary or appropriate to have an independent doctrine of frustration that automatically brings the contract to an end in certain circumstances. The alternative approach (the 'construction approach' or 'implied terms approach') argues that the consequences of a change of circumstances after the contract is made can *always* be determined by construing and interpreting the terms of the contract in the ordinary way, implying terms where appropriate. It suggests that there is no need, and indeed no room, for an independent doctrine to govern such situations. While this approach is currently wholly out of favour (see, for example, its treatment by the House of Lords in *National Carriers Ltd v Panalpina (Northern) Ltd* (1981) and the Court of Appeal in *Great Peace*), it is suggested that it may provide a better way of explaining the cases. The radical change of obligation test often fails to capture the essence of the court's reasoning. However, we will explore the cases by reference to this test, but consider throughout whether it is satisfactory.

14.10 Two modern Court of Appeal cases provide guidance on how the test works and its inter-relationship with the allocation of risk by the contract. In the first, *The Sea Angel*

(2007), a salvage firm called Tsavliris chartered from Global a ship called the *Sea Angel* in order to assist Tsavliris in salvage operations concerning an oil tanker that had run aground near Karachi, causing a major pollution incident. The charter was to last for 20 days from 25 August to 15 September 2003. Having done its salvage work, Tsavliris gave notice to Global on 9 September that it would redeliver the *Sea Angel* at the redelivery port in the charter agreement, expecting that the ship would be able to leave the port of Karachi that day. However, in fact the Karachi port authority refused to issue the necessary certificate allowing the ship to leave, a certificate stating that all port charges had been paid: it was using this as a bargaining chip in its demand for compensation for the oil pollution damage. It became clear by 13 October that a commercial solution between Tsavliris and the port authority was not going to be possible, and following litigation by Tsavliris, the port authority was forced to release the vessel on 26 December. In response to Global's claim for payment for the hire of the vessel in respect of the period after 15 September until eventual redelivery, Tsavliris claimed that it was not liable to pay past 13 October because the contract was frustrated on this date, it being clear that there would be a delay of at least three months in releasing the vessel, which was far longer than the charter period of 20 days. The Court of Appeal rejected this argument.

14.11 Rix LJ helpfully explained how he thought that the 'radical change of obligation' test should be applied in practice, and how important in applying it the allocation of risk by the contract was:

> In my judgment, the application of the doctrine of frustration requires a multi-factorial approach. Among the factors which have to be considered are the terms of the contract itself, its matrix or context, the parties' knowledge, expectations, assumptions and contemplations, in particular as to risk, as at the time of contract, at any rate so far as these can be ascribed mutually and objectively, and then the nature of the supervening event, and the parties' reasonable and objectively ascertainable calculations as to the possibilities of future performance in the new circumstances. Since the subject matter of the doctrine of frustration is contract, and contracts are about the allocation of risk, and since the allocation and assumption of risk is not simply a matter of express or implied provision but may also depend on less easily defined matters such as 'the contemplation of the parties', the application of the doctrine can often be a difficult one. In such circumstances, the test of 'radically different' is important: it tells us that the doctrine is not to be lightly invoked; that mere incidence of expense or delay or onerousness is not sufficient; and that there has to be as it were a break in identity between the contract as provided for and contemplated and its performance in the new circumstances.

14.12 It was therefore too simplistic just to compare the anticipated delay with the length of the contract. When a ship is chartered for a specific period, the risk that something will happen to delay it being returned is generally on the charterer, because it agrees to pay hire until redelivering the vessel. Therefore, the court held, it would require something very serious to require the owner (Global) to share this risk by denying it its right to hire charges for the period from 13 October until redelivery. Such a factor was not present here, principally because the port was merely refusing to let the ship leave until the dispute over its release could be resolved, the problem only occurred at the tail-end of the charter after Tsavliris had carried out the salvage operation, and there was a foreseeable risk of a vessel being detained in the midst of a serious pollution incident.

14.13 The second relevant Court of Appeal decision is *Graves v Graves* (2008) (noted by Capper (2008)). In *Graves*, an ex-husband allowed his wife (who lived with their children) to rent one of his properties. She had few resources and therefore both parties wanted to be sure that she was entitled to housing benefit, because this was intended to finance 90 per cent of her rent payments. She asked the council whether she was entitled, and they responded in the affirmative, so—having told her ex-husband of the result of her enquiry—she entered into the lease, paying a £12,000 deposit in the process. However, it turned out that the council's advice was incorrect. She could not pay the rent and so her ex-husband sought possession. In response, she claimed that the lease was void for mistake or alternatively frustration, and sought the return of the deposit that she had paid.

14.14 The Court of Appeal held that both parties contracted on the basis that Mrs Graves was entitled to the housing benefit and that this would be used to provide 90 per cent of the rent. Without this assumption, neither party would have contemplated entering the contract. Mrs Graves did not *promise*, whether expressly or impliedly, that she was entitled to the housing benefit: she had effectively made a joint enquiry to the council on behalf of both of them and simply relayed what the council had said. In these circumstances, the contract did not place the risk of the council's advice being wrong upon her. Instead, the court found that there was an implied condition that if the housing benefit was not payable, the tenancy would come to an end, so that when the council informed Mrs Graves that she was not entitled to the benefit, the tenancy came to an end. The term was so obvious as to go without saying, and could therefore be implied on orthodox implied term principles (see paras **7.77–7.88**). Accordingly, there was no room for any doctrines of frustration or mistake to operate.

14.15 One might feel that the decision was a little favourable to Mrs Graves—ordinarily if you promise to pay for something, it is your problem if it turns out you cannot, so the risk should be on you. However, putting this to one side, there is a more important point here. *Graves* shows how easily the courts can use orthodox implied terms principles to deal with frustration cases if they want to, without the need to resort to an independent doctrine of frustration.

Was there a radical change in the obligation?

14.16 While we should be wary of splitting the cases into rigid categories, because each case turns on the construction of the particular contract, such categories are at least useful as a starting point.

Non-occurrence of an event

14.17 The situations that cause most difficulty are where an event *fails* to occur that at least one party assumed would occur. We shall start with two cases that are famously difficult to explain or reconcile. While they have sometimes been criticised and are borderline cases, it is submitted that they *may* both be correctly decided and at the very least tell us a lot about how the doctrine of frustration should operate.

14.18 The first case is *Krell v Henry* (1903). The defendant agreed to hire from the claimant a flat in Pall Mall for 26–27 June, when King Edward VII's coronation procession was scheduled to take place and pass along Pall Mall. The flat would offer a particularly good view of the procession. The contract contained no express reference to the coronation procession, or to any other purpose for which the flat was taken. However, it did say that the defendant was only to have the use of the room during the day, and not during the night. A deposit was paid when the contract was entered into. As a result of the King's serious illness, the procession was postponed, so the defendant declined to pay the balance of the agreed rent. The Court of Appeal held that the taking place of the procession on the days originally fixed along the proclaimed route was regarded by both contracting parties as the foundation of the contract, so the contract was frustrated and the defendant did not have to pay the balance.

14.19 Two passages from the judgment of Vaughan Williams LJ are particularly crucial to understanding the court's reasoning. First, he explained why he had come to the decision that the contract was frustrated:

> [T]he plaintiff exhibited on his premises, third floor, 56A, Pall Mall, an announcement to the effect that windows to view the Royal coronation procession were to be let, and that the defendant was induced by that announcement to apply to the housekeeper on the premises, who said that the owner was willing to let the suite of rooms for the purpose of seeing the Royal procession for both days, but not nights, of June 26 and 27. In my judgment the use of the rooms was let and taken for the purpose of seeing the Royal procession. It was not a demise of the rooms, or even an agreement to let and take the rooms. It is a licence to use rooms for a particular purpose and none other. And in my judgment the taking place of those processions on the days proclaimed along the proclaimed route, which passed 56A, Pall Mall, was regarded by both contracting parties as the foundation of the contract.

14.20 Second, he distinguished the situation in *Krell* from a hypothetical example, discussed in the course of argument, where frustration would not apply:

> [I]f a cabman was engaged to take some one to Epsom on Derby Day at a suitable enhanced price for such a journey, say £10, both parties to the contract would [not] be discharged in the contingency of the race at Epsom for some reason becoming impossible ... for I do not think that in the cab case the happening of the race would be the foundation of the contract. No doubt the purpose of the engager would be to go to

see the Derby, and the price would be proportionately high; but the cab had no special qualifications for the purpose which led to the selection of the cab for this particular occasion. Any other cab would have done as well ... Whereas in the case of the coronation, there is not merely the purpose of the hirer to see the coronation procession, but it is the coronation procession and the relative position of the rooms which is the basis of the contract as much for the lessor as the hirer ...

14.21 Many have had difficulty in understanding the decision in *Krell* and how the case can be distinguished from *Herne Bay Steam Boat Co v Hutton* (1903) (see para **14.26**). Some judges have even criticised it (for example, in *Larringa & Co Ltd v Societé Franco-Américaine des Phosphates de Medulla, Paris* (1929) and *Maritime National Fish Ltd v Ocean Trawlers Ltd* (1935)). Nonetheless, while the result in *Krell* was certainly an exceptional one the decision is surely correct and the court's reasoning illuminating. Let us begin with the previous cab example. In the example, the person hiring the cab hired it for the purpose of going to the Derby. He assumed that the Derby would take place. So the first thing the example shows is that it is not enough that one party entered into the contract for the purpose of seeing the Derby: the fact that one party makes an assumption which subsequent events show to be incorrect (in the cab example that the Derby would take place) is not enough to frustrate the contract. The starting point is that if a bargain turns out badly for you, this is your bad luck: the risk is on you. The motives of the person who takes the cab for entering into the contract are not the business of the other party. So if your assumptions and expectations are disappointed, that is your bad luck and nothing to do with me. You need a good reason to be able to shift the risk, to get out of the bargain.

14.22 The second point about the cab example is that the cabman knows that the passenger wants the cab to go and see the Derby (he charges a high price for this very reason). He knows that the other party is assuming that the race will go ahead. So the second lesson to be drawn is that even if one party makes an assumption that is subsequently shown to be incorrect *and* the other party knows of this assumption at the time of contracting, this is still not enough to bring the contract to an end.

14.23 So what extra ingredient was there on the facts of *Krell*, not present in the cab example, that led the Court of Appeal to discharge the contract for frustration? In *Krell*, the defendant's motive for contracting was to see the procession and the plaintiff knew this. However, the cab example shows that something more is needed. Why could the claimant in *Krell* not say that the defendant's motives were not his business? Three answers can be given. First, he advertised that he was selling a view of the royal procession, rather than simply letting the room. Secondly, the claimant only offered the use of the room in the day, not during the night. Thirdly, the claimant was not in business hiring out his room regularly—unusually, and unlike the cabman in the Epsom Derby example, he only contracted because of the coronation procession. These factors show that the claimant was not merely hiring out a room for ordinary use; he was selling a view of the procession and nothing more. Therefore, crucially, we can say that *both* parties assumed that the procession would go ahead; there was a joint assumption as to this important matter, and it was this that allowed the Court of Appeal to say the contract should be discharged.

14.24 What is noticeable about *Krell* is how little use the later 'radical change' test is in explaining the decision or helping to decide what result should be reached. The court simply asked whether both parties had contracted on the assumption that the procession would take place; whether this was important to both parties or just the concern of one.

14.25 This reasoning looks extremely similar to asking whether a term should be implied, and seems governed by very similar rules (see paras **7.77–7.88**). We look at the assumptions and expectations *shared* by the parties. A similar approach is taken to implied terms, where we look at what assumptions the parties shared that they specifically failed to advert to and put expressly into the contract.

14.26 The second case to be examined is *Herne Bay Steam Boat Co v Hutton* (1903). A Royal naval review was due to take place at Spithead on 28 June 1902. The claimants and the defendant agreed in writing that the claimants' steamship *Cynthia* should be 'at the disposal' of the defendant on 28 June to take passengers from Herne Bay 'for the purpose of viewing the naval review and for a day's cruise round the fleet; also on 29 June for similar purposes: price £250 payable, £50 down, balance before ship leaves Herne Bay.' On signing the agreement the defendant paid the £50 deposit. On 25 June the review was cancelled, whereupon the claimants contacted the defendant, stating that the ship was ready to start and requesting payment of the balance. Receiving no reply, the claimants used the ship for their own purposes on 28 and 29 June. During these two days the fleet remained anchored at Spithead. The claimants sought to recover the balance less the profits made by their use of the ship during the two days, and the defendant pleaded frustration. The Court of Appeal, composed of exactly the same judges as in *Krell*, held that the hiring of the ship was the defendant's venture and the risk of things not going as the defendant intended was his risk alone. Accordingly, the contract was not frustrated.

14.27 Again, two passages are crucial to understanding the decision. First, Vaughan Williams LJ set out his reasoning as follows:

> *Mr. Hutton, in hiring this vessel, had two objects in view: firstly, of taking people to see the naval review, and, secondly, of taking them round the fleet. Those, no doubt, were the purposes of Mr. Hutton, but it does not seem to me that because, as it is said, those purposes became impossible, it would be a very legitimate inference that the happening of the naval review was contemplated by both parties as the basis and foundation of this contract, so as to bring the case within the doctrine of Taylor v Caldwell. On the contrary, when the contract is properly regarded, I think the purpose of Mr. Hutton, whether of seeing the naval review or of going round the fleet with a party of paying guests, does not lay the foundation of the contract within the authorities … I see nothing that makes this contract differ from a case where, for instance, a person has engaged a brake to take himself and a party to Epsom to see the races there, but for some reason or other, such as the spread of an infectious disease, the*

races are postponed. In such a case it could not be said that he could be relieved of his bargain. So in the present case it is sufficient to say that the happening of the naval review was not the foundation of the contract.

Second, Romer LJ set out the core of his reasoning in the following passage:

[I]t is a contract for the hiring of a ship by the defendant for a certain voyage, though having, no doubt, a special object, namely, to see the naval review and the fleet; but it appears to me that the object was a matter with which the defendant, as hirer of the ship, was alone concerned, and not the plaintiffs, the owners of the ship ... The ship (as a ship) had nothing particular to do with the review or the fleet except as a convenient carrier of passengers to see it: any other ship suitable for carrying passengers would have done equally as well. Just as in the case of the hire of a cab or other vehicle, although the object of the hirer might be stated, that statement would not make the object any the less a matter for the hirer alone, and would not directly affect the person who was letting out the vehicle for hire.

14.28 The court took the view that the reference in the agreement to the purpose of the hire only expressed Hutton's motive for entering into the contract. Therefore, as in the cab example, Hutton's purpose was to see the review: he assumed that the review would take place. Moreover, the defendant knew that this was Hutton's assumption, because it was mentioned in the agreement itself. However, this is not enough in itself, as we saw from the cab example in *Krell*. As in the cab example, there is nothing to make it the defendant's business as well: it does not care about whether the review takes place. So the assumption made here is not a *joint* one. There is not the extra ingredient that there was in *Krell*: the defendant was in business hiring out a boat, and did not care what Hutton used it for.

14.29 Having examined these two cases, we can see that in order for the contract to be frustrated, we must ask whether the contract was based on an assumption made by *both* parties. It is not enough that one party's motives or assumptions are disappointed, or even that the other knows of the former's motives; the assumption must be a joint one.

Let us examine whether this approach applies to other types of situation in which the contract is commonly held to be frustrated.

Destruction of subject matter of the contract

14.30 One of the most extreme cases is where the subject matter of the contract does not exist. Generally, the parties both assume that the subject matter of the contract will continue to exist. So, for example, in *Taylor v Caldwell* (1863), the defendant agreed to hire out some premises to the claimant for staging a performance, but the premises burnt down the day before the performance was to take place. The claimant argued that the defendant was in breach of contract in failing to supply the premises and claimed damages, but Blackburn

J held that the parties contracted on the basis that the premises would continue to exist, so the contract was frustrated. Similarly, in *Appleby v Myers* (1867), the claimant agreed to erect machinery on the defendant's premises, but the premises and machines were destroyed by fire before the work was completed. It was held that the contract was frustrated.

However, it is still ultimately a matter of construction of the contract as to whether it places the risk of destruction on one party. In *Bunge SA v Kyla Shipping Co Ltd* (2012), a chartered ship was damaged severely while chartered through no fault of the owner or charterer. It was held that the owner was promising that it would supply a seaworthy vessel and that, as it was insured for the cost of repair, the contract placed the risk on the owner of the ship being damaged in a way that he could repair at the cost of the insurers. Therefore, contrary to the owner's argument, the contract was not frustrated.

Increased expense

14.31   It is clear that, if the contract has just become more expensive to perform for one party, this does not frustrate the contract. For example, in *Davis Contractors Ltd v Fareham UDC* (1956), Davis agreed to build 78 houses for £94,000, the work to be completed within eight months. In fact, the work took 22 months and cost £17,000 more than anticipated. Davis (cheekily) claimed that the contract was frustrated (and that accordingly, they were entitled to a reasonable sum for the work that they had done). The House of Lords held that the fact that performance of the contract had proved more onerous than Davis had anticipated was insufficient to frustrate the contract. This can be easily explained using the same reasoning. One party enters into a contract because he thinks he can make a profit; if it turns out to be more expensive than he thought, his assumption is proved incorrect. However, his assumptions and reasons for entering into the contract are not the business of the other party; the other party makes no such assumptions.

14.32   The courts generally assert that increased expense will *never* frustrate a contract: *Tsakiroglou & Co Ltd v Noblee Thorl GmbH* (1962) (except for Lord Reid, who reserved his position in respect of extreme increases in expense). Beatson (1996) argues that this absolute bar is unjustified; he argues that while a clear, certain rule is important, we should not single out situations of increased expense for special treatment by laying down an absolute rule, when we do not do this in other contexts. However, one argument for the absolute bar is that stated earlier: increased expense is the business of one party alone. As stated in the context of mistake by Toulson J at first instance in *Great Peace*, 'it cannot properly be the function of the law to relieve a party from such a bargain if it turns out to have been not merely bad, but very bad.'

14.33   In *Tandrin Aviation Holdings v Aero Toy Store LLC* (2010) the defendant attempted to argue that the 'credit crisis' of 2007–8 (which it described as an 'unanticipated, unforeseeable and cataclysmic downward spiral of the world's financial markets') triggered the *force majeure* clause in a contract for the sale of a jet aircraft. (Notice that frustration was not strictly in issue, but the judge recognised that the construction of the *force majeure* clause presented an analogous issue.) The judge unhesitatingly rejected the defendant's argument, pointing out that it is 'well established under English law that a change in economic/market circumstances, affecting the profitability of a contract or the ease with which the parties' obligations can be performed, is not regarded as being a *force majeure* event. Thus a failure of performance due to the provision of insufficient financial resources has been held not to amount to *force majeure*.' Nor would it amount to a frustrating event in the absence of the clause. (The defendant was also unsuccessful in its attempt to argue that a provision for forfeiture of its deposit on default amounted to a penalty clause, on which see further Chapter 17.)

14.34   Following on from this reference to the financial crash, another hugely significant political event (and one which itself might produce an equivalent effect on financial markets) deserves a brief mention. Following the Brexit referendum result and the triggering of Article 50, it is clear that the deal by which the United Kingdom eventually leaves the European Union has the potential to impact significantly on commercial contracts. As MacMillan (2016) points out, 'the comparatively sudden development of even the prospect of Brexit' suggests that existing commercial contracts are unlikely to include provisions dealing with that eventuality. 'While *force majeure* clauses often provide against the possibility of insurrection, Brexit presupposes a legal rather than a violent revolution.' This in turn means that, at least for those contracts entered into before the referendum was mooted, many parties are likely to invoke the doctrine of frustration. As MacMillan suggests, it might be desirable for Parliament to address the position of such contracts as part of the legislative apparatus of withdrawal. Time will tell how the courts and Parliament respond to this issue, but in the meantime anyone drafting commercial contracts will, from now on, be wise to make appropriate provision for the possible impact of Brexit.

Forced alteration of manner of performance/impossibility of performance by the defendant

14.35   If a subsequent event merely prevents one party performing in the manner that she had originally envisaged, this does not frustrate the contract: generally, it is her business how she performs the contract and not that of the other party. So in *Blackburn Bobbin Co Ltd v Allen (TW) & Sons Ltd* (1918), the seller agreed to supply Finnish timber to the purchaser. The outbreak of war cut off its source of supply from Finland, so when the purchaser sought damages for breach of contract, the seller claimed that the contract had been frustrated. It was held that the contract was not frustrated: the seller might have regarded the source of supply as important, but it was not the concern of the purchaser. As Pickford LJ commented:

> Why should a purchaser of goods, not specific goods, be deemed to concern himself with the way in which the seller is going to fulfil his contract by providing the goods he has agreed to sell? The sellers in this case agreed to deliver the timber free on rail at Hull, and it was no concern of the buyers as to how the sellers intended to get the timber there.

14.36 Taking this a stage further, the fact that the defendant's supplier chooses not to supply to the defendant, rendering it impossible for the defendant to perform its contractual obligations, does not frustrate the contract, as the Court of Appeal confirmed in *CTI Group Inc v Transclear SA* (2008). In *CTI Group*, the defendant seller had contracted to sell some cement to the claimant as part of the claimant's attempt to import it into Mexico in breach of a cartel operated by a local company, Cemex. The defendant knew that this was the claimant's goal, but when it came to try to provide the cement, it found that Cemex had 'got to' its intended supplier and the supplier was no longer willing to provide the cement. The defendant did not have a binding contract with the supplier and therefore could not insist on performance from it, so claimed that the contract with the claimant had become impossible of performance and was frustrated. The court rejected this argument. It is the defendant's business how he goes about performing his obligations, and the risk that he cannot do so, as matters turn out, is a risk that he must bear, not the other party to the contract.

Illegality

14.37 If the contract becomes illegal to perform, this may frustrate the contract if it has a serious enough effect on the contract: parties normally both assume that the majority of the contract can be lawfully performed. Whether the effect is serious enough will normally depend on how long the legal restriction applies for compared with the term of the contract (for example, see *Cricklewood Property and Investment Trust Ltd v Leighton's Investment Trust Ltd* (1945)). As mentioned in para **14.8**, illegality is the one area where the parties' agreement to allocate risk will not be effective to save the contract. This is because, as Beatson J said in *Islamic Republic of Iran Shipping Lines v. Steamship Mutual Underwriting Association (Bermuda)* (2010), quoting Treitel (2015) it is:

> well recognised that when considering supervening illegality, the court is concerned not only with allocating or distributing the loss caused by the supervening event and 'reaching a solution which may do justice between the contracting parties'. The court 'is also concerned with the public interest that the law is observed'.

The outbreak of war

14.38 The outbreak of war often affects the performance of the contract; whether it will frustrate it depends on the nature of the effect it has on the contract. If it just affects the way in which one party intended to perform the contract, generally this will not be the business of the other party: he will not have made any assumptions about how the contract must be performed. Therefore, the contract will not be frustrated. Good examples are found in the context of the war between Britain and Egypt in 1956 following Egypt's nationalisation of the Suez Canal. This led to the blockage of the canal, with consequent delays for many charter and international sale contracts. In *Tsakiroglou & Co Ltd v Noblee Thorl GmbH* (1962), Viscount Simonds commented that '[t]here is no evidence that the buyers attached any importance to the route. They were content that the nuts should be shipped at any date in November or December.' This is very similar to the reasoning in the Epsom Derby example discussed in *Krell v Henry*—only one party's assumptions are affected by the supervening event.

14.39   However, if both parties assumed that performance would occur in a particular way, and it now cannot because of the war, this may frustrate the contract, because both parties have made the assumption. So if the assumption is an important enough one, this will frustrate the contract. In *Tsakiroglou* it was suggested that if it had been important to the buyers that the nuts were shipped via the Suez Canal, for example because the 'nuts would deteriorate as the result of a longer voyage and a double crossing of the Equator' then the result might have been different. Similarly, if both parties agreed that a particular ship would be supplied, but it is requisitioned by a government, this will frustrate the contract, depending on how long it is requisitioned for (compare *Bank Line Ltd v Arthur Capel Ltd* (1919) with *FA Tamplin Steamship Co Ltd v Anglo-Mexican Petroleum Products Co Ltd* (1916)), because both parties assume that the ship will be available for at least a certain amount of the contract term. Notice that, in such a case, it might be more natural for the court to interpret the agreement to the effect that it was subject to an implied condition that the ship continued to be available.

Delay or temporary interruption

14.40   As indicated in para **14.11**, the question of whether an event, such as the requisition of a ship, frustrates the contract depends in part on the length of the interruption compared with the length of the contract. Of course, this poses a problem for contracting parties, because it is impossible to know in advance (without the benefit of hindsight) how long the interruption will last, yet they need some way of calculating when they can safely assume that the contract is frustrated and walk away. Chitty (2016) says: 'To frustrate a contract, the delay must be so abnormal, in its cause, its effects, or its expected duration, so that it falls outside what the parties could reasonably contemplate at the time of contracting.'

14.41   This highlights that the length of the delay is, as the Court of Appeal emphasised in *The Sea Angel* (see paras **14.10-14.12**), only one factor to take into account. In determining whether the parties should be made to share the risk of the delay, one must also take into account factors like the circumstances in which it arose, how foreseeable it was, and how the contract distributes the risk of these sorts of events occurring.

Contracts for personal services

14.42   Contracts for the provision of personal services, such as contracts of employment, may be frustrated if one party is unable to perform through death, illness, or incapacity. Even a contract with a builder to carry out work on a house has been held to constitute a contract for personal services where a family knew him, had built up a relationship of trust with him, and were obtaining his services for substantially less than the market rate (*Atwal v Rochester* (2010)).

14.43 Both parties generally must expect that the party in question may be occasionally ill or incapacitated, but they assume that he will be able to perform a certain amount of the contract. Therefore, the court looks at matters such as how long he is unable to perform for, how long the contract was for, and the terms of the contract (*Marshall v Harland & Wolff Ltd* (1972)). The court will also take a close look at whether the illness or incapacity really does make the contract impossible to perform, or whether it is possible for someone acting on the person's behalf to continue performance of it. In *Blankley v Central Manchester & Manchester Children's University Hospitals NHS Trust* (2015), the Court of Appeal held that a 'no win no fee' agreement between a client and solicitor survived the client's incapacity because the court had appointed someone to act for the client. This avoided the unattractive conclusion that the solicitors were deprived of part of their fee for getting a good settlement of the litigation for the client just because the client had to have someone acting on her behalf for the latter part of the case.

The relevance of foreseeability

14.44 The fact that parties have foreseen the event in question normally precludes frustration. Usually, if the event is foreseeable but the parties do not expressly state what should happen if the event occurs, the inference will be that it was only the business of one party, that the contract has placed the risk on that party. I might contract to buy some beans from you, and we both know that it is a real possibility that civil war might break out in the country where the beans are grown, driving prices up. If we do not expressly say in the contract what should happen in that event, the inference may well be that if war breaks out it is your problem, not mine, so the contract should continue to bind you. Similarly, in *The Sea Angel* (paras **14.10–14.12**), the foreseeability of the ship being detained was an important factor in determining whether the contract was frustrated.

14.45 However, this will not always be the case. For example, in *Tatem v Gamboa* (1939), a ship was chartered during the Spanish Civil War, in order to evacuate the civilian population from north Spain. The ship was chartered for 30 days and the hire rate was three times the normal rate. The ship was seized by a Nationalist ship just under halfway through the charter and was not released until well after the charter had ended. It was held that even on the assumption that the parties had foreseen that this might happen, the contract was still frustrated. The reason for this is that both parties contracted on the basis that the ship would be available to evacuate the civilians. So if both parties contract on the basis that an event will not occur, and this assumption is crucial to both parties, then the contract will be frustrated, even if the event was foreseeable. The situation in *The Sea Angel* fell on the other side of the line, not least because the port authority in that case was doing something less serious to the ship (detaining it until the dispute could be resolved) and the problem did not prevent the charterer carrying out his salvage operation because it had already been completed.

14.46 Of course, it is important to be clear about what is meant by 'foreseeable' here. In the tortious sense of the word, virtually anything could be deemed to be foreseeable (for example, the King being ill on his coronation day satisfies the *Wagon Mound* test of foreseeability), but we are concerned here with contract, not tort. The issue which the courts have to consider is whether or not one party or the other has assumed the risk of the occurrence of the event. As Treitel (2015) puts it: 'Foreseeability will support the inference of risk-assumption only where the supervening event is one which any person of ordinary intelligence would regard as likely to occur.' This approach was approved by the Court of Appeal in *The Sea Angel*.

Self-induced frustration

14.47 Where you have brought things on yourself, the case for relief is less strong. So if it was your act that caused the event which you allege frustrates the contract, you (though not the other party) will often be prevented from claiming that the contract was frustrated. As Bingham LJ asserted in *The Super Servant Two* (1990):

> The essence of frustration is that it should not be due to the act or election of the party seeking to rely on it ... A frustrating event must be some outside event or extraneous change of situation.

For example, in *Melli Bank plc v Holbug Limited* (2013), an Iranian bank claimed fees for a particular credit facility that it provided for a customer. The customer claimed that the fees were not due because the contract was frustrated, since the bank's assets were frozen as part of the sanctions against Iran. However, she could have applied for a licence from the Treasury to allow her facility to continue to operate, so the court rejected the customer's frustration defence on the basis that it was within her power to make the contract capable of performance, and gave summary judgment for the bank.

14.48 The two most interesting cases in this area are *Maritime National Fish Ltd v Ocean Trawlers Ltd* (1935) and *The Super Servant Two* (1990). In the former, Maritime National Fish Ltd (MNF) chartered a trawler fitted with an otter trawl from Ocean Trawlers Ltd (OT), both parties being aware at the time of contracting that a licence was required to use an otter trawl. MNF was operating five trawlers, three of its own, the one it had chartered from OT and one that it had chartered from someone else. It applied for licences but was informed that only three would be granted, and was asked to choose three of the trawlers to obtain licences for. MNF chose not to nominate the trawler chartered from OT, and then claimed that the contract with OT was frustrated because it could not legally fish with the trawler. The Privy Council held that the contract was not frustrated because the inability of MNF to legally fish with the trawler had come about because of MNF's decision not to nominate the trawler chartered from OT.

This seems fair: MNF could have legally used both of the trawlers that it chartered, and it was only MNF's decision that prevented this. The merits are less straightforward in the next case.

14.49 In *The Super Servant Two*, the defendants contracted to transport the claimants' drilling rig using one of their two barges, the Super Servant One and the Super Servant Two. The defendants had also entered into two similar contracts with other parties. They intended to use the Super Servant One for these other two contracts and the Super Servant Two for the contract with the claimants. Unfortunately, before the time came to transport the claimants' rig, the Super Servant Two sank. The defendants refused to use the Super Servant One for the job, so the claimants sued for breach of contract, in response to which the defendants claimed that the sinking of the Super Servant Two discharged the contract because of a *force majeure* clause, or failing that, frustrated the contract. On the trial of four preliminary issues of law, the Court of Appeal, applying *Maritime National Fish Ltd*, held that the contract would not be frustrated. The defendants could have still performed the contract despite the sinking of the Super Servant Two: they simply chose not to. So it was the defendants' choice not to use the Super Servant One to transport the claimants' rig that made them unable to perform the contract.

14.50 The correctness of this decision is hotly debated. The problem is that the defendants had overstretched themselves: as a result of events after the time of contracting they were unable to perform all of the three contracts that they had entered into. As McKendrick (1990) notes, the decision puts people such as the defendant in a very difficult position: they are not allowed to get out of any of the contracts (unless the contracts provide that they can do so) so they have to choose which of the contracts to breach. Indeed, Beatson, Burrows, and Cartwright (2016) argue that the decision is wrong. Most importantly, 'it is likely to lead to practical difficulties', by which they seem to mean that it is overly harsh on a defendant. An alternative point of view is that the other party to the contract should not lose out (by the defendant being able to invoke the doctrine of frustration) just because the defendant has overstretched himself by entering into more contracts than he should have. This is the defendant's business alone, so we should say that the contract normally places the risk on the defendant in such circumstances. Moreover, a defendant can protect himself by inserting a *force majeure* clause to remove its liability in such circumstances. Indeed, in *The Super Servant Two* itself, the defendant had inserted such a clause and it was accepted that it could be invoked providing that the sinking of the Super Servant Two occurred without any negligence on the defendant's part.

14.51 So far we have been dealing with acts where the defendant is aware of the consequences of his act: for example, the defendants in *The Super Servant Two* knew that by choosing not to use The Super Servant One for the contract with the claimants, they would be unable to perform the contract. What if the act was inadvertent? Think again about the example about renovation of my house from para **14.4**, but let us change the facts slightly. Imagine that the day before you are due to start work, the house burns down as a result of my *negligence*: should this prevent me claiming frustration? *The Super Servant Two* says '[a] frustrating event must take place without blame or fault on the side of the party seeking to rely on it', but the standard of fault necessary to prevent frustration is not completely clear. However, while the matter is not free from doubt and was left open by the House of Lords in *Joseph Constantine Steamship Line Ltd v Imperial Smelting Corpn Ltd* (1942), the better view is that negligence is sufficient to prevent frustration.

14.52 One final comment can be made on the relevance of fault to frustration. If the principal focus is on how radical the change of obligation is (as the current test suggests), it is difficult to see why fault should be relevant. Fault has no impact on how radical the change of obligation is. In contrast, fault can be relevant to whether, and what sort of, a term should be implied.

What are the effects of frustration?

14.53 We must begin by examining the effects of frustration at common law. As we shall see, the common law was in some respects unfair to one party or the other, and so a statutory scheme was put in place—the Law Reform (Frustrated Contracts) Act 1943 ('the Act')—to redress some of the more undesirable effects of the common law in this area.

Common law

14.54 Under the common law rules, the frustration of a contract had four main effects:

- On frustration the contract was brought to an end automatically.

- The parties were released from obligations that would have fallen due after the occurrence of the frustrating event. This requires further explanation. Imagine I contracted to pay you 12 monthly instalments of £100, the first to be paid on 1 January 2011, in return for your supplying me with bananas, but the contract was frustrated on 20 February. The third instalment would have only fallen due on 1 March, but the frustration of the contract before this date means that I am released from paying this (and the later) instalments.

- The parties were *not* released from obligations that should have been performed before the frustrating event occurred. So in our example, if I had not paid the second instalment which fell due on 1 February, I would still have to pay this instalment even though the contract was later frustrated. As we shall see, in respect of obligations to pay money (as in the example), the Act changes this common law rule.

- At common law you could only recover the value of the benefit that you had transferred if the other party had performed *none* of his obligations, that is, if there was a 'total failure of basis' (see para 18.9). So in *Fibrosa Spolka Akcyjna v Fairbairn Lawson Combe Barbour Ltd* (1943), the appellant, a Polish company, had paid £1,000 under a contract for the supply of machinery. The respondent did considerable work under the contract but the contract was frustrated when Germany occupied Poland. It was held that the respondent's obligations under the contract were to deliver the goods, which he had not done, so there was a total failure of basis and the money could be recovered.

14.55 The common law position was unfair in at least two respects. For one thing, a party could not recover the value of the benefit that he had transferred where the other party had performed some of his contractual obligations. In addition, where one party could recover the value of the benefit that he had transferred, no account was taken of the fact that the other party might have incurred expenditure in preparing to perform the contract. For example, in *Fibrosa*, no account was taken of the time, effort, and money expended by the respondent in making the machinery. The Act was passed to alleviate these problems.

The Law Reform (Frustrated Contracts) Act 1943

14.56 The Act applies to contracts governed by English law that have 'become impossible of performance or been otherwise frustrated' (s 1(1)). If the contract makes provision for what should happen in the situation that has occurred, the Act cannot operate in a manner inconsistent with this (s 2(3)). Section 1(2) of the Act deals with obligations to pay money, while s 1(3) deals with other obligations.

14.57 Section 1(2) provides as follows:

> *All sums paid or payable to any party in pursuance of the contract before the time when the parties were so discharged (in this Act referred to as 'the time of discharge') shall, in the case of sums so paid, be recoverable from him as money received by him for the use of the party by whom the sums were paid, and, in the case of sums so payable, cease to be so payable:*

> *Provided that, if the party to whom the sums were so paid or payable incurred expenses before the time of discharge in, or for the purpose of, the performance of the contract, the court may, if it considers it just to do so having regard to all the circumstances of the case, allow him to retain or, as the case may be, recover the whole or any part of the sums so paid or payable, not being an amount in excess of the expenses so incurred.*

It deals with situations where you either have paid or owe money to the other party. If you have paid money to the other party before the frustrating event occurred, you can get the money back, subject to an allowance for the expenses that the other party has incurred in or for the purpose of performing his side of the deal. If you owe money under an obligation that fell due before the time of discharge, you do not have to pay it. However, the other party can recover a sum in respect of the expenses that he has incurred (up to the amount that you owed).

14.58 The key issue here is how much the other party should get in respect of the expenses that he has incurred. One thing is clear: the onus of proof is on the recipient to demonstrate that he should be allowed to recover or retain some of the money because of the expenses that he has incurred. The courts have held that they have a broad discretion to decide on an appropriate figure. In *Gamerco SA v ICM/Fair Warning (Agency) Ltd* (1995), the claimant, a Spanish concert promoter, contracted with the first defendants, the agency organising the European tour of Guns N' Roses, a rock group, and the second defendants, the corporate persona of the group, to promote their concert in Madrid. The venue was declared unsafe by the local authority, frustrating the contracts. The claimant sued for the $412,500 that it had paid the second defendants, but the second defendants had spent $50,000 in relation to performing their side of the contract. Garland J held that all of the $412,500 could be recovered. The court, he said, had a broad discretion to do what was just in all the circumstances, and on the facts it was just for the claimant to recover all of the money that it had paid over. (Garland J was distinctly unimpressed with the defendant's evidence, which may explain his decision!)

14.59 Turning to the performance of obligations other than the payment of money, each party is still obliged to perform those obligations which fell due before the occurrence of the frustrating event. So for example, if I was obliged to deliver some goods to you on 14 July but failed to do so, and the contract was frustrated on 18 July, this would not release me from my obligation to deliver the goods. So by failing to do so, I am still in breach of contract.

14.60 If I have performed obligations other than the payment of money to the other party (for example, by providing services or supplying goods), I may be able to recover money in respect of this performance under s 1(3) of the Act, which reads:

> Where any party to the contract has, by reason of anything done by the other party thereto in, or for the purpose of, the performance of the contract, obtained a valuable benefit (other than a payment of money to which the last foregoing subsection applies) before the time of discharge there shall be recoverable from him by the said other party such sum (if any), not exceeding the value of the said benefit to the party obtaining it, as the court considers just, having regard to all the circumstances of the case and, in particular,
>
> (a) the amount of any expenses incurred before the time of discharge by the benefited party in, or for the purpose of, the performance of the contract, including any sums paid or payable by him to any other party in pursuance of the contract and retained or recoverable by that party under the last foregoing subsection, and
>
> (b) the effect, in relation to the said benefit, of the circumstances giving rise to the frustration of the contract.

So where I have conferred a 'valuable benefit' on the other party (other than by paying money), I can recover such sum as is 'just' in all the circumstances. To work out the just sum, we must first value the benefit received by the other party. This is the maximum figure that the court could allow me to recover. In order to arrive at the 'just sum', this figure may need to be reduced to take account of factors such as those listed in paras (a) and (b), one of which is the amount that the other party has spent in performing or preparing to perform his side of the contract.

14.61   Accordingly, the first issue is how we should value the benefit that I have conferred. The first difficulty we encounter here is to *identify* the benefit in question. This is a problem in relation to the provision of services. If I build some machinery for you, is the benefit in question the machinery that I have built or the services that I have provided? In other words, is the value of the benefit the value of the machines to you or the amount that I have spent in providing my services? It was held by Goff J in *BP Exploration Co (Libya) Ltd v Hunt (No 2)* (1979) that generally we should look at the value of the end-product of the services, not the services themselves. Goff J recognised an exception to this rule in situations where there is no end-product, for example where I just contract to offer you advice. In such situations, we must place a value on the services themselves. He also emphasised that it is the value to the other party that counts, so if you contract with me to have your wall painted a horrible colour, this painted wall has value to you, even if it would not to the average person.

14.62   The principal problem that has arisen under s 1(3) is where the factors in limbs (a) and (b) fit in. These factors require us to take into account the effect of the frustrating event on the benefit that I have conferred and the expenses that the other party has incurred in relation to performing his side of the deal. It appears from the wording of the section that they should be taken into account in working out the just sum, not in the valuation of the benefit. Imagine I start work on building an extension to your house; I get halfway through, so the house has risen in value by £10,000, when the house burns down through no fault of either of us. From the wording of s 1(3), you would think that we would say that the value of the benefit I conferred on you was £10,000. *Then* we would take into account the effect of the frustrating event (the house burning down) and any expenses incurred by the other party, when working out whether this figure should be reduced to reach the 'just sum' that I can recover. This seems fair: it allows the court some flexibility in taking account of the house burning down. It does not have to award £10,000: it can award any figure between £10,000 and £0.

14.63   However, Goff J complicated matters in *Hunt* by holding the contrary: that we take into account limbs (a) and (b) of s 1(3) at the earlier stage of valuing the benefit, rather than at the stage of working out whether this figure needs to be reduced to reach the 'just sum'. In other words, we value the benefit not at the time that the benefit was received, but after the frustrating event has occurred. So in our example, we would have to take account of the effect of the house burning down on the benefit when valuing the benefit received; that is, we would value my work *after* the house has burnt down. This would mean that the value of the benefit would be £0, so I would recover nothing. There are two problems with this interpretation. First, the wording of s 1(3) suggests that the factors mentioned in limbs (a) and (b) are to be taken into account when determining the just sum, not the value of the benefit (Virgo (2015)). Second, this interpretation also allows the court greater flexibility, as the example illustrates, in deciding what effect the frustrating event should have on the sum that the claimant can recover. It seems unfair, and contrary to the intention of the Act, that I should automatically receive nothing for my work in the example.

14.64 Having calculated the value of the benefit, how do we work out what sum it would be just to award the claimant? Goff J suggested in *Hunt* that the guiding principle here must be the need to prevent 'the unjust enrichment of the defendant at the [claimant]'s expense'. While the Court of Appeal in *Hunt* declined to interfere with the way that Goff J had worked out the just sum, they made a thinly veiled criticism of Goff J for reading words into the Act that were not there. They also suggested that the trial judge had a very broad discretion in deciding what was 'just'. If the arguments in para **14.63** are correct, we should take into account limbs (a) and (b) in working out what sum it would be just to award. These factors are not exhaustive (s 1(3) just requires regard to be had to these two factors 'in particular'). It would seem fair to look at the conduct of the parties; however, this factor was held to be irrelevant by Goff J. It is submitted that the matter might require reconsideration: for example, if one party had an opportunity to reduce the loss he would suffer but did not take it, it is suggested that this should be taken into account (Virgo (2015)).

14.65 It should be noted that not all work done by one party in performing or preparing to perform the contract will fall under s 1(3), because of the requirement in the section that the work confer a valuable benefit on the other party. For example, if I contract to build you a factory and I have to buy particular tools and machinery to do so, but the contract is frustrated before I begin building. Despite the fact that I have spent money to put myself in a position to start work, I cannot recover in respect of this under s 1(3) because I have not conferred a valuable benefit upon you.

14.66 By way of conclusion, we have seen that there are problems in deciding how much the other party should get in respect of the expenses he has incurred, and problems in working out how to value benefits other than the payment of money. These difficulties stem at least in part from the difficulty of working out what the rationale behind the Act is: what is its purpose? Its purpose may be to apportion the loss suffered by the parties. This would suggest that we look at the loss incurred by the parties and determine how much it is fair to expect each party to bear. However, the Act does not achieve this aim perfectly: for example, not all work done falls within the scope of s 1(3) (see para **14.60**). Alternatively, the purpose of the Act may be to prevent the unjust enrichment of the other party, as suggested by Goff J in *Hunt*. Yet this interpretation too is strained. There is a need for clearer legislation that provides more guidance to judges as to how it should be interpreted. The issue is what rationale should underpin such legislation. There are a number of advantages in basing it on loss apportionment, as McKendrick (1990) argues: neither party is at fault so why should one party be left worse off as a result of circumstances beyond their control? Inevitably, though, there are a number of problems with this concept as well (Virgo (2015)). Perhaps we must accept that there is unlikely to be a perfect solution to the remedial implications of a frustrated contract!

OVERVIEW

1   Issues of frustration arise where circumstances change after the contract has been entered into, which show that an assumption held by both parties at the time of contracting no longer applies. As in the case of common mistake, English law is very reluctant to let a party escape from a bargain where there has not been any wrongdoing by the other party. So the doctrine of frustration is a narrow one.

2   The currently favoured test requires three conditions to be fulfilled in order for a change of circumstances after the time of contracting to frustrate the contract:

   ●   the event must make performance of the contract 'radically different' from the performance that was contracted for;

   ●   the contract must not deal with what should happen on the occurrence of such an event; and

   ●   the event in question must not have been caused by either party: they must not have brought it on themselves.

3   It is arguable that the 'radical change' test is not extremely helpful in explaining the case law. It seems that what lies at the heart of the cases is the issue of whether the parties made a joint assumption when contracting that has turned out to be incorrect, or whether it was only one party who made the assumption. Only in the former case will the contract be frustrated.

4   Frustration only applies when an event occurs for which the parties have not allocated the risk in their contract. Commonly, a contract will expressly provide what is to happen when something unlikely occurs, for example by means of a *force majeure* clause, or else it is possible to imply a term allocating the risk to one party or the other. In such cases, there is no room for the doctrine of frustration, which is why in practice cases of frustration are very rare.

5   Where a contracting party has brought things on herself, the case for relief is not strong. So if it was the contracting party's act that caused the event which she now alleges has frustrated the contract, she will often be prevented from successfully claiming that the contract has been frustrated. If a contracting party's act is deliberate, this will certainly prevent frustration. If the act was merely negligent, the answer is less clear, but it appears that in an appropriate case this may also prevent frustration.

6   Frustration automatically brings a contract to an end. The parties are released from obligations that would have fallen due after the frustrating event occurred but are still bound by those obligations that fell due before the date of frustration (although this latter proposition is qualified by the Law Reform (Frustrated Contracts) Act 1943 in the case of the obligation to pay money).

7   A contracting party can recover sums paid before the date of frustration, subject to a possible deduction for the expenses incurred by the other party in performing or preparing to perform the contract (s 1(2) of the 1943 Act). If she owed money to the other party under an obligation that fell due before the date of frustration, this money is no longer

payable, but the other party may be able to recover a sum to reflect the expenses he has incurred in performing or preparing to perform the contract (s 1(2)).

8   If the contracting party has conferred a 'valuable benefit' on the other party before the date of frustration (other than by paying him money), she can recover such sum as is 'just', having regard to all the circumstances, particularly those factors mentioned in s 1(3)(a) and (b) of the Act (s 1(3)). The court has a broad discretion to decide what sum is 'just'.

FURTHER READING

Beatson 'Increased Expense and Frustration' Chapter 6 in *Consensus Ad Idem* (1996)

Capper 'More Muddle on Mistake' [2008] LMCLQ 264

Morgan *Great Debates in Contract* (2015) pp 128–39

Smith 'Contracts—Mistake, Frustration and Implied Terms' (1994) 110 LQR 400

SELF-TEST QUESTIONS

1   When will a contract be discharged for frustration?

2   Do you think that the 'radical change of obligation' test is a helpful way of explaining the cases? If not, what would you replace it with?

3   Was *The Super Servant Two* (1990) correctly decided?

4   How do you work out whether you can recover under s 1(3) of the Law Reform (Frustrated Contracts) Act in respect of the services that you have provided before the contract was frustrated?

5   Hotdog contracts with Ivor to hire him his reception suite and to provide the catering for 200 guests for the wedding of Ivor's daughter Judy to Keith, which is to be held on the afternoon of 1 May. Ivor makes a pre-payment of £2,000 and agrees to pay the balance of £5,000 on the morning of the wedding. On 25 April, by which time Hotdog has made the wedding cake and procured supplies of champagne but has not prepared any of the food for the reception, Keith is very seriously injured in a road accident and admitted to hospital, where he lies in a coma. Ivor telephones this news to Hotdog on the same day and tells him that the wedding is off. Hotdog replies: 'That's your business: you are paying me to put on a reception and so far as I'm concerned the show goes on.' Hotdog prepares the food and makes all the other arrangements for the reception, but no guests come. (a) Is Ivor entitled to the return of the £2,000, or any other sum? (b) Is Hotdog entitled to claim the £5,000, or any other sum?

For hints on how to answer question 5, please see the online resources at **www.oup.com/uk/sullivan8e/**.

15 Discharge of a contract for breach

SUMMARY

This chapter considers how a contract can be discharged by one party following breach or in-complete performance by the other party. It explores situations in which the specified order of performance makes one party's performance conditional on performance by the other party of certain obligations (entire obligations). It then considers the classification of terms into conditions and innominate terms, the difference between them, how to distinguish them, and their respective advantages and disadvantages. It covers repudiation and anticipa-tory breach, the innocent party's option to elect whether to accept or reject the repudiation, and the implications of both choices.

15.1 Breach of contract always gives the innocent party the right to claim damages (see Chapter 16). However, the innocent party may in certain circumstances *also* have the option of withholding his own performance or bringing the contract to an end because of the other party's breach. Three introductory points are worth remembering. First, breach of contract does not automatically bring a contract to an end, however serious it may be. It merely gives the innocent party an *option* to terminate the contract (although in practice he may not have much choice in the matter). This was described in *Soares v Beazer Investments Ltd* (2004) as 'a fundamental principle of the law of contract'. In fact it is just one of a number of situations in the law of contract in which one party must make an election of some kind; the general principle of election at common law was summarised by Lord Goff in *The Kanchenjunga* (1990). Second, termination of a contract for breach is not the same as 'rescission'. As we saw in Chapter 9, rescission means setting a contract aside *ab initio* because of a defect in its formation, such as misrepresentation, whereas terminating a contract for breach is *prospective* only. It is important not to con-fuse the two, as the Court of Appeal reaffirmed in *Howard-Jones v Tate* (2011). The use of the term 'rescission' in this context is confusing and should be avoided. Third, it is not always easy to tell if one party has breached the contract. This will require analysis of the express terms of the contract, which may be strict or may set a lesser standard (such as requiring the contracting party to exercise reasonable care), and also consideration of the question of implied terms (see paras **7.69–7.97**).

Withholding performance

Conditions precedent

15.2 Sometimes one party's obligation is *conditional* on something else: put another way, his obligation to perform is subject to a *condition precedent*. Often, this condition precedent is something the other party has promised to achieve, so that failure to perform the condition is itself a breach of contract, but other times the condition precedent is something separate. For example, I might promise to sell you goods if you obtain an export licence for them: you have not *promised* that you will obtain an export licence, so I cannot sue you for damages if you do not. But nor am I obliged to sell you the goods, because the condition for my obligation has not been satisfied. The concern is whether I must perform, not whether I can sue for damages.

15.3 The modern meaning of 'condition' has become divorced from this sense of the order of performance (see paras **15.15-15.19**), but the traditional approach remains important in unusual cases where a contractual obligation is interpreted as being 'entire', which simply means it must be performed in full as a condition of the other party's obligations arising at all.

Entire obligations

15.4 Sometimes the appropriate interpretation of what the parties have agreed is that one party must completely finish before the other's obligation (usually to pay the price) arises. 'If a man engages to carry a box of cigars from London to Birmingham, it is an entire contract and he cannot throw the cigars out of the carriage half-way there and ask for half the money' (*Re Hall & Barker* (1878) per Sir George Jessel). But it is relatively rare for an obligation to be construed as 'entire', not least because this puts all the risk onto one party, who must perform in full before the other side has to perform or, more commonly, pay anything at all. For example, in *Re Hall & Barker* itself, the judge refused to construe a solicitor's retainer to act in relation to winding up a bankrupt's estate in that way. The parties cannot have intended 'that a solicitor should engage to act for an indefinite number of years, winding up estates, without receiving any payment on which he can maintain himself.' So whether an obligation is entire depends on what the parties must have intended, judged objectively, looking at all the circumstances.

15.5 In *Cutter v Powell* (1795) a slave ship was sailing from Kingston (Jamaica) to Liverpool. Before the voyage, the master engaged C as second mate, promising to pay him 30 guineas ten days after arriving in Liverpool, provided he did his duty as second mate for the whole voyage. C died a couple of weeks before arriving in Liverpool and the court held that his estate was entitled to nothing, not even a proportion of the 30 guineas. Serving as second mate as far as Liverpool was a 'condition precedent' of his earning the lump sum—in other words, it was an entire obligation. Even in 1795 this conclusion was unusual, since sailors were normally engaged for a weekly wage; it may be that the master deliberately offered C a lump sum of more than the usual wage but on an 'entire' basis, to discourage desertion (see Dockray (2001) for a detailed study of the case in context).

15.6 Notice that C's death was not itself a breach of contract, but it did prevent him ful-filling an entire obligation (today a remedy would be available under the Law Reform (Frustrated Contracts) Act 1943). More commonly, failure to perform an entire obli-gation will be a breach of contract. For example, in *Sumpter v Hedges* (1898), a builder contracted with D to build two houses plus stables on D's land for the sum of £565. The builder did part of the work (valued at £333), then ran out of money and abandoned the job. D finished the work at his own expense (using some building materials the builder had left behind). The builder sued for the price, or alternatively for a reasonable sum for the work completed, but the Court of Appeal held that he was entitled to nothing apart from a small sum for his building materials (see para **15.11**), because his obligation was entire and he had not completed it.

15.7 As has been said, the question of whether an obligation is entire is a matter of construing the contract and it is common for contracts to be drafted so as to make it clear that a particular obligation is *not* intended to be entire. For example, building contracts often make provision for instalment payments at different stages of the work. The courts will construe obligations in this way if they can, but sometimes the wording of the contract and the type of obligation make such a construction out of the question. But the courts have also developed another weapon—the so-called 'doctrine of substantial perform-ance'—to mitigate some of the hardship of construing an obligation as entire.

An exception for 'substantial performance'?

15.8 The builder in *Sumpter v Hedges* abandoned the work just over halfway through, but in other cases, it is more accurate to say that work subject to the entire obligation has been finished, but finished badly. In such cases, the courts tend to say that the entire obligation has been *substantially* performed, triggering the other party's obligation to pay the price, but subject to a reduction for damages for the defects. *Dakin & Co Ltd v Lee* (1916) was such a case. Pickford LJ said:

> What the plaintiffs have done is to perform the work which they had contracted to do, but they have done some part of it insufficiently and badly; and that does not disentitle them to be paid, but it does entitle the defendant to deduct such an amount as is suf-ficient to put that insufficiently done work into the condition in which it ought to have been under the contract.

15.9 This was applied in *Hoenig v Isaacs* (1952), where H was an interior decorator and furni-ture designer, who had a contract to renovate I's flat. When the work was done, I refused to pay the outstanding balance, alleging that the work was defective and thus H's entire obligation had not been performed. The Court of Appeal held that the defects were very minor, so gave judgment for the outstanding price less a small deduction, since H's obligation had been 'substantially performed'. The court observed that the result in *Cutter v Powell* would have been different if the sailor had completed the whole voyage but 'possibly through inadvertence, failed on some occasion in his duty as mate whereby some damage had been caused'.

15.10 Substantial performance is usually regarded as an 'exception' to the principle of entire obligations, but Treitel (2015) rationalises the law in a different way. He distinguishes between different obligations, explaining, for example, that a contract to build a house involves both an obligation as to quantity (a 'whole house'), which is entire, and an obligation as to quality, which is not. In other words, he regards the very notion of substantial performance of an entire obligation as contradictory—the meaning of 'entire' requires nothing less than full performance. This argument is attractive: after all, a builder who built nine-tenths of a house could not rely on substantial performance to claim nine-tenths of the price, whereas the defects in *Hoenig v Isaac* cost about one-tenth of the purchase price to repair, yet the price was earned. The problem is that, in practice, it is hard to disentangle 'not finishing' from 'finishing badly'. For example, in *Bolton v Mahadeva* (1972) Bolton completed the installation of a heating system, but it did not heat adequately and gave out fumes. The Court of Appeal held that Bolton was not entitled to any part of the contract price: the work was so defective as not to amount to substantial performance at all. For Sachs LJ, 'It is not merely that the work was shoddy, but it is the general ineffectiveness of it for its primary purpose that leads me to that conclusion.' Generally, the courts do use the notion of substantial performance of entire obligations when they want to prevent one party from wriggling out of paying anything for work by alleging trivial defects in it.

Acceptance of partial performance

15.11 Where the innocent party has actually *accepted* the partial performance, he will not be able to rely on the entire obligations rule to resist paying for it, but only where the innocent party actually had a choice in the matter—it then makes sense to imply that he must be willing to pay a reasonable price for it. In *Munroe v Butt* (1858) Lord Campbell contrasted a contract to make a piece of furniture with a contract to do building work on land. If the furniture maker does not comply with an entire obligation but the purchaser decides to accept the furniture anyway, he must pay for it. But it is very different where the contract involves building work:

> What is he [the owner] ... supposed to do? The contractor leaves an unfinished or ill-constructed building on his land ... yet it may be essential to the owner to occupy the residence.

This explains why the defendant in *Sumpter v Hedges* was obliged to pay for the materials left on the site but not for the building work itself. As the court said, 'the circumstances must be such as to give an option to the defendant to take or not to take the benefit of the work done.' The same reasoning is seen in s 25 of the Consumer Rights Act 2015 (CRA) which provides that, in a consumer sale of goods contract, where the seller delivers a quantity of goods less than he contracted to sell, the buyer may reject them, but if the buyer accepts the goods he must pay for them at the contract rate. Non-consumers have equivalent protection in s 30 of the Sale of Goods Act 1979, except that a non-consumer buyer has no right to reject if the shortfall is so slight that it would be unreasonable to do so.

Should the law be reformed?

15.12 Many commentators dislike the notion of entire obligations, pointing out that in *Sumpter v Hedges* the consequence of construing the builder's obligation as entire was that he earned absolutely nothing for doing at least part of the work: the owner received the benefit of a partly completed building, with no obligation to pay anything for it. So perhaps, to prevent such 'unjust enrichment' in this situation, the builder should be entitled to receive a reasonable sum for the work he did. The Law Commission's Report *Pecuniary Restitution on Breach of Contract* (No 121 (1983)) agreed, recommending that the party who has not fully performed an entire obligation and who therefore cannot claim the price, should nonetheless be entitled to a reasonable sum, regarded as a restitutionary remedy to reverse the owner's unjust enrichment. Unusually, this Report (which has never been implemented) was not unanimous, but contained a 'dissent' by Brian Davenport QC.

15.13 Despite the hardship caused to contractors if an obligation is held to be entire, it is suggested that Mr Davenport was right to dissent. First, more is needed for a restitutionary remedy than merely identifying that someone has been 'enriched'. There must also be a ground of restitution (like mistake)—put another way, the enrichment must be 'unjust'. One suggestion is that the builder could rely on 'failure of consideration', because he received nothing for the work, but there is no failure of consideration if this outcome is what the contract provided. A related objection (seen in the reasoning in *Cutter v Powell*) is that restitutionary remedies must be subsidiary to, and must not subvert, the contractual regime. It is obvious that, if a contract *expressly* provides that payment is not due unless the work is finished in full, a restitutionary remedy for partial performance would be out of the question. But if an obligation is interpreted as entire, the effect is that the contract means precisely the same. Finally, there are practical reasons not to give defaulting contractors a remedy in such cases. Most written building contracts provide for the builder to be paid in stages and so entire obligations are only likely to feature in informal domestic building jobs, where there is a major practical problem of 'cowboy' builders leaving jobs unfinished. The Law Commission's proposals would take away the aggrieved householder's only bargaining weapon in such a case, of withholding payment until the job is finished.

15.14 The status of the entire obligations approach derived from the rule in *Sumpter v Hedges* was considered by the Court of Appeal in *Multiplex Constructions (UK) Ltd v Cleveland Bridge UK Ltd* (2010), where it was argued that the court should not follow *Sumpter v Hedges* on the basis that it had been subject to academic criticism and that the law of restitution had moved on considerably since it was decided. But the Court of Appeal did not agree. As Sir Anthony May P put it:

> I am quite unpersuaded that this court should disregard Sumpter v Hedges. True it is that it has been subjected to academic criticism and was the subject of recommenda- tions from the Law Commission. But the Law Commission recommendations have not been taken into legislation and, as importantly, the [subsequent restitutionary case law] ... cannot possibly be taken as overruling Sumpter v Hedges.

For further cogent arguments against a restitutionary remedy for part performance of an entire obligation, see McFarlane and Stevens (2002).

Termination of the contract for breach

15.15 There are two distinct situations in which an innocent party can terminate a con- tract because of the other party's breach. The first involves straightforward breach, in the sense of defective performance or non-performance. Here, the question of whether the innocent party can terminate the contract, as well as claiming damages, depends on the *classification* of the term which has been breached. The second cat- egory is generally called 'repudiation' of the contract, which means that one party has pulled out of or 'renounced' the contract, either by words or by conduct. This second category has an interesting extra dimension, because it is possible to repudi- ate a contract *in advance of* the time fixed for performance (known as 'anticipatory breach').

Breach of condition or serious breach of an innominate term

15.16 One of the peculiarities of English law is that the question of whether the innocent party can terminate the contract because of the other party's breach is usually said to depend on what sort of *term* has been breached. The original Sale of Goods Act (1893) reflected this, dividing terms in sale of goods contracts into two distinct categories: 'conditions', any breach of which gave the innocent party the option to terminate the contract, and 'warranties', breach of which never gave the innocent party the option to terminate the contract. Over time, this came to be regarded as a comprehensive way of categorising contractual terms generally.

15.17   However, the idea that all terms could be rigidly and exhaustively divided into these two categories was probably a nineteenth-century misreading of earlier law. Before then, the relevant division was between different forms of action, not different types of term. In the Middle Ages, a party alleged that a 'condition' had not been performed so as to resist paying the price (in the sense discussed at para **15.2**), but brought a trespassory action for 'breach of warranty' to claim damages. As Ibbetson (1999) points out, terms would not have been defined '*ab initio* either as conditions or as warranties; some warranties were conditions and some conditions were warranties, and whether a term was described as one or the other depended wholly on the remedy that the party was seeking'. Moreover, by the eighteenth century at least, the courts allowed a party to escape from a contract for a very serious failure in performance (one that 'went to the root of the contract'), and this did not depend on the prior categorisation of the term breached as a 'condition'. Indeed, the test was the same even if the failure of performance was not itself a breach.

15.18   In the seminal case of *Hong Kong Fir Shipping Ltd v Kisen Kaisha Ltd* (1962) the Court of Appeal demonstrated convincingly that the Sale of Goods Act twofold distinction between 'conditions' and 'warranties' had never been, and should not be regarded as, exhaustive. There is, in addition, a third category of term, breach of which does not automatically entitle the innocent party to terminate the contract, but only if the *consequences* of the breach are very serious, labelled 'innominate' or 'intermediate' terms. In *Hong Kong Fir*, D chartered a ship from the owners for 24 months. It was a term of the charter contract that the owners promised that the ship was seaworthy. In fact the ship was not seaworthy, because it was undermanned, the engine-room staff were incompetent, and the engine needed repairs (hire was not payable for any period during which the ship was being repaired). D purported to terminate the charter, arguing that the term as to seaworthiness was a *condition*. But the Court of Appeal did not agree, observing that the seaworthiness term 'can be broken by the presence of trivial defects easily and rapidly remediable as well as by defects which inevitably result in a total loss of the vessel.' In other words, it would be unsatisfactory if the only choice as to the categorisation of the term were between 'condition', which would entitle D to terminate the contract however trivial the breach, and 'warranty', which would never entitle D to terminate the contract, however serious the breach. As Diplock LJ explained:

> There are, however, many contractual undertakings of a more complex character which cannot be categorised as being 'conditions' or 'warranties' ... Of such undertakings all that can be predicated is that some breaches will and others will not give rise to an event which will deprive the party not in default of substantially the whole benefit which it was intended that he should obtain from the contract; and the legal consequences of a breach of such an undertaking ... depend upon the nature of the event to which the breach gives rise and do not follow automatically from a prior classification of the undertaking as a 'condition' or a 'warranty' (emphasis added).

15.19 So we now have three categories:

Condition:	breach *always* gives innocent party option to terminate contract and claim damages;
Innominate term:	innocent party can always claim damages and *might* also be able to terminate contract if the *effect of breach is serious enough*;
Warranty:	breach *never* gives innocent party option to terminate contract; he can *only* claim damages.

Deciding whether a term is a condition or an innominate term

15.20 The decision as to the appropriate categorisation of a term presents a stark choice between the 'certainty + inflexibility' of a condition *versus* the 'flexibility + uncertainty' of an innominate term. A good starting point is to adopt the four categories identified by the Court of Appeal in *BS & N Ltd v Micado Shipping Ltd (The 'Seaflower')* (2001), in which a term is likely to be categorised as a condition.

15.21 First, a term will be a condition 'if it is expressly so provided by statute'. The most common example involves various terms which are implied into contracts for the sale of goods by statute. Non-consumer sale of goods contracts are governed by the Sale of Goods Act 1979, and the statute itself designates certain implied terms as conditions (for example, that goods sold by description comply with the description under s 13(1), and, for business sales, that the goods are of satisfactory quality under s 14(2) and are reasonably fit for the buyer's purpose under s 14(3)). This means that, however minor the breach, the buyer is entitled to reject the goods (unless under s 15A the breach is so slight that it would be unreasonable for the buyer to do so). For consumer sale of goods contracts, the label 'condition' is no longer used in the Consumer Rights Act 2015 regime, but this does not matter as the CRA now provides a comprehensive set of remedies for the buyer in the event of the seller's breach, including the right to reject.

15.22 In *Arcos Ltd v EA Ronaasen & Son* (1933), buyers contracted to buy a quantity of timber staves, to be used for making cement barrels. The staves were sold by description, namely that they were to be half an inch thick. In fact most were 9/16ths of an inch and the buyers rejected them. The breach was trivial, in that the staves were still perfectly adequate for making barrels and the buyers' real reason for rejecting the staves was that their market price had fallen below the contract price. But the House of Lords held that this did not matter, because the statutory implied term that goods comply with their description is a condition. If the facts of *Arcos* arose today, it would be caught by s 15A of the Sale of Goods Act, which restricts the right of a (non-consumer) buyer to reject goods for breach of condition (see para **15.21**). But this is not tantamount to changing the statutory implied conditions into innominate terms, since the buyer only loses the right to reject the goods where the breach is so slight that it would be unreasonable to reject, whereas breach of an innominate term would only give such a right where the breach was very serious.

15.23 Secondly, a term will be a condition 'if it has been so categorised as the result of previous judicial decision (although it has been said that some of the decisions on this matter are excessively technical and are open to re-examination by the House of Lords).' Commercial contracts often contain standard terms, so that the same clauses regularly appear in contracts of the same type. Where a standard term has been categorised as a condition in a prior precedent, it makes commercial sense to stick to that. For example, a standard term in international sale of goods contracts requires the buyer to give the seller a specified minimum number of days' notice that the shipping vessel is ready to load. In *Bunge Corpn v Tradax Export SA Panama* (1981), the House of Lords held that this 'notice of readiness' obligation is a condition, so that a seller may terminate the contract even if the buyer is only slightly late in giving notice and this delay causes no prejudice to the seller. One important reason was that earlier precedents had categorised the same standard term as a condition, so commercial assumptions would be unsettled by any change to its categorisation. The Court of Appeal in *The Mihalis Angelos* (1971) had earlier adopted similar reasoning, when an equivalent standard clause in a ship charterparty was construed as a condition, noting that the leading book on charterparties for practitioners described the term as a condition, without criticism.

15.24 Thirdly, a term will be a condition 'if it is so designated in the contract or if the consequences of its breach, that is, the right of the innocent party to treat himself as discharged, are provided for expressly in the contract.' So the parties can in principle elevate a term to the status of condition by expressly providing as such in their contract, although the courts require very clear evidence that this was what the parties intended. It is relatively straightforward where, as in *Stocznia Gdynia SA v Gearbulk Holdings Ltd* (2009), the parties spell out that breach of the relevant term entitles the other party to terminate the contract. In *Stocznia*, the question in issue was whether that express contractual right to terminate also carries the right to damages for loss of bargain, as are available where the claimant terminates at common law following a repudiation, which the Court of Appeal unanimously answered in the affirmative.

15.25 However, the mere use of the word 'condition' is unlikely to suffice, particularly where the rest of the terms and surrounding circumstances point away from this interpretation. For example, in *Schuler AG v Wickman Machine Tool Sales Ltd* (1973) a minor term (clause 7) was described as a 'condition'. But the contract also contained another common clause, clause 11, allowing either party to terminate the contract if the other committed a *material* breach of any term. W breached clause 7, but not in a material way, so the express contractual right to terminate in clause 11 was not triggered. Could S terminate in any event, on the basis that clause 7 was described as a 'condition'? The House of Lords held that the parties did not intend the word 'condition' in clause 7 to have its technical meaning, since this would be inconsistent with the regime in clause 11. In other words, its meaning is not considered in a vacuum, but by reference to the document as a whole:

> The fact that a particular construction leads to a very unreasonable result must be a
> relevant consideration. The more unreasonable the result, the more unlikely it is that the

parties can have intended it and if they do intend it the more necessary it is that they shall make that intention abundantly clear.

15.26 A good example of express stipulation by the parties is where an obligation specifies the time of performance *and* provides that 'time is of the essence'. This wording means that the time stipulation is a condition, so that even a negligible delay in performance entitles the innocent party to terminate the contract. For example, in *Union Eagle Ltd v Golden Achievement Ltd* (1997) the contract for the sale of a flat provided that completion must take place before 5 p.m. on a particular date, that time was of the essence and that if the purchaser failed to comply, the seller could retain the purchaser's deposit. The purchaser was ten minutes late with the cheque, the seller refused to accept it, and forfeited the purchaser's deposit. This may seem harsh, but the Privy Council agreed that the seller was entitled to do so. Indeed, their Lordships' sympathy was with the seller, which had been unable to resell the flat for years while the purchaser's claim was litigated.

15.27 Interestingly, even if the contract does not specify it initially, following a breach time can effectively be made 'of the essence' by the innocent party serving notice to this effect, as long as the other party is given a reasonable time within which to remedy the breach (see *Behzadi v Shaftesbury Hotels Ltd* (1992), *Sentinel International Ltd v Cordes* (2008), and *North Eastern Properties v Coleman* (2010)). This commonly arises in a land transaction, where the purchaser has failed to complete the purchase on the contractual date and the vendor serves a 'notice to complete', and is an incredibly useful device. Despite the view of the Court of Appeal in *Urban 1 (Blonk Street) Ltd v Ayres* (2013) to the contrary, this is almost universally regarded as 'making time of the essence'. This does not mean that one party, here the vendor, can unilaterally alter the categorisation of a contractual term into a condition, but it comes to much the same thing in practice because it means that if the purchaser still fails to complete after the date specified in the notice, the vendor can terminate the contract immediately (see Carter, Courtney, and Tolhurst (2017)). The (*obiter*) suggestion in *Samarenko v Dawn Hill House Ltd* (2011) that, on serving such a notice, the innocent party will still only be entitled to terminate if the other party's failure to comply with the notice within a reasonable time is itself a serious breach, seems equally out of line with principle, defeats the object of the notice regime, and is hard to reconcile with the weight of authority, as Carter (2013) explains.

15.28 Fourthly, a term will be a condition 'if the nature of the contract, of the subject-matter or the circumstances of the case lead to the conclusion that the parties must, by necessary implication, have intended that the innocent party would be discharged from further performance of his obligations in the event that the term was not fully and precisely complied with.' So another reason for the results in *The Mihalis Angelos* and *Bunge v Tradax* was that, in each case, the commercial nature of the contract (an international sale contract) and the obligation (a time stipulation) and all the other circumstances suggested that the parties intended that it should be a condition. The courts thought it would be intolerable if the innocent party had to guess whether the other was *sufficiently* late to entitle it to terminate, and unlikely to be what the parties intended. For similar reasons, in *Samarenko v Dawn Hill House Ltd* (2011) the Court of Appeal held that a term in a contract for the sale of land obliging the purchaser to pay a deposit once planning permission was obtained was a condition, as such terms would almost invariably be, entitling the vendor to terminate the contract immediately, an analysis approved by the Court of Appeal in *Firodi Shipping Ltd v Griffon Shipping LLC* (2013).

15.29 However, even in the commercial context, the courts sometimes decide that the circumstances point to an innominate term. *Bunge v Tradax* was distinguished in *Spar Shipping A/S v Grand China Logistics Holding (Group) Co Ltd* (2016), in which the Court of Appeal suggested obiter (see para **15.40** for the actual decision in the case) that the obligation on charterers to pay the charter hire punctually is an innominate term—unlike international sales, where a chain of contracts tends to be involved that means certainty is the most important value, here Gross LJ could not 'conceive that the parties intended … that a single payment of hire a few minutes late would entitle Spar to throw up a five- or three-year charterparty and claim loss of bargain damages'. The innominate term categorisation is particularly tempting for the court where an innocent party is relying on a trivial breach in order to terminate for an ulterior reason. In *The Hansa Nord* (1975) a contract for the sale of citrus pulp pellets (which buyers planned to use as animal feed) contained an express term whereby the seller promised that the shipment would be made in good condition. On arrival, some of the pellets were damaged, although still perfectly adequate for use as animal feed. But the market price of citrus pulp had fallen since the date of the contract, so the buyers asserted that the term was a condition and rejected the goods. The Court of Appeal held the express term was not a condition, merely an innominate term. The main reason was that, like the seaworthiness term in *Hong Kong Fir*, it could be breached in an array of different ways, some trivial, some serious. Since the cargo was still perfectly satisfactory as animal feed, the breach did not deprive the buyers of substantially the whole benefit of the contract. Indeed the buyers, having rejected the cargo, had immediately bought it back from the sellers for less than a third of the contract price and used it for animal feed as planned. Notice that the term in issue in the case was an *express* promise of good condition, not the Sale of Goods Act implied term as to the quality of goods. That implied term *is* a condition, but the Court of Appeal held that it had not been breached on the facts, a conclusion criticised by Weir (1976).

15.30 Finally, there may be other good commercial reasons for construing a particular obligation as a condition (discussed in *The Seaflower* (2001) itself). For example, in a contract giving one party the option to acquire goods of very fluctuating market value, the time for performance is likely to be construed as a condition even if the parties have not expressly specified this (see *Hare v Nicholl* (1966), concerning an option to purchase shares).

Advantages and disadvantages

15.31 As has been said, the difference between conditions and innominate terms represents a clear point of tension between opposing values of certainty and flexibility. The 'rediscovery' of innominate terms in *Hong Kong Fir* was applauded, since as Diplock LJ observed, many terms are complex, so termination might be justified for one sort of breach but not for another sort: it is unduly simplistic to imagine that the answer can always be found in the prior classification of the type of term. Categorisation of a term as a condition means that the innocent party has the right to terminate for a trivial breach of condition, even (as in *Arcos*) cynically for an ulterior motive, which troubles those who argue for a more general principle of good faith in contractual dealing. On the other hand conditions have considerable advantages over innominate terms in the commercial context. First, it is much harder for the innocent party to decide how to react to breach of an innominate term than breach of a condition. As Weir (1976) noted:

> when the right to reject depended on the nature of the term in the contract which was broken, the innocent party simply had to go to the filing cabinet, consult the contractual document and then decide whether the term broken was a very serious one or not; this final step admittedly called for judgment, and there could be two views, but at any rate the requisite data were immediately and presently available. Now that the right to resile turns on the gravity of the consequences of the breach, the necessary data are not words but events, which might be in the South China Sea rather than in the head office where decisions are taken, and one will probably have to wait for them, since consequences tend to occur after their causes.

15.32   Second, where an innominate term is breached, an innocent party who regards the consequences as serious enough to justify termination of the contract runs the risk that, years later, the court might rule that he had misjudged the situation and that the breach was *not* sufficiently serious. This in turn means that the innocent party's purported termination was itself a repudiatory breach.

Any role for warranties?

15.33   The Sale of Goods Act (as amended by the CRA) preserves a third category of term, the 'warranty' (defined in s 61(1)), but outside this statutory context there may be very few true warranties. It is rare for a term to be so peripheral that it is impossible to imagine circumstances in which breach of it might have very serious consequences, so in practice the choice tends to be between conditions and innominate terms. Many old cases applied the label 'warranty' when deciding that the innocent party was not entitled to terminate the contract, but adopted reasoning that focused on the consequences of breach, so that the term would today be regarded as an innominate term. Other cases are unhelpful because the claim is merely for damages, so the label 'warranty' says nothing about the potential availability of a right to terminate. Nonetheless, the courts and commentators generally refer to a threefold categorisation of terms, so it is safest to do the same.

How to tell if breach of an innominate term justifies termination

15.34   As *Hong Kong Fir* makes clear, only a very serious breach of an innominate term will entitle the innocent party to terminate the contract. 'Serious' here refers to the consequences of the breach for the innocent party (rather than the deliberateness or manner of the breach), which must 'deprive the innocent party of substantially the whole benefit which it was intended that he should obtain from the contract'. Many students express surprise at the conclusion in *Hong Kong Fir* that the breach was not sufficiently serious to justify termination, pointing out that the ship needed significant repairs *and* had an incompetent crew. But the repairs were not going to take more than four months out of the two-year charter and, crucially, the charterers were not obliged to pay hire for any repair period. One way to explain the result is to say the charterers' expectations from the contract were still largely achievable. In contrast, *Aerial Advertising Co v Batchelors Peas Ltd (Manchester)* (1938) shows how the consequences of breach of a very minor term might, on unusual facts, be wholly prejudicial to the innocent party. A made a long-term contract with B to advertise B's product by flying a small plane over residential districts trailing the banner 'Eat Batchelors' Peas!'. A breached a term in the contract that it would confirm its route with B. Breach of this term would normally be inconsequential, but on this occasion A flew the plane over the centre of Salford, during the two-minute silence on Armistice Day! The adverse publicity had a disastrous effect on B's sales and the court held that B was entitled to terminate the contract. B's expectations from an advertising contract had been wholly dashed.

15.35   The test is slightly more difficult to apply where the innocent party wishes to terminate the contract because of lots of small breaches, arguing that they add up to a substantial failure of performance, but in essence the courts decide what the combined effect of the breaches is on the innocent party, taking into account the conduct of the defaulting party, as seen in *Decro Wall v Practitioners in Marketing* (1971). For example, in *Alan Auld Associates v Rick Pollard Associates* (2008) the Court of Appeal held that A's invariably late payments of the defendant's monthly invoices for technical services added up to repudiation of the agreement, which the defendant had accepted. The court took into account the fact that the breaches as to the time of payment were 'substantial, persistent and cynical' and that the defendant had complained repeatedly, but to no effect. In contrast, in *Valilas v Januzaj* (2014) the claimant dentist's failure to pay licence fees on time to the defendant (for occupying a room in the defendant's practice) did not amount to a repudiation, because it was always clear to the defendant that the claimant would pay once his NHS income was finalised, plus the defendant was unable to show any serious disadvantage from the delay. See also *Force India Formula One Team Ltd v Etihad Airways PJSC* (2010), where the Court of Appeal held that a series of steps to re-brand a racing car and replace the sponsor's logo was an 'accumulation of breaches' of the sponsorship agreement, amounting to a 'cumulative, continuing and accelerating repudiation'.

Repudiation and anticipatory breach

15.36   The other sort of situation in which the innocent party is entitled to terminate the contract is if the other party 'repudiates' it, which means wrongfully abandoning or renouncing the contract altogether. This may involve express words (like 'I want nothing

more to do with our contract'), or may be implied from conduct that is wholly inconsistent with the contract or renders performance impossible. Repudiation of this kind
was found by the Privy Council in *Sentinel International Ltd v Cordes* (2008), where
the claimant's conduct 'evinced an intention no longer to be bound by the contract' and
'showed a disregard … of its basic obligations which went to the root of the contract'.

15.37 Renunciation by express words is straightforward. A good example is *Frost v Knight*
(1872), dating from a time when an engagement to be married was a legally enforceable
contract. A young man got engaged, promising to marry his fiancée on the death of his
father, but later broke off the engagement. This undoubtedly amounted to an express
renunciation of the contract to marry his fiancée (the only live issue being whether the
fiancée could bring her action while the man's father was still alive, which it was held she
could do: see paras **15.41–15.44**).

15.38 Of course, the contract might give the parties the *right* to cancel in certain circumstances—in practice, express termination rights are common and extremely important
commercially—but a valid exercise of a contractual right to terminate is not a repudiation. Repudiation means a *wrongful* cancellation of the contract. It seems that, even
where a party misinterprets a contractual right to cancel and is not entitled to cancel
on the facts, the court will be reluctant to construe the party's cancellation as a repudiation of the contract. As Lord Wilberforce said in *Woodar Investment Development v
Wimpey Construction UK Ltd* (1980):

> It would be a regrettable development of the law of contract to hold that a party who bona
> fide relies upon an express termination clause should, by that fact alone, be treated as
> having repudiated his contractual obligations if he turns out to be mistaken as to his rights.

Likewise in *Eminence Property Developments Ltd v Heaney* (2010) the vendor of property served a contractual notice giving the purchaser ten working days to complete, but
by mistake miscalculated the date on which the notice expired, so purported to terminate the contract and forfeit the deposit after only eight working days. The purchaser argued that this was itself a repudiation by the vendor, but the Court of Appeal disagreed.
What the claimant had done had obviously been a mistaken application of the contract,
which would have been viewed as such by any reasonable person—it had not demonstrated an unequivocal intention to abandon the contract, required for a repudiation.

15.39 The same might sometimes not apply (as we saw in para **15.31**) where a contracting
party purports to cancel the contract thinking he is entitled to do so because of the
other party's breach (assuming either that a condition has been breached, or that it is an
innominate term and the breach is serious enough). If the court later takes a different
view of the facts, the innocent party's cancellation might itself be treated as a wrongful
repudiation, for which he must compensate the party originally in breach.

15.40 It is also possible to renounce a contract by implication, although this will not be lightly
inferred. The test was described in *General Billposting Co v Atkinson* (1909) as: 'Do the

acts and conduct of the party evince an intention no longer to be bound by the contract?' and in *Universal Cargo Carriers Corpn v Citati* (1957) as: 'whether the party renouncing has acted in such a way as to lead a reasonable person to the conclusion that he does not intend to fulfil his part of the contract.' As ever, this turns on the intention of the party, judged objectively. The test is strict: the conduct must be clear and give the impression that the contractor is renouncing all (or all his important) obligations in the contract. Otherwise almost any instance of defective performance or failure to perform an obligation would be construed as a renunciation of the whole contract. But in an appropriate case, this may well be the conclusion, as in *Spar Shipping A/S v Grand China Logistics Holding (Group) Co Ltd* (2016) in which charterers persistently failed to pay the charter hire punctually and there was little prospect of them ever being able to do so because the market had moved against them—judged objectively, this evinced an intention not to perform in a way which deprived the owners of substantially the whole benefit from the contract. This reminds us that renunciation is not about the defaulting party's subjective intention. Gross LJ in *Spar Shipping* cited a pithy dictum of Devlin J from *Universal Cargo Carriers*, 'Willingness in this context does not mean cheerfulness; it means simply an intent to perform. To say: "I would like to but I cannot" negatives intent just as much as "I will not".'

15.41 Repudiation by conduct may also involve one party making it *impossible* for himself to perform or continue to perform his obligations. For example, in *Lovelock v Franklyn* (1846) F contracted to assign his leasehold interest to L within seven years. Before the end of seven years, F assigned the lease to someone else and the court held this breach was a repudiation, since F's conduct had made it impossible for him to perform his contract with L. As in *Frost v Knight*, L was not obliged to wait until seven years had elapsed, but could terminate the contract and bring his action for damages immediately.

The anticipatory angle

15.42 It is clear from the cases already considered that repudiation can occur *before* the time fixed for performance, in which case it is known as an 'anticipatory breach'. Indeed, most of the authorities on repudiation involve anticipatory breach, a label which can be confusing. The relevant breach, which gives the innocent party the option to discharge the contract, is the *repudiation* itself, not the other party's eventual non-performance of the contract. And, as Dawson (1981) demonstrates, the repudiation is a breach of an *implied* term not to hinder or prevent the other party complying with its obligations under the contract, not the principal term containing the obligation to perform, pay the price or whatever. This is why, if the innocent party decides to terminate the contract, he or she may do so immediately, without the need to wait for the (now redundant) due date for performance to come and go before terminating and claiming damages.

15.43 A well-known example is *Hochster v De La Tour* (1853): D engaged H on 12 April to act as his courier and accompany him on an overseas tour, starting on 1 June. On 11 May D wrote to H saying he no longer required his services, an express renunciation of the contract. The court held that this repudiation gave H the right to terminate the contract and bring an action for damages immediately, even though performance was not due for three more weeks:

> It is surely much more rational, and more for the benefit of both parties, that, after the renunciation of the agreement by the defendant, the plaintiff should be at liberty to consider himself absolved from any future performance of it, retaining his right to sue for any damage he has suffered from the breach of it.

15.44 The rationale is to encourage mitigation. Potential losses are kept to a minimum by allowing the innocent party the option of terminating the contract as soon as it is clear that the other party is not going to perform when the time comes and claiming damages immediately. This occasionally gives rise to problems of *calculating* damages, since damages are being awarded in advance of the date for performance. For example, in *The Golden Victory* (2007) the House of Lords, by a majority, decided that damages payable to the shipowner for the charterer's repudiation before the end of the charter period should reflect the possibility that the charterer would, as things turned out, have terminated lawfully before the end of the charter anyway, pursuant to a war clause. For detailed analysis of this decision, see Mustill (2008). *The Golden Victory's* overriding compensatory approach to assessing damages for repudiation was applied in *Glory Wealth Shipping Pte Ltd v Korea Line Corpn* (2011), and by the Supreme Court in *Bunge SA v Nidera BV* (2015), discussed by Dawson (2016). In *Bunge*, sellers of Russian wheat crop purported to cancel the contract as soon Russia introduced an embargo on exports of wheat; although this amounted to a repudiation, because it was technically premature, the embargo continued and so the contract could have been lawfully cancelled under a 'prohibition clause' by the time delivery was due. The Supreme Court held that the buyers had therefore lost nothing, applied *The Golden Victory's* overriding compensatory principle and awarded no damages.

Innocent party's option to terminate contract

15.45 As *Hochster* makes clear, in theory the innocent party is *at liberty* to bring the contract to an end following a breach of condition, serious breach of an innominate term or a repudiation (together often referred to as a 'repudiatory breach'), but is not *obliged* to do so. This right to elect either to terminate or not to terminate is, in theory, a completely unfettered choice, just as where there is an *express* right to cancel in the contract, which the cancelling party can exercise as it pleases, without having to consider the interests of the other party, discussed by Foxton (2016). In practice, however, the innocent party may have little option but to terminate the contract. In many cases the innocent party will be unable to honour his continuing obligations without the cooperation of the party in breach. For example, if a landowner wrongfully orders a builder to cease work on his land, the builder simply cannot opt to continue to perform the contract, as to do so would amount to trespass (see *Hayes and another (t/a Orchard Construction) v Gallant* (2008)); similarly where an employer dismisses an employee in breach of contract, the employee cannot realistically elect to keep the contract alive and continue to present herself for work every morning. As the Court of Appeal explained in *Soares v Beazer Investments Ltd* (2004): 'in the real world of employment there is usually no room for debate about whether an employer's repudiation has been accepted by the employee.' But this does not mean that an employment contract is terminated automatically by the employer's repudiation—the employee may have no realistic choice but to accept the repudiation, but it is still her act of acceptance that terminates the contract, which remains alive until that choice is exercised, as the Supreme Court clarified in *Société Générale, London Branch v Geys* (2012).

15.46   A couple of complications should just be mentioned briefly. The first is the suggestion by Lord Reid in *White & Carter (Councils) Ltd v McGregor* (1962) that, even if the innocent party is able to perform their obligations without the cooperation of the other party, they may nonetheless not be entitled to keep the contract alive when they have 'no legitimate interest, financial or otherwise' in performance'. This dictum is very controversial, since it suggests a restriction on the innocent party's otherwise unfettered right to elect to keep the contract alive, and only applies in wholly exceptional circumstances. Its significance is remedial—whether an innocent party with no such legitimate interest, who nonetheless opted to keep the contract alive, is confined to a claim for damages rather than being entitled to claim the price—and for this reason is considered in more detail at paras **17.15–17.21**.

15.47   Secondly, we should note the Court of Appeal's controversial suggestion in *MSC Mediterranean Shipping Co SA v Cottonex Anstalt* (2016), that on the exceptional facts of the case, the contract terminated *automatically* in circumstances that amounted to a repudiatory breach. Cottonex hired containers owned by MSC to transport cotton to Bangladesh. The purchaser of the cotton paid for it but failed to collect it, and the port authorities in Bangladesh impounded the containers, which meant that Cottonex was unable to return them. MSC alleged that the contract required Cottonex to keep paying the hire fee until the containers were returned. This stalemate lasted for years, by which time the hire fee was more than four times the value of the containers. Leggatt J at first instance held that Cottonex had eventually repudiated the contract and although MSC had purportedly opted to reject it and keep the contract alive, it had no legitimate interest in doing so (applying Lord Reid's dictum mentioned in para **15.46**) and confined MSC to a claim for damages. The Court of Appeal reached the same conclusion by a different, unorthodox route: MSC's delay in redelivery had been so prolonged that the original contract had become 'incapable of performance' and so 'the innocent party simply cannot treat the contract as subsisting because it is no longer capable of performance as agreed'. Morgan (2017) has convincingly criticised this reasoning as being a 'difficult fit with supposedly basic propositions', since it envisages a peculiar hybrid between frustration (inapplicable on the facts because the contract allocated the risk of the relevant event onto the repudiating party) and 'true' repudiation which we know gives the innocent party the choice to keep the contract alive, and as placing reliance on Lord Sumption's dissent in *Société Générale* rather than the reasoning of the majority.

15.48 Returning to the usual position, you may find the language of the cases somewhat confusing. If the innocent party does not wish to terminate the contract, he is said to 'reject' the other party's repudiatory breach, but this does not mean that he is waiving it entirely, in the sense of treating it as if it were not a breach for all purposes, because he may still claim damages. In contrast, if the innocent party decides to terminate the contract, he is said to 'accept' the other party's repudiatory breach. Each option will be considered in turn.

Electing to 'reject the breach' and keep the contract alive

15.49 Until the innocent party decides what to do, the contract remains on foot, but once he has elected to keep the contract alive, that decision is irrevocable. So the court will not infer this drastic step lightly: only an unequivocal decision, in full knowledge of the circumstances of the repudiatory breach, will suffice. In *Yukong Line Ltd of Korea v Rendsburg Investments Corpn of Liberia* (1996) charterers purported to cancel the charter contract, prompting a telex from the owners urging the charterers to reconsider and honour their obligations. This was held not to be an election to affirm the contract. On the facts, the telex was a cry of protest and, far from unequivocally rejecting the repudiation, was merely stating how unacceptable the charterers' conduct was. Likewise, the Court of Appeal held in *Stocznia Gydnia SA v Gearbulk Holdings Ltd* (2009) that the claimant had not affirmed a shipbuilding contract, when the shipyard had failed to deliver the ships, by bringing a claim on an express 'refund guarantee' contained in the contract—the parties intended the refund guarantee to operate precisely when the contract was terminated and so relying on it did not represent an unequivocal decision by the claimant to affirm the contract. In contrast, in *Re Simoco Digital UK Ltd* (2004), the applicant contracted with the company to purchase telecommunications software, but later alleged that the company had repudiated and that it had elected to terminate the contract. However, after the alleged repudiation the applicant paid a further instalment of £15,000 towards the purchase price, which the judge held to be 'wholly inconsistent with it treating the contract as at an end and operated as an election to affirm the contract'.

15.50 It was famously declared in *Howard v Pickford Tool Co Ltd* (1951) that an 'unaccepted repudiation is a thing writ in water'. This vivid metaphor is almost entirely accurate. If the innocent party elects to keep the contract alive, it is as if the repudiation never occurred. Of course, where there has been an anticipatory breach and the contract is not terminated, the repudiating party is likely to breach again by not performing on the due date. For example, if one party says in January that he is pulling out of a contract due for performance in June and, when June comes round, he duly refuses to perform, the innocent party may claim damages. However, in the meantime, the contract is alive and the innocent party runs the risk of breaching his own obligations, whereupon he may (to use a colloquial phrase) 'kick himself' that he did not accept the other party's repudiation in January. He may likewise regret his decision to reject the repudiatory breach if the contract is subsequently frustrated, as in *Avery v Bowden* (1855). If this situation arose today, the innocent party might be able to argue that, had he opted instead to accept the repudiation and terminate the contract, the 'frustrating' event might have occurred anyway and thus should be taken into account in reducing his damages, since the reasoning in *The Golden Victory* (2007), discussed at para **15.44**, could in an appropriate case cover frustration as well as a contractual 'war clause'.

15.51 Finally, an innocent party who rejects a repudiation and keeps the contract alive runs the risk that the other party will later be able to invoke an express contractual right to terminate the contract, of which a good example is *Fercometal SARL v Mediterranean Shipping Co (The Simona)* (1989). A ship charterparty contract gave the charterers the express option to cancel if the vessel was not ready to load on or before 9 July. On 2 July, the owners requested an extension of the loading date to 13–16 July (this request for indulgence was not itself a repudiation). In response, the charterers purported to cancel the contract; this amounted to an anticipatory breach. However, the owners then telexed that the ship would indeed be ready to load on 8 July, thereby unequivocally electing *not* to accept the charterers' repudiation. Unfortunately for the owners, the ship was not ready to load on 8 July and so the charterers cancelled on 12 July pursuant to the express option in the contract. The House of Lords held that the charterers' cancellation was valid:

> The anticipatory breaches by the charterers not having been accepted by the owners as terminating the contract, the charter party survived intact with the right of cancellation unaffected. The vessel was not ready to load by close of business on the cancellation date viz. 9 July and the charterers were therefore entitled to and did give ... an effective notice of cancellation.

15.52 However, very occasionally, the courts will take some notice of the fact that one party committed a repudiatory breach, even where the innocent party opted to keep the contract alive. For example, an innocent party who *knows* of the other party's intention not to perform on the due date for performance (because he earlier purported to repudiate the contract) may be able to persuade the court to give a decree of specific performance in advance of the due date, as in *Hasham v Zenab* (1960). Of course, if it is the sort of contract for which specific performance is available, the innocent party's option to keep the contract alive in the face of a repudiatory breach is much more meaningful than normal.

15.53 A second, and more difficult, exception is rationalised on estoppel principles. In *The Simona*, Lord Ackner said:

> Of course it is always open to A, who has refused to accept B's repudiation of the contract, and thereby kept the contract alive, to contend that in relation to a particular right or obligation under the contract, B is estopped from contending that he, B, is entitled to exercise that right or that he, A, has remained bound by that obligation. If B represents to A that he no longer intends to exercise that right or requires that obliga-

tion to be fulfilled, then clearly B cannot be heard thereafter to say that he is entitled to exercise that right or that A is in breach of contract by not fulfilling that obligation.

Carter (1995) points out that this estoppel principle sits uncomfortably with the theory, reiterated in *The Simona* itself, that the innocent party must choose between just two options following a repudiatory breach, of either accepting the breach and terminating the contract, or rejecting the breach and keeping the contract alive. Lord Ackner is essentially concerned with the gap following a repudiatory breach, but before the innocent party has decided to keep the contract alive, clarifying that the innocent party (A) will not later be prejudiced if, during that interim period, B's repudiation caused A to fail to perform his own obligations. Carter argues that this is a strained solution and that it would be simpler to acknowledge openly that repudiation entitles the innocent party to suspend performance of his own contractual obligations. This theory has a number of attractions. First, it mirrors (and generalises) the regime discussed at para **15.4** whereby one party is entitled to withhold performance until the other party has fully performed a condition precedent or entire obligation. Second, it provides a theoretical explanation for the status of outstanding contractual obligations pending the innocent party's final response to the breach. Finally, it better reflects commercial parties' attitudes when faced with a repudiatory breach, since 'good business practice suggests that cancellation is preceded by an attempt to preserve the bargain'. However, for the time being English law preserves the theoretical position that there is no halfway house between outright acceptance and irrevocable rejection of a repudiatory breach, although the notion that there may in practice be a gap while the innocent party decides what to do was recognised by the Court of Appeal in *Force India Formula One Team Ltd v Etihad Airways PJSC* (2010), where Rix LJ said:

> *The present case concerns a complex and medium term relationship, which a takeover has destabilised, and where it necessarily and legitimately takes time for the consequences to become clearer and for the innocent party to consider his position. That is the middle ground between acceptance of a repudiation and affirmation of a contract.*

Electing to 'accept the breach' and discharge the contract

15.54 Acceptance of a repudiatory breach must be clear and unequivocal, but need not be by express words. As the court said in *Heyman v Darwins* (1942):

> *The other party may ... 'accept the repudiation' by so acting as to make it plain that, in view of the wrongful action of the party who has repudiated, he claims to treat the contract as at an end, in which case he can sue at once for damages.*

This acceptance must generally be communicated to the other party (described as a 'basic and well known principle' by the Privy Council in *Sookraj v Samaroo* (2004)) or at least 'overtly evinced' to him, but can the innocent party accept the repudiation by mere failure to perform its future obligations? In *State Trading Corpn of India* (1989), the Court of Appeal suggested not, since 'such conduct would be equivocal and equally consistent with a decision not to exercise the right to treat the contract as repudiated'.

15.55 However, the House of Lords subsequently explained in *Vitol SA v Norelf Ltd (The Santa Clara)* (1996) that this is not a rigid rule of law. It is just that, in most cases, 'doing nothing' will be too equivocal to count as an election to terminate the contract but, in exceptional circumstances, the innocent party's failure to perform its future obligations may suffice. *The Santa Clara* involved an international sale of a cargo of propane gas. The buyers sent a telex to the sellers rejecting the cargo while it was still being loaded: this was an anticipatory breach. Thereafter, neither party did anything more towards this contract. The sellers carried on loading, resold the cargo to someone else and claimed damages representing the difference between the two prices (the price of propane was volatile: the contract price was $400 per ton but the resale price a few days later was $170 per ton). The buyers argued that the sellers had never accepted their repudiation, asserting that mere non-performance can never, as a matter of law, amount to an acceptance of repudiation. The House of Lords disagreed. As Lord Steyn explained:

> Postulate the case where an employer at the end of the day tells a contractor that he, the employer, is repudiating the contract and that the contractor need not return the next day. The contractor does not return the next day or at all. It seems to me that the contractor's failure to return may, in the absence of any other explanation, convey a decision to treat the contract as at an end.

On the facts, the sellers' failure to perform was sufficiently unequivocal (and the buyers never had any genuine doubt that their repudiation had been accepted). There is an analogy with the acceptance of offers at the stage of *forming* a contract, where, exceptionally, silence may be sufficient for acceptance of an offer (see paras **2.81–2.89**). More to the point, the analogy is not perfect. At the formation stage, neither party starts from the position of being 'innocent' or 'in default'. Moreover, the formation rule that silence does not constitute an acceptance is to protect the offeree from being bound unless he goes to the trouble of rejecting the offer. Where the relevant acceptance is of a repudiatory breach by the other party, protection of the offeree may well (as in *The Santa Clara*) necessitate *allowing* acceptance by silence.

15.56 Up to now, we have referred to the innocent party's election to accept a repudiation as having the effect of *terminating* the contract, but in fact the proper analysis is that the contract does not 'disappear' and is not 'unravelled' or 'undone' (as, for example, when a contract is rescinded for misrepresentation). Strictly, the parties' outstanding *primary* obligations (to perform, pay the price, and so on) are discharged and replaced automatically by *secondary* obligations (principally, the obligation on the party in breach to pay damages, subject to the innocent party's 'duty' to mitigate). Lord Diplock made this clear in *Photo Production Ltd v Securicor Transport Ltd* (1980) (see para **8.13**). The context was to explain that 'termination' of a contract for repudiatory breach did not have the effect of destroying or nullifying the exclusion clause in the contract (since it was not a primary obligation). For the same reason other contractual obligations, such as liquidated damages clauses and arbitration clauses, continue to operate following acceptance of a repudiatory breach. If this was the intention of the parties, the courts will give effect to that intention, an approach applied by the Court of Appeal in *Stocznia Gdynia SA v Gearbulk Holdings Ltd* (2009), discussed at para **15.23**.

15.57 Likewise, because acceptance of a repudiatory breach is not the same as rescission, contractual obligations and rights that have already *accrued* by the date a repudiatory breach is accepted survive, and in fact it makes no difference which party has the accrued obligation or right. So if a building contract is 'terminated' by the owner because the builder commits a repudiatory breach, but at that point an earlier instalment of the price has already accrued and is due to the builder, it remains due, although of course in practice it will be set off against any damages the builder must now pay the owner (see *Hyundai Heavy Industries Co Ltd v Papadopoulos* (1980)).

15.58 Generally, acceptance of a repudiation discharges the whole contract—in other words, all the outstanding primary obligations. It is, however, possible for a contract to be construed as having severable obligations, so that, for example, in a contract for the sale of goods by instalments the buyer may accept a repudiation as to one instalment without effect on the rest of the contract, but this is unusual (see *Friends Provident Insurance v Sirius* (2005)). Moreover, even in an instalment contract it is possible that breach of one instalment might amount to a repudiation of the whole contract. A useful guide is that the courts take into account, 'first the ratio quantitatively which the breach bears to the contract as a whole, and secondly the degree of probability or improbability of such breach being repeated' (*Maple Flock v Universal Furniture Products* (1934)).

15.59 A final point to bear in mind is that it does not generally matter if the innocent party purports to terminate the contract for a 'bad' reason that does not entitle them to terminate, but it subsequently transpires that, unbeknown to them, there was another 'good' reason. Nor does it matter if the innocent party was aware of the 'good' reason for termination but did not mention it at the time. This is subject to two exceptions, spelt out in *Glencore Grain Rotterdam BV v Lebanese Organisation for International Commerce* (1997). These were, first, if the 'good reason' might have been 'put right' by the party in breach, had he had notice of it and, second, if estoppel could be established, in the sense of an unequivocal representation by the innocent party that they were not going to rely on the 'good reason'.

OVERVIEW

1   Breach of contract always gives the innocent party the right to claim damages, but in certain circumstances the innocent party might also be able to bring the contract to an end from then on. This is not the same as rescission for vitiating factors like misrepresentation.

2   Where one party's performance is subject to a condition, that party need not perform until the condition is satisfied. Sometimes, performance of the other party's obligations is the condition. An obligation construed in this way is said to be 'entire', which means that if the entire obligation is not completely performed, the obligations that were conditional on it (commonly to pay the price) do not come into effect (unless part performance is voluntarily accepted). This is mitigated by a principle of substantial performance, though only where an entire obligation is performed completely but defectively (the distinction between incomplete and defective performance is not always easy to draw). The Law Commission once proposed that a party who does not fully perform an entire obligation should be entitled to recover a reasonable sum, but this proposal is very problematic and has not been taken any further.

3   There are two sorts of situation in which the innocent party can terminate the contract for the other party's breach. The first depends on the categorisation of the term broken. Breach of a term designated a condition always entitles the innocent party to terminate, however trivial the breach. Most other terms are now designated as innominate terms, breach of which will entitle the innocent party to terminate if its consequences are serious enough. The distinction between conditions and innominate terms reveals a fundamental tension between two inconsistent values, certainty versus flexibility.

4   In addition, repudiation of the contract (where one party renounces the contract or renders the other party's performance impossible) allows the innocent party to terminate. Repudiation involves breach of an implied term not to do anything to hinder the other party in rendering performance, not breach of the actual performance obligations in the contract, and thus can occur in advance of the due date for performance (anticipatory breach), which can give rise to difficulties in the quantification of damages.

5   In both categories, the innocent party has in theory a choice, the option of whether to accept the breach and bring the contract to an end, or reject the breach and keep the contract alive (though the latter option may not be feasible in practice). Once a repudiatory breach has been rejected, the contract continues and the innocent party cannot 'resurrect' the repudiatory breach later. Strictly, it is misleading to think in terms of 'terminating' the contract for breach, because the correct analysis is that the primary performance obligations in the contract are discharged and replaced with secondary remedial obligations.

FURTHER READING

Dawson 'Metaphors and Anticipatory Breach of Contract' [1981] CLJ 83

McFarlane and Stevens 'In Defence of *Sumpter v Hedges*' (2002) 118 LQR 569

Morgan 'Repudiatory Breach: Inability, Election and Discharge' [2017] CLJ 11

Mustill '*The Golden Victory*—Some Reflections' (2008) 124 LQR 569

Weir 'Contract—The Buyer's Right to Reject Defective Goods' [1976] CLJ 33

SELF-TEST QUESTIONS

1   What is meant by an 'entire obligation'?

2   What are the advantages and disadvantages of innominate terms?

3   Is it correct to say that an unaccepted repudiation is a 'thing writ in water'?

4   Should English law allow the innocent party to suspend its obligations when faced with a repudiatory breach?

5   What is the effect on the contractual regime of acceptance of a repudiatory breach?

6   Alice contracts with Book-a-Month Ltd, a mail order company, to buy the 12-volume Knowall Encyclopedia on an instalment basis. The company agrees that it will post one volume to her on the first of every month, and she agrees to send the price of £20 on receipt of each volume 'by return of post'. Consider each of the following alternative situations:

   (a)   Alice has received the first three volumes on 4 January, February and March, and the company has received in return a cheque for £20 posted on 11 January and another cheque for £40 posted on 25 March. On 27 March, Book-a-Month asks your advice.

   (b)   Alice has been sent the first three volumes but not Volume 4. On 4 May she receives Volume 5, together with a note from the company explaining that, because of editorial difficulties, Volume 4 has been cancelled and will not now be produced. Advise Alice.

   For hints on how to answer question 6, please see the online resources at **www.oup.com/uk/sullivan8e/.**

16   Remedies I: compensatory damages

SUMMARY

This chapter covers the principal remedy for breach of contract, compensatory damages. It deals with:

- Has the claimant suffered any loss and how is that loss converted into financial damages: loss of a chance, expectation measure of damages (cost of cure or difference in value), reliance measure of damages?
- Has the claimant suffered an actionable type of loss: financial loss, consumer surplus, distress?
- Causation: did the breach cause the claimant's loss?
- Remoteness of damage: was the type of loss (and liability for the type of loss) within the reasonable contemplation of the parties?
- Mitigation: has the claimant mitigated their loss?
- Contributory negligence: did the claimant's fault contribute to their loss?

Introduction

16.1   What remedies should the victim of a breach of contract have against the other party? This is a surprisingly difficult question to answer. At the time that a contract is made, each party hopes that the other will perform their side of the agreement. Therefore, often neither party has thought about or agreed with the other what should happen if one party breaches the contract. This means that the principal determinant of the appropriate remedies for a breach of contract cannot be the parties' intentions at the time that the contract was entered into (see Atiyah (1986), Hedley (1995), and Dagan (2000)).

16.2   Instead, the remedies granted broadly reflect the value of the interest that we are seeking to protect, here the party's contractual right to performance and the objects that he wants to achieve by contracting, as well as the defendant's conduct (Cane (1997); see also Rotherham (2007)). The greater the value that we place on the right to have the contract performed and the interest that a party has in having the contract properly performed, the greater the remedy we should award to reflect this. Similarly, the worse we consider the defendant's conduct in breaching the contract to be, the more severe the remedy necessary to reflect this. There are other factors which shape the remedies awarded for breach of contract, such as the idea that each party should have some regard to the interests of the other, which is increasingly conceptualised as a requirement of 'good faith', but the two mentioned are arguably the most important.

16.3 It is convenient for present purposes to group remedies into three categories: compensatory damages, other exceptional measures of damages, and specific remedies. Compensatory damages aim to award the claimant the loss that he has suffered as a result of the breach, and form the subject matter of this chapter. Occasionally other measures of damages are awarded, not immediately focused on compensation of loss, and are dealt with in Chapter 18. Specific remedies, at least on the traditional view, directly enforce the defendant's obligations: they get him to build the house that he promised to, deliver the goods he contracted to, and so forth. These remedies are examined in Chapter 17. However, it is important not to place too much emphasis on the categorisation of a particular type of remedy, particularly whether it is compensatory or not. There are cases where it is difficult to fit a particular remedy easily into any of these three categories. As the question that is ultimately being asked is what remedy is appropriate to reflect the value of the interest and the severity of the defendant's conduct, and the parties' intentions do not determine or constrain the type of remedy that is being awarded, the answer will sometimes be a remedy that does not look like a typical example of *any* of these three types of remedy.

16.4 The subject matter of this first remedies chapter is compensatory damages. Damages for breach of contract are generally compensatory (*Addis v Gramophone Co Ltd* (1909)). However, this principle is coming under increasing attack, as the scope of non-compensatory damages expands. The reasons for this expansion have not always been clear: is it to better reflect the defendant's conduct where he has acted particularly badly, to better protect the claimant's right to performance, or something else? As we shall see in Chapter 18, the failure to think about precisely why such expansion is necessary means that in some cases, there is a danger that this expansion has gone too far.

16.5 The theme of this chapter is also one of expansion. There is a trend towards greater protection of a party's non-financial interests, by an increasing willingness to place a monetary value on such interests and award damages in respect of them (see *Hamilton Jones v David & Snape* (2004)). This has been caused, at least in part, by an increasing appreciation of the fact that people, particularly consumers, often have non-financial reasons for entering into a contract as well as financial ones. They often enter into a contract for pleasure, security, privacy, and peace of mind, not just to make a profit. However, as in the case of non-compensatory damages, it will be suggested that this expansion has gone too far in one respect.

16.6 This expansion of compensatory damages has also thrown into sharp relief that once we move beyond the most obvious, classic case of compensatory damages—namely where the defendant has clearly caused the claimant a readily ascertainable *financial* loss—determining when damages should and should not be awarded becomes considerably less straightforward. Are *non*-financial losses (such as mental distress) deserving of protection by damages? When should we hold the defendant responsible for damages if someone else (or even the claimant) is partly responsible for the loss? When should a third party stepping in to redress the consequences of the defendant's acts, whether as a matter of obligation (as in the case of an insurance company) or voluntarily (as in the case of a friend), let the defendant escape responsibility for these consequences? In each of these cases, we must make a number of value judgements to answer these questions (Tettenborn (2007)).

16.7 Questions about compensatory damages can be approached in the following six stages:

    (1)   Has the claimant suffered any loss?

    (2)   Has the claimant suffered an actionable type of loss?

    (3)   Causation: did the breach cause the claimant's loss?

    (4)   Remoteness: was the type of loss too remote?

    (5)   Mitigation: has the claimant mitigated the loss?

    (6)   Did the claimant's fault contribute to the loss?

We shall take each in turn.

1. Has the claimant suffered any loss?

16.8 The claimant must show not only that a breach of contract has occurred, but also that he has suffered loss as a result. The general rule is that the claimant can only recover for his own loss (affirmed in *Alfred McAlpine Construction Ltd v Panatown Ltd* (2000)), although, as discussed in Chapter 6, there has been increasing scrutiny of when exceptions to this rule should be made.

16.9 In general, difficulty of assessment is no bar to recovering compensatory damages: the court will make an attempt to assess how much a claimant has lost (*Simpson v London & North Western Railway Co* (1876)). Even where all the claimant has lost is the chance to obtain a benefit, the court will sometimes attempt to put a value on this, providing that the claimant can show that she has lost a real or substantial, not merely a speculative, chance. In *Chaplin v Hicks* (1911), the claimant was one of 50 finalists in a competition to win a job as an actress. The prize-winners were to be determined by the defendant, who was the organiser of the competition, after an appointment with each of the finalists, but he breached the contract with the claimant by not giving her a fair opportunity to arrange a convenient appointment. This deprived her of the chance of competing for one of the 12 prizes. It was held that she was entitled to recover substantial damages, despite the fact that it was difficult to calculate the value of her lost chance with any precision. Three points should be noted about this approach.

16.10   First, in *Chaplin*, had the contract not been breached, it would have been up to the defendant to decide whether the claimant should be awarded a prize. However, in *Allied Maples Group Ltd v Simmons & Simmons* (1995) it was suggested that damages will only be awarded for loss of a chance where it was the action of a *third party* that would have determined whether the claimant would have made the gain had the contract been properly performed (see also *Equitable Life v Ernst & Young* (2003) and Lord Hoffmann in *Gregg v Scott* (2005)). The phrase 'action of a third party' does not seem to include the defendant, so how can the two cases be reconciled? The Court of Appeal in *Allied Maples* mistakenly thought that *Chaplin* supported their decision (see the Court of Appeal decision in *Bank of Credit and Commerce International SA (in liquidation) v Ali (No 2)* (2002)) and therefore did not focus on what would happen where it is the defendant's actions that are relevant. One answer that has been suggested is that if there are limits on the defendant's discretion, such as that it must be exercised in good faith, then there is a chance that the defendant would have decided in the claimant's favour and so loss of a chance damages are available (*Clark v Bet* (1997)). Where, on the other hand, the defendant has an unfettered discretion, we must assume that he would have decided against the claimant and so loss of a chance damages are not available (see Treitel (2015)). The reason is that we must assume that the defendant would have performed his legal obligations in the way least onerous to himself and least beneficial to the claimant (see para **16.17**). However, in *Dandara Holdings Ltd v Co-operative Retail Services Ltd* (2004), Lloyd J, relying on *Chaplin*, simply held that loss of a chance damages could in principle be awarded where it is the actions of the defendant that are relevant, without drawing any distinction based on the nature of the defendant's discretion.

16.11   Secondly, the Court of Appeal has since explained that even where the uncertainty relates to what a third party would have done had the contract been performed, one must not fall into the trap of assuming that the loss of a chance approach will always apply to determine what damages are recoverable. Often, it may be clear that the third party would have had to carry out a particular exercise and the court feels comfortable in determining (whether with the benefit of expert evidence or otherwise) how he would have done it, such as valuing certain assets. In such a case, the court will feel able to apply the ordinary approach of working out what would have happened and not need to resort to the loss of a chance approach. In *Law Debenture Trust Corpn plc v Elektrim SA* (2010), the bond agreement between the claimant and defendant provided that in certain events, the defendant would have to pay the claimant a sum to be determined by a third party, the sum to be calculated by reference to the assets of the defendant. In breach of contract, the defendant failed to put the calculation process in train, so the claimant sued for the sum that it said that it should have received. The court held that it should decide what valuation would have been arrived at and award a sum accordingly, rather than apply the loss of a chance approach. The two factors that influenced the court in taking this approach were:

- the question of which valuation approach should be taken turned largely on legal questions, so the court felt able to choose between the approaches;

- the loss of a chance approach is difficult to operate, and therefore a less attractive method, where there are more than two possible relevant outcomes. In *Chaplin*, the contestant would either have one of the 12 prizes or she would not, so one could apply the loss of a chance approach simply by assessing her chances of winning. However, where (as in *Elektrim*) there were a number of different possible valuation approaches and therefore a number of different calculation results, the loss of a chance approach would not work so well, because it would be necessary to work out the chance of each different approach being applied to calculate what result each different approach would have yielded.

16.12 Thirdly, even where the court identifies a chance dependent on the hypothetical actions of a third party, lost as a result of the defendant's breach, and applies *Chaplin* and *Allied Maples* to assess the percentage chance lost, it must also consider whether that lost chance was too remote (see para **16.94**). For an example of a lost chance claim falling at the remoteness hurdle, see *Wright v Lewis Silkin LLP* (2016) discussed further at para **16.94**.

16.13 When ascertaining whether the claimant has suffered a loss, and if so, how much, damages will be assessed as at the date of the breach, unless this would be unjust, in which case the court can fix any other date that would be appropriate (*Johnson v Agnew* (1980)). In practice, the most important context in which the courts are willing to depart from the breach date is the anticipatory repudiation of a contract some time before the contract would otherwise have come to an end, which has already been discussed at para **15.44**.

16.14 The most important issue is how we should work out the extent to which the claimant is worse off as a result of the breach. To do this, we must know what we are comparing the claimant's current position with, for the purpose of working out the extent to which they are worse off. There are two possibilities:

- We could compare their current position with the position they would have been in had the contract been performed in accordance with its terms. This is known as the *expectation measure*. For example, if in breach of contract Carla has been supplied with a radio worth £40 and had the contract been performed properly she would have received a radio worth £100, the expectation measure of damages would allow her to recover £60. Notice that 'worse off' is a slightly misleading phrase in this context—it really means 'the extent to which the claimant would have been *better off* had the contract been performed', even if they have suffered no loss in the tortious sense as a result of the breach (for example if the contract price Carla paid for the radio was only £20).

- Alternatively, we could compare the claimant's current position with their position before the contract was entered into: how much money have they spent in preparing to perform and then performing the contract which is now wasted as a result of the breach? This is known as the *reliance measure*. For example, if a TV company spends £100 promoting a new show and the presenter then pulls out in breach of contract, the reliance measure allows the company to recover the wasted £100.

16.15 As we shall see, the expectation measure is the primary measure of damages and the reliance measure is in a sense subordinate to it. Why should the former be the primary measure? This has generated a large amount of academic discussion, notably the seminal article by Fuller and Perdue (1936–7). It is suggested the answer is that it is the expectation measure that best signifies what is wrong about breaching a contract. Imagine that the primary remedy for a breach of contract was removing the profit that the defendant had made from breaching the contract. This would signify that what is wrong about breaching contracts is that you make a profit from it. Alternatively, if the primary remedy for a breach of contract was reliance damages, this would signify that what is wrong about breaching a contract is that you have made the other party incur reliance costs. Neither of these captures the essence of what is wrong about breaching a contract. Having a primary remedy for breach of contract that aims to place the claimant in the position that he would have been in if the contract had been performed signifies that what is wrong about breaching a contract is that you have failed to carry out the obligations that you undertook, that you have not done what you promised you would (for related arguments see Friedmann (1995a), Kimel (2003), and Smith (2004)).

Expectation measure

16.16 The aim of the expectation measure is to put the claimant in the position that he would have been in had the contract been performed in accordance with its terms (*Robinson v Harman* (1848)). As we shall see, the measure falls short of achieving this aim in a number of ways: for example, contract law does not compensate for all types of loss, it requires the type of loss to be reasonably foreseeable, it lays down certain causation requirements, and the claimant may be unable to recover if they have not taken sufficient steps to minimise the loss they suffer. However, this should not necessarily be a cause for concern. All this tells us is that values other than the protection of the claimant have a role to play here. Therefore, English contract law does not make damages the exact financial equivalent of performance. This has two effects. From the perspective of the party about to receive performance of a particular obligation, it means that performance is better than damages in a number of ways. Conversely, from the perspective of the party who is about to be obliged to perform a particular obligation, there is an incentive to breach the contract.

16.17 Two issues need examination here. First, and less importantly, expectation damages are calculated on the basis that the defendant would have performed his obligations under the contract, but *would not have done anything that he was not legally obliged to* (*Lavarack v Woods of Colchester Ltd* (1967)). However, care is needed in identifying the defendant's legal obligations where a contract provides him with a discretion as to whether to pay money or do something, as it may be that the contract places an obligation on him to properly consider in bona fide and rational fashion whether and how much to pay or whether to do the act in question. For example, in *Horkulak v Cantor Fitzgerald* (2004), the Court of Appeal held that an employer at an investment bank had a legal obligation to properly consider whether to award a discretionary bonus.

16.18 Likewise the Court of Appeal in *Durham Tees Valley Airport Ltd v Bmibaby Ltd* (2010) decided that the general rule in *Lavarack* does not hold true in a case where the defendant is required to do something but is under a discretion as to how he does it. The facts are set out in para **4.12**. When the airport sued for damages, Bmibaby argued that the contract was too uncertain to be enforced because it did not specify how many flights would be operated. As we have seen in Chapter 4, this argument was rejected by the Court of Appeal. However, the court then had to assess the correct level of damages. The question was whether the court should attempt to ascertain, as in *Lavarack*, the minimum obligations of the defendant, here the minimum number of flights that Bmibaby was required to operate, and then only award the airport the profit that it would have generated on these flights, or award a measure of damages that was not restricted in this way.

16.19 The Court of Appeal held that damages should not be so restricted. It was held that where the defendant is under a single obligation (such as to fly two or more aircraft for ten years) but the contract gives him a discretion as to how to perform it (such as by not providing for the number of flights), then the court should ask how the contract would have been performed had it not been breached, rather than asking what was the minimum level of performance that the claimant could get away with under the contract. *Lavarack*, it held, was not this type of case, because that case concerned whether a wrongfully dismissed employee was entitled to damages representing the bonus that he might have received, where there was no obligation at all to provide the bonus; here, in contrast, there *was* an obligation but one that gave the defendant a discretion as to its exercise. In asking how the defendant would have performed the contract, it should assume that the defendant would act in good faith and not have acted uncommercially merely to spite the claimant, and therefore the level of performance assumed may well exceed the minimum level of performance contracted for.

16.20 The decision is a slightly difficult one. Toulson LJ, who dealt with the point in most depth, was influenced in his choice of approach by the practical problems he saw in determining what the minimum level of performance would have been on the facts, compared with the easier task of determining how the contract would actually have been performed if Bmibaby had continued to run two aircraft (using past performance as a helpful guide in this regard). Therefore, it is important to consider whether the approach would have been different if the contract had specified a minimum number of flights. Toulson LJ appears to have considered that the defendant would in such a situation have been limited to damages based on the minimum level of performance. He suggested that it might be appropriate to take different approaches depending on whether the parties had chosen to lay down themselves a minimum level of performance, but it does have the odd consequence that if the claimant manages to persuade the defendant to agree to include a term in the contract promising a minimum level of performance, the claimant will be worse off in the event of breach because he will be limited to claiming damages on the basis of minimum performance. Therefore, it is suggested that the approach taken in *Bmibaby* should be limited to situations where it is not possible for the court to work out in advance what the minimum level of performance would be for the remainder of the contract (and therefore the court is forced to adopt a different approach), rather than any situation where the parties have not provided for one.

16.21 The second, and often more important, issue in relation to the expectation measure is how we convert expectation loss into money and put the claimant into the position that he would have been in had the contract been performed. There are two methods of doing this:

- The first is to award the difference between the value of the performance that was actually provided and the value of the performance that should have been provided. This is known as the *difference (or 'diminution') in value* approach. For example, if the defendant breaches the contract by supplying me with a bath worth £200 when he should have supplied me with one worth £300, the difference in value is £100. We see this rule in s 53(3) of the Sale of Goods Act 1979, for example, which states that the measure of damages for a breach of warranty is '*prima facie* the difference between the value of the goods at the time of delivery to the buyer and the value they would have had if they had fulfilled the warranty'.

- The other method awards the defendant the cost of 'curing' the breach, that is, how much it would cost the claimant to get a third party to perform the contract or to rectify the breaches caused by the defendant. This is known as the *cost of cure* approach. So if Darlene breaches her contract with me by redecorating my bedroom in a defective manner, the cost of cure approach would award me the cost of getting these defects remedied.

16.22 Often the two measures produce the same result: for example, if goods are not delivered, the cost of cure in purchasing a substitute in the market is equal to the value of the goods. Therefore, the diminution in value measure is perfectly satisfactory where substitute performance can readily be obtained in the market and where the claimant's reason for contracting is basically commercial, that is, to make a profit. Therefore it makes sense that the difference in market value rule is used as the prima facie measure throughout the Sale of Goods Act 1979. Notice, however, that it is only prima facie. In certain circumstances it will not be the best assessment of what the claimant has actually lost, whereupon it will be displaced, as it was in *Bence Graphics v Fasson UK Ltd* (1998), although this departure from the general rule in *Bence* is convincingly criticised by Treitel (1997).

16.23 However, the diminution in value approach is not so satisfactory where the claimant has contracted in part for non-financial reasons, for example, to obtain relaxation. In such circumstances, the diminution in value may be extremely small, so this measure is inadequate to compensate the claimant properly. An example makes the point. Imagine I contract to have a deluxe bird-watching hut built in my garden, so I can spend relaxing afternoons gazing at birds in comfort, but the hut will not increase the market value of my house at all. In breach of contract, the defendant builds the hut in a shoddy manner.

The diminution in value approach will give me little if any damages, because the market value of the house would not have been any greater had the contract been performed properly. All I can recover on this approach is a small sum in respect of my loss of enjoyment (the 'consumer surplus': see para **16.35**). The cost of having the hut 'done up' properly, the cost of cure, may be far greater than this sum.

16.24 Where the cost of cure exceeds the diminution in value, as in the example, the starting point is that the claimant is allowed to opt for the cost of cure measure. He has been the victim of the breach, so he should be allowed to have the breach rectified even if this is expensive. However, he will be prevented from recovering the cost of cure if it would be unreasonable for him to do so (*East Ham Corpn v Bernard Sunley & Sons Ltd* (1966)). The House of Lords stressed in *Ruxley Electronics & Constructions Ltd v Forsyth* (1996) (the facts of which are discussed at para **16.39**) that an important factor in deciding whether it would be unreasonable is whether the cost of cure is 'wholly disproportionate' to the diminution in value (the words of Lord Mustill).

16.25 Four points flow from this. First, where the cost of cure is wholly disproportionate to the diminution in value, the claimant will be unable to recover the cost of cure. Secondly, to work out whether the cost of cure is wholly disproportionate, we are comparing the cost of cure to the difference in market value plus the consumer surplus (see para **16.35** for the meaning of the latter). Thirdly, the word 'wholly' suggests that the claimant will usually be able to claim the cost of cure. However, in *Ruxley* itself, where the cost of cure (£21,650) was 8.5 times more than the diminution in value when the lost 'consumer surplus' is taken into account (£2,500), it was held that the cost of cure was wholly disproportionate. This gives us some idea of how the test will be applied. Finally, whether the claimant genuinely intends to have the consequences of the breach rectified is highly relevant to the issue of whether it would be unreasonable to allow cost of cure damages. If the claimant does not intend to do so, he is highly unlikely to be able to recover the cost of cure (see *Tito v Waddell (No 2)* (1977) and *Ruxley* itself). On the other hand, even if the claimant does intend to have the breach rectified, this is not a sufficient condition for cost of cure damages: *Ruxley* seems to have reduced the role of intention here (see O'Sullivan (1997)).

16.26 O'Sullivan (1997) argued that a test focusing on whether the cost of rectifying the breach is disproportionate might be flawed in two respects. First:

> the principle seems to mean 'the cost of cure is very high', which of course is usually because it includes an element of undoing the original work. This is unacceptable—it makes the owner's damages depend not on the extent of the defect or the degree of deviation from specification, but on the technical difficulty and thus cost of undoing the breach.

Furthermore:

> it conveys the wrong signal to contractors. Assume, for example, a contractor doing domestic building work where, as in Ruxley, the employer is not on site supervising

his every move. If the contractor monitors the work properly, keeping the employer informed at every stage, he risks spotting mistakes and defects which he will then have to spend money remedying. If, however, he ploughs on with the work, quickly burying any defects deeper in the fabric of the construction, he maximises the chances that the cost of curing any such defects will be high and thus rejected as disproportionate? ... [T] he principle encourages a culture of inefficiency and provides no incentive, indeed a positive disincentive, for builders to monitor work or keep the employer informed.

16.27 A better approach, and one that affords greater protection to consumers, might be that of Lord Jauncey in *Ruxley*, who focuses on whether there has been a total failure of the contractual objective, that is, on the extent of the deviation from the contractual specification, the scale of the defect. The greater the scale of the defect, the greater the chance of being awarded cost of cure damages.

16.28 A helpful case law illustration of the difficulty of comparing the cost of rectifying the problem with the diminution in value is provided by the High Court of Australia decision in *Tabcorp Holdings Ltd v Bowen Investments Pty Ltd* (2009). In breach of a term of the lease prohibiting alterations to the commercial premises without prior landlord consent, the tenant, well aware that it was in breach of contract, destroyed the existing foyer (that the claimant landlord had very carefully chosen) and replaced it with a new one. This only diminished the value of the premises by AUS$34,820 but it would have cost AUS$580,000 to restore it to its original condition (coupled with a AUS$800,000 loss of rent while the restoration was being carried out). In this situation, it would surely be unthinkable to limit damages to the diminution in value, leaving the claimant with a foyer that it did not want and had not originally chosen, particularly in circumstances where the defendant had acted with contempt for the claimant's rights and its own contractual obligations. The court understandably had no difficulty in awarding the costs of reinstatement, coupled with lost rent, dismissing any suggestion that the remarks in *Ruxley* about proportionality prevented such a remedy.

Reliance measure

16.29 As mentioned, the aim of reliance damages is to put the claimant back in the position he was before the contract was made. It allows him to recover the expenses he has incurred in performing or preparing to perform his side of the contract. Such damages can only be claimed as an alternative to the expectation measure (*Cullinane v British 'Rema' Manufacturing Co Ltd* (1954)). Generally, the contract will be profitable for the claimant, so in the event of a breach, it would be more advantageous for him to be put in the position he would have been in had the contract been properly performed than being put back in the position he was in before the contract was made.

16.30 Sometimes however, the claimant will enter into a bad bargain, and so giving the claimant back the expenses he has incurred would put him in a better position than if the contract had been properly performed. So damages for reliance loss would give him more than the expectation measure of damages. For example, I spend £100 preparing to build a house for Dirk, but in breach of contract he throws me off his land before I can begin actually building the house. Imagine that I have made a bad choice in entering into the contract, because if the contract had been fully performed by both parties, I would have made only £40 gross profit, so made a net loss of £60. My reliance loss is £100, the money I have spent preparing to perform. However, my expectation loss is £40: I would only be £40 better off if the contract had been fully performed. If the *defendant* can show that the expectation measure would give the claimant less than the reliance measure, then the claimant is limited to the expectation measure (*C & P Haulage v Middleton* (1983), affirmed in *Omak Maritime Ltd v Mamola Challenger Shipping Co Ltd* (2010), which contains a thoughtful analysis of the basis for the rule). So the rule is that the claimant can get the reliance measure of damages unless the defendant can show that this would exceed the claimant's expectation loss, in which case the claimant is limited to his expectation loss. In other words, the defendant can use the expectation measure to cap the claimant's damages here. However, it may be difficult for the defendant to show this: the onus is on him to show that the expectation measure would yield less damages.

16.31   Bearing this qualification on claiming reliance damages in mind, when will it be most advantageous for the claimant to rely on the reliance measure? Two situations can be identified: first, where it is impossible to show what would have happened had the contract been properly performed, as, for example, in *McRae v Commonwealth Disposals Commission* (1951) discussed at para **13.15**, where it would have been impossible to speculate how much profit would have been made from salvaging a wreck that never existed. Secondly, it might be advantageous to claim the reliance measure in order to recover pre-contractual expenditure, as in *Anglia Television v Reed* (1972), although this suggestion is a little controversial, since it is arguable that any pre-contractual outlay was at the claimant's risk.

16.32   It is worth considering what the rationale for this cap on reliance damages is. It seems to be that because the loss results from having entered into a bad bargain, the courts do not want to put the claimant in a better position than he would have been in had the contract been properly performed (*C & P Haulage*). The expectation measure is the primary measure (see para **16.15** for the reason for this), so we do not want it to be undermined by allowing the claimant to escape from a bad bargain. Put another way, the loss results not from the *breach* of contract but from the contract itself.

2. Has the claimant suffered an actionable type of loss?

16.33   As a matter of principle, it might seem that contract law should afford the same protection to non-financial loss (such as disappointment and distress) that it gives to financial loss. However, while there is movement in this direction, English contract law is still unwilling to award compensation for some types of non-financial loss.

Financial loss

16.34 Here, I am worse off, or rather, I am not as well off, as I would have been had the contract been performed. For example, if the house that you have built badly for me is worth £1.5 million, when it should have been worth £2 million if properly built, then my house is worth £500,000 less than it should have been. There is no controversy here: such loss can be recovered (as long as the loss is not too remote and other such conditions are fulfilled).

The consumer surplus

16.35 This type of non-financial loss first came to the attention of contract lawyers in an article by Harris, Ogus, and Phillips (1979) and can be defined as the amount by which the particular plaintiff values performance of a particular obligation over and above its market value.

16.36 Let us try to unpack what this means. People often enter into contracts for partly non-financial reasons. For example, I may want a wall built along the boundary of my land to ensure that I have privacy (as in *Radford v de Froberville* (1977)), or to have a swimming pool that is particularly deep because I am a tall man (as in *Ruxley* (1995)), or to go on a beautiful holiday in order to relax me (as in *Jarvis v Swan Tours Ltd* (1973) and *Jackson v Horizon Holidays Ltd* (1973)), or to find out how much aircraft noise would be experienced in a particular house in order to ensure that I can relax in peace if I buy the house (as in *Farley v Skinner* (2001)). In each of these examples, if the contract is breached, I have missed out on something that is important to me, something that I contracted for: privacy, quiet, relaxation, etc. These things are not financial matters, but they are of value to me, which is why I entered into a contract for the purpose of attaining them. Therefore I have suffered a loss in such circumstances. The loss is the value that I place on having peace and quiet, or relaxation, or whatever else I may want. It is not the fact that I am worse off financially than I should be that we are focusing on here; indeed, sometimes the fact that the house is noisy (in *Farley*) or the swimming pool not deep enough (in *Ruxley*) will not affect the value of my property, so I will have lost nothing financially. It is the value that *I place* on having a deep pool or a quiet house that matters, hence the definition put forward.

16.37 While there has been some judicial support for the concept at the highest level, it is not clear that it is yet completely accepted. The existence of a similar but narrower category was recognised in *Watts v Morrow* (1991). After confirming that damages generally cannot be awarded for distress caused by a breach of contract, the Court of Appeal recognised two exceptions to this rule, the former of which was set out in the following terms by Bingham LJ:

> *Where the very object of a contract is to provide pleasure, relaxation, peace of mind or freedom from molestation, damages will be awarded if the fruit of the contract is not provided or if the contrary result is procured instead.*

16.38   This category is arguably slightly narrower than the consumer surplus. The consumer surplus approach views the situation from the victim's situation (what value did the *claimant* place on the performance of the obligation?), whereas the *Watts* approach requires that regard be had to the expectations of *both parties* in order to determine what the 'object' of the contract was.

16.39   However, it did not take long for some judges to suggest a broader approach. In *Ruxley*, the builder contracted with Mr Forsyth to build a swimming pool at the latter's home. It was agreed that the pool would have a maximum depth of seven feet six inches. Apparently Mr Forsyth was a tall man and wished to avoid hitting his head while diving. However, the pool built by the builder had a maximum depth of only six feet six inches. Accordingly, when sued for payment, Mr Forsyth counterclaimed for breach of contract, claiming the cost of rebuilding the pool to the specified depth, approximately £21,650. The trial judge found that the missing inches made no difference to the value of the property and that Mr Forsyth's stated intention of rebuilding the pool would not outlive the proceedings. As discussed, the claim for cost of cure was rejected on the ground that it was wholly disproportionate to the diminution in value. However, the trial judge awarded £2,500, an award affirmed by the House of Lords. What is of interest here is *why* this award was made. In the House of Lords, Lord Mustill viewed the award as representing the consumer surplus: even though having a deeper swimming pool would have no effect on the market value of the property, it was something that was important to Mr Forsyth. Lord Lloyd, on the other hand, took a narrower view, regarding the award as compensating Mr Forsyth for his loss of amenity under the *Watts* exception.

16.40   The House of Lords had a chance to deal with the concept again in *Farley v Skinner* (2001). The claimant was interested in purchasing a property near Gatwick airport as a quiet, relaxing place to spend his retirement. Keen to check that the property was suitable, he employed the defendant surveyor to look over the property and expressly asked him to report on whether aircraft noise was likely to be a problem. In breach of contract, the surveyor reported back that it was unlikely that the property would be very noisy. Therefore, the claimant bought the house, only to find to his horror that the property was noisy. Despite the fact that the trial judge found that the price the claimant paid reflected the aircraft noise problem (so his financial loss was nil), he nevertheless awarded the claimant £10,000 for his discomfort. This award was affirmed by the House of Lords, although some of the Lords thought the amount awarded was at the high end of what was appropriate. Each judge upheld the award on two separate grounds. The second ground is discussed at paras **16.45–16.47**. In respect of the first ground, Lord Scott took the most radical approach, unhesitatingly endorsing the concept of the consumer surplus and allowing relief on this basis: the defendant's breach prevented the claimant from obtaining the peace and quiet that were extremely important to him. Lord Steyn, on the other hand, rested his decision on the 'object of the contract' exception from *Watts*. It is slightly unclear which approach Lords Hutton and Clyde favoured, and Lord Browne-Wilkinson simply stated that he agreed with the speeches of Lords Scott and Steyn. It is important to note that those adopting the *Watts* test all interpreted the test in a broad way (or actually widened the test, depending on your taste): it was sufficient that an important object of the contract was to give pleasure, relaxation, or peace of mind and it was unnecessary to show that this was the sole or dominant object.

16.41 Therefore, while the consumer surplus concept is not yet fully accepted in English law, there is at the very least a move towards its acceptance. Although not all of the Lords in *Farley* explicitly endorsed the concept, those who did not do so nevertheless moved closer to it in substance by broadening the *Watts* test. On the other hand, lower courts at least may feel more comfortable relying on the words of the *Watts* test rather than the consumer surplus approach (see, for example, *Hamilton Jones v David & Snape* (2004)). It is submitted that the consumer surplus concept should be accepted: unlike businesses, consumers often contract for goods and services for the pleasure that they confer, and as a starting point at least these non-financial interests deserve the same protection that we afford to financial ones. An example of the principle in operation (although not one that uses the phrase 'consumer surplus') is the Court of Appeal decision in *Newman v Framewood Manor Management Co Ltd* (2012). Mrs Newman purchased a flat in a development and was keen to use the communal swimming pool and jacuzzi, especially when her grandchildren came to stay, but the defendants in breach of contract replaced the jacuzzi with a sauna. The court awarded Mrs Newman £2,500 damages for 'loss of amenity' on the basis that a reasonable person would not regard a sauna as a substitute for a jacuzzi, particularly those with young children or grandchildren. Therefore, the court looked at Mrs Newman's personal preferences and also to the value that a reasonable person might place on these non-financial matters.

16.42 Three further points need to be made. First, awards for non-financial loss will be modest in size (reiterated in *Farley*). This approach applies equally to the types of non-financial loss examined later. Secondly, as will be discussed, it will often be difficult for a claimant to show that his consumer surplus loss was sufficiently foreseeable to be recoverable: for example, people normally do not care too much if their swimming pool is six feet six inches or seven feet six inches in depth. Thirdly, some have argued that even recognition of the consumer surplus may not on its own offer adequate protection to the claimant's non-financial reasons for contracting (see O'Sullivan (1995) and McKendrick (1999)). The limitations on the availability of the cost of cure measure (see para **16.24**) means that there may no longer be any way for a claimant to recover enough money to have the consequences of the breach rectified. Where the cost of cure measure is deemed wholly disproportionate to the diminution in value, the claimant will be unable to recover enough to repair the defect even if it is extremely important to him to have the defect rectified.

Distress caused by an unwelcome sensory experience

16.43 Recovery for distress must be distinguished from recovery on the consumer surplus basis, as O'Sullivan (1997) explains:

> Mental distress is like death or personal injury—one of the negative results that flow from a breach [of contract] or a tort that leave you worse off than you were before you

started. In contrast, the consumer surplus is part of the expectation—you are not actually worse off, you simply have not become better off to the extent that you were promised.

16.44   Unfortunately, the decision in *Farley* (2001) has left it slightly unclear when a claimant can recover for distress. Before *Farley*, the circumstances in which you could do so were those laid down by the Court of Appeal in *Watts* (1991):

> *[A claimant can recover] for physical inconvenience and discomfort caused by the breach and mental suffering directly related to that inconvenience.*

In *Watts* itself, the defendant surveyor in breach of contract failed to mention various defects in the house he was reporting on. The husband and wife claimants bought the house in reliance on the report and had to have extensive repairs done. They each recovered £750 for the physical inconvenience and mental distress consequent upon it from living at weekends in the house while it was undergoing such repairs.

16.45   In *Farley*, the second ground on which the House of Lords upheld the trial judge's award was on the basis that it compensated the claimant for his distress under the category from *Watts*. All of the Lords except Lord Scott were happy to apply the *Watts* test (although the test did receive some criticism from Lord Clyde: '[i]t does not seem to me that there is any particular magic in the word "physical"'). They held that the aircraft noise caused the claimant physical inconvenience.

16.46   Lord Scott opted for a more radical approach to uphold the £10,000 award. He criticised the distinction drawn in *Watts* between physical and non-physical interference:

> *[T]he adjective 'physical', in the phrase 'physical inconvenience and discomfort', requires, I think, some explanation or definition. The distinction between the 'physical' and the 'non-physical' is not always clear and may depend on the context. Is being awoken at night by aircraft noise 'physical'? If it is, is being unable to sleep because of worry and anxiety 'physical'? What about a reduction in light caused by the erection of a building under a planning permission that an errant surveyor ought to have warned his purchaser-client about but failed to do so?*

Instead, he suggested that a different distinction should be drawn:

> *In my opinion, the critical distinction to be drawn is not a distinction between the different types of inconvenience or discomfort of which complaint may be made but a distinction based on the cause of the inconvenience or discomfort. If the cause is no more than disappointment that the contractual obligation has been broken, damages are not recoverable even if the disappointment has led to a complete mental breakdown. But, if the cause of the inconvenience is a sensory (sight, touch, hearing, smell etc) experience, damages can, subject to the remoteness rules, be recovered.*

Therefore, the question to be asked was whether the distress was caused by an unwelcome sensory experience or not. Arguably, this category is broader than that laid down in *Watts*. On the facts of *Farley*, the breach caused the claimant to suffer unwanted noise, which constituted an unwelcome sensory experience. Therefore, he could recover for the discomfort that he had suffered.

16.47 Lord Scott's approach should be preferred to the old *Watts* test, for two reasons. First, as he pointed out, the distinction drawn in *Watts* between physical and non-physical inconvenience is often a difficult one to draw. Second, and more importantly, if he has indeed broadened the range of circumstances in which damages can be recovered for distress, this is a move that should be supported. If non-financial loss is as deserving of protection as financial loss, at least as a starting point, then Lord Scott's alteration of the law takes us one step closer to that position.

16.48 Unfortunately, a number of problems can also be identified. First, despite the argument of Capper (2002) to the contrary and hints in Lord Clyde's speech that his view may be similar to Lord Scott's, it is questionable whether Lord Scott's speech represents the ratio on this issue, given that the other Lords followed the *Watts* test without altering it. Secondly, Lord Scott fails to provide any reasons why, as a matter of policy, the correct distinction to draw is between distress caused by an unwelcome sensory experience and distress caused merely by disappointment that the contract has been breached. The reason behind it might be that people are usually disappointed that a contract has been broken, so we do not want to allow a claim for disappointment to be added onto every breach of contract claim (see paras **16.51–16.57**). Thirdly, as will be discussed (at para **16.55**), it is arguable that Lord Scott should have gone even further than he did, by allowing recovery even where the distress does not result from an unwelcome sensory experience. If we really believe that non-financial loss is as worthy of protection as financial loss, that would be the logical position to adopt. Finally, it is slightly unclear how wide the category of 'unwelcome sensory experience' is. This, however, can be resolved in future cases if Lord Scott's approach is followed.

16.49 One matter remains to be dealt with—namely the exact relationship between the consumer surplus and distress caused by an unwelcome sensory experience. While it is important to distinguish the two concepts (see para **16.43**), there is a large overlap between them in practice. Often, one can recover using either approach. Where this is the case, they are simply different ways of viewing the same situation. For example, Lord Scott said that the claimant in *Farley* could recover on either approach. The consumer approach would run as follows: the claimant contracted for accurate information from the surveyor about aircraft noise but did not get it; such information was important because he wanted to buy a house that was peaceful, so he lost something of value to him. The distress approach would run like this: the claimant was distressed by living in a noisy house; this distress was caused by an unpleasant sensory experience (noise) as required by Lord Scott, so the claimant can recover for this distress. One proviso made clear in *Farley* should be noted: because the different approaches often cover the same ground, you cannot recover twice over for the same situation.

16.50 *Haysman v Mrs Roger Films* (2008) provides a good example of the overlap. Mr Haysman lent his retro-themed house to a production company for filming, including as a term of the contract that the company would indemnify him against any loss caused by their actions. The film company damaged the house and driveway, denting Mr Haysman's pride in his carefully kept house and deterring him from going ahead with his usual annual charity events at the house. In addition to awarding the remedial costs, the court was happy to award £1,000 damages for non-pecuniary loss on two alternative bases. First, one of the objects of the contract and the term was to provide peace of mind to a home-owner allowing his property to be used for filming. Second, the court adopted Lord Clyde's comments in *Farley* about taking a broad approach to physical inconvenience and held that the interference with his enjoyment of the property sufficed for these purposes. The case also suggests that the courts may well feel more comfortable adopting Lord Clyde's more orthodox approach in *Farley* than that of Lord Scott.

Distress caused by disappointment that the contract has been breached

16.51   As discussed, Lord Scott held in *Farley* that damages would not be recoverable for mere disappointment at the breach of contract. The same is true of other non-financial losses caused by the breach of contract. For example, the claimant cannot claim for loss of reputation unless he can show that he has suffered financial loss as a result of this damage to his reputation (*Malik v BCCI SA* (1998), applied in *Bank of Credit and Commerce International SA (in liquidation) v Ali (No 1)* (2001)). The issue to be discussed here is whether this absolute bar is too harsh. What is so special about an unwelcome sensory experience that means that damages should only be recoverable if the distress is caused by such an occurrence? Indeed, as Lord Scott acknowledges, the consequence of his approach is that a claimant who suffers a complete mental breakdown as a result of his disappointment at the breach will be unable to recover anything. Can it be right that a defendant who foresees that his breach will have this effect should escape compensating the claimant for it?

16.52   There are two competing viewpoints here (see Burrows (2004) and Chandler and Devenney (2007) for general discussions). The first is concerned that allowing non-financial loss to be generally recoverable (subject to satisfying the remoteness rules) would lead to claims for distress to be tacked onto a large number of breach of contract claims. This potential increase is considered a bad thing, particularly in the commercial context. What underlies the courts' reluctance to award damages for mental distress is, despite the argument of McDonald (1994) to the contrary, something more fundamental than mere difficulty in valuing how much such distress is worth in monetary terms. As Staughton LJ commented in *Hayes v James & Charles Dodd* (1990):

> I would not view with enthusiasm the prospect that every shipowner in the Commercial Court, having successfully claimed for unpaid freight or demurrage, would be able to add a claim for mental distress suffered while he was waiting for his money.

Similarly, Lord Cooke suggested in *Johnson v Gore Wood & Co* (2002) that '[c]ontract-breaking is treated as an incident of commercial life which players in the game are expected to meet with mental fortitude'. Therefore, it is thought by many that there are good policy reasons for placing greater limits on the recovery of damages for non-financial loss than for financial loss (for example, Bingham LJ in *Watts*).

16.53   The other viewpoint starts from the position that non-financial loss is every bit as deserving of protection as financial loss. So providing such loss is sufficiently fore-seeable and not too remote (see paras **16.63–16.95**), it should be recoverable. To place the claimant in the same position as if the contract had been performed, we must take account of the mental distress that the breach has caused him (McDonald (1994)). Therefore, in the example given by Lord Scott in *Farley* of someone who suffers a complete mental breakdown as a result of his disappointment at the con-tract being breached, damages should be recoverable providing this type of harm was sufficiently foreseeable. Importantly, this viewpoint suggests that liability for non-financial loss can be kept within acceptable limits by the use of limiting fac-tors such as foreseeability and remoteness (Chandler and Devenney (2007); see also Phang (2003)). As Linden J commented in the Canadian case of *Brown v Waterloo Regional Board of Commissioners of Police* (1982):

> Normally, in ordinary commercial situations, it is not contemplated that mental suffer-ing will result from a breach of contract; however, where the contract affects 'personal, social and family interests', the likelihood of mental suffering in the event of breach may be foreseen.

16.54   There have been times when it seemed that English law (*Dunk v George Waller & Son Ltd* (1970) and *Cox v Philips Industries Ltd* (1976)) and New Zealand law (*Rowlands v Collow* (1992)) would adopt this broader viewpoint, but both systems of law have rejected it. A good example of this is *Wiseman v Virgin Atlantic* (2006). Having purchased a return ticket from Gatwick to Nigeria, presented his return ticket to Virgin's employees at the airport in Nigeria, and been asked for a bribe to enable him to board the aircraft (which he refused to pay), Dr Wiseman was wrongly accused of having a fake passport, ridiculed by various members of staff in front of friends from his church who had come to see him off, and accused of being a crim-inal! Eventually he was permitted to return on a flight 12 days later. Despite the fact that the breach had caused him mental distress (and distress that would seem clearly foreseeable), he was held not to be entitled to recover anything for that element of his claim. Therefore, the courts seem to be reluctant to award damages where the loss is not linked to something that they regard as tangible, be it physical discom-fort, a swimming pool of a different depth (*Ruxley*) or a sauna rather than a jacuzzi (*Newman*–see para **16.41**).

16.55   Which approach is better? There is much to be said for the second approach. It accepts that non-financial loss is equally as deserving of protection as monetary loss. It seems simpler, as it avoids the drawing of difficult distinctions like physical/non-physical in-convenience and unwelcome sensory experience/mere disappointment at the breach. Moreover, a number of factors can be used to keep liability within acceptable limits: the foreseeability requirement, insisting that where the claimant is a company it would be unable to claim for distress, and keeping the quantum of any awards modest (*Farley*). However, there are two problems with it. First, the broader approach also requires difficult distinctions to be drawn, between situations in which distress is sufficiently foreseeable and situations in which it is not. This is far from easy to do. Second, it is not certain that this approach would, as the quote from *Brown* in para **16.53** claims, prevent recovery for distress in ordinary commercial situations: for example, is it not foreseeable that a businessman may be extremely distressed if in breach of contract he does not receive goods that are vital for the running of his family business? The reason for not allowing recovery in such situations seems to be based more on the 'stiff upper lip' mentality in commercial dealings than on lack of foreseeability.

16.56   It is interesting to observe how the Canadian courts have dealt with the issue. In *Fidler v Sun Life Assurance Co of Canada* (2007), the Supreme Court held that damages for mental distress could be awarded as long as they were reasonably foreseeable, stating that this was the only limiting factor on relief. However, the court was keen to emphasise that 'in normal commercial contracts, the likelihood of a breach of contract causing mental distress is not ordinarily within the reasonable contemplation of the parties. It is not unusual that a breach of contract will leave the wronged party feeling frustrated or angry. The law does not award damages for such incidental frustration.' Therefore, ultimately the court ended up saying that in order to award damages for mental distress, it had to be satisfied:

> *(1) that an object of the contract was to secure a psychological benefit that brings mental distress upon breach within the reasonable contemplation of the parties; and (2) that the degree of mental suffering caused by the breach was of a degree sufficient to warrant compensation.*

Accordingly, while professing to prefer the second, broader approach, the court felt the need to restrict the ambit of this approach to the extent that it ended up with a specific test little different to the English approach.

16.57   Finally, one way to reconcile the desire to treat mental distress on an even footing with other types of loss while keeping relief within reasonable bounds is suggested by the House of Lords decision in *Transfield Shipping Inc v Mercator Shipping Inc ('The Achilleas')* (2008), discussed in detail at paras **16.72-16.84**. There, the majority of the House of Lords held that the correct test was not whether the type of loss was reasonably foreseeable at the time of entering into the contract, but whether it was a type of loss which the parties reasonably contemplated that the defendant would assume responsibility for. Focusing on assumption of responsibility allows one to take into account the extent to which parties to commercial contracts should be expected to put up with the rough and tumble of contract breaking, and therefore provides a more effective limiting factor than reasonable foreseeability. There are some hints of a very similar approach in *Fidler* itself. Therefore, this may provide a viable way forward.

3. Did the breach cause the claimant's loss?

16.58 Some link between the breach of contract and the loss suffered by the defendant must be shown in order to recover compensation. However, the exact nature of the link required is controversial. A much quoted version of the test is that stated by the Court of Appeal in *Galoo v Bright Grahame Murray* (1994):

> The test ... that it is necessary to distinguish between a breach of contract which causes a loss to the plaintiff and one which merely gives the opportunity for him to sustain the loss, is helpful but still leaves the question to be answered, 'How does the court decide whether the breach of duty was the cause of the loss or merely the occasion for the loss?' ... The answer in the end is 'By the application of the court's common sense'.

16.59 The court's unwillingness to set down any hard and fast rules reflects the difficult value judgements that we have to make in deciding whether we can say that the defendant 'caused' the claimant's loss—can we really hope to set out in advance when the intervention of a third party should let the defendant off the hook? However, it is submitted that this approach based on common sense is nevertheless unsatisfactory: to the same effect, see *Equitable Life v Ernst & Young* (2003) and Lord Hoffmann's extra-judicial comments (Hoffmann (1999)). As the Court of Appeal conceded, 'not all judges regard common sense as driving them to the same conclusion'. Therefore, such an approach lacks certainty and provides insufficient guidance to judges. A far better approach is to divide causation into two requirements, factual and legal causation, an approach famously pioneered by Hart and Honoré (1985) but rejected in some of the Australian decisions referred to in *Galoo*.

16.60 In order to establish a sufficient causal link between the breach and the claimant's loss, both factual and legal causation must be shown. Factual causation requires the claimant to show that but for the breach of contract, they would not have suffered the loss in question. Legal causation requires the breach of contract to be the direct cause of the loss. Putting this second requirement another way, in certain circumstances, intervening acts, whether by the claimant or a third party, may relieve the defendant of liability.

16.61 Where the intervening actor is the claimant, the courts tend to look at how reasonable their actions were: were they so unreasonable that it would be right to entirely relieve the defendant of liability (for example, *Compagnia Naviera Maropan SA v Bowaters Lloyd Pulp and Paper Mills Ltd* (1955))? A court will be reluctant to find that the claimant, who is a victim of the defendant's wrongdoing and has suffered loss as a result, is the main cause of their own loss. So some really unreasonable conduct on the part of the claimant is needed to relieve the defendant; just as in tort, mere negligence will not normally suffice here, as the Court of Appeal made clear in *Stacey v Autosleeper Group Ltd* (2014). If the claimant's acts are not so unreasonable as to completely relieve the defendant of liability, it might be thought appropriate to reduce the defendant's liability on account of the claimant's fault. Indeed, often the fairest solution would be to make the defendant pay for some but not all of the claimant's loss because the claimant is at fault as well. The problem is that frequently this cannot be done because contributory negligence is not available for all types of breach of contract (see paras 16.106-16.114). Therefore, often the solution will be overly blunt. A better way might be to increase the circumstances in which the defence of contributory negligence can be used, as will be argued.

16.62 Where the intervening actor is a third party, whether the defendant will be relieved of liability depends on a number of factors, namely how likely it was that the intervening act would happen (*Monarch Steamship Co Ltd v Karlshamms Oljefabriker (A/B)* (1949)), whether the claimant had a duty to prevent the act occurring (*Stansbie v Troman* (1948)), and how reasonable the intervening act was: was it just a reasonable response to a difficult situation caused by the defendant, or was it unreasonable?

4. Remoteness of damage: was the type of loss (and *liability for* the type of loss) within the reasonable contemplation of the parties?

16.63 By breaching a contract, a defendant exposes the claimant to a risk of consequential loss. The defendant may well not know the extent of the loss (if any) that the claimant will suffer—for example, a defendant computer shop that contracts to supply computers to the claimant company and, in breach of contract, delivers them slightly late, may not know precisely what the company intends to use the computers for, or what projects the claimant needs to use the computers to fulfil. We may instinctively think at first glance that this is the defendant's problem—if the computer shop wants to avoid the risk of being liable for the profits that the claimant would have made from an extremely urgent, once in a lifetime, extraordinarily lucrative project, it should perform its contract with the claimant properly and deliver the computers on time. However, there are countervailing considerations. The claimant had the opportunity of telling the defendant computer shop of the special importance of having the computers delivered on time. Moreover, the defendant may not have breached the contract negligently or deliberately (remember that most contractual obligations are strict)—its delivery vans might have broken down or been stolen, for example. Further, the amount of loss suffered by the claimant might be out of all proportion to the severity of the breach.

16.64 Given these countervailing considerations, the courts wish to impose some limits on the claimant's ability to recover from the defendant losses that the latter has caused. Sometimes—harsh though it may seem—the claimant must bear some of the loss. However, one can see from these countervailing considerations that it is difficult to articulate precisely what limits one should place on the claimant's right to recover.

What is the right test?

16.65 The court's original answer to this question was that a claimant can only recover actionable loss caused by a breach if it was within the reasonable contemplation of the parties at the time that the contract was entered into that the claimant might sustain this type of loss as a result of such a breach. For convenience this test will be referred to as one of 'reasonable foreseeability', though be aware that the concept is rather different from the equivalent remoteness of damage test in tort cases.

16.66 The test was laid down by Alderson B in the famous case of *Hadley v Baxendale* (1854). The claimant's mill ground to a halt as a result of a broken crank-shaft. Having no replacement, the claimants needed to obtain a new one, so they engaged the services of the defendant to transport the crank-shaft to someone who could make a new one using the old one as a pattern. At the time of the contract, the defendant had not been told that the mill could not function without the new crank-shaft. In breach of contract, the crank-shaft was not delivered on time, so the claimant sued for the loss of profit that he had suffered as a result of the delay. Alderson B regarded the test as comprising two limbs:

> *Where two parties have made a contract which one of them has broken, the damages which the other party ought to receive in respect of such a breach of contract, should be such as may fairly and reasonably be considered, either arising naturally, i.e. according to the usual course of things from such breach of contract itself, or such as may reasonably be supposed to have been in the contemplation of both parties, at the time they made the contract as the probable result of the breach of it.*

16.67 The first limb states that the claimant will be able to recover such loss as would usually be caused by the breach. Therefore, the claimant does not have to bring such usual types of loss to the defendant's attention in order to recover in respect of them. However, the first limb will not catch other types of loss, losses that one would not ordinarily expect someone to suffer as a result of the breach. For example, people do not usually mind greatly if their swimming pool has a maximum depth of six feet six inches rather than seven feet six inches, so Mr Forsyth in *Ruxley* was unable to recover under the first limb. The second limb deals with such unusual losses. Such loss will only be recoverable if it was reasonably foreseeable to the defendant at the time the contract was made. Usually, this means that the claimant must bring to the defendant's attention that he may suffer such losses before or at the time that the contract was entered into, as did Mr Forsyth in *Ruxley* (by making it clear that the depth of the pool was important to him) and the claimant in *Farley* (by asking the defendant surveyor to specifically investigate how noisy the property was). However, we should not draw too sharp a distinction between the two limbs. Both limbs were commonly regarded as part of a more general test, namely whether the type of loss was reasonably foreseeable in light of the actual knowledge of the defendant at the time of contracting, or the knowledge that they should have possessed (see *Jackson v Royal Bank of Scotland* (2005)).

16.68 Before the modern refinement of *Hadley* by the House of Lords (discussed in paras **16.72–16.84**), the case had been considered in a number of appellate authorities, in particular *Victoria Laundry (Windsor) Ltd v Newman Industries Ltd* (1949), *Koufos v Czarnikow Ltd, The Heron II* (1969), *Parsons v Uttley Ingham & Co Ltd* (1978), and *Brown v KMR Services Ltd* (1995). In the first of these, the claimants contracted to buy a boiler from the defendants to help with the expansion of their business. The defendants were aware at the time of contracting that the claimants wanted to use the boiler immediately. Despite this, and in breach of contract, the defendants were late in delivering the boiler. The claimant sought to recover the ordinary loss of profits that it had suffered, and the profit it had lost from exceptionally lucrative dyeing contracts that it could have otherwise obtained. It was held that the two limbs of the *Hadley* formula could be combined into one test: was the loss reasonably foreseeable? On the facts, it was held that only the ordinary loss of profits satisfied this test, because the defendant could not have been expected to know of the exceptional profits that the claimant could have made from the dyeing contracts. This view that the two limbs of *Hadley* form part of a single test was also taken in *The Heron II*.

16.69 As to what it is that must be reasonably foreseeable at the time of contracting, it was held in *Parsons* that only the type of loss, and not its extent or exact nature, need be foreseen. This approach was followed in *Brown* and reaffirmed subsequently by the House of Lords, although perhaps not in such explicit terms as it might have done, in *Jackson v Royal Bank of Scotland* (2005). What is less clear is whether *Victoria Laundry* can be regarded as correctly decided in light of this development. At first glance, it appears that the type of harm that was reasonably foreseeable in that case was the business profits of the claimant, and that this type of harm included both the ordinary and the exceptional losses of profit that the claimant suffered. While the Court of Appeal in *Brown* attempted to reconcile *Victoria Laundry* with this new approach, its attempts were not wholly convincing.

16.70 The discussion of *Victoria Laundry* highlights the discomfort that courts feel in awarding levels of damages that may have been entirely unforeseeable to the defendant and where the breach may have been inadvertent. Trying to use the doctrine that the 'type' of loss must be foreseeable to stop such damages awards is problematic, because the court would be forced to define the type of loss in extremely narrow terms. Moreover, dealing with the issue in this way hides the full range of policy considerations that are likely to motivate the court's conclusions. The court is trying to allocate the risk of unforeseeable losses between the two parties, and it is understandable that it may—implicitly or otherwise—take account of not only how foreseeable the type of loss was but also the quantum of the loss suffered compared to the benefit that the defendant derived from the contract, whether the breach was deliberate or negligent, general practice in the industry in question, and so forth.

16.71 As a result of this, some commentators (for example, Tettenborn (2007a)) suggested that the *Hadley* test was due an overhaul and that one should ask more explicitly whether—in light of the nature and object of the contract—it is reasonable to require the defendant to assume responsibility for such losses. Therefore, in the case of *Victoria Laundry*, one might reach the same result, but on the basis that the purpose of the contract as both parties would have understood it was to supply the claimant with goods to use in its business. If the claimant planned to use them in an incredibly profitable manner, that is a function of the claimant's business practices, and the defendant should not be required to assume responsibility for losses over and above the ordinary amount of profit that someone would make from using its goods.

16.72 An opportunity for the House of Lords to evaluate the *Hadley* test and apply it in modern conditions came in *Transfield Shipping Inc v Mercator Shipping Inc ('The Achilleas')* (2008). A charterer of a ship was obliged to return it to its owners by 2 May. By April market rates had more than doubled, so the owners arranged a new six-month charter with Cargill, promising delivery of the ship no later than 8 May, at the rate of $39,500 a day. The ship was delayed on its last voyage and so the original charterer did not return the ship until 11 May. By this time, market rates had plummeted, so in light of the fact that the owner could not deliver the ship to Cargill on time, it had to renegotiate the contract with Cargill to provide it with the ship at a reduced daily rate of $31,500. The owner sued the charterer for the difference in the daily rate for the period of the six-month charter, which came to over $1.3 million. The charterer argued that it was only liable for damages at the market rate *for the period of the delay in returning the ship*, which came to just over $158,000.

16.73 The critical point was that the claimant had only suffered a loss by virtue of having concluded an extremely profitable contract when the market rates had surged, and the market rate then quickly plummeting, so, as Rix LJ commented in the Court of Appeal, '[i]t requires extremely volatile conditions to create the situation which has occurred here'. Moreover, the defendant did not intend to breach the contract, the delay was relatively short and had occurred in the course of a sub-charter that the owner could probably have vetoed if it risked delaying the return of the vessel. The loss by comparison was extremely high, and the court was told that industry practice was that a charterer was only liable for damages for the period of delay in such cases. However, it was foreseeable at the time that the charter was entered into with the defendant that the claimant might charter it out to someone else and need the return of the ship in order to charter it out again, so if foreseeability of the *type* of loss was the only limiting factor, one might think the claimant would be liable for the full damages.

16.74 Faced with this dilemma, all five members of the House of Lords found that the charterer's liability was limited to damages for the period of delay. However, there were (at least) two different routes to this conclusion. Lords Hoffmann, Hope, and Walker held that the question was whether the loss was outside the scope of the liability which the parties would reasonably have contemplated that the charterer was *assuming responsibility for*. Foreseeability by itself was not sufficient—one had to go further and identify whether it would reasonably have been contemplated not just that the type of loss was reasonably foreseeable, but that the defendant was *assuming responsibility* for *liability* for the type of loss that had occurred. Here, the charterer could not control or know of the extent of his potential liability for late delivery at the time he entered into the contract (and nor could the owner even inform him of the risk since the loss resulted from subsequent market increases and then drops). Moreover, the owner had the ability to protect himself against the risk of being unable to meet its obligations under future charters by refusing to allow last voyages to go ahead where they would place the return date in jeopardy. Accordingly, the defendant could not be taken to have assumed responsibility for this type of loss.

16.75 For Lord Hoffmann (and Lord Walker), this explained *Victoria Laundry*: '[t]he vendors of the boilers would have regarded the profits on those [particularly lucrative dyeing contracts] as a different and higher form of risk than the general risk of loss of profits by the laundry' and therefore would not be taken to have assumed responsibility for them.

16.76 The remaining two judges decided the case on the more orthodox basis that the extraordinary type of loss suffered here was not reasonably foreseeable, because the loss only occurred as a result of the extremely volatile market conditions, namely the increase in market rate that allowed the owner to conclude the lucrative future charter, and then the drop in market rate that required the owner to renegotiate this charter to get Cargill to accept the ship upon its late delivery.

16.77 There are three main difficulties with the minority approach. First, one gets the feeling from *Transfield* and the earlier cases that the courts do want to take—and *are taking*—into account factors other than the foreseeability of loss, the sort of factors referred to in para **16.70**. If such factors are to be taken into account, this should be done openly. Secondly, the minority approach requires one to take a rather counter-intuitive view of what the 'type of loss' was in *Transfield* (and *Victoria Laundry*) in order to reach what both courts felt was the right result in those cases. The arbitrators had found that it was 'not unlikely' that a delay in returning the ship would cause missing dates for a subsequent charter. The simplest way of defining the type of loss is as loss of profits derived from future charters that the claimant had entered into. To split up the loss of profits by saying that certain aspects of this loss of profits arise from volatile market movements seems more to distinguish the *reason* why the loss has arisen rather than the *type* of the loss. Thirdly, on the facts of *Transfield*, it was the volatile market movements that caused the loss that the claimant was held to be allowed to recover—the difference between the charter rate and the market rate during the period of the delay—every bit as much as the loss that the claimant was held *not* to be allowed to recover, the difference between the original and revised charter rate for the six-month period (Foxton (2008)).

16.78 Turning to the majority approach, it must be acknowledged that the range of factors that one may take into account in deciding whether the defendant can be taken to have *assumed responsibility* for the type of loss causes problems for this approach, and in determining what result its application will yield in a particular case. Indeed, Baroness Hale was clearly concerned about this consequence, and given the uncertainty that concepts of assumption of responsibility have led to in tort law, one can well understand this. Against this, the process of examining carefully the nature and object of the contract is far from novel in contract law, being one that the courts have to undertake (often with equal difficulty) in cases of common mistake and frustration (see Chapters 13 and 14), so it is suggested that this objection is not necessarily a fatal one. The second objection to the majority approach is that—contrary to a number of suggestions in the judgments of Lords Walker, Hope, and Hoffmann—it is submitted that there is little support in pre-existing authorities for such an approach. However, it was far from clear that the previous test was actually explaining the full range of considerations that the courts instinctively wanted to take into account.

16.79 Ultimately, as in so many areas of contract law, one is left with a choice between a more certain 'brightline' rule that can sometimes wreak unfairness (at least on one view), and a more subtle route that is less certain in its application. It is suggested that the courts want to take a broader range of factors into account than the reasonable foreseeability test allows, and, this being the case, the majority approach is on balance to be preferred. Moreover, it is easy to understand why the courts wish to preserve this flexibility rather than tying themselves to a test that only takes into account how likely the loss is to result from the particular breach. For example, imagine a taxi driver who is told by a customer getting into his cab that the customer is on his way to a critical business meeting to conclude a huge deal that will give him a profit of £100 million, but (through no fault of his own) he will lose the deal if he does not get there in 30 minutes, and through the negligence of the taxi driver the ride takes 40 minutes when it should have taken only 20. In these circumstances, despite the breach of contract by the driver, one may have reservations about holding him liable for the lost profit, whether because there is not a realistic opportunity for him to bargain to negotiate specifically to limit his liability in this respect, because responsibility for this huge potential loss is unlikely to be factored into the price, or otherwise (see for example Peel (2009)). On the other hand, the danger of this more subtle approach is that the courts do not articulate clearly and precisely what factors are to be used to determine the result. Without such articulation, the courts may depart too readily from the foreseeability test so as to deny the claimant's recovery, such as on the basis of general understandings in the market in question that particular types of loss are not recoverable (such general understandings being asserted and accepted in *Transfield*), even though they are rarely in practice particularly concrete. This danger is, if anything, accentuated by the use of the concept of assumption of responsibility as a dividing line, because one is dealing with cases where the parties have not turned their mind to the recoverability of particular loss (Harris (2012)).

16.80 Lord Hoffmann has since expanded extra-judicially on the rationale for his approach, emphasising a theme picked up in both his and Lord Hope's judgments in *Transfield*, namely that the question of whether the loss is too remote is 'part of the interpretation of the obligations imposed by the contract rather than the application of a foreseeability rule' (Hoffmann (2010)). You construe the contract objectively to determine whether the defendant has assumed responsibility for the loss in question.

16.81 However, it is suggested that this is not a sound basis for the approach. First, in many contracts the parties (or reasonable persons in their shoes) are unlikely to focus on the precise measure of liability if the contract is breached in each of the different ways that it could be, so it is artificial to regard determining whether the loss is too remote as an exercise in construction. While Lord Hoffmann suggests in his article that this point is met by the fact that interpretation is judged objectively, so that it does not matter whether the parties actually had these points in mind, reading into the contracts terms dealing with whether a specific type of loss caused by a specific type of breach is recoverable does seem rather artificial and unnecessary to justify the approach that Lord Hoffmann wishes to take. One of the main criticisms of the old foreseeability test is that it masks what the courts are really doing, so one must be careful before replacing it with a test that risks doing the same by portraying it as a matter of construction. Second, it is possible to seek to justify all of the rules on remedies, whether for compensating loss or disgorging profit, as being based on what the parties would reasonably have agreed had they thought about it, and therefore treat it as an exercise in construction. However, using what the parties would reasonably have agreed as a touchstone tells you very little about what the detail of these rules should be, and therefore does not really get to the root of how to determine the content of these rules. Indeed, Lord Hoffmann's assumption of responsibility approach in *Transfield* drew on his similar earlier approach to the tort of negligence in the *South Australia* case (see para **9.56**), where the parties' intentions are not used as a guiding principle.

16.82 The question of which of the approaches taken in *Transfield* should be followed was considered by Toulson LJ in *Supershield Ltd v Siemens Building Technologies FE Ltd* (2010). In substance he took the approach of Lords Hoffmann and Hope, holding that a party should only be held liable for loss if he can 'reasonably be taken to have assumed a responsibility to protect the victim', suggesting that this approach was based on the 'presumed intention' of the parties. That case also provides a helpful illustration of how this approach works in practice.

16.83 Siemens had contracted to supply and install the sprinkler system in a new office building occupied by a city law firm, and it had subcontracted the installation of the system to Supershield. The valve in the plumbing apparatus installed by Supershield failed and water from a storage tank for the sprinkler system overflowed into the basement of the office building. There were drains in the floor of the room in which the tank stood, but they became blocked or partially blocked by material on the floor. Water then flowed outside the tank room, reaching electrical equipment in the basement and causing substantial damage. The valve had failed because it had not been installed correctly by Supershield. Siemens settled claims brought by its contractor (in due course the settlement made its way up the chain of contracts to the law firm), then sought an indemnity from Supershield.

16.84 One of Supershield's arguments was that Siemens should not have agreed to pay anything by way of settlement, because it had a good defence on the basis that the damage to the electrical equipment was too remote. This was because the blockage of all the drains was a 'most unfortunate and unlikely occurrence', which prevented the water from running away as it would have done in the normal course of events. But the Court of Appeal disagreed. The loss was not too remote, because irrespective of how unlikely it was that the breach would cause the loss, the purpose of installing the valve was to provide the first means of protection against flooding, and therefore protecting against flooding was what the installers were assuming a responsibility to do. Toulson LJ explained that *Transfield* is:

> authority that there may be cases where the court, on examining the contract and the commercial background, decides that the standard approach would not reflect the expectation or intention reasonably to be imputed to the parties. In those two instances the effect was exclusionary; the contract breaker was held not to be liable for loss which resulted from its breach although some loss of the kind was not unlikely. But logically the same principle may have an inclusionary effect. If, on the proper analysis of the contract against its commercial background, the loss was within the scope of the duty, it cannot be regarded as too remote, even if it would not have occurred in ordinary circumstances.

What remains of reasonable foreseeability after *Transfield*?

16.85 Another question arising out of *Transfield* is what role remains for the requirement that the type of loss be reasonably foreseeable on the approach of Lords Hoffmann, Hope, and Walker. It appears from Lord Hoffmann's speech and the way that he formulated the question before the court that he considered that:

> the rule that a party may recover losses which were foreseeable ... is ... a prima facie assumption about what the parties may be taken to have intended, no doubt applicable in the great majority of cases but capable of rebuttal in cases in which the context, surrounding circumstances or general understanding in the relevant market shows that a party would not reasonably have been regarded as assuming responsibility for those losses.

In other words, he considered that reasonable foreseeability is just a part—albeit an extremely important and normally decisive part—of the assumption of responsibility test. The same appeared to be the view of Lords Hope and Walker.

16.86 This has been clarified by the Court of Appeal decision in *John Grimes Partnership Ltd v Gubbins* (2013). The case concerned whether the defendant engineer, whose breaches of contract had caused the delay of the claimant developer's development scheme, could be held liable for the loss suffered by the claimant as a result of the market value of the property dropping in the meantime. The court held that, in deciding a remoteness question, its role was effectively to imply a term as to what losses the defendant was accepting potential liability for on breach. Importantly, it held that in normal circumstances this term would accept liability for reasonably foreseeable types of losses, unless (as in *Transfield*) there was evidence that the nature of the contract and the commercial background, or indeed other relevant special circumstances, rendered that implied assumption of responsibility inappropriate. Therefore, normally reasonable foreseeability governs, but there may be special reasons why it is not enough to allow the claimant to recover.

The degree of foreseeability required–comparison with tort and concurrent liability

16.87   Another knotty issue—even after *Transfield*—is the precise degree of foreseeability required and, in particular, how this standard compares to that required in tort. *The Heron II* explains that a higher degree of foreseeability is required in contract. Lord Reid gives the following explanation for this difference:

> In contract, if one party wishes to protect himself against a risk which to the other party would appear unusual, he can direct the other party's attention to it before the contract is made, and I need not stop to consider in what circumstances the other party will then be held to have accepted responsibility in that event. But in tort there is no opportunity for the injured party to protect himself in that way, and the tortfeasor cannot reasonably complain if he has to pay for some very unusual but nevertheless foreseeable damage which results from his wrongdoing.

16.88   Take a paradigm case of negligence: Bertha is knocked down by a car driven negligently by Desmond, a complete stranger. Imagine that Bertha is an investment banker, earning £10 million a year, but she is no longer able to work as a result of the tort. Because Bertha and Desmond had no dealings with each other before the tort occurred, Bertha could not be expected to bring her unusually high salary, and thus massive potential future loss of earnings, to Desmond's attention. So the remoteness test in the tort of negligence is incredibly generous—a defendant takes the claimant as he finds her, and only wholly unforeseeable types of loss are irrecoverable. In contrast, take a paradigm contract case. In this case, the parties have dealt with each other: they have concluded a contract. Therefore, if one party has some peculiar vulnerability, such as a lucrative potential sub-contract or that they care greatly that a pool is of a certain depth, they have the opportunity to bring this fact to the other party's attention before the contract is entered into. The upshot of this is that we require a claimant in contract to establish a higher degree of foreseeability because of this opportunity.

16.89   Prior to *Transfield*, it was considered that the tighter test of foreseeability in contract was a sufficient restricting factor on contractual damages. As seen, this has now been rejected. However, in this section, we are concerned with a different issue. The problem that arises is this: what happens where the parties were in a pre-existing relationship with each other before a tort was committed? In such a case, unlike in the paradigm tort case discussed previously, the claimant has the opportunity to inform the other party of his exceptional vulnerabilities before the tort is committed. This typically occurs where there is concurrent liability in tort and contract, such as where one party provides services to the other. Here, the assumption of the contract paradigm case still holds true (the parties have previous dealings with each other), but the assumption of tort paradigm does not, so the latter should give way: the contract standard of foreseeability should apply. In such a situation, the claimant should have to establish the higher standard of foreseeability whether his claim is in tort or in contract.

16.90 This issue was tackled in *Parsons*, but the Court of Appeal failed to resolve it in a wholly satisfactory manner. Lord Denning MR stated that the degree of foreseeability required should depend on the type of loss suffered, rather than on whether the claim was brought in tort or contract: the higher standard was required for economic loss and the lower standard for personal injury and property damage. For the reasons given in the two preceding paragraphs, it is suggested that this is not the correct distinction to draw. Orr and Scarman LJJ rejected the distinction drawn by Lord Denning. Most interesting of all are the comments of Scarman LJ. In some passages, he suggests that where the parties are in a contractual or similar relationship, the same test should be applied. Scarman LJ found it difficult to articulate the exact situations in which the same degree of foreseeability should be required in contract and tort. However, it appears that he was getting extremely close to the pre-existing relationship test mentioned previously, which it is suggested is the appropriate distinction to draw. Scarman LJ also did not make it clear which test should apply in such situations: the higher standard or the lower standard. For the reasons given, it is submitted that the higher standard should apply.

16.91 Immediately after *Transfield* the courts continued to adopt the somewhat illogical position that, in cases of concurrent liability in contract and tort, the remoteness tests are different depending on whether the claim was phrased as tort or breach of contract. The Court of Appeal in *Yapp v Foreign and Commonwealth Office* (2015) assumed the correctness of this distinction in a physical harm case, where an employee suffered psychiatric illness as a result of the defendant's negligent breach of his employment contract, triggering potential concurrent liability in contract and tort. The court unanimously held that the psychiatric illness was unforeseeable even under the more generous tort test, and was therefore definitely irrecoverable for breach of contract, which was said to have a stricter version of the test.

16.92 Happily, the issue has since been resolved by the Court of Appeal, at least in the much more significant context of negligent professional advice causing pure financial loss, where the defendant is concurrently liable for breach of contract and in the tort of negligence. It is now clear that, in such a case, the contractual test applies. In *Wellesley Partners LLP v Withers LLP* (2015) the defendant solicitors acted for the claimant, a firm of executive head hunters, in connection with an investment of capital by a bank. The deal was that the bank was to have the option to withdraw half its capital exercisable after 42 months (ie not within the first 41 months), but defendants negligently drafted the investment agreement so as to give the bank the option within the first 41 months. Sure enough, the bank exercised the option and withdrew half its capital after only 12 months, which meant that the claimant could not pursue a lucrative opportunity to expand its business in the USA. The Court of Appeal held that the appropriate remoteness test was the *Transfield* contractual test, rather than the more generous tort test. As Floyd LJ said:

> *The parties are assumed to be contracting on the basis that liability will be confined to damage of the kind which is in their reasonable contemplation. It makes no sense at all for the existence of the concurrent duty in tort to upset this consensus, particularly given that the tortious duty arises out of the same assumption of responsibility as exists under the contract.*

16.93   On the facts, the claimant's losses were recoverable even under the stricter contractual test. The defendants were given express instructions to draft a clause which would prevent the bank from withdrawing half its capital within the first 41 months. Floyd J saw 'nothing unfair or unreasonable, or inconsistent with the purpose of the duty in holding that damage which is the consequence of the unavailability of that capital should be the responsibility of [the defendants]'. Moreover, the 'fact that the extent of loss cannot be predicted at the date of the formation of the contract cannot by itself amount to a sufficient reason for holding that the contract breaker has not assumed responsibility for it.'

16.94   Finally notice that the claimant was not certain to have made a profit in the USA, even if the defendant had drafted the investment agreement properly and the bank's capital had been locked in. What the claimant lost was the *chance* of obtaining the relevant business, which depended on the hypothetical action of the potential US counterparty (see para **16.12**), assessed at 60 per cent. This reminds us that the remoteness test applies just as much to lost chance cases as all others. In contrast to *Wellesley*, the claimant in *Wright v Lewis Silkin LLP* (2016) established that the defendant solicitor's negligence (in omitting to include a clause in an agreement between parties based in India to confer exclusive jurisdiction on the English courts) allowed the other party to the agreement (Deccan) to challenge the jurisdiction of the English courts; this caused a year's delay before the English courts accepted jurisdiction and gave judgment for the claimant; the delay in turn meant that the claimant lost a (20 per cent) chance of recovering £10 million from Deccan, which had got into financial difficulties during the year's delay. The Court of Appeal awarded the claimant a small amount of damages to reflect the additional costs incurred because of the absence of an exclusive jurisdiction clause, but decided that the £2 million (20 per cent of £10 million) was too remote: 'as a result of the delay caused by defective contract drafting, the claimant lost a 20 per cent chance that Deccan would honour the judgment debt voluntarily. In my view that loss is not damage of a kind that either party … would have had in mind as not unlikely to result from the omission of an exclusive jurisdiction clause.'

What happens where the actual type of loss of profit is unforeseeable but a lesser type of loss of profit would have been foreseeable?

16.95   One last point deserves mention. If the actual loss of profit suffered by the claimant is not reasonably foreseeable, he can still recover a lesser sum measured by the loss of profit that would have been foreseeable (*Cory v Thames Iron Works Co* (1868), discussed by Burrows (2004)). So for example, if the defendant's breach meant that the claimant had missed out on an extraordinarily lucrative contract, and this extraordinary loss of profit was not reasonably foreseeable, the claimant can still recover the ordinary loss of profit that the defendant could reasonably have foreseen.

5. Has the claimant mitigated his loss?

16.96 A claimant must take reasonable steps to minimise the loss caused by the defendant's breach. This is often known as the 'duty to mitigate', although strictly the reference to a 'duty' is incorrect because a claimant is free not to mitigate his loss without incurring any liability to the defendant (as Bridge (1989) explains). Mitigation can be broken down into three sub-rules: see Harris, Campbell, and Halson (2002).

16.97 First, the claimant cannot recover damages in respect of any part of his loss that he could have avoided by taking reasonable steps (*British Westinghouse Electric Co Ltd v Underground Electric Railways Co of London Ltd* (1912)). So if Stella is dismissed from her job in breach of contract and is offered an identical job by another company for the same amount of money, she will probably be unable to claim loss of wages from the moment at which she should have started at her new place of work. It has been held that under some circumstances, the reasonable steps test will require the claimant to offer to enter into a new contract with the defendant on the same terms as the old one (*The Solholt* (1983)). However, as Bridge (1989) points out, requiring the claimant to enter into a new contract with the defendant renders the claimant's right to terminate the original contract for the defendant's breach 'utterly illusory', because the moment that he terminates, he has to offer to enter into a new contract with the defendant on the same terms! This reasonable steps requirement placed on the claimant is not quite as onerous as it first appears, for two reasons. In deciding whether the claimant has taken reasonable steps, the court will take into account that he may have been placed in a tight spot by the wrongful conduct of the defendant, so the court will be reluctant to allow a wrongdoing defendant to say that the victim of breach should have acted differently (*Banco de Portugal v Waterlow* (1932)). Moreover, the claimant is offered some protection by the fact that it is the defendant who bears the onus of showing that the claimant has failed to take such reasonable steps to minimise his loss, rather than the claimant having to show that he has mitigated his loss.

16.98 The second sub-rule is that the claimant can recover for any expenses that he incurs in making reasonable efforts to reduce the loss that he will suffer, even if these efforts are not successful (*Wilson v United Counties Bank* (1920)). So in our example, Stella would be able to recover for travel expenses that she incurred in attending interviews in an attempt to find a new job, even if these interviews were unsuccessful.

16.99 The third sub-rule is that, if the claimant has in fact avoided the potential loss likely to result from the defendant's breach of contract, he cannot recover the loss that he has avoided suffering. Returning again to our example, if Stella accepted the new job, she could not recover loss of wages from the date that she started the new job. So if the claimant receives a benefit that wipes out the loss that he would have otherwise suffered, he cannot recover. However, not all benefits can be taken into account. For example, if Stella won the lottery the week after losing her job, this benefit should not be taken into account when deciding whether she should be allowed to recover her lost wages because it has nothing to do with her being sacked or her loss of wages. The issue is, therefore, when will a benefit received by the claimant be taken into account when working out whether the claimant has avoided the loss caused by the breach of contract?

16.100 One way of approaching the question is to ask, as in *Hussey v Eels* (1990), whether the benefit was 'part of a continuous transaction of which the [defendant's fault] was the inception', that is, whether the fault that caused the loss also caused the gain. This approach was applied by the Court of Appeal in *Primavera v Allied Dunbar Assurance plc* (2002). However, as Midwinter (2003a) points out, the test is problematic:

> *Every day there are countless examples of benefits received by a claimant that mitigate or avoid his loss but could in no way be said to be part of a continuous transaction caused by the defendant's acts ... It is obvious, for example, that a claimant whose arm is broken by the defendant's negligent act cannot recover for the loss of the use of the arm for the rest of his life if his arm has been repaired by a surgeon. Yet it is impossible to say that the effects of the surgeon's skill are caused by the defendant's act: they are the voluntary acts of a third party with whom the defendant has no connection.*

A better test, he suggests, would be to ask simply whether the subsequent gains are referable to the loss. As in the case of causation, the difficulty in formulating in advance a satisfactory test to determine when such 'compensating' benefits should be taken into account reflects the multitude of situations in which such benefits can crop up and the slightly different considerations that might apply in each of them. Accordingly, while the proposed 'referability' test is a slightly more accurate one than the 'continuous transaction' tests, one is still faced with the same difficult value judgements in deciding whether the gains are 'referable' to the loss in question.

16.101 The Supreme Court has recently examined this issue in two separate cases. In the complex financial case of *Lowick Rose LLP v Swynson Ltd* (2017), the claimant company invested in a company, E Co, which the defendant accountant negligently failed to spot was financially insecure. The claimant lent money to E Co to try, unsuccessfully, to avert its collapse. Eventually (for tax reasons) the claimant's controlling shareholder lent money to E Co, to enable it to repay the loans to the claimant. Did this reduce the amount of the claimant company's loss that could be claimed from the defendant, or was it a collateral benefit? The Court of Appeal thought it was collateral and thus to be disregarded, but the Supreme Court disagreed. Lord Sumption set out a general approach as follows:

> *The general rule is that loss which has been avoided is not recoverable as damages, although expense reasonably incurred in avoiding it may be recoverable as costs of mitigation. To this there is an exception for collateral payments (res inter alios acta),*

which the law treats as not making good the claimant's loss. It is difficult to identify a
single principle underlying every case. In spite of what the Latin tag might lead one to
expect, the critical factor is not the source of the benefit in a third party but its character.
Broadly speaking, collateral benefits are those whose receipt arose independently of the
circumstances giving rise to the loss. Thus a gift received by the claimant, even if occa-
sioned by his loss, is regarded as independent of the loss because its gratuitous character
means that there is no causal relationship between them.

16.102 This test of 'independence' is easier to state than to apply, but the Supreme Court unanimously held that there was nothing independent going on here—E Co had itself repaid
what it owed the claimant and thus the claimant's loss was reduced. The *source* of funds
that enabled E Co to do so was irrelevant, even though the reality was that the claimant's
controlling shareholder provided the money, and thus suffered an equivalent loss by an
indirect route—that was his choice.

16.103 The benefit under consideration in the second Supreme Court decision fell the other
side of the line and was regarded as collateral. In *Globalia Business Travel SAU v Fulton
Shipping Inc* (2017) the charterer repudiated a charter contract two years before the expiry date and the ship owners accepted this repudiation (see para **15.54**). Prima facie,
this gave the owners the right to claim damages for the lost profits on the hire it would
have earnt for the remaining two years, subject of course to its requirement to mitigate
its loss. The owners managed to sell the ship for over $23 million at that point, whereas
it would only have been worth $7 million at the end of the term two years later. The
Supreme Court had to decide whether this capital profit was obtained by mitigation, so
as to reduce the owners' damages claim against the charterers, or an independent collateral benefit. The court expressed the general test in slightly different terms from the
previous decision, but with the same emphasis on causal connection or independence:

> *The essential question is whether there is a sufficiently close link between the two and*
> *not whether they are similar in nature. The relevant link is causation. The benefit to be*
> *brought into account must have been caused either by the breach of the charterparty or*
> *by a successful act of mitigation.*

16.104 On the facts, the benefit of selling the vessel before it fell in value was 'irrelevant because the owner's interest in the capital value of the vessel had nothing to do with the
interest injured by the charterers' repudiation of the charterparty.' For the same reason,
the owners would not have been able to claim any additional loss if they decided to sell
the vessel only to find its market value would have risen over the next two years. Either
way, they were 'making a commercial decision at their own risk'. Both *Lowick Rose* and
Globalia remind us that describing a rule as one of 'causation' or independence' should
not disguise the value judgement the court has to make about the scope of a contractual
obligation and where commercial risk ought to lie.

16.105 Having examined the detail of the mitigation rules, it seems pertinent to ask why we
should impose this requirement on the claimant to take reasonable steps to minimise his

loss in the first place—what is the purpose behind this rule? The mitigation requirement is one of the doctrines that prevents expectation damages putting the claimant in as good a position as he would have been in had the contract been performed. In other words, it helps to render damages inferior to getting full performance from the claimant's perspective. This demonstrates that contract law embodies values other than protecting the claimant, because the doctrine of mitigation reduces the scope of this protection. This begs the question, what other values are at play here? This is actually quite a difficult question to answer, as Bridge (1989) demonstrates in his examination of the possible rationales for mitigation. The prevention of the waste of resources is often put forward as an explanation, but Bridge (1989) disagrees with this argument. A more radical yet convincing explanation is that of Friedmann (1995b), who argues that it is based on notions of good faith, in the following sense:

> [Mitigation] is predicated on the ground that if properly carried out, [it] will benefit the wrongdoer without harming the victim. The requirement duly to consider the interest of another is thus an application of the concept of good faith.

6. Did the claimant's fault contribute to the loss that he suffered?

16.106   Where the claimant's fault has contributed to the loss that she has suffered, then the amount of damages that he can recover for the breach of contract may be reduced on account of her contributory negligence. In extreme cases, where the claimant has acted wholly unreasonably, the causation requirement may not be satisfied so the defendant may be relieved of liability entirely (see para **16.61**). This section deals with less extreme situations, where the claimant's fault may merely lead to a reduction in the damages that she can recover. The statutory basis for a reduction for contributory negligence is s 1 of the Law Reform (Contributory Negligence) Act 1945. Unfortunately, liability for breach of contract does not appear to have been at the forefront of the minds of those responsible for the Act, so it is not clear from its wording when, if ever, contributory negligence should be available as a defence to an action for breach of contract.

16.107   As a result of the Court of Appeal decision in *Forsikringsaktieselskapet Vesta v Butcher* (1988), affirming the categorisation adopted at first instance by Hobhouse J, three situations must be distinguished:

> (1) Where the defendant's liability arises from some contractual provision which does not depend on negligence on the part of the defendant.

> (2) Where the defendant's liability arises from a contractual obligation which is expressed in terms of taking care (or its equivalent) but does not correspond to a common law duty to take care which would exist in the given case independently of contract.

(3) Where the defendant's liability in contract is the same as his liability in the tort of negligence independently of the existence of any contract.

16.108 It was stated by the Court of Appeal in *Butcher*, albeit by way of *obiter dicta*, that contributory negligence would only be available in situation (3). This categorisation and approach has been followed on many occasions, for example by the Court of Appeal in *Barclays Bank plc v Fairclough Building Ltd* (1994), where it was held that the defence was not available in situation (1). However, the approach has not been followed in Australia: the High Court of Australia held in *Astley v Austrust Ltd* (1999) that contributory negligence should never be available for a breach of contract.

16.109 When should contributory negligence operate as a defence to breach of contract? It is suggested that *Butcher* was correct to allow its operation in situation (3). Otherwise, unfair circumstances could follow. In situations where there is concurrent liability in tort and contract, the same result should be reached whether the claim is brought in contract or in tort, because the substance of the claim is the same in both cases (Cane (1997)). This was implicitly acknowledged by the House of Lords in *Parsons*, discussed in the context of foreseeability (see para **16.68**). If this is the case, it would be wrong for the defence to be available in relation to the tort claim but not the contractual one, because it would allow the claimant to recover more on the contract claim.

16.110 There are also powerful arguments for allowing the application of the defence in situations (1) and (2). Taking situation (2) first, it is hard to see why this situation should be treated differently from situation (3): why should the presence of concurrent liability (in situation (3)) make such a difference? Burrows (2004) makes a telling criticism of allowing the defence to operate in situation (3) but not in situation (2):

> *[I]t encourages an odd reversal of roles in that a blameworthy plaintiff will be better off, as regards contributory negligence, if he can establish that the defendant was merely liable for breach of a contractual duty of care (or the breach of a strict contractual duty) and was not also liable for the tort of negligence. In other words, so far as contributory negligence is concerned, the plaintiff will be trying to show that the defendant was not also liable in the tort of negligence, while the defendant will be trying to show that he was also liable in the tort of negligence.*

16.111 For this reason, the proposal of the Law Commission in Law Com Report No 219 (1993) to allow the application of the defence in situation (2) should be followed. Indeed, in *Butcher* itself, O'Connor LJ, while feeling compelled by the words of the 1945 Act to limit the defence to situation (3), said that he saw 'great force in the contention that the same rule should apply to claims whether they are based in contract or tort where the act complained of involves the breach of a duty of care'. Notice, though, that the practical significance of category (2) is now greatly reduced. At the time of *Butcher*, concurrent liability in contract and tort was rare, but since *Henderson v Merrett Syndicates* (1995) concurrent liability in tort has been the default position where the contractual obligation is one of reasonable care, so category (2) has effectively been swallowed up by category (3).

16.112 Moreover, there are also strong arguments for allowing the defence in situation (1) as well. The principal objection to doing so is that outlined by the Law Commission in their consultation paper, namely that it would turn many straightforward contractual disputes into more complex disputes about comparative blameworthiness. Indeed, this reasoning was employed by the High Court of Australia in *Astley* to reject the possibility of contributory negligence ever operating as a defence to claims for breach of contract. However, Burrows (2004) puts forward a forceful counterargument:

> If the plaintiff's unreasonable conduct can sometimes result in his recovering no damages, through the principles of intervening cause or mitigation, it must be sensible for there to be a mid-position where his negligence results in a mere reduction of damages.

16.113 As O'Sullivan (2017b) has argued, Burrows' position is on balance correct. Without having this 'mid-position', the courts are forced into an overly blunt solution, either allowing the claim in full or, more worryingly, rejecting it in full (for example, by concluding that the claimant's conduct broke the chain of causation), whereas the course that would best reflect the degree to which the claimant was at fault would be the much more nuanced option of partial reduction for contributory negligence. It is also noteworthy that in a completely different strict liability context, the tort regime for strict liability for defective products under the Consumer Protection Act 1987, the defence of contributory negligence is available. Finally, fears that claimants will be under-protected if contributory negligence were to be available in situation (1) can be met by ensuring that the defence is only invoked where the claimant is truly partially to blame—so if the claimant did not take steps to protect her own position because she was justifiably relying on the defendant's strict warranty, the claimant is not at fault.

16.114 If the claim does fall into situation (3), the defendant must show two further things in order to invoke the defence. First, he must show that the claimant was at fault, and second, he must prove that this fault was a factual cause (see para **16.60**) of the loss that the claimant sustained. The court will then reduce the amount recoverable 'to such extent as the court thinks just and equitable having regard to the claimant's share in the responsibility for the damage' (s 1(1) of the 1945 Act).

OVERVIEW

1   Parties often do not agree in advance what should happen if the contract is breached. Contract law fills this gap by allowing the victim of a breach a number of remedies against the other party, one of which is compensatory damages.

2   The more protection we want to give to the victim's rights to performance, the more willing we should be to award compensation in respect of the harm that he suffers as a result of the breach. The current trend in English law is to increase the protection of the victim's non-financial interests, by expanding the circumstances in which she can recover for non-financial loss.

3   In general, the claimant can only recover for loss that he has suffered, and not for loss that another party has sustained. Difficulty of assessment is generally no bar to recovering damages. Damages are generally assessed as at the date of the breach, although the court has a power to choose a different date where justice demands.

Measures of damages

4   There are two ways of measuring how much the claimant has lost:

- The expectation measure: aims to put the claimant in the same position as if the contract had been properly performed. There are two ways of doing this. First, to award the claimant the cost of rectifying the breach (the 'cost of cure') or second to award the difference between the value of the performance actually given and the value of the performance that should have been given (the 'difference in value'). The latter will only give a small amount of damages where the claimant entered into the contract for non-commercial reasons, such as to obtain enjoyment or relaxation. In these circumstances, it will be advantageous to claim the cost of cure. The cost of cure can be recovered unless it would be 'unreasonable' to do so. If the cost of cure is 'wholly disproportionate' in size to the difference in value, it will be unreasonable to recover the cost of cure.

- The reliance measure: aims to put the claimant in the position she was in before the contract was entered. This allows the claimant to recover the money she spent in preparing to perform the contract and in actually performing it. However, if the defendant can show that the reliance measure exceeds the expectation measure, the claimant will be limited to recovering the expectation measure.

Actionable types of loss

5   While there is a greater willingness to award damages for non-financial loss, contract law still does not allow compensation to be recovered for some types of non-financial loss. Therefore, we must ask whether the loss is one of the following types of actionable loss:

- Financial loss: this is straightforwardly recoverable, as is personal injury and property damage (more usually associated with tort claims).

- The consumer surplus: this concept has received some judicial support but is not yet fully accepted. It means the amount by which the claimant values performance of a particular obligation over and above the market value. I may enter into a contract for reasons other than to make money, such as to get pleasure or relaxation. If the contract is breached, I may lose little financially, but might have lost something that I value greatly, like peace and quiet, or relaxation. An award of damages should be available for my consumer surplus.

- Distress caused by an unwelcome sensory experience: again, this category is controversial. The category was originally known as 'physical discomfort and mental distress consequent upon it'. However, it is unclear which approach currently represents the law.

6   If the loss is of a different type from those outlined (such as loss of reputation or distress caused by mere disappointment that the contract has been breached), damages will not be recoverable in respect of it.

Causation

7   Some causal link between the breach of contract and loss suffered must be shown. The exact nature of the link required is quite controversial. The current approach is said to be one based on 'common sense' but this gives little guidance and arguably should be replaced by a two-limbed test of factual and legal causation.

Remoteness

8   Traditionally, the claimant had to show that it was (a) within the reasonable contemplation of the parties (b) at the time the contract was entered into that (c) the claimant would suffer the type of loss that he has in fact sustained. However, this test has been re-analysed by the House of Lords in the *Transfield* case and the test is now whether the defendant is to be taken to have assumed responsibility for the type of loss in question.

Mitigation

9   The claimant must take reasonable steps to minimise the loss caused by the breach. This breaks down into three sub-rules:

- The claimant cannot recover damages in respect of any part of her loss that she could have avoided by taking reasonable steps.

- The claimant can recover for any expenses that she incurs in making reasonable efforts to reduce the loss that she will suffer, even if these efforts are unsuccessful.

- If the claimant has in fact avoided the potential loss likely to result from the breach, she cannot recover the loss that she has avoided suffering.

Contributory negligence

10   Contributory negligence can only be used as a defence to an action for breach of contract where (a) the defendant is in breach of a contractual duty of care, such as to take reasonable care, to use reasonable skill etc; and (b) he is also in breach of a tortious duty of care. The defendant must also show that the claimant was at fault and that this fault was a factual cause of the loss that the claimant suffered.

FURTHER READING

Bridge 'Mitigation of Damages in Contract and the Meaning of Avoidable Loss' (1989) 105 LQR 398

Chandler and Devenney 'Breach of Contract and the Expectation Deficit: Inconvenience and Disappointment' (2007) 27 LS 126

Coote 'Contract Damages, *Ruxley* and the Performance Interest' [1997] CLJ 537

Enonchong 'Breach of Contract and Damages for Mental Distress' (1996) 16 OJLS 617

Harris 'Fairness and Remoteness of Damage in Contract Law: A Lexical Ordering Approach' (2012) 28 JCL 122

Hoffmann '*The Achilleas*: Custom and Practice or Foreseeability?' (2010) 14 Edin LR 47

Kramer 'An Agreement-Centred Approach to Remoteness and Contract Damages' in *Comparative Remedies for Breach of Contract* (2005) 249

McDonald 'Contractual Damages for Mental Distress' (1994) 7 JCL 134

McKendrick 'Breach of Contract and the Meaning of Loss' [1999] CLP 37

O'Sullivan 'Loss and Gain at Greater Depth: The Implications of the *Ruxley* Decision' Chapter 1 in *Failure of Contracts* (1997) 1

O'Sullivan 'Damages for Lost Profits for Late Redelivery: How Remote is Too Remote?' [2009] CLJ 34

O'Sullivan 'Contributory Negligence and Strict Contractual Obligations Revisited' Chapter 11 in *Defences in Contract* (2017) 215

Pearce and Halson 'Damages for Breach of Contract: Compensation, Restitution and Vindication' (2008) 28 OJLS 73

Peel 'Remoteness Re-visited' (2009) 126 LQR 6

Robertson 'The Basis of the Remoteness Rule in Contract' (2008) 28 LS 172

Tettenborn 'What is a Loss?' Chapter 17 in *Emerging Issues in Tort Law* (2007) 441

Tettenborn (2007a) '*Hadley v Baxendale* Foreseeability: A Principle Beyond its Sell-by Date?' (2007) 23 JCL 120

For an excellent account of many of the areas covered, see Burrows (2004) Chapters 1–4 in *Remedies for Torts and Breach of Contract*

SELF-TEST QUESTIONS

1   Is non-financial loss equally deserving of protection as financial loss? What stance does English law take on this issue?

2   What does the 'consumer surplus' mean?

3   Should a breach itself count as a loss for which compensation should be awarded?

4   How do the tests of foreseeability for contract and tort differ? Are there any circumstances in which the same test should be applied for both?

5   Why should a claimant have to 'mitigate' his loss?

6   When, if ever, should contributory negligence be a defence to an action for breach of contract?

7   Jonty owns a vintage Bentley, which is his pride and joy. He contracts with Knightley Ltd, a company specialising in restoring and preserving vintage cars, for repairs to the engine of the car. In particular, Jonty specifies in the contract that Knightley must use authentic parts from another vintage Bentley for repairing the interior of the engine, and that the car must be ready for collection by 30 June. He mentions in general terms that he uses the Bentley for film and television work, but gives no further details. Despite strenuous efforts, Knightley find it impossible to locate authentic parts from another vintage Bentley to repair the engine, but are hugely relieved to locate a source of authentic parts from a vintage Rolls Royce, which fit perfectly into the Bentley when welded into place and which are identical to the untrained eye.

The delay in sourcing the parts means that the car is not ready for collection until 2 July. Jonty is distraught, because the delay has meant that he missed a lucrative opportunity to show his car on 1 July to a film director who was 'auditioning' vintage Bentleys for an exceptionally lucrative film role. Moreover he is mortified to discover that the car now contains non-authentic engine parts and believes he will never be able to show his face again at the Vintage Bentley Enthusiasts Club, of which he is chairman, a realisation that causes him to lapse into depression. Advise him as to the measure of damages he can expect for breach of contract.

 For hints on how to answer question 7, please see the online resources at **www.oup.com/uk/sullivan8e/**.

17 Remedies II: specific remedies

SUMMARY

This chapter considers specific remedies for breach of contract:

- Action for an agreed sum, including performance of entire obligations, whether the price can be claimed following repudiation, liquidated damages, and penalty clauses.
- Specific performance, including the test for specific performance, when specific performance will and will not be available, and when it will be barred.
- Injunctions, mandatory and prohibitory, and damages in lieu.

17.1 Aside from being compensatory, the remedies discussed in Chapter 16 share two common features. First, they place an obligation on defendants to pay damages rather than actually perform their side of the contract: the primary obligation to perform is converted into a secondary obligation to pay damages. Second, they impose obligations on the parties that they had not agreed to or intended: as was commented, parties often do not think or agree on what will happen if one party breaches the contract. The remedies forming the subject matter of this chapter do not have the first feature and are traditionally thought not to possess the second feature either. As traditionally understood, they require defendants to *perform* their side of the bargain, as both parties agreed at the outset. So if the defendant contracted to build a house for the claimant, a specific remedy will enforce the primary obligation to perform, for example, by ordering the defendant to build the house, rather than pay damages. However, as we shall see (paras **17.56–17.57**), this traditional distinction may not be correct, and in fact, damages and specific remedies may not be as different as is commonly thought.

17.2 Specific remedies can be divided into two groups, those that place 'positive' duties on the defendant and those that place 'negative' duties. By a positive duty, we mean that the defendant is placed under a duty to *do* something: to pay the money, to deliver the goods, etc. By a negative duty, we mean that the defendant is placed under a duty *not to do* something: not to sing for another record label, not to work for another law firm, etc. There are three types of specific remedies that impose positive duties on a defendant: the action for an agreed sum, specific performance, and the mandatory injunction. In the other camp there is only one remedy, the prohibitory injunction.

17.3 As we shall see, this is a helpful way of dividing specific remedies, because the courts are often markedly more willing to award specific remedies placing only a negative duty on the defendant than those that place a positive duty on her. This brings us neatly to an important issue that runs through this chapter: how willing should we be to award specific remedies? As Burrows (2000) notes, we might expect that a claimant would always be able to obtain a specific remedy as an alternative to getting damages, because 'the specific remedies more directly protect the claimant's right not to be the victim of a wrong than does compensation': they place a duty on the defendant to actually do what he promised, rather than just pay the financial equivalent. This argument seems even stronger when we consider that performance will often be better than damages to a claimant, given the presence of doctrines like mitigation and remoteness that limit the damages recoverable (see Chapter 16). However, as we shall see, English law is often reluctant to award specific remedies for an actual or potential breach of contract. Why is this? In particular, the appropriate scope of specific performance has proved particularly controversial. We shall return to this question after an examination of each of the specific remedies in turn.

The action for an agreed sum

17.4 This common law remedy can be conveniently sub-divided into the award of an agreed *price* and the award of other types of agreed sums (see Burrows (2000)).

Award of an agreed price

17.5 The award of an agreed price allows the claimant to recover a sum of money that is due to him under the terms of the contract. It is important to note that it is a claim for the payment of a *debt*, not a claim for damages. In other words, the claim arises because the obligation breached is an obligation to pay money and one to which the defendant has agreed. Two consequences follow from this. First, there is no need for the claimant to establish that he has suffered a loss: the issue is whether any sum is owing to him under the contract. It should, however, be noted in passing that if the claimant has suffered loss exceeding the sum that is due to him under the terms of the contract, he can make a claim for damages in respect of the excess (*Overstone Ltd v Shipway* (1962)). Second, there is no requirement of mitigation. However, as we shall see, there is increasing pressure for the development of a principle analogous to mitigation, to require the claimant to pay some regard to the interests of the defendant after the contract has been breached.

17.6 In order to claim the agreed price, two requirements must be made out. First, the sum in question must be due under the terms of the contract. Second, the sum must be owed to the claimant: he cannot recover a sum owing to someone else (*Beswick v Beswick* (1968), discussed in para **6.44** and criticised in this respect by Andrews (1988)).

17.7 Whether or not the claimant is entitled to the price requires careful construction of the terms of the contract. One possible construction is that the claimant will not be entitled to the sum until she has completely performed some or all of her obligations under the contract. This is known as the 'entire obligations' rule: complete performance of an obligation or of some obligations is required before a party can recover under the contract. This can be harsh to a claimant, as we saw in our discussion of *Cutter v Powell* (1795) (see para **15.5**).

17.8 The courts have found a number of ways to alleviate this harshness. First, the courts have been reluctant to construe an obligation as being 'entire' (see *Ministry of Sound (Ireland) Ltd v World Online Ltd* (2003) for a good modern example). They have tried to interpret contracts as only requiring substantial rather than complete performance of an obligation in order for the price to fall due, as for example, in *Hoenig v Isaacs* (1952) (discussed at para **15.9**). However, as we have seen, this solution will not always allow the claimant to recover the price (remember *Bolton v Mahadeva* (1972) discussed at para **15.10**).

17.9 Secondly, if the defendant stops the sum becoming due, for example, by preventing the work being completed, the claimant will be allowed to recover in respect of the work that she has done (*Hoenig*). So if, for example, the defendant throws the claimant off his premises before the claimant can finish building the house that she was contracted to build, the claimant can recover a sum representing the value of the work that she has done.

17.10 Thirdly, if the claimant has only partially performed his obligations, the defendant must nevertheless pay for this performance, providing that the defendant has a chance to reject the work done by the claimant but opts to accept it (discussed at para **15.11**). The key requirement here is that the defendant must have had a chance to decide whether to accept or reject the claimant's performance. For example, in *Hoenig*, the defendant had a choice whether or not to use the defective furniture. He chose to, so he had to pay for it.

17.11 Having discussed the three requirements for the action for an agreed price, we must now turn to an important limit on recovery. This limit applies to situations where the claimant has either started or continued to perform *after the defendant has repudiated the contract*. So despite the defendant telling the claimant that the defendant wants nothing more to do with the contract, the claimant elects to keep the contract open (as is his right, see para **15.11**) and begins or carries on performing. The claimant then claims the sum due to him for the performance that he has carried out since the repudiation.

17.12 The most important decision on this issue is the controversial House of Lords decision in *White & Carter (Councils) Ltd v McGregor* (1962). The claimant was an advertising contractor, who agreed with the defendant, the owner of a garage, to renew a contract to display advertisements for his garage for three years. On the same day that the contract was renewed, the defendant wrote to the claimant in an attempt to pull out. The claimant refused to terminate the contract and, as permitted by the contract, performed and sued for the full contract price. By a 3–2 majority, the House of Lords allowed the claimant to recover the full price. The reasoning of the majority was that the claimant had a choice as to whether to keep the contract open, and he elected to do so. There was no mitigation requirement for an action for the agreed price, so the fact that the claimant had performed despite knowing that this performance was unwanted did not prevent him claiming the price. The minority, on the other hand, were motivated by the conviction that the claimant had acted unreasonably by ignoring the defendant's wishes and so should be limited to a claim in damages (see para 15.46).

17.13   Importantly, Lord Reid, a member of the majority, put forward two qualifications on the claimant's entitlement to recover the agreed price. It is important to understand the effect of these qualifications: as emphasised in *The Alaskan Trader* (1983) they limit the claimant's ability to claim the *remedy* in question (the agreed price), not her right to keep the contract open (although the practical effect of limiting the claimant's entitlement to the remedy may be to make it pointless to keep the contract open). Moreover, they affect her ability to bring an action for an agreed sum but *not* her claim for damages. Therefore, if one of the qualifications applies, she will have to show that she has suffered loss as a result of the defendant's breach in order to recover any money.

17.14   The first qualification laid down was the 'cooperation qualification': in 'most cases by refusing co-operation the party in breach can compel the innocent party to restrict his claim to damages'. This is not really an exception to the general rule, just the practical recognition that if the claimant is only entitled to a particular sum under the contract if he performs certain services and he is unable to perform these services by reason of the defendant's failure to cooperate, then the claimant will not be entitled to the sum under the terms of the contract (see *Ministry of Sound (Ireland) Ltd v World Online Ltd* (2003)). Imagine Dave has contracted to do some work inside Paula's factory and Dave is only entitled to payment upon completion of the work. If Paula refuses to let him into the building, Dave cannot do the work and so cannot become entitled to the money under the contract. He may have suffered loss, in which case he can bring a claim for damages, but he is not able to bring an action for the agreed sum. Similarly, if I am dismissed from my job in breach of contract, in theory I have the right to opt to keep the contract alive (see para 15.45), but in practice this is not meaningful or possible: I cannot turn up to work the next day and earn my wage if my former employer has confiscated my security pass. It has been suggested that the cooperation test is a simple one which just requires the court to ask whether the claimant could claim the sum without the need for the defendant to do anything other than the contract (*Isabella Shipowner SA v Shagang Shipping Co Ltd* (2012)). We shall return to this decision later.

17.15   The second qualification from *White & Carter* is the much more controversial 'legitimate interest' qualification:

> if it can be shown that a person has no legitimate interest, financial or otherwise, in performing the contract rather than claiming damages, he ought not be allowed to saddle the other party with an additional burden with no benefit to himself ... just as a party is not allowed to enforce a penalty, so he ought not to be allowed to penalise the other party by taking one course when another is equally advantageous to him.

It is not entirely clear what this legitimate interest qualification means. If the idea of a 'financial' interest is interpreted literally, the claimant would always have a legitimate interest. The reason for this is that it will invariably be advantageous for a claimant to get the contract price rather than a claim for damages, because of the many limitations on the latter, such as the mitigation requirement (see Nienaber (1962) and Carter, Phang, and Phang (1995)).

17.16   Moreover, while the courts have not taken this literal interpretation of the qualification, they have had difficulty establishing a uniform interpretation. For example, in *Attica Sea Carriers Corpn v Ferrostaal Poseidon Bulk Reederei GmbH ('The Puerto Buitrago')* (1976), Lord Denning MR focused on the adequacy of damages to the claimant, suggesting that the qualification applied where 'damages would be an adequate remedy'. On the other hand, in *The Alaskan Trader* (1983), Lloyd J suggested that 'wholly unreasonable' conduct was required. While it has been stated that there may be little difference in practice between these approaches (*Stocznia Gdanska SA v Latvian Shipping Co* (1995) per Clarke J), it is suggested that the subtle shift of focus from the legitimate interests of the claimant to whether his actions are reasonable may reduce the protection to the claimant.

17.17   In *The Alaskan Trader*, for example, a ship was chartered for 24 months. There was a serious engine failure after one year so the charterers indicated that they no longer wanted it, but the owners ignored this and went ahead with expensive repairs, costing $800,000 and taking five months. They told the charterers that the ship was ready again, but the charterers weren't interested. However, the owner refused to treat the charterers' conduct as a repudiation (see para **15.35**) and kept the ship at anchor and fully ready to sail until the charter ran out seven months later. The owner sued for the seven months' hire, but the charterers resisted the action on the ground that the owner should have accepted the repudiation. The arbitrator agreed with the charterers, holding that there was no legitimate interest in performance. Applying his 'wholly unreasonable' test, Lloyd J refused to interfere with this finding. This decision is mildly troubling. The main reason for the decision of the arbitrator was the 'commercial absurdity' of keeping the ship ready for seven months when the owner knew that the charterer no longer wanted the ship. However, it was accepted that it would have been difficult to re-let the ship elsewhere, so why was this not a legitimate financial interest? As Carter and Marston (1985) put it:

> it does not appear that the arbitrator found that the owner's motive was to cast a gratuitous burden on the charterers: rather the owners were faced with one of those commercial risks which are inherent in the trade, namely a sudden fall in the freight market leading to a surplus of tonnage, and would have regarded the continued payment of hire as a means to enable them to ride out the economic storm.

17.18   Sometimes it is obvious that the claimant has a legitimate interest, such as where she has an interest in protecting her relationships or potential relationships with third parties. So, for example, if the claimant needs to perform in order to protect her reputation or to honour agreements with third parties, then this should constitute a legitimate interest: see Carter, Phang, and Phang (1995). But in other cases it is not so obvious: how stubborn should the claimant be permitted to be?

17.19   There are two principal schools of thought on the legitimate interest qualification. The first notes that the agreed price is very often better to the claimant than damages, because of the various limitations on the latter (such as mitigation). Therefore, as she is the victim of the breach whom we should be protecting, we should allow her to opt for whichever of the two remedies is the more advantageous to him. Equally importantly, an action for debt comes extremely close to directly enforcing the debtor's primary obligation under the contract to pay money and the creditor's primary right to be paid the money (see para **17.1** for the distinction between 'primary' and 'secondary' rights and obligations). Therefore, if we say that the claimant must act reasonably in order to bring a debt claim, then we are getting dangerously close to saying that the parties must act reasonably in performing the contract itself. We should be extremely unwilling to qualify the parties' primary rights and obligations under the contract in this way, because they have freely agreed to them.

17.20   The second school of thought suggests that the claimant should be made to have some re- gard to the interests of the defendant: the claimant should not be able to increase the liabil- ity of the defendant by performing against his wishes without good reason (for example, Friedmann (1995a) and Morgan (2015)). The argument is that this rationale underlies the mitigation requirement where the claim is for damages, so why should this rationale not apply equally to the action for the agreed sum. Leggatt J in *MSC Mediterranean Shipping Company SA v Cottonex Anstalt* (2015) at first instance defended the second view by say- ing that the 'no legitimate interest' qualification should be seen in a wider context of a principle of good faith in contractual performance that underlay a number of more spe- cific rules, in particular the rule that a contractual discretion must be exercised in good faith for the purpose that it was conferred and must not be exercised capriciously, arbi- trarily, or unreasonably (see para **7.73**). The suggestion that there is an underlying prin- ciple of good faith in English law is unorthodox and has been considered elsewhere (see paras **4.27, 7.73, and 8.78**), but in any event the analogy is unsatisfactory—there is a clear difference between imposing restrictions on the exercise of a discretionary power given in the contract to one of the parties, and restricting the remedies available to the inno- cent victim faced with the *other* party's discretionary decision to repudiate the contract. When the case reached the Court of Appeal (*MSC Mediterranean Shipping Company SA v Cottonex Anstalt* (2016)), the appeal was resolved on another ground (see para **15.47**), but *obiter* the court disapproved of Leggatt J's approach:

> In my view the better course is for the law to develop along established lines rather than to encourage judges to look for what the judge in this case called some 'general organising principle' drawn from cases of disparate kinds. For example, I do not think that decisions on the exercise of options under contracts of different kinds, on which he also relied, shed any real light on the kind of problem that arises in this case. There is in my view a real danger that if a general principle of good faith were established it would be invoked as often to undermine as to support the terms in which the parties have reached agreement

17.21   What does seem clear is that any move to water down the claimant's protection should be resisted. It should only be in exceptional circumstances that the claimant is condemned as behaving unreasonably, where all she is doing is seeking to keep the contract alive, perform her side of the bargain, and claim what she is entitled to, in the face of a serious repudiatory breach by the defendant. One such exceptional situation might be where the contract does not otherwise have a mechanism for it to end (such as arose in *The Puerto Buitrago* (1976)), so that the claimant is effectively seeking to keep the contract alive *in perpetuity*, an un-palatable stalemate that the courts rightly refuse to countenance (see O'Sullivan (2017c)). But in standard cases, the confirmation by the Court of Appeal in *Reichman v Beveridge* (2006) that the category of cases where the innocent party will be deprived of his ability to bring an action for the agreed sum is 'very limited' is to be welcomed. A good example is *Isabella Shipowner SA v Shagang Shipping Co Ltd* (2012), where the defendant chartered a ship from the claimant shipowner and tried to insist that the claimant take re-delivery of the ship early. The claimant refused to do so and claimed the hire fee for the full charter period, saying that it was under no obligation to accept such re-delivery. Cooke J over-turned the arbitrator's finding that the claimant was limited to damages. He emphasised that the claimant's conduct had to be *wholly* unreasonable for him to be denied his rights under the contract to insist on performance of the contract, and that it was important not to overlook the difficulties which the defendant's breach of contract could foist upon the claimant against his will if he was forced to accept the defendant's defective performance (such as requiring the claimant to go out to find another hirer of the ship in a difficult market and to bring a damages claim against a defendant that was in financial difficulty and might run out of funds before the damages claim could be made good). Cooke J also resisted any move to water down the claimant's protection by use of the cooperation quali-fication (see para **17.14**), explaining that if, as here, the contract entitled the claimant to the fee without the need for the defendant to do anything, then contractual performance did not require cooperation for the purposes of the test.

Award of other agreed sums—liquidated damages and the penalty jurisdiction

17.22 Rather than saying that a particular sum is due in return for the other side *performing* the contract, the contract may state that a particular sum is payable if one party *breaches* the contract. This type of term is generally construed as a 'liquidated damages' clause: it takes the form 'if you breach the contract, you must pay £X'. Such clauses are generally viewed as a good thing: if the parties can estimate in advance the loss that they will suffer as a re-sult of a breach and insert such a clause, they can save themselves money by avoiding hav-ing to go to court in the event of a breach to work out how much the victim can get, and can save the court time. Moreover, they allow each party to know in advance how much they will have to pay for breaching the contract and help to prevent disputes in regard to how much a party should pay on breach. Problems arise, however, where the clause states that the defendant will have to pay a sum much higher than any loss the claimant might conceivably suffer from a breach. Such a clause may be classed as a 'penalty clause' rather than a liquidated damages clause, and struck down. So while we want to encourage par-ties to specify the amount payable on breach, the law has traditionally imposed limits to ensure that such clauses are not overly harsh on one party.

17.23   Detailed guidelines as to when such a clause would be struck down as a 'penalty' were given by Lord Dunedin in *Dunlop Pneumatic Tyre Ltd v New Garage and Motor Co Ltd* (1915). The most important guideline is that if the clause is a genuine attempt to pre-estimate the loss that may be caused by a breach, then the clause is acceptable. However, if the sum laid down in the clause is 'extravagant and unconscionable in amount in comparison with the greatest loss that could conceivably be proved to have followed from the breach', then it will be struck down as a penalty clause. Other guidelines include:

- Whether or not the clause is a penalty clause is to be judged at the time that the contract is made, not the time that it is breached, in light of the circumstances existing at that earlier time.

- If the parties use the phrases 'penalty' or 'liquidated damages', this is relevant, but not conclusive.

- If the breach consists in not paying a sum of money, and the sum stipulated in the clause is a greater sum, then the clause will be a penalty clause.

- When a single lump sum is expressed to be payable by way of compensation on the occurrence of one or more or all of several events, some of which may cause serious harm and others which may cause trivial harm, then there is a presumption that it is a penalty clause. So if the clause stated that £250 was to be payable upon any breach of the agreement (as in *Ford Motor Co v Armstrong* (1915)), there is a presumption that this is a penalty clause. The reason for this is that it suggests that the parties are not taking account of the likely loss caused when fixing the figure to be paid on breach.

- The fact that it is hard to estimate in advance the consequences of the breach does not make the clause a penalty clause. This consideration often points in the opposite direction to the previous consideration; indeed, Downes (1996) comments that it 'risks contradicting' it. If it is hard to work out how much loss the breaches may cause, that might make it helpful for the parties to agree that the same lump sum would be payable for any breach (as in *Dunlop* itself).

17.24   In recent years, the courts have been increasingly unwilling to find that a clause is a penalty clause, particularly in commercial transactions. This attitude can be seen in the Privy Council decision in *Philips Hong Kong Ltd v AG of Hong Kong* (1993), where Lord Woolf emphasised that the courts should be reluctant to strike down clauses where the parties are of roughly equal bargaining power and are professionally advised because '[a]ny other approach will lead to undesirable uncertainty especially in commercial contracts'. In other words, the parties do not need paternalistic protection from their own freely negotiated deals—freedom of contract should prevail. A similar attitude is increasingly taken in many other areas of the common law of contract where the parties' are sophisticated non-consumers (see, for example, paras **8.49-8.51** discussing UCTA in relation to commercial contracts).

17.25   Consistent with this trend, the rules on penalty clauses were reviewed by the Court of Appeal in *Murray v Leisureplay* (2005). While all three judges agreed that the clause was not a penalty clause, there was an interesting divergence of opinion on how to apply the *Dunlop* 'genuine pre-estimate of loss' test. Arden LJ favoured a test which required the court to ask how much by way of damages the claimant would be able to claim for the breach of contract in the absence of the liquidated damages clause, and if the liquidated damages clause gave a greater amount to look for some justification for the discrepancy. Buxton LJ, supported by Clarke LJ, thought this introduced too much rigidity into what should be a broader enquiry into whether the provision was unconscionable—for example, there might be good commercial reasons for a very large payment, much greater than the potential total loss, to be specified. Buxton and Clarke LJJ also helpfully supported the re-casting of the *Dunlop* 'genuine pre-estimate of loss' test in more modern terms: at the time that the contract was entered into, was the 'predominant function of the clause in question to deter a party from breaking the contract or to compensate the innocent party for the breach'? Unless it is clear that the clause was intended as a deterrent, it should not be condemned as a penalty clause.

17.26   All previous case law on the question of whether a clause is an enforceable liquidated damages clause, or an unenforceable penalty, must now be read in the light of the hugely important decision of the Supreme Court in *Cavendish Square Holdings BV v El Makdessi* (2015). *Cavendish* involved a clause in a share sale agreement whereby the seller lost the right to receive the final two instalments of the purchase price from the purchaser (up to $44 m) if he committed a breach of restrictive covenants in the agreement by competing with the business of the company that had been sold. The seller did indeed compete in breach of covenant, so the purchaser relied on the clause and withheld the final instalments of the price, whereupon the seller argued that the clause was an unenforceable penalty. Notice that both sides were of equal bargaining strength and advised by city law firms, who negotiated the complex commercial agreement; moreover, there was a good commercial reason for the clause to be included, which was to protect the goodwill in the company from competition from the seller. Nonetheless, very controversially (see O'Sullivan (2014)), the Court of Appeal (reversing Burton J at first instance) held that there was no commercial justification for the clause and that it was therefore an unenforceable penalty. While the clause was there to try to protect goodwill, the court felt that the potential financial downside for the seller was so much larger than the actionable damage the purchaser could suffer that it strayed firmly into the territory of deterrence (principally because of a strange company law rule that barred the purchaser, rather than the company being sold, from recovering damages for the seller's wrongful competition).

17.27   The Supreme Court unanimously allowed the purchaser's appeal in *Cavendish*, and overturned the Court of Appeal's decision that the clause was a penalty. For Lord Sumption, Lord Dunedin's presumptions from the *Dunlop* case should not be treated as a rigid code. Instead, the validity of a clause providing for the consequences of a breach of contract depends on whether the innocent party can be said to have a *legitimate interest* in performance which extends beyond the recovery of pecuniary compensation, a concept which features more broadly in the law of remedies for breach of contract (see, for example, cases like *AG v Blake* (2001) and *Experience Hendrix LLC v PPX Enterprises Inc* (2003) discussed in Chapter 18). As Lord Sumption explained:

> [32] The true test is whether the impugned provision is a secondary obligation which imposes a detriment on the contract-breaker out of all proportion to any legitimate interest of the innocent party in the enforcement of the primary obligation. The innocent party can have no proper interest in simply punishing the defaulter. His interest is in performance or in some appropriate alternative to performance. In the case of a straightforward damages clause, that interest will rarely extend beyond compensation for the breach, and we therefore expect that Lord Dunedin's four tests would usually be perfectly adequate to determine its validity. But compensation is not necessarily the only legitimate interest that the innocent party may have in the performance of the defaulter's primary obligations. This was recognised in the early days of the penalty rule, when it was still the creature of equity ... It was reflected in the result in Dunlop. And it is recognised in the more recent decisions about commercial justification.

Lord Mance adopted a similar approach, explaining that the first step is to consider whether any (and if so what) legitimate business interest is served and protected by the clause, and if so secondly, whether the way in which the clause provides for that interest is 'extravagant, exorbitant or unconscionable'.

17.28   On the facts of *Cavendish*, the Supreme Court was not convinced that the clause in issue was a liquidated damages clause at all, in that it might better be characterised a 'price adjustment clause' that defined the parties' primary obligations, and thus not strictly subject to the penalty jurisdiction. Nonetheless the Supreme Court was 'prepared to assume, without deciding, that a contractual provision may in some circumstances be a penalty if it disentitles the contract-breaker from receiving a sum of money which would otherwise have been due to him'. Applying the law to the facts, the Supreme Court unanimously decided that the purchaser had a legitimate interest in the observance of the restrictive covenants, to protect the goodwill of the company and the wider corporate group, and the clause was a justified way of protecting that interest:

> As Burton J graphically observed..., once Cavendish could no longer trust the Sellers to observe the restrictive covenants, 'the wolf was in the fold'. Loyalty is indivisible. Its absence in a business like this introduces a very significant business risk whose impact cannot be measured simply by reference to the known and provable consequences of particular breaches. It is clear that this business was worth considerably less to Cavendish if that risk existed than if it did not. How much less? There are no juridical standards by which to answer that question satisfactorily. We cannot know what Cavendish would have paid without the assurance of the Sellers' loyalty, even assuming that they would have bought the business at all. We cannot know whether the ... price ... would have been the same if they were not adjustable in the event of breach of the restrictive covenants. We cannot know what other provisions of the agreement would

have been different, or what additional provisions would have been included on that hypothesis. These are matters for negotiation, not forensic assessment (save in the rare cases where the contract or the law requires it). They were matters for the parties, who were, on both sides, sophisticated, successful and experienced commercial people bargaining on equal terms over a long period with expert legal advice and were the best judges of the degree to which each of them should recognise the proper commercial interests of the other.

17.29 In advance of the Supreme Court's decision, some commentators argued that English law should abandon the common law penalty clause jurisdiction altogether and allow freedom of contract to prevail. After all, the penalty jurisdiction is the only corner of the English common law that allows someone to get out of a bad bargain on the ground that the contract is *substantively* disadvantageous to them (contrast the common law's hawkish attitude if the contracting process was disadvantageous by virtue of misrepresentation, duress, and other vitiating factors). In the event, regrettably the Supreme Court declined to go this far, preferring instead to clarify the penalty jurisdiction and limit its remit. One of the most convincing arguments in favour of abolition of the common law jurisdiction was that penalty clauses are only really objectionable in *consumer* contracts, but the courts have a specific *statutory* tool to deal with this problem in the CRA (see paras **8.52–8.78**). Indeed, the indicative grey list of unfair terms includes the following: 'A term which has the object or effect of requiring a consumer who fails to fulfil his obligations under the contract to pay a disproportionately high sum in compensation' (Sch 2, para 6). The application of the penalty jurisdiction to consumer cases, and the equivalent statutory protection in the Regulations that pre-dated the CRA, were considered by the Supreme Court in the other case heard on appeal with *Cavendish*, namely *ParkingEye Ltd v Beavis*. Mr Beavis parked in a car park (operated for the landowner by ParkingEye) pursuant to a contractual licence on the terms of notices prominently displayed, which said that the parking period was limited to two hours and imposed a fee of £85 for overstaying the period. Mr Beavis parked for nearly three hours, so ParkingEye demanded payment of the £85 fee. He argued that it was unenforceable as a penalty, and also an unfair term under the Unfair Terms in Consumer Contracts Regulations 1999 (the predecessor of the CRA), arguments that were rejected both by the judge at first instance and by the Court of Appeal.

17.30 The Supreme Court dismissed Mr Beavis' appeal. So far as the penalty jurisdiction is concerned, the court held that the jurisdiction was engaged, but that the £85 fee was not a penalty. As Lord Sumption said: 'The reason is that although ParkingEye was not liable to suffer loss as a result of overstaying motorists, it had a legitimate interest in charging them which extended beyond the recovery of any loss' which involved receiving income to meet the legitimate costs of running the parking scheme, which was itself a legitimate way for the landowner to regulate the efficient use of the car park. The figure of £85 was not disproportionate, and the wording of the charge was clearly and prominently displayed. The majority of the Supreme Court reached the same result on the question of whether it was an 'unfair term' under the Regulations, regarding the charge as not being 'contrary to the requirement of good faith'; Lord Toulson dissented on this question.

17.31   Before concluding our examination of liquidated damages clauses and penalties, a number of further issues need to be addressed. First, as discussed, the jurisdiction to strike down a clause as a penalty clause only applies to the secondary obligations under the contract; at common law the courts cannot interfere with the parties' primary obligations under the contract just because they are unfair. This means the penalty clause jurisdiction operates only if the sum is to be payable in the event of a *breach*. So if a sum is expressed to be payable on the occurrence of some event other than a breach, it cannot be struck down as a penalty clause. Lord Sumption in *Cavendish* suggested that this should not be a problem in practice:

> However, the capricious consequences of this state of affairs are mitigated by the fact that, as the equitable jurisdiction shows, the classification of terms for the purpose of the penalty rule depends on the substance of the term and not on its form or on the label which the parties have chosen to attach to it.

17.32   Nonetheless this feature has sometimes been used to circumvent the rules on penalties. A good example is *Alder v Moore* (1961), where the defendant, a footballer by the name of Brian Moore, had suffered an eye injury and been forced to stop playing the beautiful game. As a result, he was paid £500 under his insurance policy. However, in return for getting the money, he covenanted that '[i] n consideration of the above payment I hereby declare and agree that I will take no part as a playing member of any form of professional football and in the event of infringement of this condition I will be subject to a penalty of [£500].' He started playing football again professionally, so the insurers sued for the £500. The Court of Appeal (somewhat surprisingly) held by a majority that Moore was under no contractual obligation not to play professional football again, so he did not breach the contract by resuming his football career. Therefore, the sum was payable on the occurrence of an event other than breach of contract, so it could not be struck down as a penalty clause.

17.33   This all seems a little unsatisfactory. It means that someone who breaches a contract is in a better position than someone who does not, because only the former will be able to invoke the protection of the penalty clause rules. Indeed, the Law Commission tentatively recommended some years ago that such clauses be subject to the same protection as clauses specifying a sum to be payable on breach (Law Com Working Paper No 61 (1975)). Despite this, the English courts have, in the past, been unwilling to extend the protection of the penalty clause rules (for example, see *Else (1982) Ltd v Parkland Holdings Ltd* (1994)) and the Supreme Court in *Cavendish* declined to do so.

17.34   In the first instance commercial case of *M&J Polymers Ltd v Imerys Minerals Ltd* (2008) (a case that was not mentioned by the Supreme Court in *Cavendish*) Burton J was prepared to hold that, as a matter of principle, the penalty clause rule might apply to a clause in a long-term supply contract requiring the buyer to pay a minimum amount each month even if it had not ordered the minimum amount in a given month (a 'take or pay' clause), although on the facts the clause was commercially justifiable and had been freely negotiated. Moreover, there are some hints that the courts will at least be vigilant to identify attempts by the parties to disguise penalty clauses as clauses requiring the payment of a sum on the occurrence of an event other than breach (in, for example, *Interfoto Picture Library Ltd v Stiletto Visual Programmes Ltd* (1980) discussed at para **7.35**).

17.35   In Australia, the High Court in *Andrews v ANZ* (2012) (noted Davies and Turner (2013)) suggested that one must look more to the substance of the matter in determining whether a clause is a penalty, meaning that a clause can be a penalty even if the sum is payable other than on breach. They held that 'a stipulation *prima facie* imposes a penalty on a party ("the first party") if, as a matter of substance, it is collateral (or accessory) to a primary stipulation in favour of a second party and this collateral stipulation, upon the failure of the primary stipulation, imposes upon the first party an additional detriment, the penalty, to the benefit of the second party'. The Supreme Court in *Cavendish* considered whether to follow the *Andrews* approach but decided against it. As Lord Sumption said: 'we cannot accept that English law should take the same path, quite apart from its inconsistency with established and unchallenged House of Lords authority' and proceeded to give reasons, historical and of principle, why this route did not appeal. This therefore means that it remains vital to tell the difference between a secondary obligation (to which the penalty jurisdiction applies) and a primary obligation (to which it does not). Yet this is not always straightforward, as the Supreme Court's uncertainty about the proper characterisation of the clause in *Cavendish* reminds us.

17.36   A related issue is that, to come under the penalty clause jurisdiction, a clause must create a new liability: it must impose a duty on the other party to pay a sum where previously he was under no obligation to do so. Therefore, if the clause only accelerates an existing liability, then it will not be a liquidated damages clause or penalty clause (*Protector Loan Co v Grice* (1880)). Accordingly, this is another method of avoiding the penalty clause rules. Such a clause says for example that a sum is due at the time the contract is made but that the debtor can pay at some future date so long as certain conditions are met. If these conditions are not met, then the debtor has to pay the whole amount immediately. The 'acceleration rule' is open to criticism. Breaching the conditions set out in the clause puts the debtor in a worse position than he was previously, even though technically he is not subject to any new liability, because he has to pay up immediately rather than at some future date. In substance, then, the effect is exactly the same as a liquidated damages clause. Again, it should be noted that some protection in respect of such clauses in consumer contracts is offered by the CRA.

17.37   Another conundrum is whether the party who is entitled to *receive* liquidated damages should ever be allowed to claim that the relevant clause is a penalty? She might want to do this where it turns out that the actual loss she sustains on breach exceeds that which the liquidated damages clause requires the other party to pay. The law currently provides no clear answer to this. While *Wall v Rederiaktiebolaget Luggude* (1915) suggests that such a course of action is permissible, the issue was left open in *Cellulose Acetate Silk Co Ltd v Widnes Foundry Ltd* (1933) and regarded as unclear by one member of the Court of Appeal in *Robophone Facilities Ltd v Blank* (1966). A claimant should not be allowed to do this, because the penalty rules are designed to protect the defendant from unfairness;

here, there is no such unfairness. In practice, the point is highly unlikely to arise, given how draconian a clause has to be before it will be regarded as penal after *Cavendish*—it is almost impossible to imagine circumstances in which the claimant's actual loss would exceed the amount specified in such a clause.

17.38 Finally, notice that *Cavendish* is unlikely to be the last word on penalty clauses. As well as the 'primary v. secondary' distinction just discussed, the courts can expect to face litigation about what it means to have a 'legitimate interest' in preventing breach and when will a clause be regarded as 'extravagant, exorbitant or unconscionable'. Commercial drafters are likely to try and keep one step ahead of the law, inserting clauses that purport to explain why there is a legitimate interest in enforcing the clause or (echoing the contractual estoppel reasoning discussed in para **9.88**) simply recite that both parties agree the interest is legitimate. For detailed discussion of unresolved issues in the law of penalties since *Cavendish*, see Summers (2017).

Specific performance

17.39 In contrast to the action for an agreed sum, specific performance usually applies where the obligation of the defendant that you are seeking to enforce is other than to pay money.

17.40 The traditional understanding of specific performance is that, unlike damages, it enforces the primary duty of the defendant to perform the contract. Damages, on the other hand, replace this primary duty to perform with a secondary duty to pay money. While we will examine whether this understanding is really correct at the end of the chapter, it will suffice for present purposes. One point should be noted, however: While a claimant normally has to show that the defendant has breached the contract in order to obtain specific performance, it is technically possible to obtain the remedy even before a breach has occurred, where circumstances can be shown which would justify the intervention of the court—see *Hasham v Zenab* (1960) discussed at para **15.52**.

What is the test for granting specific performance?

17.41 Originally, a claimant had to show that damages would be inadequate in order to obtain the remedy (*Ryan v Mutual Tontine Westminster Chambers* (1893), for example). However, it appeared few decades ago that the test was being relaxed, and that it would be sufficient to show that specific performance was the 'appropriate remedy' (see, for example, *Beswick v Beswick* (1968) and *Tito v Waddell (No 2)* (1977)). This test allowed factors other than the adequacy of damages to be considered in deciding whether specific performance should be granted. This period of expansion, however, was to be checked by the House of Lords in *Co-operative Insurance Society Ltd v Argyll Stores (Holdings) Ltd* (1998).

17.42 The defendants, Argyll, found themselves in deep financial trouble by 1995, and so decided to close down a number of supermarkets, one of which was located in a large shopping centre in Hillsborough and was the shopping centre's 'anchor tenant'. This action breached a clause in the lease requiring the defendant to keep the premises open. The lease still had 19 years to run, so the claimant landlord sought specific performance. The House of Lords, reversing the Court of Appeal's decision, refused to make such an order. Lord Hoffmann, giving the only judgment, took into account a number of factors in coming to his decision. First, keeping the supermarket open would cause massive losses to the defendant. Second, the obligation in question was insufficiently precise. If specific performance of such an obligation were granted, this would increase the likelihood of wasteful litigation over compliance and the oppression caused by having to run a business under the threat of contempt proceedings for breach of the order. Third, tied to the second reason was the fact that the court would have to supervise and police the order for 20 years. Fourth, the order would enrich the claimant at the expense of the defendant. Finally, it would not be in the public interest for the courts to require someone to carry on a business at a loss if there is any plausible alternative by which the other party can be given compensation.

17.43 Lord Hoffmann focused a great deal on the harm that granting specific performance would cause to the defendant, and it is arguable that he should have given greater weight to the interests of the claimant. As Jones (1997) notes, it is difficult to envisage how the claimant in *Argyll* could ever prove what loss it suffered from the breach of covenant. Should the court's primary concern not have been to protect the rights to performance of the victim of the breach? Indeed, *Argyll* seems out of line with the trend discussed in Chapter 16 towards greater protection of the claimant's right to performance. One explanation for Lord Hoffmann's approach seems to have been that he looked far more kindly on the defendant's conduct than did the Court of Appeal, which considered that the defendant had acted with 'gross commercial cynicism'.

17.44 Has the expansion of specific performance been halted by *Argyll*? The first instance decision in *Rainbow Estates v Tokenhold* (1999) suggests not. It was held for the first time that specific performance could be available for breach of a tenant's repairing obligations. However, the judge also seemed to suggest at one point that there may be little difference between the old adequacy of damages test for granting specific performance and the more modern test based on appropriateness. Nonetheless, the broad range of factors taken into account in *Tokenhold* perhaps suggests that adequacy of damages is no longer the exclusive test, though it remains the starting point for any discussion of specific performance. An interesting recent example of specific performance being potentially available, in circumstances that echo the broader reasoning in Beswick, is *Latin American Investments Ltd v Maroil Trading Inc* (2017), where the contractual obligation was to pay money, not to the promisee but to a third party, a joint venture company. Teare J approved the statement from Chitty (2016) that 'as a general principle, the promisee should be able to obtain specific performance in favour of the third party whenever that is the most appropriate method of enforcing the contract which was actually made.'

Some specific examples

17.45 A good example of a situation where specific performance is often granted is where damages are an inadequate remedy because the claimant is unable to obtain a substitute for
the promised performance. Traditionally, the paradigm example of a contract which will
be specifically enforced is a contract for the sale of land, because each parcel of land is
unique. Of course in practice this is not invariably true, as where an investment purchaser
buys an industrial unit or flat, not to occupy but purely for the income it generate. Here
damages would be a perfectly adequate substitute if the vendor breaches the contract and
refuses to transfer the property, but at present English law still awards specific performance in all land contracts (and because it is available as against the vendor, the principle
of 'mutuality' requires that the purchaser's obligation to pay the price can be specifically
enforced). The same rationale applies to contracts for the sale of unique goods. Even in
the case of generic goods, like petrol, specific performance may exceptionally be ordered
where such goods cannot be obtained other than from the defendant (for example, where
there is an oil crisis, as in *Sky Petroleum Ltd v VIP Petroleum Ltd* (1974)).

Bars to specific performance

17.46 As a discretionary remedy, there are a number of factors that may cause a court to refuse
to order specific performance:

- Specific performance would require constant supervision by the court. This bar was
  reaffirmed by Lord Hoffmann in *Argyll*. He explained that the bar had been misunderstood: the evil that it sought to guard against was the possibility of the court
  having to give an indefinite series of rulings on whether the rule has been breached.
  He drew a distinction between orders to carry on activities and orders to achieve
  results, suggesting that it was only the former that fell foul of the bar, because of
  the possibility of the claimant making repeated applications to the court claiming
  that the defendant was failing to comply with the order. *Argyll* is an example of the
  former, because the order would have had to be policed by the court for the duration of the lease, while *Wolverhampton Corpn v Emmons* (1901), where the contract was for a one-off project to build eight houses, is an example of the latter. Lord
  Hoffmann also suggested that when considering whether the bar should apply, the
  court should take into account how precise the contractual obligation in question is.
  The more precise it is, the less likely it is that disputes will arise over whether or not
  it has been breached, so the less likely it is to fall foul of the constant supervision bar.
  It is suggested that Lord Hoffmann overstated the problem of constant supervision:
  the court has various devices at its disposal to overcome it, such as the appointment
  of a receiver to perform the acts in question. Moreover, a court should be reluctant
  to take away the claimant's rights simply to reduce its workload.

- The contract in question is a contract involving personal service, such as a contract of employment. The reason for this bar is that it is thought to be difficult and
  inappropriate to try to force unwilling parties into a personal relationship. In the

context of employment, there is a statutory bar preventing an employee being compelled to perform a contract of employment (s 236 of the Trade Union and Labour Relations (Consolidation) Act 1992). This general bar is increasingly coming under fire on the ground that employment is increasingly a less personal relationship than it used to be, due to the presence of large organisations. Indeed, the courts have been increasingly willing to force the employer to reinstate an employee, *Hill v CA Parsons Ltd* (1972) being a good example. However, these cases nearly all involve compelling an employer to reinstate a worker, and it is submitted that the objections to forcing a worker to return to work carry far more weight.

- The obligation in question is insufficiently precise (as was the case in *Argyll*). As discussed, the certainty of the term in question is also relevant to whether the constant supervision bar applies.

- The defendant has acted particularly badly. As with all remedies having their root in the equitable jurisdiction of the Court of Chancery, a claimant must 'come with clean hands' and so his conduct may affect the availability of specific performance, as for example, in *Shell UK Ltd v Lostock Garages Ltd* (1976).

- Severe hardship would be caused to the defendant by granting specific performance. An example of the application of this bar is *Patel v Ali* (1984), where specific performance of a contract for the purchase of a house was refused because one of the vendors, who was living in the house, was disabled and extremely ill and removing her from the house would deprive her of the daily assistance of her neighbours on which she depended. It was held that severe hardship could operate as a bar even where the hardship was not caused by the claimant and had been suffered after the contract was entered into.

- The claimant has delayed too long in seeking specific performance and this delay would make it unjust in all the circumstances to award the remedy. In these circumstances, the equitable doctrine of laches will bar the claim.

17.47 In summary, the trend towards greater availability of specific performance has been slowed but not halted by *Argyll*. We have already noted that it may be desirable for this trend to continue, because *Argyll* seems to offer insufficient protection to the claimant's interests in having the contract performed. The issue of whether specific performance should be as freely available as damages will wait until the conclusion of the chapter.

Mandatory injunctions

17.48 Where the defendant has breached a negative covenant, that is a covenant prohibiting him from doing something, the claimant may be able to get a mandatory injunction to compel the defendant to undo the effects of his act. For example, imagine there is a term in a contract stating that you will not build any huts on the land you are using, but you ignore this and build some huts. The other party might be able to get a mandatory injunction to make you tear down these huts.

17.49 However, such injunctions will rarely be available, only where a strict balance of convenience test is satisfied, namely that the prejudice to the defendant in having to undo the effects of the breach would be far greater than the benefit to the claimant of having this done (*Sharp v Harrison* (1922)). For a case where this test was made out, see *Charrington v Simons & Co Ltd* (1971).

Prohibitory injunctions

17.50 Such injunctions are normally granted as a matter of course to stop the defendant breaching a negative obligation, that is, an obligation not to do something. A common example is a non-competition clause, such as where the defendant sells her business to the claimant and promises not to compete in the same line of business, usually for a limited time and geographic area. Technically, the claimant is required to show that damages are inadequate, but this is very easily done. A good example of the court's approach is *Araci v Fallon* (2011), where the Court of Appeal granted an injunction on Derby day against the jockey Kieren Fallon, who had promised not to ride any horse other than one of Mr Araci's horses, Native Khan, barring Mr Fallon from riding a rival horse for another owner.

17.51 There are two main grounds on which courts tend to refuse to grant such injunctions, the first of which is that it would be oppressive to do so, as it was in *Jaggard v Sawyer* (1995). Here the defendant had built a house that could only be accessed by breaching a covenant. An injunction to prevent the breach of this covenant was refused, on the ground that it would have been in blatant disregard of the defendant's rights, and therefore oppressive. Second, a prohibitory injunction will not be granted if it would have the effect of compelling the defendant to perform the contract in circumstances where specific performance would have been refused. This has caused most difficulty in the context of contracts for personal services, which as a general rule are not specifically enforceable. Imagine I contracted to work for Big Bucks Ltd and agreed never to work for anyone else or to go into business on my own account. Granting a prohibitory injunction in such circumstances would force me to perform my contract with Big Bucks Ltd or else starve!

17.52 The principles governing the granting of such injunctions in the context of contracts for personal services where the defendant has a particular skill were well summarised by Nourse LJ in *Warren v Mendy* (1989):

> In such a case the court ought not to enforce the performance of the negative obligations if their enforcement will effectively compel the servant to perform his positive obligations under the contract. Compulsion is a question to be decided on the facts of each case, with a realistic regard for the probable reaction of an injunction on the psychological and ma-

terial, and sometimes the physical, need of the servant to maintain the skill or talent. The longer the term for which an injunction is sought, the more readily will compulsion be inferred. Compulsion may be inferred where the injunction is sought not against the servant but against a third party, if either the third party is the only other available master or if it is likely that the master will seek relief against anyone who attempts to replace him. An injunction will less readily be granted where there are obligations of mutual trust and confidence, more especially where the servant's trust in the master may have been betrayed or his confidence in him has genuinely gone.

17.53 In *Warner Brothers Pictures Inc v Nelson* (1937), the defendant film star Bette Davis had a contract with Warner Bros to render her exclusive services as a movie and stage actress to them and to perform exclusively for them. She came to England after two years and wanted to act in a film for another company. Warner Bros sought an injunction. The judge accepted that an injunction would not be granted if it would have the indirect effect of compelling performance: of forcing her to either work for Warner Bros or starve. However, he held that this was not the case here: she was only being prohibited from working in film or on stage. Therefore, an injunction was ordered, but only for three years.

17.54 However, in *Warren v Mendy* (1989), while refraining from saying *Nelson* was wrongly decided, Nourse LJ commented that:

> On a first consideration, that learned judge's view that Miss Bette Davis might employ herself both usefully and remuneratively in other spheres of activity for a period of up to three years appears to have been extraordinarily unrealistic. It could hardly have been thought to be a real possibility that an actress of her then youth and soaring talent would be able to forego screen and stage for such a period.

Therefore, caution is required in applying *Nelson*.

Damages in lieu of an injunction

17.55 The High Court and Court of Appeal have power to award damages in addition to, or in substitution for, an injunction or specific performance (s 50 of the Senior Courts Act 1981). The same principles apply as for common law damages (*Johnson v Agnew* (1980)).

Concluding thoughts

17.56 To return to the two issues left unresolved at the beginning of the chapter, do specific remedies actually enforce the *primary* obligations under the contract that the defendant has agreed to, or do they replace these obligations with subtly different *secondary* obligations? As mentioned, the traditional understanding of specific remedies is that unlike damages, they enforce the primary duty of the defendant to perform the contract. Damages, on the other hand, replace this primary duty to perform with a secondary duty to pay money. It substitutes the duty to pay money in place of the primary duty, so it is known as a 'substitutionary' remedy. However, this sharp distinction between the two has been challenged by McKendrick (2016). He argues that even in the case of specific performance, the court is replacing the primary duty to perform with a duty imposed by the court, the latter being different from the former in content, so specific performance is also a substitutionary remedy:

> [I]n the vast majority of cases, the defendant is not ordered 'specifically' to perform a contractual obligation. The obligation that the defendant is ordered to perform generally differs in some way from the initial obligation that was undertaken in the contract. Most claimants do not seek specific performance until the defendant has already broken the contract, although it is not strictly necessary for a claimant seeking a specific performance order to demonstrate that the defendant has already broken the terms of their contract. In such a case, the defendant obviously cannot perform exactly in accordance with the original contractual obligation in that, at the least, performance will take place at a different time from that originally agreed. On this basis it can be argued that specific performance is a substitutionary and not a specific remedy.

17.57 McKendrick is correct to suggest that specific performance is a substitutionary remedy. However, his reasoning is not completely convincing in one respect. McKendrick's reasoning seems to be that specific performance is substitutionary because the content of the obligations placed on the defendant by the court order is different from those that he originally undertook under the contract. However, this will not always be the case: for example, in those cases where specific performance can be sought before the defendant breaches the contract, the content of the obligations will be the same. More importantly, even though the *content* of the obligations imposed by the order may sometimes be the same as those imposed by the original contract, the obligations imposed by specific performance are obligations imposed by the *court*, not the original contract, with different sanctions for non-compliance, namely criminal sanctions. The point is well made by Barker (1998) in the context of the right to get your money back in the law of restitution:

> The order replicates the content of the primary right, but this does not make it the same thing. In truth, the right to the order is a subtle substitute for the primary right, albeit a clever and, to the casual eye, indistinguishable one.

Therefore, specific remedies and damages are not so different after all: they are both substitutes for performance under the contract.

17.58 This is all very interesting, but why does it matter? To answer this, we must turn to the second issue left unresolved earlier on, namely why are specific remedies, and specific performance in particular, not available as of right against a defendant who has breached a contract? If specific remedies are just enforcing the claimant's primary rights, those rights that the other party freely undertook, then it is very difficult to see why the court is ever entitled to refuse a specific remedy. On the other hand, once we see that specific remedies replace the claimant's primary rights with subtly different secondary rights, secondary rights that the parties have not agreed to (see para **16.1**), then it becomes clear why the court is entitled sometimes to refuse the claimant a specific remedy. Put simply, a claimant who seeks a specific remedy is not merely asking the court to declare that the defendant is obliged to do something *under the contract*; she is asking for the court to order that the defendant do something, and back this order with the threat of *criminal sanctions*. The claimant and defendant never agreed that such an order should be made in event of breach, so the court has a choice as to whether it would be appropriate to make it.

17.59 Having explained why a court is *entitled* to refuse to award a specific remedy, we must address why it would *want* to do so as a matter of policy. Starting with specific remedies in general, we have seen from our examination the courts' unwillingness to award positive remedies and their greater willingness to award negative remedies. The reason for this is that it is a greater intrusion upon your autonomy and freedom to order you to do something than it is to order you not to do something (in the context of the criminal law, see Ashworth (1989) for the same point). The former type of restriction cuts off more of your options: for example, placing a duty on you to go to Berlin leaves you with only one way to comply with the duty, whereas ordering you not to go to Berlin leaves you with many other things you could do without breaching the duty.

17.60 This in turn provides us with a clue as to why we are unwilling to allow specific performance to be available for all breaches of contract. While Beatson, Burrows, and Cartwright (2016) provide two good reasons for limiting the availability of the remedy, namely that it avoids the policy of the mitigation rule and that the courts are increasingly willing to award appropriate levels of compensation for a breach of contract (see Chapter 16), it is submitted that there is a more fundamental one. Allowing the defendant to decide between performing and paying compensation is far less intrusive to a defendant than ordering him to perform his side of the bargain. As Kimel (2002 and 2003) points out, we should only limit the defendant's liberty to the extent that this is necessary to protect the claimant. So where damages would be an adequate substitute for performance, specific performance should not be granted:

> [P]erhaps all that is needed is, to use Joel Feinberg's language, 'a general presumption in favour of liberty'. Given that specific performance is a more intrusive remedy than damages—at any rate, that enforced performance amounts to a greater interference with personal freedom compared to allowing the party in breach to choose between performance and compensation for non-performance—such a simple presumption suffices to recommend the latter in all those cases where the innocent party ... would not in any way be worse off as a result.

OVERVIEW

1   Unlike damages, specific remedies order the defendant to actually perform his side of the bargain. Again unlike in the case of damages, this is an obligation to which the parties have agreed.

2   Specific remedies can be divided into two groups: those that place 'positive' duties on the defendant (duties to do something) and those that place 'negative' duties on him (duties not to do something). There are three types of the former: the action for an agreed sum, specific performance, and the mandatory injunction. There is only one type of the latter: the prohibitory injunction. The courts are (the action for an agreed sum aside) much less willing to grant a specific remedy placing a positive duty on the defendant than a negative one because it constitutes a larger intrusion upon his liberty.

Action for an agreed sum

3   There are two types of this action: the action for an agreed price and the action for other types of agreed sum.

4   In order to bring a successful action for an agreed price, it must be shown that the sum in question is due to the claimant under the terms of the contract. Whether or not the sum is due requires careful construction of the contract. One possible construction is that the claimant is not entitled to the price unless he has completely performed an obligation or some obligations (the 'entire obligation rule'). However, this can be harsh on the party claiming payment, so the courts have developed a number of ways to alleviate this harshness.

5   If the claimant has started or continued to perform the contract after the defendant has repudiated it, he may be precluded from claiming the agreed price if he had no legitimate interest in performing the contract, although this limitation should be very restrictively interpreted.

Award of other types of agreed sum

6   The sum may be expressed in the contract to be payable on breach of the contract or on the occurrence of another event. If it is payable on breach, it will either be a liquidated damages clause or a penalty clause. It will be construed as a liquidated damages clause if it is a genuine attempt to estimate in advance how much the claimant will lose from the breach, but the innocent party may sometimes have a legitimate interest in performance which extends beyond the recovery of pecuniary compensation; a clause will be struck down as a penalty clause only if it is extravagant and exorbitant, such that its adverse impact significantly exceeds the innocent party's legitimate interest. The courts are increasingly reluctant to strike down clauses in this way, especially in commercial transactions, but the Supreme Court has declined to abolish the penalty clause jurisdiction altogether, even though there is separate statutory jurisdiction to regulate unfair penalty clauses in consumer contracts.

Specific performance

7   This remedy usually applies to obligations other than to pay money. Originally, a claimant had to show that damages would be inadequate to obtain specific performance, but it seems that the test has been relaxed, so that the claimant must now merely show that specific performance would be the appropriate remedy. The courts are becoming increasingly willing to award this remedy, although this trend was checked by the House of Lords decision in *Co-operative Insurance Society Ltd v Argyll Stores (Holdings) Ltd* (1998). A good example of a situation where specific performance is often awarded is where the claimant cannot get equivalent performance from someone else, such as where the subject is unique, like land or a painting, or in short supply.

8   There are a number of grounds on which the remedy can be refused:

- Specific performance would require the constant supervision of the court. This will be the case where the order is to carry on an activity (like running a business) as opposed to achieving a result.

- The contract is a contract for personal service, such as a contract of employment.

- The obligation in question is insufficiently precise.

- The defendant has acted particularly badly.

- Severe hardship would be caused to the defendant by granting specific performance.

- The claimant has delayed too long in seeking the remedy and this would make it unjust in all the circumstances to grant specific performance.

Mandatory injunctions

9   Where the defendant has breached a negative covenant, a covenant not to do something, the claimant may, in rare situations, be able to get a mandatory injunction to compel the defendant to undo the effects of his act.

Prohibitory injunctions

10   Such injunctions are normally granted as a matter of course to stop the defendant breaching a negative covenant. The courts will refuse to grant such an injunction if it would be oppressive to do so, or if it would have the effect of compelling the defendant to perform the contract in circumstances where specific performance of the contract would have been refused.

FURTHER READING

Carter, Phang, and Phang 'Performance Following Repudiation: Legal and Economic Interests' (1999) 15 JCL 97

Davies and Turner 'Relief Against Penalties Without a Breach of Contract' (2013) 72 CLJ 20

Kimel 'Remedial Rights and Substantive Rights in Contract Law' (2002) 8 Legal Theory 313, 320–37

Summers (2017) 'Unresolved Issue in the Law on Penalties' LMCLQ 95

SELF-TEST QUESTIONS

1   What is the 'entire obligations rule' and when can its application be avoided?

2   What limits are placed upon the availability of the action for an agreed price? What, if any, limits should be placed upon it?

3   When will a clause specifying an amount to be payable in the event of breach be struck down as a penalty clause? Should such clauses ever be struck down?

4   When should specific performance be available? Did the House of Lords in *Co-operative Insurance Society Ltd v Argyll Stores (Holdings) Ltd* (1998) give an overly restrictive answer to this question?

5   Tom entered into a written contract with Una to sell her a building plot which is presently part of the garden of Tom's house. What remedies are available in each of the following cases?

(a)   The contract contains a promise by Una to build a stone wall six feet high along the new boundary. When she learns after completion of the purchase that the cost of such a wall will be £10,000, Una refuses to build it, arguing that it will make little, if any, difference to the value of either property.

(b)   The contract contains a promise by Una that she will not erect any fence or wall along the new boundary. When Tom returns from holiday, he finds that Una has nearly completed building a stone wall which will cost her £10,000, though it will make little, if any, difference to the value of either property.

 For hints on how to answer question 5, please see the online resources at **www.oup.com/uk/sullivan8e/.**

18

Remedies III: other non-compensatory or exceptional remedies

SUMMARY

This chapter considers other non-compensatory or exceptional remedies for breach of contract: restitution of money paid in advance for total failure of basis, pre-payments and deposits, the 'user principle' or 'negotiating damages' and recovery of a reasonable sum, disgorgement of defendant's profits and whether punitive damages should be available.

Why might a non-compensatory remedy be desirable?

18.1 Non-compensatory damages are more controversial than compensatory damages, because they may involve giving the claimant more than they have lost as a result of the breach of contract. In other words, they may place the claimant in a better position than if the contract had been properly performed in accordance with its terms. This begs the question: why would we ever want to do this?

18.2 The US case of *City of New Orleans v Fireman's Charitable Association* (1891) helps to provide an answer. The claimant paid the defendant to provide a fire-fighting service for five years, with the contract specifying how many men and horses should be kept available and how much hosepipe. At the end of the contract period, the claimant discovered that the defendant had failed to keep available as many men or horses as specified, or the length of hosepipe that had been promised, thereby saving itself over $40,000. However, the claimant could not show that the breach had prevented the defendant extinguishing any fires, so the Supreme Court of Louisiana held that the claimant had suffered no loss and thus was not entitled to damages.

18.3 Most people feel unease about this result. The important issue is what exactly is wrong with the decision. We might conclude that the claimant did in fact suffer a loss. It got an inferior level of service to that for which it contracted. On this view, compensatory remedies can deal with the problem, as long as we adequately measure the claimant's expectation interest. Another view is that the claimant overpaid: he paid for a certain number of firemen but got less than he paid for. Therefore, he should be able to get back some of the money that he paid (see paras **18.6–18.20**). Alternatively, we may feel that it is wrong for the defendant to have made a profit from his breach of contract, and that the appropriate thing to do is to strip him of any profit that he has made (see paras **18.34–18.47**). Finally, we may feel that the defendant has acted badly by deliberately providing a lower level of service than he promised, and that he should be punished for this by having to pay punitive damages that reflect his bad conduct (see paras **18.48–18.58**).

18.4 In light of this, it is unsurprising that the cases and academic commentary present a number of different reasons for awarding non-compensatory remedies: because compensatory damages do not adequately protect the claimant's interest in performance, because the defendant's conduct is reprehensible, because the defendant should not be allowed to profit from breaching the contract, and because we want to deter others from breaching their contracts, to name but four. As we shall see, often the cases have not resolved this question satisfactorily. The current trend in English law is to expand the circumstances in which non-compensatory damages are available, but in some cases, it may have gone too far.

18.5 In this chapter, we shall examine four types of remedies for breach of contract that are not straightforwardly compensatory: restitution for total failure of basis; the 'user principle', now often known as 'negotiating damages' (although this is best understood as an unusual form of compensation); disgorgement of profits; and punitive damages. The scope of these categories is a matter of some controversy. Indeed, the last of these, punitive damages, is not recognised in English law in respect of breaches of contract, although some argue that English law should move towards recognising this type of damages.

Restitution of money for total failure of basis

18.6 Where A transfers money to B under a contract, A transfers it on the condition that B does something in return. For example, if I contract to have a house built for me for £5,000, the money to be paid up front, I transfer the money on the condition that the other party builds the house for me. So my intent to transfer the benefit is *qualified*: I only intend the other party to have the money if he does something in return for me. If he doesn't do what he promises to do (in our example, if he fails to build the house), I don't intend him to have the money. As it was put by Lord Wright in *Fibrosa Spolka Akcyjna v Fairbairn Lawson Combe Barbour Ltd* (1943):

> There was no intent to enrich [the defendant] in the events which happened ... The payment was originally conditional. The condition of retaining it is eventual performance. Accordingly, when that condition fails, the right to retain the money must simultaneously fail.

18.7 In such a situation, we say that there has been a 'failure of basis', because the basis on which I transferred the benefit has not been fulfilled, and the law allows me to recover the money that I transferred. We call this recovery of the benefit that I transferred 'restitution' (because the defendant will be 'unjustly enriched' if allowed to retain the benefit), so the remedy is known as restitution for failure of basis. It is often referred to as restitution for failure of consideration, but such terminology is confusing because 'consideration' bears a different meaning here than it does in the context of formation of a contract ('when one is considering the law of failure of consideration ... it is, generally speaking, not the promise which is referred to as the consideration, but the performance of the promise' *Fibrosa* (1943)). For the meaning of 'consideration' in the context of contract formation, see Chapter 5.

18.8 In most cases this remedy has no advantage over claiming damages, because where the claimant has made a good bargain, it is better for her to be put in the same position as if the contract had been performed than to be returned to the position that she was in before it was formed. However, the remedy is attractive to a claimant where she has made a bad bargain, that is, a contract that she would have made a loss from even if it had been properly performed. Imagine that I agree to buy a car from you for £10,000. In fact, the car is only worth £4,000, so I have made a bad bargain. I pay you the price but you never hand over the car. Because I have made a bad bargain, I cannot recover very much in the way of expectation damages (only £4,000). I will be far better off if I can just get my money back and escape from the bargain. Restitution for failure of basis sometimes allows me to do this. It is for this reason that the argument of Stevens and Neyers (1999)—that this remedy is really a claim for expectation loss for breach of contract—is misconceived. It is often clear that the claimant has suffered little expectation loss, and that allowing him to get restitution for failure of basis would allow him to recover a far greater sum. In short, restitution for failure of basis is not a damages claim.

18.9 Currently, a claimant has to fulfil two conditions to recover restitution for failure of basis:

- The failure of basis must be 'total' (*Whincup v Hughes* (1871)). This is why the remedy is often referred to as 'restitution for *total* failure of basis'. This requirement means that the defendant must not have performed a single one of her obligations under the contract (*Stocznia Gdanska SA v Latvian Shipping Co* (1998)). To work out whether this is the case, close examination of the terms of the contract and the obligations that it imposes upon the defendant is necessary in order to tell precisely what steps the defendant is required to take in return for the payment and therefore determine whether the defendant has performed (a) none of these steps (in which case there will be a total failure of consideration); (b) some of these steps (in which case there will be a *partial* failure of consideration); or (c) all of these steps (in which case there will be no failure of consideration at all).

- For example, if the contract is one that only requires the defendant to supply goods, there will be a total failure if the defendant fails to deliver the goods, even if they spent a great deal of time and money manufacturing them (*Fibrosa* (1943)), so the case will fall into category (a) (see the *Systech International Ltd* case at para **18.15** for another example of category (a)). On the other hand, if the contract places an obligation on the defendant to manufacture and then deliver the goods, then if the defendant starts to manufacture the goods but fails to complete or deliver them, then there will not be a total failure of consideration, because the defendant has started to perform the contract by beginning to manufacture the goods (*Hyundai Heavy Industries Co Ltd v Papadopolous* (1980)), so the case will fall into category (b). If a claimant purchaser of property pays a deposit to have the property taken off the market but then does not go through with the purchase, there will be no failure of consideration at all, because he has received the benefit for which the deposit was paid (*Sharma v Simposh Ltd* (2013)), so the case will fall within category (c).

- The contract must be terminated, void, or unenforceable (*Thomas v Brown* (1876)). Here, we shall focus on restitution following the *termination* of the contract. For when a contract can be terminated for breach, see Chapter 15.

18.10 The first requirement has come under heavy attack from commentators. The reason for this is that the rationale behind allowing restitution for failure of basis suggests that the remedy should be available even if the failure is partial rather than total, that is, even if the defendant has performed some of her obligations under the contract. The rationale for the remedy is that the claimant only intended the defendant to keep the benefit transferred to her by the claimant if the defendant did *everything* that she was meant to do under the contract. So it should not matter whether the defendant performed none of her contractual obligations, or whether she performed some but not all of them. Why then do we still have the rule that the failure be total? There are two possible reasons.

18.11 First, the courts are unwilling to force themselves to place a value on the defendant's part performance, a task that they would have to carry out if restitution for partial failure of basis was allowed. Take the house-building example again. If the law allowed me to recover this sort of restitutionary remedy despite the defendant having built some of the house, I wouldn't be allowed to get all my money back: the defendant would be allowed to keep some of it because of the work that he had done. To work out how much he should be allowed to keep, the courts would have to work out how much his partial performance of the contract was worth, something they do not like doing! As Birks (1996) argues, this is a poor reason for keeping the 'total failure' requirement. For one thing, the courts are happy to value part performance in other contexts, such as where a partly performed contract is rescinded for misrepresentation.

18.12 A more convincing reason for the requirement is provided by Jaffey (1998). He argues that it is only where the defendant has taken no steps to perform their side of the bargain that the claimant should be allowed to get out of the bargain by obtaining restitution for failure of basis. Notice that where the claimant has made a good bargain, a remedy that just lets her recover money paid in advance will not be terribly attractive, because expectation damages will allow for greater recovery (if the contract had been performed, the claimant would have made more profit than merely covering her up-front payment). In a bad bargain, it will be very attractive for the claimant to recover the upfront payment and the law allows this. Notice that this is out of step with the position of a claimant who claims reliance damages to avoid a bad bargain, who is restricted to the expectation measure (see para **16.30**). This is how we might defend the 'total' requirement, because it justifies allowing claimants to escape bad bargains in this way. It is only in a *total* failure case, i.e. where the defendant has performed *no part* of the bargain, that the defendant should be barred from invoking the contractual allocation of risk so as to limit the claimant to expectation damages. On the other hand, this argument is not without its problems. It is generally accepted that a contract is binding from the moment that it is entered into, not just from the time that performance begins, so a party can normally invoke the contractual allocation of risk as soon as the contract is made. Moreover, should it really make such a difference that the defendant has performed one trivial bit of the contract?

18.13 What stance does the case law take on this issue? The law still requires the failure to be total: see *Stocznia Gdanska* for confirmation of this. Interestingly, however, the courts are increasingly finding methods to circumvent the rule. Three techniques can be identified. First, the court may construe the contract in a way that allows them to say that despite appearances, the defendant has performed none of his obligations. For example, in *Rowland v Divall* (1923), D sold a stolen car to R for £334. Despite the fact that D's actions had allowed R to use and enjoy the car for four months, the Court of Appeal held that D had not performed any of his obligations under the contract, in particular to give R good title to the car. Second, the court may be able to *apportion* the benefit transferred by the claimant between different bits of performance of the defendant (*Goss v Chilcott* (1996)). In other words, the court may in effect be able to divide the contract up into smaller contracts. For example, I agree to pay Dave £100 for 100 tons of corn, the money to be paid up front. After I pay, he only delivers 30 tons, which I eagerly accept. The court will say that £30 of my money bought 30 tons of the corn, and the other £70 represented the 70 tons that Dave did not deliver. So in respect of this £70, I have got nothing in return, so there has been a total failure in respect of this sum. The courts are willing to do this in the context of sale of goods contracts (see s 30 of the Sale of Goods Act 1979) and contracts of loan (see *Goss* itself) but not yet in the context of a contract for services (see the Australian case of *Baltic Shipping Co v Dillon* (1993)). Third, on at least one occasion the courts have all but ignored the rule. In *D O Ferguson v Sohl* (1992), one party had paid £26,738.75 to builders to carry out some work on shop premises. In breach of the contract, the builders walked out, having only done £22,065.76 worth of work. The Court of Appeal allowed the recovery of the balance, £4,673, on the ground that there had been a total failure of basis in respect of this amount. Clearly, however, any failure of basis was partial (see *Ministry of Sound (Ireland) Ltd v World Online Ltd* (2003)), because the builders had done a great deal of work under the contract.

18.14 There are two problems with the courts' stance of purporting to maintain the rule but then finding ways to avoid its application. It causes needless uncertainty, because it is hard to predict when the court will attempt to circumvent the rule, and when they will not. Second, it is slightly intellectually dishonest to purport to follow the rule but then find cunning ways to avoid doing so by the back door. Therefore, it would be better for the courts to confront the issue head on and either abolish the rule or state that it must be properly respected. There are hints that the former may happen: see *Westdeutsche* (1996) per Lord Goff (although contrast his more cautious words in *Stocznia Gdanska*).

18.15   The Court of Appeal grappled with the question of failure of consideration in *Systech International Ltd v PC Harrington Contractors Ltd* (2012). There, the claimant and defendant had paid an arbitrator to decide their dispute but the arbitrator had made errors in his determinations that rendered it invalid, so the claimant sought to recover the fees paid. The court held that the question was not whether there had been a total failure of consideration but whether the arbitrator had performed the services necessary to make payment due, which turned on whether he had to provide a *valid* decision in order for the fees to be due. It held that he had not. This is a slightly odd way of viewing the issue—the question whether there is a failure of consideration for the payment turns on precisely the issue that the court identified, namely whether the payment was for a valid decision or just for any decision, but does not prevent the need to apply the doctrine of failure of consideration, because this is what explains why the claimant is entitled to restitution of the money paid. Therefore, the case is better explained on orthodox total failure principles.

18.16   Turning to the second requirement, that the contract be terminated, there has been no criticism of this in the cases. However, some commentators have questioned whether such a requirement is justifiable: see Smith (1999), Tettenborn (2002), and for a similar, but slightly more cautious view, Beatson (1999). Imagine that I have an agreement for 12 batches of eggs to be delivered, one batch each month, £100 to be paid the day before delivery each month. Things proceed smoothly for three months but despite my paying the fourth instalment, no delivery is made in the fourth month. I paid the fourth instalment on condition that the fourth batch was delivered, so why shouldn't I be able to get the fourth instalment back and carry on with the contract for the remaining eight months? However, it is important to remember when a claimant would want to use such a remedy. If she has entered into a good bargain, she will simply claim damages without terminating the contract. It is where she has entered into a bad bargain that a restitutionary remedy will be useful, and it is far from certain that we should allow claimants to 'get out of' unwise contracts in such circumstances.

18.17   Finally, what happens when the party who has *breached* the contract seeks restitution for failure of basis? In general, the remedy is equally available. Although at first sight this might seem surprising, it must be remembered that the victim of the breach will have a damages claim for breach of contract which he can set off against the restitutionary claim. One particular situation where a party in breach may seek this remedy is where he has paid money before the other party commences performance. This payment will either be construed as a *deposit* or an *advance payment*, using the normal rules of contractual interpretation (see para **7.43**). If it is construed as a deposit, this means the payor intends the other party to have the money whether or not the payor fulfils his side of the bargain. The essence of a deposit is that you intend the other party to keep it even if you later pull out of the bargain: it is security for your performance. Therefore, if the payor fails to fulfil his side of the bargain, he cannot claim that there has been a failure of basis, because he intended the other party to keep the money in these circumstances (*Howe v Smith* (1884)). On the other hand, if the payment is construed as an advance payment, the payor only intended the payee to have the money if the other side of the bargain is performed, so if it is not, he can get the money back, even if he is the party in breach. For example, in *Dies v British and International Mining and Finance Corpn Ltd* (1939), the purchaser paid £100,000 of the purchase price in advance but, in breach of contract, refused to take delivery of the goods. It was held that he could recover the £100,000 (minus the amount of any damages suffered by the seller from the breach of contract) on the basis that he had not received the goods for which he had contracted.

18.18 A deposit is similar to a liquidated damages clause (see para **17.22**): in both cases, the contract stipulates that the claimant will lose a sum of money if she breaches the contract. The main difference is a that the former has been paid in advance, so the defendant simply keeps the money that the claimant has already paid (known as 'forfeiting' the deposit), whereas the latter only requires the claimant to pay the money over once she has breached the contract. In light of the similarities between the two concepts, it is no surprise that similar rules have evolved to protect against unfair deposits, albeit with different historical routes. For deposits, the principle is that the court has a jurisdiction to give 'relief' against the defendant's 'forfeiture' of the deposit. The similarities between the two principles were expressly noted by the Privy Council in *Workers Trust & Merchant Bank Ltd v Dojap Investments Ltd* (1993), where a vendor of land was not permitted to retain a whopping 25 per cent deposit when the purchaser did not complete the purchase, and by the Supreme Court in *Cavendish Square Holdings BV v El Makdessi* (2015), although their precise relationship remains somewhat unclear. Certainly, the Supreme Court envisaged some overlap between the two, although the issue was not before the court of the facts of the case. Lord Mance said that 'a case may raise for consideration both the penalty doctrine and the power of the court to relieve against forfeiture. In my opinion, that is both logical and correct in principle under the current law.'

18.19 The jurisdiction to give relief against forfeiture is phrased in similar terms to the penalty jurisdiction—a court will not allow a defendant to forfeit (i.e. retain) a deposit if it would be oppressive and unconscionable for the defendant to do so (*Stockloser v Johnson* (1954)). There is some doubt as to whether this protection extends to all types of contracts, or only those concerning the transfer or creation of proprietary or possessory rights (this limitation was suggested in *The Scaptrade* (1983)), but it certainly extends beyond monetary deposits in land transactions. In *Cukurova Finance International Ltd v Alfa Telecom Turkey Ltd* (2013), the Privy Council granted relief against forfeiture, in exceptional circumstances of unconscionability by the lender, where the lender had taken security over shares and was seeking to forfeit them.

18.20   Statute also offers some protection in this area for consumer contracts, in the shape of the Consumer Rights Act 2015 ('CRA') and the Consumer Credit Act 2006. Indeed, the indicative grey list of unfair terms in the CRA includes the following: 'A term which has the object or effect of permitting the trader to retain sums paid by the consumer where the consumer decides not to conclude or perform the contract, without providing for the consumer to receive compensation of an equivalent amount from the trader where the trader is the party cancelling the contract' (see further paras **8.55–8.56**).

The user principle/'negotiating damages'

18.21   There has traditionally been a remedy available where the defendant breaches a duty to the claimant by using the claimant's property without the claimant's consent: in certain circumstances the claimant can claim a *reasonable sum* for the defendant's use of it. This is sometimes called the 'user principle' (*Inverugie Investments v Hackett* (1995)) and is available outside the law of contract, such as where the defendant has committed the tort of trespass to land. Our focus here is on breach of contract, where the principle has expanded beyond its proprietary origins and is now of more general application, where the defendant has breached a contractual obligation without the claimant's consent, thereby depriving the claimant of the opportunity to charge a reasonable sum for the release of that obligation. Two issues arise: when is this remedy available and why should it be available?

18.22   It used to be thought that, in order to get this remedy in the contractual setting, it was necessary (although not sufficient) to show that the defendant's breach of contract also violated a proprietary right of the claimant, such as a restrictive covenant. The classic example is *Wrotham Park Estate Co Ltd v Parkside Homes Ltd* (1974), where the defendant built houses on its land in breach of a restrictive covenant given to the claimant forbidding it from doing so except in particular circumstances. A restrictive covenant is a proprietary right, so by building the houses, the defendant had infringed the claimant's proprietary rights. But the claimant could not point to any obvious financial loss from the breach, for example in the form of diminution in the value of the claimant's retained land. Therefore, the claimant was awarded the sum that the claimant might reasonably have demanded for relaxing the covenant, which was held to be five per cent of the defendant's anticipated profits. In *AG v Blake* (which is discussed in depth at paras **18.34–18.47**), however, it was held that there is no justification for confining this remedy to breaches of contract that also involve violation of proprietary rights. Lord Nicholls stated:

> It is not easy to see why, as between parties to a contract, a violation of a party's contractual rights should attract a lesser degree of remedy than a violation of his property rights ... it is not clear why it should be any more permissible to expropriate personal rights than it is permissible to expropriate property rights.

18.23 In other words, it should not be necessary to show that the defendant's breach of contract violated the claimant's proprietary rights. Although some commentators did not support this development, arguing that proprietary rights are generally more important than non-proprietary rights and therefore more deserving of the protection offered by the user principle (see Dagan (2000)), the *Wrotham Park* remedy is now no longer seen as confined to proprietary breaches of contract, an expansion that was unequivocally accepted by the Court of Appeal in *One Step (Support) Ltd v Morris-Garner* (2016). In the light of this change, the 'user principle' label is no longer apt, because the remedy is available in cases beyond those where the defendant is using the claimant's property without consent. The Privy Council adopted the label 'negotiating damages' in *Pell Frischmann Engineering Ltd v Bow Valley Iran Ltd* (2009) and this seems preferable, since the sum awarded represents the hypothetical amount that would have been negotiated between the parties, if the defendant had negotiated for a release from the claimant, rather than gone ahead and breached the contract. It should be noted that the Court of Appeal held in *Devenish Nutrition Ltd v Sanofi-Anetis SA* (2008) that the 'proprietary' requirement remains for torts, though it should also be noted, as emphasised by the Court of Appeal in *One Step (Support) Ltd v Morris-Garner* (2016), that the claimant in *Devenish* was claiming an 'all or nothing' disgorgement remedy, in other words an account of all the defendant's profits, not a tortious version of the negotiating damages remedy.

18.24 What, then, is it necessary to establish in order to be able to claim negotiating damages? The Court of Appeal decision in *Experience Hendrix LLC v PPX Enterprises Inc* (2003) sheds some light on this issue without resolving it in a completely satisfactory manner. In breach of a settlement agreement, the defendant released unlicensed recordings of Jimi Hendrix. The defendant should have obtained the claimant's consent before doing so. The defendant did not violate any proprietary rights of the claimant: it merely used its own recordings in breach of the terms of the settlement. The claimant was awarded negotiating damages, a reasonable sum for the use of the material, such sum as might reasonably have been demanded by the claimant in return for the claimant granting the licences. The guidance provided by the case as to when negotiating damages will be available is vague. As in the case of the much more exceptional remedy of 'disgorgement of profits' (see paras **18.34–18.47**), a guide will be whether the claimant has 'a legitimate interest in preventing the defendant's profit making activity'. A deliberate breach and difficulty in establishing that the claimant has suffered financial loss will both be relevant. So if all these factors are made out, how do we tell whether negotiating damages or disgorgement is the appropriate remedy? This question will be explored in more detail in paras **18.41–18.47**, but for now the short answer seems to be that if the breach took place in a 'commercial' context, negotiating damages will be awarded. If, on the other hand, it takes place outside the commercial context, in a situation where something more important than money is at stake, for example a contract of employment with the intelligence services as in *Blake*, where matters of national security were thought to be at stake, then disgorgement might exceptionally be awarded. The rationale for this distinction is presumably that only money is at stake in the commercial context, so a lesser remedy is warranted than in cases where matters of national security and other such important interests are at risk.

18.25   What clearly emerges is that removing the 'proprietary rights' requirement for negotiating damages means that some other criteria are necessary to keep the remedy within reasonable limits, and unfortunately the *Experience Hendrix* 'legitimate interest' test is inherently vague and has the potential for confusion between this remedy and disgorgement of profits.

18.26   The Court of Appeal has explored the criteria for the award of negotiating damages in *One Step (Support) Ltd v Morris* (2016). Here the defendants used to own and run the claimant company, One Step, which provided supported living services to children leaving care and vulnerable adults. They resigned from One Step and entered into a contract with it, containing restrictive covenants not to compete with its business or solicit its clients or customers. Unbeknown to One Step, the defendants had already set up a rival company, called Positive Living, prior to resigning, and then breached the covenants by operating in competition and poaching several customers and clients of One Step. One Step sought negotiating damages, but the defendants argued (somewhat disingenuously) that they should only be available where the claimant suffered no financial loss in a mainstream sense, like the claimant in *Wrotham Park*. The trial judge and a unanimous Court of Appeal disagreed, awarding negotiating damages based on the amount One Step might reasonably have demanded to release the covenant. According to Christopher Clarke LJ, the test is whether the award of negotiating damages would be a 'just response' or appropriate 'what is required to avoid injustice'. That was the case here, because One Stop would face considerable difficulty in establishing damages on the ordinary basis:

> there would seem to me to be very real problems in showing what placements One Step lost or might have lost because of the appearance of Positive Living on the scene... the whole exercise would, as it seems to me, in practice be fraught with difficulty. In addition any loss of goodwill is inherently difficult to measure.

18.27   The defendants had argued that an award of *Wrotham Park* damages on these facts 'would make the exception the norm.' It is undeniably true that, in many cases 'it may be difficult to say what business the contract breaker has obtained which the innocent party would have obtained; and even more so to say what has been the effect on the goodwill and reputation of the innocent party, and what business the innocent party might, but for the competition, have secured (both in the period of restraint and thereafter).' The Court of Appeal expressed sympathy with this concern, but were not persuaded by it. On the particular facts (including the defendants' cynical conduct as well as the difficulties of proving conventional loss), justice required the award of negotiating damages. Nor did it matter that these were likely to be considerably higher than any plausible figure for conventional loss. This is to be welcomed. The claimant is being compensated, not for the loss that did or did not ultimately ensue, but for the lost opportunity to demand a fee to release the covenants. (See para **18.32** for a discussion of how such damages are quantified.)

18.28 As to why negotiating damages should ever be available, some see their purpose as compensating the claimant for a loss suffered (for example *Jaggard v Sawyer* (1995) and Waddams (1997)), others as removing a gain made by the defendant, in that he has saved money by obtaining for himself the free use of something for which he should have paid (for example, Goodhart (1995)). A third view is that the remedy is neither exclusively compensatory nor exclusively restitutionary (a view expressed by the Privy Council in *Inverugie Investments v Hackett* (1995)). In *Inverugie*, the court supported the need for the remedy, adopting the dictum of the Lord Chancellor in *Mediana (Owners of Steamship) v Comet (Owners of Lightship)* (1900) that 'it is no answer for a wrongdoer who has deprived the plaintiff of his chair to point out that he does not usually sit in it or that he has plenty of other chairs in the room' but did not feel it important to place the remedy in either the compensatory or the non-compensatory category.

18.29 At first glance, the claim does not seem to fit perfectly into either the first or second category. Many commentators suggest that the claimant often suffers no loss, because often he would not have sold the thing in question or allowed someone else to use it for any price, so he has not lost the money that he would have obtained through selling it. On the other hand, the claim does not seem to focus on the profit made by the defendant either, because a reasonable sum is awarded whether the defendant has made a loss from his breach of contract or a huge gain. Judicial opinion pre-*Blake* differed on the appropriate categorisation of the claim (though with a clear majority of judges favouring compensatory reasoning), but *Blake* preferred the restitutionary explanation (removing the defendant's gain). *Experience Hendrix* is equivocal on this point, but *One Step* firmly favours a compensatory analysis, as Christopher Clarke LJ said:

> *Wrotham Park damages are a form of compensatory damages, although not of the ordinary type. As a result "compensatory damages" is a phrase sometimes used to mean damages calculated in the ordinary way by assessing the actual financial loss incurred, e.g. a profit that would have been obtained, and sometimes to mean compensation in the form of the price which would be agreed in a hypothetical bargain with the claimant for the right to use property which has been appropriated without permission, or to be released from a burdensome negative covenant. The sum that the claimant could have obtained is what he may be taken to have lost: see Lord Hobhouse in Blake and the price for what amounts to the compulsory acquisition by the wrongdoer of the right per Lord Nicholls.*

18.30 It is suggested that *One Step* is right to treat negotiation damages as primarily compensatory. As will be suggested in the context of disgorgement, taking a broad notion of loss can solve many of the problems in this area. As Waddams (1997) explains:

> *the plaintiff's loss is a real one. A defendant who has helped himself to the plaintiff's property cannot argue that it has no value because the plaintiff would not have sold it voluntarily. In the absence of a market value the court must, after the wrong has been done, do its best to estimate a reasonable value on the basis of a hypothetical transaction.*

In other words, if you take something of mine or use it without my consent, then I have suffered loss even though I would never have sold the thing in question. Indeed, the fact that I would not have sold it suggests that it is *particularly* valuable to me, so it is counterintuitive to suggest that I have suffered no loss in such circumstances. Imagine that I have lost my legs as a result of the defendant's negligence and bring a personal injury claim. The fact that I would not have sold my legs for any amount of money does not prevent us saying that I have suffered a loss—quite the contrary! The same applies outside the proprietary terms of the example, to important covenants that matter a lot to the claimant and that the claimant would not have released at any price.

18.31 However, one can readily understand the Privy Council's view in *Inverugie* that negotiating damages are neither compensatory nor restitutionary. The important point, whichever view is taken, is that sight is not lost of the underlying need to ensure that the remedy reflects the interest in question and the defendant's conduct. This should be the focus, not the somewhat academic question of how we classify the remedy.

18.32 A final issue, more important in practice than the precise nature of the remedy, is the question of how the court quantifies what a reasonable fee would be when awarding negotiating damages. *Pell Frischmann Engineering Ltd v Bow Valley Iran Ltd* (2009) explained that the award is to be worked out by envisaging a hypothetical negotiation between a willing buyer and seller over how much should be paid for the release of the contractual right in question, *even if* the parties themselves would never have been willing to have such a negotiation. The Court of Appeal in *One Step* provided a little more detail. It clarified that the sum that might reasonably have been demanded in advance to release the covenant might exceed the actual financial loss eventually suffered by the claimant, since this hypothetical negotiation is, by definition, conducted without hindsight about the actual profits eventually made by the defendant from the breach (this must be true, when you reflect that the claimant in *Wrotham Park* itself suffered no obvious financial loss in the form of diminution in the value of the retained land). Christopher Clarke LJ said:

> The amount taken as the reasonable sum for the relaxation of restrictive covenants, even if it is a modest percentage of future profits, may represent more, perhaps far more, than the loss realistically to be regarded as, in the event, suffered by their breach ... In the present case, some of the evidence suggests that One Step may in fact have suffered little or limited loss from the competition of Positive Living. Further, the assessment of a reasonable price may involve consideration of several imponderables, such as the likely effect of future competition ...

18.33 Nonetheless, although the focus is normally on a hypothetical negotiation happening at the date of breach, *One Step* recognised that exceptionally:

> justice may require and entitle the court to take into account facts and events after the date of the hypothetical negotiation, although they would normally be irrelevant,

or, if justice requires it, take a post breach valuation date. One possible circumstance when such events might be relevant is where the nature of the competition which in fact occurred was less than might have been possible if there had been no restrictive covenants at all.

Disgorgement of profit

18.34 When, if ever, should a claimant be allowed to claim the *profit* that the defendant has made by breaching the contract between them? In *Blake*, the House of Lords allowed the claimant to do so for the first time. The remedy, the removal of the defendant's profits, is known as 'disgorgement', or an 'account of profits', or 'restitutionary damages'. As for the negotiating damages remedy just discussed, two issues require attention: when *does* the law currently allow the claimant to obtain this remedy? And when, if ever, *should* the claimant be allowed this remedy?

18.35 The facts of *Blake* were that George Blake worked for the British intelligence services from 1944 to 1961. From 1951 until 1961, he was a double agent of the Soviet Union. After being convicted for his treachery in 1961, he escaped from Wormwood Scrubs prison to Moscow in 1966. In 1989 he wrote his autobiography, *No Other Choice*, which contained some information relating to his days in British intelligence. While the information was no longer confidential by this time, nor was its disclosure damaging to the public interest, its release was held to breach Blake's duty under his employment contract 'not to divulge any official information gained by [him] as a result of [his] employment, either in the press or in book form.' Jonathan Cape secured the exclusive rights to publish the book for £150,000, to be paid in three instalments. By the time of trial, Blake had already received £60,000 of this, which was in practice unrecoverable, as Blake was living in Russia. The Crown brought proceedings to get its hands on the remaining £90,000. By a 4–1 majority, the House of Lords held that the Crown could recover the profits made by the defendant from his breach of contract. Accordingly, a declaration was granted that the Crown was entitled to recover a sum equal to that owing under the publishing agreement.

18.36 Lord Nicholls, giving the principal judgment for the majority, sought to set out the circumstances in which disgorgement for breach of contract would be available, but found it extremely difficult to lay down anything but vague guidelines:

> *Normally the remedies of damages, specific performance and injunction, coupled with the characterisation of some contractual obligations as fiduciary, will provide an adequate response to a breach of contract. It will only be in exceptional cases, where those remedies are inadequate, that any question of accounting for profits will arise. No fixed rules can be prescribed. The court will have regard to all the circumstances, including the subject matter of the contract, the purpose of the contractual provision that has*

been breached, the circumstances in which the breach occurred, the consequences of the breach and the circumstances in which the relief is being sought. A useful general guide, although not exhaustive, is whether the plaintiff had a legitimate interest in preventing the defendant's profit-making activity and, hence, in depriving him of his profit. It would be difficult, and unwise, to attempt to be more specific.

18.37   Two points emerge from this: first, that Lord Nicholls considered the legitimate interest test to be a helpful guide in working out whether disgorgement is appropriate and, second, that he only intended this test to be satisfied in exceptional circumstances. Why was this case an exceptional one where the claimant had such a legitimate interest? Lord Nicholls answered this as follows:

The present case is exceptional. The context is employment as a member of the security and intelligence services. Secret information is the lifeblood of these services. In the 1950s Blake deliberately committed repeated breaches of his undertaking not to divulge official information gained as a result of his employment. He caused untold and immeasurable damage to the public interest he had committed himself to serve.

He also made it clear that in order to establish a legitimate interest, it is insufficient to show that the defendant deliberately breached the contract, or that the defendant breached in order to enter into a more profitable contract. It seems that to have a legitimate interest, the claimant must stand to lose something more than merely money from the breach. Some extremely important non-financial interest must be at stake, such as national security.

18.39   Lord Hobhouse dissented. One of his reasons for doing so was the danger of introducing an element of uncertainty into commercial transactions, because it would be hard for parties to predict in advance when such a remedy would be awarded:

I must also sound a further note of warning that if some more extensive principle of awarding non-compensatory damages for breach of contract is to be introduced into our commercial law the consequences will be very far reaching and disruptive.

This danger had earlier been pointed out by the Law Commission in Law Com No 247 (1997) and its earlier Consultation Paper No 132 (1993).

18.40   How real and important is this danger of uncertainty? Edelman (2002) suggests that it is not a problem at all:

Nor is the award arbitrary or any more uncertain than compensatory damages. A prospective defendant will know precisely what the award will be; the amount of profits made as a result of the breach.

However, this misses the point slightly. The real uncertainty is not the measure of damages, but *when* disgorgement will be awarded. In the case of compensatory damages, you know compensatory damages will be awarded against you when you breach a contract, providing that the claimant can show that she has suffered loss as a result (unless the loss is too remote or there is a defence). In the case of disgorgement, it is far more difficult to say when a defendant will be required to hand over the profits made from a breach of contract. Therefore, unless it is clear when the remedy will be available, uncertainty is a real problem.

18.41 Have subsequent cases clarified when disgorgement will be available? *Esso v Niad Ltd* (2001), the first case to apply *Blake*, vindicated those fears of uncertainty, because disgorgement was awarded in a run-of-the-mill commercial situation. Esso ran a 'price-watch' scheme, whereby those running Esso garages, such as the defendant, would reduce their prices when told to do so by Esso in order to remain competitive with local rivals, and in return for doing this, the garages would receive fuel from Esso at a discounted price. The defendant failed to reduce the prices as recommended by Esso, so Esso sued. One of the remedies that it claimed was an account of profits. It was held that the claimant had a legitimate interest because the defendant had breached the contract deliberately, it was difficult to ascertain the amount of financial loss that the claimant had sustained as a result of the breach, and the obligation breached, requiring the implementation of Esso's recommended prices, was 'fundamental' to the agreement. Yet these three features are often found in the commercial context, and are hardly 'exceptional' (see Beatson (2002a), McMeel (2002), and Sandy (2003)). This is not what Lord Nicholls intended!

18.42 *Blake* was subsequently considered by the Court of Appeal in *Experience Hendrix* (see para **18.24**). Disgorgement was refused on the facts. The judgment of Mance LJ restores some certainty by articulating what made *Blake* the sort of exceptional case where disgorgement would be awarded:

> The exceptional nature of Blake's case lay, first of all in its context—employment in the security and intelligence service, of which secret information was the lifeblood, its disclosure being a criminal offence. Blake had furthermore committed deliberate and repeated breaches causing untold damage, from which breaches most of the profits indirectly derived in the sense that his notoriety as a spy explained his ability to command the sums for publication which he had done. Thirdly, although the argument that Blake was a fiduciary was not pursued beyond first instance, the contractual obligation he had given was 'closely akin to a fiduciary obligation, where an account of profits is a standard remedy in the event of breach'.

He went on to explain that none of these conditions was made out on the facts. And in *One Step (Support) Ltd v Morris-Garner* (2016) Christopher Clarke LJ summarised the difference by saying that although the test for negotiating damages 'is not whether the case is exceptional but what does justice require. The position is different in relation to an account of profits which is, truly, an exceptional remedy.'

18.43 Sales J in *Vercoe v Rutland Fund Management Ltd* (2010) gave a useful explanation of how to identify exceptional cases where disgorgement of profits is warranted from those where the claimant should only receive negotiating damages, as follows:

> *In some situations, where the rights of the claimant are of a particularly powerful kind and his interest in full performance is recognised as being particularly strong, there may well be a tendency to recognise that the claimant should be entitled to [choose whether to seek disgorgement of the defendant's profits]. There are indications in the authorities that this may more readily be found to be appropriate in cases involving infringement of property rights ... This may reflect the particular importance usually attached to property rights and the extent of protection they are to be afforded in law—although one might think that in relation to ordinary rights in relation to property of a kind which is regularly bought and sold in a market, damages assessed by reference to a notional buy-out fee may often represent an appropriate and fair remedy, and it is possible that the law may develop in that way. By contrast, it may be more appropriate to award an account of profits where the right in question is of a kind where it would never be reasonable to expect that it could be bought out for some reasonable fee, so that it is accordingly deserving of a particularly high level of protection (such as the promise to keep state secrets which was in issue in Blake, which was classified as an exceptional case meriting such an award, and rights to protection under established fiduciary relationships, where trust between the parties rather than a purely commercial relationship is regarded as central to the obligations in question).*

18.44 It seems that we are beginning to reach some clarity as to when disgorgement might, exceptionally, be awarded. One problem remains: the status of *Niad*. On the reasoning in *Experience Hendrix, Niad* was wrongly decided: none of the three conditions set out applied. However, at the very least, no adverse comment was made of *Niad* when it was discussed in *Experience Hendrix*, and indeed the court comes close to implicitly approving it. In conclusion, providing the status of *Niad* can be cleared up, it is suggested that the objection based on commercial uncertainty is not a decisive one.

18.45 Is *Blake* therefore correct to suggest that disgorgement should sometimes be awarded for a breach of contract? It is suggested that it is not. A helpful way of assessing the decision is to adopt the approach of Cane (1997). He suggests that in order to determine what the appropriate remedy should be in a situation, we should look at the defendant's conduct and the importance of the interest of the claimant that we are seeking to protect. So the worse the conduct, or the more important the protected interest, the more severe the remedy. For example, if the defendant deliberately physically injures the claimant, his conduct is bad and the protected interest (the claimant's personal security) is important, so the remedy should be severe to reflect this. As we shall see, this approach largely coincides with the reasoning employed in *Blake*.

18.46 The protected interest here is the right to contractual performance by the other party. Lord Nicholls argued that damages for loss are sometimes insufficient to protect this interest and so can leave the claimant undercompensated, particularly when his losses are non-financial in nature. The answer to this failure to compensate properly, he argued, was to allow the claimant to recover the defendant's profit in such situations. (Notice that the reasoning in *Blake* is explicitly restitutionary—or concerned to reverse the defendant's unjust enrichment—although the Court of Appeal in *World Wildlife Fund for Nature v World Wrestling Federation Entertainment Inc* (2007), the Court of Appeal puzzlingly characterised the remedy as compensatory.) There are a number of problems with Lord Nicholls' reasoning:

- If the problem is failure to compensate properly for loss suffered, the solution is to compensate better, by expanding the situations in which we recognise that the defendant has suffered a loss for which he can claim damages. The problem should be tackled directly: if the problem is failure to compensate properly, the answer is to expand the notion of loss to enable the law to compensate more fully (see Mitchell (1999) and O'Sullivan (2002)). In short, as Worthington and Goode (2000) put it, '[t]here is no sense in complaining that compensation is inadequate and then adopting a strategy which is unrelated to solving that problem'.

- Indeed, as seen in Chapter 16, the recent trend in English law is to expand the situations in which the claimant can recover for non-financial losses. Therefore, English law is tackling this problem without the need to resort to allowing the defendant to be stripped of his profit (see O'Sullivan (2002)).

- Allowing the defendant to be stripped of his profit will not always solve the problem of undercompensation, because the defendant will not always have made a profit. If in *City of New Orleans*, the defendants had supplied all of the promised firemen but in breach of contract most of them sat around eating cakes all day, the defendants wouldn't have made a profit, because they wouldn't have saved any money, so allowing the claimant to recover the defendants' profit would have been of no assistance. This highlights that the problem of undercompensation should be tackled directly.

- It is not clear that there was a problem of undercompensation on the facts of *Blake*. As Hedley (2000) points out, the breach was not that serious; it was Blake's treachery in earlier times that was the serious act. The information he released in breach of contract was not confidential, so it is hard to see that the government suffered any real loss that needed redressing.

18.47   Let us turn now to the defendant's conduct. While not stated explicitly in any of the majority judgments in *Blake*, it was clearly intended that the severe remedy awarded should reflect the defendant's bad conduct and perhaps deter others. Lord Hobhouse recognised this in his dissent. Indeed, it is evident right from Lord Nicholls' opening sentence, '[m]y Lords, George Blake is a notorious, self-confessed traitor'. There are a number of problems with using disgorgement as a remedy to reflect how bad the defendant's conduct is:

- The remedy is too blunt. It only allows the *exact* amount of the defendant's profit to be taken from him, not a penny more, not a penny less. If the remedy is meant partly to reflect the defendant's conduct, sometimes the conduct will be appalling, for example, and we would need to take more from the defendant than just the profit he has made (Jaffey (1995)). Similarly, his conduct may not be quite so bad after all, so stripping him of *all* his profits might be too harsh a remedy to reflect his conduct. To accurately reflect the defendant's conduct, we would need to allow recovery of punitive damages for breach of contract, which English law currently does not (see the words of the Supreme Court of Canada in *Whiten v Pilot Insurance* (2002): '[p]unitive damages serve a need that is not met either by the pure civil law or the pure criminal law'). Whether it would be appropriate to allow punitive damages for breach of contract is discussed later. Such damages are designed specifically to reflect how badly the defendant has acted. Disgorgement is simply too inflexible to do this (see Hedley (2001a and 2001b)).

- Again, what if the defendant has acted badly but made no profit or only a small profit? Here, disgorgement cannot come close to reflecting the gravity of the defendant's conduct. As Worthington and Goode (2000) note, '[i]f a particular type of breach is unacceptable and warrants a deterrent remedy, then it is unacceptable whether or not the defendant makes a collateral profit.'

- There is a danger that the remedy will reflect conduct *other than* the breach of contract. The remedy is not meant to reflect how well or badly the defendant has lived his whole life: it is just meant to reflect how bad his breach of contract was. In *Blake*, the defendant was really being punished for his previous treachery, rather than his breach of contract, which was not so bad. As Lord Hobhouse notes in his dissent in *Blake*, it is all too easy to fall into this trap: Blake had escaped just punishment for his crimes. There was no prospect of ever bringing him back into the jurisdiction to make him serve out his prison sentence. Now he had an asset in the jurisdiction, that at least should be withheld from him; the asset had a connection with the crimes which he had committed.

Punitive damages for breach of contract?

18.48   Punitive damages are awarded to reflect the fact that the defendant has acted particularly badly when committing the civil wrong in question. The amount awarded may well exceed the amount of loss suffered by the claimant or the profit made by the defendant. The reason for this is that such damages have a different purpose: to signify the gravity of the defendant's conduct.

18.49   English law has set its face against allowing such damages for breach of contract. For example, Lord Bridge commented in *Ruxley* (1995) that '[t]here is no question of punishing the contract breaker'. However, as the discussion of disgorgement and restitution for failure of basis illustrates, English law is increasingly willing to allow non-compensatory damages. In light of this, two issues merit our attention. First, is English law slowly moving towards recognising punitive damages for breach of contract? Second, should such damages be made available?

18.50 As to the first issue, Edelman (2001) seems to suggest that English law is moving in this direction. He argues that English law has finally unequivocally recognised in *Blake* that compensatory damages will sometimes be inadequate to reflect the defendant's bad conduct or to deter others, and accordingly that damages need not be limited to what the claimant has lost. This is true. However, it is important to remember that punitive damages were described as 'anomalous' by Lord Nicholls in *Blake*. Second, Edelman points to the expansion by the House of Lords in *Kuddus v Chief Constable of Leicestershire Constabulary* (2001) of the circumstances in which punitive damages can be awarded against someone who has committed a tort. However, as we shall see, it is one thing to award punitive damages for tort, quite another to do so for breach of contract. As discussed in the context of disgorgement, commercial certainty is extremely important, so we should at the very least be more reluctant to award punitive damages for a breach of contract than we would for a tort. Therefore, if English law is moving towards recognition of punitive damages for breach of contract, it is suggested that it is doing so more slowly than Edelman suggests.

18.51 Should we recognise such a remedy? Some academic opinion suggests an answer in the affirmative (for example, McBride (1995), Edelman (2001), Hedley (2001a and 2001b), McKendrick (2003), and Phang and Lee (2003)). The argument offered for recognising such damages is simple: the remedy granted should reflect the protected interest of the claimant at stake and the defendant's conduct (Cane (1997)). To reflect the defendant's conduct accurately when the defendant has acted very badly, the argument is we need to award punitive damages.

18.52 There are a number of objections to taking such a course. First, it is often said that it is not the role of the civil law to punish; punishment is the role of the criminal law alone. This is put in stronger and more coherent terms by Beever (2003), who argues that punishment is simply foreign to the structure of private law. On the other hand, the civil law already reflects the defendant's conduct in the remedies that it awards (Cane (1997)). For example, a more severe remedy is granted for a fraudulent misrepresentation than a wholly innocent one (see paras **9.54–9.60**). Similarly, most vitiating factors take into account the defendant's bad conduct in pressuring, influencing, taking advantage of, or misleading the claimant and we are rarely prepared to let the claimant undo the contract where the defendant has done nothing wrong. If the remedy reflects in part the conduct of the defendant, then punitive damages might not be ruled out as a matter of general principle.

18.53 Second, it is often argued that it would be wrong to punish defendants without affording them the same safeguards that the criminal law would grant them, such as requiring proof beyond reasonable doubt, rather than just on the balance of probabilities. This objection could be countered in two ways. We can argue that such safeguards are unnecessary because the punishments inflicted by punitive damages are inherently less serious than those inflicted by the criminal law. As Edelman (2002) puts it 'the criminal law creates an offence against the state', whereas punitive damages do not have this effect. Alternatively, we could accept that such safeguards are necessary and allow the defendant to have them in cases where punitive damages may be awarded, though this is unimaginable in a commercial contractual dispute, which leads us on to the last objection.

18.54   The last objection is a practical one and is, it is suggested, compelling. The objection is that allowing such damages would cause unacceptable uncertainty in the commercial context. In the commercial sphere, certainty is all-important: commercial parties need to be able to predict what liability they would incur by committing a particular breach of contract. As Steyn LJ remarked in the context of disgorgement in *Surrey CC v Bredero Homes Ltd* (1993):

> [Such remedies] will lead to greater uncertainty in the assessment of damages in commercial and consumer disputes. It is of paramount importance that the way in which disputes are likely to be resolved by the courts must be readily predictable ... such a widespread availability of restitutionary remedies will have a tendency to discourage economic activity in relevant situations. In a range of cases liability would fall on underwriters who have insured relevant liability risks. Inevitably underwriters would have to be compensated for the new species of potential claims. Insurance premiums would have to go up. That, too, is a consequence which mitigates against the proposed extension.

18.55   This objection is dismissed by a number of academic commentators (McBride (1995 and 1996), Jaffey (2000), and Hedley (2001a)) on the ground that those who breach contracts do not deserve certainty. It is suggested that this view does not fit into the commercial context. Elsewhere, English law does not take such a serious view of those who breach their contracts in the commercial context: for example, it allows them to keep at least some of the profit that they have made from their breach (because disgorgement does not apply: see the discussion of *Blake* at paras **18.34–18.47**). So some degree of certainty is both necessary and desirable.

18.56   The reason for the potential uncertainty here is that judges find it very difficult to evaluate how bad conduct is in the commercial arena, because a certain amount of self-interested conduct is acceptable and, indeed, encouraged. A good example of this is the case of *Co-operative Insurance Society Ltd v Argyll Stores Holdings Ltd* (1997) (discussed further at para **17.41–17.47**). Argyll's breach of the covenant in its lease to keep open its store in the Hillsborough shopping centre was described as 'gross commercial cynicism' by the Court of Appeal, but was viewed in a far kinder light by Lord Hoffmann in the House of Lords. Even outside the purely commercial context, where only one of the parties is a business, there is a still a problem. Two examples will suffice for present purposes. First, take the Canadian decision in *Whiten v Pilot Insurance* (2002). After the appellant's house had burnt down, the respondent insurance company refused to pay out and claimed without any substance whatsoever that the family had torched its own home! The jury awarded $1 million punitive damages for the breach of contract, which the appeal court reduced to $100,000, before the Supreme Court reinstated the $1 million award. The point for present purposes is that the three courts disagreed by a factor of ten on how bad the defendant's conduct was. A similar picture emerges from both of the two subsequent Supreme Court of Canada decisions in *Fidler v Sun Life Assurance Co of Canada* (2007) and *Honda Canada Inc v Keays* (2008). In *Fidler*, the trial judge's decision not to award punitive damages was overturned by the Court of Appeal, who awarded $100,000, but their decision was in turn overruled by the Supreme Court, which restored the original decision on the point. Similarly, in *Keays* the judge awarded punitive damages of $500,000, reduced on appeal to $100,000 and set aside by the Supreme Court entirely.

18.57 The second example is *Bank of Credit and Commerce International SA v Ali (No 1)* (2001). In negotiating contracts of release with some employees whom it had made redundant, BCCI chose not to disclose the corrupt way that it had been running its business. The Court of Appeal viewed this non-disclosure as extremely bad conduct, holding that to enforce the contract would 'reward dishonesty at the expense of the innocent'. The House of Lords took a very different view of BCCI's non-disclosure, Lord Nicholls remarking that 'there can be no question of BCCI having indulged in anything approaching sharp practice in this case'. Furthermore, these problems in evaluating the conduct of a commercial actor are highlighted by the Law Commission in their examination of the area:

> Many breaches of contract are made for commercial reasons and it is difficult to draw the line between 'innocent' breach, for which there would only be compensation, and 'cynical' breach ... This would lead to greater uncertainty in the assessment of damages in commercial and consumer disputes (Law Com No 247, para 3.46).

18.58 In conclusion, while there may be arguments of principle in favour of punitive damages for breach of contract, there are formidable practical problems in taking this course. The issue is whether the potential uncertainty can be kept within acceptable limits, by limiting or structuring the discretion the court would have. Edelman (2002) suggests that this can be done by guideline judgments and a list of factors to consider. However, this discussion and the examples given suggest that the problem may be more deep-rooted: courts simply have great difficulty agreeing on what constitutes bad conduct on the part of a commercial actor. The same response can be offered to the argument made by McBride (1995) that those who seek 'in good faith not to breach their contracts' can rest easy that they will not be subject to punitive damages if they do breach. The lack of certainty over what constitutes 'good faith' in the commercial sphere would make it extremely difficult for someone to be sure in advance that they would not be subject to punitive damages. Overall, as Scott (2007) concludes, punitive damages for breach of contract 'should be avoided'.

OVERVIEW

1   Non-compensatory remedies are more controversial than compensatory damages, because they may involve giving the claimant more than he has lost as a result of the breach of contract. The current trend in English law is to increase the circumstances in which they are available.

2   There are three types of non-compensatory financial remedy for breach of contract:

- restitution for total failure of basis;
- a reasonable sum awarded by way of 'negotiating damages'; and
- disgorgement of profit.

3   In addition, some commentators argue that punitive damages should be available for breach of contract and that English law is slowly moving towards this, but this is a minority view.

4   Restitution for total failure of basis allows the claimant to get back money that he transferred to the other party under the contract. Normally, a claimant will prefer to seek expectation damages as these will exceed the amount of the claimant's price (where the claimant would have made a profit if the contract had been performed), so the separate restitutionary remedy is most useful where the claimant made a bad bargain. Currently, two conditions must be fulfilled for this remedy to be available:

- the other party must have performed none of his obligations under the contract; and
- the contract has been terminated.

The first condition has been heavily criticised by academics and the courts are increasingly finding ways to get around it. However, it is still currently a requirement and may be justifiable in view of the fact that this remedy allows the claimant to avoid his own bad bargain, so should be reserved for cases where the defendant has performed no part of his contractual obligations.

The second condition has begun to be attacked by some academics.

5   Where the defendant breaches the contract by doing something without the claimant's consent, in certain circumstances the claimant can claim a reasonable sum in damages. The breach will usually involve the defendant using the claimant's property, but this no longer need be the case. The claimant is effectively being compensated for the defendant's failure to negotiate and thus pay a fee for the claimant's consent; therefore this remedy is commonly called 'negotiating damages' and, although sometimes calculated by reference to a proportion of the defendant's hypothetical profits, is best understood as an exceptional loss-based measure.

6   Where the claimant has a legitimate interest in preventing the defendant's profit-making activity, the claimant will be allowed to recover the profit that the defendant has made from breaching the contract (*AG v Blake*). This is known as disgorgement or an account of profits. This legitimate interest will only be satisfied in utterly exceptional circumstances, where some important non-financial interest is at stake, such as national security. The circumstances in which this remedy should be available, indeed whether it should ever be available, and what its proper categorisation is, remain hotly contested issues.

7   Punitive damages are designed to reflect how badly the defendant has acted and often greatly exceed the loss caused to the claimant. They are unavailable in English law for breaches of contract, for good reason.

FURTHER READING

Birks 'Failure of Consideration' Chapter 9 in *Consensus Ad Idem* (1996)

Campbell and Wylie 'Ain't no Telling (Which Circumstances are Exceptional)' [2003] CLJ 605

Edelman 'Exemplary Damages for Breach of Contract' (2001) 117 LQR 539

Jaffey 'The Use Claim' Chapter 4 in *The Nature and Scope of Restitution* (2000) (note that this pre-dates *Blake*)

McBride 'A Case for Awarding Damages in Response to Deliberate Breach of Contract' (1995) Anglo-Am LR 369

McKendrick 'Total Failure of Consideration and Counter-Restitution: Two Issues or One?' Chapter 8 in *Laundering and Tracing* (1995)

Mitchell 'Remedial Inadequacy in Contract and the Role of Restitutionary Damages' (1999) 15 JCL 133

O'Sullivan 'Reflections on the Role of Restitutionary Damages to Protect Contractual Expectations' Chapter 12 in *Unjustified Enrichment* (2002)

Rotherham 'The Conceptual Structure of Restitution for Wrongs' [2007] CLJ 172

Rotherham '*Wrotham Park* Damages and Accounts of Profits: Compensation or Restitution?' [2008] LMCLQ 25

Rotherham 'Gain-Based Relief in Tort after *AG v Blake*' (2010) 125 LQR 102

Willmot-Smith 'Reconsidering 'total' failure' [2013] CLJ 414

SELF-TEST QUESTIONS

1   When, if ever, is it justified to award the claimant more than he would have received had the contract been properly performed?

2   When, if ever, should restitution for failure of basis be available?

3   Why would we ever want to allow the claimant to recover the defendant's profit from the breach of contract? Why are other remedies inadequate for this task?

4   Should we ever award punitive damages for a breach of contract? If not, why not?

5   Xizzi runs an elite model agency for children and often has to employ chaperones to accompany the children to assignments. Acutely conscious of the importance of child protection and that she has little time to undertake checks herself, Xizzi enters into a two-year contract with Yvonne's Chaperone Agency, paying the contract price of £50,000 upfront. Although Yvonne's services are very expensive, Xizzi does not mind paying because she is very impressed with the promises made in return: Yvonne undertakes to conduct exhaustive checks on her chaperones, not just with the criminal records bureau but with numerous other sources of information, formal and informal, describing the agency's service

as 'equivalent to MI5 levels of scrutiny'. When the two years have elapsed, however, Xizzi is contacted by Zoot, a disgruntled former employee of Yvonne, who tells her that absolutely no checks are carried out, that the chaperones are all out-of-work actor friends of Yvonne, at least one of whom is a convicted paedophile, and that Yvonne has used the money paid by Xizzi to make hugely profitable investments in the gold market. Xizzi is absolutely horrified to learn this, although fortunately all her child models have been safely chaperoned throughout the two-year period, and seeks your advice as to whether she can recover the profits made by Yvonne in order to punish her.

For hints on how to answer question 5, please see the online resources at **www.oup.com/uk/sullivan8e/**.

Appendix: Additional chapters on the Online Resource Centre

Available to download from the accompanying Online Resource Centre at www.oxfordtextbooks.co.uk/orc/osullivan8e/are two additional chapters: 'Incapacity' and 'Illegality and public policy'. These chapters provide complete coverage for students who wish to explore these areas of contract law. Both are fully indexed and referenced in the book itself as W1 and W2. Short summaries of the two chapters are provided below.

W1 Incapacity

This chapter considers how the law deals with contracting parties who lack capacity, or full capacity, to contract: minors, those who lack mental capacity, companies and public authorities.

W2 Illegality and public policy

This chapter considers the complex effect of illegality on contracts, including criminal and civil wrongdoing and other activities regarded as contrary to public policy such as contracting in restraint of trade. For example, some statutes prohibit particular contracts per se, while elsewhere an otherwise lawful contract may be performed in a manner that breaches a statute. The common law will not enforce an illegal contract, but other remedies may in certain circumstances still be available, such as recovery of money paid in advance or vindication of underlying property rights. There is a tension between the rigid application of the illegality rules for policy reasons and a more flexible, case-by-case discretionary approach, which makes the law somewhat confused and unpredictable. The Supreme Court last year decided a very important decision on this issue, in the context of a claim for restitution, with important implications for contractual illegality. Time will tell whether this decision produces greater clarity on how to resolve this tension.

Bibliography

Adams (1983) 'The Battle of Forms', JBL 297

Adams, Beyleveld, and Brownsword (1997) 'Privity of Contract—the Benefits and the Burdens of Law Reform', 60 MLR 238

Adams and Brownsword (1988) 'The Unfair Contract Terms Act: A Decade of Discretion', 104 LQR 94

Al Ibrahim, Ababneh, and Tahart (2007) 'The Postal Acceptance Rule in the Digital Age', 2(1) J Int' Commercial L & Tech 47

Andrews (1988) 'Does a Third Party Beneficiary have a Right in English Law?', 8 LS 14, 29

Andrews (2001) 'Strangers to Justice No Longer: The Reversal of the Privity Rule under the Contracts (Rights of Third Parties) Act 1999', 60(2) CLJ 353

Andrews (2017) 'Interpretation of Contracts and "Commercial Common Sense"', 76(1) CLJ 36

Arden (2013) 'Coming to Terms with Good Faith', 30 JCL 199

Ashworth (1989) 'The Scope of Criminal Liability for Omissions', 105 LQR 424

Atiyah (1957) '*Couturier v Hastie* and the Sale of Non-Existent Goods', 73 LQR 340

Atiyah (1976) 'When is an Enforceable Agreement not a Contract? Answer: When it is an Equity', 92 LQR 174

Atiyah (1982) 'Economic Duress and the 'Overborne Will'', 98 LQR 197

Atiyah (1986) *Essays on Contract* (Oxford: Clarendon Press)

Atiyah (1986a) 'The Hannah Blumenthal and Classical Contract Law', 102 LQR 363

Atiyah and Smith (2006) *Atiyah's Introduction to the Law of Contract* (6th edn, Oxford: Clarendon Press)

Atiyah and Treitel (1967) 'Misrepresentation Act 1967', 30 MLR 369

Ball (1983) 'Work Carried Out in Pursuance of Letters of Intent—Contract or Restitution?', 99 LQR 572

Bamforth (1995) 'Unconscionability as a Vitiating Factor', LMCLQ 538

Barker (1998) 'Rescuing Remedialism in Unjust Enrichment Law: Why Remedies are Right', 57(2) CLJ 301

Barker (2003) 'Coping with Failure—Reappraising Pre-Contractual Remuneration', 19 JCL 105

Beale (1980) *Remedies for Breach of Contract* (London: Sweet & Maxwell)

Beale (1995) 'Legislative Control of Fairness: The Directive on Unfair Terms in Consumer Contracts' in J Beatson and D Friedmann (eds) *Good Faith and Fault in Contract Law* (Oxford: Clarendon Press) 231

Beale (2010) 'A Review of the Contracts (Rights of Third Parties) Act 1999' in A Burrows and E Peel (eds) *Contract Formation and Parties* (Oxford: Oxford University Press) 225–50

Beale and Goriely (2005) 'An Unfairly Complex Law', 155 NLJ 318

Beatson (1996) 'Increased Expense and Frustration' in F Rose (ed) *Consensus Ad Idem* (London: Sweet & Maxwell) 121

Beatson (1999) 'The Temptation of Elegance: Concurrence of Restitutionary and Contractual Claims' in W Swadling and G Jones (eds) *The Search for Principle* (Oxford: Oxford University Press) 143

Beatson (2002a) 'Courts, Arbitrators and Restitutionary Liability for Breach of Contract', 118 LQR 377

Beatson, Burrows, and Cartwright (2016) *Anson's Law of Contract* (29th edn, Oxford: Oxford University Press)

Beever (2003) 'The Structure of Aggravated and Exemplary Damages', 23(1) OJLS 87

Benson (2001) 'Outline of a Theory of Contracts' in P Benson (ed) *The Theory of Contract Law* (Cambridge: Cambridge University Press) ch 4

Bigwood (1996) 'Undue Influence: Impaired Consent or Wicked Exploitation?', 16(3) OJLS 503

Bigwood (2001) 'Economic Duress by (Threatened) Breach of Contract', 117 LQR 376

Birks (1983) 'Restitution and the Freedom of Contract', 36(1) CLP 141

Birks (1989) *An Introduction to the Law of Restitution* (revised edn, Oxford: Clarendon Press)

Birks (1990) 'The Travails of Duress', LMCLQ 342

Birks (1996) 'Failure of Consideration' in F Rose (ed) *Consensus Ad Idem* (London: Sweet & Maxwell) 179

Birks (1997) 'Unjust Factors and Wrongs: Pecuniary Rescission for Undue Influence', RLR 72

Birks and Chin (1995) 'On the Nature of Undue Influence' in J Beatson and D Friedmann (eds) *Good Faith and Fault in Contract Law* (Oxford: Clarendon Press) 57

Braithwaite (2016), 'The Origins and Implications of Contractual Estoppel', 132 LQR 120

Bridge (1989) 'Mitigation of Damages in Contract and the Meaning of Avoidable Loss', 105 LQR 398

Bridge (2001) 'The Contracts (Rights of Third Parties) Act 1999', 5 Edin LR 85

Bridge (2015) *Personal Property Law* (4th edn, Oxford: Clarendon Press)

Bright (2000) 'Winning the Battle against Unfair Terms', 20 LS 331

Brown and Chandler (1992) 'Deceit, Damages and the Misrepresentation Act 1967, s 2(1)', LMCLQ 40

Brownsword (2006) *Contract Law—Themes for the Twenty First Century* (2nd edn, Oxford: Oxford University Press)

Buckley (1993) '*Walford v Miles*: False Certainty About Uncertainty—An Australian Perspective', 6 JCL 58

Burrows (1983) 'Contract, Tort and Restitution: A Satisfactory Division or Not?', 99 LQR 217

Burrows (1996) 'Reforming Privity of Contract: Law Commission Report No 242', LMCLQ 467

Burrows (2000) 'Judicial Remedies' in P Birks (ed) *English Private Law* (Oxford: Oxford University Press) ch 18

Burrows (2001) 'No Damages for a Third Party's Loss', 1 Univ of Oxford Commonwealth LJ 107

Burrows (2004) *Remedies for Torts and Breach of Contract* (3rd edn, Oxford: Oxford University Press)

Burrows (2010) *The Law of Restitution* (3rd edn, Oxford: Oxford University Press)

Buxton (2010) 'Construction and Rectification after *Chartbrook*', 69(2) CLJ 253

Calnan (2017) *Principles of Contractual Interpretation* (2nd edn, Oxford: Oxford University Press)

Campbell and Wylie (2003) 'Ain't No Telling (Which Circumstances are Exceptional)', 62(3) CLJ 605

Cane (1996) 'Exceptional Measures of Damages: A Search for Principles' in P Birks (ed) *Wrongs and Remedies in the Twenty First Century* (Oxford: Clarendon Press) 301

Cane (1997) *The Anatomy of Tort Law* (Oxford: Hart Publishing)

Capper (1998) 'Undue Influence and Unconscionability: A Rationalisation', 114 LQR 479

Capper (2002) 'Damages for Distress and Disappointment—Problem Solved?', 118 LQR 193

Capper (2008) 'More Muddle on Mistake', LMCLQ 264

Capper (2009) 'Common Mistake in Contract Law', 51 Singapore J Legal Stud 457

Capper (2010) 'The Unconscionable Bargain in the Common Law World', 126 LQR 403

Carter (1995) 'Suspending Contract Performance for Breach' in J Beatson and D Friedmann (eds) *Good Faith and Fault in Contract Law* (Oxford: Clarendon Press) 485

Carter (2013) 'Deposits and "Time of the Essence"', 129 LQR 149

Carter and Courtney (2016) 'Good Faith in Contracts: Is there an Implied Promise to Act Honestly', 75(3) CLJ 608

Carter, Courtney, and Tolhurst (2017) 'An Assimilated Approach to Discharge for Breach of Contract by Delay', 76(1) CLJ63

Carter and Marston (1985) 'Repudiation of Contract—Whether Election Fettered', 44(1) CLJ 18

Carter, Phang, and Phang (1995) 'Performance Following Repudiation: Legal and Economic Interests', 15 JCL 97

Cartwright (1993) 'An Unconscionable Bargain', 109 LQR 530

Chandler and Devenney (2007) 'Breach of Contract and the Expectation Deficit: Inconvenience and Disappointment', 27 LS 126

Chen-Wishart (1995) 'Consideration: Practical Benefit and the Emperor's New Clothes' in J Beatson and D Friedmann (eds) *Good Faith and Fault in Contract Law* (Oxford: Clarendon Press) 123

Chen-Wishart (2009) 'Contractual Mistake, Intention in Formation and Vitiation: the Oxymoron of *Smith v Hughes*' in JW Neyers, R Bronaugh and SGA Pitel (eds) *Exploring Contract Law* (Oxford: Hart Publishing) 341

Chitty (2016) *Chitty on Contracts* (31st revised edn, London: Sweet & Maxwell) (ed Beale)

Christensen (2001) 'Formation of Contracts by Email—Is it Just the Same as the Post?', 1(1) Queensland Univ of Tech L & Justice J 22

Clarkson, Miller and Muris (1978) 'Liquidated Damages v Penalties: Sense or Nonsense?', Wisconsin LR 351

Cohen (1995) 'Pre-Contractual Duties: Two Freedoms and the Contract to Negotiate' in J Beatson and D Friedmann (eds) *Good Faith and Fault in Contract Law* (Oxford: Clarendon Press) 25

Collins (1994) 'Good Faith in European Contract Law', 14(2) OJLS 229

Coote (1971) 'The Instantaneous Transmission of Acceptances', 4 NZULR 331

Coote (1978) 'Consideration and the Joint Promisee', 37(2) CLJ 301

Coote (1997) 'Contract Damages, *Ruxley* and the Performance Interest', 56(3) CLJ 537

Coote (2001) 'The Performance Interest, *Panatown* and the Problem of Loss', 117 LQR 81

Coote (2004) 'Consideration and Variations: A Different Solution', 120 LQR 19

Corbin (1930) 'Contracts for the Benefit of Third Parties', 46 LQR 12

Dagan (2000) 'Restitutionary Damages for Breach of Contract: An Exercise in Private Law Theory', 1 TIL 115

Davies (2009) 'The Illegality Defence—Two Steps Forward, One Step Back?', 3 Conv PL 182

Davies (2010) 'Bank Charges in the Supreme Court', 69(1) CLJ 21

Davies (2010a) 'Contract and Unjust Enrichment: A Blurry Divide', 126 LQR 175

Davies (2010b) 'Anticipated Contracts: Room for Agreement', 69(3) CLJ 467

Davies (2011) 'Negotiating the Boundaries of Admissibility', 70(1) CLJ 24

Davies (2012) 'Rectifying the Course of Rectification', 75(3) MLR 387

Davies (2015) 'The Meaning of Commercial Contracts' in PS Davies and J Pila (eds) *The Jurisprudence of Lord Hoffmann* (Oxford: Hart Publishing)

Davies (2016) 'Rectification versus Interpretation' 75(1) CLJ 62

Davies (2017) 'Interpretation and Rectification in Australia' 76(3) CLJ 000 (forthcoming)

Davies and Turner (2013) 'Relief Against Penalties Without a Breach of Contract', 72(1) CLJ 20

Dawson (1981) 'Metaphors and Anticipatory Breach of Contract', 40 CLJ 83

Dawson (2016) 'Damages for Anticipatory Breach', LMCLQ 6

Denning (1952) 'Recent Developments in the Doctrine of Consideration', 15 MLR 1

Dietrich (2001) 'Classifying Precontractual Liability: A Comparative Analysis', 21 LS 153

Dixon (1994) 'Looking up a Remedy for Inequitable Conduct', 53(2) CLJ 232

Dockray (2001) '*Cutter v Powell*: A Trip Outside the Text', 117 LQR 664

Downes (1996) 'Rethinking Penalty Clauses' in P Birks (ed) *Wrongs and Remedies in the Twenty First Century* (Oxford: Clarendon Press) 249–69

Edelman (2000) 'Restitutionary Damages and Disgorgement Damages for Breach of Contract', RLR 129

Edelman (2001) 'Exemplary Damages for Breach of Contract', 117 LQR 539

Edelman (2002) *Gain-based Damages* (Oxford: Hart Publishing)

Enonchong (1996) 'Breach of Contract and Damages for Mental Distress', 16(4) OJLS 617

Enonchong (2000) 'Illegal Transactions: The Future', RLR 82

Fifoot (1949) *History and Sources of the Common Law: Tort and Contract* (London: Stevens & Sons)

Fleming (1952) 'Common Mistake', 15 MLR 229

Foxton (2008) 'Damages for Late or Early Redelivery under Time Charterparties', LMCLQ 461–7

Foxton (2016) 'A Good Faith Goodbye? Good Faith Obligations and Contractual Termination Rights', LMCLQ 360

Freeman (1996) 'Contracting in the Haven: *Balfour v Balfour* Revisited' in R Halson (ed) *Exploring the Boundaries of Contract* (Farnham: Ashgate Dartmouth) 68

Fried (2015) *Contract as Promise* (2nd edn, New York: Oxford University Press, USA)

Friedmann (1995a) 'The Performance Interest in Contract Damages', 111 LQR 628

Friedmann (1995b) 'Good Faith and Remedies for Breach of Contract' in J Beatson and D Friedmann (eds) *Good Faith and Fault in Contract Law* (Oxford: Clarendon Press) 399

Fuller and Perdue (1936–7) 'The Reliance Interest in Contract Damages', 46 Yale LJ 52

Furmston and Tolhurst (2015) *Privity of Contract* (Oxford: Oxford University Press)

Gardner (1992) 'Trashing with Trollope: A Deconstruction of the Postal Rules in Contract', 12(2) OJLS 170

Giliker (2017) 'The Consumer Rights Act 2015—a Bastion of European Consumer Rights?', 37 LS 78

Goetz and Scott (1977) 'Liquidated Damages, Penalties and the Just Compensation Principle: Some Notes on an Enforcement Model and a Theory of Efficient Breach', 77 Col LR 548

Goff and Jones (2016) *The Law of Unjust Enrichment* (London: Sweet & Maxwell) by C Mitchell, P Mitchell, and S Watterson

Goodhart (1941) 'Mistake as to Identity in the Law of Contract', 57 LQR 228

Goodhart (1995) 'Restitutionary Damages for Breach of Contract: The Remedy That Dare Not Speak Its Name', RLR 3

Gower (1952) 'Auction Sales of Goods without Reserve', 68 LQR 457

Grant (2004) 'Unfair Terms sent on Vacation', 154 NLJ 486

Häcker (2008) 'Mistakes in the Execution of Documents: Recent Cases on Rectification and Related Doctrines', 19 KLJ 293

Halson (1990) 'Sailors, Sub-contractors and Consideration', 106 LQR 183

Halson (1991) 'Opportunism, Economic Duress and Contractual Modifications', 107 LQR 649

Halson (1999) 'The Offensive Limits of Promissory Estoppel', LMCLQ 257

Hare (2003) 'Inequitable Mistake', 62(1) CLJ 29

Harpum and Lloyd Jones (1979) 'Contracts to Contract—Some Answers; Some Questions', 38(1) CLJ 31

Harris (2012) 'Fairness and Remoteness of Damage in Contract Law: A Lexical Ordering Approach', 28 JCL 122

Harris, Campbell and Halson (2002) *Remedies for Breach of Contract* (2nd edn, Cambridge: Cambridge University Press)

Harris, Ogus and Phillips (1979) 'Contract Remedies and the Consumer Surplus', 95 LQR 581

Hart and Honoré (1985) *Causation in the Law* (2nd edn, Oxford: Oxford University Press)

Hedley (1985) 'Keeping Contract in its Place—*Balfour v Balfour* and the Enforceability of Informal Agreements', 5(3) OJLS 391

Hedley (1995) 'Unjust Enrichment', 54(3) CLJ 578

Hedley (1998) 'Work Done in Anticipation of a Contract which does not Materialise: A Response' in W Cornish, R Nolan, J O'Sullivan, and G Virgo (eds) *Restitution: Past, Present and Future* (Oxford: Hart Publishing) 195

Hedley (2000) 'Very Much the Wrong People: The House of Lords and Publication of Spy Memoirs (*AG v Blake*)', Web JCLI

Hedley (2001a) *Restitution: Its Division and Ordering* (London: Sweet & Maxwell)

Hedley (2001b) *A Critical Introduction to Restitution* (Oxford: Oxford University Press)

Hedley (2001c) Book review, Edin LR 248

Hedley (2004) 'Implied Contracts and Restitution', 63(2) CLJ 435

Hepple (1970) 'Intention to Create Legal Relations', 28(1) CLJ 122

Hill (2001) 'Flogging A Dead Horse—The Postal Acceptance Rules and Email', 17 JCL 151

Hilliard (2002) '*Re Hastings-Bass*: Too Good to be True?', 16 TLI 202

Ho (2000) 'Undue Influence and Equitable Compensation' in P Birks and F Rose (eds) *Restitution and Equity Volume One: Resulting Trusts and Equitable Compensation* (London: Mansfield Press/LLP) 193

Hoffmann (1999) 'Common Sense and Causing Loss', Lecture to the Chancery Bar Association, 15 June 1999

Hoffmann (2010) '*The Achilleas*: Custom and Practice or Foreseeability?', 14 Edin LR 47

Hooley (1991) 'Damages and the Misrepresentation Act 1967', 107 LQR 547

Hooley (2014) 'Implied Terms after *Belize Telecom*', 73(2) CLJ 315

Hooley and O'Sullivan (1997) 'Undue Influence and Unconscionable Bargains', LMCLQ 17

Hoskins (2014) 'Contractual Obligations to Negotiate in Good Faith: Faithfulness to the Agreed Common Purpose', 130 LQR 131

Hopkins (1990) 'Privity of Contract: The Thin End of the Wedge?', 49(1) CLJ 21

Hudson (1966) 'Retraction of Letters of Acceptance', 82 LQR 169

Hudson (1968) '*Gibbons v Proctor* Revisited', 84 LQR 503

Hudson (1974) 'Penalties Limiting Damages', 90 LQR 31

Ibbetson (1999) *A Historical Introduction to the Law of Obligations* (Oxford: Oxford University Press)

Jaffey (1995) 'Restitutionary Damages and Disgorgement', RLR 30

Jaffey (1998) 'Failure of Consideration and Reliance in Contract', RLR 157

Jaffey (2000) *The Nature and Scope of Restitution* (Oxford: Hart Publishing)

Jaffey (2000a) 'Restitution, Reliance and Quantum Meruit', RLR 270

Jansen and Zimmermann (2010) 'A European Contract Code in All But Name': Discussing the Nature and Purpose of the Draft Common Frame of Reference', 69(1) CLJ 98

Jones (1997) 'Specific Performance: A Lessee's Covenant to Keep Open a Retail Store', 56(3) CLJ 488

Kennedy (2016) 'Unnecessary Complications', LMCLQ 190

Kimel (2002) 'Remedial Rights and Substantive Rights in Contract Law', 8 Legal Theory 313

Kimel (2003) *From Promise to Contract* (Oxford: Hart Publishing)

Kincaid (2000) 'Privity Reform in England', 116 LQR 43

Kramer (2005) 'An Agreement-Centred Approach to Remoteness and Contract Damages' in E McKendrick and N Cohen (eds) *Comparative Remedies for Breach of Contract* (Oxford: Hart Publishing) 249

Leggatt (2015) 'Making Sense of Contracts: the Rational Choice Theory', 131 LQR 454

Macdonald (2011) 'Incorporation of Standard Terms in Website Contracting', 27 JCL 198

MacMillan (2000) 'A Birthday Present for Lord Denning: The Contracts (Rights of Third Parties) Act 1999', 63 MLR 721

MacMillan (2002) 'Evolution or Revolution? Unfair Terms in Consumer Contracts', 61(1) CLJ 22

MacMillan (2010) *Mistakes in Contract Law* (Oxford: Hart Publishing)

MacMillan (2016) 'The Impact of Brexit upon English Contract Law' 27 Kings Law Journal 420

Marks (1992) 'Loss of Profits in Damages for Deceit', 108 LQR 386

Mason (2000) 'Contract, Good Faith and Equitable Standards in Fair Dealing', 116 LQR 66

McBride (1995) 'A Case for Awarding Punitive Damages in Response to Deliberate Breaches of Contract', 24 Anglo-Am LR 369

McBride (1996) 'Punitive Damages' in P Birks (ed) *Wrongs and Remedies in the Twenty First Century* (Oxford: Clarendon Press) 175

McCaughran (2011) 'Implied Terms: The Journey of the Man on the Clapham Omnibus', 70(3) CLJ 607

McDonald (1994) 'Contractual Damages for Mental Distress', 7 JCL 134

McFarlane and Stevens (2002) 'In Defence of *Sumpter v Hedges*', 118 LQR 569

McKendrick (1988) 'The Battle of the Forms and the Law of Restitution', 8(2) OJLS 197

McKendrick (1990) 'The Construction of *Force Majeure* Clauses and Self-Induced Frustration', LMCLQ 153

McKendrick (1995) 'Total Failure of Consideration and Counter-Restitution: Two Issues or One?' in P Birks (ed) *Laundering and Tracing* (Oxford: Clarendon Press) 217

McKendrick (1998) 'Work Done In Anticipation of a Contract which does not Materialise' in W Cornish, R Nolan, J O'Sullivan and G Virgo (eds) *Restitution: Past, Present and Future* (Oxford: Hart Publishing) 163

McKendrick (1999) 'Breach of Contract and the Meaning of Loss', 52(1) CLP 37

McKendrick (2003) 'Breach of Contract, Restitution for Wrongs and Punishment' in A Burrows and E Peel (eds) *Commercial Remedies* (Oxford: Oxford University Press) ch 10

McKendrick (2016) *Contract Law: Text, Cases and Materials* (6th edn, Oxford: Oxford University Press)

McKendrick and Graham (2002) 'The Sky's The Limit: Contractual Damages for Non-Pecuniary Loss', LMCLQ 161

McLauchlan (2005) 'Parol Guidance and Contract Formation', 121 LQR 9

McLauchlan (2008) 'The 'Drastic' Remedy of Rectification for Unilateral Mistake', 124 LQR 608

McLauchlan (2009) '*Chartbrook Ltd v Persimmon Homes Ltd*: Commonsense Principles of Interpretation and Rectification?', 125 LQR 8

McLauchlan (2012) 'The Entire Agreement Clause: Conclusive or a Question of Weight?', 128 LQR 521

McLauchlan (2014) 'Refining Rectification', 130 LQR 83

McMeel (2002) 'Note on *Esso v Niad Ltd*', RLR 166

McMeel (2006) 'Interpretation and Mistake in Contract Law', LMCLQ 49

Megarry and Wade (2012) *The Law of Real Property* (8th edn, London: Sweet & Maxwell), by C Harpum, S Bridge, and M Dixon

Meikle (2003) 'Partial Rescission—Removing the Restitution from a Contract Doctrine', 19 JCL 40

Midwinter (2003a) 'Causation, Loss and Double Recovery', 62(1) CLJ 23

Midwinter (2003b) '*The Great Peace* and Precedent', 119 LQR 180

Miller (1972) '*Felthouse v Bindley* Revisited', 35 MLR 489

Millett (1976) '*Crabb v Arun District Council*—A Riposte', 92 LQR 342

Millett (1998) 'Equity's Place in the Law of Commerce', 114 LQR 214

Mitchell (1999) 'Remedial Inadequacy in Contract and the Role of Restitutionary Damages', 15 JCL 133

Mitchell and Phillips (2002) 'The Contractual Nexus: Is Reliance Essential?', 22(1) OJLS 115

Morgan (2015) *Great Debates in Contract Law* (2nd edn, London: Palgrave Macmillan)

Morgan (2017) 'Repudiatory Breach: Inability, Election and Discharge', 76(1) CLJ 11

Mouzas and Furmston (2008) 'From Contract to Umbrella Agreement', 67(1) CLJ 37

Mustill (2008) '*The Golden Victory*—Some Reflections', 124 LQR 569

Nahan (1997) 'Rescission: A Case for Rejecting the Classical Model?', 27 ULWALR 66

Nicholls (2005) 'My Kingdom for a Horse: The Meaning of Words', 121 LQR 577

Nienaber (1962) 'The Effect of Anticipatory Repudiation: Principle and Policy', 20(2) CLJ 213

Nolan (2010) 'Offer and Acceptance in the Electronic Age' in A Burrows and E Peel (eds) *Contract Formation and Parties* (Oxford: Oxford University Press) 61

Neuberger (2014) 'The Impact of Pre- and Post-Contractual Conduct on Contractual Interpretation' speech to the Banking Services and Finance Law Association Conference, Queenstown, available at www.supremecourt.uk/docs

Oldham (1995) 'Neither a Borrower nor a Lender Be—The Life of *O'Brien*', 7 CFLQ 104

O'Neill (1992) 'A Key to Lock-out Agreements?', 108 LQR 405

O'Sullivan (1995) 'Contract Damages for Failed Fun—Taking the Plunge', 54(3) CLJ 496

O'Sullivan (1996) 'In Defence of *Foakes v Beer*', 55(2) CLJ 219

O'Sullivan (1997) 'Loss and Gain at Greater Depth: The Implications of the Ruxley Decision' in F Rose (ed) *Failure of Contracts* (Oxford: Hart Publishing) 1

O'Sullivan (1998) 'Undue Influence and Misrepresentation after *O'Brien*: Making Security Secure' in F Rose (ed) *Restitution and Banking Law* (Oxford: Mansfield Press) 42

O'Sullivan (2000) 'Rescission as a Self Help Remedy: A Critical Analysis', 59(3) CLJ 509

O'Sullivan (2002) 'Reflections on the Role of Restitutionary Damages to Protect Contractual Expectations' in D Johnston and R Zimmermann (eds) *Unjustified Enrichment* (Cambridge: Cambridge University Press) 327

O'Sullivan (2009) 'Damages for Lost Profits for Late Redelivery: How Remote is Too Remote?', 68(1) CLJ 34

O'Sullivan (2014) 'Lost on Penalties', 73(3) CLJ 480

O'Sullivan (2016a) 'Silence is Golden: Implied Terms in the Supreme Court', 75(2) CLJ 199

O'Sullivan (2017a) 'Unconsidered Modifications', 133 LQR 191

O'Sullivan (2017b) 'Contributory Negligence and Strict Contractual Obligations Revisited' Chapter 11 in A Dyson, J Goudkamp and F Wilmot-Smith (eds) *Defences in Contract* (Hart, Bloomsbury) 215

O'Sullivan (2017c) 'Repudiation: Keeping the Contract Alive' Chapter 3 in G Virgo and S Worthington (eds) *Commercial Remedies: Resolving Controversies* (Cambridge: CUP) 51

Palmer (1992) *The Paths to Privity* (San Francisco, CA: Austin and Winfield)

Paterson (2011) 'Consumer Contracting in the Age of the Digital Natives', 27 JCL 152

Pearce and Halson (2007) 'Damages for Breach of Contract: Compensation, Restitution and Vindication', 28(1) OJLS 73

Peden (2001) 'Policy Concerns behind Implication of Terms in Law', 117 LQR 459

Peel (2001) 'Reasonable Exemption Clauses', 117 LQR 545

Peel (2009) 'Remoteness Re-visited', 126 LQR 6

Peel (2010) 'Agreements to Negotiate in Good Faith' in A Burrows and E Peel (eds) *Contract Formation and Parties* (Oxford: Oxford University Press) 37–60

Phang (1993) 'Implied Terms in English Law—Some Recent Developments', JBL 242

Phang (1998) 'Implied Terms, Business Efficacy and the Officious Bystander—A Modern History', JBL 1

Phang (2003) 'The Crumbling Edifice? Contractual Damages for Mental Distress', JBL 341

Phang (2005) 'The Frontiers of Contract Law—Contract Formation and Mistake in Cyberspace—The Singaporean Experience', 17 Singapore Academy of L J 361

Phang and Lee (2003) 'Restitutionary and Exemplary Damages Revisited', 19 JCL 1

Phang and Tjio (2002) 'The Uncertain Boundaries of Undue Influence', LMCLQ 231

Rawlings (1979) 'The Battle of Forms', 42 MLR 715

Robertson (2008) 'The Basis of the Remoteness Rule in Contract', 28 LS 172

Ronan (2006) 'Challenged but not Defeated by Technology: Why the Postal Rule Should Apply to Contracts Formed by E-mail', paper delivered at 61st Annual ALTA Conference, July

Rotherham (2007) 'The Conceptual Structure of Restitution for Wrongs', 66(1) CLJ 17

Rotherham (2008) 'Wrotham Park Damages and Accounts of Profits: Compensation or Restitution?', LMCLQ 25

Rotherham (2010) 'Gain-Based Relief in Tort after AG v Blake', 125 LQR 102

Ruddell (2014) 'Common Intention and Rectification for Common Mistake', LMCLQ 48

Sandy (2003) 'Spies, Rock Stars and Restitutionary Damages', 153 NLJ 723

Saprai (2017), Balfour v Balfour and the Separation of Contract and Promise, 37 LS 468

Scott (2007) 'Damages', LMCLQ 465

Slade (1952) 'Auction Sales of Goods without Reserve', 68 LQR 238

Slade (1953) 'Auction Sales of Goods without Reserve', 69 LQR 21

Slade (1954) 'The Myth of Mistake in the English Law of Contract', 70 LQR 385

Smith (1979) 'The Law of Contract—Alive or Dead?', 13 The Law Teacher 73

Smith (1994) 'Contracts—Mistake, Frustration and Implied Terms', 110 LQR 400

Smith (1994a) Annual Review: Contract Section, 47 CLP Vol 1

Smith (1997) 'Contracting under Pressure: A Theory of Duress', 56(2) CLJ 343

Smith (1997a) 'Contracts for the Benefit of Third Parties: In Defence of the Third Party Rule', 17(4) OJLS 643

Smith (1999) 'Concurrent Liability in Contract and Unjust Enrichment: The Fundamental Breach Requirement', 115 LQR 245

Smith (2004) Contract Theory (Oxford: Clarendon Press)

Smith (2007) 'Rectification of Contracts for Common Mistake, Joscelyne v Nissen and Subjective States of Mind', 123 LQR 116

Spence (1999) Protecting Reliance (Oxford: Hart Publishing)

Spencer (1973) 'Signature, Consent and the Rule in L'Estrange v Graucob', 32(1) CLJ 104

Staughton (1999) 'How do the Courts Interpret Commercial Contracts?', 58(2) CLJ 303

Stevens (2004) 'The Contracts (Rights of Third Parties) Act 1999', 120 LQR 292

Stevens and Neyers (1999) 'What's Wrong with Restitution?', 37 Alberta LR 221

Steyn (1997) 'Contract Law: Fulfilling the Reasonable Expectations of Honest Men', 113 LQR 433

Stoljar (1989) The Law of Quasi-Contract (2nd edn, Sydney: The Law Book Co)

Summers (2017) 'Unresolved Issue in the Law on Penalties', LMCLQ 95

Summers and Kramer (2017) 'Deceit, Difference in Value and Date of Assessment', 133 LQR 41

Tettenborn (1994) 'Contract, Bailment and Third Parties—Again', 53(3) CLJ 440

Tettenborn (1996) 'Third Party Contract—Pragmatism from the Law Commission', JBL 602

Tettenborn (2002) 'Subsisting Contracts and Failure of Consideration—A Little Scepticism', RLR 1

Tettenborn (2007) 'What is a Loss?' in JW Neyers, E Chamberlain, and S Pitel (eds) Emerging Issues in Tort Law (Oxford: Hart Publishing) 441

Tettenborn (2007a) 'Hadley v Baxendale Foreseeability: A Principle Beyond its Sell-By Date?', 23 JCL 120

Tettenborn (2011) 'Agreements, Common Mistake and the Purpose of Contract', 27 JCL 91

Thal (1988) 'The Inequality of Bargaining Power: The Problem of Defining Contractual Unfairness', 8(1) OJLS 17

Tiplady (1983) 'Concepts of Duress', 99 LQR 188

Trebilcock (1976) 'The Doctrine of Inequality of Bargaining Power: Post-Benthamite Economics in the House of Lords', 26 Univ of Toronto LJ 359

Trebilcock (1980) 'An Economic Approach to Unconscionability' in B Reiter and J Swan (eds) *Studies in Contract Law* (Toronto: Butterworths) 381

Treitel (1997) 'Damages for Breach of Warranty of Quality', 113 LQR 188

Treitel (2002) *Some Landmarks of Twentieth Century Contract Law* (Oxford: Oxford University Press)

Treitel (2015) by Edwin Peel, *The Law of Contract* (14th edn, London: Sweet & Maxwell)

Trukhtanov (2009) 'Misrepresentation: Acknowledgment of Non-Reliance as a Defence', 125 LQR 648

Unberath (2003) *Transferred Loss* (Oxford: Hart Publishing)

Unger (1953) 'Self-Service Shops and the Law of Contract', 16 MLR 369

Virgo (1995) 'Anticipatory Contracts—Restitution Restrained', 54(2) CLJ 243

Virgo (2015) *The Principles of the Law of Restitution* (3rd edn, Oxford: Oxford University Press)

Vorster (1987) 'A Comment on the Meaning of Objectivity in Contract', 103 LQR 274

Waddams (1997) 'Profits Derived from Breach of Contract: Damages or Restitution', 11 JCL 115

Waddams (2009) 'Principle in Contract Law: The Doctrine of Consideration' in J Neyers, R Bronaugh and S Pitel (eds) *Exploring Contract Law* (Oxford: Hart Publishing) 51–76

Weir (1976) 'Contract—The Buyer's Right to Reject Defective Goods', 35(1) CLJ 33

Weir (1997) *Economic Torts* (Oxford: Clarendon Press)

Weir (2000) *A Casebook on Tort* (9th edn, London: Sweet & Maxwell)

Whittaker (2009) 'A Framework of Principle for European Contract Law?', 125 LQR 616

Williams (1945) 'Mistake as to Party in the Law of Contract', 23 Can Bar Rev 271

Willmot-Smith (2013) 'Reconsidering "Total" Failure', 72(2) CLJ 414

Winfield (1939) 'Some Aspects of Offer and Acceptance', 55 LQR 499

Worthington and Goode (2000) 'Commercial Law: Confining the Remedial Boundaries' in D Hayton (ed) *Law's Future* (Oxford: Hart Publishing) 281

Index